IIS 6:
The Complete Reference

Hethe Henrickson
Scott Hofmann

McGraw-Hill/Osborne

New York   Chicago   San Francisco
Lisbon   London   Madrid   Mexico City
Milan   New Delhi   San Juan
Seoul   Singapore   Sydney   Toronto

The McGraw·Hill Companies

McGraw-Hill/Osborne
2100 Powell Street, 10th Floor
Emeryville, California 94608
U.S.A.

To arrange bulk purchase discounts for sales promotions, premiums, or fund-raisers, please contact **McGraw-Hill**/Osborne at the above address. For information on translations or book distributors outside the U.S.A., please see the International Contact Information page immediately following the index of this book.

IIS 6: The Complete Reference

1234567890 DOC DOC 019876543

ISBN 0-07-222495-9

Publisher
  Brandon A. Nordin

Vice President & Associate Publisher
  Scott Rogers

Acquisitions Editor
  Jane Brownlow

Project Editor
  Jody McKenzie

Acquisitions Coordinator
  Jessica Wilson

Technical Editor
  Steve Wright

Copy Editor
  Lisa Theobald

Proofreader
  Susie Elkind

Indexer
  Jack Lewis

Composition
  Carie Abrew
  Tara A. Davis

Illustrators
  Kathleen Fay Edwards
  Melinda Moore Lytle
  Michael Mueller
  Lyssa Wald

Series Design
  Peter F. Hancik

This book was composed with Corel VENTURA™ Publisher.

To my wife, Andra, and my children, Jaymie, Zach, and Ashleigh.
—Hethe Henrickson

For Lori, Jacob, Matt, and Katie.
—Scott Hofmann

About the Authors

Hethe Henrickson has been a professional Windows Server administrator since 1997. Currently, he is a Windows Server lead for a large multinational corporation. He is an MCSE in both Windows 2000 and Window NT 4. His IIS work started in 1997 with IIS 3.0, and he's worked on well more than 100 web sites since that time. He has worked extensively with Windows NT 4, Windows 2000, and Windows 2003 servers.

Hethe has been a book technical editor, and he was a technical instructor at National American University, where he taught Windows NT and Windows 2000 MCSE classes. He has also been a columnist for swynk.com.

Hethe's big drive in the Windows Server arena is to automate processes and maintenance of servers so mammals don't have to keep touching servers. He strives to automate many of the ordinary tasks that administrators do each day, especially if it involves scripting with VBScript.

Hethe lives in Wisconsin with his wife and children.

Scott Hofmann has been involved in more than a dozen significant enterprise web application efforts that consisted of $1 million–plus development efforts. Among these projects, ownerconnection.com and Rapportnet.com were the most notable. With more than ten years of programming experience, Scott has served in many efforts as a programmer and has led most projects as a senior system architect and development manager, overseeing design, code production, and maintenance. Scott writes code using C++, Visual Basic, JavaScript, SQL, VBScript, Pascal, and Java on server hosts running Windows NT 4, Windows 2000, and Windows 2003 Server; Solaris; Red Hat, Debian, and Mandrake Linux; and FreeBSD.

Scott has been a technical editor for IDG Books, Hungry Minds, and Wiley Publishing. Among his written works is a whitepaper for Microsoft called "Interoperation Using .NET" and an article about using ESRI's MapObjects in Visual Basic. Scott earned a bachelor's degree in engineering from Michigan State University in 1991 and obtained a Microsoft MCSD certification in 1998.

Scott lives with his wife and children in Michigan. Scott may be contacted through his web site, mapobject.com, or via e-mail at scott@mapobject.com.

About the Technical Editor

Steve Wright is a consultant with 15 years experience for Planet Consulting Inc. in Omaha, Nebraska. He holds many current certifications from Microsoft, including MCDBA, MCSD, MCSE, MCAD, and MCSA. He is primarily an architect and technical lead for line-of-business application projects using Microsoft technologies. Steve has also worked for Microsoft developing demonstration applications for unreleased products. Steve holds bachelor's degrees in math and computer science and a master's degree in computer science.

Contents

Part II

IIS Administration

Part III

IIS Programming

Part IV

IIS Extras

Acknowledgments

I would like to thank Scott Hofmann for joining me on this project; it would not have been nearly the book it is without your work. I would also like to thank my agent, Neil Salkind, and also Mitch Tulloch, for introducing me to Neil and getting me started in this business.

I would like to thank my editor, Jane Brownlow, for leading me through this project. I'd also like to thank everyone at McGraw-Hill/Osborne, including Jessica Richards, Jessica Wilson, Jody McKenzie, Lisa Theobald, Michael Mueller, Steve Wright, Tana Allen, and Tracy Dunkelberger. Thanks to Bernie Berg for all his help with encryption.

I would also like to thank some of the people in my life who have inspired me: Jesus, Orv and Linda Henrickson, Pres and Di Moerman, Ralph Schuler, Audie Baker, Rich Adcock, Carol Brenner, Dan Hacking, Rocky Larson, and many others that I don't have the space to name here.

I would like to thank my wife, Andra, who is my biggest fan, and my children, who went through this process with me and understood during all those days when I couldn't come outside and play.

—Hethe Henrickson

I would like to thank Hethe Henrickson for inviting me to join him in this project and Jane Brownlow for having me on this project. I would also like to thank my agent, Neil Salkind, for believing in me and introducing me to Hethe and Jane. I am truly grateful to all of you for having been granted the opportunity to participate in this project.

I would like to thank the folks who were involved with this book. The material is honed and beautified through their talents and expertise. Without them, the book would not be what it is. Specifically, I would like to thank the following editors: Jody McKenzie, for all of the late-night, last-minute edits; Jessica Wilson; Tracy Dunkelberger; Steve Wright; Tana Allen; Jessica Richards; and Lisa Theobald. I know there are also many others who participated, and I thank all of you as well.

I would like to acknowledge my late friend, Russ Cripe, who inspired me never to duck a challenge. Anytime the technology seemed too sophisticated or the project seemed too impossible to build, he would say, "Why not us? Someone has to do it. What makes them any better then us?"

I would like to thank my friend Jim Russell, who challenged me to write a book and read Machiavelli. We survived living and driving in Turkey for a few years, and I look forward to another adventure somewhere—sometime.

I would also like to thank my wife, Lori, for her support on this project. I cannot do good work without a good partner.

—*Scott Hofmann*

Introduction

When we set out to write this book, we wanted it to cover all the bases: serious technical detail and background about the technologies involved in the Internet and a wealth of information about IIS administration and programming for IIS. We envisioned a book that would be a one-stop shop for everything you need to know to get a web site off the ground and running.

This book came from our desire to have that information all in one place. Traditionally, administration and programming are at opposite ends of the spectrum. But some of us want to do both programming and administration. Some administrators want to know enough programming to make a good web site, and some programmers want to know enough administration to get their web server configured correctly.

We also strove to include background and in-depth technical details about the technologies that make IIS work. As you read each of the chapters, such as "Authentication" (Chapter 7) and "Encryption" (Chapter 10), you'll notice that we cover not only the component, but also the background of the technology and how it works in technical detail.

We hope that as you read this book, you'll see the effort we put into making this an excellent resource for what you need to get your Internet site up, from start to finish, and that it is truly a resource that allows you to see both the programming and administration sides of IIS.

About the Book

This book is organized into four sections.

Part I is about basic IIS services. We cover each of the major IIS services in detail, including how to administer and configure each of the IIS services and what each of the options do.

Part II is about IIS administration and the supporting technologies for IIS. We cover security, encryption, TCP/IP, DNS, and authentication. In this section, we also cover the administration of IIS through scripts and programming interfaces, so you don't have to use the GUI all the time.

Part III is about programming for IIS. We have included something for everyone. Many of the common Microsoft platform technologies, ranging from ASP to .NET, are featured, using a variety of the programming languages associated with those technologies. ASP, the biggest application technology in IIS, is demonstrated with VBScript, XML, and ADO. COM and ASP web programming are featured with ADO in Visual Basic 6. We also demonstrate .NET web programming in C# by featuring the use of ADO .NET in ASP .NET web forms and web services. If you're really feeling like you want to tackle the high-performance technologies, we also cover ISAPI technology and ATL Server using C++.

Part IV is about the IIS extras that help you bring everything together and that have a full-featured Internet presence. In fact, Chapter 19 walks you through building a fully featured web site from the ground up. Good programming just doesn't happen; you need to plan for it, so Chapter 18 goes through how to set up the methodology for writing the code for software. Chapter 20 covers what to do when something goes wrong.

Bonus Material

Content for the book is available at **http://mapobject.com/iis6/**. The web page includes a link to download a zip file that contains all of the source code and other referenced material produced by the authors. Most of the content is source code for the programming chapters featured in Part III: Chapters 12, 13, 14, 15, 16, and 17. The documents referenced in Chapter 18 are also included.

The Complete Reference

IIS 6

Part I

Basic IIS Services

The
Complete
Reference

IIS 6

Chapter 1

IIS Fundamentals

Internet Information Services (IIS) is Microsoft's suite of applications for the Internet. With support for the web, File Transfer Protocol (FTP), Network News Transfer Protocol (NNTP), and Simple Mail Transfer Protocol (SMTP) for e-mail, IIS is much more than just a web server. Because it is fully integrated at the operating system level, it integrates well with Microsoft .NET applications, and it allows organizations to add Internet capabilities that weave directly into the rest of their infrastructure.

As the Internet becomes more prevalent in our daily lives, the infrastructure behind it becomes more complicated, and the knowledge of how to support that infrastructure becomes more valuable. This chapter will introduce you to Windows Server 2003 (WS03) and the features of IIS 6. It also covers the *metabase* (which holds all the configuration information for IIS) and the architecture of IIS 6. Let's get started.

About Windows Server 2003

IIS 6 is the latest version of Microsoft's web server, and it's packaged with Windows Server 2003, which comes in four flavors: Web Server, Standard Server, Enterprise Server, and Datacenter Server.

Web Server is a limited functionality version. It gives you everything you need to run a web server, including network load balancing, but it can't act as a domain controller. It also can't act as a certificate authority and issue certificates. The upside? Lower price.

Standard Server is your garden-variety server operating system. It offers the standard functionality and is the version most people run.

Enterprise Server gives you everything Standard Server does, plus the ability to make a four-node cluster network configuration. In addition, if the hardware supports it, you can add memory while the server is running. Enterprise Server also allows you to cluster servers together for fault tolerance, rather than just balancing traffic across servers. Enterprise Server will also be released in a 64-bit edition.

Datacenter Server, the big dog of the family, supports the most processors and the most RAM, all at a greater cost. It also offers Microsoft's Datacenter support program. Datacenter Server includes support for up to eight-node clusters. Like Enterprise Server, Datacenter Server will be released in a 64-bit edition.

Hardware Support in Windows 2003

The big draw of a more expensive version is its hardware support. The following table details the hardware supported by each version of WS03; as you can see, the more expensive the version, the more memory and processors it can support.

	Web	Standard	Enterprise	Datacenter
Max RAM	2G	4G	32G*	64G*
Max Processors	2	2	8	32

*The Itanium processors support twice the RAM in these versions.

Installing Windows 2003

The installation of WS03 is similar to the installation of previous versions of the OS, and since this is a book about IIS, we won't go into detail about the install. However, here are a few tips to remember about installing WS03:

- **Use NTFS partitioning** Remember to use NTFS partitioning, because an IIS server is typically exposed to the outside world. Even if that's not the case, the server still needs to be secure. Use NTFS on every partition on the IIS server.

- **Separate OS files from data files** Use more than one partition. With Windows 2003, you can create a really big C drive to store everything, but why would you want to? Multiple partitions help you keep everything more organized, and if you do lose your OS partition, your data has a better chance of surviving.

- **Use TCP/IP** Since the Internet is based on TCP/IP (Transmission Control Protocol/Internet Protocol), you must be using TCP/IP as a network protocol for IIS to work.

A Little History

Before we get started installing IIS, let's take a trip down memory lane and cover the history of IIS.

Version 1   IIS 1 was available as an add-on to Windows NT 3.51. It didn't have many features, but it included the standard web, FTP, and gopher services.

Version 2   IIS 2 was included with Windows NT 4. It wasn't tremendously different from IIS 1.

Version 3   IIS was upgraded to version 3 when Service Pack 3 for Windows NT 4 was installed. It included new features, such as Active Server Pages (ASP).

Version 4   IIS 4 was available with the Windows NT 4 Option Pack. It was a major overhaul of IIS, removed the Gopher service, and greatly enhanced the feature set of IIS.

Version 5   IIS 5 was included with Windows 2000 Server. It was not a major upgrade from IIS 4.

Version 6   IIS 6 represents a fundamental shift in the web services product offering from Microsoft. While the FTP, SMTP, and Network News Transfer Protocol (NNTP) services are not extremely different, the web server component of IIS 6 has a new focus on security and fundamental changes in the way it behaves at its core.

Installing IIS

In Windows 2000 Server, IIS was part of a default installation. However, in WS03, you must install IIS manually. With Microsoft's new mindset of "off by default," IIS is no longer part of a default installation.

Here's how to install IIS:

1. In the Control Panel, click Add Or Remove Programs to open the Add Or Remove Programs dialog box.

2. Click the Add/Remove Windows Components icon on the left. The Windows Components Wizard will pop up.

3. Click Application Server, and then click the Details button.

4. The IIS components are located in the Internet Information Services area.

If you click the IIS checkbox, only the default components will be installed. To install optional components (subcomponents), you must select them manually.

The IIS Subcomponents

As indicated in step 3 in the preceding section, you'll click Details to see the subcomponents of IIS, which are shown in Figure 1-1.

Choose all the subcomponents you want to install, and then click OK three times to get back to the main Windows Components screen. When you click Next, you may be prompted for the Windows 2003 CD, if it's not already in the drive.

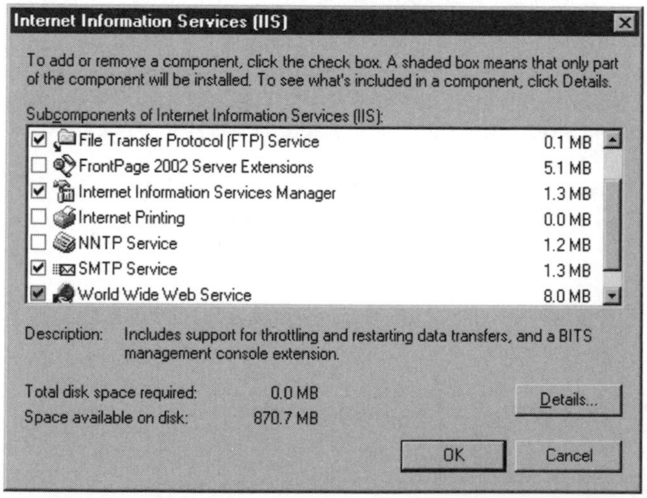

Figure 1-1. *Subcomponents of IIS*

Background Intelligent Transfer Service (BITS) Server Extensions

The BITS Server Extensions contains two components: an Internet Server Application Programming Interface (ISAPI) filter to allow BITS uploads, and the server extensions snap-in.

Note *An ISAPI filter is basically a dynamic link library (DLL) that gets first crack at incoming Hypertext Transfer Protocol (HTTP) code. ISAPI technology is covered in detail in Chapter 17.*

BITS allows files to be transferred in the background so as not to interrupt any active users on a system. File transfers are throttled to limit their bandwidth use. If a file is interrupted because of a broken connection, it will continue transferring when the connection is reestablished. When the file is completely transferred, the application requesting that file is notified.

BITS is installed with Windows 2003 and Windows XP, and it is available as an add-on for Windows 2000.

Common Files

You must install this component or IIS won't work.

File Transfer Protocol (FTP) Service

This component is not installed by default. The FTP service allows for the creation of an FTP server, where users can upload and download files.

FrontPage 2002 Server Extensions

Selecting this component installs the software necessary for users to upload their web sites to the server directly through Microsoft FrontPage or Visual InterDev. This allows web page authors a greater degree of control on your web server, and installing it can also be considered a security risk.

Internet Information Services Manager

This component installs the Microsoft Management Console (MMC) snap-in that allows you to administer IIS. Like Common Files, it's mandatory.

Internet Printing

This component installs the options that allow you to configure and share printers over HTTP. This option is the same as the Windows 2000 Server web printing options. In WS03, it is now an optional service.

NNTP Service

This component installs the News Server, which allows the creation of newsgroups.

SMTP Service

This installs the SMTP Service, which allows the IIS server to send e-mail. It's useful for those web sites that let visitors send e-mail.

World Wide Web Service

The World Wide Web Service is the one you've been looking for. It provides HTTP services and comprises several subcomponents.

Active Server Pages   The Active Server Pages subcomponent installs the ASP DLL and other files that support ASP for your web server. This option is always installed, although it is disabled by default.

Internet Data Connector   Internet Data Connector (IDC) allows for database connectivity in your web site. This option is always installed.

Remote Administration (HTML)   Installing this option enables you to administer IIS remotely through a web browser. This is different from the previous HTML administration options for IIS, with which you could administer only the same server.

Remote Desktop Web Connection   This installs the ActiveX control that allows Internet Explorer web browsers to connect to a terminal server session using the pages provided. This was available in Windows 2000 as the Terminal Services Advanced Client.

Server Side Includes   This provides support for server-side includes and is always installed.

WebDAV Publishing   WebDAV stands for Web-based Distributed Authoring and Versioning. It is a set of extensions to HTTP that allows users to access and manage files on WebDAV published directories on your web server. It is always installed.

World Wide Web Service   This component installs the core WWW service application. Without this, many IIS components won't function.

IIS Services

Several services run to support IIS; each is listed in the services control panel for WS03. The services that appear depend on which components of IIS are installed. If a component isn't installed, the associated service will not appear in the services control panel.

IIS Admin Service   This is the main administration service for IIS. All the other services depend on this service, so if this service is stopped, all other IIS services will stop as well.

FTP Publishing   This is the service behind the FTP server component of IIS.

World Wide Web Publishing   This is the service behind the web server component of IIS.

Simple Mail Transfer Protocol (SMTP)   This is the service behind the SMTP server component of IIS.

Network News Transfer Protocol (NNTP)   This is the service behind the NNTP server component of IIS.

HTTP SSL   This is the service that enables the WWW Publishing service to perform SSL (Secure Socket Layer) certificate functions. The WWW Publishing service depends on this service.

| Tip |
Service dependencies allow services to be linked so that a service that needs another service won't be started without its partner. Dependencies can be viewed in the Dependencies tab of the Properties window for a service.

The IIS Directory Structure

The core components of IIS are stored at *%systemroot%\System32\inetsrv*. The directory structure under *inetsrv* is shown in the following table:

Directory	Explanation
ASP Compiled Templates	If you use an ASP template for your site, it is stored here.
History	The history folder for the metabase changes, which allows you to roll back the metabase.
iisadmpwd	Contains ASP pages dealing with IIS Admin authentication.
MetaBack	The default directory for metabase backups.

| Note |
For more information on the metabase, see the section "The Metabase" later in this chapter.

The Administration Web Site

In IIS 6, the administration web site allows you to administer your entire Windows server from a local or remote web browser. The administration web site is located at *%systemroot%\System32\ServerAppliance*. It runs over SSL on port 8098, by default. To access the administration web site, type in **https://*machinename*:8098** (where *machinename* stands for the name of the machine you wish to administer) in your web browser's address line.

IIS Help Files

All the help files in IIS 6 have been moved to a central location, along with all other Windows help files. They are located at *%systemroot%\help\iishelp*. The best way to access IIS help is to choose Help | Help Topics in the MMC.

The Inetpub Directory

The *Inetpub* directory is the main content directory of IIS. Under *Inetpub* are all the content directories for each service installed. The default path for the *Inetpub* directory is *C:\Inetpub*.

The content directories under *Inetpub* are shown in the following table:

Directory	Description
AdminScripts	Contains some Visual Basic scripts for use in administering your IIS server
ftproot	The top level directory for the FTP service
mailroot	The top level directory for the SMTP service
nntpfile	The top level directory for the NNTP service
wwwroot	The top level directory for the default web site

Accounts Used by IIS

Because everything in WS03 has to run within a security context, and an account is required for access, IIS installs two accounts and one group to your account database for its use. These allow IIS to run code and worker processes and allows people to access your site. These accounts and group are discussed next.

IUSR_COMPUTERNAME

This user account grants anonymous access to a web site when a user connects to a web page without any security information of his or her own. This user is not a member of any group other than Guests, by default.

IWAM_COMPUTERNAME

This user account is used to launch worker processes. It is a member of the IIS_WPG group.

IIS_WPG

The members of this group can run worker processes. Any user account that runs worker processes needs to be a member of this group. This is a low security account that has the rights of Network Service. Processes using the Network Service level of rights can access the server as though they were running from outside the server, so they don't have direct access to the operating system.

You can view these in the Computer Management MMC, in the Administrative Tools group. Here's how to open Users and Groups:

1. At the Start menu, click Administrative Tools and then Computer Management.

2. In the Computer Management MMC, users and groups are listed separately under Local Users and Groups.

3. However, if this computer is a *domain controller*, users and groups are located in the Active Directory Users And Computers under Administrative Tools.

Navigating IIS

IIS is managed through an MMC snap-in. The MMC is a framework that allows for a common look and feel across applications. IIS 6 is managed by, simply enough, the IIS snap-in. The IIS MMC is located under Administrative Tools in the Start menu.

The Microsoft Management Console

The IIS Manager snap-in (or MMC), shown in Figure 1-2, allows you to manage all the FTP sites, application pools, web sites, SMTP virtual servers, and NNTP virtual servers on this machine or any other machine to which you connect. By default, you are connected to the local computer: if you right-click your local computer and choose Connect, you can choose to connect to and manage another computer.

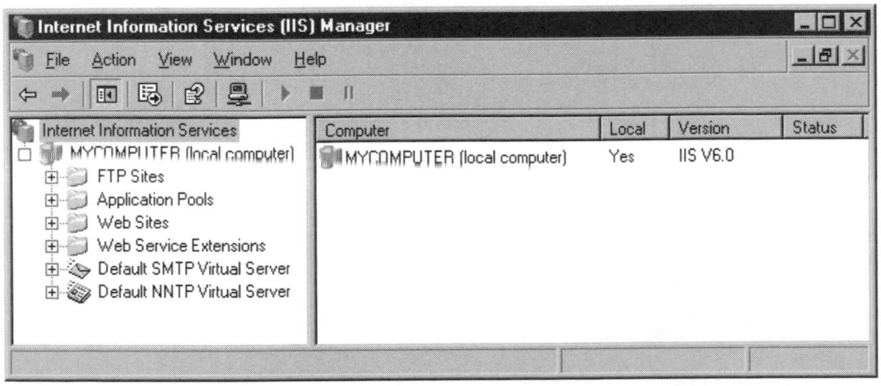

Figure 1-2.   *The IIS Manager snap-in*

Managing a Site with the MMC

Across the top of the IIS Manager is a toolbar that allows you to perform basic functions on your site. Above the toolbar, the menu bar contains all the management commands. It's important that you understand that the MMC is a separate program from IIS, and that not all the options here deal with IIS. They may configure portions of the MMC instead. The toolbar and menu bars will change, depending on what is selected in the left pane of the IIS Manager window.

Typically, the easiest way to manage a component is to use the shortcut menu that appears when you right-click a component. All valid administration commands are listed on this menu. Most of the configuration options are listed under the Properties command.

Local Computer Properties The properties for the local computer allow you to change the options that globally affect all components of IIS. To access the local computer properties, right-click *computername* (Local Computer) in the IIS MMC, and then choose Properties. You'll see the Properties window shown in Figure 1-3.

Changing something here requires that IIS be restarted after you make the change. Two options affect IIS as a whole: Enable Direct Metabase Edit and Encode Web Logs In UTF-8.

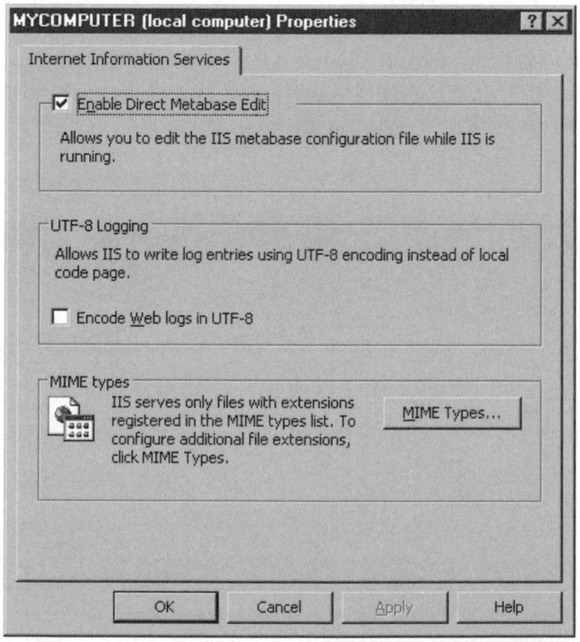

Figure 1-3. *Local computer Properties window*

The Enable Direct Metabase Edit option allows you to edit the metabase while IIS is running. In previous IIS versions, the metabase was a binary file that could be accessed only with a resource kit utility. Now, as an XML (eXtensible Markup Language) file, you can edit the metabase with Notepad. You can cut and paste the configuration, save, and it will take effect immediately. This does require the metabase history to be enabled, but since that's the default, it shouldn't be a problem.

The Encode Web Logs In UTF-8 option sets the web and/or FTP logs to log in the UTF-8 standard rather than in the local character set. *UTF-8* is a standard for encoding text with 8-bit encoding of Unicode characters. One to six octets are used to represent each character. UTF-8 uses a universal character set and preserves the ASCII text for backward compatibility.

The Metabase

The metabase is roughly equivalent to the registry for IIS: it holds all the configuration information for IIS. In previous versions, the metabase was a binary file that could be edited only by the metabase editor, part of the resource kit. In IIS 6, the metabase is a good old XML text file (as shown in Figure 1-4) that can be edited with Notepad. Even though the metabase in IIS 6 is completely different, it is still completely compatible with the IIS 5 metabase, so all the same APIs and scripts still work.

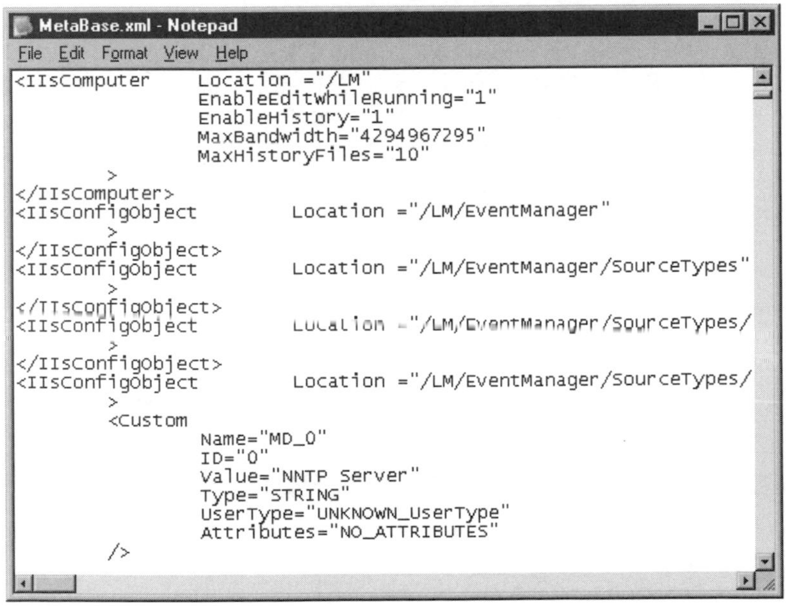

Figure 1-4. *View of a metabase file*

The metabase is stored in *%systemroot%\system32\inetsrv* and is called, appropriately enough, *MetaBase.xml*. The schema for the metabase is called *MBSchema.xml*. Because the metabase is a text file, it can easily be edited with any text editor, and it is less likely to be corrupted. Even if the metabase does experience corruption, it can easily be fixed or recovered.

Metabase History

The metabase is backed up and "versioned" periodically by IIS. Two version numbers are used for the metabase: a major version number and a minor version number. The name of the backup files are *MetaBase_[10 digit major version number]_[10 digit minor version number].xml* and *MBSchema_[10 digit major version number]_[10 digit minor version number].xml* (for example, *MBSchema_0000000160_0000000000.xml*).

By default, ten copies of the metabase files are stored. This allows the metabase to be rolled back to any of these previous versions. The number of metabase versions kept is configurable by editing the `MaxHistoryFiles` property in the metabase. As a general rule, you shouldn't configure less that ten copies of the metabase history to be kept. Each time the metabase is saved, a backup copy of the metabase and corresponding schema are made in the *history* folder. IIS checks to see how many history file pairs are present, and if more files are present than the value of `MaxHistoryFiles`, IIS deletes the oldest pair.

History Folder Location

By default, the *history* folder is located at *%systemroot%\system32\inetsrv\history*. This is configurable by changing the registry key under *HKEY_LOCAL_MACHINE\Software\Microsoft\InetMGR\Parameters*. Add a new string value named `MetadataFile`. The value of the `MetadataFile` key should be the absolute pathname of the location to which you want to store the metabase files (for example: *D:\IISMetadata\ThisIsMyMetabase.xml*).

Caution *As always, editing the registry is a dangerous thing, and the usual warnings apply. Be very, very careful.*

When you change the location of the metabase files, make sure all the metabase files are moved to the new location, or else when IIS starts up, it will create the default metabase in the new location. The changes to the metabase location will not take effect until the IIS Admin and World Wide Web Publishing service are restarted.

Backing Up and Restoring the Metabase

While you can use history files to restore metabase configuration files, performing a backup of the metabase has some advantages. For one, metabase history files can be used only on the computer on which they were created, while backups can be restored to another computer. The metabase can be backed up on demand through the IIS MMC.

The metabase can be fully backed up and restored using the Backup/Restore Configuration option in the IIS MMC. To access it, highlight the computer in IIS, and choose Action | All Tasks | Backup/Restore Configuration.

From the Configuration Backup/Restore dialog box shown in Figure 1-5, you can choose to back up, restore, or delete a metabase backup. All the metabase backups appear here.

The Backup Option

When you create a backup, you must specify a backup name. The backup file is located in *%systemroot%\System32\Inetsrv\MetaBack*. The metabase has a *.MD0* extension, and the schema has a *.SC0* extension. Each backup with the same name will increment the number in the extension to preserve the previous backup. The password option encrypts the backup with the password you specify. It can be decrypted only with the same password. This allows a web site to be moved from one computer to another, while keeping the metabase secure.

Caution *Moving the metabase to another computer works well only if the drive configuration is the same on the new computer. Because pathnames are stored in the metabase, if your content is on a different drive, the web site won't work properly. Extra care must also be taken if the site has an SSL certificate.*

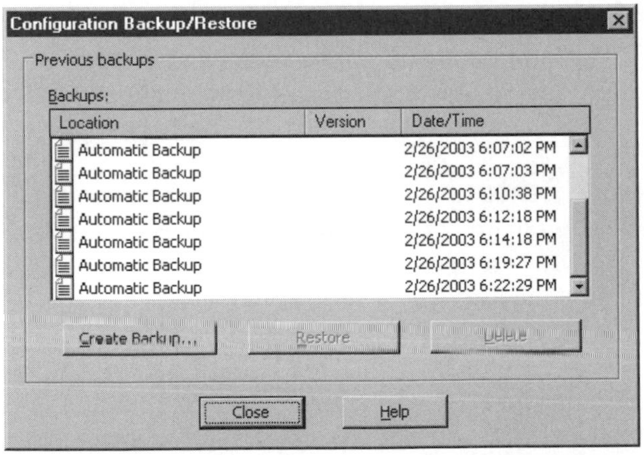

Figure 1-5. *Backup/restore configuration*

The Restore Option

To restore a configuration, choose that configuration, and then click the Restore button. When you click Restore, a warning will pop up, informing you that all your settings will be wiped out (they'll be restored to the saved configuration) and that all the services will be stopped and restarted. This action is not to be undertaken on a whim.

The Delete Option

To delete a metabase backup, choose the backup and click Delete. You will be asked if you are sure you want to delete, and if you say Yes, the backup is deleted.

Metabase Snapshots

Another way to back up the metabase is to use Windows Backup Utility. The Backup Utility uses the Metabase Snapshot Writer automatically to make sure the *MetaBase.xml* and *MBSchema.xml* files are successfully backed up.When the Backup Utility detects that the drive to be backed up contains the metabase, it writes the in-memory metabase to the files and prevents anything from being added to the in-memory metabase for up to two minutes.

> **Tip**   *The Metabase Snapshot Writer is not used during Backup Utility restores. If you are going to restore the metabase files, make sure that you stop the IIS services first, so you don't risk data loss.*

Editing the Metabase

When the Enable Direct Metabase Edit option is enabled in the Properties window (see Figure 1-3), you can use a few different methods to modify the metabase while IIS is running.

Notepad or Text Editor

A favorite for those of you who like doing things by hand, a text editor can be used to edit the metabase directly. Just open the *MetaBase.xml* file, make the changes, and save. They'll take effect immediately.

IIS WMI Provider

Microsoft has a new push for all its programs to be accessible to Windows Management Instrumentation (WMI). So you should be able to use WMI to access the same configuration items you could through the user interface. WMI edits the saved copy of the metabase on the disk.

IIS ADSI Provider

ADSI, the Active Directory Scripting Interface, edits the copy of the metabase in memory. ADSI creates an instance of the metabase object that you can manipulate programmatically.

Editing the metabase is explained in further detail and some examples are given in Chapter 9.

The Metabase Schema

The metabase *schema* is loaded into memory with the metabase when IIS initializes. It contains the definitions for all the properties that can be written to the keys in the metabase. The schema also enforces these definitions to a certain extent. As long as a property is written as an in-schema property, it works because it has been defined. This can be overridden by using a custom property in the *MetaBase.xml* file, which is essentially creating your own definition for a property. The goal here is to define all the properties used, rather than limiting you to a certain few variables. While editing the metabase isn't difficult, editing the metabase schema isn't recommended.

IIS 6 Architecture

If you've worked with previous versions of IIS, you'll notice some significant improvements with IIS 6. Version 6 is designed to be much more stable and secure than previous versions. As you're going through this information, keep in mind that this is referring to the web server component of IIS. In IIS 6, FTP, SMTP, and NNTP still run in the *inetinfo.exe* process.

Previously in IIS (see Figure 1-6), everything ran in the *inetinfo.exe* process or *out of process* in *dllhost.exe*. An errant web site running in *inetinfo.exe* could take down the entire web service, causing an outage. IIS 6 separates web-server code from application-handling code with a kernel-mode HTTP listener, *http.sys*, and the Web Administration

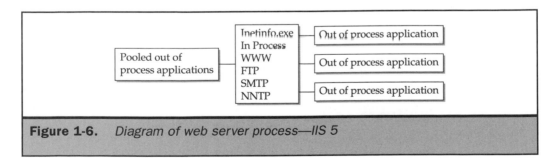

Figure 1-6. *Diagram of web server process—IIS 5*

Service (WAS), which is a user-mode configuration and process manager (see Figure 1-7). These programs don't run any third-party code, so they can't be affected by an errant web site. The code is run in a worker process. These worker processes are run by the application *w3wp.exe*. Each copy of *w3wp.exe* is another worker process. These worker processes are separate from each other and from the kernel so that they can be isolated from the operating system.

Tip	In process *refers to code that runs in the same process as the parent.* Out of process *refers to code that is run in a separate process.*

Worker Process Isolation Mode

The IIS 6 web service runs all application code in an isolated environment. This is called Worker Process Isolation Mode. This type of functionality was previously available in IIS, but it inflicted a significant performance penalty. Since everything in IIS 6 is run out of process by design, there is no performance hit. Previous versions of IIS also relied on user mode processes to route requests to each other. In IIS 6, requests are pulled directly from the kernel, completely isolating worker processes from each other. This helps when two applications need to be isolated from each other for security reasons. For now, other IIS services (such as FTP and SMTP) still run in *inetinfo*, just as in IIS 5. Perhaps the next version will introduce worker process isolation for these services, but at the present time, they do have the ability to affect the *inetinfo* process.

IIS 5.0 Isolation Mode

Sometimes, worker process isolation can cause issues with applications that need to access data across instances or perform in an IIS 5 application pool environment. In this case, IIS can switch to what's called *IIS 5 isolation mode*. This mode operates like IIS 5 and allows these applications to perform in the IIS 5 application pool environment, while still allowing the kernel mode *http.sys* to queue and cache requests.

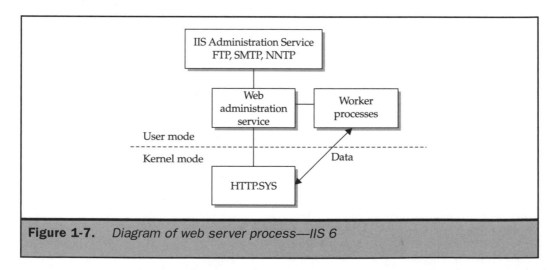

Figure 1-7.   *Diagram of web server process—IIS 6*

Most web sites will work just fine under IIS 6, but a few events would force you to use isolation mode and abandon worker process recycling:

- Multi-instance ISAPIs that are written to be used multiple times simultaneously by different processes
- Read raw-data filters that would try to grab all the data before it hits a web site
- In-process session state variables, because they are lost every time a worker process is recycled
- Applications that farm out work to their own worker processes

Enabling IIS 5.0 Isolation Mode   Enabling isolation mode must be done at the root level for the *Web Sites* folder in the IIS MMC. This is done for all web sites on this server as a whole—you cannot enable it on a per-web-site basis. Here's how it's done:

1. Open the IIS MMC.
2. Right-click the *Web Sites* folder and choose Properties.
3. Click the Service tab. Note that this tab is available only at this level.
4. Place a check mark in the box to Run WWW Service In IIS 5.0 Isolation Mode.
5. Click OK to return to the IIS MMC.

Application Pools

IIS introduces a whole new way of handling applications. *Application pools* allow code to be run in an isolated environment. Each application pool is serviced by one or more worker process. When IIS starts, the Web Administration Service initializes the *http.sys* namespace routing table with one entry for each application. This routing table determines to which application pool an application should be routed. When *http.sys* receives a request, it asks WAS to start up one or more worker processes to handle that application pool. This isolation of processes makes the web server as a whole more stable.

Health Monitoring

The WAS is able to keep IIS healthy by keeping track of the worker processes and monitoring their health. It can control these processes to keep them from causing IIS to stop responding. WAS keeps track of worker processes by *pinging* them at periodic intervals. If a worker process fails to respond to a *ping*, WAS terminates the process and starts a new one. This enables the system to keep responding to requests, even when a worker process gets hung up. If a process crashes and the worker process hangs, *http.sys* will queue up the requests until WAS starts a new worker process to handle that application pool. The end user will experience a temporary loss of service with applications in that application pool, while the core web services and any other applications will continue to function.

Orphaning Worker Processes

WAS can also be configured to orphan a worker process instead of merely terminating it. This allows the bad worker process to be examined to determine what happened.

WAS can be configured to run a command on the worker process (such as a debugger) when it orphans a worker process. Worker processes can be periodically restarted in addition to being automatically restarted on failure. This allows the system to reduce the effect of memory leaks by periodically reinitializing the environment and returning that memory to the system. When WAS restarts a worker process, it creates a new worker process and tells the existing one to finish what it's doing in a certain time frame and then shut down. This allows the application to stay up, while refreshing the worker processes behind it. If the worker process does not shut down within the allowed time frame, it is terminated.

Worker processes can be restarted based on the following criteria:

- Elapsed time
- Number of requests
- Time of day
- Memory usage
- Idle time
- CPU time used

Scalability

Worker process isolation mode also allows for better scaling of the web server. Thousands of sites can exist on a server with this configuration. Each application pool can be throttled individually, limiting the individual application pool to a certain amount of processor time.

Web Gardens

Multiple worker processes can be set up to handle a single application pool. This is called a *web garden*. Web gardens allow for better multiprocessor scalability, since each worker process can have an affinity for a single processor, to increase the cache hits on that processor. If one worker process gets bogged down, the other ones can take up the slack. It also reduces the need to reboot the server, even when upgrading components, because the application pool can merely be restarted.

The number of requests that should be queued for each application pool can be set in *http.sys* when running in worker process isolation mode. When this limit is reached, new requests to the full application pool are not processed, and the user gets an HTTP 503 error.

Note   *For more details on application pools and these options, see Chapter 2.*

Chapter 2

The WWW Service

The WWW service, the most widely used service in the IIS suite, serves up web pages. This chapter covers the options available for a web site at the site, directory, and file levels. It tells you how to use the WWW service to set up a web site of your own.

Using the IIS MMC

First, you need to get familiar with the IIS Microsoft Management Console (MMC) snap-in. Open the IIS MMC by choosing Start | Administrative Tools | Internet Information Services (IIS) Manager. From the MMC, you can configure all the IIS components you have installed. Web sites are configured through the Web Sites folder in the left pane of the MMC. When you click to expand the Web Sites folder, you'll see a list of all the web sites on this server, and basic information about each site will appear in the right pane, as shown in Figure 2-1.

Web Site Directories

When you click a web site in the left pane of the MMC, a listing of all the files and directories on that site will appear in the right pane. You can navigate in the MMC as you would in Windows Explorer. You can also access the NTFS permissions for a directory here. You cannot, however, configure any of the NTFS permissions for files. The MMC allows you to see what files are available in the configured directories.

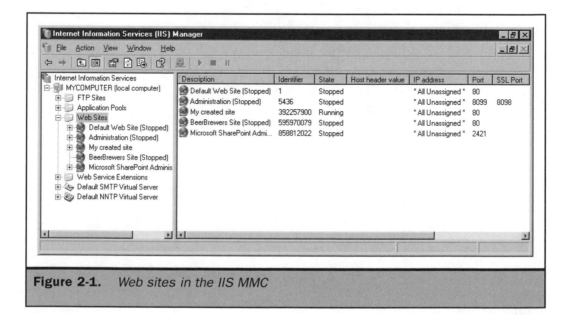

Figure 2-1.   *Web sites in the IIS MMC*

Web Site Identifier

The first site is the Default Web Site. Each site has a randomly generated *identifier* associated with it, and the Default Web Site's identifier is always 1. This identifier is used in the metabase configuration file to reference this site, and any programmatic interfaces—such as Windows Management Instrumentation (WMI) and Active Directory Scripting Interface (ADSI)—will use this same identifier.

Web Site Service Controls

The Windows service that web sites run in is called the World Wide Web Publishing Service. This service controls all the web sites on the server, and if it is stopped, all web sites are stopped. You can also stop, start, and pause individual web sites on a server from the MMC.

To start, stop, or pause a site, you click the site, and then use the toolbar buttons that correspond to the actions you wish to perform. These toolbar buttons look like the play, stop, and pause buttons you see on a VCR or DVD player. The State column in the right pane of the MMC displays whether a site is running, stopped, or paused:

- **Running** The web site is currently enabled.
- **Stopped** This web site is not serving clients and will not respond to requests.
- **Paused** The web site is not accepting new requests. Processes that existed before the web site was paused will conclude, and then end. This is useful if you want to stop the site but not cut off clients abruptly.

Addressing for Sites

Each site that is running needs to have a unique address associated with it. Three types of addressing are available, and only one of the three of the addresses needs to be unique. You can decide which one of the following three is unique:

- Host header value
- IP address
- Port number (not the SSL port; this doesn't count)

We'll cover how to configure these settings in the "Setting up an Address for Your Web Site" section later in this chapter. If you attempt to start a web site that does not have a unique address in one of these three types of addressing, you will receive an error message.

Creating Virtual Directories

In addition to physical directories, you can also configure a virtual directory in the MMC. Virtual directories allow you to point a client to another directory, Uniform Resource Locator (URL), or even a share on another machine, and the directory appears to the client to be just another directory.

Creating a virtual directory is a straightforward process:

1. Open the IIS MMC by choosing Start | Administrative Tools | Internet Information Services (IIS) Manager.

2. In the left pane of the IIS MMC, highlight the web site or directory under which you want the virtual directory to be created.

3. Choose Action | New | Virtual Directory.

4. The Virtual Directory Creation Wizard will open. Click Next.

5. In the Virtual Directory Alias dialog box, type in the alias, or name, that you want to use for this virtual directory. This is the name clients will use when accessing this directory. Click Next.

6. In the Web Site Content Directory dialog box, type in or browse to the path that you want to use for this site. If you want to redirect to a URL, choose any path here—you can change it later if you need to. Click Next.

7. In the Virtual Directory Access Permissions dialog box, choose the level of permissions you wish to enable for this virtual directory. Your choices are Read, Run Scripts, Execute, Write, and Browse. Click Next.

8. Click Finish to exit the wizard.

Saving a Web Site Configuration to a File

When you have configured a web site the way you want it, you can save that web site's configuration to a file. The file is a metabase XML (eXtensible Markup Language) configuration file. By saving, you can create other sites just like this one on other servers without having to reconfigure all the options. You can also save virtual directories, File Transfer Protocol (FTP) sites, and application pools.

1. In the IIS MMC, highlight the site that you want to save.

2. Choose Action | All Tasks | Save Configuration To A File.

3. In the Save Configuration To A File dialog box, type in the name of the file you wish to use.

4. Type in or browse (by clicking the Browse button) to the location to which you wish to save this configuration.

5. Choose whether or not you want to encrypt the export file. Since this is an XML metabase file, information may be included here that you don't want others to see or access, so encryption might be a good idea.

6. If you choose to encrypt the configuration, choose a password to protect the encrypted contents.

7. Click OK.

Creating a New Site

You can create many sites on a server, as long as each site is unique. To create a new site, you can use the Web Site Creation Wizard or use a file you've saved from another site. Here's how to create a site using the Web Site Creation Wizard:

1. Highlight Web Sites in the left pane of the MMC.
2. Choose Action | New | Web Site.
3. In the Web Site Creation Wizard, click Next.
4. Type in the description of the site you want to create. This should be a friendly name (a descriptive name that means something to you) so that you can easily identify the site in the MMC.
5. Enter the IP Address, TCP Port, and (optionally) the Host Header Name for this site. The value (All Unassigned) will configure this site to use any IP address that is not specifically used by another site. Only one (All Unassigned) site can be running on a Transmission Control Protocol (TCP) port at one time.
6. Click Next.
7. Type in or browse to the directory you want to use for this site. (You should have created this directory ahead of time; you can't do it from here.)
8. Check whether or not you want to allow anonymous access to your site. Click Next.
9. Choose the level of permissions you wish to enable for this web site. Your choices are Read, Run Scripts, Execute, Write, and Browse.
10. Click Next, and then click Finish to exit the wizard.

If the site has an addressing conflict with another site, you will still be allowed to create the site, but it will not start.

Here's how to create a site using a file:

1. Highlight Web Sites in the MMC left pane.
2. Choose Action | New | Web Site (From File).
3. In the Import Configuration dialog box, type in or browse to the file that contains the configuration you wish to use.
4. Click Read File to see the configuration for that file. The configuration description will appear in the Location section below.
5. In the Location section, highlight the configuration you wish to import, and then click OK.
6. If this site already exists, you will be prompted to create a new site or replace the existing one.

7. If you choose to create a new site, it will have the same name and configuration, but a different Identifier number.

8. Click OK to create the site and exit.

Accessing Configuration Tabs

To access properties and configuration tabs for global web sites, web sites, directories, or files shown in the left pane of the MMC, right-click the object in the left pane, and then choose Properties. You'll see a Properties window appear.

Configuration tabs are located in the Properties window for each of these hierarchies. This chapter steps through the tabs found at each hierarchical level, starting with the web site level, since that's the level that has most of the tabs in it, and the one you generally use most.

The Web Site Properties Tabs

To access the Properties window for a particular web site, right-click the web site name in the left pane of the MMC and choose Properties. The following tabs display information that appears when the BeerBrewers Site properties are accessed.

Web Site Tab

When you open the Properties window for any web site, the Web Site tab opens by default, as shown in Figure 2-2. Here you can set the Internet Protocol (IP) address and port information for the site, as well as configure connection timeouts and logging.

The following options are configurable on this tab.

Creating a Description

What you enter in the Description field shows up in the Description column of the IIS MMC. Here, you can distinguish the web site by typing in a descriptive name. This name is not visible to users of the web site.

Setting up an Address for Your Web Site

Each web site must have a unique address to which traffic associated with that site is sent. You can differentiate your web site from others in three ways: via IP address, TCP port, and host header name. From an addressing perspective, any combination of these can be used to differentiate your site, but at least one of them must be unique for the machine on which the site is located.

IP Address   The IP Address editable drop-down box lets you set the primary IP address for this web site. You may either choose an IP address from the drop-drop box or type in one. Choosing (All Unassigned) allows this web site to respond to any IP address on the machine that is not being used by another web site.

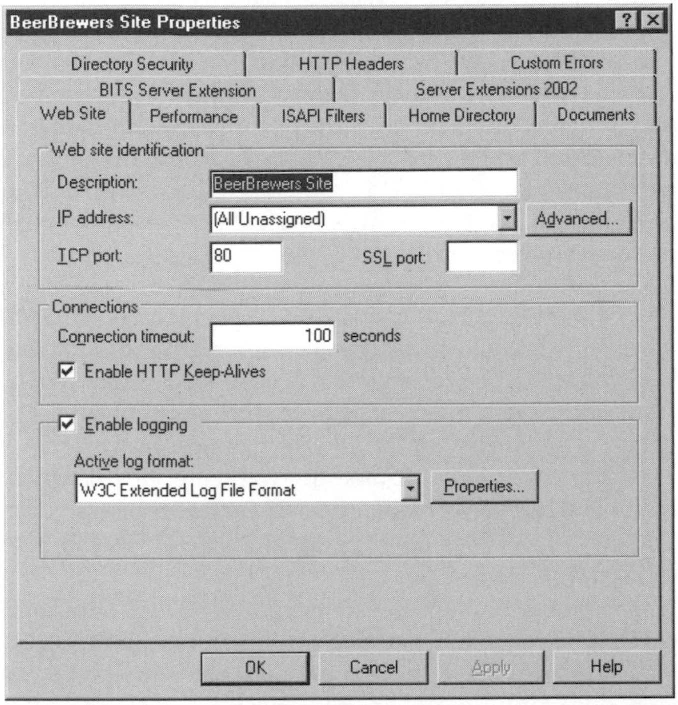

Figure 2-2. *The Web Site tab*

Tip *When you are typing in an IP address manually, the system does not check to see whether this IP address is already assigned on the system. It checks only that the IP address as typed is a valid, real IP and that the address is not being used on another web site. As long as an address is a valid IP address and is not defined on another web site, you can type in any IP you want here. Therefore, it's possible to type in an IP address that is not even available to the machine. Keep this in mind when you're troubleshooting connection issues.*

TCP Port   In the TCP Port field, you set the port number on which this web site will listen. You can choose any port that is not being used by another service. While IIS will not stop you from choosing a port that's already in use, communications problems with that other service will occur when you try to use the port.

For example, you can set a web site to use port 25, which conflicts with the Simple Mail Transfer Protocol (SMTP) service that's running on the same box and using the same port. When a packet comes in for port 25, the machine won't know which service gets that packet. Most likely, since the SMTP service was there first, it would receive the web request and would not know what to do with it. Make sure that if you choose a port other than 80, it is not being used by another service.

By default, web browsers always look for port 80 if no port is specified in the address field in the browser window. If you change the port to something other than 80, clients will need to add the port number after the URL so that the browser knows to ask for the web server at that port. For example, if you changed your web site to listen on port 1500, clients would have to type in **http://www.beerbrewers.com:1500** instead of just **http://www.beerbrewers.com** to get to your web site.

SSL Port   In the SSL Port field, you choose which port the Secure Sockets Layer will listen on for this web site. SSL allows you to encrypt and/or authenticate data as it travels between the client and the server—this is described in detail in Chapter 10.

As with the TCP port, if you change this from the default of 443, clients will need to type in the port number along with the URL to access your web site. If you changed the port to 1543, for example, clients would have to type in **https://www.beerbrewers .com:1543**, instead of just **https://www.beerbrewers.com**, to access your web site.

Advanced Button

Clicking the Advanced button opens the Advanced Web Site Configuration page, where you can set up multiple addresses and multiple identities for this web site. Multiple identities allow your site to have more than one address so that people can access the site using one of multiple addresses. This is a useful feature if you want to point people typing in the URL for one web site to another site on the same machine, and you don't want to use Domain Name System (DNS). (You can read more about DNS in Chapter 8.) In this page, you can also enter host header names for this web site, so you can use the same IP address and port for multiple web sites.

About Host Headers   Host headers let you differentiate one of your web site addresses from another. Basically, host header names allow you to configure different web sites on the same IP address and port. A host header is the full DNS name that's typed into the browser's address bar to access this site. Host headers are extremely handy when you want to use the same IP address for all your web sites to conserve address space, or when you have only one IP address to use. When an Hypertext Transfer Protocol (HTTP) 1.1 web browser requests a web page, the first part of the request looks like this:

```
GET./.HTTP/1.1
Accept:.image/gif,.image/x-
xbitmap,.image/jpeg,.image/pjpeg,.application/vnd.ms-
powerpoint,.application/vnd.ms-excel,.application/msword,.*/*
Accept-Language:.en-us..Accept-Encoding:.gzip,.deflate..
Use61 r-agent:.Mozilla/4.0.(compatible;.MSIE.6.0;.Windows.NT.5.2)
Host: www.mywebsite.com
```

The part after *Host* is the host header name—*www.mywebsite.com*. IIS will use this header to send the message to the appropriate web site, based on that name.

Host header names were introduced in the HTTP 1.1 protocol, and all browsers that are HTTP 1.1–compliant can use them. Older browsers don't pass the host header, so they will always reach the default web site for any IP address.

Tip *If you want to provide support for older browsers, you can make the default page for that IP address include a list of all the web sites and use cookies to direct people to those web sites. Because every release of Internet Explorer after version 3 and every Netscape version after 2 supports host headers, I won't go into detail about how to do this. The Microsoft web site offers documentation that explains how to accomplish this.*

Note *Because host header names are part of the HTTP 1.1 protocol, you can't use host headers on FTP, mail, or news sites in IIS. If you want to use multiple sites on the same server, you'll have to get multiple IP addresses or use different ports. Host headers are also not available on your web page when you use SSL, since the header is in the encrypted request.*

Adding Another Identity   A web site has the ability to have multiple addresses associated with it. It will respond to requests on any and all of these addresses. Each address that is identified with this web site is called an *identity*. To add another identity to the web site, click the Add button in the Web Site Identification section on the Web Site tab. The Advanced Web Site Identification dialog box, as shown in Figure 2-3, will open.

Each identity must use one of the three addresses (IP address, TCP port, or Host header value) to be unique; otherwise, you can type in any legal IP addresses, port, or host header name. As with the IP Address field of the Web Site tab, the system does not check to see whether the address you are typing is in use on that machine, so you can type in anything that is legal—though it may not be useful if the machine can't find the site at that address.

Removing Identities   To remove an identity, highlight that identity and click Remove. You will not be allowed to remove all the identities for the site on this page. (Technically, you can remove them all, but the OK button will then be disabled.)

Editing Identities   To edit an identity, highlight that identity and click Edit. You can then modify the properties for that identity.

Assigning Multiple SSL Identities   You can also assign multiple SSL identities to your web site. Because host headers don't exist in SSL, you may edit only the IP address and port number. If you don't have a certificate installed on this site, all the options for SSL identities will be disabled.

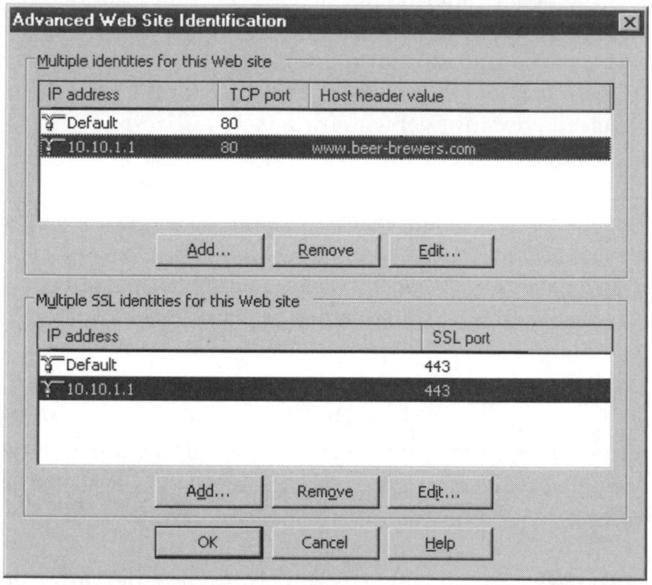

Figure 2-3.   *The Advanced Web Site Identification dialog box*

Adding Multiple SSL Identities   To add another SSL identity to this web site, click the Add button. You can add multiple identities; just remember that SSL certificates are based on the name of the site, not the IP address. Any IP address you type in must be resolvable through a DNS name. If you try to access the site through the IP address, it will be unavailable.

Removing SSL Identities   To remove an SSL identity from this web site, highlight it and click the Remove button. You cannot remove all the SSL identities from a site.

Editing SSL Identities   To edit an SSL identity for this web site, highlight it and click the Edit button. You can then modify the properties for that identity.

Connection Timeout

The Connection Timeout setting, back in the Web Site tab, lets you configure how long, in seconds, the server will keep open a connection for a client. Normally, the web browser will ask the server to keep a connection open for the client. This is called an HTTP *keep-alive*. The client can use this connection for multiple requests of elements, and the client and server don't have to go through all the overhead of establishing a connection for each request. This greatly enhances performance for both the client and the server, especially over high-latency connections. When the client is done with its requests, it lets the server know to close this connection and free up those resources.

If, for some reason, the client fails to close the connection, the connection will stay open indefinitely, unless the server knows to close it. This Connection Timeout value controls that time interval.

Enable HTTP Keep-Alives

The Enable HTTP Keep-Alives box is checked by default. This lets the server know to accept HTTP keep-alive requests from clients. If this box is not checked, performance on both the client and the server will be degraded.

Enable Logging

By default, logging is enabled on web sites. The default log type is the W3C Extended Log File Format. If you wish to disable logging or change the type of logging for this site, you can do that here. Logging is covered in more detail in Chapter 11.

The Performance Tab

On the Performance tab of the Web Site Properties window, shown in Figure 2-4, you can configure bandwidth throttling and the number of connections this site will accept.

Bandwidth Throttling

The Bandwidth Throttling setting lets you configure the maximum amount of bandwidth the machine can devote to this web site, in kilobytes per second. For bandwidth throttling to function, IIS needs to install the Windows Packet Scheduler, a Quality Of Service (QOS) application that determines whether a packet can be sent on the network. It queues up data and sends it across the network at a specified rate. IIS will automatically install the Windows Packet Scheduler when you click OK after you set up a maximum bandwidth.

When you configure this setting, it's important that you keep in mind that although your LAN connection may be 10, 100, or 1000 Megabits per second (Mbps), typical Internet speeds are much slower. For example, a full T1 line is 1.544 Mbps. If you take the default setting of 1024 (that's kilobytes, folks), that's much more than the speed of your T1 line.

| **Note** | *A byte is 8 bits. A kilobyte is 8192 bits.* |

Web Site Connections

The Web Site Connections radio buttons allow you to configure the number of client connections allowed on this site. The default is Unlimited. If you choose Connections Limited To, you can enter in any number between 0 and 2,000,000,000.

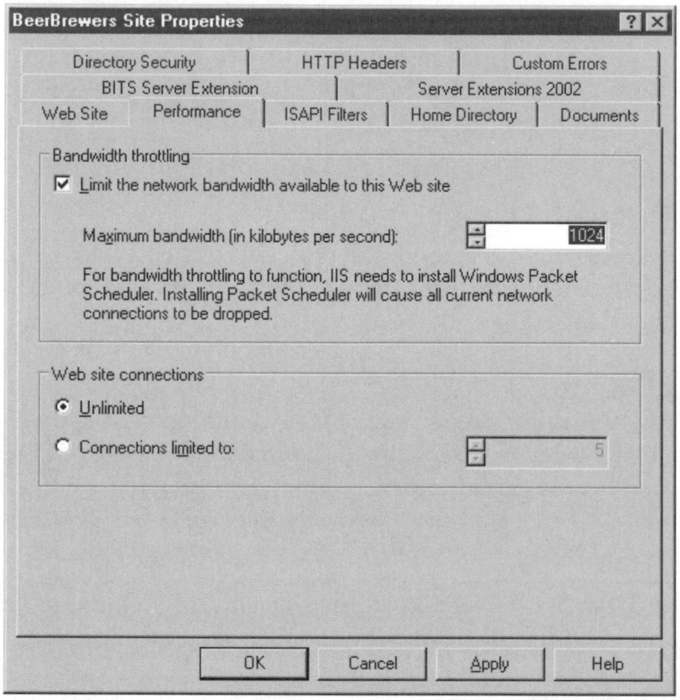

Figure 2-4.   *The Performance tab*

The ISAPI Filters Tab

The ISAPI Filters tab, shown in Figure 2-5, is where you add Internet Server Application Programming Interface (ISAPI) filters for this web site. All HTTP traffic to this site will be directed to these ISAPI filters in the order designated here. While an ISAPI extension applies to just the extension for which it's mapped, an ISAPI filter applies to all the traffic on this site. This can result in huge performance hits to your site, especially if the ISAPI filter isn't properly written and has memory leaks. (For more about ISAPI technology, see Chapter 17.)

Each ISAPI filter has a status. A red down arrow means that the filter is currently disabled. A green up arrow means that the filter is currently enabled.

Adding an ISAPI Filter

To add an ISAPI filter, click the Add button. Name the filter, and then choose the executable through which the traffic is to be filtered. The filter name is a friendly name.

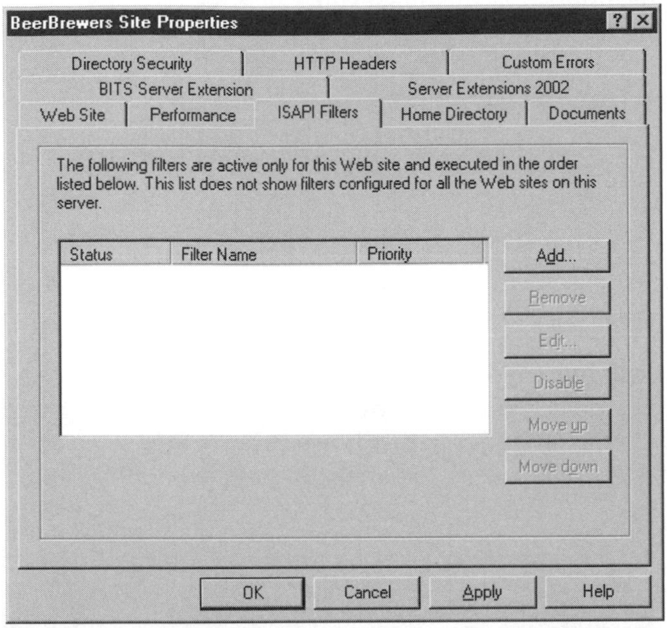

Figure 2-5.   *The ISAPI Filters tab*

Deleting an ISAPI Filter

To delete an ISAPI filter, highlight the filter and click the Remove button.

Editing an ISAPI Filter

To edit an ISAPI filter, highlight the filter and click the Edit button. Note that you may only edit the executable to which the filter is pointing. You may not change the name of the filter.

Enabling/Disabling an ISAPI Filter

If a filter is currently active, you may disable it by highlighting it and clicking the Disable button. If a filter is currently inactive, you may enable it by highlighting it and clicking the Enable button. Disabling a filter allows you to take it out of service without deleting the filter from the list.

Changing the Execution Order

ISAPI filters are executed in order. If multiple filters are used, you will most likely want them to be applied to data in a particular order. You can determine that here. To make a filter higher in the priority list, highlight it and click the Move Up button. To make a filter lower on the priority list, highlight it and click the Move Down button.

The Home Directory Tab

In the Home Directory tab, shown in Figure 2-6, you configure where this site points to and how it handles data.

Pointing IIS to the Content Location

To tell IIS where to get content, you must choose the appropriate radio button where the data is located.

A Directory Located on This Computer   Choose this radio button, and the Local Path text box below it lets you type in any local drive and directory where the content for this site is located. You can click the Browse button to browse to the directory where the content is located, or you can type the path in the box.

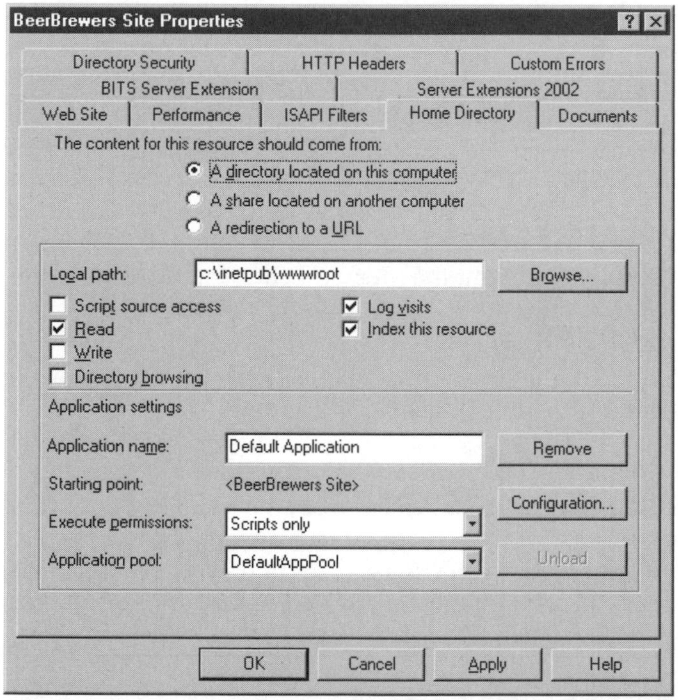

Figure 2-6.   *The Home Directory tab*

A Share Located on Another Computer   When you choose this radio button, the text displayed in the Home Directory tab changes, and the Local Path text box changes to be a Network Directory text box. The Browse button also changes to become a Connect As button. Type in the path using the Universal Naming Convention (UNC) path name (*servername**sharename*). Click the Connect As button that appears to enter a username and password that IIS will use to connect to this share in the Network Directory Security Credentials dialog box. This is necessary because when the server is logged off, it does not have a token to be able to access shared network resources. This username/password allows IIS to authenticate to a network share.

You may also configure IIS to use the username and password that the client used to authenticate to the site by checking the box labeled Always Use The Authenticated User's Credentials When Validating Access To The Network Directory, which appears in the Network Directory Security Credentials dialog box. If the client's credentials do not allow it to access that remote network share, it will not be able to access that share in IIS either.

A Redirection to a URL   Choose this radio button, and in the Redirect To text box that appears below it, you can type in a URL that clients will be sent to when connecting to this resource. Check one of the following three options after you choose this button:

- **The Exact URL Entered Above**   This option redirects the client to the URL in the Redirect To box, without modifying the URL. Choosing this option means that a fully qualified URL needs to appear in the box.

- **A Directory Below URL Entered**   This option will send the client to a child directory under the parent that the client entered in their browser. When you choose this option, simply type in a subfolder name, prefixed by a slash (/).

- **A Permanent Redirection For This Resource**   Use this option when you are moving a site from one URL to another. This option sends the client a "HTTP 301 Permanent Redirect" message. Some clients can then automatically update their bookmarks when receiving this message.

Home Directory Options

When you choose either A Directory Located On This Computer or A Share Located On Another Computer as the option for resource content, the following options become available in the Home Directory tab. Remember that IIS sits on top of the file systems, so for these permissions to work, the logged in (or anonymous) user must have rights at the file-system level to perform these actions.

Script Source Access Checkbox   When checked, the Script Source Access checkbox allows clients to access the source code for scripts, such as Active Server Pages (ASP) scripts, if the appropriate read/write permissions are set. Because scripts are processed server-side, there is no need for the client to access the source code for scripts. Therefore, this option should not be checked.

Read Checkbox   When checked, allows clients to read files. If unchecked, clients will not be able to read files. If you're trying to serve up web content with this site, not checking this box is a bad thing. You would want to disable Read only if you're allowing clients to upload files with the write option, and you don't want them to be able to read the files they upload (see the corresponding tech note).

Write Checkbox   When checked, allows clients with a HTTP 1.1 browser that supports the *PUT* function to upload files to this directory.

Caution	*If you allow both the Read and the Write options on a directory, anyone will be allowed to upload a file and then execute it. If scripts are enabled, they are processed server-side, so someone could upload a malicious ASP file, execute it, and have your server do bad things to itself.*

Directory Browsing Checkbox   Checking this box enables directory browsing, which lets the client see all the files in this directory. If a default page is defined and that page exists, the client will see that default page. If no default page is defined, the client sees a listing of all the files and directories on that site. Virtual directories do not show up in this listing, however, since they do not exist on the file system. Enabling directory browsing can be considered a security risk, since it allows anyone to see the files and directory structure on your site.

Log Visits Checkbox   When this box is checked, any visits to this directory will be logged, provided IIS logging is enabled.

Index This Resource Checkbox   When this box is checked, this directory will be indexed by the Microsoft Indexing Service, provided Indexing Service is installed and enabled.

Application Settings

The Application Settings section configures applications for the purposes of defining application boundaries. When you create an application, you can choose to run it in an application pool that you have created. This allows you to separate applications from each other and configure worker processes for more troublesome applications, scripts, or content to be isolated from the rest of your applications.

Application Name   Here, you type in the name of the application you want to create. If the text box is grayed out, and a Create button is visible, no application has been defined. If the text box has text in it and the Remove button is visible, an application has been defined for that directory, and the application name will appear in the Application Name text box.

Execute Permissions   The Execute Permissions drop-down box allows you to configure the types of content that will be enabled in this site. There are three settings here:

- **None**   The default setting for IIS 6, this is a huge change in the way IIS is configured out of the box. Previously, scripts (such as ASP) were enabled in an IIS default installation. This caused problems, especially because IIS was installed in a Windows default installation. So, right out of the box, Windows was configured to run IIS and allow scripts to run in IIS. Now, turning scripts off in a default installation puts IIS in its most secure setting right out of the box.

- **Scripts Only**   This setting allows scripts, such as ASP, to run on this site. Enabling scripts does open the door so that all kinds of scripting can be run on this site, so enable scripts only if you must.

- **Scripts And Executables**   This setting allows executables in addition to scripts to run on the site. This includes file types such as executables (*.exe*), dynamic link libraries (*.dll*), and Common Gateway Interface (*.cgi*) scripts. This setting allows any type of file to be accessed or executed. Again, enable this only if you need the functionality.

Caution   *Be sure that the NTFS Write permissions and IIS Write access are turned off for any directory that has anything other than None for the Execute Permissions.*

Application Pool   The Application Pool drop-down box allows you to choose which application pool you wish this content to run in. This list is populated from the Application Pools created in the IIS MMC. If you do not have an application defined for this home directory, this box will be grayed out.

Unload Button
Clicking the Unload button allows you to unload an isolated application from memory. If you have the application loaded into memory, and you make a configuration change, you must unload the application for the change to take effect. If this button is grayed out, the application is not loaded or you are not in the starting point directory for that application.

Configuration Button
Clicking the Configuration button allows you to change the application configuration options for this directory. You can configure several options in the Application Configuration window that appears (shown in Figure 2-7), which concern how this directory deals with scripting and executable content.

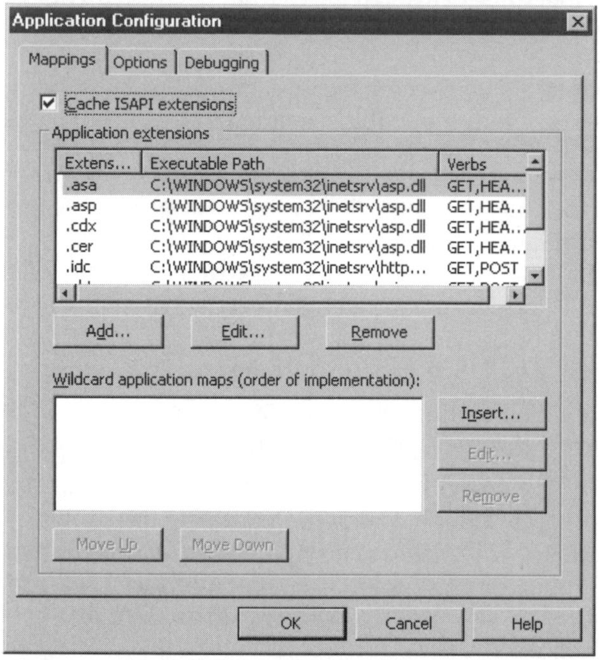

Figure 2-7. *The Application Configuration window*

The following tabs appear in the Application Configuration window.

The Mappings Tab Here you configure which file extensions map to which Internet Server API DLLs. By default, all the ASP (*.asa*, *.asp*, *.cdx*, *.cer*), Database connector (*.idc*), and server-side include DLLs (*.shtm*, *.shtml*, *.stm*) are mapped. When a request comes in, this list is checked to see which corresponding DLL the content should be sent to, based on the extension of the file being requested.

When the Cache ISAPI Extensions option is checked, the ISAPI DLLs are cached in memory so that IIS can process requests for the associated extensions without loading the DLL again. This results in performance enhancements for most ISAPI applications, including ASP. By default, this option is checked, and it is highly recommended that you leave it that way. If you uncheck this option, IIS will need to load *ASP.DLL* and create the application and session state objects each time an ASP page is requested. IIS then unloads *ASP.DLL* immediately after the request is processed. If a client requests an ASP page while the application is being unloaded, an error could occur. Basically, the only time you would need to turn this off is if you are testing an *ISAPI DLL* and you want it to be reloaded each time because you're testing code.

You can add your own ISAPI DLLs and map them here. Here's how to add and configure a DLL for use:

1. Click the Add button. The Add/Edit Application Extension Mapping dialog box will appear.

2. Type in the name of or browse to the executable you wish to run this content through.

3. Type the name of the extension. It is not necessary to include a period before the extension.

4. Choose whether you want all of the HTTP verbs, or just certain verbs to be passed to the application. To limit the verbs, type in the verbs that you want to enable in comma-separated format.

5. Leave the Script Engine and Verify That File Exists boxes checked, unless you have a good reason not to. We'll cover their functionality in a minute.

   ■ **Limiting HTTP Verbs**   HTTP clients use *verbs* to request actions of the server. These verbs, or methods, are defined in the W3C Specification for HTTP. The most common methods you will see are *GET*, *HEAD*, *POST*, and *TRACE*, although others can also be used, such as *PUT* and *DELETE*. It is recommended that you limit the HTTP verbs to those that will be used, to reduce vulnerability to attack. For example, the mapping for ASP limits the verbs to *GET*, *HEAD*, *POST*, and *TRACE*. When you limit verbs, only the verbs in the list will be passed on to the application for processing.

   ■ **Script Engine**   This box is enabled by default. This instructs IIS to run this content as a script, rather than as an executable. This prevents you from having to enable execute permissions on a directory, since the scripts are mapped to an interpreter.

   ■ **Verify That File Exists**   When this box is checked, IIS will make sure that the script file does exist, and that the user has access rights to the file before sending that content to the interpreter. Since each script has to be opened twice, once for verification and again for reading and sending to the engine, enabling this option results in a performance hit. This was not enabled by default in IIS 5, and like many other changes from IIS 5 to IIS 6, it's disabled for security purposes.

Note   *Even though you have ISAPI extensions mapped and enabled, they will not run unless you have at least Script Only selected in the execute permissions for this directory. If you are not running these extensions in the script engine, you must have Scripts And Executables enabled for this content to run successfully.*

To edit an application mapping, highlight the extension, and click the Edit button. The same screen that appears after clicking the Add button appears. The options are the same as well.

To remove an application extension mapping, highlight the extension and click the Remove button. You will be prompted to confirm the deletion.

Wildcard Application Maps allow you to set an ISAPI application mapping for all file extensions. You may be thinking "Hey, can't you just use an ISAPI filter?" There are some differences between an ISAPI filter and a wildcard application map, however. At the administration level of ISAPI, the difference between ISAPI filters and ISAPI extension mappings is that ISAPI filters apply to the web site as a whole, while ISAPI extensions can be configured on a per-directory basis. A subdirectory will inherit the wildcard application script mappings from a parent directory if it does not contain its own mappings; otherwise, those mappings configured on the directory override the parent mappings.

To add an application map, click the Insert button. You may then type in or browse to the executable you want content to be run through. The Verify That File Exists option has the same effect as it does for extension mappings and is a security feature.

To edit an application map, highlight the extension and click the Edit button. The same Add screen appears. The options are the same as well.

To remove an application map, highlight the extension and click the Remove button. You will be prompted to confirm the deletion.

The Move Up and Move Down buttons allow you to set priority on the ISAPI application maps. Requests will be run through each of the defined application maps in the order specified here.

The Options Tab   The Options tab, shown in Figure 2-8, allows you to set the configuration for this application, determine how sessions are handled, and configure the scripting engine used to process code.

The Enable Session State option configures ASP to create a server-side session for each client session to the server. This applies only to regular ASPs, since the session state is configured in *web.config* for ASP.NET applications. In this session, data can be stored about the user that transcends across each page that user accesses. Programmatically, the data is stored in variables in the session object. While powerful, session variables should be used sparingly on high-traffic sites, because misusing that power can result in performance problems, since all those session variables can take up lots of memory.

The Session Timeout setting controls the length of time a session can remain idle before it is terminated. You can enter in any number between 1 and 2,000,000,000 minutes. Who knows, you may need that session variable 3800 years from now.

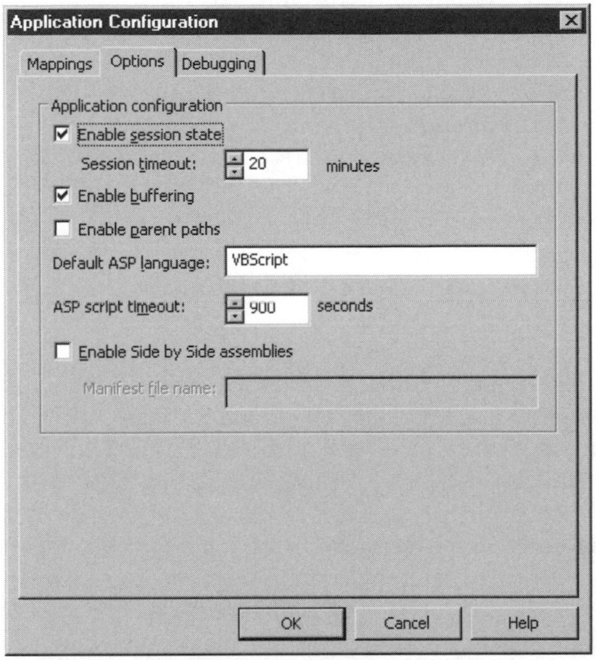

Figure 2-8. *The Options tab of the Application Configuration window*

Tip   *Using session state can be tricky, especially when you have an ASP web farm or you are using worker process recycling. In an ASP web farm, each time the user connects to the web site, they may get a different server. Since the session state was created on a different server than the user is currently logged on to, that session state information is lost. Session state information is also lost when the worker process containing that session information is recycled. For these reasons, it's a good idea either to find a way around using session state or use ASP.NET.*

Click Enable Buffering to configure the server to cache the entire contents of the ASP script output before sending it to the browser. This sends the output all at once, rather than line by line. If, however, you have a long script, and you want the page to draw as the content is processed, disable this option.

Parent paths allow you to reference directories using relative pathnames in your ASP code. A script in the parent directory can be referenced by double dots (..). This applies only to dynamic content, such as include files. Static content can always be referenced by relative pathnames. The Enable Parent Paths checkbox is disabled by default because it is a security risk to allow dynamic content to be run from one page without specifying the directory structure to get there.

Note	*In IIS 6, parent paths are now disabled by default. If you have relative pathnames in your code that previously ran under a previous version of IIS, you will need to modify your code or check the Enable Parent Paths option to get your dynamic content to run in IIS 6.*

The Default ASP Language option specifies the language that processes all scripting content. Scripting content is marked by the <% and %> tags. Two languages come with IIS 6 out of the box: Microsoft Visual Basic Scripting Edition (the default) and Microsoft JScript. You may install any ActiveX scripting engine you wish to interpret content on your site.

ASP Script Timeout specifies the maximum time a script can run; without a timeout setting, a poorly written script could run indefinitely, causing issues on the server. When the timeout is reached, the script is stopped, and processed content is sent to the browser with an error message at the end stating that the maximum time was reached. You may specify any value between 1 and 2,000,000,000 seconds (that's 63 years!).

Choosing Enable Side By Side Assemblies allows your ASP application to use a specific version of an application to run code. This allows you to have the latest version of an application installed on your server, but still run this specific application code in an older version of the DLL or EXE. To configure side by side assemblies, you must first have a manifest file, which is an XML file that has the configuration, location, and COM registration information in it. It points IIS to the correct component to use. You need to add this manifest file to each virtual directory that uses the side-by-side assembly.

The Debugging Tab The Debugging tab of the Application Configuration window, shown in Figure 2-9, helps you troubleshoot ASP scripts—which is very helpful when you are testing code. When enabled, IIS uses the Microsoft Script Debugger to check code. You can configure IIS to debug both server-side and client-side scripts. Enabling server side scripting comes with a performance hit, so you shouldn't enable it on a production site unless you must. You may also configure the error message sent to clients when a script error occurs.

■ **Enable ASP Server-Side Script Debugging** Checking this box will configure IIS to use the script debugger to check code as it is processed.

■ **Enable ASP Client-Side Script Debugging**   Checking this box will configure IIS to allow the client to debug ASP pages with the Microsoft Script Debugger. When an error occurs, the client will receive a message asking whether the error should be debugged.

■ **Send Detailed ASP Error Messages to Client**   The default setting, this sends the standard error message with the filename and relative path, the specific error message, and the line number where the error occurred. This does give clients some detailed information about the setup of the site, so you may want to choose to send another error message.

■ **Send the Following Text Error Message to Client**   Check this option and type in the specific error message you would like to send to the client when an ASP script error occurs. For example, you can type in a message with an e-mail address to use for reporting errors.

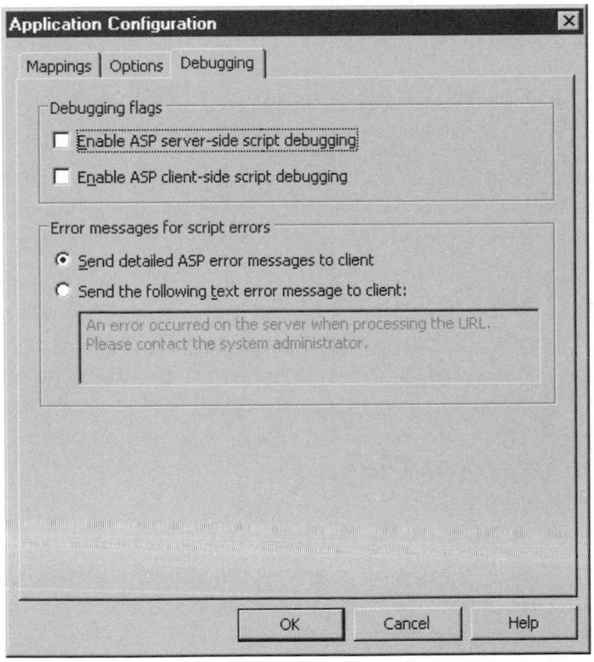

Figure 2-9.   *Debugging tab*

Creating a Side-by-Side Assembly

Let's make a manifest file that allows an application to use an older version of a DLL. The manifest file is the heart of a side-by-side assembly, so we'll start there. This manifest file tells IIS which GUID to use for the COM object that is being loaded. This file, which we'll call *Myapp.xml*, needs to be included in each virtual directory that will use this DLL.

```
<?xml version="1.0" encoding="UTF-8" standalone="yes"?>
<assembly xmlns="urn:schemas-microsoft-com:asm.v1" manifestVersion="1.0">
<assemblyIdentity publicKeyToken="XXXXXXXXXXXXXX" type="win32"
name="MyApp4Testing" version="1.0.0.0" processorArchitecture="x86"/>
<file name="MyApp.dll" hash="b654b4565d654a54f65465e645e564" hashalg="SHA1">
<comClass clsid="{12345678-0123-4567-89AB-123456789ABC}" progid="My.TestApp"
threadingModel="apartment"/>
<typelib tlbid="{12345678-0123-4567-89AB-123456789ABC}" version="1.0"
helpdir=""/>
</file>
</assembly>
```

The next step is to tell IIS to use the side-by-side assembly. In the Options tab, check the box to Enable Side By Side Assemblies. Then type **Myapp.xml** in the Manifest File Name box. Because the manifest file exists in the same directory, you do not need to provide a path—just the filename.

The Documents Tab

The next tab in the Web Site Properties window is the Documents tab, shown in Figure 2-10. Here, you configure the default pages for the web site and any footer you wish to place on each page.

Enable Default Content Page

This check box enables and disables the use of a *default page*, which is returned if no document is specified in the URL of a request. For example, when a client types *http://www.microsoft.com* in the browser, the IIS web server checks to see whether a default document is configured for that site. If so, it returns that document. This prevents clients from having to know and specify a document for each site they visit. If the default document is not enabled, and the client does not specify a document, what happens next depends on whether or not directory browsing is enabled.

- **Directory browsing enabled**   The server sends a listing of the contents of the directory.

■ **Directory browsing not enabled**   The server sends an error message stating "This Virtual Directory does not allow contents to be listed."

Adding and Removing Default Content Pages

The names of pages listed here are those that IIS looks for if no page is specified in a query. The entire filename must match, so make sure the extension is included, and correct, here as well—*Default.htm* is not the same thing as *Default.html*. To add a name to the list, click the Add button and type in the name of the page. To remove a name from the list, highlight the name and click Remove. You are not prompted to confirm the deletion.

Sorting Default Content Page Order

When searching for a default content page, IIS checks this list in the order in which it appears here. IIS uses the first matching page it finds. To modify this list, highlight a page name and use the Move Up and Move Down buttons to change the order.

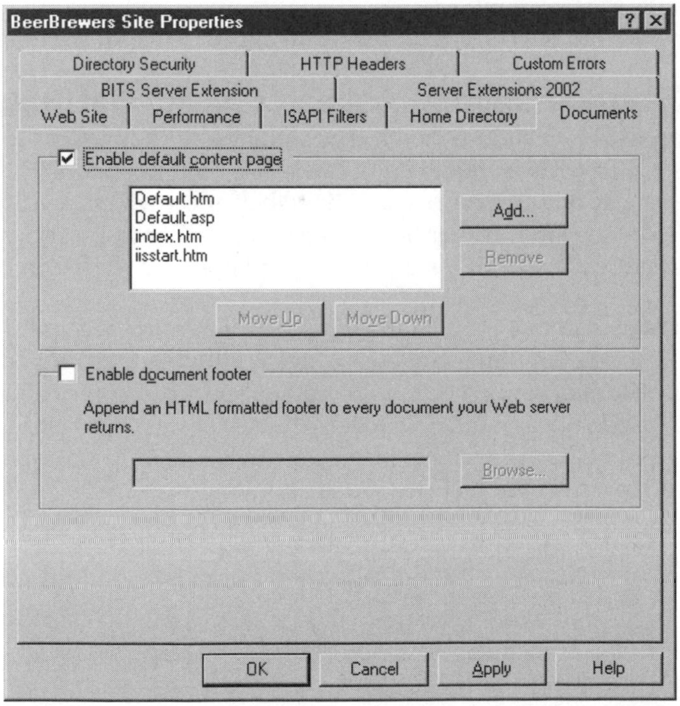

Figure 2-10.   *The Documents tab*

Enable Document Footer

To enable a document footer, place a checkmark in this box. The document footer is an HTML document that contains code you want to appear at the bottom of each page. This is useful if you want some legal or contact information to appear on your entire web site, for example, without putting the code (or an include file) on each sheet. This HTML document only needs to have the specific code in it that you want to display, and it does not need the opening <HTML> tag; only tags that format the text displayed in the footer need to be used. Unfortunately, document footers can only be used on your static content (HTML) pages.

Once you have enabled the document footer, click the Browse button to select the document you wish to use. While the code in the document has to be HTML compatible (no scripting content), you may use any document you wish (the file does not have to end in .HTM).

The Directory Security Tab

The Directory Security tab, shown in Figure 2-11, allows you to configure the security options for the site. You can configure how IIS authenticates clients, which clients can connect, and how secure the communication between client and server are.

Editing Authentication and Access Control Settings

This section enables you to choose the type of authentication for this site when security is required. This can be tricky sometimes, because you need to understand the interaction between NTFS security and IIS security, and how they affect which user is authenticated to a web page. To change the Authentication and Access Control settings, click the Edit button. The Authentication Methods dialog box will open, as shown in Figure 2-12.

Enable Anonymous Access   When the Enable Anonymous Access checkbox is checked, it allows a user to connect to a web page without submitting any logon information. Because everything needs to be run in a security context, the Internet Guest account is used. This account is created when IIS is installed and is named *IUSR_<computername>*, where *<computername>* is the name of the computer. This option allows you to set up the security for all anonymous users using this specific user account. If you do not wish to use the Internet Guest account, you may use any account you wish—either local or on a trusted domain.

> **Tip**   *Any account used to access web pages will need to have permission to access the files at the NTFS level. For more information on how to set these permissions, see Chapter 6.*

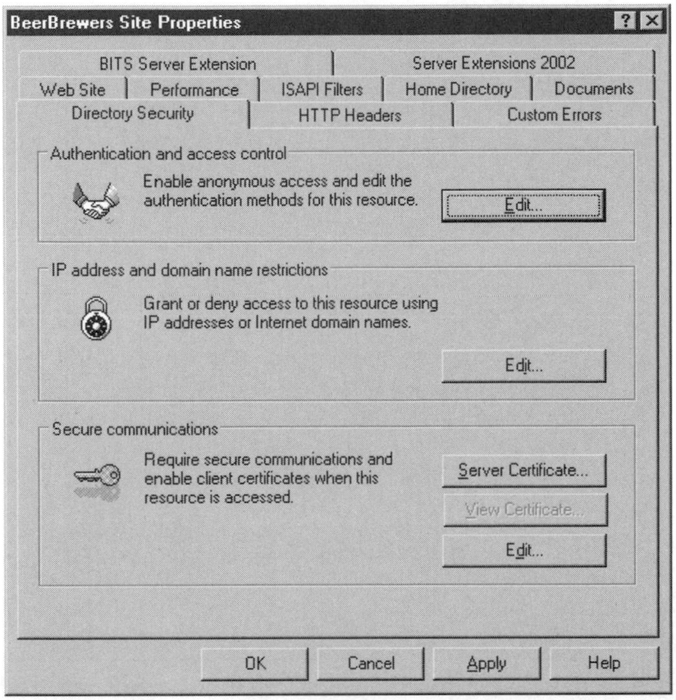

Figure 2-11.   *The Directory Security tab*

To choose the account you want to use for anonymous access:

1. Type in the name of the account in the Authentication Methods dialog box. If it is a domain account, use the *domainname\username* naming convention.

2. If you want to search for the name instead, click the Browse button. The standard Windows 2003 object selection screen will appear.

3. Here, you can select the name of the user account and location you wish to use, or you can search for it by clicking the Advanced button.

4. Once you have chosen the user account, click the OK button.

5. Then type in the password for that account in the Password text box. When you click OK, you will be prompted to confirm the password.

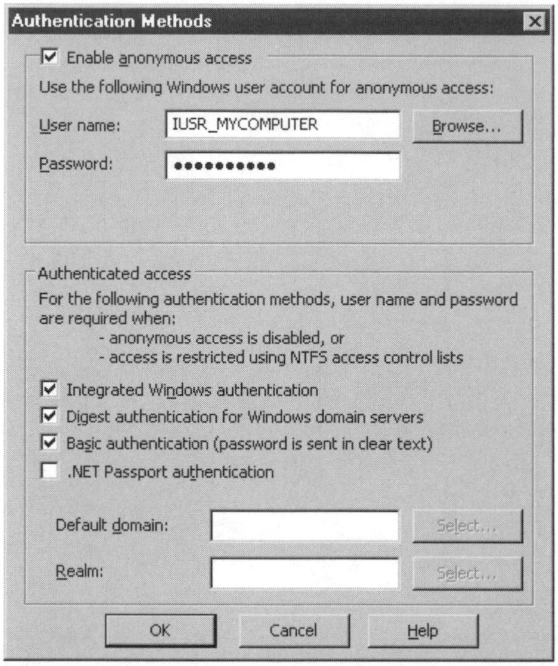

Figure 2-12. *The Authentication Methods dialog box*

When you type in a username and password, IIS does not check to see whether the username/password combination is correct. If it is not, IIS will behave as though anonymous access is disabled, and you will not be able to access the web site anonymously. This can be tricky to detect, because Internet Explorer will automatically fail over to the other types of authentication, if available, and try to authenticate you with your logged-in credentials. As an administrator, you will most likely have rights to access resources that the guest account will not. The way to see which user is being authenticated is to check the IIS log file for this site. If you are being authenticated as anyone other than the anonymous user, it will show up in the log file. If you are not using an account that has access to this resource, you will be prompted for authentication credentials.

Authenticated Access The Authenticated Access section of the Authentication Methods window shows the types of authentication that are enabled for this site. When the IIS guest account does not have access to a resource, IIS checks to see what types of authenticated access are available. Four types of authenticated access are available:

■ **Integrated Windows Authentication**   The most secure means of authentication, this is great if you're using all Internet Explorer browsers and you're not using an HTTP proxy. It has been built into all IE browsers since version 2.0. Other types of browsers, such as Netscape, do not support this authentication method. On the back end, Integrated Windows authentication uses NT challenge/response, or the Kerberos protocol. If the client and server support Kerberos, and a trusted Key Distribution Center (KDC) is available, Kerberos is used; otherwise, IIS falls back to NT challenge/response.

■ **Digest Authentication for Windows Domain Servers**   Digest authentication is available if you are using Active Directory accounts, and although some security risks are associated with it, it is a more secure means of authentication than Basic authentication. It is not intended to be a complete answer to security on the web; it is designed only to avoid the problems of Basic authentication. In addition to Active Directory, Digest authentication requires use of HTTP 1.1, so it will work only with newer browsers that support that protocol. Digest authentication requires that the domain controller keep a plaintext copy of each password, so it can check that password against the hash sent by the client. Therein lies the security risk. Having plaintext passwords stored anywhere is a security risk, so if you choose this form of authentication, you will need to make sure that the domain controller is secure from intrusion, or passwords can be compromised. The upside to using Digest authentication is that the password is not sent across the network in plaintext, unlike Basic authentication.

Because digest authentication is a simple hash, it works across firewalls and proxy servers. It is also available on Web-based Distributed Authoring and Versioning (WebDAV) directories. Since Digest authentication requires a domain, when you choose this type of authentication, the Realm box becomes available. If Digest (or Basic) authentication is not enabled, the Realm box is grayed out. Otherwise, in this box you can select which user account database to authenticate against. To choose the realm, type in the realm name in the box, or use the Select button to choose from a list of realms.

■ **Basic Authentication**   This is the simplest (and most universal) type of authentication; the username and password are sent across the network in clear text. Since there is no encryption, this is easy to crack. The benefit of using Basic authentication is that it is pretty much universally accepted. As with Digest authentication, you can select which user account database to authenticate against. Type in the realm name in the Realm text box, or use the Select button to choose from a list of realms.

■ **.NET Passport Authentication**   This is a new form of authentication used by Microsoft technologies. It allows clients to use a single sign-in to

Passport-enabled web sites. To have Passport-enabled sites, you must have a .NET Passport central server running. You can download the .NET Passport server from Microsoft's MSDN web site (http://msdn.microsoft.com). When you select .NET Passport authentication, the Default Domain box becomes active. In order for Passport authentication to work, the IIS server must be a member of a domain, and a default domain for authentication must be specified. To choose the default domain, type in the domain name in the box, or use the Select button to choose from a list of domains.

Restricting Access by IP or Domain Name

In IIS, you can restrict who has access to a site without using a username and password. By restricting access through IP address, you can target a certain population to have access or be denied access to your site. This can be useful if you have specific needs, such as the following:

- You want a certain target audience to be able to access content.

- You know exactly who the audience is, IP address-wise.

- You want to prevent other people from accessing the site.

- You don't necessarily want to use authentication as a means of controlling access, or you want to use another restriction on top of authentication.

If you decide IP address restrictions are a good idea for your site, you need to set up some restrictions. Click the Edit button in the Directory Security tab's IP Address And Domain Name Restrictions area. When you click on the Edit button, the IP Address and Domain Name Restrictions dialog box, shown in Figure 2-13, will open. Here, you need to decide whether you want to start from a restrictive perspective and grant specific people access, or start from a permissive perspective and deny specific people access. If you choose the Granted Access radio button, you will be permissive, and if you choose the Denied Access radio button, you will be restrictive.

Modifying IP Address Restrictions   To add an IP address to the list, click the Add button. The Grant Access or Deny Access box will appear, depending on which radio button you chose.

Choosing to grant or deny access is an all-encompassing action. You cannot choose to deny some IPs and grant access to others. It's all or nothing. You can choose from among three types of access:

- **Single Computer**   Allows you to input an IP address into the access list. You may enter multiple computers, one at a time, in this fashion. If you do not know the IP address of a machine, you can click the DNS Lookup button to obtain the IP address using the name.

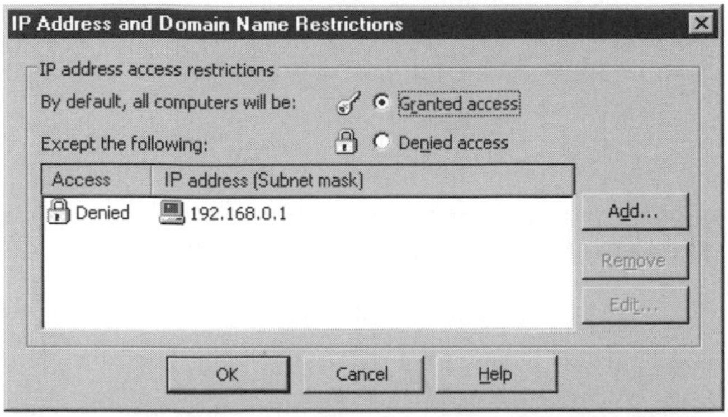

IP Address and Domain Name Restrictions

IP address access restrictions

By default, all computers will be: ⊙ Granted access

Except the following: ○ Denied access

Access	IP address (Subnet mask)
🔒 Denied	💻 192.168.0.1

Add...

Remove

Edit...

OK   Cancel   Help

Figure 2-13.   *The IP Address and Domain Name Restrictions dialog box*

- **Group Of Computers**   Allows you to enter a network ID and subnet mask to add computers to the list. Using variable length subnet masks, you can get fairly granular with the IPs in the list.

- **Domain Name**   Allows you to enter a domain name to deny access to. Be cautious of using this, because it will cause the server to do a reverse lookup on each client that connects to the server to see if it is a member of that domain. This is a performance hit, and using it will cause delays in the client getting authenticated while the server performs the reverse lookup. Reverse lookups are generally not speedy operations.

Once you have selected and configured the type of access, click OK to cause that entry to appear in the list.

To remove an entry, highlight it and click Remove. To modify an entry, highlight it and click Edit.

Secure Communications

The Secure Communications section of the Directory Security tab allows you to set up how the server will use certificates for authentication and encryption. Here, you can create certificate requests; assign, export, import, and back up certificates; and set up how the server will interact with client certificates.

To set up a server certificate on this server, click the Server Certificate button. The Web Server Certificate Wizard will appear. Click Next, and you'll see the options for assigning a certificate for this site:

- **Create A New Certificate**   Allows you to set up a request to send to a certificate authority (CA—covered in detail in Chapter 10). When you create a request, you have the option of sending it to an online CA or saving it to a file and sending that file to a CA through its registration process. To send a request to an online CA, you must have Certificate Services installed on a server.

> **Tip** *Enterprise CAs are located in Active Directory and will have an SRV record in DNS, so you can find them. For more information on SRV records and DNS, see Chapter 8. If you have a standalone CA installed on this same computer, IIS will not recognize it. This is not necessarily a problem because you can manually approve and install the certificate, as detailed in Chapter 19. It's also a good idea to have your CA in a secure location, and an exposed web server probably isn't the best place for that.*

To create a request for sending to a CA later:

1. Choose Create A New Certificate, and click Next.

2. Choose Prepare The Request Now, But Send It Later, and click Next.

3. Type the name you wish to use for this certificate. You may use any name.

4. Choose the bit length of the certificate. You can choose 512, 1024, 2048, 4096, 8192, or 16384 bits for the complexity of the hash.

5. If you want to choose which cryptographic service provider (CSP) is used to generate this certificate, check the box provided. A CSP is an algorithm that is used to generate the certificate.

6. Type the name of your organization and the organizational unit. Remember that if you are using a commercial CA, this will need to be your official business name. Click Next.

7. Type in the common name of the site. This must match the DNS or NetBIOS name that you will be using for this site. Since certificates are name-specific, the certificate is good for that name only. If you use a different DNS or NetBIOS name for your site, you will need to get a new certificate. Click Next.

8. Type in your City, State, and Country. You must not abbreviate anything. Click Next.

9. Type in the name and location of the file where you wish to place this request. Remember this, because you will be using it to request the certificate. Click Next.

10. The next screen is the summary screen. Make sure that all the information is correct. If so, click Next.

11. Click Finish to exit the wizard.

- **Assign An Existing Certificate**   Allows you to take a valid certificate on this machine and assign it to a resource. The resource in this case is the web site.

When you select this option, you will be presented with a list of the valid certificates on this machine. Click one of the certificates to select it, and then click Next. You will then need to choose the SSL port for this site. The default (443) is listed here. Don't change this port unless you have a good reason to, because clients will look for SSL communications on port 443 by default as well. After you have chosen the port number, go through the summary screens and finish the wizard. At this point, you have a certificate installed for your web site. It will be available for immediate use by clients.

- **Import A Certificate From A Key Manager Backup File**   This option allows you to import a certificate that you have exported using the Windows NT 4.0 Key Manager. When you choose this option, you browse to the location at which the *.key* file is stored and select it. After you have chosen the *.key* backup file, choose the SSL port for this site, go through the summary screens, and finish the wizard.

- **Import A Certificate From A .pfx File**   This option allows you to import a certificate file that uses the Personal Information Exchange Syntax Standard, otherwise known as PKSC #12. This is a standard for storing or transporting certificates in a portable format. If you want to be able to back up or export this certificate after you import it here, you will need to check the Mark Cert As Exportable box. After you choose the *.pfx* file, you will need to provide the password used to secure the file when it was exported. Then you will choose the SSL port for this site, go through the summary screens, and finish the wizard.

- **Copy Or Move A Certificate From A Remote Server Site To This Site**   You can now get certificates from another web site. This prevents you from having to export the certificate to a file, which can be a security risk. To copy or move a certificate from a remote web server:

  1. In the IIS Certificate Wizard, choose the Copy Or Move A Certificate From A Remote Server Site To This Site option, and click Next.

  2. In the Copy/Move Certificate dialog box, choose whether to copy or to move a certificate to this web site.

  3. Choose whether you want the certificate to be exportable from this web site. Click Next.

  4. Type in or browse to the computer from which you wish to import the certificate.

  5. Type in the credentials of a user with sufficient permissions to access this certificate, and then click Next.

  6. Enter the instance of the site from which you want to import the certificate. Clicking the Browse button allows you to select an instance from a list. Click Next.

7. Check the summary screen to make sure you have imported the correct certificate.

8. Click Next, and then click Finish.

Processing a Certificate   After you've received the certificate response from a CA, you can then process that pending certificate request. To process the request:

1. Start the Web Server Certificate Wizard again by clicking on the Server Certificate button in the Directory Security tab.

2. In the Server Certificate dialog box, choose Process The Pending Request and install the certificate. Click Next.

3. Type in or browse to the location of the response file from the CA, and then click Next.

4. Type in the SSL port this site should use. Click Next.

5. View the summary screen and make sure the information is correct.

6. Click Next, and then click Finish.

You now have a valid certificate for this site, and can start using it on the port number you specified when installing the certificate response file. If you don't get a response, you'll need to delete the pending request.

To delete the pending request:

1. Select Delete The Pending Request in the Web Server Certificate Wizard. The next dialog box in the wizard lets you know that you will not be able to process any future responses regarding this request if you continue, and gives you a chance to back out.

2. Click Next to delete the request.

3. Click Finish to complete the wizard.

Viewing the Details of an Installed Certificate   When you have an installed certificate, you can view the certificate information by clicking on the View Certificate button in the Directory Security tab.

■ **General tab**   This tab includes the information about the certificate. It contains the intended purpose of the certificate, the issuer of the certificate, who the certificate was issued to, and the valid dates of the certificates.

■ **Details tab**   Includes the nitty-gritty details of the certificate. Here you can see all the properties of the certificate, and you can start the Certificate Export Wizard, enable/disable purposes for this certificate, and set up cross-certificate downloads, which allow you to specify multiple download locations from different CAs. This is what allows unrelated CAs to "trust" each other.

- **Certification Path tab**   Allows you to view the CA certification hierarchy for this certificate. It also displays whether or not the certificate is valid.

Editing Secure Communications   Clicking the Edit button allows you to edit certificate mappings and trust lists, as shown in Figure 2-14. You can also force SSL usage here.

In the Secure Communications window, checking the Require Secure Channel checkbox allows you to force the use of SSL on this site. Any browser that does not "speak" SSL will not be able to access this site.

Checking the Require 128-Bit Encryption checkbox allows you to force the use of strong encryption. Forcing this will prevent browsers with weaker encryption from accessing this site. Internet Explorer 128-bit upgrades are available from the Microsoft web site (http://www.microsoft.com/ie), and they can be downloaded by anyone except in a U.S.-embargoed country (since Microsoft is a U.S.-based company).

The use of client certificates allows the site to identify the users connecting to this site. The client certificates can be used as a means of access control. You can choose from three settings:

- **Ignore**   The default option. Any client certificate presented will not be used.

- **Accept**   Allows the certificate, and you can set up client certificate maps, but they are not mandatory. Any browser without a client certificate will still be able to access the site.

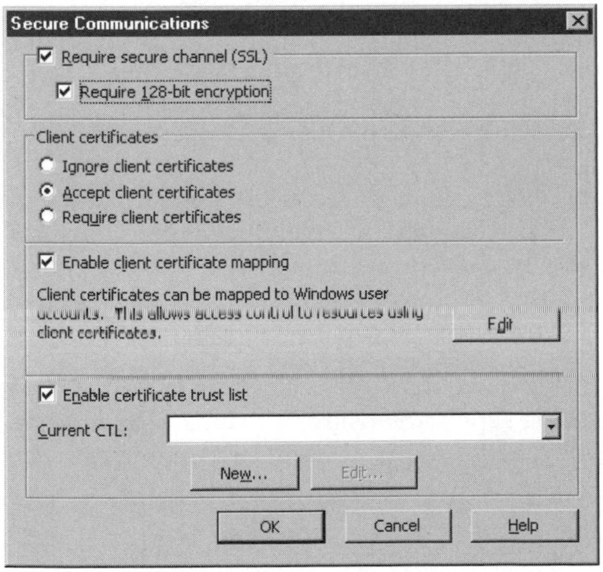

Figure 2-14.   *The Secure Communications window*

■ **Require**   Forces the use of certificates. Any client without a certificate will not be allowed access to the site. To choose this option, you will need to check the Require Secure Channel checkbox.

Client certificate mapping is used to authenticate a client machine to a Windows user account. There are two types of mappings: one-to-one and many-to-one.

■ **One-to-one mappings**   Used when each user account has its own certificate. A user account can have more than one certificate, but each account has to have at least one unique certificate to use this feature. You import the certificate and tie it to a user account, and then the certificate can be used to authenticate the user.

■ **Many-to-one mappings**   Used when multiple certificates are tied to a user account. You provide the wildcard client certificate matching criteria, in which you provide some information about that certificate, like an organizational unit or organization name. If it matches, the specified account is used.

The HTTP Headers Tab

The HTTP Headers tab of the web site Properties window, shown in Figure 2-15, allows you to configure content expiration, content ratings, and MIME types in addition to adding HTTP headers.

Enable Content Expiration

This option sets an expiration date on the files on a web site and is used when you want to make sure time-sensitive content doesn't stay cached after a certain period of time. The expiration date is given along with the content when it is requested. You can use the *RESPONSE* object with the *CACHECONTROL* or *EXPIRES* property to set the caching and expiration time on ASP pages, but that doesn't help you much with graphics. This option can do it all via the following three settings:

Expire Immediately   Expire Immediately tells the requester not to cache the data—period. This is great to use on a test or development site, since you can make code changes and you know the old code isn't stuck in the IE cache somewhere. This is also useful when your site has a page with dynamically changing content, when each time the user will get a different result and you want to make sure it's not cached somewhere down the line.

Expire After   Choosing Expire After will allow you to set a timeout period in minutes, hours, or days. You can choose any value between 1 minute and 32,767 days (that's just shy of 90 years).

Expire On   Expire On will set the content to expire at a specific time and date. You can't choose an expiration date before today's date. You can, however, choose any date up to December 31, 2035. Since the expiration data is processed by the client, it's driven

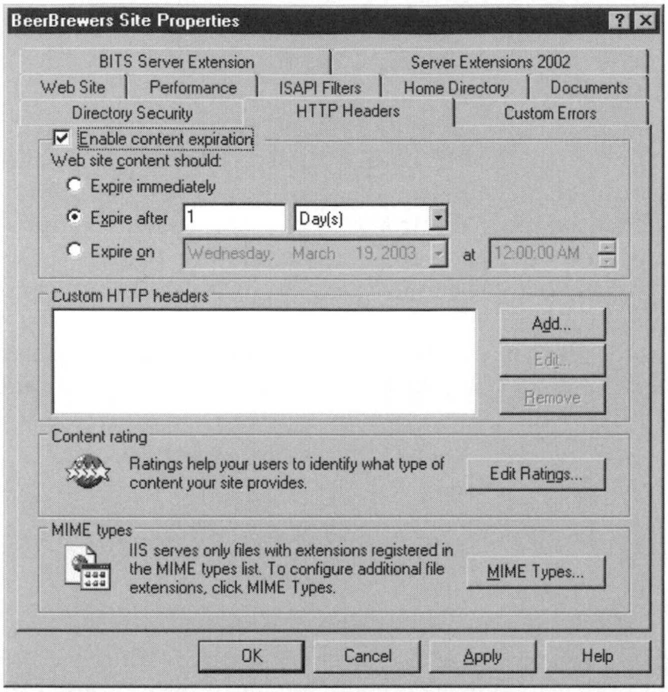

Figure 2-15.   *The HTTP Headers tab*

by the client's time zone, so there can be some variation in exactly when the content is expired, based on where the client is located.

Custom HTTP Headers

This section allows you to configure a custom HTTP header to be sent to the client. This header supplements the header that the client normally receives from the server. This header can be used for additional custom data that you want to send to the client that it will find useful. You can also use it to add additional functionality to HTTP—for example, to support a new HTTP standard that IIS 6 doesn't natively support.

To add a custom header:

1. Click the Add button. The Add/Edit Custom HTTP Header dialog box appears.

2. Type in the custom header name in the box provided.

3. Type in the custom header value in the box provided.

4. Click OK.

You can modify the header by clicking the Edit button and delete it by clicking the Remove button. You are not prompted when choosing to remove a custom header.

Content Rating

You can enable content ratings for your site in this area. Content ratings are a voluntary system developed by the Internet Content Rating Association (ICRA). ICRA is a nonprofit, independent organization that aims to give parents data to make informed decisions about what their children see in electronic media. This system comprises two parts: part one occurs when the webmaster gives the site a rating (ICRA does not do the actual rating), and part two is when the end user sets the browser settings to block certain sites based on ratings content.

Two standards for content ratings are used: the older RSACi standard and the newer ICRA system. IIS 6 supports the legacy RSACi system, which rates content by four categories.

- Violence
- Sex
- Nudity
- Language

After you rate your system, you also provide an e-mail address of the person rating the content, so you can get feedback on perceptions of ratings. You can also set an expiration date for ratings. Once the expiration date has passed, the ratings will no longer apply.

Enabling Content Ratings for Your Site   Here's how to set up content ratings:

1. Open the Content Ratings dialog box by clicking the Edit Ratings button in the HTTP Headers tab.
2. In the Content Ratings window, click the Enable Ratings For This Content checkbox.
3. Click the rating you wish to set.
4. Use the sliding bar to set that rating to level 0–4.
5. Set any or all of the other ratings if so desired.
6. Type an e-mail address into the box provided. A generic role-based account is usually best (something like *webmaster@thisdomain.com*).
7. Add an expiration date on this data. You can't choose anything before today, but you can choose any date up to December 31, 2035.
8. Click OK.

MIME Types

The Multipurpose Internet Mail Extensions (MIME) are the definitions of the file types that IIS will serve to clients. IIS 6 will serve only file types that are either script mapped or have a MIME type defined. If IIS encounters an extension for which it has no MIME mapping, the client will get a 404 not found error, and the server will log a substatus code of 3.

Note *There's one exception to the MIME rule: Text files with a .txt extension, while not MIME or script mapped, will still be served by IIS.*

You can set up MIME types on a global, web site, or directory level, and those types are inherited down the chain. Let's go through an example of adding a MIME map.

Let's say you want to web publish a logfile directory. All the log files have a *.log* extension and are in plaintext format. IIS does not have a MIME mapping for *.log* files out of the box, so we'll have to add one.

1. Click the MIME Types button in the HTTP Headers tab at the appropriate level (globally, site, or at the directory level, per your choice in the MMC).

2. Click New.

3. In the MIME Type dialog box, type the extension of the file you wish to add in the Extension box. In this case, type **.log**.

4. Type the MIME type in the text box provided. Since we're dealing with a plaintext file, the appropriate MIME type would be **text/plain**.

5. Click OK. You will see your extension has been added.

6. Click OK again, and then once more.

Your server/site/directory is now configured to serve out *.log* files. Clients choosing a file in that directory will now see it in their browsers. You can edit and remove MIME type mappings here as well.

If you don't set up the MIME type properly, IIS will still serve up the file, but it won't know what to do with it. IE users will be prompted to choose which program to use to open this file.

Note *Where do we find out what is the proper MIME type to put in for our file? RFC2045 and RFC2046 specify the fields for MIME types and that they are assigned and listed by IANA. (Yup, the same people who determine IP addresses.) The full list with subtypes is on their web site at http://www.iana.org.*

The Custom Errors Tab

The Custom Errors tab, shown in Figure 2-16, allows you to change the default error messages sent out by IIS. A mapping for each HTTP error and substatus code appears here. This allows you to have custom errors or scripts run when clients encounter an error.

When you modify the custom errors, you can then use them for error reporting and to help you resolve issues. For example, you can make the message type be an ASP script that alerts the webmaster, logs the incident, shows a message on the screen for the end user that lets them know an issue occurred, and redirects the user to the default page. Or you can take the user back to the previous page they were viewing. Since you can use scripts, you can actually make the error messages useful, and the messages can actually help you to diagnose issues with your web site.

You can choose from three types of messages:

- **Default** The default error that IIS has programmed. This allows you to reset a custom error quickly if you don't want to use it anymore.

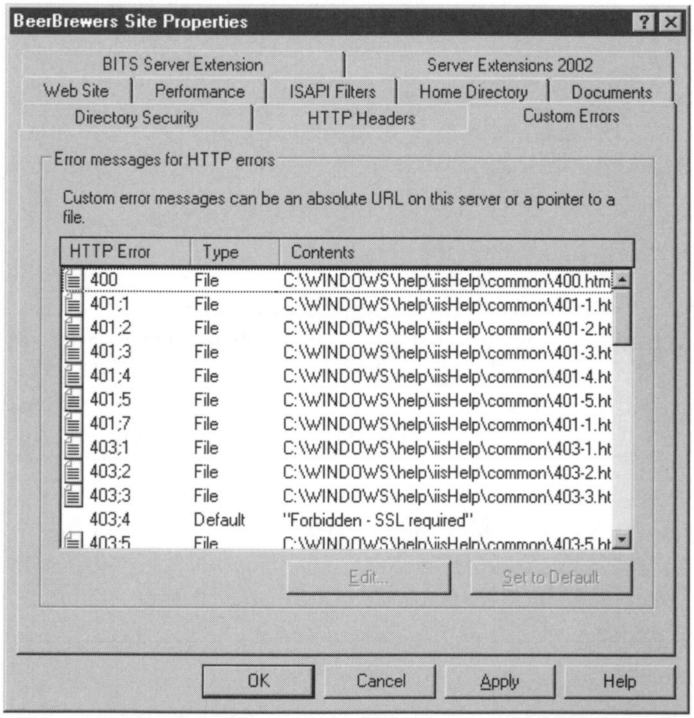

Figure 2-16. *The Custom Errors tab*

- **File**   Allows you to choose a file using the fully qualified filename (such as *C:\Windows\help\errors\iiserror404.asp*).

- **URL**   Allows you to direct the client to a page on this site using the absolute URL pathname (from the top of the site). So the HTTP error pages have to be on the same site, although they can be on a virtual directory. If you try to type in a URL that's not in the proper format, you will get a pop-up error.

Modifying the Custom Error Properties

To modify the custom error properties:

1. Highlight the HTTP error that you want to modify, and click Edit. The Edit Custom Error Properties window appears.

2. From the drop-down box, choose the message type you would like to use for this error.

3. If using a file, type in or browse to the file location.

4. If using a URL, type in that absolute pathname.

5. If choosing Default, there is nothing to configure.

6. After you have selected and configured the option, click OK.

7. Click OK again.

Some Error Messages Can't Be Mapped to URLs

Some error messages cannot be mapped to URLs, because if an error of this type exists, that URL might not exist either. The following error messages can't be assigned to URLs:

- 401.1 Unauthorized: Access is denied due to invalid credentials

- 401.2 Unauthorized: Access is denied due to server configuration favoring an alternate authentication method

- 401.3 Unauthorized: Access is denied due to an ACL set on the requested resource

- 401.4 Unauthorized: Authorization failed by a filter installed on the Web server

- 401.5 Unauthorized: Authorization failed by an ISAPI/CGI application

- 407: Proxy Authentication Required

- 502: Bad Gateway

The BITS Server Extension Tab

The Background Intelligent Transfer Service (BITS) allows you to transfer a large amount of data slowly over a long period of time. It transfers data when the network is not being used, so it doesn't impact network performance. The BITS Server Extension tab (Figure 2-17) is available only when that component is installed. (This option is in Add/Remove Windows Components. See Chapter 1 for more information.) IIS uses the BITS server extensions to receive client uploads to a virtual directory. The client must have the software that allows them to upload using bits; IIS just configures the server to accept the BITS transfers. When a transfer is initiated, BITS will manage that transfer as long as a network connection exists. If a network connection is dropped, BITS will suspend the transfer and pick up right where it left off when the connection is re-established. So the data can be transferred over multiple disconnects and reboots. BITS will monitor the network usage on the client, and it will only transfer when excess bandwidth allows.

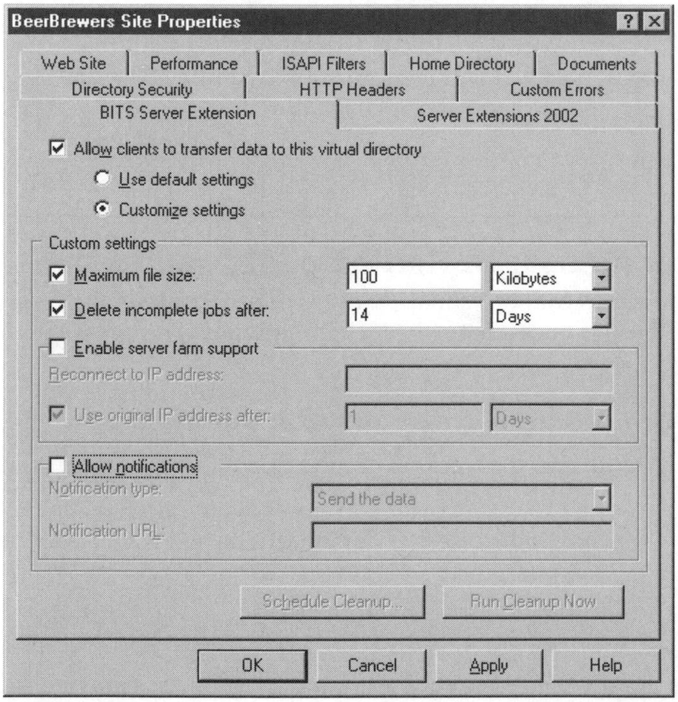

Figure 2-17. *The BITS Server Extension tab*

Allow Clients to Transfer Data to This Virtual Directory

This option configures this virtual directory to accept BITS transfers. If you choose Use Default Settings, you cannot configure any of the options in this tab. The Customize Settings option allows you to modify the settings. These settings are inherited from the web site level to the virtual directories that are enabled for BITS transfers. Likewise, a subvirtual directory will inherit settings from its parent virtual directory.

Custom Settings

In the Custom Settings area, you can configure the Maximum File Size that BITS can accept. This is the maximum size of a single file, and you can choose a value between 1 byte and 16,777,215 terabytes. (So this will hold you until those new 16 exabyte hard drives come out.) You can also configure how long to keep incomplete transfers until they can be deleted by the cleanup process. You can choose any time between 1 second, which will delete any incomplete job when the cleanup process is run, and 49,710 days, at which time that 16 exabyte hard drive will be old news.

Enable Server Farm Support

A BITS server *farm* is a group of servers to which a client can upload. You can configure file storage for a server farm in two ways:

- The servers can all share a single network share for the virtual directory. Since they are all virtual directories, you can point them all to the same network share.

- The servers can all use their own local storage for the upload directory.

If you choose the second option, these server farm support options come into play:

- **Reconnect To IP Address**   Lets the client know which IP address to reconnect to when resuming transfers. If your servers use local storage, the client is going to want to reconnect to the same server so that it can resume the existing file, rather than creating a new one on a different server. You can use DNS names here, but only if there is a single A record for that name (round-robin DNS will send the client to multiple servers, defeating the purpose of the reconnect).

- **Use Original IP Address After**   Configures the timeout for reconnection. This setting is usually in sync with the cleanup time period. If the incomplete transfer file has been cleaned, reconnecting to the same server doesn't help. The client will have to reconnect using the original URL after this time period has been reached. You can configure any time period between 1 second and 49,710 days.

Allow Notifications

This option, when checked, enables notifications for this virtual directory. Notifications allow you to send a message or data to a URL so that an application can be alerted that a transfer has completed. Two settings appear here:

- **Notification Type** Configures what to send. If you choose to send the filename, the server sends the full path for the file to the notification URL. If you choose to send the data, the file is sent by the server to the notification URL using the HTTP POST method.

- **Notification URL** This is where you type in the URL that you wish to use to send notifications when a transfer occurs. You can use a fully-qualified URL or a relative URL here.

Cleanup of Incomplete Files

Sometimes, a transfer won't complete, and the client never finishes the file. Rather than leaving the file there forever, IIS can "scrub" the directories periodically to make sure those incomplete files don't take up space. The trick is to leave the time period long enough that infrequently connected clients can finish their upload, but short enough so that the drive doesn't fill up with incomplete files that will never be finished.

- **Schedule Cleanup** Allows you to create a scheduled task that runs periodically to check the incomplete files. If an incomplete file is found, the date on the file is compared to the timeout value that you configured in the Delete Incomplete Jobs After boxes. If the file is older than the timeout value, the file is deleted, and the job is canceled.

- **Run Cleanup Now** Starts the cleanup task immediately. It behaves exactly like a scheduled cleanup otherwise.

The Server Extensions 2002 Tab

This tab, shown in Figure 2-18, is available only at the web site level, and only if the FrontPage 2002 Server Extensions have been loaded with the Add/Remove Windows Components wizard. By default, when you open this tab, a message tells you that server extensions have not been enabled for this web site.

1. In the IIS MMC, choose Action | All Tasks | Configure Server Extensions 2002.

2. Internet Explorer pops up and asks for login information. You'll need to provide credentials with Administrator rights.

3. The web site to enable FrontPage Server Extensions 2002 opens.

4. Make sure the account that appears in the Administrator box is the one you want to use, and then click Submit.

5. In the Server Administration web site that opens, you can configure FrontPage Server Extensions.

After Server Extensions have been enabled, the Server Extensions 2002 tab displays a Settings button that you can click to open the Server Administration web site.

The Server Administration Web Site

In the Server Administration web site, you configure the FrontPage server extensions. When you open the Server Extensions 2002 tab shown in Figure 2-18, you will see a Settings button, and no configuration options are available in the IIS MMC. Press the Settings button to go to the FrontPage Server Administration site, shown in Figure 2-19. The first page you will see is the Change Configuration Settings page. At the top of the page, there are hyperlinks for Administration, which take you to the site administration page, and Help.

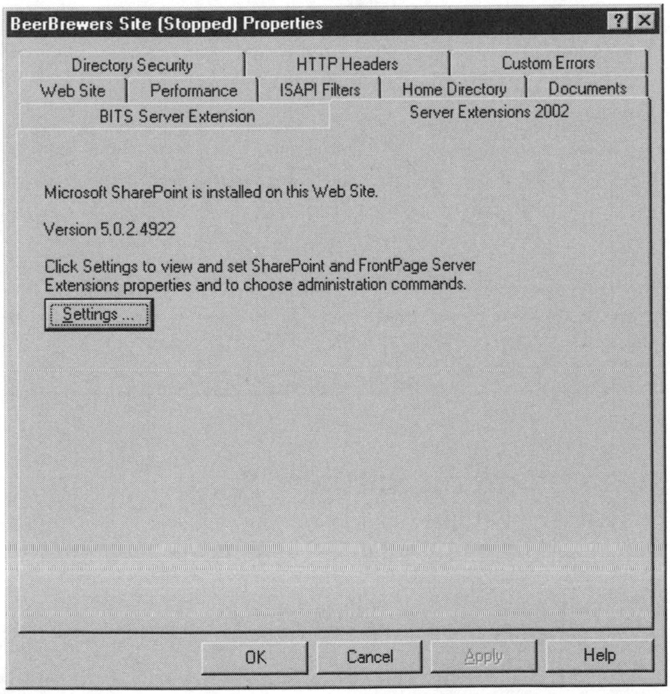

Figure 2-18. *The Server Extensions 2002 tab*

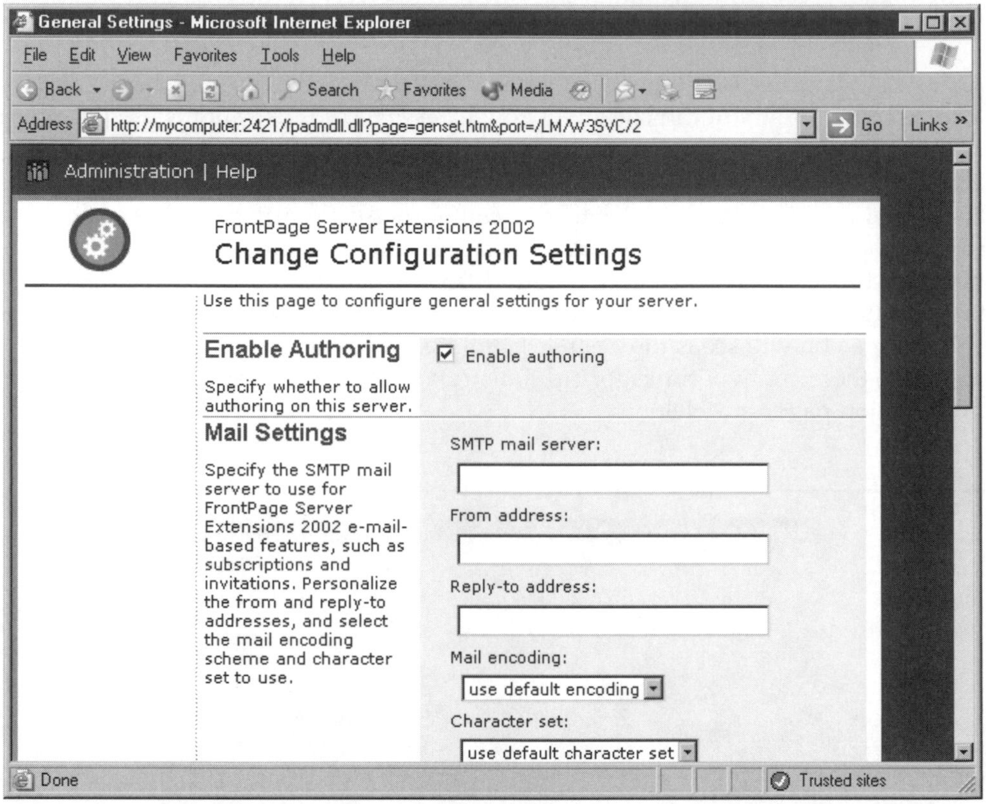

Figure 2-19. *The FrontPage Server Administration site Change Configuration Settings page*

The Change Configuration Settings Page

In the Change Configuration Settings page, you can configure the general settings for all the sites on this server. You must be a member of the local Administrators group on the server to make these changes.

The Enable Authoring Checkbox   Click the Enable Authoring checkbox to configure whether or not clients can use FrontPage to upload content to their respective web sites. This is enabled by default when you install Server Extensions 2002. Removing the checkmark will prevent authors from publishing new content. This is useful when you are performing maintenance or upgrades, and you don't want any new content published while you're working. Or, from a more secure perspective, this should not be turned on at all in production except during scheduled maintenance periods when content is going to be uploaded.

Mail Settings   In the Mail Settings area, you configure FrontPage's use of e-mail services for this server. When you configure the SMTP settings, you specify the SMTP server name or IP address. There is no option to provide a username and password, so make sure the server you're using accepts messages without that. You can also set the From and Reply-to addresses. That way, clients can reply to the messages. Lastly, you can configure the mail encoding and character set if you're using an e-mail server that has different settings.

Performance Tuning   The FrontPage Server Extensions 2002 allow you to configure caching for your web sites. When you have a large number of pages and documents on your site, caching can help improve the overall response time of the site. Changing one of the following settings in this area lets you configure the size of the cache:

- < 100 pages
- 100–1000 pages
- 1000 pages
- Custom

If none of these choices fits your site's needs, or you want to modify the caching settings, you can choose Custom and provide your own values.

Client Scripting   The Client Scripting section lets you choose the language you will allow for client scripting on this server:

- No scripting
- JavaScript
- VBScript

If you choose no scripting, client scripting will be disabled for this server.

Security Settings   In the Security Settings section, you configure the security for the FrontPage Server Extensions for this server.

- **Log Authoring Actions** Sets up logging for all authors publishing content to this server. That way, you can track who uploads what, and if someone overwrites files on a server, you can find out who did it.

- **Require SSL For Authoring And Administration** Mandates that the client use an SSL channel. This will encrypt the traffic and make it more difficult for a third party to "listen in" on the traffic between the client and the server.

■ **Allow Authors To Upload Executables**   Enables publishing of executable programs to the server. By default, this is disabled, because someone could upload a destructive executable to the server and then run it at the server.

The Server Administration Page

The Server Administration page, shown in Figure 2-20, shows you the list of virtual servers and lets you set user information.

Set List Of Available Rights   Clicking this hyperlink takes you to a page that allows you to configure the permissions for this server, which are in two categories: web design rights and web administration rights. With these rights, you can granularly control how authors can access this site.

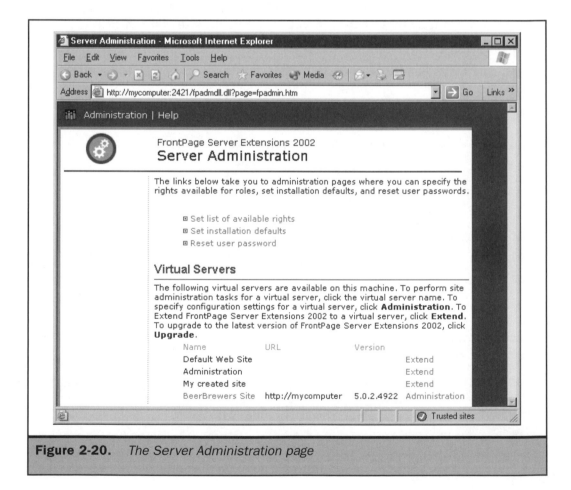

Figure 2-20.   *The Server Administration page*

Set Installation Defaults   Click this hyperlink to set the default settings for all new web sites on this server. You can configure the mail settings and the security settings. This page is the same as the Configuration Settings page, except you cannot set the mail encoding and character set here. The security settings are the same.

Reset User Password   Click this hyperlink to access the page that allows you to change an author's password for a site.

1. In the Virtual Server drop-down list, choose the site that contains the user account.
2. In the Web Name box, type in the name of the web site of which the user is a member.
3. In the User Name text box, type in the username for which you wish to reset the password.
4. In the New Password and Confirm New Password text boxes, type in the new password.

Note   *You do not need to know the old password in order to change it.*

Virtual Servers   The Virtual Servers section shows you a list of all the web sites on this server. If the FrontPage Server Extensions have been enabled on this site, you will see the URL and the version number of the extensions. If not, the word Extend will appear, and you can click it to enable the FrontPage Server Extensions on this site.

Administering a Virtual Server

When you click a site name in the Virtual Servers section, the Site Administration page opens, where you can administer that site. You can perform various tasks related to site administration:

- Change whether or not anonymous access is allowed
- Manage user accounts
- Manage roles for those user accounts
- Send an invitation to a user (only if SMTP has been set up)
- Check the health and security settings for this site
- Check the hyperlinks in a site to make sure they are valid
- Configure whether this site uses version control, to be able to roll back changes
- Create a subweb

Global Web Sites Properties Tabs

Many of the options that are set on an individual web site can also be set on a global basis so that they apply to all web sites on this server. Right-click the Web Sites folder in the left pane of the MMC, and choose Properties to access the Properties window. At the global level, all the same tabs appear in this window, with one addition: Service. If you change a setting on one of these tabs, it applies to all web sites, and some settings can't be made at the global level.

The Service Tab

The Service tab, shown in Figure 2-21, includes the options for setting IIS isolation mode and setting HTTP compression.

Isolation Mode

IIS 5.0 isolation mode allows for backward compatibility with applications that don't work under worker process isolation. These types of applications are rare, but IIS does

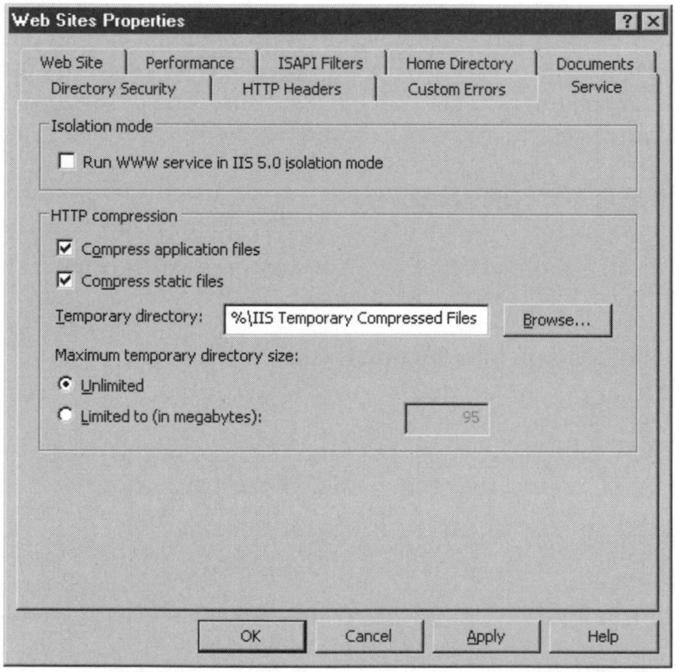

Figure 2-21. *The Service tab*

support them in this mode. Here are some reasons why you'd need to use IIS 5.0 isolation mode:

- Multi-instance ISAPIs that are written to be used multiple times simultaneously by different processes.
- Read raw data filters that would try to grab all the data before it hits a web site.
- In-process session-state variables, because they are lost every time a worker process is recycled. If you're using ASP.NET, this issue doesn't exist.
- Applications that farm out work to their own worker processes.

Because isolation mode is applied at the global level, it applies to all web sites on this server. Therefore, if you enable isolation mode, you lose all the cool functionality that worker process recycling gives you. If you absolutely must use a certain application that doesn't play well with worker process isolation mode, you may want to consider putting it on a web server by itself, so your other web sites can take advantage of this.

HTTP Compression

Most of you have probably experienced the excruciatingly slow web surfing experience of a 56K modem. You can have the biggest, baddest web server around with dual DS3 lines plugged in, but typically the weakest link in the chain leads to the client's browser—this is what's known as the "last mile," or the copper in between the telephone company's distribution point and the end user's computer. There's not a whole lot you can do about that, but you can enable HTTP compression.

HTTP compression is supported through the HTTP content-encoding standard. Most HTTP 1.1–compliant browsers support content encoding. When compression is enabled, IIS sends compressed files to the client. Note that this is different from compressing the data stream. With IIS compression, the headers are still uncompressed; just the files are compressed. The files are then decompressed by the client and interpreted by the browser.

Note *HTTP compression takes extra CPU cycles on both the client and the server, because the content has to be compressed by the server and then decompressed by the client. This shouldn't affect the actual performance, though. Needless to say, CPU time is generally not the limiting factor on the server, and especially not on the client.*

These compressed files have a content expiration date of January 1, 1997, which prevents proxy servers and browsers from caching these files. This can be a downside to compressing files, since the cache on proxy servers and browsers speeds up the overall speed of browsing on frequently visited sites. When HTTP compression is enabled, after IIS receives a request, it goes through this process to get data to the client:

1. IIS checks to see whether the browser supports compression.

2. If it doesn't support compression, the data is sent normally.

If it does support compression, IIS checks the type of file being requested to see whether it is static or application content.

- If the file is a dynamic-content file, IIS compresses the file and sends it. Dynamic files are not stored in the temporary compression directory.

- If the file is a static-content file, IIS checks to see whether the file is stored in the temporary compression directory.

- If the file exists in the temporary compression directory, the file is sent from there.

- If the file does not exist in the temporary compression directory, IIS sends the client an uncompressed file, and then compresses the file to the temporary compression directory for the next user.

Compress Application Files   When you choose this option, all application content files are compressed before being sent across the wire. This includes ASP, CGI, and executables. Even though scripting content, such as ASP, is just regular HTML when it is sent to the client, it is differentiated from static content because of the processing that occurs on the server side. Because the response is compressed every time it is requested, it pretty much throws the whole ASP caching thing out the window. Caching dynamic content files has a much greater impact on system performance than caching static content files, because dynamic files are not cached to the temporary compression directory. To compress application files, you have to enable compression on static files as well. Although, interestingly enough, the GUI will let you do this without any prompting or error messages, it just doesn't work.

Compress Static Files   Selecting this option will configure IIS to compress all static files. The static files are stored in the temporary directory and served up to the client when requested. When a client requests a file, and compression is enabled for that file type, the file is sent from the temporary compression directory if that file exists.

Temporary Directory   The temporary directory that IIS uses is configured here. You can either type in the directory name or click Browse and choose it there. The default location is *%windir%\IIS Temporary Compressed Files*. The temporary directory location must be on the local system, and it must also be on an NTFS partition. It's also a good idea not to have the directory be compressed with NTFS compression—not that it would hurt anything, but compressing already compressed files doesn't give you any benefit and wastes CPU time.

Maximum Temporary Directory Size   If you wish, you can limit the size of the directory that IIS uses for compressed files. You can estimate how big this directory can get by sizing up all the files for which you have compression enabled. The directory size won't be any bigger than the size of all the files, and it will probably be less, because they are compressed. If you have the space, there is no need to limit the size. If you do limit size here, when IIS runs out of space in the temporary directory, it automatically makes more space by deleting the files that are used the least. You can choose a value between 1 and 1024 MB.

Other Tabs

The other tabs that are available at the global level are the same as those at the individual web site level. Here's a description of what is and is not available for each of them.

Web Site Tab   At the web site level, the web site identification options are not available, since they set the IP address and port information for the web site. The connection timeout, keep alive, and logging options are all available.

Performance Tab   All options are available in the Performance tab.

ISAPI Filters Tab   The ISAPI filter options are available. Adding an ISAPI filter here applies to all web sites. You cannot view any ISAPI filters installed here at the individual site level.

Home Directory Tab   On the Home Directory tab, you can configure the execute permissions for all sites. You can also enable or disable Read, Write, Directory Browsing, Log Visits, and Index This Resource for all web sites. All of the options available from the Configuration button are active as well.

You cannot configure any application pools at this level. You also cannot set up where the content comes from, since that is very site-specific.

Documents Tab   All options are available in the Documents tab.

Directory Security Tab   On the Directory Security tab, you can configure authentication and access control for all sites. You can also set up IP address and domain name restrictions for all sites. In place of the Server Certificate wizard is a checkbox called Enable The Windows Directory Service Mapper. This configures Directory Service client certificate mapping, and it is available only at the global level. Directory Service mapping is available only if the web server is a member of an Active Directory domain, and it precludes the use of one-to-one and many-to-one mappings for client certificates. Directory Service mapping stores all the certificates in Active Directory tied to the user account. This way, you need only one certificate mapping for all sites, and you can access resources without supplying a username and password.

HTTP Headers Tab   All options are available in the HTTP Headers tab.

Custom Errors Tab   All options are available in the Custom Errors tab.

Directory Level Properties Tabs

You can also configure sites at the directory level. Modifying a directory affects all files in that directory, and the properties are inherited by subdirectories. When you make a modification, if any of the subdirectories have conflicting settings, you are given a chance to accept the changes or not to have those subdirectories inherit the settings. The directory level tabs are fewer than at the web site level.

Directory (or Virtual Directory) Tab   The Directory tab has all the same options that the Home Directory web site tab has, with one exception. If this is a physical directory, the choice to have the content come from a share located on another computer is disabled. If it is a virtual directory, the name of this tab is Virtual Directory, and all three content choices are available.

Documents Tab   All options are available in the Documents tab.

Directory Security Tab   All options are available in the Directory Security tab.

HTTP Headers Tab   All options are available in the HTTP Headers tab.

Custom Errors Tab   All options are available in the Custom Errors tab.

BITS Server Extensions Tab   This tab is available only on virtual directories. It is not available on regular directories. On virtual directories, all options are available in the BITS Server Extensions tab.

File Level Properties Tabs

You can also modify settings at the individual file level. At this level, the properties apply only to the chosen file, and there is no inheritance. The file level also has the most limited number of tabs of any of the configuration levels.

File Tab   The File tab has a limited set of options to configure. You can have the content come from the file (the default), or you can redirect the content to a URL. You can also enable and disable the options for Script Source Access, Read, Write, and Log Visits.

File Security Tab   All options are available in the File Security tab.

HTTP Headers Tab   All options are available in the HTTP Headers tab.

Custom Errors Tab   All options are available in the Custom Errors tab.

Application Pools

Application pools, as discussed in Chapter 1, are used when IIS is running in worker process isolation mode. Application pools make worker process isolation mode work with the applications by tying applications to worker processes. Application pools help maintain the health of IIS, since an application can be tied to one or more worker processes. Also, since worker processes are separated, if one fails, the others aren't affected, ensuring your other applications are available.

You access the Application Pools node from the IIS MMC, as shown in Figure 2-22.

Creating an Application Pool

The default application pool is called *DefaultAppPool*. Each site created will use the *DefaultAppPool* unless otherwise configured. To make a new application pool:

1. Highlight Application Pools in the IIS MMC.

2. Choose Action | New | Application Pool. The Add New Application Pool dialog box appears.

3. Type in the Application Pool ID in the text box. This should be a friendly name.

4. If you want to use another application pool as a template, instead of the default settings, click the Use Existing Application Pool As Template radio button and choose that application pool from the list.

5. Click OK.

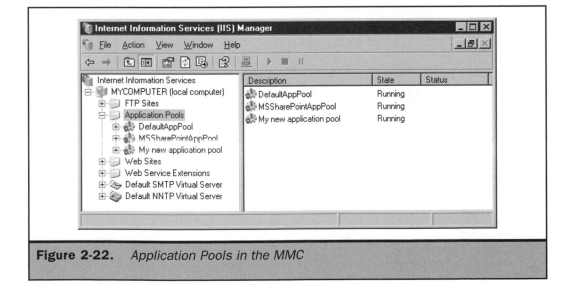

Figure 2-22.   *Application Pools in the MMC*

Application Pool Properties

After you have created a new application pool, you can configure its options. To access the Application Pool Properties window, highlight the application pool in the MMC and choose Action | Properties. The Properties window will open, where you'll be able to configure this pool. You can also configure all the application pools globally. Just highlight the Application Pools level instead of the individual pool. The options are the same.

The Recycling Tab

On the Recycling tab, shown in Figure 2-23, you configure memory and worker process recycling. Recycling worker processes helps keep IIS healthy by terminating the worker process and launching a new one, thereby returning all the memory that a worker process used.

You can set five criteria for recycling processes. You can use one or all of them at the same time.

■ **Recycle Worker Processes (In Minutes)**   Allows you to configure the number of minutes that a worker process will be active before it is terminated and a new one is launched in its place. You can choose any value between 1 and 4,000,000 minutes. At 1 minute, you'll be recycling so often that your server will be doing that more than anything else. At 4,000,000 minutes (7.6 years), you may as well not recycle at all. From a memory leak perspective, the frequency needed to recycle depends on the technology the site is using. ASP/COM applications have many more memory leak problems than ASP.NET or CGI applications. The volume of requests on the site is also an important consideration. Each application is different, so it's best to evaluate how the application handles itself to determine how often you need to recycle it.

Dealing with Memory Leaks

Memory leaks are caused by applications that run and don't return all the memory used back to the system. Each time that application is run, a little more memory is lost. Eventually, there isn't enough memory left for the system to run. Memory leaks are very easy to create. For example, the following ASP code will cause a memory leak:

```
SET MyBadApp = Server.CreateObject("SomeApp.ThisHurts")
MyBadApp.DoSomething
```

Normally, you should close out your application by setting *MyBadApp* to Nothing by adding the line *SET MyBadApp = Nothing*. By not making this setting, that memory is not returned.

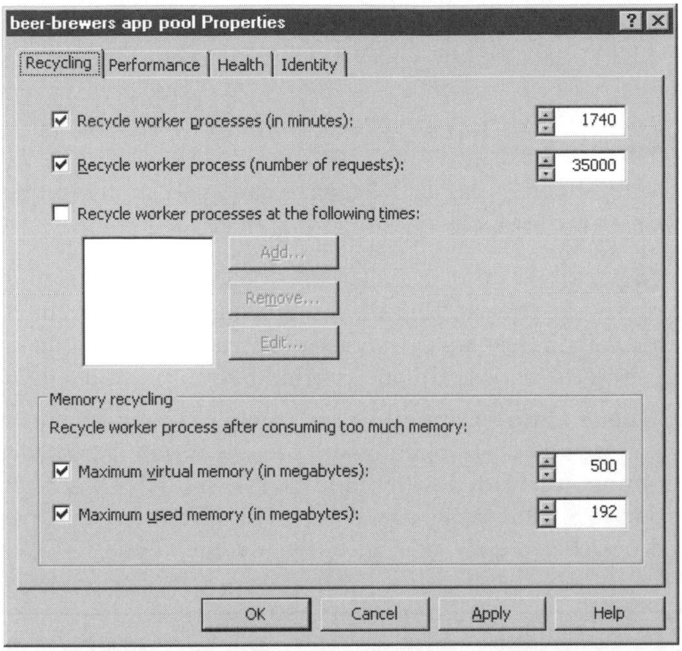

beer-brewers app pool Properties   ? ×

Recycling | Performance | Health | Identity

☑ Recycle worker processes (in minutes):   1740

☑ Recycle worker process (number of requests):   35000

☐ Recycle worker processes at the following times:

    Add...

    Remove...

    Edit...

Memory recycling

Recycle worker process after consuming too much memory:

☑ Maximum virtual memory (in megabytes):   500

☑ Maximum used memory (in megabytes):   192

OK   Cancel   Apply   Help

Figure 2-23.   *The Recycling tab*

- **Recycle Worker Processes (Number Of Requests)**   Allows you to configure how many requests a worker process processes before recycling. You can choose any value between 1 and 4,000,000 requests.

- **Recycle Worker Processes At The Following Times**   Will configure certain times of the day, each day, that the worker processes are recycled. You can add, remove, and edit the times here.

Memory Recycling   You can also recycle based on memory usage. This is a great way to prevent memory leaks from taking over the system, since you can recycle as soon as a predefined threshold is reached.

- **Maximum Virtual Memory (In Megabytes)**   Will recycle the worker process after the threshold is reached. This is measured against the system's virtual memory. Valid choices are between 1 and 2,000,000 MB. Note that you can enter a number much larger than the actual amount of virtual memory you have available (about 1.9 terabytes), and, of course, 1 MB will pretty much always be hit, so you'll be recycling constantly.

■ **Maximum Used Memory (In Megabytes)** Will recycle based on physical memory usage, instead of virtual memory usage. The valid choices again are between 1 and 2,000,000 MB, which is far more memory than your average Windows Server has.

The Performance Tab

The Performance tab, shown in Figure 2-24, enables you to configure the options that keep IIS from taking over the CPU.

■ **Idle Timeout** Allows you to configure how long a worker process can stay idle before it is shut down. This allows more applications to be hosted on a server, especially if they are frequently idle, since they won't use CPU time when idle. You can choose any time period between 1 and 4,000,000 minutes.

■ **Request Queue Limit** Configures the number of requests that this application pool will queue up before rejecting any new requests. This prevents the server from becoming overloaded with requests. When the limit is reached, the server will respond to all new requests with an HTTP 503 "Service Unavailable" error. You can choose between 0 and 65,535 items in the queue.

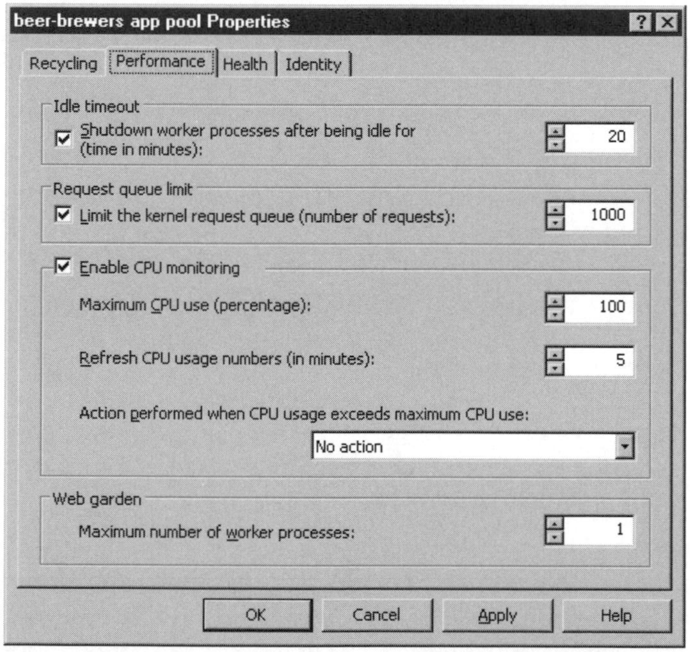

Figure 2-24.   *The Performance tab*

- **Maximum CPU Use (Percentage)**   Prevents this application pool from using a certain percentage of the CPU time. This uses CPU accounting to track the CPU time, and it is not done in real time. You can set any value between 1 and 100 percent.

- **Refresh CPU Usage Numbers (In Minutes)**   Configures the refresh time for CPU accounting. The CPU process numbers are updated at this interval. You can select any time between 1 and 1440 minutes.

- **Action Performed When CPU Usage Exceeds Maximum CPU**   You have two options: No Action or Shutdown. No Action just writes an event to the event log. Shutdown sends a shutdown request to the worker processes in this application pool.

Web Gardens   Web gardens allow you to farm out requests to more than one worker process in this application pool, which allows an even greater degree of performance and reliability, since this application will be using multiple worker processes and an error in one process will not affect the other worker processes. The Maximum Number Of Worker Processes setting allows you to set the number of worker processes in this application pool. You can choose between 1 and 4,000,000 worker processes for this application.

| Caution |

Setting too many worker processes can hurt your system's performance, since each one takes about 5 MB just to start. Keep this in mind when choosing how many worker processes to run on your server.

The Health Tab

The Health tab, shown in Figure 2-25, allows you to configure options that keep this application pool healthy or to detect when problems occur.

- **Enable Pinging**   Configures the system to ping the worker process periodically. If the worker process fails to respond, something is wrong with it, so IIS terminates that process and creates a new one. You can choose any value between 1 and 4,000,000 seconds.

Rapid-Fail Protection   Rapid-fail protection protects the server by monitoring failures in the worker processes. If a service fails a certain number of times in a certain time period, IIS shuts down this application pool to protect the server. The server will respond to all new requests with an HTTP 503 "Service Unavailable" error.

- **Failures**   Configures the number of failures that the server will allow before triggering the rapid-fail protection. You can choose any number between 1 and 4,000,000 failures.

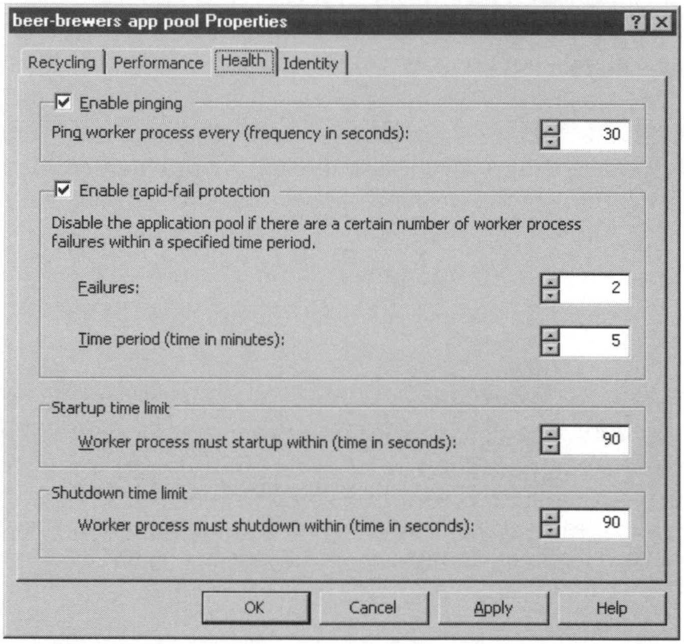

Figure 2-25. *The Health tab*

- **Time Period (Time In Minutes)** Configures the period of time in which these failures must take place before the rapid-fail protection takes place. You can choose any time period between 1 and 4,000,000 minutes.

Here's how it works:

1. The worker process fails.
2. IIS writes an event to the application log stating that the process terminated unexpectedly, and issues a process ID number and an exit code.
3. IIS restarts the worker process automatically when another request comes in.
4. This continues until the threshold is reached.
5. When the threshold is reached, IIS writes an event to the application log stating that the application pool is being automatically disabled due to multiple failures.
6. All clients attempting to use that application pool will receive a 503 "Service Unavailable" error.
7. This will continue until the application pool is stopped and restarted.

Startup and Shutdown Time Limits   Worker processes are not necessarily killed immediately when terminated, and they need time to start up as well. When a worker process needs to be stopped, it is sent a terminate request, and then it is given time for the current activities to finish and drain out of the queue before the process is terminated. If it's being recycled, the new process is up and running before the old one is stopped so that there is no interruption in service. Sometimes, a worker process doesn't stop very well or has problems starting up. These timeouts are used to configure how long IIS waits before determining that a problem exists.

- **Startup Time Limit**   Configures how long IIS will wait for a worker process to start. You can set a time between 1 and 4,000,000 seconds.

- **Shutdown Time Limit**   Configures how long IIS will wait for a worker process to stop gracefully. You can set a time between 1 and 4,000,000 seconds.

The Identity Tab

The Identity tab, shown in Figure 2-26, allows you to choose which security account the worker processes in this application pool will use. By default, worker processes will run as a Network Service, giving them limited rights to the operating system.

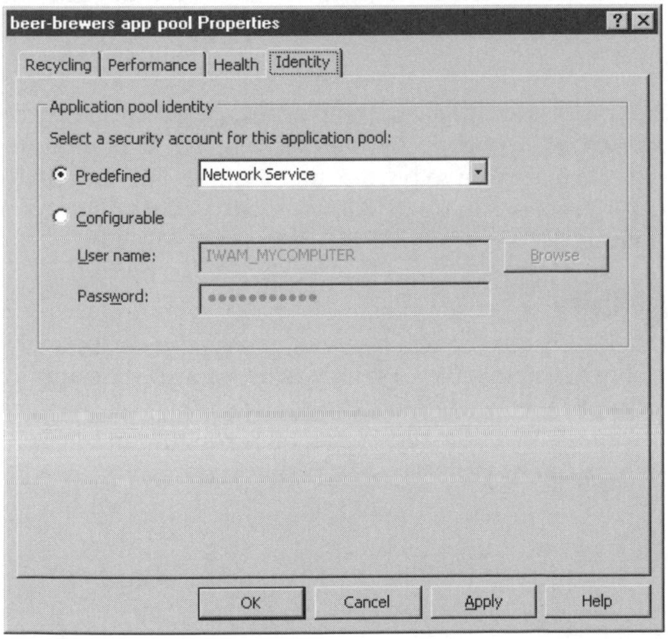

Figure 2-26.   *The Identity tab*

Here, you can choose which identity they will use. You can choose from a predefined identity, or choose a user account. Choosing a user account can be a security risk, since they typically have greater access to the operating system.

- **Network Service** This is the default choice, it's the most secure choice, and it's a good choice to run worker processes. It can't directly access the operating system and can't exert any control over it.

- **Local Service** Has more rights to the system than Network Service. It can access the operating system, but it can't access anything outside the server. It also can't interact with the desktop.

- **Local System** Has more rights than Local Service. In fact, Local System has full rights to the entire system.

All three accounts are part of the *IIS_WPG* group, which is on the local system to which you can assign rights. If you find you need to grant the worker process more rights than it currently has, you can grant those rights to the *IIS_WPG* group. If you configure an account for this worker process, you must make sure it is a member of the *IIS_WPG* group for it to run.

- **Configurable** Allows you to choose an account under which to run these worker processes. You can either type in the account or click the Browse button and select it there. You also need to provide the password and confirm it to use an account here.

When a worker process is launched, it has a token for the identity it is configured with. It uses this token when performing actions. When a client request comes through, that thread uses the client's token to process that request. This is called *impersonation*, and it allows worker processes to run at a low security level while still performing higher level operations.

Processor Affinity

When you have multiple processors in a server, you can tie an application pool to a processor. This allows you to have CPUs set aside for a specific application pool, guaranteeing that application more processing power. This option is available only if there are multiple processors in the server and IIS is running in Worker Process mode.

The
Complete
Reference

IIS 6

Chapter 3

The FTP Service

File Transfer Protocol (FTP) is a service that Internet Information Services (IIS) 6 offers with Windows Server 2003 (WS03). A number of FTP features enable the administrator to configure multiple FTP sites on a server and define the web user's interaction with the service. Administration may be performed by using the Microsoft Management Console (MMC) snap-in for IIS or by using a script.

Managing the FTP Service

The *Computer Management* MMC snap-in is a good choice for administering the FTP service in WS03, because it offers many other snap-ins useful for performing other WS03 administrative tasks in addition to administering IIS. A VBScript named *iisftp.vbs* is also provided with IIS, which offers command-line control over the FTP services.

Computer Management should be used by administrators who are accustomed to using the MMC for managing their Windows servers. The Computer Management snap-in may be used to administer a server remotely since it can run on a workstation and connect to the server that needs to be administered.

The *iisftp.vbs* script provides nearly the same functionality to the administrator as the IIS mode of the Computer Management MMC snap-in, including the ability to manage a host remotely. The *iisftp* script allows the administrator to automate tasks via the script or in conjunction with other scripts. The script may be used to make programmatic manipulations of the FTP server based on scripted logic and may be launched from the scheduler or user interaction.

Let's get started with the Computer Management MMC snap-in:

1. From the Start menu, choose All Programs | Administrative Tools | Computer Management.

2. Click the Services And Applications icon.

3. Click the Internet Information Services (IIS) Manager, and then click the folder icon labeled FTP Sites.

4. If the FTP Sites folder does not appear in the MMC, then the FTP service probably hasn't been installed. Installing the FTP services is required as a deliberate undertaking, as it is not a default selection while installing IIS on WS03. To add FTP services, first open the Control Panel.

5. Choose the Add And Remove Programs applet in the Control Panel.

6. Choose Add And Remove Windows Components from the left side of the Add And Remove Programs applet. The Windows Component Wizard will start.

7. Select Application Server in the list of Components in the Windows Component Wizard. Then click the Details button.

8. In the Application Server window, select Internet Information Services from the list of Subcomponents Of Application Server. Then click the Details button.

9. In the Internet Information Services window, File Transport Protocol (FTP) Service will appear as a selection in the list of Subcomponents Of Internet Information Services. Click this selection to install FTP Services.

You can expand all related icons for the nodes of interest in the MMC to expose the hierarchical relationship of the services and the instances of site configurations. Once the FTP service is installed, you can expand the FTP Sites node to reveal the FTP sites created on the host. Click on any of the FTP site nodes (if any exist) and you will see virtual directories for the respective FTP site, if any exist. When the FTP services are initially installed, a default FTP site named *Default FTP Site* is created for you.

To use the *iisvbs.vbs* script, open a command window by choosing Start | Run, type **CMD**, and click OK. Run the iisvbs script in the command window that opened. If you run the *iisftp.vbs* script directly from the Run window, the command window will open, execute the command, and close when it is completed, thereby offering no feedback as to the success or failure of the usage. Opening the command window first and entering the iisvbs command will enable the script to print feedback of the execution status to the command window. It will remain open after execution is complete so that you can see the execution feedback.

In the command window, type **iisftp** along with the switches and arguments that follow the name of the script and define what the script should do. Because the *iisftp.vbs* script file resides under the *\Windows\System32* directory, the *PATH* variable set for the server covers that location, so you don't need to type the full path to the script. To obtain help on iisftp, the expected switches, their arguments, and what they cause iisftp to do, run iisftp along with the switch and argument, /?, as shown next. The script, iisftp, will display help in the command window and define the script's switches, expected arguments for the switch, and what they cause the iisftp script to do.

```
iisftp /?
```

Windows Script Host Background

Windows Script Host (WSH) is the software on a Windows operating system that processes scripts. Scripts may be executed to produce output that is written to pop-up dialog windows or to command windows. The WSH executable that processes a script using a windowed output is called *Wscript.exe*. The WSH executable that processes a script using a command window output is called *Cscript.exe*. Windows will use either *Wscript.exe* or *Cscript.exe* as the default WSH executable for processing scripts. The default may be changed at any time using the following command syntax:

```
<WSH script executable> //h: <WSH script executable>
```

For example, to set WSH to use command windows as the default script executable, run the following command:

```
CScript //h: CScript
```

Some scripts require the use of one script executable versus the other. For the administrator, the *CScript* executable is the likely preferred choice. For the *iisftp* script, however, the use of the *CScript* is a requirement. As a result, if the WS03 server is set to use *Wscript* by default, a dialog box may appear when *iisftp* is run for the first time, which indicates that the script cannot be run using *WScript* and that it requires *CScript*. A second dialog box will appear after the first is closed, offering to change the default setting of the WS03 server to use *CScript* as the default. If you click the Yes button, the *CScript* executable will be set as the default WSH executable and the *iisftp* script will run the next time *CScript* is run.

Viewing FTP Service Status

In MMC Detail view, as shown in Figure 3-1, the right pane displays detailed information about the item selected in the left pane. List view, the default view setting, shows only icons and names representing the items subordinate to the selected node in the left pane of Computer Management.

Here's how to change the view setting: Right-click the right pane to open the context menu. Then choose View | Detail, and the right pane should change to show more details about the subordinate entities to the selected node in the left pane.

If, for example, the node for FTP Sites is selected in the left pane, as shown in Figure 3-1, the right pane will display all the FTP sites that are created on the host, plus the following information:

- **Description**   Name of the FTP instance
- **Identifier**   The ID number assigned to the FTP instance by IIS
- **State**   If the site is running, whether it's stopped or paused
- **IP Address**   IP address assigned to the FTP instance
- **Port**   Port of the FTP instance
- **Status**   Information about the configuration of the FTP instance

The *iisftp* script provides a query function that will offer output similar to that offered by clicking the FTP Sites node and viewing the right pane of the MMC in Detail view. Run the iisftp script with the following syntax to determine the status of the FTP sites:

```
iisftp /query
```

The resulting output from this command for the server shown in Figure 3-1 is shown in Figure 3-2. A tabular listing appears in the command window for all the FTP sites configured on the host. A description of each site is provided, along with the IIS ID number, status, assigned IP address, and the port for each respective FTP site instance.

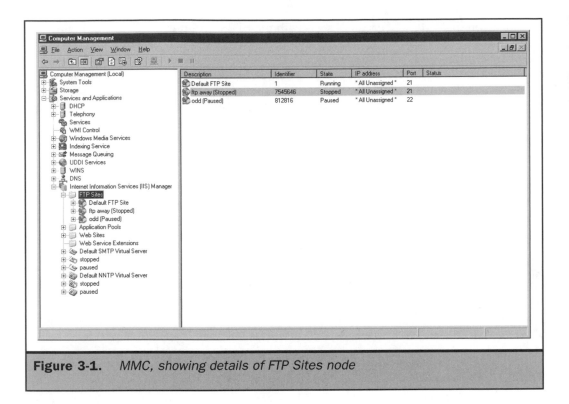

Figure 3-1.   *MMC, showing details of FTP Sites node*

Starting and Stopping FTP Sites

FTP sites are identified by "earth-globe" icons under the FTP Sites folder icon in the MMC. As shown in Figure 3-1, the FTP sites named *Default FTP Site*, *FTP away*, and *odd* have these earth-globe icons. If the FTP site is not running, the icon displays a small, red

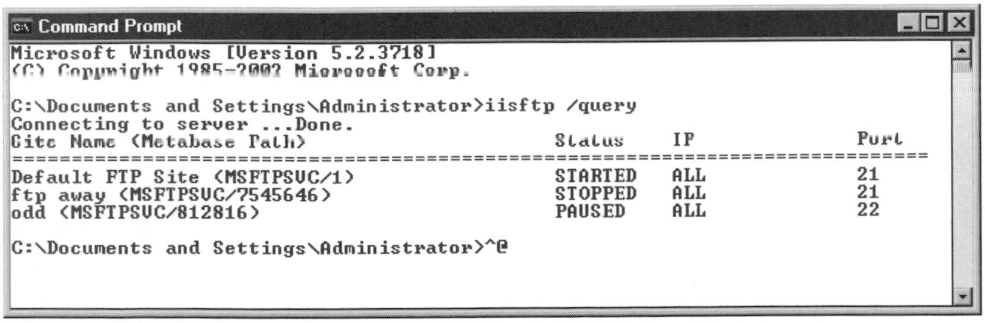

Figure 3-2.   *Results of iisftp script querying the local host*

"x-globe" on the earth-globe icon as seen with the FTP site named *FTP away* in Figure 3-1. You can *start*, *stop*, or *pause* FTP sites by right-clicking the site node in the MMC, and then choosing Start, Stop, or Pause to perform the respective action to the FTP site selected.

Starting an FTP site enables the server to respond to requests to log in, access resources, or place resources. If the FTP instance is *stopped*, it will refuse any request for a connection, which means that any user requesting to open a session with the FTP server will not be allowed to log in and the server will not respond with any message. If users are currently logged in and engaged in uploading or downloading files and the site is stopped, all transactions will cease immediately.

Selecting *Pause*, on the other hand, will acknowledge a connection when a user attempts to connect, but the connection will immediately be closed before the user can log in. If Pause is selected while users are connected, transactions will be allowed to complete and users logged in will be able to engage in new transactions, but users requesting access to the site will not be allowed access to the server.

You can also use the *iisftp* script to start, pause, and stop an instance of an FTP site, using the respective */start, /pause, or /stop* switch. For example, to start the FTP site named *default FTP site*, the following command can be used, and the script will return a message indicating a successful start or indicating the nature of the failure:

```
iisftp /start "default ftp site"
```

Current Sessions

In an FTP site's User Sessions window, which can be accessed from the MMC, you can determine who is logged in and manage existing sessions. Here's how to access the window that provides session maintenance:

1. Open the properties for a given FTP site by right-clicking the FTP site node in the MMC and choose Properties.

2. In the Properties window, choose the FTP Site tab.

3. Click the Current Sessions button near the lower-left corner of the window to open the FTP User Sessions window, where all current connections are displayed.

4. In this window, the administrator can disconnect a selected user or all of the users, as shown in Figure 3-3. This window can remain open indefinitely, and clicking the Refresh button will cause the MMC to update the current users displayed and the time that they have been connected.

Note   *The* iisftp *script offers no capability to manage current sessions. All the administration of current sessions must be handled through the MMC.*

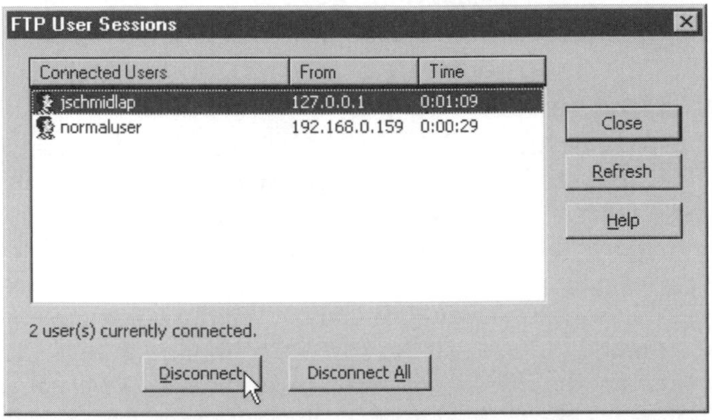

BASIC IIS SERVICES

Figure 3-3. *FTP User Sessions window, showing a few active sessions*

Managing FTP Site Contents Using the MMC

If the node for an FTP site is selected in the left pane of the MMC, the right pane will display virtual FTP sites, if any have been configured. The files or contents of the selected FTP site are not displayed in the right pane (even though this might be expected, since this is the native functionality found with a web site node in the MMC).

An administrator can examine and manage the contents of a given FTP site instance within the MMC using a number of the following functions:

- **Explore** Displays files in the MMC right pane, similar to how Windows Explorer would display the files

- **Open** Opens an instance of Windows Explorer at the physical file path

- **Permissions** Opens the Windows File Permissions dialog box

- **Browse** Displays files in the right pane of the MMC as the respective service would display

- **Export List** Saves a list of filenames, pathnames, and their respective status to a text file

These functions are all accessible in the MMC by right-clicking the FTP site or a node subordinate to an FTP in the left pane of the MMC. In the context-sensitive menu that appears, the first four commands manage the content of the FTP site. The Export List command is not grouped with the other commands and resides further down the menu.

Note   *The preceding list is not a comprehensive list of commands within the context-sensitive menu. The menu also offers other commands that aid in the administration of IIS FTP.*

Explore and Browse

The Explore and Browse commands of the MMC let you view and manage content. The Explore command causes the MMC to act as a proxy to the Windows Explorer. Files in the selected FTP site node are displayed using the display properties for the currently logged on user's Explorer settings. In addition, file attribute data indicates whether the file is archived or read-only. The display of content using this command is similar to the display the user sees when viewing contents in Windows Explorer.

The Browse command differs from the Explore command in that it displays the contents in the context of the *IIS service permissions* and *configurations* that apply to the selected node. In the case of FTP, file information is provided based on the attributes that FTP uses, such as filename, type, and modified date. Windows security or attribute information is not provided when the files are displayed using the Browse command, as they would be when using the Explore command. If a given FTP site does not allow anonymous access, the credentials for accessing the site may be requested when the Browse command is selected.

Open

The Open command extends the Explore command slightly so that an instance of Windows Explorer is opened for the physical file location on the server for the selected node.

Permissions

When a user logs in to an FTP site, he or she either authenticates as anonymous or uses a specific login name and password. Access to a given resource on the FTP server is dictated by the FTP service in conjunction with the Windows file permissions. If an FTP site allows anonymous access, a user will access resource under the credentials of a Windows account assigned as the surrogate user for anonymous users. If a user accesses an FTP site under specific domain, login, and password credentials, the server will verify these credentials against the indicated domain and enforce access based on the settings for the user's credentials and the Windows file permissions.

The FTP service does provide some access control, given that users can be allowed read or write privileges. Windows security operates as a subordinate system to the FTP service; the most restrictive policies of each are enforced if conflicting settings are encountered.

Export List

The Export List command saves a list of FTP sites or virtual directories at the currently select node into a tab-delimited text file. You can export a list from the FTP Sites node or from a given FTP site node or virtual directory node. The fields of the export file correlate to the view for the selected node in the right pane of the MMC. For example, in the case of a virtual directory, the fields are as follows:

- **Name**   Name of the file or virtual directory
- **Path**   Physical path of the file or virtual directory
- **Status**   Status of the file or virtual directory (for example, error message related to virtual directory)

Choosing the Export List command on the FTP Sites node will list all the FTP sites on the host. The following example shows the output for the FTP Sites node on a server:

```
Description    Identifier    State    IP address    Port    Status
Default FTP Site (Stopped)   1    Stopped    * All Unassigned *    21
ftp away (Stopped)    7545646    Stopped    * All Unassigned *    21
odd (Stopped)    812816    Stopped    * All Unassigned *    22
doc site    984253357    Running    * All Unassigned *    21
```

The Export List file will not list files or content located in a subdirectory of the physical path of the FTP site or virtual directory. This feature offers an administrator a means for documenting the contents of a system and communicating the content to others via e-mail or printed hard copy.

Refresh

Whenever the status of a given FTP site changes, the MMC may not reflect the exact status of the host. If sites are being changed or added via a script or other programmatic means, the view may not reflect the most accurate information and should be refreshed. In this case, you can refresh the Detail view by right-clicking the right pane and selecting the Refresh command. The host's status will be queried when the Refresh command is invoked to make sure that the view in the right pane is valid.

Creating and Configuring FTP Sites

Creating FTP sites on WS03 can be performed

- by using *iisftp* script,
- by processing a definition file, or
- by using the MMC FTP Site Creation Wizard.

Regardless of the means used to create the FTP site, the following information is required:

- Physical file path for the FTP root on the host server
- Name of the FTP instance used to identify the FTP site

An FTP site must also have an IP address and port that it will use. Knowing the site's IP address and port is not required, because it will be assumed if the administrator does not actively set these values.

The MMC provides configurations in addition to those provided by the *iisftp* script. *Iisftp*, for example, does provide the ability to configure important parameters required to support the major tasks that are core to managing FTP sites. The MMC offers additional FTP site creation features such as the following:

- The ability to configure the properties that all FTP sites can inherit using the FTP Sites node
- The ability to export definition files of FTP sites that can be used to create an identical FTP site

Virtual directories may also be used to enhance management of a given FTP site. When using virtual directories, an abstraction can exist between the physical file structure on the host and the structural organization as it appears to the FTP consumer.

FTP Site Creation Wizard

The MMC's FTP Site Creation Wizard walks the user through the creation of an FTP site. Every property for a given FTP site, except the User Isolation Mode, can be changed after the site's creation using the MMC Properties window.

Here's how to use the MMC FTP Site Creation Wizard:

1. Right-click any node subordinate to the FTP Sites node in the left panel of the MMC, and choose New | FTP Site from the context-sensitive menu.

2. The FTP Site Creation Wizard opens with a window introducing the wizard. Click the Next button, and the wizard will prompt for the site description, as shown in Figure 3-4.

3. Enter a descriptive name for the FTP site. Then click Next.

Set Up IP Address and Port

Next, you'll set up the site's IP address and port.

1. Set the site's IP address and the port in the IP Address And Port Selection window. By default, the port is set to 21, the standard port number used for FTP, although the port could be set to any number ranging from 1 to 65535. The default IP setting is (All Unassigned), but a specific IP will be selected, as shown in Figure 3-5.

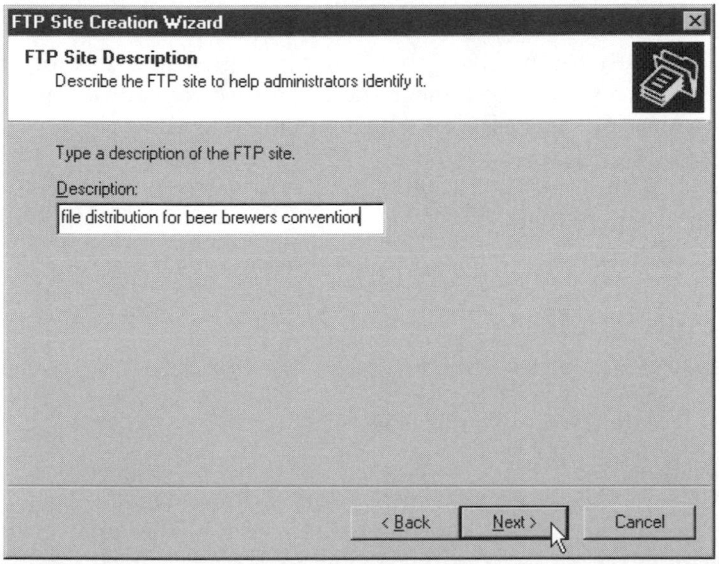

FTP Site Creation Wizard

FTP Site Description
Describe the FTP site to help administrators identify it.

Type a description of the FTP site.

Description:

file distribution for beer brewers convention

< Back   Next >   Cancel

Figure 3-4.   Site Description window for the FTP Site Creation Wizard

FTP Site Creation Wizard

IP Address and Port Settings
Specify an IP address and port setting for the FTP site.

Enter the IP address to use for this FTP site:

192.168.0.159

Type the TCP port for this FTP site (Default = 21):

65535

< Back   Next >   Cancel

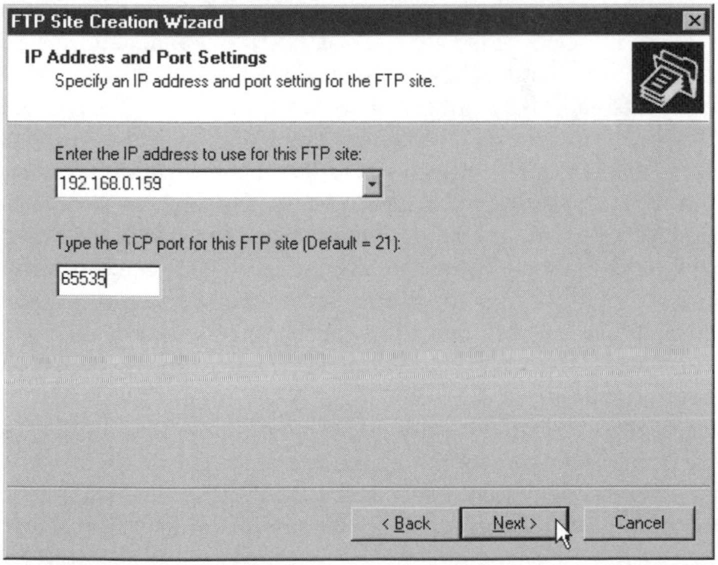

Figure 3-5.   IP Address And Port Settings window

2. Choose (All Unassigned) to cause IIS to choose the IP address that is to be used, by allowing all IP addresses for the server not otherwise assigned to be used for another purpose for the given port, to support the FTP site being created. For any given server, the port number and IP address must be unique. On a server having a single IP address, the (All Unassigned) setting is ideal. If the server has more than one IP address, select the desired IP address. Explicitly assigning an IP address will reduce the risk that at some future date another IP address will be added to the FTP site.

3. Click Next to open the FTP User Isolation window.

User Isolation Modes

You can choose from among three modes for user isolation:

- **Do Not Isolate Users**   No intrinsic access control based on a user's home directory exists.

- **Isolate Users**   Users authenticate to local or domain accounts of the FTP host server, and intrinsic access control exists that establishes directories for users and excludes other users from accessing other users' directories.

- **Isolate Users Using Active Directory**   Users authenticate to an active directory, and intrinsic access control exists that is based on a FTP root file path and the user's home directory file path obtained for the user from an active directory server.

Each mode is identified on the FTP User Isolation dialog box as an option selection. The default option is the Do Not Isolate Users. Choose the Isolate Users option if you want to create an FTP site that has home directories without the support of an active directory server. The Isolate Users option most closely resembles the native functionality found on a UNIX server when FTP is enabled. The Isolate Users Using Active Directory option offers the greatest extendibility, because the authentication takes place on a separate server and the location of the user's home directory can be different for each user. The Isolate Users option limits the physical location of the user's home directory to the physical host. Using the Isolate Users Using Active Directory option on the FTP site, user's home directories can exist on many physical hosts, and the active directory can serve the credentials and configurations for many physical hosts.

An active directory server is not available for this example, since it requires a special configuration that is beyond the scope of this chapter. As shown in Figure 3-6, the Isolate Users mode is selected for this site. This mode will authenticate users to the local host or a domain. Before users can access the site, a directory must be created for them; otherwise, logon will fail. For users authenticating to the local host, a directory called *LocalUser* must be created in the FTP root. Subordinate to that directory is a directory named for the user's login name. For example, if the FTP root was located at *C:\schmidlap_beer_FTP* and a user with the login *jschmidlap* needed to access the site, the home directory for jschmidlap would need to be created at: *C:\schmidlap_beer_FTP\ LocalUser\jschmidlap*. If the users authenticate to a domain controller, the *LocalUser* directory would be replaced with the respective domain controller name in the file

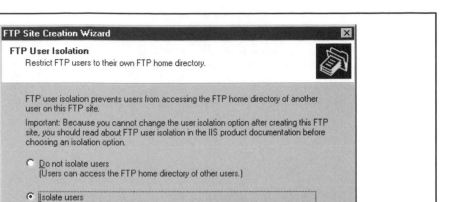

Figure 3-6.   *FTP User Isolation window*

path. For example, if the login *jschmidlap* needed to access the site and *jschmidlap* authenticated to the *Clowns* domain, the home directory that would need to be created is *C:\schmidlap_beer_FTP\Clowns\ jschmidlap*.

Home Directory

After you set up user isolation modes in the wizard, click Next to open the FTP Site Home Directory window, as shown in Figure 3-7. The path for the FTP root must be entered here. This path represents the physical path on the host where the FTP-related content and home directories for users reside. Users accessing the FTP site will not have access to file paths above or outside of this directory.

Site Access Permissions

After you click the Next button, the FTP Site Access Permissions window opens, where you'll indicate whether the site will enable *read* or *write* access permissions. The choices are not mutually exclusive, so either or both options may be selected. As shown in Figure 3-8, both Read and Write are selected so that users can download, upload, and delete files from the server. The Write permission allows users to upload and delete files from the FTP site. The Read permission provides access for files to be downloaded. The FTP server permissions are still subject to the Windows files permissions established by the host on the file system. The FTP server permissions will function as expected in so much as they do not conflict with the existing Windows file permissions.

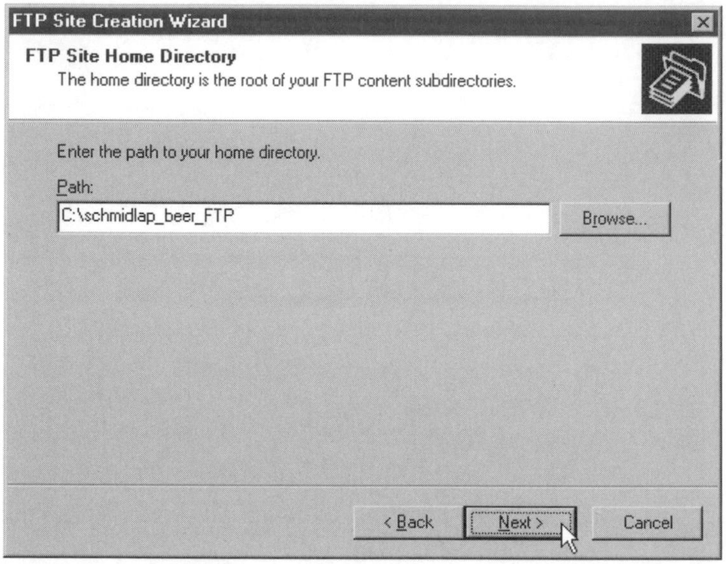

Figure 3-7. FTP Site Home Directory window

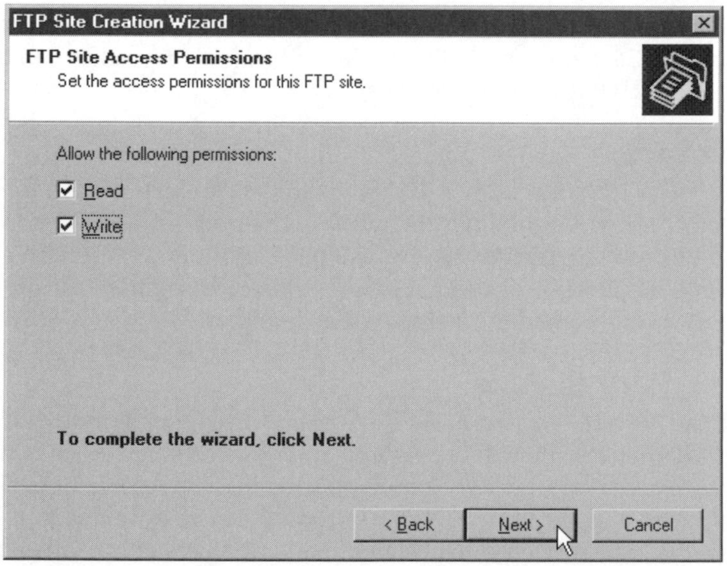

Figure 3-8. FTP Site Access Permissions window

Note *Oddly enough, it is possible not to select either option, which will result in an FTP site that will run but will not allow any users to log in because they do not have access to the site.*

Click the Next button, and you'll see the FTP Site Creation Wizard's final screen, which indicates that the FTP site will be created after you click the Finish button. After the wizard completes the creation of the site, the site node is added to the nodes of the existing FTP site listed subordinate to the FTP Sites node in the MMC.

Creating FTP Sites Using the iisftp Script

Using the *iisftp* script, an administrator can create an FTP site on a host to which he or she has console access or on a remote host to which the administrator has administrative permissions. The script provides the same functionality as the FTP Site Creation Wizard of the MMC. The script supports the following syntax:

```
iisftp [/s <server> [/u <username> [/p <password>]]]
/create <root> <name> [/b <port>] [/i <ip>] [/dontstart]
[/isolation <isomode> [/ADDomain <domain>
/ADAdmin <admin> /ADPass <password>]]
```

iisftp Switches and Arguments Used in FTP Site Creation

The primary switch that is unique to the creation of an FTP site is the */create* switch, which requires a root argument for the physical file path of the FTP root and a name argument for the name of the FTP site. Optionally, the port and IP address may be specified using the */b* and */i* switches, respectively. If neither the */b* or */i* switch is specified, the port is assumed to be port 21 and the IP address will be set to (All Unassigned).

If the */dontstart* switch is passed, the site will not be started after creation; otherwise, the site will be started automatically after creation. The optional */s*, */u*, and */p* switches are common to every command supported by the *iisftp* script for providing credentials that the script should utilize during execution. If the */s* switch is not specified, the local server will be assumed as the host on which the script will create the FTP site. The */u* and */p* switches are the user name and password credentials, respectively, that the script runs under. If the */u* and */p* switches are not specified, the credentials of the current user are assumed.

If the */isolation* switch is passed, either the argument *local* or *AD* must be passed to specify whether the user isolation mode should use the local system or domain controller accounts or an active directory. In the absence of the use of the */isolation* switch, no user isolation is assumed during the creation of the FTP site. When the */isolation* switch is set with the *AD* argument, the credentials for the active directory server must be set using the */ADDomain*, */ADAdmin*, and */ADPass* switches along with the respective arguments for each switch.

For a summary of the switches and their usage, refer to Table 3-1.

Switch	Argument	Required	Description	Default
/s	Server Name	No	Name of server hosting the FTP site	Local host
/u	Username	No	Username under which to execute the request; may be specified in the form *<domain>\<username>* or *<username>*	Current user's login
/p	Password	No	Password for the username specified	Current user's password
/create	Root file path	Yes	File path on the physical host to the root of the FTP site; path is created if it does not already exist	N/A
/create	Site Name	Yes	Name of the FTP site maintained by IIS for administrative purposes; this name is displayed in MMC and must be in quotes	N/A
/b	Port	No	Number of the port that the FTP site will utilize	21
/i	IP address	No	IP address that the FTP site will utilize	(All Unassigned)
/dontstart	N/A	No	Indicates that the site should not be started after creation if it is passed	Site is started after creation
/isolation	Local or AD	No	Sets the site to use user isolation mode	Site does not support user isolation

Table 3-1. *Summary of iisftp Script Switches for Creating an FTP Site*

Switch	Argument	Required	Description	Default
/ADDomain	Domain name of AD	No	Specifies the active directory domain name to be used if the isolation mode is set to AD.	N/A
/ADAdmin	Username for AD	No	Specifies the active directory administrative username to be used if the isolation mode is set to AD	N/A
/ADPass	Password for AD	No	Specifies the active directory administrative username's password to be used if the isolation mode is set to AD	N/A

Table 3-1.   *Summary of iisftp Script Switches for Creating an FTP Site* (continued)

To see an example of the script making a simple FTP site named *doc site* with a root located at *C:\FTPSites\docs*, refer to Figure 3-9.

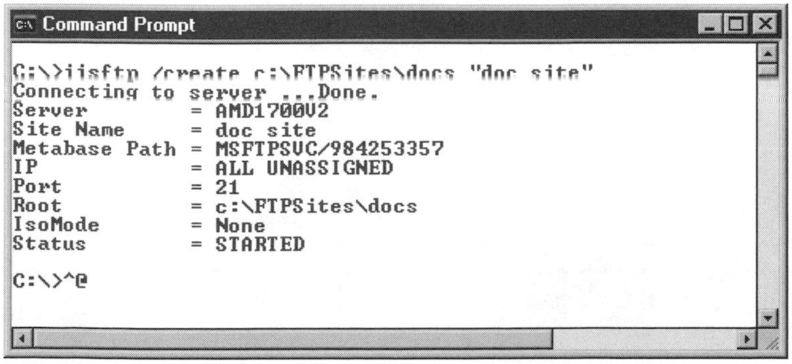

Figure 3-9.   *Creating a simple FTP site using iisftp script*

Using Export Definition Files

The MMC allows you to export the information required to produce an FTP site into an XML file. Here's how to make a configuration file: Right-click the FTP Sites node in the left panel of the MMC, and choose All Tasks | Save Configuration To A File. A window prompting for a filename will open. As shown in Figure 3-10, the option to protect the data by encrypting the file content with a password is also available. The encryption will not affect all of the element or attribute data. The XML element and attribute identifiers are also not encrypted.

Select a file, and then click the OK button. The prompt is dismissed, and the XML file is created. In the example shown in Figure 3-10, the file was named *AllFTPSites*.

An individual FTP site node or virtual directory site node can also be saved to a configuration file. The MMC will export the configuration for the selected node in the MMC and all subordinate configurations.

Here's how to create a site from a configuration file:

1. Right-click any node subordinate to the FTP Sites node in the left panel of the MMC. Then choose New | FTP Site (From File).

2. In the Import Configuration window, choose the file *AllFTPSites*, which was exported previously. Then click the Read File button. As shown in Figure 3-11, the existing FTP sites that were hosted when the configuration file was produced are listed.

3. After selecting a site to create, the OK button will become enabled; click it to close the dialog.

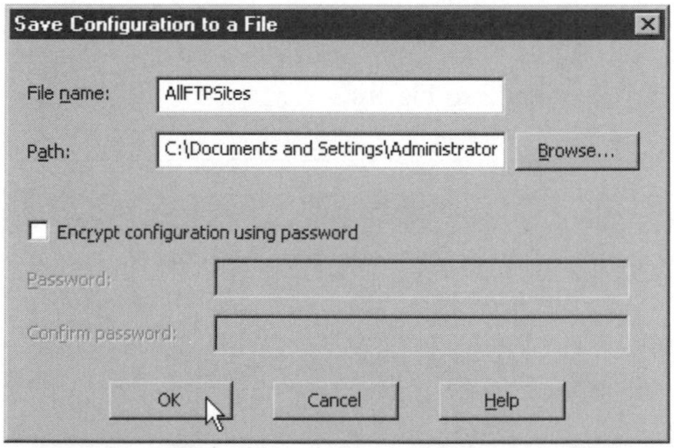

Figure 3-10. *Save a configuration to a file*

Import Configuration   ☒

File:

| C:\Documents and Settings\Administrator | Browse... | Read File |

Select a configuration to import:

Location
Default FTP Site
file distribution for beer brewers convention
doc site1
ftp away
odd
doc site

OK   Cancel   Help

Figure 3-11.   *Import Configuration window with an FTP site selected*

4. Because the site already exists within the host on which this example is being performed, a window appears, asking whether a new site should be created or whether the existing site should be replaced. As shown next, the option to create a new site is selected.

5. Click OK, and the site will be created; this site will be identical to the original site in every aspect, except that it will likely not run because it is assigned the same port and IP as the existing site on the same host, thereby causing a binding conflict to occur. If the configuration file were used to create a site on a different host that was not already occupying the same port or IP for a use, it would function after executing the file prompt.

Creating Virtual FTP Directories

Virtual directories may be created under existing FTP sites or virtual directories. Virtual directories allow an FTP site to emulate the existence of a physical path being subordinate to the FTP root when it does not physically exist subordinate to the FTP root. To the FTP site user, the virtual directory appears as another directory, even though the host file structure may not be organized that way.

The virtual directory in an FTP site can also support a configuration that may be different from that of the parent FTP site. The configurations for a virtual directory are as follows:

- **Physical File Path of Virtual Directory**   Local file path on the host or network path using the Universal Naming Convention (UNC) path
- **Read Permissions**   Permissions to download files from the directory
- **Write Permissions**   Permission to upload files to the directory or delete files from the directory
- **Log Visits**   Access to the virtual directory will be logged if the FTP site logging is enabled
- **Directory Security**   IP restriction may be established such that users from a given IP may or may not be allowed access to the virtual directory

The MMC must be used to create or configure the virtual directories, since this functionality is not available in the *iisftp* script. To create a virtual directory, the Virtual Directory Creation Wizard must be invoked unless you generate the virtual directory from a file. Except for the screen prompting for the user isolation mode and a screen prompting for IP address and port number, the same steps used to create an FTP site using the FTP Site Creation Wizard are used in the Virtual Directory Creation Wizard.

1. To start the MMC Virtual Directory Creation Wizard, right-click the FTP site node or virtual directory site node in the left pane of the MMC to which the intended virtual directory should be subordinate.

2. Choose New | Virtual Directory.

3. The Virtual Directory Creation Wizard will open with a window introducing the wizard and the purpose of the wizard. Follow the steps described in the section "FTP Site Creation Wizard" earlier in this chapter. Skip the steps under "User Isolation Modes" and "Set Up IP Address and Port."

If you make a mistake in the Virtual Directory Creation Wizard, you can change any of the properties of the virtual directory. Right-click on the virtual directory, select Properties, and configure any of the properties using the Properties window.

FTP Sites Node Configuration

The FTP Sites node in the MMC provides a means for you to set the properties that affect all the existing FTP sites for the FTP server host through *inheritance*. To access the FTP Sites properties, right-click the FTP Sites node in the left panel of the MMC and choose Properties. The Properties window for the FTP Sites node is identical to the Properties window of a given FTP site. Some properties for the FTP Sites node cannot be edited, because inheriting the values would not make sense—for example, the following items are not editable at the FTP Sites level:

- **Name** Name of the FTP site in the MMC
- **IP Address** IP address that the FTP site uses
- **Port** Port number for the FTP site
- **Root Path** Physical file path for the FTP root

By configuring properties for the FTP Sites node, existing sites can inherit the settings and all future FTP sites created will inherit the settings. As expected, individual FTP sites can be configured with alternative property configurations that differ from the FTP Sites node properties if they are configured separately.

For example, a welcome banner may be set in the FTP Sites node that differs from the existing welcome banner used in many of the existing FTP sites. Some of the FTP sites may not have a welcome banner specified at all. The sites that do not have a banner specified will get the new banner placed in the FTP Sites node property for the welcome banner when it is entered and applied. When the welcome banner is set in the FTP Sites Properties window by clicking OK or Apply, a prompt appears, indicating that existing FTP sites include a value for the welcome banner. The prompt will ask whether the existing values should be changed or remain unchanged. The FTP sites that should have their welcome banner changed should be selected in the prompt, and those sites that do not require the change should not be selected. When the prompt is dismissed, the changes will be applied to the selected sites.

Advanced IIS MMC Configurations

In addition to the settings required to create or configure an FTP site, you can set other properties in the MMC that affect the way that a given FTP site interacts with the user or the host.

Connections

IIS provides automated management of connections for a given FTP based on a connection timeout and a maximum number of connections that will be supported by the server. The connection timeout property for a given FTP site determines the amount of time that can pass when a user is disconnected from the site due to inactivity. If the time period for the connection timeout property elapses from the last request a user makes to the FTP site, the user will be automatically disconnected and will have to reauthenticate to the FTP site to continue to interact with the FTP site.

To set the connection timeout or maximum number of connections for a given FTP site, right-click the FTP Site node of the MMC, and then choose Properties. In the Properties window for the selected FTP site, the FTP Site tab is open by default. About halfway down is FTP Site Connections. The maximum number of FTP site connections can be set here. You can also specify a maximum amount of time a user is allowed to maintain a connection to the server. After the value is changed, click OK or Apply to set the change.

Directory Security—IP Address Restrictions

IIS supports IP address–based access control for the FTP Sites node, a given FTP site, or a virtual directory. Users who have a given IP address may be excluded or exclusively provided access to a given FTP site or virtual directory.

Here's how to set IP address restrictions for the FTP Sites node, an FTP site, or a virtual directory:

1. Right-click the respective node in the left pane of the MMC, and select Properties.

2. In the Properties window for the selected FTP site, choose the Directory Security tab. You'll see a list box labeled Except Those Listed Below, which lists the exceptions to the exclusive options identified as Granted Access and Denied Access.

3. If you select Granted Access, the list box shows the IP addresses that are not allowed access to the FTP site. If you select Denied Access, the list box shows the IP addresses that are granted access.

4. If you want to exclude all users except for a few with a given IP address or subnet, choose the Denied Access option and enter the IP address or subnet for those users who should be allowed into the FTP site.

5. If you want to allow all users except for a few with a given IP address or subnet, choose the Granted Access option and enter the IP addresses or subnets for those users who should be denied access.

6. After you make your selection, click OK or Apply to set the property setting.

Directory Listing Style—MS-DOS or UNIX

IIS allows a server to act like a UNIX server FTP site or a DOS server site—but only in how the files are listed in the server directory. The UNIX mode causes the file-listing format to look like the style of a UNIX server listing. The MS-DOS mode causes IIS to list files as though the `dir` command had been called in a command window on a Windows operating system.

Here's how to set the directory listing style for the FTP Sites node or a given FTP site:

1. Right-click the respective node in the left pane of the MMC, and choose Properties.

2. In the Properties window that opens for the selected node, choose the Home Directory tab.

3. Near the bottom of the tab under Directory Listing Style are two options called UNIX and MS-DOS. To set the desired style for the FTP node, select the respective option for the desired style and click the OK or Apply button to set the new property.

Messages

Messages that are presented to the user at the login or exit of the FTP site may be set for a given FTP site or the FTP Sites node. To set the messages presented for the FTP Sites node or a given FTP site, right-click the respective node in the left pane of the MMC and choose Properties. In the Properties window, choose the Messages tab, as shown in Figure 3-12.

The following messages may be set:

- **Banner**   Text message displayed when a user opens the FTP site
- **Welcome**   Text message displayed after a user successfully authenticates to the FTP site
- **Exit**   Text message displayed when a user exits the FTP site
- **Maximum Connections**   Text message displayed when a user attempts to open the FTP site and access is denied because the maximum connections have been met

Refer to Figure 3-13 for a sample dialog box showing an FTP server that is configured with the messages set in Figure 3-12.

Logging Configuration

IIS maintains logs of FTP events and interactions with an FTP server for a given user. A single log is generated for each FTP site by default. IIS enables an administrator to choose to log or not to log, the log style, the file location or database for the log, and the data included in the log. Please see Chapter 11 for more information about IIS logging.

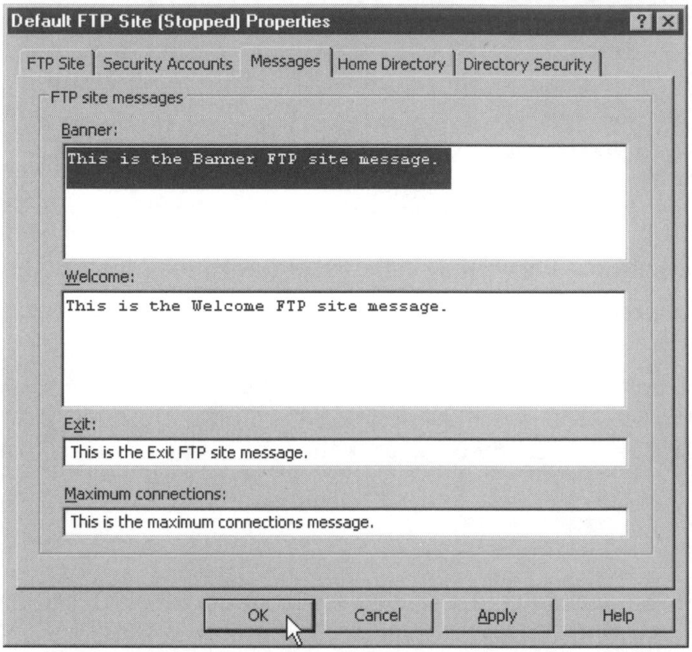

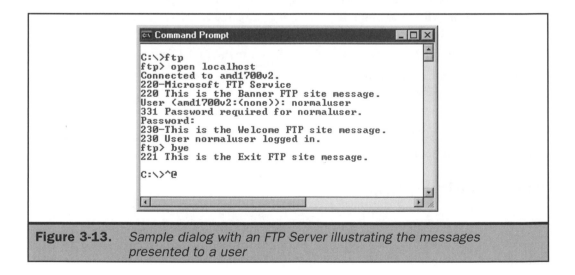

Figure 3-12. *Messages tab of the Properties window for an FTP site*

Figure 3-13. *Sample dialog with an FTP Server illustrating the messages presented to a user*

Here's how to configure the logging for the FTP Sites node or a given FTP site:

1. Right-click the respective node in the left pane of the MMC, and choose Properties.

2. In the Properties window, choose the FTP Site tab.

3. At the bottom of the tab, as shown in Figure 3-14, you can check the Enable Logging checkbox. The Active Log Format drop-down list determines whether the log is written to a database table or text file format.

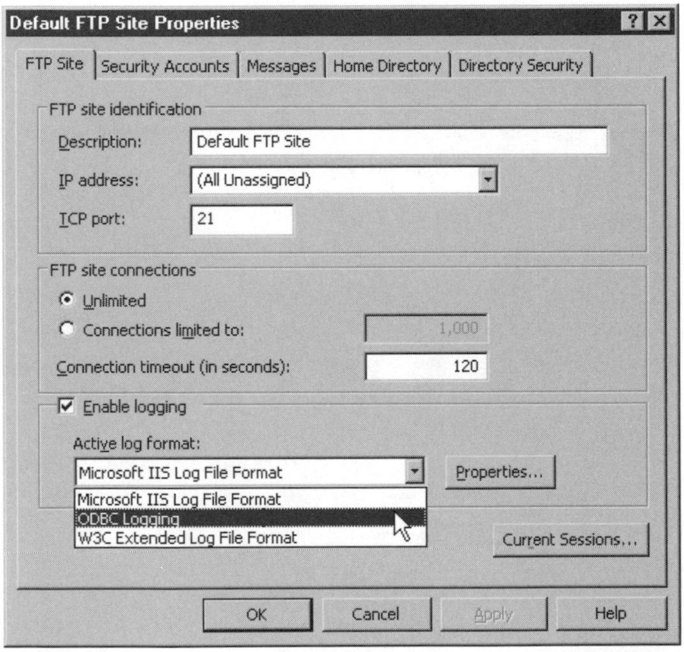

Figure 3-14. *FTP Site tab for FTP Site Properties window*

The
Complete
Reference

IIS 6

Chapter 4

The SMTP Service

IIS 6 provides the Simple Mail Transport Protocol (SMTP) service. SMTP allows one computer to send messages to another; incoming messages are routed to a mailbox on the host, if the messages' destination is the host server. If a message's intended destination is not for a mailbox or user account on the host, the SMTP server forwards the message to the intended destination.

When the SMTP server is forwarding a message from a client, it contacts the next host prior to accepting delivery from the client. If the next host cannot be contacted or refuses acceptance for some reason, the SMTP server will not accept the message from the client and will send the client an error message indicating a *non-delivery event*. An SMTP server, by default, directly contacts the server hosting the domain to which the intended message is addressed. SMTP servers may be configured in a variety of ways to offload the resources of authenticating a client, maintaining connection state, and forwarding messages. In some cases, the next host may not be configured to accept any messages, because some administrators establish SMTP servers that are devoted to sending messages to remove the burden from the SMTP servers that are receiving messages from clients. Despite its name, SMTP is not always so simple.

Using the IIS 6 administration tools, the SMTP server may be configured to distribute messaging services across various hardware and network topographies. Message *routing*, *encryption*, and *authentication* configurations can be customized to accommodate the unique characteristics of a particular network and organization.

Given this overall architecture, the administrator will likely want to control the following:

- How a client authenticates to the SMTP server prior to sending messages
- How messages are transported to the SMTP server from a client
- How messages are transported from the SMTP server
- How messages are routed from the SMTP server
- SMTP configurations for a given SMTP domain

Managing the SMTP Service

The Computer Management Microsoft Manager Console (MMC) snap-in is a good choice for administering SMTP on Windows Server 2003 (WS03), because it offers many additional snap-ins for other WS03 administrative tasks.

Here's how to get started with the Computer Management MMC snap-in:

1. Choose Start | All Programs | Administrative Tools | Computer Management.

2. In the Computer Management MMC, click the Services And Applications node.

3. Click the Internet Information Services Manager node to open it.

Unlike many of the other services under IIS, the SMTP service does not have a monolithic node in the MMC that may be used to administer all instances of the service. For example, the File Transfer Protocol (FTP) service has the FTP Sites node in the MMC that you may use to make configuration changes that affect all of the FTP sites. Instead, SMTP virtual servers are created independently and subordinate to the IIS node. Just as any other service has a node in the Services section of the MMC, so too does the SMTP service. The SMTP service applet can be opened to administer the SMTP service.

Viewing SMTP Virtual Server's Status

If the Computer Management MMC is set to *Detail view*, the right pane will display more information about the item selected in the left pane. *List view* is the default view setting, which shows only icons and names representing the items subordinate to the selected node in the left pane. To change the view setting, right-click the right pane and select View | Detail. If the node for IIS is selected in the left pane, as shown in Figure 4-1, the right pane will display all the SMTP virtual servers that are created on the host and the following information:

- **Name** Name of the SMTP virtual server
- **Status** Whether the SMTP virtual server is running, paused, or stopped

Starting, Pausing, and Stopping SMTP Virtual Servers

Starting an SMTP virtual server will enable it to respond to requests. After an SMTP virtual server is created, it is started; however, it would *not* be started if the SMTP virtual server was intentionally stopped or paused or if the server failed to start due to a configuration conflict. *Pausing* an SMTP virtual server will prevent it from responding to new requests for sending messages, but the server will continue to process existing requests. Pausing an SMTP virtual server allows the administrator to change configurations on that server, without having to stop it to make the changes. Stopping an SMTP virtual server, on the other hand, prevents it from responding to any requests or processing any message queues that may exist prior to the stop command being issued.

SMTP virtual servers are identified by envelope icons under the IIS icon in the Computer Management MMC, as shown on the SMTP virtual server named "Default SMTP Virtual Server" in Figure 4-1. If an SMTP virtual server is not running, the icon displays a small, red "x-globe" on the envelope icon, as shown on the SMTP virtual server named "stopped" in Figure 4-1. If an SMTP virtual server is paused, its envelope icon is marked by two parallel vertical lines, as seen on the SMTP virtual server named "paused" in Figure 4-1. SMTP virtual servers may be started, paused, or stopped by right-clicking the node in the Computer Management MMC and choosing Start, Pause, or Stop to perform the respective action.

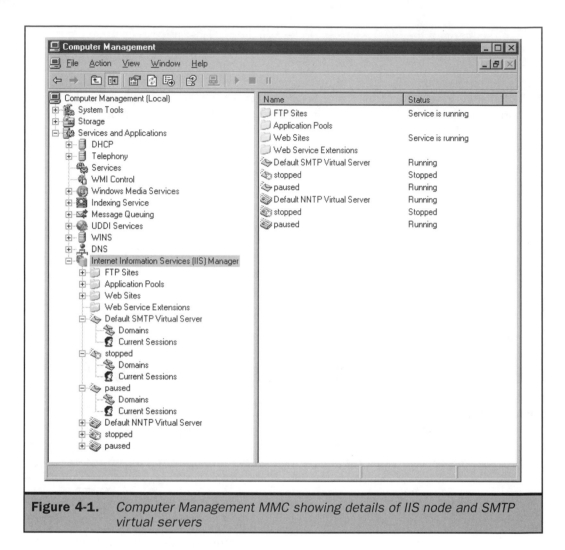

Figure 4-1.   *Computer Management MMC showing details of IIS node and SMTP virtual servers*

Starting, Pausing, and Stopping SMTP Service

Starting, pausing, or stopping the SMTP service will affect all SMTP virtual servers that reside on the host. As expected, stopping the SMTP service will cause all SMTP virtual servers to stop. If you stopped the SMTP server, starting the SMTP service will cause all SMTP virtual servers to start automatically that were started or paused prior to the stop command being issued. Any SMTP virtual servers that were stopped prior to the SMTP service being shut down will remain stopped after the SMTP service is started. Pausing the SMTP Service causes all the SMTP virtual servers to pause if they were started or paused previous to the pause command being issued. If any of the SMTP virtual servers were stopped prior to the pause command being issued to the SMTP service, they will remain unaffected in a stopped state. Oddly enough, starting the SMTP service after it was paused by using the resume command causes all the SMTP virtual servers to return to their original operating status, which is slightly different than the behavior exhibited when the SMTP service is started from a stop command. When the SMTP service is started from a stop command, all SMTP virtual servers are started, including SMTP virtual servers that were paused prior to the stop being issued. For a summary of the start and stop behavior for the SMTP service and the effects on the virtual servers, please refer to Table 4-1.

Controlling the SMTP service is accomplished via the SMTP service applet opened from the MMC under the Services node. To access the SMTP service applet, expand the Services And Applications node in the left pane of the Computer Management MMC and select the Services node. A "gear-to-gear" icon represents a service as well as the services node in the MMC snap-in, as seen in Figure 4-2. If the Computer Management MMC was previously opened to access the IIS node, the Services node is located on the same level of the tree as the IIS node.

With the Services node selected in the MMC's left pane, the services loaded on the host server are displayed in the right pane alphabetically; the SMTP service will be close to the bottom of the list unless the name column heading is clicked to reverse the sorting, as shown in Figure 4-2. After you select an SMTP service from the list in the right pane, the MMC snap-in provides links in the upper-left corner of the right pane; these are used for starting, stopping, or pausing the selected service.

Command Issued to SMTP Service	SMTP Service Prior to Command	SMTP Virtual Server State Prior to Command	SMTP Virtual Server's State Post Command
Stop	Started	Started	Stopped
Stop	Started	Paused	Stopped
Stop	Started	Stopped	Stopped
Start	Stopped	Started	Started
Start	Stopped	Paused	Started
Start	Stopped	Stopped	Stopped
Start	Paused	Started	Started
Start	Paused	Paused	Paused
Start	Paused	Stopped	Stopped

Table 4-1. *Start and Stop Behavior for the SMTP Service and Effects on the Virtual Servers*

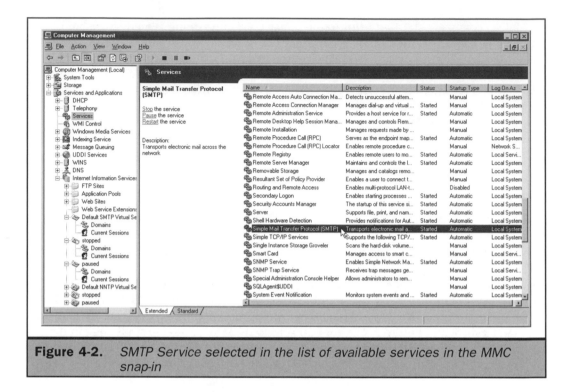

Figure 4-2.   *SMTP Service selected in the list of available services in the MMC snap-in*

Startup Type for the SMTP Service

Double-click the SMTP service in the right pane of the MMC to open the SMTP service applet, which provides the same capabilities for starting, stopping, and pausing the service as the links at the upper-left corner of the right pane. The SMTP service applet also provides configuration settings for how the service should start and run.

By default, the SMTP service is set to start automatically when the host is booted. You can change the configuration of the SMTP service in the General tab's Startup Type area so that it starts manually or so that it's disabled entirely: Choosing Automatic as the Startup Type setting causes the SMTP service to start when the host boots. The Disabled startup type disables the SMTP service, and the Manual startup type requires that an administrator start the SMTP service deliberately after the host boots.

Creating and Configuring SMTP Virtual Servers

To allow a WS03 server to send e-mail using SMTP, the SMTP service must first be installed and running on the server. If the SMTP service is installed and running, an SMTP virtual server must be created to enable use of the SMTP service. By default, an SMTP virtual server is created on a WS03 server when the SMTP service is installed.

If another SMTP virtual server must be added, the Computer Management MMC provides a wizard that walks the administrator through the process of defining a basic configuration of the SMTP virtual server. Unlike the FTP and web servers that are a part of IIS, SMTP virtual servers cannot be created from or exported to a configuration file. A script to administer SMTP and create SMTP virtual servers is also not available, so the New SMTP Virtual Server Wizard is the only option an administrator can use to create an SMTP virtual server.

New SMTP Virtual Server Wizard

Every property for a given SMTP virtual server except the home directory value can be changed at a later date using the Properties window of the Computer Management MMC. Entering an incorrect value in the wizard is not difficult to correct after the virtual server is created. Here's how to start the New SMTP Virtual Server Wizard:

1. Right-click the Internet Information Services Manager node in the left pane of the MMC and choose New | SMTP Virtual Server.

2. The New SMTP Virtual Server Wizard will open, prompting you for the site name, as shown in Figure 4-3. Enter a descriptive name that will be useful for identifying the SMTP site. The value you enter will be displayed next to the node for the SMTP virtual server in the Computer Management MMC.

3. Click the Next button to continue.

4. The next screen prompts for the IP address that the virtual server should use, as shown in Figure 4-4. Messages that are sent and received from the host server

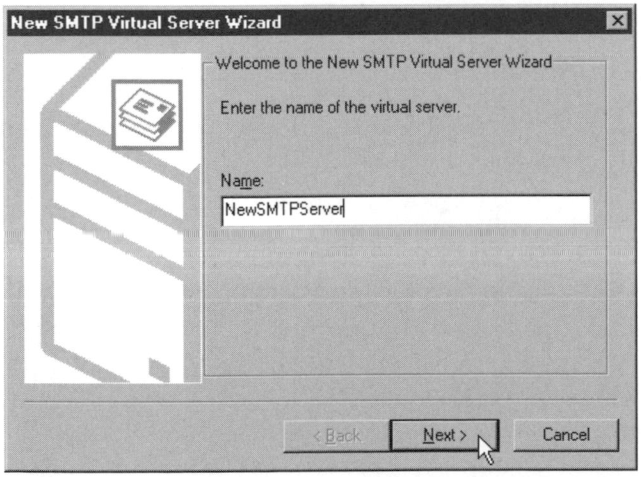

Figure 4-3.   *SMTP virtual server name prompt of the New SMTP Virtual Server Wizard*

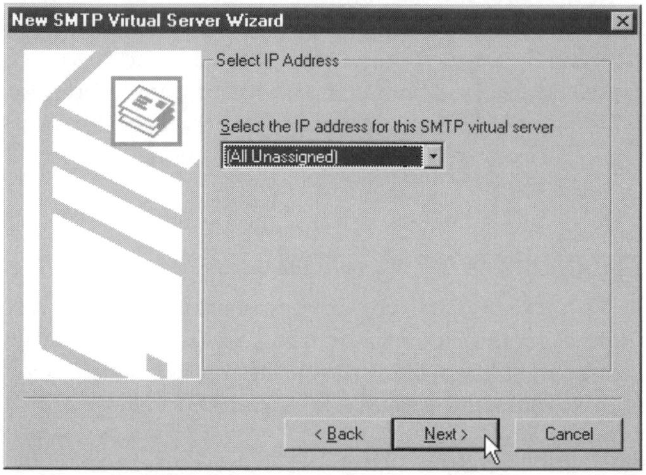

Figure 4-4. *Select IP Address screen of the wizard*

will use this IP address. The default value is (All Unassigned), but if multiple IP addresses exist, they will appear in the drop-down list. Because the list is an "exclusive" selection type, if the selection does not appear here, an administrator cannot type it into the box. For a host server with only one IP address (as in this example), the value (All Unassigned) is the only selection allowed. Allow the (All Unassigned) value to remain and click the Next button.

5. The New SMTP Virtual Server Wizard will next display the Select Home Directory screen. The home directory for an SMTP virtual server is the file path on the host server where the messages and SMTP virtual server–related files are written by the SMTP service. The following subdirectories are created subordinate to the chosen home directory for any SMTP virtual server:

■ **BadMail**   Directory in which messages are placed when they are returned with a non-delivery report

■ **Drop**   Directory in which all incoming messages for a given domain are written

■ **Pickup**   Directory in which messages are written that are to be picked up by a given messaging service

■ **Queue**   Directory on the server in which e-mail is queued for pickup in a remote triggered delivery when a remote domain is being supported

Select a file path, as shown in Figure 4-5, for the SMTP virtual server to use as the home directory. Click the Browse button to locate the path, if necessary.

IP Address and Port Conflict

If an SMTP virtual server is already configured on the server host and the IP address that is used for the existing SMTP virtual server is the same address chosen in the Select IP Address screen, the error message shown in the following illustration is displayed. When in doubt, clicking Yes will cause no problems in the current services for the SMTP server virtual directories, and the IP and port for the new SMTP virtual directory may be changed at a later date. If the IP address chosen for a new SMTP server conflicts with an existing SMTP virtual server, the new virtual server will be stopped after it is created and will not cause any disruption in the existing SMTP virtual directory's service.

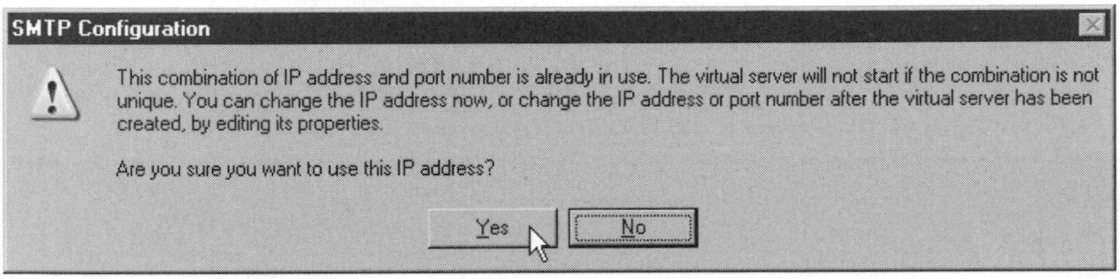

6. After selecting the file path, click the Next button to reveal the Default Domain screen. The default domain is the domain name appended to a given account name during authentication. Enter a value in the text box, as shown in Figure 4-6, and click the Finish button. The wizard will generate the new SMTP virtual server.

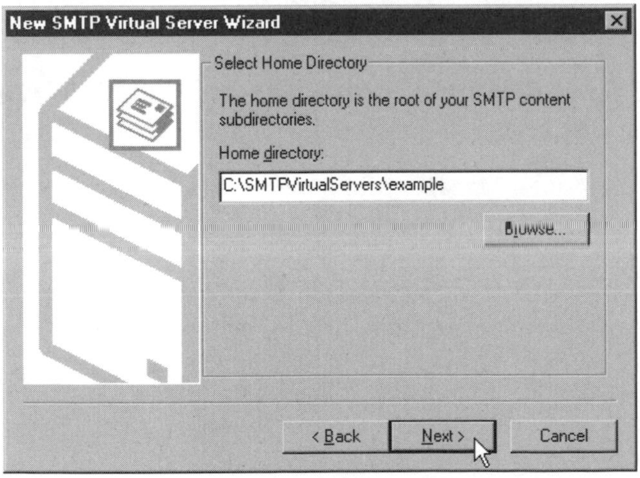

Figure 4-5.   *Choose home directory screen of the new SMTP virtual server wizard*

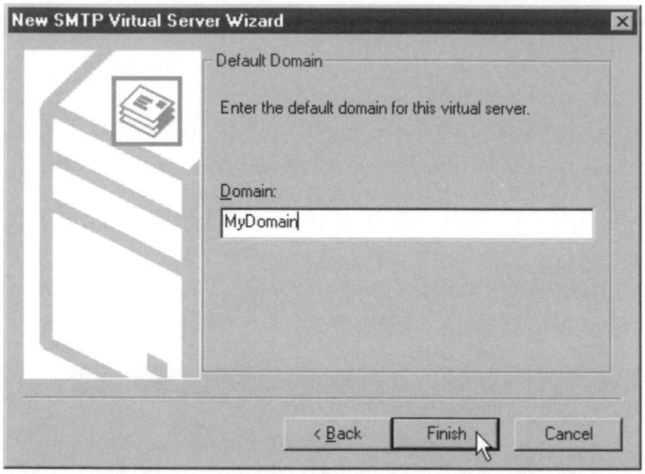

Figure 4-6. *Set the default domain name*

Configuring an SMTP Virtual Server

After the new SMTP virtual server has been created, the administrator will likely need to edit some of its functions. Configurations can be set in an SMTP virtual server in two ways: a Properties window is available for the SMTP virtual server itself, and Properties windows are available for each domain within an SMTP virtual server. Using these windows, an administrator can configure the SMTP virtual server to meet an organization's messaging requirements with SMTP.

Opening the Properties Window for an SMTP Virtual Server

Here's how to open the Properties window for an SMTP virtual server:

1. Open the Computer Manager MMC snap-in, and click the Services And Applications node in the left pane to expose the available subordinate nodes.

2. The Internet Information Services Management node should be found subordinate to the Services And Applications node. Click the Internet Information Services Management node to expand the subordinate nodes.

3. Right-click the SMTP virtual server node in the left pane and select Properties. The Properties window will open, where you can administer configuration options for the SMTP virtual server to which the window pertains.

Opening the Properties Window for a Domain in an SMTP Virtual Server

Here's how to open the properties window for the domain of an SMTP virtual server:

1. Open the Computer Manager MMC and navigate through the nodes to the SMTP virtual server to which the domain pertains.

2. Click the SMTP virtual server node in the left pane of the MMC to reveal the nodes subordinate to the SMTP virtual server. You'll see two subordinate nodes to each SMTP virtual server, called *Domains* and *Current Sessions*.

3. Click the Domains node to reveal the domains that are used in the SMTP virtual server, which are listed in the right pane.

4. Right-click the respective domain name in the right pane of the MMC, and then choose Properties to open the Properties window.

Connection Settings

An SMTP server is primarily designed to send and receive messages for a specified domain. The number of concurrent connections supported by an SMTP virtual server and the allowable connection timeout can have a great impact on the host server's overall resource utilization. If too many clients are simultaneously attempting to send or receive messages from the server, the server may not be able to support other important tasks. Limiting the number of concurrent connections that an SMTP virtual server can support also protects the server from Denial-of-Service (DoS) attacks that are designed to attack the server by wasting its resources in processing an overwhelming number of bogus requests. The number of concurrent connections that the SMTP virtual server can support is set by limiting the number of maximum connections allowed and the maximum time allowed for a connection to remain open while inactive. Setting a connection timeout will cause the server to terminate connections with clients that remain inactive for the allotted time period, thereby eliminating connections that are unfruitful for both the client and the server.

Connections for Inbound Messages

Here's how to set the number of connections that an SMTP virtual server can support for clients that desire to send messages:

1. Open the Properties window for the SMTP virtual server, as described previously.

2. By default, the General tab is open. On this tab, you'll see a checkbox below the IP address for the SMTP virtual server labeled Limit Number Of Connections To. Check it to enable a text box to its right.

3. Enter a number in the text box that represents the maximum number of concurrent connections the server will allow to connect to send messages. By default, no limit on the number of concurrent connections is imposed. Enter a value between 1 and 1999999999 as a maximum number of connections. It is difficult to suggest a good limit because it is largely dependent on many factors exclusive to the environment, such as server usage, network, and server resource.

4. The default connection timeout is set at 10 minutes. This setting is also located on the General tab of the Properties window below the Limit Number Of Connections To checkbox. Enter a value in the text box labeled Connection Time-Out (Minutes) to specify the maximum amount of time the server will allow a connection to be maintained without any activity. Clients may initiate a connection and due to connectivity failures, may not be able to complete the request or properly close the connection. Without the timeout setting, the SMTP server could wait indefinitely to respond to a connection request for a client that cannot complete the request; with a timeout set, the SMTP server will terminate the connection after the specified time.

Connections for Outbound Messages

A limit for the number of connections for outbound messages may be set using the Properties window for the SMTP virtual server.

1. Open the Properties window and select the Delivery tab.

2. Click the Outbound Connections button at the bottom of the window to open the Outbound Connections window.

3. The Limit Number Of Connections To checkbox is checked by default and set to 1000 connections, and Time-Out (Minutes) is set to 10. Set a limit on the number of connections for outbound messages.The range of valid limits is the same as it is for inbound messages: 1 through 1999999999.

4. In the Outbound Connections window, the administrator can set the number of connections for a given domain and the port number that is used to handle outbound connections. Set the number of connections for a given domain to a number less than the total number of connections allowed for outbound connections. The port used for outbound connections is 25 by default, which is the same port used for inbound. If you need to change the port for security or other restriction conditions, choose a port different from the port used for inbound messaging.

Logging Configuration

As is the case with WWW (World Wide Web) and the FTP (File Transfer Protocol) services, IIS also maintains logs of SMTP events and interactions with an SMTP virtual server for a given connection. A single log is generated for each SMTP virtual server if logging is enabled. Using the Properties window for a given SMTP virtual server, the administrator can choose to log or not to log, the log style, the file location or database for the log, and the data to be included in the log.

Here's how to configure logging for an SMTP virtual server: Open the Properties window. At the bottom of the General tab, you'll see the Enable Logging area and checkbox. Check the Enable Logging checkbox to turn on logging and enable log configuration. By default, the Enable Logging checkbox is not checked, so logging is not turned on. The Active Log Format drop-down box determines whether the log is written to a database table or text file format. Please see Chapter 11 for more information about setting up logging.

Managing Inbound Messages

Configurations based on message parameters may also be set for an SMTP virtual server. Depending on the characteristics of a given message, the SMTP virtual server can handle a message in a particular way. The message configurations may be set as follows:

- **Limit Of Message Size**   Maximum message size accepted by the SMTP virtual server. Messages that are larger than this size are not accepted, and the client will received an error message from the SMTP virtual server.

- **Limit On Session Size**   Maximum size of all messages' bodies added up for a given connection allowed by the SMTP virtual server.

- **Limit On The Number of Message For A Given Connection**   Maximum number of messages allowed by the SMTP virtual server for a given connection.

- **Limit On The Number of Recipients Per Message**   Maximum number of recipients per any given message being handled by the SMTP virtual server.

- **Address For Sending A Non-Delivery Report To**   E-mail address that all non-delivery reports for the SMTP virtual server will be sent.

- **Directory For Storing Non-Delivery Reports**   File path on the host server that all non-delivery reports for the SMTP virtual server will be written.

To change any of the message configurations, open the Properties window for the SMTP virtual server, as described previously. Choose the Messages tab, as shown in Figure 4-7, to access the settings that pertain to message parameters.

Setting Message Size Limits

The message size limit is set to 2048K by default. The minimum value that can be set is 1K. This value is the maximum size for a single message that the SMTP virtual server will accept. The SMTP virtual server will reject messages larger than the set size and send an error to the client that sent the message. The value for this setting is identified in the Limit Message Size To (KB) field on Messages tab, as shown in Figure 4-7. If you don't want to set a limit, uncheck this checkbox and none will be imposed.

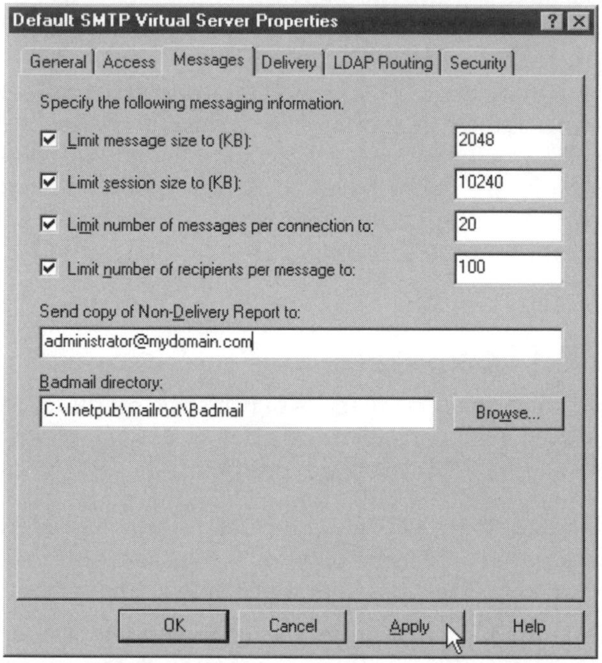

Figure 4-7. *Messages tab of the Properties window for an SMTP virtual server*

Size restrictions may also be imposed based on session. A message session size is the sum of all message bodies for a given connection. The Limit Session Size To (KB) field identifies the maximum size in kilobytes that the SMTP virtual server will allow for a given connection. The default value is 10240K. The minimum value must be larger than the Limit Message Size setting. To impose the session size, the checkbox must be selected. To remove any restrictions on session size, uncheck the checkbox. If the setting is exceeded in a given session, the SMTP virtual server will respond with an error to the client and will fail to complete the transaction requested by the client.

Limiting the Number of Messages per Connection

The number of messages sent for a given connection may also be used as a restrictive measure for limiting resource utilization on a given server. Using the amount indicated in the Limit Number Of Messages Per Connection To setting, the SMTP virtual server will process up to the maximum number of messages for a given connection. If the number of messages being sent exceeds the set limit, a new connection will be established and the remaining messages will be processed in the subsequently created session as long as the number of remaining messages does not exceed the limit allowed for a given connection. This behavior forces the SMTP server to process smaller batches of messages, which reduces the overall resource utilization for a given server. By default, this restriction is turned on and set to a value of 20 messages.

The total number of recipients on a message can also be limited for a given connection. The Limit Number Of Recipients Per Message To checkbox turns on the ability for the SMTP virtual server to process the number of recipients up to the limit specified before another connection will be created to complete the remaining number of recipients. By default, this setting is checked and therefore enabled. The default value is 100, which means that up to 100 recipients will be processed for a given message on a given connection. If more than 100 recipients occur, the SMTP virtual server will create another connection and complete sending the messages to the recipients specified.

Non-delivery Reports

When a failure occurs in sending a message, depending on the nature of the failure, a non-delivery event may occur. When non-delivery event occurs, a report may be generated that describes the failure. Non-delivery reports may be forwarded to an e-mail address specified in the Send Copy Of Non-Delivery Report To field. If no e-mail is specified in the field, no non-delivery report is forwarded.

When a message cannot be delivered or returned to the sender, the message itself is stored in the file directory specified as the *badmail* directory. The *badmail* directory is a file path specified on the host server's file system, typically subordinate to the SMTP virtual server home directory. Examining the messages in the *badmail* directory is a useful endeavor for the administrator to determine whether security problems exist with a given client or other types of systematic failures occur with the messaging system, such as a client that is constructing the message incorrectly.

Managing Message Delivery

In addition to receiving messages, the SMTP service *sends* messages. To send messages, an SMTP virtual server establishes a connection with another server and validates that the receiving server is prepared to accept the messages. The configurations that affect the way the SMTP virtual server sends a message are found on the Delivery tab of the Properties window for the SMTP virtual server, as shown in Figure 4-8.

Configuring Retry Attempts and Intervals

All the settings found in the Outbound area of the Delivery tab relate to message delivery. The First Retry Interval (Minutes) setting indicates the number of minutes the server will wait to retry delivery of a message that failed on the first delivery attempt. The default value is 15 minutes, and the valid range for this setting is 1 through 9999. If a message fails to be delivered on the second attempt, the server will wait until the amount of time indicated in the Second Retry Interval (Minutes) setting is reached. The default setting for the second retry interval is 30 minutes, and the allowable range for the value is from 1 through 9999. If a message fails to be delivered on the third attempt,

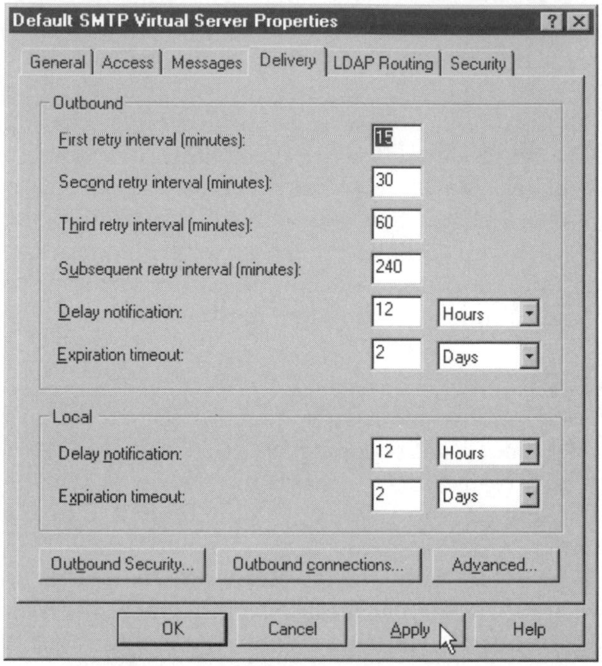

Figure 4-8. *Delivery tab for an SMTP virtual server Properties window*

the server will wait until the amount of time indicated in the Third Retry Interval (Minutes) setting is reached. The default setting for the third retry interval is 60 minutes, and the allowable range for the value is between 1 and 9999.

The retry attempts are customizable for the first three message delivery failures. After three failures, only one retry configuration can be set for all subsequent retries using the Subsequent Retry Interval (Minutes) setting—also found in the Outbound area of the Delivery tab. The default value for the subsequent retry interval is 240 minutes, and the allowable range for setting the value is between 1 and 9999 minutes. Since a message may be undeliverable regardless of the number of retry attempts, a maximum duration of time may be set for the subsequent retries to occur within. Using the Expiration Timeout value and the applicable units for the expiration value, the subsequent message delivery retries may be ended after a given period of time. The expiration timeout may also be set for the local network by editing the setting in the Local area. The default value is two days, during which the message subsequent retries will be performed. If the message is delivered, the delivery notification can be delayed to accommodate network delays. Since the delays on a local network may be considerably different from the delays experienced on a network otherwise, the Delay Notification may be set for either type of network independently of the other. Use the Delay Notification setting in either the Local or Outbound area on the Delivery tab to set a time period that must expire before the delivery notification is sent. The default setting is 12 hours.

Configuring Advanced Delivery Settings

Configuring advanced settings for message delivery is achieved by clicking the Advanced button located at the bottom left of the Properties window's Delivery tab. After you click the Advanced button, a window will open, where the administrator can set the following configurations:

- **Maximum Hop Count**   Maximum number of routers on which a message is allowed to travel.

- **Masquerade Domain**   Domain name to replace the local domain name in the message From line.

- **Fully-Qualified Domain Name**   Name that should be used for a mail exchange (MX) record lookup other than the network identification name of the host.

- **Smart Host**   Server specified for all outbound messaging. The SMTP server may be set to attempt direct delivery prior to using a smart host server.

- **Reverse DNS Lookup**   Verifies that the client's domain or IP address matches the identified IP or domain described in the EHLO or HELO command.

Note   *EHLO and HELO are SMTP commands that are used to communicate with a given SMTP virtual server. HELO is short for Hello, and EHLO is an advanced version of HELO. After a client successfully authenticates and connects to an SMTP server, the command is issued with a domain name for the message sender's SMTP server.*

If a message is sent through more routers than the limit set in Maximum Hop Count, a non-delivery report is generated and the message will not be sent. The message and the non-delivery report will be sent to the sender. The default value is 15 hops.

Setting a value in the Masquerade Domain text box causes the domain used in the From line of a message to be replaced with the value set in the text box. If a recipient replies to the message, it will be routed to an SMTP virtual server that uses the domain name set in the Masquerade Domain setting. The value replaces the domain name on the first hop only. By default, the value is blank, and no masquerade domain name is set.

The Fully-Qualified Domain Name setting enables an administrator to have greater control of the Domain Name Service (DNS) lookup that takes place when a message is sent. The value in the Fully-Qualified Domain Name setting is the same name specified for the host's network identification, by default. Using the default host's network identification name works because the SMTP server must obtain the IP address and resolve the address to a domain name to perform a message delivery. The IP address of the host may be obtained from the network identification name, and that address may be used to find the address (*A*) record in the MX record. During a typical send event, however, the SMTP virtual server performs a lookup in the MX record before performing an *A* record lookup. By setting a fully qualified name for an SMTP virtual server, that value will be looked up in the MX record first, thereby eliminating the second IP address lookup effort. The MX record also enables the administrator greater control over the domain lookup, since multiple domains may be associated with the same IP address.

Setting a Smart Host value causes the SMTP virtual server to use the specified smart host to perform the message delivery. By default, the Smart Host value is not set. When a value is entered in the text box, the Attempt Direct Delivery Before Send Directly To Smart Host checkbox is enabled. Checking the box will cause the SMTP virtual server to attempt to send directly prior to using the smart host specified in the text box. The benefit an administrator can realize from configuring a smart host is the ability to offload the resources required to perform a message delivery to another host or network. The smart host assumes the burden of connecting and sending the message for the client as opposed to the SMTP server that the client connected with initially.

Specifying Reverse DNS Lookup causes the SMTP virtual server to perform a DNS lookup on the incoming messages and compare the results to the EHLO/HELO command identified DNS value. If a difference is found, the received header of the message will be marked with the value *RDNS failed*. If the DNS lookup yields no value to compare to the DNS identified in the EHLO/HELO command, the received header of the message will be marked with the value *unverified*. If the DNS lookup matches the DNS identified in the EHLO/HELO command, the received header of the message will remain unchanged. By default, the reverse DNS lookup is not enabled. Note that enabling reverse DNS lookup could cause a great resource burden on the host server.

Configuring Delivery Security

Some servers may require the SMTP server to authenticate to send a message. To access SMTP virtual server authentication configurations for sending messages, click the Outbound Security button on the Delivery tab. The Outbound Security window allows the administrator to set the required authentication for sending a message and indicate whether the message should be encrypted using transport layer security (TLS). By default, the authentication level for outbound messages is set to Anonymous Access. The other choices for authenticating during outbound messaging transactions are as follows:

- **Basic Authentication**   Specified username and password are transmitted to the host server for authentication using clear text
- **Integrated Windows Authentication**   Authentication is performed using a special Windows cryptic technique for transmitting information without sending the specified password to the host server for authentication

The selection of the authentication method is mutually exclusive, so only one type may be chosen. The receiving server host's requirements determine the needed authentication level, so if the receiving system fails using anonymous authentication, the administrator for the receiving server must be contacted to determine their authentication requirements.

If basic authentication or Integrated Windows Authentication is chosen, the username and password to be used in the authentication must be specified in the respective text boxes on the Outbound Security dialog box, as shown in Figure 4-9. Click the Browse button to open the Select User dialog box to help you choose the correct username for authentication. The credentials do not need to come from the Select User dialog box, however, and the credentials do not need to belong to the host server.

Checking the TLS Encryption checkbox will cause the SMTP virtual server to use TLS encryption, which applies to SMTP communication protocol in the same way the Secure Sockets Layer (SSL) protocol applies to HTTP communication. TLS is useful for encrypting clear text communications so that transmissions of important information between hosts cannot be intercepted. A good use for TLS would be for a situation in which an SMTP virtual server authenticating with another host was using basic authentication. The credentials sent for authentication are in the form of text, and if they were intercepted by a person of ill intent, the credentials would be compromised and could be used exploit the receiving server and possibly the sending server. By default, TLS encryption is not enabled. To use TLS encryption, key pairs must be created and key certificates must be configured. Refer to Chapter 2 for more information about setting key pairs and certificates.

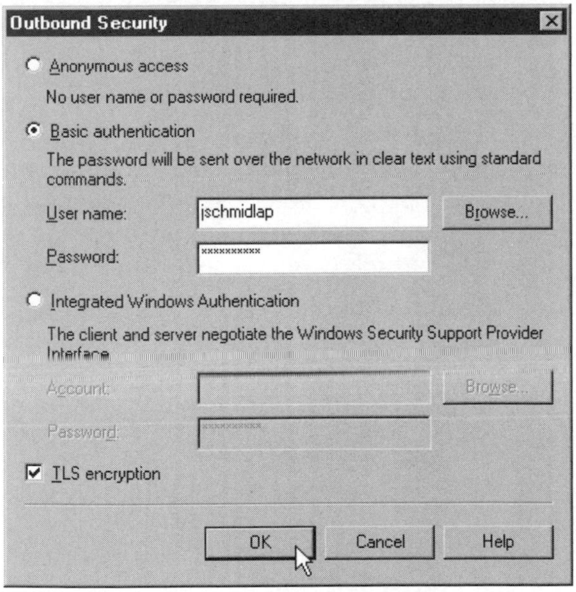

Figure 4-9.   *Outbound Security dialog box*

SMTP Server Access Security

IIS 6 offers many options and configurations for establishing SMTP security. These options relate to users performing administrative tasks for the SMTP service and clients accessing a given SMTP virtual server. Configuring these options may be performed using the Computer Manager MMC snap-in to obtain the Properties window for a given SMTP virtual server.

Security settings for performing administrative tasks may be configured using the settings on the Security tab for the Properties window. The settings that relate to clients accessing a given SMTP server are configurable under the Access tab. Refer to Chapter 2 for more information on secure communication found on the Access tab. The certificate wizard and setting key pairs and certificates tasks are the same as they are for the WWW service, and they are covered in Chapter 2 as well.

User Administrative Permissions

To enable configuration of an SMTP virtual server, permissions must be set for Windows users or groups on the host or other authenticating server that has a trusted relationship with the host server of the SMTP virtual server. The users or groups that must perform administrative tasks for the SMTP virtual server must be designated as an *operator* for the SMTP virtual server. By default, the administrators group, the Windows NT AUTHORITY\LOCAL SERVICE, and the Windows NT AUTHORITY\NETWORK SERVICE accounts are designated as operators for any given SMTP virtual server.

Here's how to designate a user as an operator for a given SMTP virtual server:

1. Open the Properties window for the SMTP virtual server in the Computer Manager MMC snap-in, and click the Security tab.

2. You'll see a list box that shows the administrators group and the users that are designated as operators. Below the list are an Add button and a Remove button. Click the Add button to open the Select Users Or Groups dialog box and select a user or group. The selected users or groups are added to the list of designated operators for the SMTP virtual server. Close the dialog by clicking OK.

3. To remove a user or group from the list, first select the user or group and then click the Remove button. The administrators group cannot be removed. Click OK when you're done.

Authenticating Incoming Connections

Clients connecting to the SMTP virtual server can be authenticated. You can configure authentication for clients sending incoming messages using the Access tab of the Properties window for a SMTP virtual server. To set the authentication for clients to be able to send messages using a given SMTP virtual server, open the Properties window, select the Access tab, and click the Authentication button found in the Access Control area. An Authentication window will open with the following settings:

- **Anonymous Access**   No credentials are required to authenticate and use the SMTP virtual server.
- **Basic Authentication**   Specified username and password are transmitted to the host server for authentication using clear text.
- **Requires TLS Encryption**   Clients connecting to this SMTP virtual server must use TLS encryption or they will not be allowed to access the server. This setting is enabled when basic authentication is selected.
- **Default Domain**   The domain name that is appended to the username during authentication when basic authentication used. This setting is enabled when basic authentication is selected.
- **Integrated Windows Authentication**   Authentication is performed using a special Windows cryptic technique for transmitting information without sending the specified password to the host server for authentication.

The authentication protocols are not mutually exclusive selections, so one or more may be selected. If the basic authentication is selected, the Requires TLS Encryption setting becomes enabled so that it, too, may be selected. The default domain setting also becomes enabled when Basic Authentication is selected so that when a user authenticates using Basic Authentication, the default domain name may be appended to the credential submitted. Anonymous Access is the default setting for authentication.

Restricting Based on IP Address or Domain Name

Computers that have a particular IP address or domain name may be restricted from using a given SMTP virtual server or exclusively allotted access to use a given SMTP virtual server. Here's how to set connection restrictions:

1. Open the Properties window, select the Access tab, and click the Connection button found in the Connection Control area.

2. In the Connection window, two explicit option selectors are listed at the top, along with a list in the middle and Add and Remove buttons below the list. The two explicit options selectors are Only The List Below and All Except The List Below. Select one option to refresh the list to show the IP addresses or domain names that apply to the given restriction.

3. Click the Add button to open a window prompting for an IP address, a domain name, or subnets that should be added to the list for the given restriction.

4. Select an option from the list and click the Remove button to remove the selected IP address or domain name.

5. When the changes are complete, click OK to save the changes; otherwise, click Cancel and no changes are made in the SMTP virtual server's configuration. By default, no restrictions are set for a given SMTP virtual server.

Restrictions for Relay from Virtual Servers

Connection restrictions may also be set for an SMTP virtual server for relaying messages. To set connection restrictions that pertain to relaying messages:

1. Open the Properties window select the Access tab, and click the Relay button found in the Relay Restrictions area.

2. The Relay Restrictions window that opens is almost identical to the Connection window. Two exclusive options are shown at the top of the window, and the list boxes function in about the same way as those in the Connection window.

Note *In this window, unlike the Connection window, a checkbox is labeled Allow All Computers Which Successfully Authenticate To Relay, Regardless Of The List Above. Checking this setting, which is checked by default, allows servers that authenticate according to the settings for authentication to relay messages regardless of the IP or domain restrictions set.*

LDAP Routing

Configuring Lightweight Directory Access Protocol (LDAP) routing will enable the SMTP virtual server to obtain settings in an LDAP to resolve senders and recipients. If groups are already established in the LDAP, likely due to the fact the LDAP is being used for other user management efforts, the e-mail addresses may be extracted from these preexisting groups and expanded by SMTP when the group name is cited in a message.

To configure an SMTP virtual server, the Computer Management MMC snap-in will be used to obtain the Properties windows for the respective SMTP virtual server. All the settings for configuring LDAP routing are located under the LDAP Routing tab of the Properties window.

On the LDAP Routing tab, the only control that is enabled is the Enable LDAP Routing checkbox. If the Enable LDAP Routing checkbox is not checked, none of the configurations will be enabled. By default, Enable LDAP Routing is not checked. After the Enable LDAP checkbox is checked, the following configurations become enabled and may be set:

- **Server** Name of the server hosting the LDAP server. If Exchange LDAP is selected, this setting is not applicable since the Exchange server will be found through self discovery by the host automatically.

- **Schema** The type of LDAP that will be utilized. Active Directory, Exchange, and Site Server are the LDAP types that may be chosen.

- **Binding** The type of authentication that will be used to connect to the directory.

- **Base** The distinguished name of a container that represents the starting point for a search in the directory.

If a binding other than anonymous or service account is chosen, the username, password, and domain configurations are made available because these bindings require credentials for authentication to be specified. In the case of service account, the credentials of the user connecting to the SMTP server are sent for authentication to the LDAP. The username credentials should be specified in the distinguished name (DN) format. For example, the DN of a user with the username *jschmidlap* working for the beer brewer's organization in the Schmitt House company might appear as follows:

```
cn=jschmidlap,ou=beerbrewer,o=SchmittHouse
```

SMTP Domains

SMTP domains should not be confused with network domains or the term *domain* as it relates to DNS or the Windows network domain. An SMTP domain's true purpose is to act as a means of organizing messages. Any given SMTP virtual server may have one or more of three types of domains:

- **Local** Messages using e-mail addresses that use the local domain name are serviced by the local server. If the local domain server is set as the default server, e-mail addresses arriving without a domain specified are appended with the local domain name.
- **Alias** A local domain that uses the same configuration as the default local domain but uses a different domain name.
- **Remote** Messages using e-mail addresses that use a nonlocal domain name are serviced by a remote server.

Each SMTP virtual server must have at least one local domain. If an SMTP virtual server has more than one local domain, the other local domains must be *aliases*. Each SMTP virtual server must also have at least one *default* domain. A default domain is a designated local domain. The default domain name is applied to e-mail addresses that do not specify a domain name. An SMTP virtual server does not need to have any remote domains. If an SMTP virtual server has only one domain, it must be a local default domain. By default, the local domain has the same name as the DNS name set in the server's TCP/IP network configuration settings.

Creating Domains

Creating domains for an SMTP virtual server is accomplished using the Computer Management MMC snap-in.

1. Open the Computer Management MMC snap-in and click the Services And Applications node in the left pane to expose the available subordinate nodes.

2. Click the IIS node, which should be subordinate to the Services And Applications node.

3. Click the SMTP Virtual Server node that requires a new domain.

4. As shown in Figure 4-10, one of the two nodes subordinate to the SMTP virtual server in the left pane of the MMC is the Domains node. Click the Domains node to expose the domains that exist for the respective SMTP virtual server.

5. To create a new domain, right-click the Domains node and choose New | Domain. The New SMTP Domain Wizard will open, prompting you for the type of new domain that should be added to the SMTP virtual server.

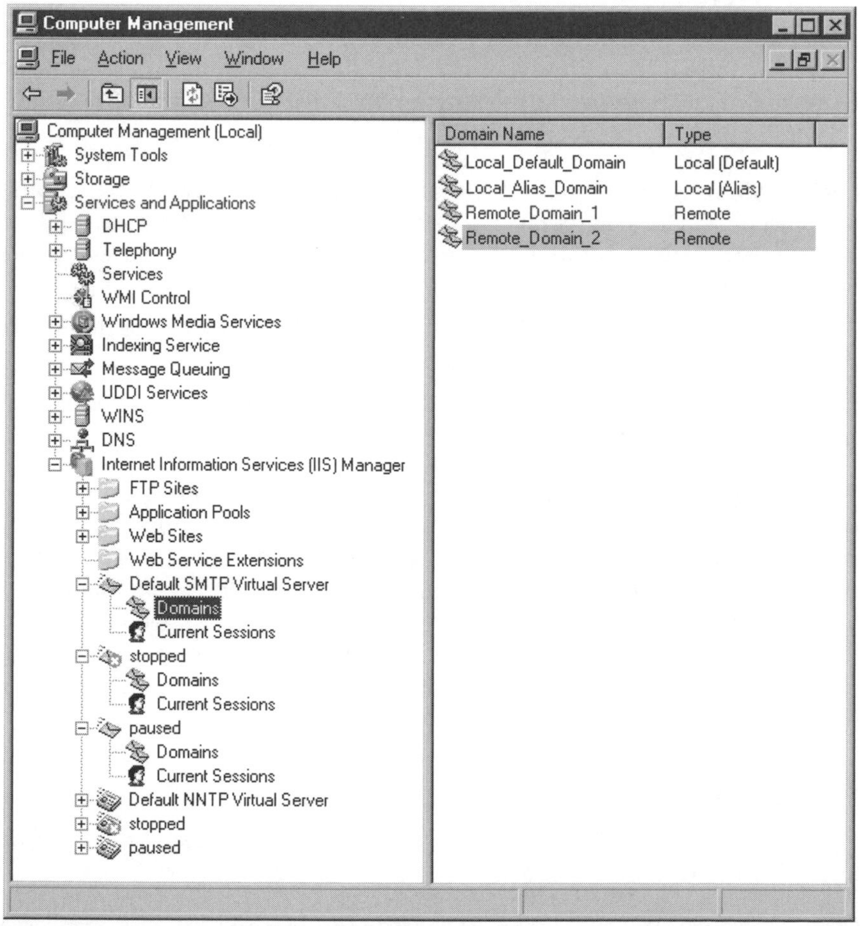

Figure 4-10. *SMTP domains displayed for the default SMTP virtual server in the Computer Management MMC*

6. Choose either Alias or Remote, and then click Next.

7. When the wizard prompts for the name of the domain, type in the name. Then click the Finished button.

Configuring Domains

An alias domain has no properties. The only edit that may be performed on an alias domain is to rename or delete it by right-clicking the domain name and choosing the appropriate command. The Properties window for an alias domain does not provide any editable attributes.

Local Default Domain Configuration

The local default domain may be configured in the Computer Management MMC by right-clicking the domain node in the right pane of the MMC and choosing Properties. The Properties window will open to the General tab and two settings options:

- **Drop Directory**   File path on the local host server, where all incoming messages will be dropped prior to processing.

- **Enable Drop Directory Quota**   The quota is ten times the size of the maximum allowable message size setting for the SMTP virtual server. If the number of messages stored in this directory exceeds ten times the maximum message size, the SMTP server will no longer accept mail and will issue an error indicating a full mailbox.

By default, the *Drop* directory is a subdirectory of the mail root directory named *Drop*. The *Drop* directory quota is enabled by default.

Configuring Remote Domains

Remote domains offer the administrator a great deal more configuration options than the local domains. Remote domains may be configured to require a client to connect using TLS, routing may be customized, and the authentication may be customized for the given domain irrespective of the SMTP virtual server settings.

To make setting changes, open the Properties window for the domain. You'll see two tabs: General and Advanced. The General tab is the default tab that is presented when the Properties window for a remote domain is opened. The following settings are presented to the administrator on the General tab for the remote domain properties window:

- **Allow Incoming Mail To Be Relayed To This Domain**   Enables the domain to relay mail. This setting will override the relay restriction that may be set for the SMTP virtual server access configuration. By default, this setting is not checked.

- **Send HELO Instead Of EHLO**   Enables the remote domain when communicating with a given client to use a HELO command instead of an EHLO. By default, EHLO is used.

- **Outbound Security**   Clicking this button opens a window identical to the Properties window shown in Figure 4-9 and is used to establish the required client authentication. By default, anonymous access is allowed.

- **Route Domain**   Allows the domain to use a smart host or send the messages directly to the server. This setting overrides the SMTP virtual server setting. The Use DNS To Route To This Domain setting is checked.

All the settings for the remote domain are also configurable for the SMTP virtual server, but they will override the SMTP virtual server settings if they conflict with the SMTP settings. The outbound security properties may be used to force a client to authenticate using basic authentication or Windows Integrated Authentication. The outbound security settings also have a TLS Encryption checkbox that, if checked, requires that the client use TLS encryption to connect.

Selecting the Advanced tab on the Properties window for a remote domain will reveal settings that pertain to using ATRN (authenticated TURN). If checked, the Queue Messages For Remote Triggered Delivery checkbox will enable a client to connect periodically and download the messages. The clients that are allowed to perform this type of activity must have a Windows user account that is listed in the Accounts Authorized To ATRN list box, which is also present on the Properties window and the Advanced tab.

To add users, click the Add button and the Windows Select Users Or Groups dialog box opens, allowing the administrator to choose the appropriate accounts that should be given the ATRN access. Removing users from the list is as simple as selecting them and clicking the Remove button.

The
Complete
Reference

IIS 6

Chapter 5

The NNTP Service

W indows Internet Information Server (IIS) offers a newsgroup server that allows consumers to access and read messages that were posted to a newsgroup established in the newsgroup server. A newsgroup server stores information about each message, such as the person who posted the message, the date and time posted, and the related message in response to which a message was posted.

You can connect and authenticate to the newsgroup server using a news reading program that displays messages similar to an e-mail program, and that lets users view, reply, and forward messages. The newsgroup server is supported by the Network News Transfer Protocol (NNTP) service, or NNTPSVC. Each given configuration of an IP address and port combination using the NNTP service running on the host server is called an *NNTP virtual server*. Typically, a host server will have only one NNTP virtual server and it will host multiple newsgroups.

An NNTP virtual server will authenticate users prior to connection, or it can be set to allow anonymous access. You will likely not want to allow anonymous access, however, unless the newsgroup is moderated, because anonymous access can result in unwanted message posting and other misbehavior. You can assign a *moderator* to validate a message before it is posted to the newsgroup. Usually, the moderator is e-mailed the message and posts it if it's deemed OK. If the moderator does not approve of the message, the message can be deleted and not posted.

Newsgroups are useful for publishing information and allowing members of the newsgroup to respond in a public forum. The newsgroup forces a consistent content format that enables efficient searching, parsing, and management of the content. Everyone who reads newsgroup postings knows that the messages posted to the newsgroup will at a minimum have the following attributes:

- Subject
- Body
- Sender
- Related message or no related message
- Date and time of posting

Installing the NNTP Service

The NNTP service is not installed by default when you install IIS; you must select the service manually during the initial server installation. After the NNTP service is installed, it will appear under the Services node of the Computer Management Microsoft Management Console (MMC) snap-in. If the NNTP service does not appear in the MMC, you can update your server by installing it, as shown in Figure 5-1.

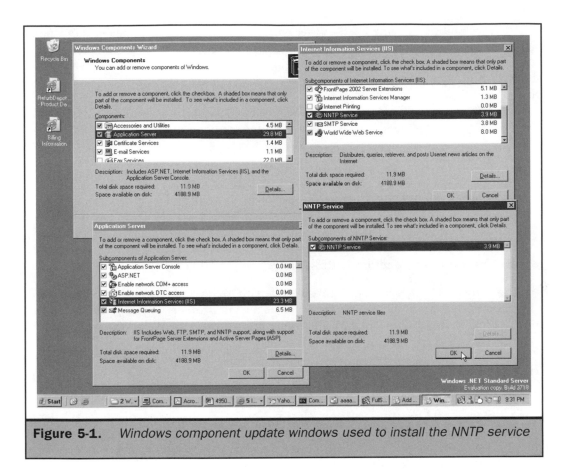

Figure 5-1.   *Windows component update windows used to install the NNTP service*

Follow these steps:

1. In the Control Panel, open the Add And Remove Program applet and choose Add And Remove Windows Components. The Windows Component Wizard will open.

2. Select Application Server from the list of Components, and then click Details.

3. The Application Server window will open. Select Internet Information Services from the list of Subcomponents Of Application Server and click the Details button.

4. The Internet Information Services Windows will open. Select the checkbox next to NNTP Service from the list of Subcomponents Of Internet Information Services.

5. Click OK several times to close the succession of windows.

After NNTP is installed, a Default NNTP Virtual Server is created and set up. The Default NNTP Virtual Server is configured with the following values:

- **IP address:** (All Unassigned)
- **Port:** 119
- **Name:** Default NNTP Virtual Server
- **Internal Files Path:** *<Inetpub root>\nntpfile*
- **Storage Medium:** File System
- **News Content Medium Path:** *<Inetpub root>\nntpfile\root*

The value *<Inetpub root>* represents the file path to the root where IIS places all of the default instances of the IIS services, such as the File Transfer Protocol (FTP) service, Simple Mail Transport Protocol (SMTP) service, and World Wide Web (WWW) service.

Administering NNTP

The NNTPSVC can be administered from the Computer Management MMC snap-in. Choose Start | All Programs | Administrative Tools | Computer Management. After the Computer Management MMC opens, click the Services And Applications node to reveal the subordinate nodes. The Services node and the Internet Information Services (IIS) Manager node include subordinate nodes with applets that are useful for administering the NNTP service and NNTP virtual servers, respectively.

Administering NNTP Service

The NNTP service can be administered globally using the NNTP Service applet found under the Services node in the Computer Management MMC snap-in. From the NNTP Service applet, you can start, pause, or stop the NNTP service and configure its launch parameters. Manipulating the NNTP service affects all of the NNTP virtual servers on the host.

Stopping, Starting, and Pausing the NNTP Service

Stopping the NNTP service will cause all NNTP virtual servers to stop. Starting the NNTP service will cause all NNTP virtual servers that were started or paused prior to the Stop command being issued to start automatically—including any NNTP virtual servers that were paused. Any NNTP virtual servers that were stopped prior to the NNTP service being shut down will remain stopped after the NNTP service is started.

Pausing the NNTP service causes all of the NNTP virtual servers to pause if they were started or paused previous to the Pause command being issued. Pausing an NNTP server or NNTP virtual servers that were stopped previous to the Pause command being issued will have no effect on the stopped virtual server, and they will remain stopped. Starting the NNTP service after it was paused by using the Resume command causes all of the NNTP virtual servers to return to their original operating status—which is slightly different from the behavior exhibited when the NNTP service is started after being stopped.

Controlling the NNTP service is accomplished through the use of the NNTP Service applet. To access the NNTP Service applet, expand the Services And Applications node in the Computer Management MMC and select the Services node. A gear-to-gear icon represents a service as well as the Services node in the MMC. When the Services node is selected in the left pane, the services installed on the host server will be displayed in the right pane, and links in the upper-left corner of the right pane can be used for starting, stopping, or pausing a selected service.

Startup Type for the NNTP Service

Double-click the NNTP Service node to open the NNTP Service applet. You can configure the NNTP service on the General tab that is open by default. The NNTP service starts by default when the host is booted, but you can change the Startup Type setting so that it starts only manually, or you can disable the service so that it is not started at all. Choosing Automatic will cause the NNTP service to start when the host boots. Choosing Disabled causes the NNTP service never to start, and choosing Manual will require that an administrator deliberately start the NNTP service after the host boots.

Administering an NNTP Virtual Server

You can use the Computer Management MMC to access and control the NNTP virtual server node. Under the Internet Information Services (IIS) Manager node, right-click the NNTP Virtual Server node you want to control and choose Start, Stop, or Pause to cause the virtual server to start, stop, or pause, as shown in Figure 5-2.

Viewing the NNTP Virtual Server's Status

In detail view in the Computer Management MMC, the right pane displays detailed information about the selection in the left pane. List view is the default view setting, which displays only icons and names representing the items subordinate to the selected node. To change the view setting to detail, right-click in the right pane and select View | Detail.

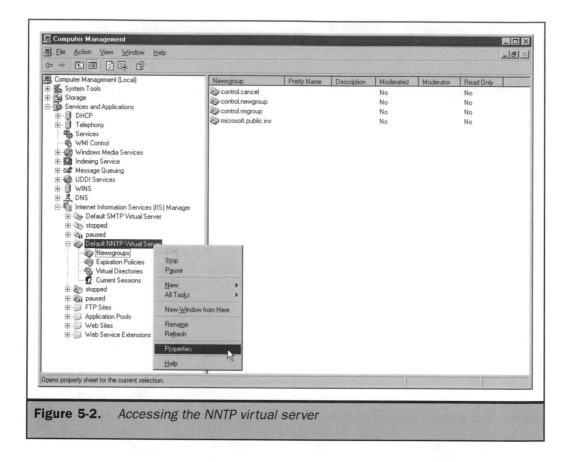

Figure 5-2. *Accessing the NNTP virtual server*

If the Internet Information Services (IIS) Manager node is selected in detail view, the NNTP virtual servers on the host and the following information will be displayed:

- **Description** Name of the NNTP virtual server
- **Status** Whether the NNTP virtual server is running, paused, or stopped

Subordinate to each node for an NNTP virtual server in the Computer Management MMC are the following nodes (see Figure 5-2):

- **Newsgroups** Contains nodes for each newsgroup hosted in the NNTP virtual server. If this node is selected in the left pane, the newsgroups are listed in the right pane.
- **Expiration Policies** Contains nodes for each of the policies that have been configured for the NNTP virtual server. If this node is selected in the left pane, policies are listed in the right pane.

- **Virtual Directories**   This node contains nodes for each of the newsgroup subtrees. Select this node in the left pane and the virtual directories will appear in the right pane.
- **Current Sessions**   This node contains nodes for each connected user; if selected in the left pane, the current connections appear in the right pane.

Opening the Properties Window for an NNTP Virtual Server

To access the Properties window for an NNTP virtual server from the Computer Management MMC, expand the Services And Applications node, and then click the Internet Information Services (IIS) Manager node to expand the subordinate nodes. Right-click an NNTP virtual server and select Properties.

Starting, Pausing, and Stopping NNTP Virtual Servers

Starting an NNTP virtual server will enable it to respond to connect requests from clients. A client's request to connect is the prelude to newsgroup interaction within the NNTP virtual server. After an NNTP virtual server is created, it is started by default.

Pausing an NNTP virtual server will prevent it from responding to new connect requests, but it will continue to allow connected users to interact with the NNTP virtual server. Pausing an NNTP virtual server provides a useful means for gracefully shutting down an NNTP virtual server that is in use. By pausing the server, you can wait until all of the current users have disconnected prior to issuing the Stop command. Stopping an NNTP virtual server prevents it from responding to any requests to connect.

NNTP virtual servers are identified by newspaper bundle icons under the Internet Information Services (IIS) Manager node in the Computer Management MMC, as shown in Figure 5-2. If an NNTP virtual server is not running, the node's icon displays a small, red "x-globe" on the newspaper bundle icon, as shown for the NNTP virtual server named "stopped" in Figure 5-2. If an NNTP virtual server is paused, the newspaper bundle icon representing the NNTP virtual server will show a quotation mark, as shown for the NNTP virtual server named "paused" in Figure 5-2.

Configuring an NNTP Virtual Server

You can view and change the configurations for an NNTP virtual server from the Properties window (as described in the previous section). The Properties window for an NNTP virtual server has the following four tabs:

- **General**   Provides configuration settings for IP and port, connection timeout, and path header
- **Access**   Provides configuration settings for how a client can establish a connection with the NNTP virtual server

- **Settings**   Provides configuration settings for how a client can interact with the NNTP server
- **Security**   Provides configuration settings for users and groups to configure the NNTP virtual server

General Tab Settings

When the Properties window is accessed initially, the General tab is open by default, as shown in Figure 5-3. The following may be configured on the General tab:

- **IP Address**   Settings for the IP address that the NNTP virtual server will use. The default value for the IP address is the (All Unassigned) value.
- **Limit Number Of Connections To**   Sets the maximum number of settings allowed to connect with the server. The default value is 5000 connections.
- **Connection Time-out**   Sets the maximum time, in minutes, that a client is allowed to remain connected during a period of inactivity. The default value is 10 minutes.
- **Path Header**   The value that will be used for each posting as the Path line. By default, no value appears in this setting.
- **Enable Logging**   Sets the logging format that the NNTP virtual server will use. By default, logging is not turned on.

NNTP Configuration Limitations

Unlike the FTP and WWW services, Microsoft does not provide a Windows Script Host (WSH) script to configure NNTP virtual servers. The MMC is the only tool available for making configuration changes. Another limitation to the NNTP configuration functionality is its inability to import or export the configuration for an NNTP virtual server. The FTP and WWW services did offer this feature, allowing you to export the configuration for an FTP virtual directory into a file and import it again on that server, or even on a different server with the exact configuration settings. This is a significant limitation. In addition, some settings can be set only during the creation of the NNTP virtual server, such as the Internal Files Path setting. If settings need to be changed at a future date, the only option, short of manually editing the NNTP configuration settings in the server's registry or metabase, is to create a new version of the NNTP virtual server with the new internal files path and manually replicate all of the settings in the new version.

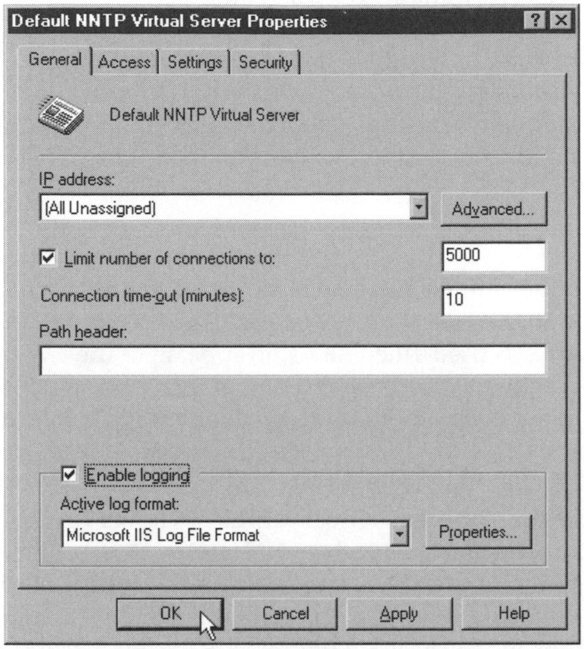

Figure 5-3.   *General tab settings*

IP Addresses and Ports

One or more combinations of IP addresses and port numbers may be specified. By default, any IP address placed in the IP Address drop-down box will use port 119. If additional IP addresses and port numbers should be specified, click the Advanced button to open the Advanced window, where you can configure multiple *identities* for the NNTP virtual server (*identity* means IP address and port combination). You can also set the port for use if the client connects using SSL and if you have your server set up with a certificate.

Connections

The number of connections that the NNTP virtual server will allow and the maximum idle connection time period for a client are both configurable. In the Limit Number Of Connections To text box, you can enter a value that will restrict the number of concurrent connections that the NNTP virtual server will handle at any one time. If a client requests a connection when the NNTP virtual server is operating at the limit, the client will be refused a connection. The Connection Time-out text box allows you to configure the maximum time that a client is allowed to remain connected while remaining idle. If the connection limit is routinely being exceeded, reducing the connection timeout property for the NNTP virtual server may improve performance of the NNTP virtual server to meet client demand.

Path Header

The value entered in the Path Header text box is placed in the path line of the message post submitted through the NNTP virtual server. The directory name service (DNS) name for the host server is used when no value appears in the text box. By default, no value appears in this setting. You can specify more than one value in the Path Header by separating the names using any type of punctuation, other than a period.

Enable Logging

NNTP logging works the same way it does for the SMTP service in IIS. IIS maintains logs of NNTP events and interactions with an NNTP virtual server for a given connection. A single log is generated for each NNTP virtual server if logging is enabled. Using the Properties window for a NNTP virtual server, the administrator may choose to log or not to log, the log style, the file location or database for the log, and the data included in the log.

To configure the logging for an NNTP virtual server, open the NNTP virtual server's Properties window. On the General tab, select the Enable Logging checkbox. In the Active Log Format combo box, choose whether the log will be written to a database table or a text file format. (See Chapter 11 for more information about setting up logging.)

Access Tab Settings

The settings on the Access tab, as shown in Figure 5-4 and described here, allow you to configure the ways that users can access the NNTP virtual server:

- **Access Control** These settings determine the way that the NNTP virtual server will allow a client to connect and the criteria used for access control.

- **Secure Communication** Wizards are provided to help set up and install SSL certificates on the server to enable SSL communication with clients. Refer to Chapter 2 for more information about this configuration.

- **Connection Control** These settings determine how a client can connect based on IP address.

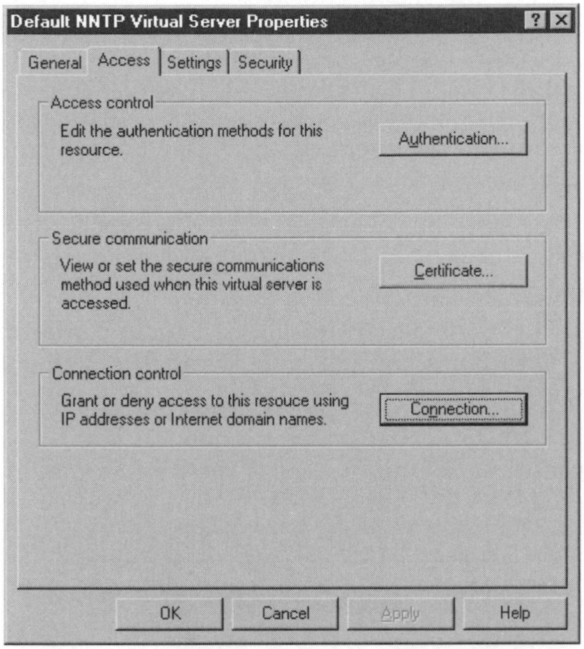

Figure 5-4.   *NNTP Virtual Server Properties Window Access tab*

Access Control

Clients connecting to the NNTP virtual server may be authenticated or allowed
to connect using anonymous credentials. Based on the credentials offered during
authentication, access to material contained within the newsgroup may be controlled
using Windows security settings for the directories that the newsgroups use to store
content. Configuration for authentication for clients requesting a connection is
performed on the Access tab. Using Windows file permissions on the directory hosting
the newsgroup data, you will be able to produce a system that provides access control
to newsgroup content.

Note   *See Chapter 7 for more information about authentication.*

To configure the server's authentication, open the Properties window, then the Access tab, and then click the Authentication button found in the Access Control area. An Authentication Methods window opens, as shown in Figure 5-5, with the following settings:

- **Allow Anonymous**   No credentials are required to authenticate and use the NNTP virtual server. This is the default setting.

- **Basic Authentication**   Specified username and password are transmitted to the host server for authentication using clear text.

- **Integrated Windows Authentication**   Authentication is performed using a special Windows cryptic technique for transmitting information without sending the specified password to the host server for authentication.

- **Enable SSL Client Authentication**   Authentication and communication protocol for the NNTP virtual server are enabled using SSL. If checked, and the host server has an SSL certificate, the client will communicate with the server using SSL.

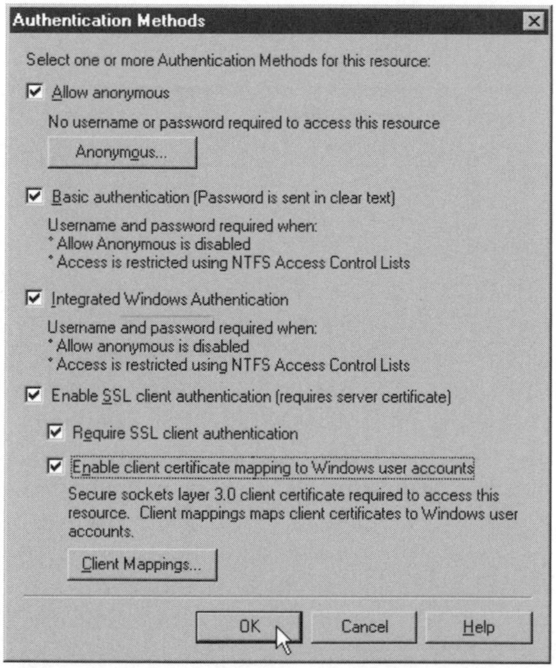

Figure 5-5.   *Authentication Methods window*

The authentication protocols are not mutually exclusive selections, so any one or more may be selected. If Enable SSL Client Authentication is selected, the Require SSL Client Authentication and Enable Client Certificate Mapping To Windows User Accounts settings become enabled so that they may be configured as well.

Allow Anonymous   Check Allow Anonymous to enable a client to connect without providing any credentials. Click the Anonymous button to open the Anonymous Account window, where you can set the Windows user credentials that anonymous users will be provided when they interact with the host through the NNTP virtual server. By default, a system account named ANONYMOUS LOGIN is used if no account is specified.

Basic Authentication   Checking Basic Authentication enables a user to connect using a login and password. The credentials supplied will be used to determine access control if newsgroups restrict access using Windows file permissions. The credentials are supplied to the NNTP virtual server via plaintext.

Integrated Windows Authentication   Checking Integrated Windows Authentication enables a user to connect using the Windows credentials that they used to access their workstation. The credentials supplied will be used to determine access control if newsgroups restrict access using Windows file permissions. The credentials are supplied to the NNTP virtual server via a special Window's cryptic technique for transmitting information without sending the specified password to the host server.

Enable SSL Client Authentication   If the Enable SSL Client Authentication box is checked, users may authenticate and communicate using SSL. The host server must have an SSL certificate to support SSL communication with a client.

Require SSL Client Authentication   If the Require SSL Client Authentication checkbox is checked, the only way a client may connect is by using SSL. If no support for access control to a newsgroup is needed, the user will have to present credentials using basic authentication or integrated Windows authentication, or client certificates may be mapped to Windows user accounts.

Enable Client Certificate Mapping To Windows User Accounts   SSL provides clients a means of transmitting data back and forth with the NNTP virtual server in an encrypted form. The SSL certificate also provides a mechanism for identifying a client uniquely. The problem with using SSL as an authentication credential is that Windows has no idea what the certificate means in terms of the Windows file permissions to determine access control. To resolve this issue, you can map Windows user accounts to SSL certificates. By checking this checkbox, the Client Mappings button becomes enabled. Click the button to open the Account Mappings window. (See Chapter 10 for more information about mapping certificates to accounts.)

Secure Communication

In the Access tab, you can click the Certificate button to open the Web Server Certificate Wizard. The wizard, and the process for setting key pairs and certificates tasks, are the same as they are for the WWW service. Refer to Chapter 2 for more information about using the Web Server Certificate Wizard.

Connection Control

Computers that have a particular IP address or domain name may be restricted from using a given NNTP virtual server or exclusively allotted access to use a given NNTP virtual server. To set connection restrictions, click the Connection button found under the Connection Control area of the Access tab. A Connection dialog box will open with two explicit option selectors at the top, a list in the middle, and Add and Remove buttons below the list. The two explicit options selectors are labeled Only The List Below and All Except The List Below. Selecting one option will refresh the list to show the IP addresses or domain names that apply to the given restriction.

Click the Add button to open a window prompting for IP address, domain name, or subnets that should be added to the list for the given restriction. Select an option in the list and click the Remove button to remove the selected IP address or domain name. When the changes are complete, click OK to set the changes; otherwise, click Cancel and no changes will be made in the configuration. By default, no restrictions are set for a given SMTP virtual server.

Settings Tab

Click the Settings tab in the Properties window to see the settings shown in Figure 5-6. The configurations on the Settings tab affect the way a NNTP virtual server functions in its routine newsgroup serving.

An NNTP virtual server may be configured to restrict client postings using the following settings:

- **Allow Client Posting**   Enables the client to post newsgroup messages to the NNTP virtual server. This is checked by default. If this configuration is not set, the NNTP virtual server will act as a read-only server.

- **Limit Post Size**   When this checkbox is checked, a maximum size for posting a message is imposed on the NNTP virtual server. By default, this setting is checked and a message no larger than 1000 KB is allowed.

- **Limit Connection Size**   This checkbox imposes a size limit of cumulative postings for a given connection. This setting is checked by default and the default cumulative posting limit is 20 megabytes (MB).

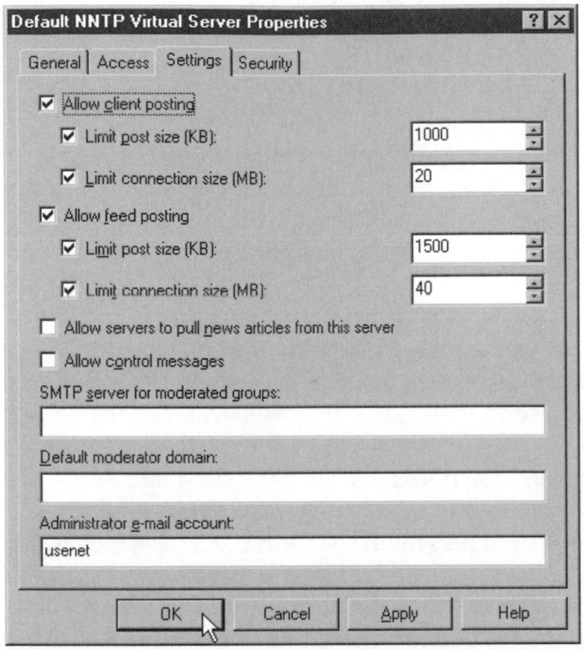

Figure 5-6.   *Settings tab in an NNTP virtual server*

An NNTP virtual server may be configured to restrict news feed postings using the following settings:

- **Allow Feed Posting**   Enables news feeds to post to the NNTP virtual server. This is checked by default.

- **Limit Post Size**   When this checkbox is checked, a maximum size for posting a message is imposed on the NNTP virtual server. By default, this setting is checked and a message no larger then 1500 KB is allowed.

- **Limit Connection Size**   Imposes a size limit of cumulative postings for a given connection. This setting is checked by default and the default cumulative posting limit is 40 MB.

The NNTP virtual server may also be restricted from allowing other NNTP servers from pulling news from your NNTP virtual server. By selecting the Allow Servers To Pull News Articles From This Server checkbox, you can enable or restrict other NNTP servers from accessing your server with a new pull feed. By default, this checkbox is not selected.

The Allow Control Messages checkbox allows messages to be posted that can create newsgroups, post messages, and delete message posts. By default, this checkbox is not selected, so control messages are not normally allowed. This feature poses a potential security risk given that it enables clients to configure your NNTP virtual server to an extent.

The NNTP virtual server can also support newsgroup moderation, in which the moderator must approve postings prior to their publication to the group. The SMTP Server For Moderated Groups text box will accept the DNS name for the SMTP server that should be used to send messages to the moderator. A local file path may also be specified, if preferred.

If a moderated newsgroup does not have a specified moderator, the Default Moderator Domain text box may be used to specify a domain to use to send moderator notifications. The e-mail messages would be sent in the form of *<news group name>@<domain name>*, where the *<news group name>* value is the name of the newsgroup that the message was posted to and the *<domain name>* is the domain name that is entered in the text box.

Nondelivery reports for e-mail notifications sent to moderators can be forwarded to an administrator using the information in the Administrator E-mail Account text box. This feature may be useful for helping to discover when a group moderator no longer exists. The e-mail address placed in the text box will be used to forward all nondelivery reports generated from a moderator posting notification failures. Entering the e-mail address alone does not enable this feature, however. An edit must be performed on the registry at the following key: *HKEY_LOCAL_MACHINE\SYSTEM\CurrentControlSet\ Services\NntpSvc\Parameters\.*

At the specified key in the registry, create a new DWORD value named *MailFromHeader* with a value of *1*, and the functionality to forward nondelivery reports generated from a moderator posting notification failures will be activated.

Security Tab

To configure any given NNTP virtual server, permissions must be set for Windows users or groups on the host or other authenticating server that has a trusted relationship with the host server of the NNTP virtual server. The users or groups that must perform administrative tasks for the NNTP virtual server must be designated as operators for the NNTP virtual server. By default, the Administrators group, the NT *AUTHORITY\ LOCAL SERVICE,* and the NT *AUTHORITY\NETWORK SERVICE* accounts are designated as operators for any given NNTP virtual server.

You can designate a user as an operator for a given NNTP virtual server in the Security tab, as shown in Figure 5-7. A list box will show the Administrators group and the users that are designated as operators. Below the list are Add and Remove buttons. Click the Add button to open the Select Users Or Groups dialog box. After selecting a user or group, click OK, and the selected users or groups are added to the list of designated operators for the NNTP virtual server. To remove a user or group in the list, select the user or group and then click Remove. The Administrators group cannot be removed.

Creating a New NNTP Virtual Server

If you need to create a new NNTP virtual server, IIS 6 provides a wizard that walks you through the process. The wizard is unfortunately the only way to create a new NNTP virtual server unless you write your own WSH script. The *internal files path* for the new

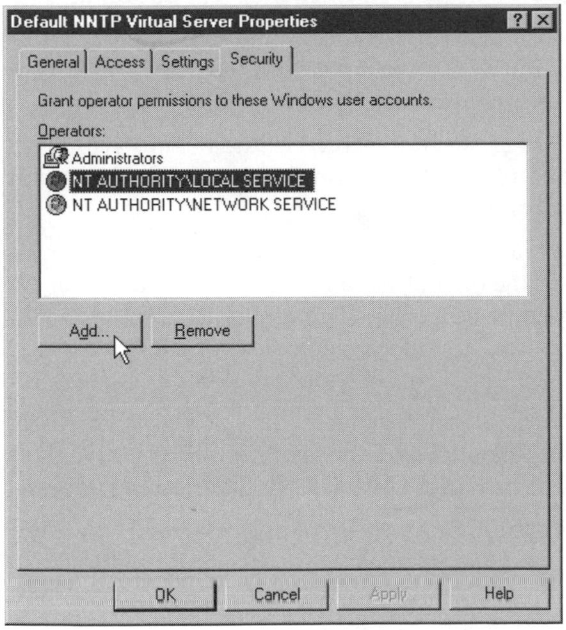

Figure 5-7.   *NNTP Virtual Server Properties Window Security Tab*

NNTP virtual server should be known prior to starting the process of creating the new NNTP virtual server, since it cannot be changed after creation.

1. To create a new NNTP virtual server, right-click the Internet Information Services (IIS) Manager node in the Computer Manager MMC.

2. Choose New | NNTP Virtual Server, and the New NNTP Virtual Server Wizard will open and display the welcome screen, prompting for a name for the new NNTP virtual server.

3. Enter a name to identify the NNTP virtual server in the MMC, and click the Next button.

4. The next screen prompts for the IP address and port that should be used for the new NNTP virtual server. The IP address has to be an existing IP address that the server is configured to support. The port default for NNTP is 119. Using a port other than 119 would require the clients to use a nonstandard port to communicate with the server. Click the Next button to continue.

5. The wizard prompts you to select an internal files path. This path cannot be changed after the NNTP virtual sever is created, so select an appropriate path and click the Next button to continue.

6. The Select Storage Medium screen of the wizard will prompt you to select where the content should be stored. Choose File System or Remote Share. Click Next to continue.

7. If you choose File System, the wizard will prompt for the news content medium file path. Enter the file path to a local drive on the server where you would like the news content to be stored. The path location selected will contain the content of the newsgroups, so you should expect that the drive medium could occupy a significant amount of storage space depending on the configurations for the NNTP virtual server. Click the Finish button to complete the wizard.

8. If you selected Remote Share in step 6, enter the Universal Naming Convention (UNC) file path to a host. Click the Next button to continue.

9. The wizard will prompt for the network credentials that should be used to access the remote share. Enter the login and password that should be used to authenticate to the remote host. Click the Finish button to complete the wizard.

After the New NNTP Virtual Server Wizard is finished, the new NNTP virtual server will have a new node added to and displayed in the MMC. If the NNTP virtual server does not have any conflicts, it should start immediately after it is created.

Newsgroups

Subordinate to any NNTP virtual server node in the MMC is a Newsgroups node, as shown in Figure 5-2. Right-click the Newsgroups node, and you can select either of the following two actions:

- **Limit Groups Enumeration**   Opens the Find Newsgroups window so that you can filter the newsgroups displayed in the right pane of the MMC.
- **Create A New Newsgroup**   Starts the New Newsgroup Wizard.

Limit Groups Enumeration

Choose Limit Groups Enumeration, and the Find Newsgroup window opens, where you can filter the newsgroups shown in the right pane of the MMC. If many newsgroups are hosted in your NNTP virtual server, it could become difficult to manage the newsgroups because you cannot find the proper newsgroup or because you are running the MMC over a limited bandwidth network connection. To help reduce the burden of listing hundreds or thousands of newsgroups to locate the one you need, you can filter using a query string that is compared to the newsgroup name. The default value for this selection is an asterisk (*), which shows all newsgroups. The maximum number of newsgroups listed can also be limited. By default, list limiting is turned on and is set to 100 newsgroups.

Create a New Newsgroup

Newsgroups may be added to the NNTP virtual server by selecting the Create A New Newsgroup command and starting the New Newsgroup Wizard.

1. Right-click the Newsgroups node in the left pane of the MMC and choose New | Newsgroup.

2. The New Newsgroup Wizard will open, prompting for the name of the newsgroup being added. Enter the name and click the Next button to continue.

3. The next screen prompts for the Description and a Pretty Name for the new newsgroup. The values you enter in these text boxes will be displayed in the respective column, identified in the right pane of the MMC. Click the Finish button and the new newsgroup will be added to the NNTP virtual server.

Newsgroups are displayed in the right pane of the Computer Management MMC when the Newsgroups node is selected for a given NNTP virtual server. Each newsgroup is identified by a newspaper icon. Fields across the top of the right pane of the MMC reflect the properties for the newsgroup and provide an easy means for checking the newsgroup's status, as shown in Figure 5-2.

Configuring Newsgroup Properties

At any time, any of the properties for a given newsgroup may be edited by right-clicking the newsgroup in the MMC and choosing Properties. In the Properties window, you can set or edit the following configurations:

- **Description**   Text box that contains optional description of the newsgroup
- **Pretty Name**   Text box that contains another name for the newsgroup that some news readers will display
- **Read Only**   Checkbox that sets the newsgroup as a read-only newsgroup; the moderator is the only person who can post messages
- **Moderated**   Checkbox that sets the newsgroup to use a moderator specified in the Moderator text box
- **Moderator**   Text box that contains the e-mail address for the moderator; if the Set Default button is clicked, the default moderator e-mail set for the NNTP virtual server will be reset

After the settings have been edited, click OK and the changes will be made to the newsgroup immediately.

Administering Newsgroups

Newsgroups may be renamed, deleted, and refreshed. To perform any of these functions, right-click the specific newsgroup node in the MMC and select the respective action. Choosing to Rename a newsgroup will enable you to edit the name displayed in the MMC. The Delete function deletes the newsgroup after you are presented a confirmation prompt. The Refresh function will cause the MMC to query the NTPP service to get the latest configurations and newsgroup status to ensure that the newsgroup is displayed with the latest status in the MMC.

Expiration Policies

As is the case with any system that enables end-user content to be contributed, considerations for expiring old data and removing it from the system should be implemented. Rules for removing content, called *expiration policies*, can be specified. Select the Expiration Policies node in the left pane of the MMC and the policies are listed in the right pane. When a new NNTP virtual server is created, expiration polices are not in place.

An expiration policy has the following properties:

- **Expiration Policy Name**   Name of the policy that is displayed in the right pane of the MMC when the expiration policies are listed
- **Newsgroups Affected**   List of wildcard characters and newsgroup names that will be used by the NNTP service to identify the newsgroups that should have the expiration policy applied
- **Order Of Execution**   Multiple rules may be set for an NNTP virtual server so the order in which they are executed may be established
- **Expiration Time Period**   The time period, in hours, for deleting the messages in the newsgroups that meet the criteria established in the expiration policy

New NNTP Expiration Policy Wizard

The New NNTP Expiration Policy Wizard is the only method available for creating a new expiration policy. Follow these steps:

1. In the MMC, right-click the Expiration Policies node and choose New | Expiration Policy to start the New NNTP Expiration Policy Wizard.

2. The wizard will prompt for the expiration policy name, which is displayed in the right pane of the MMC when the Expiration Policies node in the left pane of the MMC is selected. Click the Next button to continue.

3. You're prompted for the newsgroups that are to be affected by this policy. Newsgroups may be added by clicking the Add button. Selecting a newsgroup from the list and clicking the Remove button will remove the newsgroup immediately—without a confirmation. The Move Up and Move Down buttons will determine the order in which the newsgroups will be processed. Click the Add button to open the Add Newsgroup window.

4. In the Add Newsgroup window, you can select the option to include or exclude the newsgroup specified in the Newsgroup text box. Enter a string in the Newsgroup text box that describes the newsgroup or newsgroups that should be affected. Newsgroups may also be specified using wildcard characters—specifying the * represents all of the newsgroups. Click OK to add the newsgroup to the Newsgroups Affected wizard screen and to dismiss the Add Newsgroup window.

5. When all of the newsgroups are added to the Newsgroups Affected screen of the wizard and the execution order is specified, click the Next button.

6. The final screen of the wizard prompts for expiration time period. Enter the number of hours after which articles should be removed from the newsgroup. The maximum time that may be set is 9999 hours. Then click the Finish button.

Configuring Expiration Policies

When the New NNTP Expiration Policy Wizard is used to make the expiration policy, the policy will be listed in the MMC when the Expiration Policies node is selected. After the policy is created, the NNTP virtual server applies it immediately to content. The NNTP virtual server will routinely parse the content with each expiration policy in the order in which it is set in the list of expiration polices. Various expiration policies may apply to the same message. The policy that the NNTP virtual server is enforcing at the moment the content meets the expiration policy's qualifications will be removed before the next expiration policy is enforced. The expiration policy will cause the NNTP virtual server to take an action only after content is present in the newsgroup that qualifies based on the expiration policy's properties. Any property in an expiration policy may be edited at any time by opening the Properties window for the policy and editing the following settings, as shown in Figure 5-8:

- **Remove Articles Older Than (Hours)**   Text box that contains the time in hours after which postings should be removed from the newsgroups affected.

- **Newsgroups**   List of newsgroups that are affected by this policy. Use the Add, Remove, and Move Up and Move Down buttons to alter the policy.

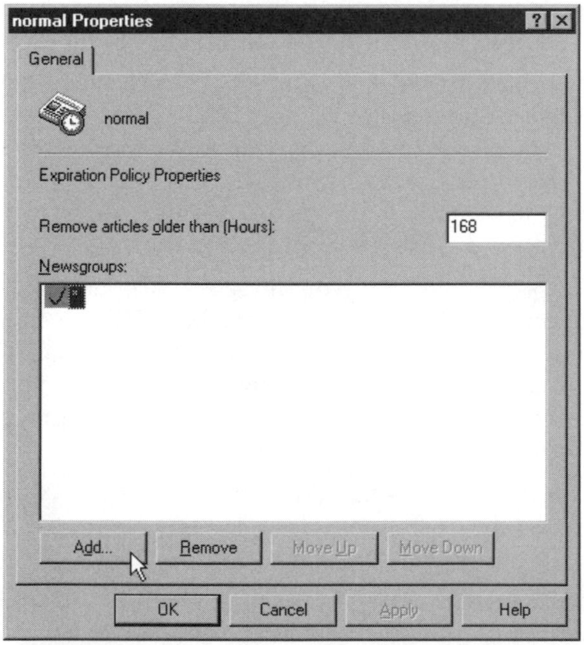

Figure 5-8.   *Expiration Policy Properties Window*

As with newsgroups, expiration policies may be renamed, deleted, and refreshed. To perform any of these functions, right-click an expiration policy node in the right pane of the MMC and choose the appropriate action. Choosing to Rename an expiration policy will enable the name to be edited as it is displayed in the MMC. The Delete function deletes the expiration policy after you are presented with a confirmation prompt. The Refresh function will cause the MMC to query the NTPP service to get the latest configurations and expiration policy status to ensure that the expiration policy is displayed with the latest status in the MMC.

Virtual Directories Node

Selecting the Virtual Directories node in the MMC lists the virtual directories configured for the NNTP virtual server. Virtual directories for an NNTP virtual server are file-storage locations either on the host or on a remote server that will contain newsgroup content. When a new NNTP virtual server is created, a file path is chosen for the location that the NNTP virtual server should store the news content. As newsgroups are added to the NNTP virtual server, the NNTP service creates directories on the file system that are named the same name as the newsgroup. If the newsgroup name includes a period, a subdirectory will be created for each segment of the newsgroup name separated by the period.

For example, the NNTP virtual server that is created automatically when the NNTP service is installed is named *Default NNTP Virtual Server*. Default NNTP Virtual Server has a newsgroup that is also added during the NNTP service installation called *microsoft .public.ins*.

The default file path for the content path of Default NNTP Virtual Server is *C:\Inetpub\ nntpfile\root*. Given this path, the content for the *microsoft.public.ins* newsgroup is stored at *C:\Inetpub\nntpfile\root\microsoft\public\ins*.

If you need to distribute content for a newsgroup across other file systems to establish unique file permissions or storage systems for newsgroups within the NNTP virtual server, virtual directories may be used. For this example, the NNTP service is placing all content on the C: drive, because that is the root file path used for the Default NNTP Virtual Server.

Let's say, for example, that the Microsoft public newsgroups contain so much information that you want to host that content on a file server elsewhere in your network that has lots of disk drive space. You can establish an NNTP virtual directory on a remote host specified by a UNC path for the subtree *microsoft.public*. The content for *microsoft.public* and all subsequent newsgroup subtrees would be written to the UNC path on the remote host specified in the NNTP virtual directory. The content for the *microsoft* subtree of the newsgroup will be stored at *C:\Inetpub\nntpfile\ root\microsoft*.

New NNTP Virtual Directory Wizard

To add a new virtual directory to an NNTP virtual directory, IIS provides a wizard that will prompt you for the newsgroup subtree and file location to store the content. Let's create a virtual directory in the Default NNTP Virtual Server for the *microsoft.public* newsgroup subtree, as described previously.

1. In the MMC, right-click the Virtual Directories node and choose New | Virtual Directory to start the New NNTP Virtual Directory Wizard.

2. The wizard will prompt for the newsgroup subtree for which the virtual directory will be created. For this example, enter **microsoft.public** and click the Next button to continue.

3. The next screen will prompt for the location at which the content should be stored. You will be presented with an option to choose File System or Remote Share. Choose File System if the file path for the content should be stored on the local host. Choose Remote Share if the content should be stored on a remote server. For this example, we will choose Remote Share. Click the Next button to continue.

4. The wizard prompts for the file path. Enter the file path and click the Next button to continue. At this point, if the File System option was chosen in step 3, the Finish button is provided. The Finish button is provided with the File System option because you have completed providing all of the information needed for the virtual directory located on the local host.

5. The final screen of the wizard prompts for the username and password credentials that are required to access the remote share path specified in step 4. After entering valid credentials that can access the share, click the Finish button and a new virtual directory for the newsgroup subtree will be created.

Configuring an NNTP Virtual Directory

As with the newsgroups and expiration policies of a virtual server, virtual directories may be renamed, deleted, and refreshed. To perform any of these functions, right-click a virtual directory node in the MMC and choose Rename, Delete, or Refresh to affect the expiration policy. Choosing Rename will enable the specified newsgroup subtree to be edited as it is displayed in the MMC. The Delete function deletes the virtual directory after you are presented a confirmation prompt. The Refresh function will cause the MMC to query the NNTP service to get the latest configurations and virtual directory status to ensure that the virtual directory is displayed with the latest status in the MMC.

The properties for an NNTP virtual directory may be edited through the Properties window, which includes only the General tab, as shown in Figure 5-9.

If you click the Contents button in the Directory Contents area, the Directory Contents window opens. Here you can edit the file system, file path, and share credential for the

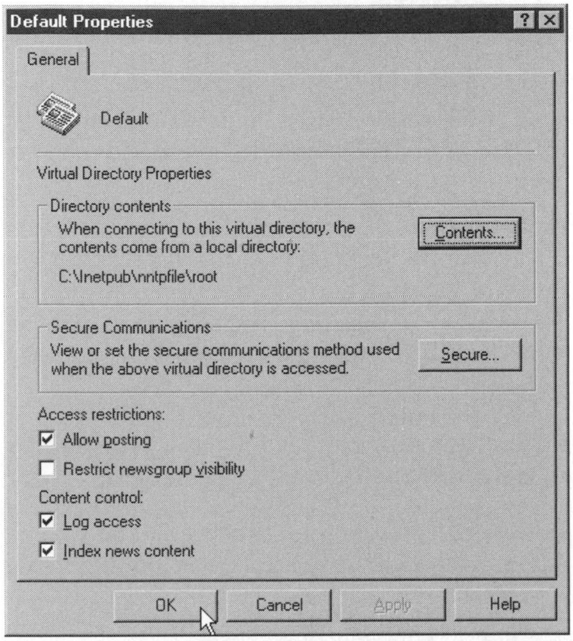

Figure 5-9. *Properties window for an NNTP virtual directory*

NNTP virtual directory. The values set in steps 3, 4, and 5 of the virtual server process can be changed from the Directory Contents window.

In the Secure Communications area, click the Secure button to open the Security window. The settings in this window affect the terms of the communication that the virtual directory will allow and engage in with a connected client. All of the checkboxes are disabled until a valid key certificate is installed on the host. If a certificate has been loaded on the host, you can select any of the following checkboxes in the Security window:

- **Require Secure Channel**   The connecting client is required to communicate using SSL.

- **Require 128-Bit Encryption**   The connecting client is required to use 128-bit SSL communication. Some clients will use 40-bit SSL, so specifying this setting will not allow anyone to connect unless they have 128-bit SSL.

Access Restrictions settings of the General tab are supported using two checkboxes. These settings provide an easy way to specify some of the access control and display, as follows:

- **Allow Posting** Allows users to post to the virtual directory; otherwise, the virtual directory is read-only. By default, this checkbox is checked, thereby allowing posting.

- **Restrict Newsgroup Visibility** Causes the virtual directory not to display newsgroups that connected users do not have access to view. This item is not checked by default. Because it adds an additional burden on the server host, it should not be selected, especially given situations in which the newsgroups allow anonymous access, because the server will be performing access control for no useful reason.

The Content Control section provides the following two checkboxes to establish logging access and indexing content to provide search capabilities:

- **Log Access** Checking this item causes access to the virtual directory to be logged. Log Access is checked by default. The logging for the virtual server must be enabled also.

- **Index News Content** This selection causes the index server to index the content. This item is checked by default. By selecting this item, the content may be searched by the client.

Current Sessions

Clicking the Current Sessions node in the MMC will cause the MMC to list the currently connected clients. A connection is created for each newsgroup that the user is using. As seen in Figure 5-10, the user *shofmann* is connected because *shofmann* is connected and downloading messages from a newsgroup in the Default NNTP Virtual Server.

You can right-click the Current Sessions node in the MMC and select the Terminate All command to close all connections with the current users. You can also right-click a user in the MMC and select the Terminate command to affect a single user.

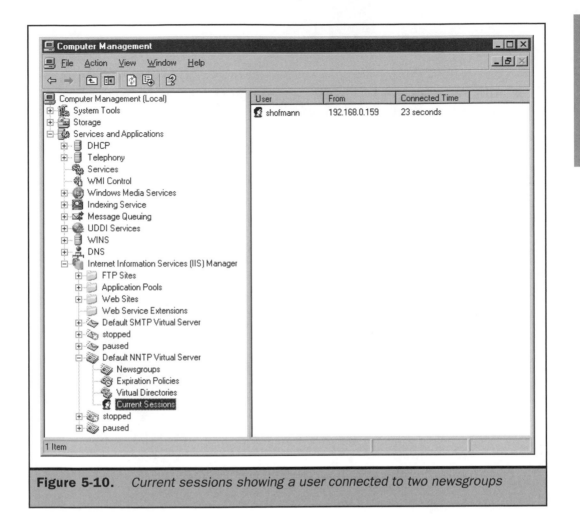

Figure 5-10.   *Current sessions showing a user connected to two newsgroups*

The
Complete
Reference

IIS 6

Part II

IIS Administration

Chapter 6

Security

Maintaining security of your web site is extremely important and getting more difficult to accomplish with each new web application or feature introduced on the market. Today's technological advances mean that you continuously need to learn and understand even more information to protect your site from vulnerabilities. Any time your system is exposed to people, you risk attack. Security involves identifying, prioritizing, and mitigating that risk. This chapter discusses the methodology behind securing your system.

Internet Security Background

The Internet was not designed to be secure; it was invented by computer techies for use by computer techies. Because the concept of having to secure the environment wasn't considered at the time, no security is built into the Internet Protocol version 4 (IPv4) stack. Since the Internet's creation, an increasing number of attacks have occurred on systems every year. With all the worms, viruses, Trojan horses, hacking, cracking, and just plain sabotage going on, it seems that no end to security issues is in sight. Diligently keeping on top of these issues is the only way to protect yourself and your system, especially if you manage high-profile servers and applications.

Why Vulnerabilities Happen

Vulnerabilities can be generated from a variety of places for a variety of reasons, including the following:

- Patch level installed on the application is insufficient for the level of protection required
- Application is misconfigured
- Virus detection software is out of date or missing
- No firewall is present
- Administrators are too trusting of personnel and permissions are set loosely
- Physical security is lacking
- Sensitive data is not encrypted

Interestingly enough, from a pure security perspective, the most *effective* attacks occur as a result of human vulnerabilities. Although worms and viruses can be destructive and can take down your system, the worst type of security problem can occur when an attacker from outside the system gains access to sensitive data by making privileged personnel believe the attacker is to be trusted. Here's an example of how that can occur:

Joe: Hello?
Hacker: Hi, this is Bob from the help desk. We're having an issue with the network, and we've traced it to your user ID.

Joe: Oh, no.

Hacker: Yes. Can you please verify your user ID for me?

Joe: Sure; it's JoeUser99.

Hacker: Yes, that's what I have here. Can I also verify your password?

Joe: Why, sure. It's Nancy, my wife's name.

Hacker: Alrighty then. Let me take care of this network issue. Thanks for all your help.

Joe: No problem.

Now the hacker has access to anything on the system to which Joe can access. The best software patching procedure in the world won't help you in such cases.

How You Can Protect Your System

First, you must have a good security methodology. While the methodology created is unique for each business, several key elements should be included:

- Identification of the types of attacks you are likely to face
- Identification of where those attacks may occur
- Identification of potential vulnerabilities
- Remediation procedures for attacks
- Implementation of an intrusion detection system (IDS)

Common Types of Security Issues

Because few good technological solutions exist to counter human security problems, we won't focus here on the human side of this equation—even though, as noted, human vulnerabilities top the list of security vulnerabilities. Instead, we'll cover some of the common programmatic types of attacks you'll encounter that you can avoid by using technological solutions.

Viruses

A *virus* is a program that "infects" the computer in some way, sometimes maliciously, by inserting itself into other, legitimate host files on your system. Two important characteristics of viruses are

- Viruses must somehow execute themselves on the target machine through a host file.
- Viruses must somehow replicate themselves.

A computer virus acts much like a regular virus, in that it attacks and weakens otherwise healthy aspects of a system. Computer viruses take over a machine frequently by replacing a valid program on that machine. It then uses that machine to help it commandeer other machines.

Trojan Horses

A *Trojan horse* is a hidden functionality that is built into a seemingly harmless program and can compromise a system. A typical example of a Trojan horse is a joke program that is passed around via e-mail. When the joke is accessed by an unsuspecting user, some "special" code is downloaded on that user's system. Once loaded onto a system, it can launch other malicious code.

Worms

A *worm* is similar to a virus, except a worm does not require the use of a host file to run on the machine. It can spread without piggybacking on another file. A worm file takes over a machine by propagating itself to such an extent that it competes with and overpowers other applications running on your system, causing your system to crash. Worms creep into other systems as well, by replicating themselves to spread to other machines. At this time, worms are the most common type of attack.

Buffer Overflows

Worms can attack a system via several methods, but the most common attack in the Microsoft world is a *buffer overflow* attack. This is how worms such as Nimda, Slammer, and Code Red attack.

A *buffer* is a temporary data storage area that programs use to hold data while it's waiting to be transferred between two locations, such as between an application's data area and another device, or waiting to be processed. Buffers are common in programming. Because lengths are defined for the data a program will receive, the buffer requirement is an exact size amount. A buffer overflow occurs when a program or process tries to store more data in a buffer than the buffer was intended to hold.

Here's an oversimplified example of a buffer overflow: Let's say two applications are talking, and the first thing they are supposed to say to one another is "Hello." As a programmer, you'd probably set the buffer to five characters, to hold the *Hello*. Now if someone's program said "Hey, what's up?" instead, the program is obviously not conforming to the standard.

If hackers weren't around, this wouldn't be an issue, because your program simply wouldn't work well with the other person's program, so it wouldn't make sense for the other programmer not to follow your standard. However, a hacker *doesn't want* the program to work with your system—and that's the whole point of hacking.

In this example, the first thing the programming standard says is that communication begins with *Hello*. Next, the data that follows tells the program what to do—in this case, let's say that the data is supposed to be 18 characters. A normal bit of data, then, might look like this:

```
HELLO
OPEN_MY_FILE_&EDIT
```

In this case, your program checks the data and follows the instructions.

Now we'll create a buffer overflow by intentionally making the data longer than it should be:

```
HELLOGRANT_ADMIN_RIGHTS
OPEN_MY_FILE_&EDIT
```

Because the first data is longer than the allowable five characters, the data has to go somewhere, so it overwrites the data in the second buffer—meaning that the data section is an instruction to grant administration rights! From there, the worm can load the malicious code on the system.

This type of attack is prevalent because lax programming practices, coupled with the buffer framework in C and C++, don't give applications the ability to handle malformed packets.

Code Red is a great example of a worm using this tactic. Here is the request with the buffer overflow that Code Red uses to get into systems using the Indexing Service:

```
/default.ida?NNNNNNNNNNNNNNNNNNNNNNNNNNNNNNNNNNNNNNNNNNNNNNNNNNNNNNNNNNNNNNNN
NNNNNNNNNNNNNNNNNNNNNNNNNNNNNNNNNNNNNNNNNNNNNNNNNNNNNNNNNNNNNNNNNNNNNNNNNNNNNN
NNNNNNNNNNNNNNNNNNNNNNNNNNNNNNNNNNNNNNNNNNNNNNNNNNNNNNNNNNNNNNNNNNNNNNNNNNNNNN
NNNNNNNNNNNNNNNNNNNNNNNNNNNNNNNNNNNNNNNNN%u9090%u6858%ucbd3%u7801%u9090%
u6858%ucbd3%u7801%u9090%u6858%ucbd3%u7801%u9090%u9090%u8190%u00c3%u
0003%u8b00%u531b%u53ff%u0078%u0000%u00=a
```

Definitions

Before you can understand how to fix security problems, you need to be familiar with a few terms. Microsoft has established definitions for *service packs*, *hotfixes*, and *security patches*.

Service Packs   Service packs are a collection of software updates that are bundled together for easy installation. They can correct problems in the code, provide product enhancements, and include driver updates. They can also add functionality to software and are typically regression tested. Service packs are cumulative, so each successive service pack contains all the fixes included in each previous service pack. This is handy, because it means that you have to install only the most recent service pack to get all the updates.

Hotfixes   Hotfixes are patches for specific products that provide specific updates. They do not go through regression testing before release, and they are not targeted at the general population for installation. Thus, you should install a hotfix only if you experience the specific critical issue that the hotfix is designed to resolve. Typically, hotfixes are created and released only if a critical issue exists and no acceptable workaround is available.

Security Patches   A security patch is basically a hotfix that fixes a specific security vulnerability. The same caution should be used for security patches as for hotfixes. However, because security patches usually fix important vulnerabilities, extra consideration should be given as to whether or not to install security patches.

Note the request to /default.ida, with a bunch of characters to overflow the buffer, and then the instructions starting with the %.

How to Protect Yourself from Attack

You can secure your system using several methods. No matter which method you choose to protect your system from attack, information is key. If you aren't *aware* of issues, it's more difficult to resolve them.

The Secure Windows Initiative

In response to attacks becoming increasingly commonplace, Microsoft launched the Secure Windows Initiative (SWI). SWI is an internal Microsoft effort that makes its products more secure from malicious attacks. The SWI team provides consulting services for developers to help them write more secure code—since most developers are not security experts and lack the training required to write secure code. In addition to identifying what code enables buffer overflows, the SWI team is well versed in other security technologies, such as encryption. Although C provides the framework for buffer overflows to happen, the security problems with it are well defined, so it's easier to write good code to prevent security vulnerabilities.

Note   *Windows is written in C++.*

This focus on security was part of the process for coding Windows Server 2003 (WS03), and it's one of the reasons IIS version 6 is much more secure than previous versions.

To Patch or Not to Patch

Although you should take seriously any security vulnerability patches that are released, you don't have to apply every patch that comes along just because it's out there. Before you decide whether or not to apply a patch, you need to consider a few factors. As you consider installing a patch, make sure that the risk of *not applying* the patch is greater than the risk of *applying* the patch. Evaluate the effectiveness and the benefit of applying the patch and the cost of not applying the patch.

Consider the urgency of applying a patch. For example, a security patch that specifically targets a bug that creates a vulnerability in your system is an urgent matter and should be considered more seriously than a feature patch that gives you added functionality.

Patching Your System

Unfortunately, no code that's millions of lines long is perfect, and security holes will always exist. One of the best ways to protect yourself is to make sure your system has the most recent patch levels installed. Rarely does a virus or worm attack a brand new vulnerability; rather, they attack known vulnerabilities for which patches exist. Typically, people who discover vulnerabilities will report them to Microsoft, and a patch is created and released along with the announcement of the vulnerability.

Note *All operating systems have vulnerabilities of one kind or another, and buffer overflows aren't indigenous only to Microsoft products. But since this book is about IIS and WS03, we are covering security only with Microsoft products.*

Administering the Patching Process

When you are administering a production environment with business-critical functions, it's extremely important that you use a controlled process to manage your patching. Here are some ideas to get you started on a patching procedure.

Implement Change Control   First and foremost, you should implement a change control process for your system. A change control process has

- Defined owners for the system, patch, and any applications
- Communication to all parties involved in the patch
- A waiting period, so that the interested and affected parties can raise objections or questions; it's often a good idea to get approval from each of the owners before applying a patch
- An audit trail and back-out plan
- A scheduled time for installation and a defined outage window

Be Consistent   When applying patches, make sure the same patch level is applied to each server—unless you have a good reason not to do this. Consistent installation is especially true for domain controllers, since out-of-sync patches could mess with replication or authentication between DCs.

Read the Documentation   Always completely read the documentation for a patch before you install it, so you can understand thoroughly what's involved. That way, you can determine whether applying the patch is going to disable some needed functionality or cause issues with a certain piece of hardware or software on your system. Reading the documentation will also educate you on which patches are necessary and which ones are not critical.

Test It Out   It is a good idea to have a test lab in your organization that tests any new patches before they're installed systemwide. When you are completely satisfied that the patch performs appropriately and have appropriate sign-off from everyone involved, target noncritical systems first for patching. If you are not comfortable patching, don't do it, especially if the patch is a feature enhancement rather than a security patch.

Be Able to Uninstall the Patch   If you can, install patches so that you can uninstall them if you need to later on. That way, you can back out of a patch if it causes problems on your system. You can usually find switches that allow for this. Also, keep a backup of the system state data on hand, plus a full backup of the system, just in case.

Make Sure the Patch Is Relevant   Always make sure that you can or should apply a patch to a system. Applying a WS03 Post SP1 patch before applying SP1 probably isn't a great idea. Also, keep in mind that you may not need to apply client patches, such as Internet Explorer patches, to a server, since Internet Explorer won't be used on the server. In addition, applying a whole service pack is usually better than applying lots of individual patches within the service pack.

Using Windows Updating

You can keep on top of the patches released in two ways:

- By visiting the Microsoft Windows Update web page (at **http://windowsupdate .microsoft.com**) every day to see if new updates are available, and by reading through everything available to see what's relevant to your system.

- By using Windows Automatic Updating, which will install updates for you.

Since most system administrators have way too much work to do, the second option is quite helpful. Windows Automatic Updating is a standard feature in WS03, and it checks the Windows Update site periodically to see whether any updates are relevant to your system.

Setting Up Automatic Updates

You can configure Windows to run Automatic Updates on your system by setting up this utility. Here's how:

1. Choose Start | Control Panel, and click the System icon.

2. In the System Properties window, click the Automatic Updates tab. Automatic Updating is enabled by default, so make sure the box next to Keep My Computer Up To Date is checked (see Figure 6-1).

3. Choose particular settings (as listed in the following sections) that indicate how and when you get your updates.

4. Click OK after you've made your selections.

> **Note** *Automatic Updates are enabled by default. You can disable Automatic Updates if you are using another package or you prefer to do your updates manually. Just click the checkbox to remove the check mark.*

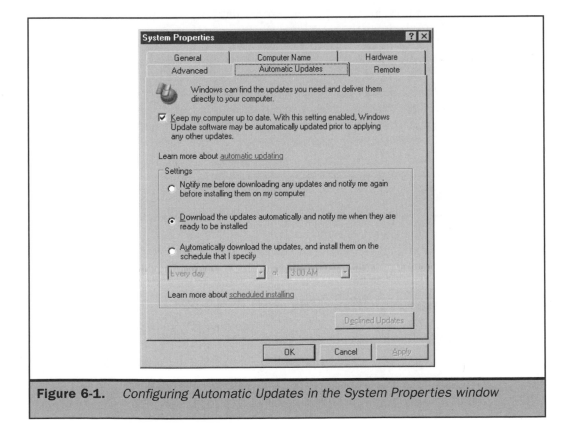

Figure 6-1. *Configuring Automatic Updates in the System Properties window*

Notify Me Before Downloading   Choosing this option will notify you of any potential updates; then, if you choose to download them, it will prompt you again when they are ready to install. It will also prompt you if a reboot is necessary to complete the installation.

Download the Updates Automatically   Choosing this option will download the updates automatically but will prompt you for any updates to be installed. It will also prompt you if a reboot is necessary to complete the installation.

Automatically Download and Install   Choosing this option will download the updates and install them automatically at the time you specify. If a reboot is necessary, the system will reboot, regardless of what is happening on the system at that time. If you are logged in to the system with administrator rights at the time, you will be given an opportunity to cancel the reboot; otherwise, your system will send out a notice to all connected users and then reboot itself.

Using the Windows Update Web Site

If you prefer, you can find out what patches are available by visiting the Windows Update site at **http://windowsupdate.microsoft.com**. The Windows Update site will install an ActiveX control that can scan your system to find out what patches are available for your configuration. You can also install product enhancements at this site.

Tip	*Even if you have a service that automatically updates your servers, it's a good idea to stay on top of security issues out there in cyberspace. One great way is to check out the CERT web site at **http://www.cert.org**. The CERT Coordination Center (CERT/CC) is a center of Internet security expertise located at Carnegie Mellon University.*

Securing IIS

Now that we've examined patching and vulnerabilities, let's take a look at how you can secure IIS. Previously, IIS was wide open by default, and this caused some security issues. IIS 6 is installed in lockdown mode by default. Even so, you can do a few things to make IIS more secure on your system.

Don't Install Components You Don't Need

Don't need the FTP service? Don't install it. Won't use the BITS Server Extensions? Don't put them on just because they sound cool. The more components you install, the more you expose your site to vulnerabilities, especially if you don't do the work of configuring those components.

Don't Turn On Directory Browsing

Directory browsing allows anyone to see a listing of the files in a directory if no default page is configured. Needless to say, letting everyone see the structure of your files and filenames is a security risk.

Lock Down cmd.exe

The command prompt is a common way for hackers to get control of a system. Typically, the *system32* directory isn't in the web site path, but a buffer overflow vulnerability *has* allowed hackers to run *cmd.exe*. Windows File Protection will make deleting or renaming *cmd.exe* difficult, but if you don't need it, just take permissions away from everyone so that no one can access it—even explicitly deny the anonymous user account. As an administrator, you can always take ownership of it and reassign permissions if you need to. This will make it more difficult for an attacker to take over the system.

Set Execute Permissions for Your Web Site

Three execute permissions settings are available: None, Scripts, and Execute. Make sure that you choose the most restrictive permissions possible for your site to help keep it secure. If you aren't using Common Gateway Interface (CGI) applications, and you are using Active Server Pages (ASP) or static content, choose the Scripts permission. If you aren't even using ASP, choose None.

None

Allows only static web pages to execute, so no scripts will be executed. This will prevent any server-side applications from running. This is the default setting for all web sites in IIS 6.

Scripts

Allows scripts, such as ASP, to run through their associated Internet Server Application Programming Interface (ISAPI) extension. Because scripts are run server-side, they have increased security risk when enabled.

Execute

Allows anything to run. Any file type can be accessed and run. This is the most permissive setting.

| Note | *Because the default permissions for all web sites are set to None out of the box, ASP pages will not work without some configuration. To get ASP scripts to work, set the permissions to Scripts. If you are developing on the same box with Visual Studio, it will set this up for you—otherwise, you'll have to do it manually. You also have to enable ASP in the Web Service Extensions section of the IIS MMC.* |

Don't Set Up Write for Your Web Site

If you have execute permissions set up for your site, don't enable write permission. If you have write enabled and permissions set for Execute, someone can upload an executable to your site and then promptly run it on your server! If you need people to write content to your web site, find another way. You don't need enabled writes unless you want people to upload files to your site through Hypertext Transfer Protocol (HTTP).

Avoid Basic Authentication

Basic authentication sends the username and password combination in clear text. This is bad, because anyone listening can pick up on that packet and get that username/ password combo. You can encrypt the traffic to get around this, but much stronger options are available, such as Windows Integrated Authentication, which uses a cryptographic exchange to verify the user's identity. In addition, Digest Authentication uses the user's Active Directory account to authenticate the user. Or you can use Microsoft's new .NET Passport authentication, detailed in Chapter 7.

Set Up Logging

It is always a good practice to set up logging for your site. This will track the IP address and username of whoever accesses content on your site. Logging will go a long way toward helping track down someone if they hack into your site.

Unmap Unneeded ISAPI Application Extensions

WS03 ships with a limited number of ISAPI applications enabled, as shown in the Mappings tab of the Application Configuration dialog box in Figure 6-2. The problematic *.htr* extensions are noticeably missing from IIS 6, as you can see in the figure. The *.htr* extensions allowed users to change their passwords via the web. These scripts were mapped to *ISM.DLL*, which had several associated security issues. Microsoft previously recommended that these extensions be disabled. Now, these extensions are completely gone and *ISM.DLL* doesn't exist anymore.

Here are the ISAPI applications that are included in IIS 6, along with their functions:

- **.asa** Associated with *asp.dll*, this extension is for ASP files that have a global or application impact. These are necessary for most ASP sites.
- **.asp** The big one, ASP is the heart and soul of Microsoft server-side web sites.
- **.cdx** These files allow for channel definition files. Channels were introduced in IE 4, and they are basically web pages with a channel definition file determining the structure.
- **.cer** These file types allow ASP to handle certificates from the certificate server.

- **.idc**   These files are used for Internet database connectivity, and they are handled by *httpodbc.dll*.

- **.shtm, .shtml, .stm**   These file types are all for server-side includes, and they are associated with *ssinc.dll*, which processes the includes.

Hide the Fact that You're Using Scripting

Here's a good way to hide the fact that you're using ASP: associate *.htm* files with *ASP.dll*. IIS could care less what the extension is—it just wants to know what to do with a particular file. Every *.htm* file will be run through *asp.dll*, and the ASP content will be processed. However, the page will appear to the end user as just a normal HTML page.

Use SSL for Sensitive Web Sites

The Secure Sockets Layer (SSL) protocol allows you to encrypt content between the browser and web server, thereby preventing anyone from seeing it. Client certificates also verify the identity of the client. SSL and certificates are covered in detail in Chapter 10.

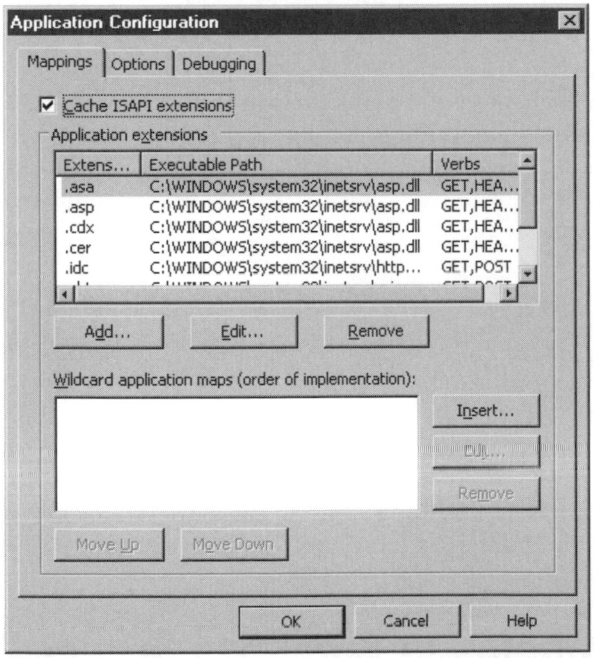

Figure 6-2.   *Mappings tab showing ISAPI application extensions*

IIS ADMINISTRATION

Always Use NTFS Permissions

This almost goes without saying. NT File System (NTFS) allows for security, and FAT (file allocation table) and FAT32 do not. Always put your web sites on NTFS partitions, and lock down the permissions. One great feature of WS03 is that it does not grant everyone full control rights by default. Identify the anonymous Internet user for that machine, and make sure that account is locked out of as much as possible at the file-system level. Unfortunately, you can't just lock the anonymous user out of everything, because some off-the-shelf programs put dynamic link library (DLL) files in the *system32* directory that the anonymous user needs to access. The answer may be to use only authenticated accounts for those types of programs.

Be on the Lookout for Hackers

Firewalls and host-based IDS software can help you identify if someone is trying to hack into your site in real time. These measures can be costly and time-consuming to set up, but if you have a high-profile site, it may well be worth the effort and expense. Firewalls, in addition to restricting what traffic can pass, can also alert you of suspicious behavior. Host-based IDS software runs on the server itself, and it also alerts based on suspicious traffic patterns. Both of these can help you stop unauthorized activity in its tracks.

Try to Hack In

You can attempt to hack into your web site and see how far you get. Applications are available that can assist in determining vulnerabilities on your site. You can use a test server configured exactly like your production server, run a hack program, and see what security vulnerabilities exist. You can then see firsthand how easy or difficult it is to break into your site.

Control IIS Servers

Lastly, one of the best ways to make sure IIS servers are hardened properly is to have them controlled by a specific team of people who are well prepared to make sure IIS servers are properly hardened, locked down, and patched. Many times, it is the "rogue" IIS servers that are the hardest hit by the latest worm to make the rounds on the Internet. Having all the servers configured by the same people ensures consistency, and it means that there is less chance of something slipping through the cracks. Again, many worms hit well-known vulnerabilities for which patches already exist.

Security Policies in Windows Server 2003

Security policies are a method of enforcing security standards on a machine. Using security templates you can enforce predefined sets of policies. You can also use security policies to enforce a certain registry key setting. If you are a member of an Active Directory domain, you can use a Group Policy Object (GPO), and all the servers in the domain will inherit those settings; otherwise, you can use a local security policy.

Creating a Local Security Policy

To modify the local security policy, choose Start | Administrative Tools | Local Security Policy. In the Local Security Settings window shown in Figure 6-3, you can directly edit your security policies.

Five main categories of policies appear in the local security policy:

- **Account Policies**   Configure the password and account lockout policies.
- **Local Policies**   Configure Audit Policy, User Rights Assignment, and Security Options:
  - **Audit Policy**   Sets up auditing for the server. You can set up to audit success and/or failure events for the following items:
    - Account Logon
    - Account Management
    - Directory Service Access
    - Logon Events
    - Object Access
    - Policy Change
    - Privilege Use
    - Process Tracking
    - System Events

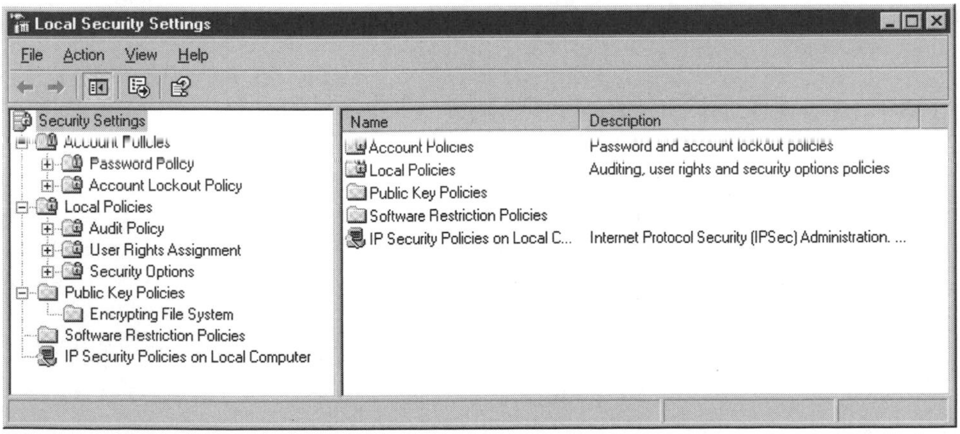

IIS ADMINISTRATION

Figure 6-3.   *Local security settings*

- **User Rights Assignment**   Specify granular user rights for specific user accounts or groups (otherwise known as objects). To add a security object to the policy, in the Local Security Settings window, right-click the policy name and choose Properties. Then click the Add User Or Group button. You can then browse to the specific security object and add it to the policy by highlighting it and clicking Add. To remove a security object from the policy, select the object and click Remove.

- **Security Options**   Specify security options for the server. While these options do not specifically deal with IIS, they can make the server more secure overall.

- **Public Key Policies**   Handle options for the Encrypting File System (EFS), which allows for encryption on the file level. If you have EFS enabled, you can set recovery agent information here.

- **Software Restriction Policies**   Enable which software can be run on a machine and which user accounts have access to run that software.

- **IP Security Policies**   Allow you to configure whether the server uses IPSEC for encrypting communication on the network. There are three settings:

   - **Client (respond only)**   Uses IPSEC if the other machine requests it.

   - **Server (request security)**   Attempts to negotiate IPSEC with a machine with which it is communicating. If that fails, it will communicate without encryption.

   - **Secure Server (require security)**   Forces IPSEC communication. If the other machine does not use IPSEC, the communication will fail.

Using the Local Security Policies

Once you have a security policy defined, you can export it from one machine and import it to another. This allows you to create a single template and apply it to any number of servers.

Importing a Local Security Policy

You can use template files to configure the local security policy by importing an *.inf* file that contains the settings. This allows you to configure multiple machines without having to check all the settings manually on each machine. Several sample security templates come with WS03 in the *%systemroot%\security\templates* directory. You can use these templates or create your own. To import a template file, click on Security Settings and choose Action | Import Policy in the menu bar. Then browse to the template file and click Open. The security policy will be imported over the top of whatever settings are configured currently.

Exporting a Local Security Policy

After you have configured a system to your specifications, you can export the security template to an *.inf* file for use on other systems. To export the security policy, click on

Security Settings and choose Action | Export Policy in the menu bar. Then browse to the directory into which you wish to save the policy, type a filename, and click Save.

Refreshing the Security Policy

When you change a setting in the security policy, it is not immediately refreshed. Instead, the policy is refreshed on bootup and every 90 minutes for non-domain controllers. Domain controllers are refreshed every 5 minutes. If you want a change to take effect immediately, open a command prompt and type **gpupdate.exe**. In WS03, that's all you need to do to refresh the security policy.

Domain Security Policies

The templates for a domain security policy are the same as for the local security policy. The difference is that domain security policies are applied to all servers in the domain instead of just the local server on which they are configured. Domain security policies are configured in the Domain Security Policy Microsoft Management Console (MMC) snap-in, which is located in the Start Menu under Administrative Tools on your domain controllers.

User Account Security

If you are using user accounts for access to resources in IIS, it is important that you make sure those accounts are protected. If a hacker were able to get a username and password, he or she would be able to access potentially sensitive data. You can protect against this happening in the following ways.

Force Strong Passwords

The strong-password standard in WS03 is the same as the standard in previous Windows Server versions. When you force strong passwords, any user changing his or her password must meet the following requirements:

- Passwords must be at least six characters long.
- Passwords must contain characters from at least three of the following four types of characters:
  - Uppercase letters
  - Lowercase letters
  - Numbers
  - Special characters, such as punctuation symbols
- Passwords may not contain the user's username or any part of the user's full name.

You can create your own password filters by writing a custom *passfilt.dll* file, which is the DLL through which password changes are run to make sure they fit a certain profile. Knowledge Base article Q151082 details how to begin writing your own *passfilt.dll* file. It can be accessed by using TechNet, or on the Microsoft Support site (**http://support.microsoft.com**) by searching on the article number.

Here's how to enable strong passwords in WS03:

1. Open the appropriate security policy (domain or local) by choosing Start | Administrative Tools | Local Security Policy (or Domain Security Policy)

2. In the Security Settings MMC, under Account Policies, choose Password Policy.

3. Double-click on Password Must Meet Complexity Requirements.

4. Set the Password Must Meet Complexity Requirements to Enabled.

5. Click OK.

You can also set the minimum password length:

1. Open the appropriate Security Policy (Domain or Local) by choosing Start | Administrative Tools | Local Security Policy (or Domain Security Policy).

2. In the Security Settings MMC, highlight Password Policy under Account Policies.

3. Double-click on Minimum Password Length.

4. Set the Minimum Password Length to a number between 0 and 14. A setting of 0 allows blank passwords.

5. Click OK.

Note	*Although users can have up to 255-character passwords in WS03, through the Local Security Policy, you can force only up to 14 characters. In addition, keep in mind that if you have enabled strong passwords, the minimum password length is 6 characters, even if you set less than that in Minimum Password Length.*

Enable Account Lockout

Enabling account lockout allows you to control how may times someone can enter an incorrect password before access is denied. After the threshold is reached, the account is no longer usable for a period of time that you can specify. This can help prevent someone from guessing passwords until he or she successfully logs in with someone else's account information.

Here's how to enable account lockout:

1. Open the appropriate Security Policy (Domain or Local) by choosing Start | Administrative Tools | Local Security Policy (or Domain Security Policy).

2. In the Security Settings MMC, choose Account Lockout Policy under Account Policies.

3. Double-click on Account Lockout Threshold.

4. Set the Account Lockout Threshold to the number of attempts you will allow before the user is locked out. You can choose any setting between 1 and 999 attempts. A setting of 0 disables this option. (A good account lockout threshold should be between three and five incorrect tries.)

5. Click OK.

6. A dialog box informs you that the lockout duration and reset counters have been set to 30 minutes.

7. Set the Account Lockout Duration by double-clicking on Account Lockout Duration. Set the amount of time you want to pass before the account is locked out. You can choose any time period from 1 to 99999 minutes. A setting of 0 will lock out the account until an administrator unlocks it.

8. Click OK

9. Set the Reset Account Lockout Counter by double-clicking on Reset Account Lockout Counter. Set the amount of time you want to pass before the lockout counter is reset. You can choose any time period from 1 to 99999 minutes.

10. Click OK.

Force Periodic Password Changes

Never changing passwords is a security risk, since people who no longer need to know a password for an account will still be able to use that account. In general, passwords should be changed every 90 to 120 days in normal environments.

Here's how to enforce a password age:

1. Open the appropriate security policy (domain or local) by choosing Start | Administrative Tools | Local Security Policy (or Domain Security Policy).

2. In the Security Settings MMC, highlight Password Policy under Account Policies.

3. Double-click on Maximum password age.

4. Set the Maximum Password Age to the number of days for which you want the password to be valid. You can choose any number from 1 to 999 days. A setting of 0 will set passwords never to expire.

5. Click OK.

Remember Past Passwords

Having the system remember previous passwords prevents a user from using the same password over and over, which defeats the purpose of changing passwords in the first place.

To enforce password history:

1. Open the appropriate security policy (domain or local) by choosing Start | Administrative Tools | Local Security Policy (or Domain Security Policy).

2. In the Security Settings windows, highlight Password Policy under Account Policies.

3. Double-click Enforce Password History.

4. Set Enforce Password History to the number of passwords you want the system to remember. You can choose any number from 1 to 24 previous passwords. Choosing 0 will set the system to not keep a password history.

5. Click OK.

Set a Minimum Password Age

If you choose to have the system expire passwords and remember a certain number of past passwords, it's a good idea to set a minimum password age as well. For example, suppose you've set up your security system policy to expire passwords every 90 days and remember 24 previous passwords. However, you don't set up a minimum password age. When 90 days rolls around, people can just change their password 24 times that morning, and then choose their old password for the twenty-fifth time, thereby defeating the purpose of remembering passwords!

To enforce a minimum password age:

1. Open the appropriate security policy (domain or local) by choosing Start | Administrative Tools | Local Security Policy (or Domain Security Policy).

2. In the Security Settings window, highlight Password Policy under Account Policies.

3. Double-click Minimum Password Age.

4. Set the Minimum Password Age to the number of days for which you want the password to be valid. You can choose any number from 1 to 1 minus the number of days for your maximum password age. A setting of 0 will enable passwords to be changed immediately.

5. Click OK.

Note *The example for minimum password age may seem a little overcautious, but some people will exploit this to get around password policies. Some problems, however, may be better addressed as a personnel issue, rather than a technical one. This is a good example of one of those types of issues.*

Tip *Sometimes, using minimum password age can be problematic. If someone changes his or her password to something that doesn't work with another application, and that application requires that the password be the same, the user would need to change the second application password. With this policy in place, the user wouldn't be able to do this without administrator intervention.*

Use One-Way Encryption for Password Storage

When enabled in the Local or Domain Security Policy, the Store Passwords Using Reversible Encryption policy stores the password using an encryption algorithm that can be used to read back the password from the security database. Normally, this is a one-way hash that is destroyed. This is essentially the same as storing the password in clear text, and it can be a security risk. Disabling this policy causes a one-way hash to be used; this is the default setting.

Don't Create User Accounts with Easy Passwords

Typically, when a user account is created, the person creating the account makes the password the same as the username or some other easy-to-remember word. Unfortunately, this default password is not always changed in a timely fashion. Even if the password is set to be changed at next logon, if the account is not used for some time, the password will be insecure for that entire time. Setting the initial password to a hardened one will reduce the risk of a new user account being hacked.

Web Service Extensions

IIS 6 is shipped in *lockdown* mode. This means that out of the box, IIS will deliver only static content, such as HTML pages. Active content, such as ASP, FrontPage, Server Side Includes (SSI), and WebDAV will not work. To make this content work in IIS, you need to use the Web Service Extensions portion of the IIS MMC. This allows you to enable and disable active content.

In the MMC, two tabs—Extended and Standard—control how you see the options of configuring the extensions. The Extended tab has buttons for Allow, Prohibit, and setting Properties, as well as hyperlinks to access to perform these tasks. On the Standard tab, you must use the menus to access those options. For this exercise, we cover the Extended tab, as shown in Figure 6-4.

A set of predefined web extensions are available, but you can define and add your own—for example, if you wrote your own ISAPI extension and wanted to add it granularly. You can add all unknown ISAPI or CGI extensions, but this is not recommended since it is a security risk.

The Web Service Extensions that are predefined are as follows:

- All Unknown ISAPI Extensions
- All Unknown CGI Extensions
- Active Server Pages
- Internet Data Connector
- Internet Printing
- Server Side Includes
- WebDAV

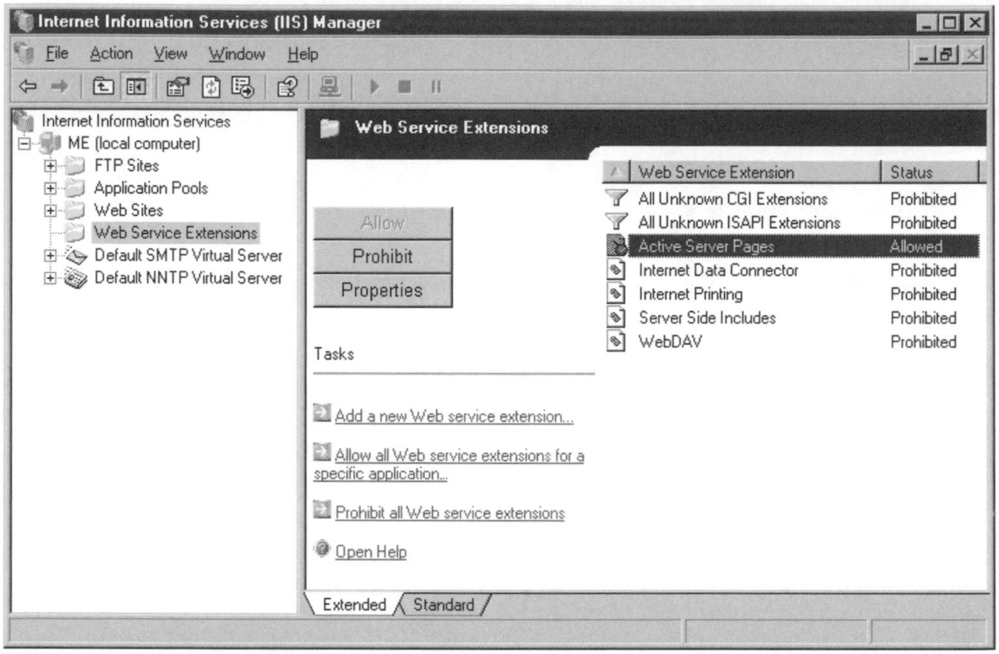

Figure 6-4.   *IIS Manager Web Service Extensions, Extended tab*

Allowing Web Service Extensions to Run

To allow a web extension to run, highlight the extension in the IIS Manager and click the Allow button. The web extension will then be allowed. If you choose to allow one of the All Unknown extensions, you will see a warning that this is a security risk. Again, it's much better to define and enable your ISAPI and CGI extensions one by one, to give you granular control over what active content is run in your site.

Prohibiting a Web Service Extension from Running

After you've enabled a web extension, you can prohibit it. Highlight the extension in the IIS Manager and click the Prohibit button. If the extension has any other extensions that depend on it, those extensions will cease to function as well. For example, Internet Printing depends on Active Server Pages. If ASP is prohibited, Internet Printing will not function.

This option can be used to prevent unwanted DLLs or executables (EXEs) from running under any circumstance. For example, you can lock out Code Red's *Admin.exe* or Nimda's *Nimda.dll* from running by adding it to the list and prohibiting it. This wouldn't prevent the buffer overflow from happening, but it would prevent any payload DLL or

EXE from running. On the other hand, an attack for IIS similar to the SQL Slammer worm, for example, would not be prevented in the Web Service Extension window, since that's a buffer overflow attack that doesn't copy any DLL or EXE file to the system.

Adding a New Web Service Extension

When you want to use an ISAPI or CGI extension that is not listed, you must add it to the list unless you have all extensions enabled. Here's how to add a new extension:

1. In the IIS Manager, click the Add A New Web Service extension hyperlink.

2. The New Web Service Extension dialog box appears. Type the name of the extension in the text box. This is a "friendly" name, so type in something meaningful to you.

3. Click the Add button to add the DLL or EXE files required to run this extension. Make sure to add all the required files.

4. If you would like the extension to be allowed right away, check the box to set it to Allowed.

5. Click OK.

Allow All Web Service Extensions for a Specific Application

If you want to enable all the extensions on which a component depends, you can use this hyperlink to enable them all at once. Here's how:

1. Click the Allow All Web Service Extensions For A Specific Application hyperlink.

2. Select the component you want to allow in the drop-down box, such as Internet Printing.

3. Note the components that will be allowed as a result of this—ASP in this case.

4. Click OK. The extensions will now show up as allowed.

Note   *If you enable extensions with a component that is dependent on other components, it will not enable the selected component's extensions, just the components it depends on to run successfully. The best use of this tool is in troubleshooting a component, to make sure that all the extensions it depends on are enabled.*

Prohibit All Web Service Extensions

To turn off all web service extensions quickly, click this hyperlink. This is useful if you want to disable all active content in one fell swoop. When you click the hyperlink, a warning/confirmation message will appear. If you click Yes, all listed extensions will be prohibited.

Modifying the Properties for a Web Service Extension

To modify the properties for a web service extension, highlight the extension in the list and click the Properties button. A box pops up with two tabs: General and Required Files.

The General tab shows you which applications use this extension. This is a good place to check if you are considering disabling this extension, because it will help you evaluate dependencies on the extension so you don't inadvertently break an application.

The Required Files tab allows you to add, remove, allow, or prohibit the files that are necessary for this component to run. You can add multiple files to your custom web service extension. The default extensions, such as ASP, are locked down, and you cannot add anything to them.

Chapter 7

Authentication

A uthentication is an important feature of any secure web site. Every time a client browses to a web site, it needs to be authenticated before it can access the resources it is requesting. By default, that authentication all takes place on the server, and the client isn't even involved. Some authentication settings can make for easy access to a web site, but sometimes you want to limit who sees what information on your site. This is where more restrictive types of authentication come in.

In this chapter, each of the following major types of IIS authentication is covered:

- Anonymous authentication
- Basic authentication
- Digest and Advanced Digest authentication
- Integrated Windows authentication
- .NET Passport authentication

Note *Certificates can also be used for authentication. They're covered in detail in Chapters 2 and 10.*

Anonymous Authentication

Anonymous authentication allows a user to access web and FTP sites without having to provide a username and password. When a client user accesses a web or FTP site, IIS uses the Internet Guest Account to authenticate that user. The Internet Guest Account is created when IIS is installed, and it is named *IUSR_<Computername>*, where *<Computername>* is the name of the host machine. Having an account to use for anonymous access allows you to configure which resources all anonymous users can access on your server. The anonymous account is also added to the Guests group when IIS is installed, so any restrictions or permissions applied to that group also apply to the account.

Note *If your computer is renamed, the Internet Guest Account does not change and continues to use the old machine name. Because user accounts use security identifiers (SIDs) to identify themselves, changing the computer name doesn't affect the account name.*

When IIS receives a request, it automatically attempts anonymous authentication first. If anonymous authentication fails, it attempts to log on the user using another logon method. If no other authentication methods are enabled, IIS sends a "403 Access Denied" HTTP error message to the client.

Tip *You can use any user account that you wish for anonymous access, including the Administrator account. You can change access settings in the item's Properties window's Directory Security tab, accessible by right-clicking the item in the IIS Microsoft Management Console (MMC) snap-in and choosing Properties. (By the way, even though you can do it, don't use the Administrator account for anonymous access.)*

Logon Types

One huge change in the way anonymous access does business is that the default logon type has been changed from *INTERACTIVE* to *NETWORK_CLEARTEXT*. Previously, every user account accessing IIS had to have the Log On Locally right. Now that *NETWORK_CLEARTEXT* is the standard, anonymous access no longer requires Log On Locally, reducing the vulnerability of IIS having too many rights.

Four main classifications of authentication are used in IIS:

- *INTERACTIVE*
- *BATCH*
- *NETWORK*
- *SERVICE*

NETWORK_CLEARTEXT is a type of *NETWORK* logon, and it is also used as the default for Basic authentication.

Subauthentication in IIS

If you've used IIS 5, you may notice that IIS 6 doesn't support automatic password synchronization. Automatic password synchronization allowed IIS to control the password of any account used for anonymous access. Needless to say, this was a security risk, because that dynamic link library (*IISSUBA.DLL*) could be used to change the password for any account. This feature was turned off by default in IIS 6. You can, however, enable this if you want, but only if the account meets the following criteria.

- The worker process configured for the application has to run as LocalSystem instead of Network Service.
- *IISSUBA.DLL* must be registered as a Component Object Model (COM) component (use *rundll32*).
- The metabase property, *AnonymousPasswordSynch*, needs to be enabled.

None of these configurations are present in a clean (default and unchanged) install of IIS 6. You notice the following if you're not using a clean install:

- If you're running in IIS 5.0 Isolation mode, the in-process applications will run as LocalSystem.
- If you upgrade from Windows 2000 running IIS 5 to Windows Server 2003 (WS03) running IIS 6, and automatic password synchronization is enabled on your IIS 5 web site, the *AnonymousPasswordSynch* metabase property will be set, but the other two configuration changes will still need to be made.

Basic Authentication

Basic authentication is a widely accepted means of authentication. Because all the information is presented and transmitted in clear text, it's easy to use and makes for easy program interoperability, but the passwords can be found out faster than you can say "security risk."

Both the web server and FTP server components in IIS support Basic authentication. Here's how it works in IIS:

1. The user enters a username and password for authentication.

2. The web browser Base64-encodes the password and sends it to the server.

3. IIS verifies that the username and password are valid, and that they have access to the resources.

Pretty straightforward, eh? Since Basic authentication is built into the HTTP specification, most browsers support it, which gives Basic authentication an edge when you're dealing with non-Microsoft browsers. You can get around the clear text password problem by using the Secure Socket Layer (SSL) protocol to encrypt all the traffic as it moves across the network.

Internet Explorer (IE) versions 2.0 and later will attempt to use Integrated Windows authentication before using Basic authentication.

Note *Base-64 refers to the system used to represent the password as a number. Other common bases are Base-10 (ordinary decimal numbers), Base-2 (binary numbers), and Base-16 (hexadecimal numbers). Base-64 encoding is detailed in RFC 1521, authored by Nathaniel Borenstein and Ned Freed. It defines a 65-character subset of the US-ASCII character set and uses 6 bits per character. The characters are uppercase and lowercase A–Z, the numbers 0–9, and the special characters + and /. The equal sign (=) is the sixty-fifth character, and it is reserved for padding at the end of data.*

Basic Authentication Tokens

IIS keeps a token cache for logons using Basic authentication. When you log on to a Windows server, an access token is created with all the SIDs for all the groups of which you are a member. This token is stored in the token cache, and IIS impersonates this token when accessing objects. This cache is used so that IIS doesn't have to authenticate you every time you access something. While this improves performance for IIS, it can be a security risk, because someone could gain access to that token in the token cache before it falls out of the cache. The default Time to Live (TTL) for a token is 900 seconds.

You can reduce this risk in two main ways:

- Don't log on using Basic authentication with any user account that has elevated rights, especially Administrator rights.

■ Set the *UserTokenTTL* setting in the registry to a lower value so that tokens expire more frequently. You can even set it to 0 so that tokens are not cached at all.

■ Obviously, not caching tokens causes a performance hit. You need to weigh this against the need to have Administrator accounts that access the server.

Note *The UserTokenTTL registry key is located at HKEY_LOCAL_MACHINE\SYSTEM\ CurrentControlSet\Services\InetInfo\Parameters\UserTokenTTL. It may not be present on your system, so you may need to add the key. As usual, editing the registry is dangerous, so be careful here.*

User Accounts and Basic Authentication

To use Basic authentication, a user account must be defined on either the local machine or on a trusted domain controller. The account-based access control is all done through the NT File System (NTFS) permissions on the file system. In the Authentication And Access Control section on the Directory Security tab of the Properties window for an object in the IIS MMC (accessed by right-clicking an object in the left pane of the MMC and choosing Properties), you simply click the Edit button and specify the type of authentication to be used and the default domain (if you're a member of a domain). You can also specify a realm, but that field doesn't mean anything on the server end— it simply displays that value to the client when the logon box pops up.

Digest Authentication

Digest authentication is available if you are using Active Directory accounts, and although it has some associated security risks, it is a more secure means of authentication than Basic authentication. Digest authentication is not intended to be a complete answer to security on the web; it is designed only to avoid the problems associate with Basic authentication. In addition to Active Directory, Digest authentication requires use of HTTP 1.1, so it will work only with newer browsers that support that protocol.

Digest authentication requires that the domain controller keep a plaintext copy of each password, so it can check that password against the hash sent by the client. Therein lies the security risk. Having plaintext passwords stored anywhere is a security risk, so if you choose this form of authentication, you will need to make sure that the domain controller is secure from intrusion, or passwords can be compromised. The upside to using Digest authentication is that the password is not sent across the network in plaintext, unlike with Basic authentication.

Here's how Digest authentication works:

1. The server sends the client a note that Digest authentication is required for this resource.

2. The server also sends the client a "nonce," some randomly generated information to include in the authentication hash. This information helps prevent replay attacks.

3. The client adds this information to its username/password combo and performs a one-way hash on it using the MD5 hashing algorithm.

4. The client sends the hash to the server. It also sends the nonce in clear text.

5. The server takes the nonce data, combines it with the local plaintext copy of the username/password combo, and performs a one-way hash on it using the MD5 hashing algorithm.

6. This hash is compared to the one received, and if they match, the authentication is accepted.

Advanced Digest Authentication

Advanced Digest authentication is exactly like Digest authentication with one important difference: In Digest authentication, passwords are stored on the domain controller as an MD5 hash, rather than as clear text. This prevents anyone from figuring out the password. Advanced Digest authentication is supported in HTTP 1.1, so any HTTP 1.1–compliant browser should work. Advanced Digest authentication is a better choice than Digest authentication because of the extra security provided.

Advanced Digest authentication has the following requirements:

- You must be running Active Directory.

- Both the IIS server and a domain controller must be running WS03.

- The clients using Advanced Digest authentication must be running at least IE 5.

- The user account must be in an Active Directory domain that is trusted to the IIS server (or the same domain).

Note   *If the domain controller and the IIS server are not both running WS03, IIS will automatically fall back to using regular Digest authentication.*

Enabling Advanced Digest Authentication

Advanced Digest authentication is enabled in the metabase, and you can apply it at any level in the W3SVC. (W3SVC is the name the Web Server Service goes by in the Metabase.) This metabase setting is inheritable by all child levels. The metabase property for Advanced Digest authentication is *UseDigestSSP*. Here's how to enable it:

1. Open the *MetaBase.xml* file in Notepad (assuming edit-while-running).

2. Go to the level at which you want to enable Advanced Digest authentication.

3. Type in **UseDigestSSP="TRUE"**, as shown in Figure 7-1.

4. Save and close the file.

5. Open the IIS MMC, and open the Authentication Methods window for the level at which you want to enable Advanced Digest authentication. To do this,

Figure 7-1. *Metabase file with UseDigestSSP*

right-click a node in the left pane of the MMC and select Properties. Then open the Directory Security tab and click the Edit button.

6. Put a check in the checkbox for Digest Authentication For Windows Domain Servers.

7. Type in the Realm, or click the Select button to choose the Realm. In Advanced Digest authentication, the realm is important and needs to match the domain or realm that will authenticate the clients.

8. Click OK.

9. Click OK again.

Following is the process that the client and server go through when using Advanced Digest authentication:

1. The server sends the client a note that Digest authentication is required for this resource (Digest and Advanced Digest use the same protocol).

2. The server also sends the realm name.

3. The client then takes the username and password, combines them with the name of the realm, and creates an MD5 hash. It then submits a request for the resource to the server, sending the MD5 hash in the header of the HTTP request.

4. The IIS server sends this hash to the domain controller for verification.

5. The domain controller verifies this hash against the hash stored in Active Directory. If they match, the domain controller sends the IIS server an acknowledgment.

Integrated Windows Authentication

Integrated Windows authentication is the most secure method of authentication, but it is available only with Internet Explorer. This authentication type had been known previously as NTLM authentication and Windows NT Challenge/Response authentication. In Integrated Windows authentication, the user's browser proves itself to the server using a cryptographic exchange during the authentication process.

Integrated Windows authentication supports both the Kerberos v5 and the NTLM (NT LAN Manager) protocols for authentication through the Negotiate package. If you are using Active Directory, and the browser supports it (IE 5 or above with Windows 2000), Kerberos is used; otherwise, NTLM is used. Both Kerberos and NTLM have limitations on their use. Interestingly enough, each one's strength is the other's weakness. Kerberos generally works with proxy servers, but it tends to have a hard time with firewalls. NTLM generally works through firewalls, but it tends to have a hard time with proxy servers.

About Microsoft Negotiate

Microsoft Negotiate is a package that serves as an interface between different security support providers. It can choose among several different authentication packages. IIS uses the Negotiate package for authentication, which currently chooses between Kerberos and NTLM. Support for future authentication packages can be added, though, which is Negotiate's strength. By default, Negotiate chooses Kerberos, because it's the more secure protocol. If, for some reason, Kerberos is not available, Negotiate falls back to NTLM.

About NTLM Authentication

NTLM is an enhancement of the old LM (LAN Manager) authentication protocol. NTLM works by using a challenge/response between the server and the client without sending the user's clear text password across the network. The client has to prove it knows the user's password by sending an encrypted hash.

Here's how NTLM works:

1. The user types in a username, password, and a domain name when logging in to the client machine.

2. The client creates a hash of this password and discards the original.

3. The client sends the server the plaintext username.

4. The server sends a 16-bit nonce to the client.

5. The client encrypts this nonce along with the hash of the user's password and sends it to the server.

6. The server then sends the username, the nonce, and the client's response to a domain controller.

7. The domain controller encrypts the nonce along with its own hash of the user's password, and it compares the value to the one sent by the server.

8. If the values match, the domain controller notifies the server that authentication is successful.

9. If the values do not match or no username matches, the domain controller notifies the server, which then sends that message to the client. The client's browser then prompts the user for login information.

About Kerberos Authentication

The original Kerberos was the three-headed dog in Greek mythology that kept people from entering the underworld. The modern day Kerberos protocol provides for secure authentication to resources. Kerberos relies on secret key authentication, in which client and server share a single key that is used for encryption and decryption. The client proves it knows the key by encrypting a message, and the server proves it knows the key by decrypting that message. It then takes part of that message, encrypts it, and sends it back to the client. If the message is intact, everybody knows who everybody else is.

Kerberos relies on a central server, called a Key Distribution Center (KDC), to provide all the keys. The KDC issues Ticket-Granting Tickets (TGTs) to clients requesting access to a server resource.

Here's how the client gets the initial TGT from the KDC:

1. The user logs in to the client with a username and password.

2. The client encrypts the password and saves it.

3. The client sends the KDC a message requesting credentials for the TGT service, along with the user's encrypted password.

4. The KDC compares the encrypted password with its master copy to make sure they match. It also checks the timestamp the client added to the request to make sure it is within five minutes of its own time.

5. If everything matches, the KDC creates the requested credentials for the TGT service by creating a logon session key and encrypting it with the user's key.

6. The KDC also creates another credential by encrypting the logon session key and a TGT for the user with its own master key.

7. The KDC then sends both credentials to the client.

8. The client decrypts the logon session key from the first credential using its encrypted password, and it stores that logon session key in its ticket cache.

9. The client also stores the TGT in its ticket cache.

Now that the client has a TGT, it can use that TGT to get tickets to access resources. Here's how that works:

1. The client asks the KDC for a ticket to access resources on a server. The client presents its TGT to the KDC along with the desired resource name and an authentication message, which is encrypted with the logon session key.

2. The KDC decrypts the TGT using the master key, extracts the logon session key, and uses that logon session key to decrypt the authentication message. If it matches, the client is verified.

3. The KDC creates a service session key for the client to present to the server when requesting resources, and it encrypts the service session key with the client's logon session key.

4. The KDC also encrypts that service session key with the server's master key into a ticket.

5. The KDC then sends both credentials to the client, which decrypts the session key using its logon session key and stores the service session key and the ticket in its cache.

Now the client has a ticket it can present to the server to gain access to resources.

1. The client sends the server the session ticket and an authentication message, which is encrypted with the service session key.

2. The server decrypts the session ticket and compares the timestamp the client put on the request to make sure it is within 5 minutes of its own time. It then gets the session key from this ticket.

3. The server then encrypts the timestamp in the session ticket with the session key and sends it to the client.

4. The client decrypts the message and compares the timestamp with the original. If it matches, everybody knows who everyone else is.

This is a very involved process, but it makes sure that the identity of everyone communicating is known and verified. Obviously, the KDC plays an important part in this, and it's important to make sure your KDC is secure.

.NET Passport Authentication

IIS 6 can use Microsoft's .NET Passport to authenticate users requesting resources from a web site or a web site virtual directory. The benefit that this solution offers is that the credentials are stored and managed on another server that you are not responsible for building or maintaining. Users can authenticate using the .NET Passport service and then be allowed access to the web site hosted on your WS03 server. The service does not provide access control or site authorization, however. The .NET Passport server can only affirm that a web consumer representing himself or herself to be the person represented by the established profile in the .NET Passport server has successfully authenticated as that person represented by the established profile.

The .NET Passport system is free for the web consumer to register with and use. Web consumers log in and log out at the Passport server, and they are directed to your web site after a successful login event. The login and logout pages may be cobranded so that they appear to be related to the web site that the user is logging in to.

Passport provides a nice system for everyone involved in a web-based transaction, because users get the benefit of a single sign-on solution for any .NET Passport authenticated web site they encounter. The web host benefits because the hosting party does not have to build and support the credentials system or server, but they must pay a fee to the Microsoft .NET Passport service to establish an account with the Passport server. After an account is set up, the web host simply needs to build the web site to respond to users who authenticate. This is the same effort that any web site with an established membership and authentication mechanism would perform regardless of where the members' credentials are hosted, except that they now deal with only authenticated users.

The problem with the .NET Passport system, however, is that many web consumers have not responded quickly to the solution. The web consumer community is apprehensive about providing personal information to the .NET Passport service. Existing web-based vendors and portals have not adopted the use of .NET Passport with great enthusiasm because they generally already have their own authentication systems in place. The benefits of providing a web single login experience are greatly minimized when the web consumer may have to authenticate to other sites that they patronize. Without wide acceptance of the use of .NET Passport by web sites using it as an authentication system, the web single login system will not benefit the web consumer.

Establishing .NET Passport Service

Before you can use the .NET Passport service, you need to prepare your site for the service. Following is a review of the steps required for establishing a .NET Passport server setup:

1. Register the web site through the .NET Passport service. Go to the following URL to begin the process: *http://www.microsoft.com/net/services/passport/ developer.asp*. Here, you'll fill out a comprehensive series of forms and complete a .NET Passport Wizard with information about yourself and your web site. Table 7-1 summarizes the information required to perform this step.

2. On successful registration, your site is assigned an ID and registered with a pending status. Microsoft will attempt to replicate the site on its server and approve your site.

3. Build the site. Microsoft provides a .NET Passport software development kit (SDK) that offers aid and support in your effort to build a .NET Passport web site. The SDK is available free for download from Microsoft's web site at *http://msdn.microsoft.com/library/default.asp?url=/downloads/list/websrvpass.asp*.

4. Petition .NET Passport services for a compliance review of the site. If your site meets the standards, you will be required to enter into a contractual agreement with .NET Passport services.

5. Launch the site. Obtain the encryption keys for the production site and roll in the production code required to support the .NET Passport integration.

The registration process identified in step 1 is rather comprehensive. You will also be presented with the .NET Passport Wizard, and you will be expected to establish a .NET Passport. After the wizard completes, you will see a series of web pages prompting you for information—some of which is mandatory to complete the process. The information requested during the registration processes is summarized in Table 7-1.

Item	Description
Your general contact information	Name, phone, address, e-mail, and so on
Name of the site	Required—Name used to identify the site in the Passport portal
Type of .NET Passport service	Required—Choose one or more of the following: Kids Passport, .NET Passport Single Sign-In, .NET Passport Express Purchase
Web Site Title	Required—Title for the web site
Domain Name	Required—The top most domain name for the site; no subdomains should be included in the name
Default Return URL	Required—The URL where customers will be redirected from the Passport server in an error event
Customer Support Phone Number	Telephone number presented to customers if they need help or support
Customer Support E-mail	E-mail address presented to customers if they need help or support
Customer Support URL	URL presented to customers if they need help or support
Privacy Policy URL	Required—URL presented to customers for your privacy policy
Cobrand URL	URL for the cobranding file that contains the JavaScript cobranding variables

Table 7-1. *.NET Passport Registration Information*

Item	Description
Cobrand CSS URL	URL for the cascading style sheet (.css) file that will be used by the .NET Passport pages to make them appear cobranded
Cobrand Image URL	Required—URL for the site's logo, which should be 468 × 60 pixels
Cobrand Image2 URL	Required—URL for the site's logo, which must be 2 × 80 pixels, and a .gif
Cobrand Image HREF	Link for the logo image
Cobrand Instruction Text	Required—Instructions that will appear at the top of the .NET Passport Credential dialog box
Registration Return URL	URL of the file that users will be redirected to after login by default
Terms of Use URL	URL for the terms of use
Edit URL	URL to the page on the web devoted to editing user's data on your site
Disable Copyright	Checkbox that will disable the Microsoft copyright link presented in each .NET Passport module
Disable Help Text	Checkbox that will disable the Microsoft help file link presented in each .NET Passport module
Disable Member Services	Checkbox that will disable the Microsoft Member Services file link presented in each .NET Passport module
Disable Privacy Policy	Checkbox that will disable the Microsoft privacy policy file link presented in each .NET Passport module
Disable Terms of Use	Checkbox that will disable the Microsoft Terms of Use file link presented in each .NET Passport module

Table 7-1.   *.NET Passport Registration Information* (continued)

Item	Description
Expire Cookie URL	Required—URL for a file that deletes the .NET Passport cookies; this URL is called when the user performs a logout function
Logout URL	URL for a file that the passport system will send customers when they sign out of .NET Passport by clicking the .NET Passport Sign Out button

Table 7-1.   *.NET Passport Registration Information* (continued)

Setting Up the Site for .NET Passport

If you set up a web site or a web virtual directory to authenticate users via .NET Passport, the users will be presented with a .NET Passport login prompt when they request a file for the first time from the web site. The circumstances under which the user will be prompted for their credentials may vary, depending on the site application's use of the .NET Passport service. After the user enters a valid login and password, they are allowed to access the requested file.

To set up IIS to provide .NET Passport authentication, follow these steps:

1. Open the IIS MMC snap-in and expand the Web Sites node in the left panel.

2. Right-click the respective web site or virtual directory that should authenticate using .NET Passport. Select Properties.

3. In the Properties window, select the Directory Security tab.

4. Click the Edit button under the Authentication And Access Control section. The Authentication Methods window will open.

5. Under the Authenticated Access section, check the .NET Passport Authentication checkbox. All other authentication methods will be disabled, since using .NET Passport authentication is a mutually exclusive option. Anonymous access can still be selected, however.

6. If you want, type a domain name in the Default Domain text box. This is the domain to which usernames will be assumed to belong on the host server after the .NET Passport server authenticates them. Realm may be used to identify the organization or domain to which users should be assumed to belong if the server participates in a non-Microsoft system.

7. Click the OK button to close the Authentication Methods window, and click the OK button to close the Properties window.

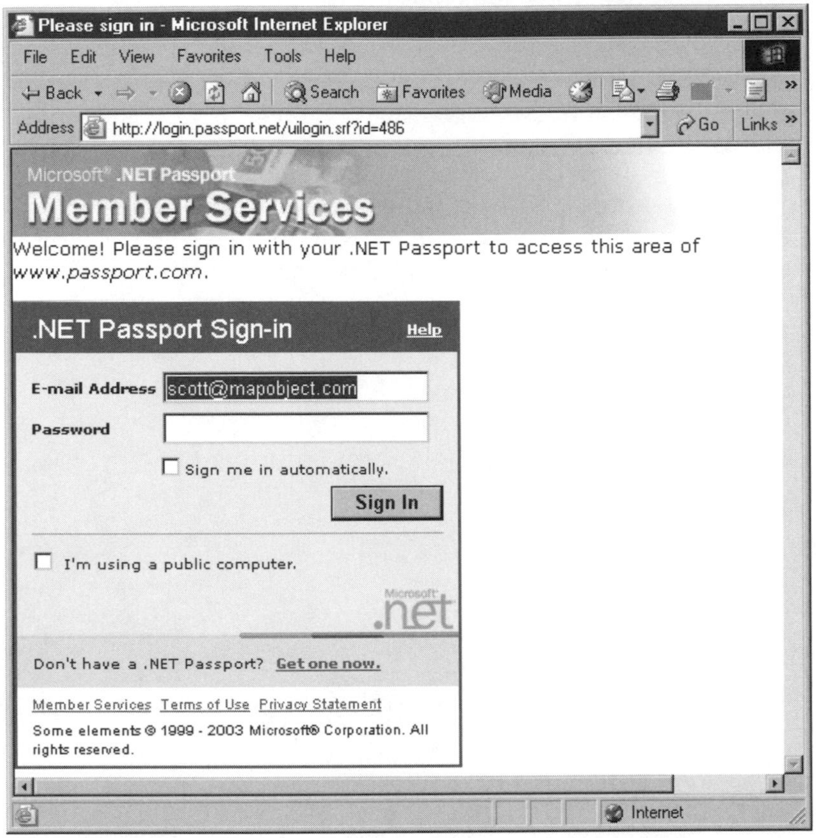

Figure 7-2. *.NET Passport login prompt with the default configurations*

If the .NET Passport service is set properly, users will be presented with a .NET Passport prompt that looks like the window shown in Figure 7-2, except the configurations described in Table 7-1 will exist in place of the default values shown in Figure 7-2.

Using Multiple Authentication Schemes

When multiple authentication schemes are in use, IIS and the client's browser will prefer certain authentication schemes over others. It attempts to use the authentication schemes in the following order:

■ If Anonymous authentication is enabled, it is always attempted first. If Anonymous authentication fails or is disabled, one of the authenticated access methods is used.

- First, Integrated Windows authentication is tried if enabled and supported by the browser.

- If Integrated Windows authentication is not available, Digest or Advanced Digest authentication is used if enabled and supported.

- Finally, Basic authentication is used as a last resort.

You may have noticed that .NET Passport authentication is not listed. That's the odd member of the bunch. If .NET Passport authentication is enabled, it disables all other forms of authenticated access (although Anonymous is still available).

The
Complete
Reference

IIS 6

Chapter 8

TCP/IP and DNS

TCP/IP, which stands for Transmission Control Protocol/Internet Protocol, is used for communicating between computers and the Internet. Without this protocol, Internet Information Services (IIS) won't function well.

The Domain Name System (DNS) is a technology that allows resolution of domain names to IP addresses. Every host on the Internet has both a domain name address, such as *www.microsoft.com*, and an IP address, such as 192.17.3.4.

This chapter delves into how TCP/IP and DNS work and how they relate to IIS. Because no respectable chapter about TCP/IP would be complete without some history, that's how this chapter starts.

The History of TCP/IP and the Internet

While most people think TCP/IP is a single protocol, it actually refers to a suite of communication protocols: the Transmission Control Protocol (TCP) and the Internet Protocol (IP) are two of the most common protocols used in the suite, but they are by no means the whole of the TCP/IP suite. Other protocols that feature TCP/IP include the User Datagram Protocol (UDP) and the Internet Control Message Protocol (ICMP).

The ARPANET

In 1968, the United States Department of Defense (DoD) Advanced Research Projects Agency (ARPA), later called the Defense Advanced Research Projects Agency (DARPA), began researching the network technology that is now called *packet switching*. TCP/IP is one of the protocols that originated from this research. The intent of TCP/IP was to facilitate communication among the DoD community without using the public-switched telephone network. This network was called the ARPANET, and it is the predecessor to today's Internet. In 1978, the separate functions of TCP and IP were formalized, and in 1983, they became standard protocols for ARPANET. In 1989, the machines on the ARPANET were switched over to the NSFnet, the National Science Foundation network, a much larger and faster network than the ARPANET. This became what is known today as the Internet. Because of the history of the TCP/IP protocol suite, it is often referred to as the DoD protocol suite or the Internet protocol suite.

Architectural Models for Communications Protocols

To provide for an environment in which communication protocols can be developed to work with each other, a framework is used to help explain and develop the protocols. This *architectural model* provides a common frame of reference and separates the functions performed by communication protocols into four layers stacked vertically: the application layer, host-to-host transport layer, Internet layer, and network access layer. Each layer in the stack performs a specific function. Any number of protocols can be written and used for that function.

Because each layer has a specific function, it can perform that function without worrying about what's happening at all the other layers. Because each layer passes data to the layer above or below it in a defined method and then forgets about the data, only its peer layer at the other end of the communication is of consequence.

Two architectural models are commonly used to describe TCP/IP communication: the DoD protocol model and the Open Systems Interconnection (OSI) protocol model.

The DoD Protocol Model

Originally, the DoD protocol model, or Internet reference model, had three layers: network access, host-to-host transport, and application. Later, a fourth layer, Internet, was added. This model is commonly used to describe how TCP/IP works. The DoD model is shown in Figure 8-1.

Each of the four layers of the DoD model has a specific function:

- **Application layer** The top layer in the model includes the protocols that process user data and manage data exchange between applications. This layer also standardizes the presentation of data.

- **Host-to-host transport layer** The next layer contains the protocols used for providing end-to-end data integrity. It also provides the controls that initiate and terminate communications.

- **Internet layer** This layer contains the protocols used for routing messages through the network. This layer puts data into a datagram.

- **Network access layer** The lowest layer in the model contains the protocols used to deliver the data physically to devices on the network. This layer puts data into a *frame*.

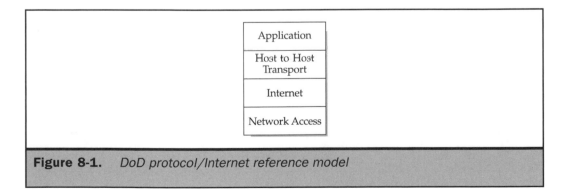

Figure 8-1.   *DoD protocol/Internet reference model*

The OSI Protocol Model

The Open Systems Interconnection (OSI) protocol model is a seven-layer model developed by the International Organization for Standardization (ISO—the same group that developed the ISO9000 standards) that corresponds to the layers in the DoD model. The OSI model was originally set up to be the universal standard for all communication protocols, but support waned for the standard. Now protocols usually loosely correspond to the OSI model, but they don't necessarily follow it exactly. The OSI model layers are shown in Figure 8-2.

Each of the seven layers of the OSI model has its own specific functions:

■ **Application layer**   This top layer supports application and end-user processes. Everything at this layer is application specific. This layer provides application services for file transfers, e-mail, and other network software services.

■ **Presentation layer**   This layer provides independence from differences in data representation. It transforms data into a usable form for the application layer.

■ **Session layer**   This layer is not concerned with the network connection. At this level, the connection is assumed. The layer contains the control structure for managing connections between applications.

■ **Transport layer**   This layer is responsible for complete transfer of data between hosts. It provides for error detection and recovery, and it ensures error-free transmission of data. The TCP and UDP protocols fall in this layer.

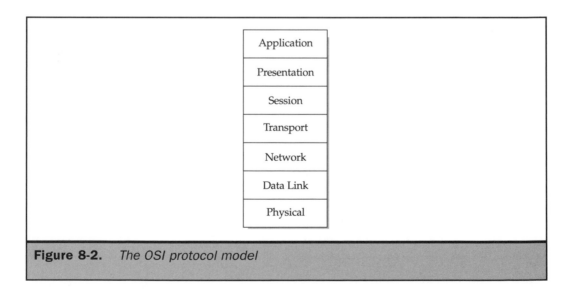

Figure 8-2.   *The OSI protocol model*

- **Network layer**   This layer is responsible for addressing and creating virtual circuits to transfer data from end to end. IP addresses fall in this layer.

- **Data link layer**   This layer is divided into two sublayers: The Logical Link Control (LLC) layer controls frame synchronization and flow control, and the Media Access Control (MAC) layer controls the addressing for the data link layer.

- **Physical layer**   This layer defines the specifications for the physical components of network communication. Bits, signaling, and cable specifications are all at this layer. This layer works with the 0's and 1's of communication.

Communicating Across the Layers

Typically, a group of protocols is written to work together within the framework of the architectural model. These protocol groups are called *stacks*. To communicate across the network, data must travel down the layers in the model on one end and then back up the layers on the other end.

Encapsulation

As data moves down the protocol stack, each layer adds its own information to the mix and encapsulates the data with its header and trailer. Each layer has its own data structure, terminology, and address mechanism. Think of it as wrapping up a box, and then wrapping that box in another box, and so on. On the other end, the boxes are unwrapped in succession; at each layer, the data is processed, and then it's sent up to the next layer in the stack. This process, called *decapsulation*, continues up the stack until the data is delivered.

Let's follow data as it travels from one machine to another. The top three layers deal with the presentation of information to the transport layer, where real network communication begins, so we'll start there. Figure 8-3 shows the path that the data takes as it travels from one machine to another.

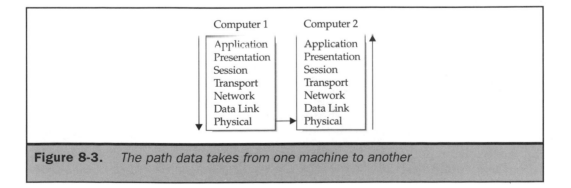

Figure 8-3.   *The path data takes from one machine to another*

At the transport layer on Computer 1, the data is encapsulated into a datagram and sent to the network layer. At the network layer, the datagram is put into a packet, with the datagram as the data portion of that packet. It is then sent to the data link layer, where the packet is put into the data portion of a frame. That frame is sent to the physical layer. At the physical layer, the frame is encoded into bits and sent across the wire to Computer 2.

On Computer 2, the bits are taken off the wire at the physical layer and sent up to the data link layer. At the data link layer, the frame header information is read for the MAC address. If it matches, the process continues, and the data (the layer 3 packet) is sent to the network layer. If it doesn't match, the data is discarded. At the network layer, the IP address is read, and if it is a match, the datagram is sent up to the transport layer. At the transport layer, the port number and protocol are read to determine who gets the data. The data is sent up to the session layer for eventual presentation to the application.

Addressing in TCP/IP

Two types of addresses are important in TCP/IP: MAC addresses and IP addresses. We'll talk about transport layer (TCP and UDP) information in the section "The TCP, UDP, and ICMP Protocols" later in this chapter.

MAC Addresses

MAC addresses reside at the data link layer of the OSI model. The Institute of Electrical and Electronics Engineers (IEEE) assigns these addresses. Every network device has a MAC address, and every MAC address is completely unique (theoretically).

MAC addresses use a 48-bit address space, which allows for millions upon millions of MAC addresses to be used on the Internet. MAC addresses have two parts: The first 24 bits are the manufacturer ID. Each manufacturer has its own prefix. That manufacturer assigns addresses, called *station IDs*, using the second 24 bits.

IP Addresses

IP addresses reside at the network layer of the OSI model. The Internet Assigned Numbers Authority (IANA) assigns these addresses and has delegated large blocks to several different authorities.

IP is considered a *routable* protocol, because IP addresses consist of the following two parts:

- **Network number** This is the first portion of the IP address that identifies the address of the devices on the network that are considered part of the same group.

- **Node number** This is the last portion of the IP address. It identifies the individual device on that network.

| Note | A subnet mask *defines the break from network number to node number in an IP address. To see the relationship at its most basic level, you have to represent the IP address and Subnet Mask in binary numbers.* |

IP Protocol Versions

Two versions of IP are in use today: version 4 and version 6. IPv4 is the existing standard that was created in the late 1970s. IPv6 is the new standard.

IPv4

Three parts are used in configuring communication with IPv4: the IP address, subnet mask, and default gateway.

IP Address

IPv4 consists of 32-bit addresses, commonly expressed as *dotted quads*—four, 8-bit parts separated by periods; for example, *192.168.0.1*. IPv4 has some problems, however, because the address space it provides is not large enough to handle the demand for addresses. This is partly due to the inefficient allocation of addresses. Many people are using private address and proxy servers to limit the number of public addresses being used. Still, with more and more machines connecting on the Internet, the IPv4 address space will run out at some point in time. IPv6 was created to resolve that problem by providing a larger address space from which to choose.

Subnet Mask

The subnet mask determines which parts of the IP address are the network and node portions. A subnet mask is another dotted quad address that "masks" the portion of the IP address to determine where the break from network address to node address occurs. A typical subnet mask looks something like this: *255.255.255.0*. Here, the first three octets are the network number and the last octet is the node number. Applying that to the IP address in our example, the following is true:

IP Address   192.168.0.1
Subnet Mask   255.255.255.0
Comparing this IP address and subnet mask, the network number is 192.168.0, and the node number is .1

For the purposes of this book, that's really all the details about IP addressing that you need to know. However, if you're curious, here's a little more technical information. The best way to represent IP addresses and subnet masks, and to understand the math behind how they work, is to represent them as binary numbers (1's and 0's):

■ The IP address 192.168.0.1 would be represented in binary numbers as 110000.10101000.00000000.00000001

■ The subnet mask 255.255.255.0 would be represented in binary numbers as 11111111.11111111.11111111.00000000

This subnet mask is also referred to as */24*, because it contains 24 bits (1's). So if you see *192.168.0.0 /24*, for example, you know the mask refers to the block of addresses from *192.168.0.0* through *192.168.0.255*, and the subnet mask is *255.255.255.0*. Now we can apply a more granular subnet mask here, remembering that the subnet mask for all devices has to be the same for them to be on the same network. The rule to follow is "different subnet mask, different network."

Default Gateway

Communicating to all the devices with the same network number is easy: just send out the packet, and it'll get there. Communicating across subnets is more involved, however, and this is where the default gateway comes in. The default gateway is an IP address of a device that resides on the same subnet. That device has more than one network connection, and it can "route" packets from one subnet to another because it is aware of different connections.

IPv6

IPv6 has a 128-bit address space, which provides enough address space so that each square foot on the planet could have its own IP address with room to spare. IPv6 does have a long way to go before it becomes the protocol of choice, however, because IPv4 is deeply ingrained into every piece of networking. IPv6 support in Windows Server 2003 (WS03) is somewhat limited.

IPv6 addresses are commonly expressed as eight sets of 16-bit hex addresses (for example, FEAD:D8F1:FFA0:FAB7:1234:5678:9012:FF1A). As you can see, it's much larger than an IPv4 address and using it will make systems such as the DNS, which performs IP address to hostname resolution, all the more important. It's hard enough to remember the 4-octect IP addresses we use today; remembering eight 16-bit hex addresses is neigh impossible.

IPv6 can be configured automatically or manually. Automatic configuration has three options:

■ **Stateless** Stateless configuration is accomplished through *router advertisement messages*. This is different than what occurs with DHCPv6. The router advertisements contain the information the client needs to set the IP address and default gateway information. This is the only type of auto configuration that WS03 supports.

■ **Stateful** Stateful configuration is accomplished through the use of a configuration protocol, like DHCPv6, to obtain all the information needed to configure the interface.

■ **Both** This option uses both a configuration protocol and router advertisements to configure the interface.

IPv6 has duplicate address detection built in. After a client gets the configuration information from the router advertisements, it performs the duplicate address detection. If that fails, the interface must be manually configured. If it succeeds, the client can use that address.

IPv6 is a rapidly developing protocol, and new Requests for Comments (RFCs) are emerging frequently. Support for IPv6 in WS03 is available, but it isn't the primary protocol WS03 was designed to use.

The TCP, UDP, and ICMP Protocols

Transmission Control Protocol, User Datagram Protocol (UDP), and Internet Control Message Protocol (ICMP) all reside at the transport layer.

TCP breaks up messages into datagrams and makes sure messages arrive at their destination. It sends acknowledgments between the devices to keep track of which datagrams have arrived. If a datagram doesn't arrive at the destination, it is re-sent. TCP also reassembles datagrams into their proper order on arrival by using a sequence number in the header of the TCP datagram.

UDP doesn't do as much as TCP. It is designed for applications for which you don't need to put together sequences of datagrams. UDP doesn't do acknowledgments, and it doesn't care whether or not a packet (datagram) has made it to the destination. Since UDP doesn't reassemble datagrams, no sequence number appears in the header. The upside to UDP is that the protocol has much less overhead than TCP, so it is useful for high-bandwidth applications that aren't upset by missing a packet or two—such as streaming video.

ICMP is used for error messages and for providing feedback about problems in the communication environment. For example, if you attempt to connect to a host, your system may get back an ICMP message saying "host unreachable." ICMP has no port numbers, because the network software itself interprets ICMP messages. Two common utilities that use ICMP are *ping* and *tracert*.

Using TCP/IP

Now that we've covered the protocol stack, let's concentrate on how TCP/IP works with WS03 and how IP addressing works with your IIS sites.

Tip   *If you're looking for some IP addresses to use for your own internal network, you can use three blocks that are not in use on the Internet:*

192.168.0.0 – 192.168.255.255
172.16.0.0 – 172.31.255.255
10.0.0.0 – 10.255.255.255

IPv4 is installed by default in WS03, so all you need to do is configure the connection. By default, WS03 uses DHCP to configure network connections. DHCP is an automatic method of configuring IP addresses, and all the settings are made on the DHCP server, rather than at each individual machine. In this book, we'll use manually configured IP addresses.

Choosing an IP Address

When choosing an IP address, you need to be aware that you cannot use two addresses in each subnet: The first IP address in a subnet is reserved for the network ID. The last IP address in each subnet is reserved for the broadcast address, which machines use when they want to talk to every machine. Both of these addresses are reserved and unusable. Here is an example of the network ID and broadcast address for two subnets:

Subnet	Network ID	Broadcast Address
192.168.0.0 /24	192.168.0.0	192.168.0.255
10.0.0.0 /8	10.0.0.0	10.255.255.255

Configuring IPv4

IPv4 is configured in the Control Panel under Network Connections:

1. Choose Start | Control Panel.

2. Double-click Network Connections in the Control Panel. Connections will be listed in the Network Connections window, as shown in Figure 8-4.

You can also configure TCP/IP settings. By accessing the advanced settings, you can have more control over the options you set. Here's how it's done:

1. In the Network Connections window, double-click the network connection you want to set. The Status window appears.

2. Click the Properties button to see the Properties window.

3. On the General tab, choose Internet Protocol (TCP/IP) from the list, and then choose Properties.

4. In the Internet Protocol (TCP/IP) Properties window, click the Advanced button to open the Advanced TCP/IP settings.

From here, you can adjust settings on the IP Settings tab.

The IP Settings Tab

On this tab, as shown in Figure 8-5, you choose which IP addresses and which default gateway to use. The IP Addresses section allows you to enter one or more IP addresses.

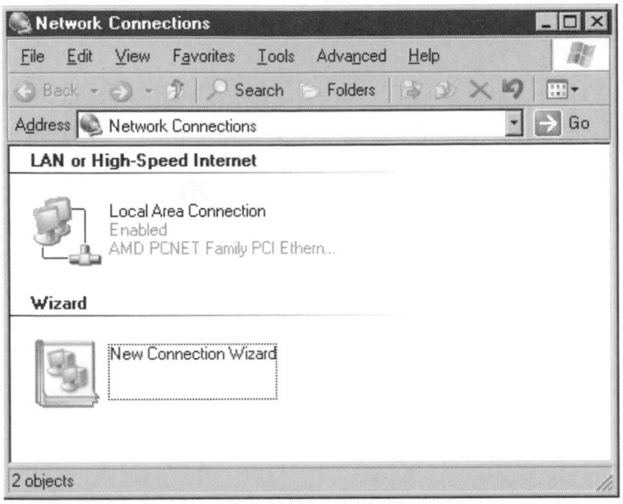

Figure 8-4.   *Network Connections window*

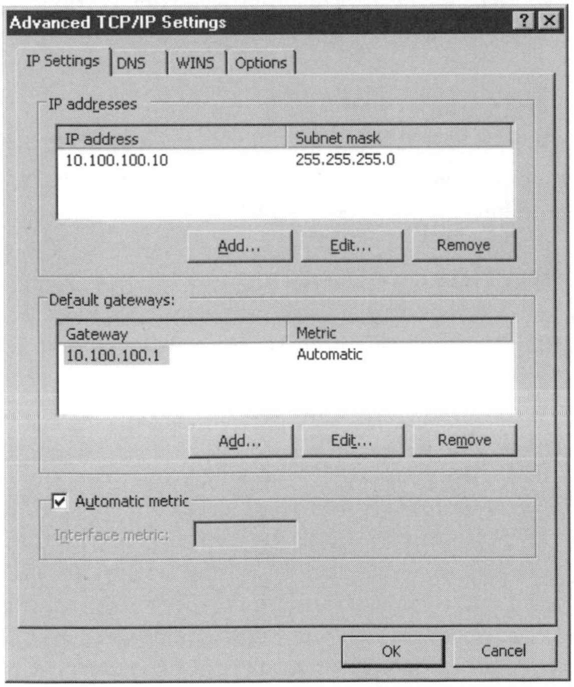

Figure 8-5.   *The IP settings tab of Advanced TCP/IP Settings*

You may need to use more than one IP address for a number of reasons—most notably, this is necessary if you want to host multiple sites on your IIS server and want each to have its own IP address. Although you can use Host Headers for web sites (see Chapter 2), you can't use them for FTP sites, so multiple FTP sites would force you to have multiple IP addresses, unless you want them to share a single IP address.

Adding IP Addresses to a Network Connection

In the IP Settings tab, click Add and type in the IP address and subnet mask. Repeat this for each IP address you want to set up. You can add any IP address here, even addresses on different networks. Since the OSI model is modular, you can run different networks over the same physical medium.

Editing and Deleting IP Addresses for this Network Connection

To edit an IP address, highlight the address you want to modify and click Edit. To delete an address, highlight the IP address and click Remove.

Adding a Gateway to this Network Connection

Click Add and type in the IP address of the gateway. Repeat this for each gateway you want to add. The metric allows you to choose more than one gateway, and you can assign a weight to each. The metric here is for the weight of each particular gateway, and it allows Windows to choose between different gateways to use for sending information.

Editing and Removing a Gateway for this Network Connection

To edit a gateway, highlight the gateway you want to modify and click Edit. To remove a gateway, highlight the gateway and click Remove.

Modifying the Interface Metric

The Interface Metric is a number that is assigned to this interface; it allows Windows to choose between different network connections on this machine to use for sending information. The lower the number, the better the connection. You can think of the metric number in terms of cost. The higher the number, the more costly (in time) it will be to use. The Automatic metric checkbox allows Windows to calculate the metric for this interface. Windows calculates the metric based solely on the speed of the connection.

The difference between the metric here on the Advanced TCP/IP Settings window and the metric in the TCP/IP Gateway Address window is that the metric here is for a network connection on this machine and the metric in the TCP/IP Gateway Address window is for the machine to use in sending data from this machine.

Consider a network connection as being tied to a network card. Each network card will get its own connection. So the gateway metric for the connection is for all gateways on that network card. The gateway metric in the TCP/IP Gateway Address window affects all network cards in the machine.

The DNS Configuration Tab

DNS is a technology that allows resolution of names to IP addresses. DNS is covered in more depth later in the section "DNS and Windows Server 2003." For now, we'll discuss just the configuration options on this tab, shown in Figure 8-6.

Adding DNS Server Addresses to this Network Connection

Click Add and type in the DNS server address. Repeat this for each address you want to add. You can enter multiple DNS server IP addresses here, instead of the two you can enter in the General tab.

Editing and Deleting DNS Server Addresses for this Network Connection

To edit a DNS server address, highlight the address you want to modify and click Edit. To delete a DNS server address, highlight the server address and click Remove.

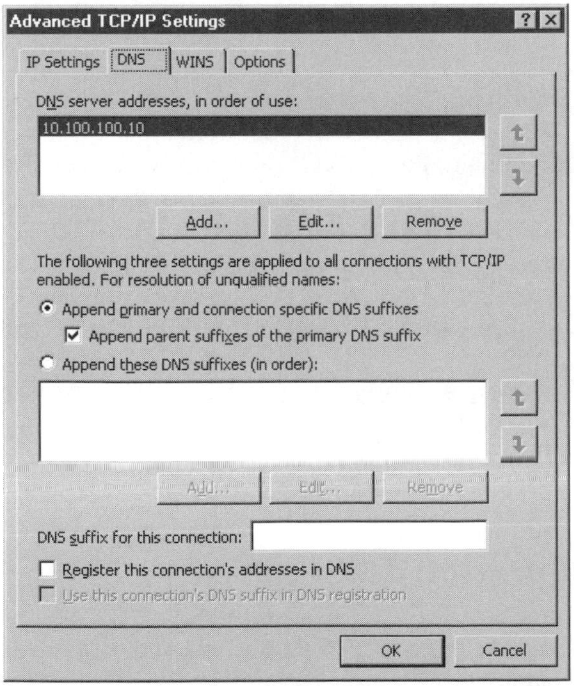

Figure 8-6. *The DNS tab of Advanced TCP/IP Settings*

Appending DNS Suffixes for Name Resolution

For DNS names to be resolved, they must be *fully qualified domain names*. For example, *myserver.mydomain.com* is a fully qualified domain name because it includes the entire domain name. Trying to resolve just *myserver* won't work with DNS. To avoid problems, you can specify a set of DNS suffixes that will be added to name-resolution queries. This enables Windows to use DNS for name-resolution queries that it normally wouldn't be able to resolve, by *assuming* the DNS suffix. You can specify the primary, parent, and connection-specific addresses, or you can specify a list of particular suffixes.

Append Primary and Connection-Specific DNS Suffixes   This option configures Windows to use the primary DNS suffix and the DNS suffix specified for this connection (as listed below in this window) for resolving names to IP addresses.

Append Parent Suffixes of the Primary DNS Suffix   This option configures Windows to use the parent DNS suffixes for resolving names to IP addresses. For example, if the primary DNS suffix is *redmond.microsoft.com*, *microsoft.com* could be used as well for DNS resolution.

DNS Suffix for this Connection   This option specifies the DNS suffix to be used for this particular network connection. This overrides the DNS suffix provided by a DHCP server.

Append These DNS Suffixes (in Order)   This option specifies a list of DNS suffixes to use for resolution. This list is processed in order from top to bottom, so if a name appears in more than one DNS domain, the first one processed would be the one resolved.

Register this Connection's Addresses in DNS

When this option is checked, the system attempts to register the fully qualified domain name with the DNS server. If the DNS server doesn't support dynamic updates, the system will attempt to update the record on the DNS server, but that operation will fail.

Use this Connection's DNS Suffix in DNS Registration

This option specifies that the connection-specific DNS suffix should be used in the dynamic registration of this computer. This is in addition to the dynamic registration of the primary DNS suffix.

The WINS Configuration Tab

Windows Internet Name Service (WINS) is a technology that also resolves names to IP addresses. WINS resolves the NetBIOS name instead of the fully qualified domain name. Because WINS and NetBIOS aren't used in IIS, we won't cover them in depth. This tab is shown in Figure 8-7.

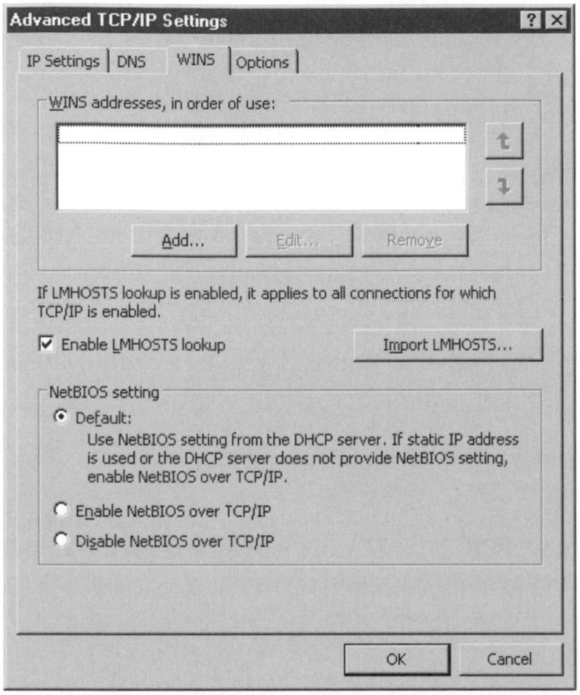

Figure 8-7.   *The WINS tab of Advanced TCP/IP Settings*

WINS Addresses, in Order of Use

The WINS servers this machine is configured to use are listed here. In this list, you add in the addresses of the WINS servers in the order that Windows uses them for NetBIOS name resolution.

Adding, Editing, and Deleting WINS Server Addresses to this Network Connection

To add an address, click Add and type in the WINS server address. Repeat this for each address you want to add.

To edit an address, highlight the WINS server address you want to modify and click Edit.

To delete an address, highlight the WINS server address and click Remove.

Enable LMHOSTS Lookup

Use this option to specify that an LMHOSTS file should be used for name resolution. An LMHOSTS file is a text file that provides name-to-IP address mappings, as WINS does. An LMHOSTS file is static, however, while WINS is dynamic.

NetBIOS Setting

Use this option to specify whether or not to use NetBIOS for network communication. Because NetBIOS resides at the session layer of the OSI model, it rides on top of TCP/IP and is not necessary for IIS to run if you are using DNS for name resolution. Most of the time, you will be using DNS.

Default   Use this option to enable NetBIOS communication, *unless* a DHCP server specifies otherwise.

Enable NetBIOS over TCP/IP   Use this option to *enable* NetBIOS communication, *even if* a DHCP server specifies otherwise.

Disable NetBIOS over TCP/IP   Use this option to *disable* NetBIOS communication, even if a DHCP server specifies otherwise.

The Options Tab

The Options tab allows you to configure the TCP/IP filtering options. TCP/IP filtering allows you to lock down Windows to use only certain ports, thereby disabling ports that you don't want open. This is all accomplished at the transport layer of the OSI model. If you enable port filtering, for example, it affects every adapter on the system. Because port filtering doesn't allow you to disable ports selectively, if you are concerned about security, a firewall may be a better option. To configure TCP/IP Filtering, click on the Properties button on the Options tab to get the TCP/IP filtering window (Figure 8-8). The following options are included in this window.

TCP Ports - Permit All or Permit Only

If you select Permit Only, you may select which TCP ports to disable. Click Add, and type in the number of the port you wish to enable. Click Remove to remove a port from the list.

UDP Ports - Permit All or Permit Only

If you select Permit Only, you may select which UDP ports to disable. Click Add, and type in the number of the port you wish to enable. Click Remove to remove a port from the list.

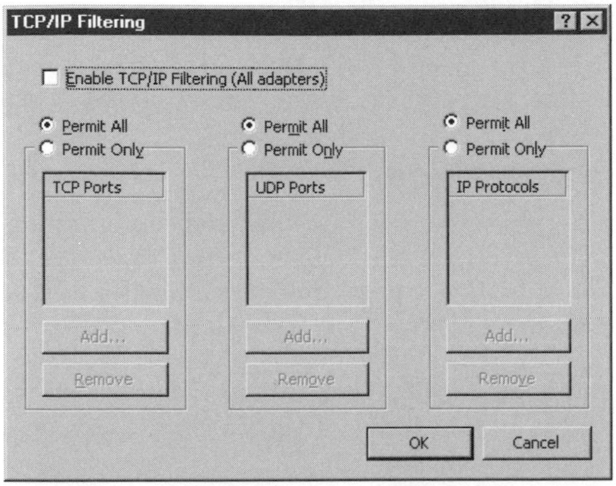

Figure 8-8. *The TCP/IP Filtering window*

IP Protocols - Permit All or Permit Only

If you select Permit Only, you may select which IP protocols to disable. Click Add, and type in the number of the protocol you wish to enable. Each protocol in TCP/IP has a numerical identifier. Click Remove to remove a port from the list.

Configuring IPv6

Although WS03 comes with IPv4 installed by default, it also provides some support for IPv6. To use IPv6, of course, it first needs to be installed.

Installing IPv6

IPv6 is installed and configured via the `netsh` command line tool. Here's how to install IPv6:

1. At a command prompt, type in **NETSH**.
2. Type **INTERFACE IPV6**.
3. Type **INSTALL**.
4. The system will enable IPv6, and you will get an OK in the command prompt window.

IPv6 is now installed on your server.

If you open a command prompt and type **IPCONFIG / ALL**, you will see that in addition to your IPv4 address, an IPv6 address is now available. Take a closer look, and you can see a mangled form of your MAC address in your IP address. Because all MAC addresses are unique, they are perfect to add to your IP address to ensure uniqueness.

Using the NETSH Interface

In the NETSH interface, you set routes, tunneling, and configuration options. Once you are in the NETSH interface, you can type **help** or **?** at any time to get help in configuring your IPv6 interface. Because IPv6 support in IIS 6 is limited, this is as deep as we're going to wade into the waters of IPv6-land. As use of IPv6 becomes more widespread, more application support will be available for it. If you do decide to use IPv6 on your web server, keep in mind that the IIS Manager does not display IPv6 addresses, and you are limited to using only Host Header names for sites (see Chapter 2 for more information on Host Header names).

Changing the Primary DNS Suffix

The Primary DNS suffix is the DNS domain of which this computer determines itself to be a member. It should match the DNS domain that this server's Address (A) record is in. Here's how to change the primary DNS suffix:

1. Open the system Control Panel by choosing Start | Control Panel | System.

2. Click the Computer Name tab.

3. Click the Change button.

4. Click More.

5. Enter the primary DNS suffix in the text box, as shown in Figure 8-9, and then click OK.

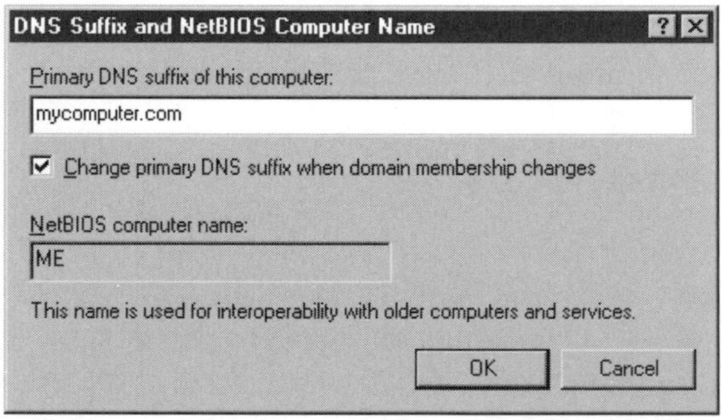

Figure 8-9. *Changing the DNS suffix*

Now that you know how to change the DNS suffix, let's get a little more into how DNS works.

DNS and Windows Server 2003

Because the Internet uses DNS as its primary name resolution method, a good working DNS setup is essential. Several DNS programs are out there, including the DNS server built into WS03.

History of DNS

DNS was developed by DARPA in the early 1980s to address problems with name resolution on the ARPANET. With DNS, computers use numbers to identify devices, like people use first and last names to identify themselves.

Originally, each host on the ARPANET had both a unique name and a unique number. An organization called InterNIC (for Internet Network Information Center) collected and distributed this information in the form of a hosts file that stored the name-to-IP address mappings. This file would be updated periodically, and each user would download a copy to his or her computer. When the user wanted to talk to another computer, the user's computer would perform the name resolution using that hosts file.

This was effective so long as every machine on the network had a unique name and the network stayed small. But when two computers tried to use the same name in the hosts file, problems ensued. In addition, people using an out-of-date hosts file wouldn't be able to resolve new machines on the network.

When DARPA standardized on TCP/IP as the protocol for ARPANET, it also looked to improve name resolution and settled on DNS, because DNS is a central database that holds only pointers to decentralized databases that hold the entries for each namespace. DARPA also chose the Berkeley Internet Name Domain (BIND) as the DNS software of choice for the project.

> **Note** *WS03 still can use a hosts file for name-to-IP address resolution. See the section "Using a Hosts File For Name Resolution" later in this chapter for the uses of a hosts file.*

A Brief Overview of DNS and TLDs

DNS is a hierarchical name resolution system that consists of several layers of naming. The first layer is called the Top Level Domain (TLD) and is the rightmost section of a DNS address. DNS addresses are read in sections, from right to left. For example, for *www.microsoft.com*, *.com* is the TLD and *microsoft* is the second level domain name. The leftmost section (*www*) is the name of a record, rather than a domain name. Domain names can be many levels deep. For example, *www.on.thursday.i.will.eat.pizza.com* could be a valid domain name. In this example, you have to wade through seven levels of domains to get to the record you're looking for.

To resolve a name, the TLD will provide the address for the DNS server that handles the second level domain. The second level domain provides the address for the DNS server that handles the third level, and so on, until you reach the last record in the chain. At that point, the entire address for that resource has been revealed. This hierarchical arrangement allows for the scalability that the Internet needs, because to resolve a name, you go to the source, and the framework is in place to get you where you want to go. A single hosts file would be unmanageable in today's Internet, because every computer on the Internet would need to be a part of that hosts file. Since there are millions of computers on the Internet, it would make for a very large hosts file, and each computer on the Internet would need a copy of that hosts file.

TLD also creates separate databases for domains, rather than just one big database, making it more difficult for a single database outage to affect large parts of the Internet. Updating name resolution information is also accomplished by thousands of different administrators. This scalability is accomplished by delegating DNS *zones* from the top down. Each layer is delegated the responsibility of handling records for that zone by the zone above it.

Because a hierarchy to the naming exists, host names can be unique, because each host name is appended to the subdomain to which it belongs. So unless two hosts have the same name in the same subdomain, there isn't a conflict if they have the same host name. If two hosts using the same name exist in the same subdomain, the conflict exists only in their subdomain instead of in the entire network.

Imagine a big database that holds all the TLDs and directs the traffic to the appropriate DNS servers for each TLD. Such a database would be the root that supports the Internet. That database exists on what are referred to as root name servers. These root name servers are in the *root-servers.net* domain. You can look them up using a *whois* search. All DNS servers know to look at the root name servers to start to resolve a name. The root name servers know about all the TLDs and can point to the DNS server that is delegated to hold the entries for a particular domain name.

How TLDs Work

The registry for all domain names on the Internet originates with IANA, the same group that hands out IP addresses. IANA holds the registry of which company hands out second level domain names in the various top level domains. Many top level domains are in use, and several companies host records for these domains. Additionally, each country has a two-letter country code TLD, as determined by the ISO code for that country. For example, the TLD for the United States is *.us*, and the TLD for the United Kingdom is *.uk*.

Original TLD List

Originally, eight TLDs were set up for use, as listed here; the last two TLDs in this list are special TLDs, because they have special purposes and are not available for ownership by organizations.

- **.com** For commercial organizations
- **.gov** For US governmental use

- **.net**   For network providers
- **.edu**   For educational institutions
- **.mil**   For the US military's use
- **.org**   For nonprofit organizations
- **.int**   For organizations created by international treaties
- **.arpa**   For reverse-DNS information

Recently Added TLDs

In November 2000, ICANN adopted seven new TLDs. Table 8-1 shows the TLDs that are in use today and the organization responsible for managing and registering domains in each namespace.

TLD	Registrar	Purpose
.aero	Societe Internationale de Telecommunications Aeronautiques SC, (SITA)	For the air transport industry
.arpa	American Registry for Internet Numbers	For reverse-DNS information
.biz	NeuLevel	For businesses
.com	Verisign	For commercial organizations
.coop	National Cooperative Business Association	For business cooperatives
.edu	Educause	For educational institutions
.gov	US General Services Administration	US government sites
.info	Afilias, LLC	Open registration
.int	IANA	For organizations created by international treaties
.mil	US DoD Network Information Center	For the US military
.museum	Museum Domain Management Association	For museums
.name	Global Name Registry, LTD	For personal names
.net	Verisign	For network providers
.org	Verisign	For nonprofit organizations
.pro	RegistryPro, LTD	Still under consideration; for professionals (doctors, lawyers, and so on)

Table 8-1.   *TLDs in Use Today*

More top level domains could be added in the future—the process is more political than technological.

Getting Your Own Domain Name

It's easy to get your own domain name; all you have to do is come up with the registration fee and fill out the appropriate forms, and you're done. Little verification occurs, unless you try to register in a restricted use domain, such as *.museum*. Each registrar has its own policies governing use and payment for domain names. Each also operates independently of the others, so if you want to register the same name in different TLDs, you may have to register with different organizations.

How DNS Names Are Resolved

A DNS server can handle queries in one of two ways: recursively or iteratively.

A *recursive* query occurs when the DNS server resolves the name, even if the server doesn't hold that information. The server will query from the root servers all the way down to get to the information. The WS03 DNS server is configured for recursive queries by default.

An *iterative* query occurs when the DNS responds that it has the information the client wants or that it does not have that information. In the latter case, it would be the client's responsibility to get that information elsewhere. The DNS server can send the address of other DNS servers as a "hint" to help the client.

> **Tip** *You can set up your DNS server to perform only iterative queries. Just change the HKEY_LOCAL_MACHINE\System\CurrentControlSet\Services\DNS\Parameters \NoRecursion key to 1. Again, modifying the registry in the wrong way can be very bad, so be careful.*

Let's follow the process of resolving a name to IP address using a recursive query:

1. The client performs some operation, such as clicking a web link, that requires a DNS name to be resolved.
2. The client machine checks the DNS cache and the hosts file on the machine to see whether the address is located there. We'll assume it's not there.
3. The client machine sends a DNS query to the first DNS server listed in the TCP/IP configuration.
4. That DNS server checks to see whether it has the name in its cache.
5. If the server has the address in its cache, it returns that information to the client.
6. If it doesn't have the address, the server looks at all the domains for which it hosts DNS and sends the query to one of the root DNS servers.
7. The root DNS server looks into its records for that domain (the second level domain), and sends back the record to the client's DNS server for the name server that handles that domain.

8. If the address record is in that domain, the client's DNS server sends its query to that destination DNS server for the address record.

9. Otherwise, if it has more levels of domains to search through, the client's DNS server keeps querying for name servers and moving down the tree until it reaches the name server that handles the domain that contains the address record.

10. When the client's DNS server reaches that name server, it queries that name server for the address record.

11. That DNS server sends back the IP address to the client's DNS server.

12. The client's DNS server caches that IP address and sends the IP address back to the client PC.

Types of Zones for Windows Server 2003

A *zone* is a part of the DNS domain. For example, the MyCompany.com domain can contain several zones, such as Sales.MyCompany.com and Corp.MyCompany.com.Typically, the term *zone* is used to refer to a part of the domain as it pertains to the DNS server. The term *subdomain* is used to describe the section of the domain that a zone handles. When only one zone exists in a domain, either term can be used.

Three types of zones are available in WS03: a primary zone, secondary zone, and stub zone.

Primary Zone   A primary zone is the master copy of a zone. This zone is authoritative for the part of the domain it manages. The zone file can be read from and written to.

Secondary Zone   A secondary zone is a read-only copy of a zone. This type of zone helps take some of the traffic off the primary server by providing name resolution just like a primary zone.

Stub Zone   A stub zone is set up to hold the authoritative name server record for that part of the domain. That way, the DNS server can keep track of which servers are authoritative for a certain domain, without having to go to the root name servers all the way down to that domain to get the information.

DNS Zone Storage

Your DNS zone information is stored in one of two places: in a text file or in Active Directory. When you create a primary or stub zone, you can choose where to store the zone file. Secondary zone files are stored only as text files.

Storing Your Zone Information in a Text File

When you choose to store zone information in a text file, it is stored by default at *%systemroot%\system32\dns*. The filename can be whatever you want—typically it is *[zone name].DNS (ex. microsoft.com.dns)*. Normally, you edit your zone file through the Microsoft Management Console (MMC) snap-in for DNS, but if you stop the DNS service, you can directly edit your text zone file. If a record spans more than one line, the line breaks must be enclosed in parentheses. Comments in the DNS zone file are preceded by a semicolon (;). Figure 8-10 shows an example DNS zone file.

The records contained in a DNS zone file are described here.

SOA Record The first record in a DNS zone file should be the Start of Authority (SOA) record. The SOA record consists of the following fields:

IN SOA <source machine> <contact email> <serial number> <refresh time> <retry time> <expiration time> <minimum time to live>

Source Machine This references the host on which this file was created.

Contact Email The e-mail address of the person responsible for this zone file. The @ in the e-mail address should be replaced with a period (.).

Serial Number The serial number of this version of the zone file database, which is used for version control.

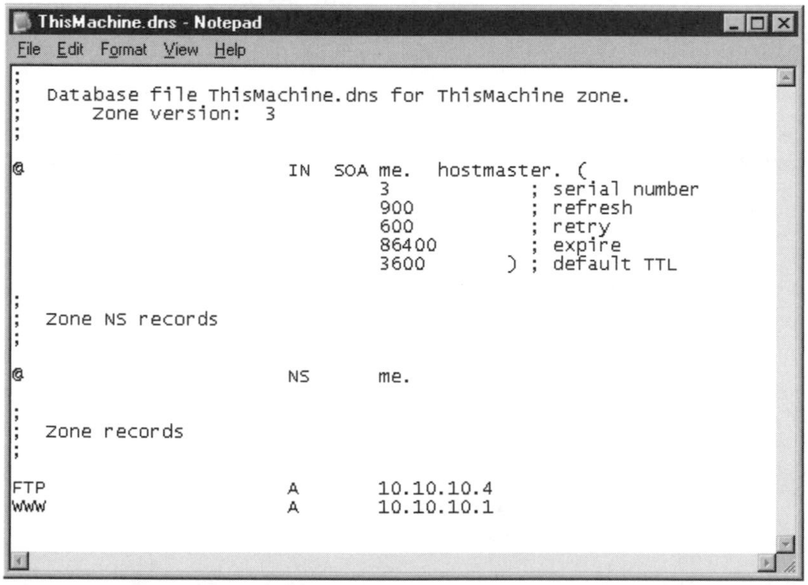

```
;
;  Database file ThisMachine.dns for ThisMachine zone.
;      Zone version:  3
;

@                         IN  SOA me.   hostmaster. (
                                  3             ; serial number
                                  900           ; refresh
                                  600           ; retry
                                  86400         ; expire
                                  3600        ) ; default TTL

;
;  Zone NS records
;

@                         NS      me.

;
;  Zone records
;

FTP                       A       10.10.10.4
WWW                       A       10.10.10.1
```


Figure 8-10. *DNS zone file*

Refresh Time   The time, in seconds, for which this information is considered current. This informs a secondary server how long to wait before downloading a new copy of the zone file.

Retry Time   In the case of a failed zone transfer, this informs a secondary server of how long to wait before attempting to retry. This field is also in seconds.

Expiration Time   The time, in seconds, for which this information is considered valid. This informs a secondary server how long to wait before discarding the data altogether. This counter is reset if a successful zone transfer occurs. So, as long as the secondary server can see the primary server, the data will not be discarded.

Minimum Time to Live   The minimum Time to Live (TTL) is presented with a name resolution request. This time is the minimum time, in seconds, in which a requester is to cache a name to IP mapping. The default minimum TTL is 1 hour. A value of 0 tells the requester not to cache the data.

Other Records   The other records in the DNS zone file inherit the TTL from the SOA Resource Record (RR), but you can override that in individual records. Let's break down the individual records. The syntax is *<name> <class> <type> <data>*.

- **Name**   The host or record name you are resolving.
- **Class**   Contains the standard text indicating the class of the resource record. *IN* indicates that the resource record belongs to the Internet class. This is the only class Windows DNS supports.
- **Type**   This record indicates the resource record type. For example, *A* indicates that the resource record stores host address information.
- **Data**   This field contains the record-specific data. The format of this record varies, depending on which record it is used for.

Storing Zone Information in Active Directory

Active Directory integrated zones are stored as a container in the Active Directory tree under the domain object container. The Active Directory database is an extensible storage engine database file named *ntds.dit*. It is placed when you create a domain controller. The container object is named after the zone you chose when creating the zone.

Benefits of Active Directory Integration

Storing your DNS zones in Active Directory is the preferred method for WS03 servers because it provides the following benefits:

Fault Tolerance   Storing DNS in Active Directory provides fault tolerance for your DNS zones, because DNS zone information is stored on every domain controller in your domain. Even though a certain domain controller may not have the DNS service running on it, it still has a copy of the database, since the Active Directory database is replicated to each domain controller. This prevents loss of the DNS database if the DNS server is lost.

Multi-Master Update   WS03 Active Directory allows for *multi-master update*, which means that several copies of the DNS database exist, and any one of them can be updated. Since Active Directory–integrated DNS zones are stored in the Active Directory database, each domain controller holds a copy of the zone. When a new domain controller is added, the DNS database is replicated to that domain controller. Any WS03 domain controller running the DNS Server service can update the master copy of the DNS zone.

This is a significant enhancement to the DNS system, which typically has a single point of failure, with the master copy of the database being in a local file on one server. Using a standard DNS server, if the primary server is not available, DNS updates cannot be made.

Security   Active Directory–integrated zones allow for the use of Access Control Lists (ACLs) to restrict access to zones or records in a zone. For example, you can restrict a zone so that only specific users or computers are allowed to update records in that zone. This is known as *secure dynamic update*, and it is the default for Active Directory–integrated zones.

Better Performance   Standard DNS zones require that the entire zone be replicated to the secondary servers when a record is changed. Active Directory–integrated zones replicate only deltas, or changes. This greatly reduces the amount of replication traffic and streamlines database replication on the network. The DNS changes are replicated using Active Directory replication, so you don't have to worry about planning for DNS zone replication. This also reduces administrative overhead.

DNS Dynamic Updates

WS03 DNS services allow *dynamic updates*, which allow clients to enter their own *A* (Address) and *PTR* (Pointer Resource) records into DNS. Traditional DNS is static, so when IP addresses change, the corresponding DNS records become out of sync. This hasn't been too much of a problem, because servers were the only machines to have DNS records, and server IP addresses were pretty much static. Besides, most name resolution was done with WINS. But now that Windows is much more DNS-reliant, it's more important than ever that all machines are in DNS. Because many clients are on DHCP and can get different IP addresses, without a means to update DNS when client IP addresses changed, things would get ugly. This is where dynamic DNS comes into play. When clients get a new IP address, they register their records, and there's no administrator overhead associated with keeping those records up to date.

When you create a DNS zone, you can choose whether or not to use secure dynamic update (you can also change it later). Let's take a look at the differences between the two types of updates: regular and secure.

Regular Dynamic Update

With dynamic updates, the clients or the DHCP server are responsible for updating the DNS *A* and *PTR* records. Because anyone can register a name, you can't stop someone from registering a rogue IP address to a name that's important. Such a predicament is inherently insecure; thus, secure dynamic update was born.

Secure Dynamic Update

Secure dynamic update is available only for Active Directory–integrated zones. It allows you to authenticate the client registering the names. Secure zones have standard Windows ACLs, so only clients that meet the security permissions can update records. This is handy, because you can lock down the zones so that only servers and your DHCP server can update their records. This prevents anyone from registering any name.

Windows Server 2003 as a Caching Server

In addition to holding zones, WS03 can also act as a *caching server*. A caching server does not hold any zone information. It simply acts as a DNS server for clients and resolves names for those clients. When it resolves a name, the caching server retains that name and IP in the cache so that information is ready for the next query.

The WS03 DNS server acts as a caching server by default. If you create zones on the DNS server, it will still perform caching—it just won't be strictly a caching server anymore.

Resource Record Types in DNS

DNS offers several different resource record types that are used to identify different types of servers or applications. The resource record types are listed here.

A   Address record. This record type is used to identify a host resource record. It maps a DNS domain name to an IPv4, 32-bit address.

AAAA   The record type to identify a host address resource record for IPv6. This maps a DNS domain name to an IPv6, 128-bit address.

AFSDB   Andrew File System Database resource record. This maps a DNS name to an AFS database server.

ATMA   Asynchronous Transfer Mode Address resource record. This maps a DNS domain name to an ATM address.

CNAME   Canonical Name resource record. This maps a DNS name to another DNS name. This is used for aliasing one name to another. The aliased DNS name must exist in that domain.

HINFO   Host Information resource record. This specifies the type of CPU and operating system for a host record. This information can be used by application protocols, such as FTP, that sometimes use different procedures with certain CPUs or operating systems.

ISDN   Integrated Services Digital Network resource record. This maps a DNS domain name to an ISDN telephone number.

KEY   Public Key resource record. This contains a public key for the zone named in this record.

MB   Mailbox resource record. This maps a domain mailbox name to a mailbox host name. The mailbox host name must be the same as a valid host address (*A*) resource record already used by a host in the same zone.

MG   Mail Group resource record. This is used to specify mailbox resource records for a domain mailing group. The mailbox (*MB*) resource records must exist in the current zone.

MINFO   Mailbox Mail List Information resource record. This is used to specify the mailbox of a responsible party for a mailbox or mailing list. The mailbox (*MB*) resource records must exist in the current zone.

MR   Mailbox Renamed resource record. This specifies a mailbox resource record that corresponds to another mailbox. An *MR* resource record is typically used to forward mail for a user who has moved to a different mailbox.

MX   Mail Exchanger resource record. This identifies a mail server that can accept mail for the current zone. A two-digit priority indicates preferred ordering if multiple exchanger hosts are specified. Each server named in an *MX* record must have a corresponding host (*A*) address resource record.

NS   Name Server resource record. This record maps a DNS domain name to a server responsible for that domain. The server specified must have a corresponding host (*A*) address resource record.

NXT   Next resource record. This is used to deny the existence of a record in a domain by creating a chain of all the owner names in that zone.

OPT   Option resource record. This adds option data to either a DNS request or a response.

PTR   Pointer resource record. This points from one name to another name in a different zone. This is used extensively for the *in-addr.arpa* domain tree to provide reverse lookups of address-to-name mappings.

RP   Responsible Person resource record. This specifies the domain mailbox name for a responsible person. This responsible person is listed as being responsible for that zone.

RT   Route Through resource record. This provides an intermediate host binding for internal hosts that do not have a direct access to an external network connection. Like the *MX* record, a two-digit preference value is used to set priority if multiple intermediate routing hosts are specified and a corresponding host (*A*) address resource record must be in the current zone.

SIG   Signature resource record. This record encrypts a resource recordset to a domain name.

SOA   Start of Authority resource record. This indicates the name of the server that is the primary name server responsible for that zone. This record is the first record in a zone. It contains the following information:

- **serial number**   The version of this zone in use
- **refresh**   The time, in seconds, that a secondary server waits before renewing the zone information from the primary server
- **retry**   The time, in seconds, that a secondary server waits before retrying a failed zone transfer
- **expire**   The time, in seconds, that a server stops responding to queries and considers its zone information invalid if a zone transfer has not taken place
- **min TTL**   The default TTL of the records in the zone

SRV   Service Locator resource record. This allows multiple servers providing a similar TCP/IP-based service to be easily located. This record maintains a list of servers for certain services so that the services can be located by using a single DNS query operation. The servers can even be ordered by preference for a DNS domain name. This is how clients locate Windows Active Directory Servers, because a *SRV* record lists the domain controllers that use the Lightweight Directory Access Protocol (LDAP) service over TCP port 389.

Several fields lie within the *SRV* record:

- **Service**   The name of the service. Well-known services have predefined names and are defined in RFC 1700. You can make any name you wish, but if a predefined name is defined, it must be used to meet standards.
- **Protocol**   Indicates the transport protocol type. By default, you can choose from TCP or UDP. RFC 1700 defines other protocols that can also be used.

- **Name**   The DNS domain name for this service record. The *SRV* resource record name is unique among other DNS record types.

- **Priority**   Sets the priority for the host specified in this record. Clients attempt to contact the first reachable host of the lowest numbered preference listed here.

- **Weight**   Sets the weight for the server specified in this record. If more than one server exists with the same priority, clients can use the weight to choose between servers. This field is optional.

- **Port**   Specifies the port used by the service indicated in the Service field. Well-known ports are specified in RFC 1700. Ports can be selected in the range of 0 to 65535.

- **Target**   Specifies the DNS domain name of the host for this service. Host names must have a valid host (*A*) record in that DNS domain.

TXT   Text resource record. This record can contain a description or additional information about the zone.

WKS   Well-Known Service resource record. This contains a list of the well-known TCP/IP services supported by a particular protocol (TCP or UDP) on a specific IP address.

X25   X.25 resource record. This maps a DNS domain name to a Public Switched Data Network (PSDN) number.

Installing DNS on Your WS03 Server

Many, many different DNS servers are out there, and Windows can run lots of them. The server that comes with WS03 is Microsoft's DNS server. DNS is not installed by default with WS03. Here's how to install it:

1. In the Control Panel, click to open the Add/Remove Programs window.

2. Click Add/Remove Windows Components.

3. Click Networking Services to highlight it, and then click Details.

4. Check the box for Domain Name System (DNS).

5. Click OK, and then click Next.

6. Insert the CD, if prompted to do so.

7. If you are using any DHCP-assigned IP addresses, you will be given an opportunity to change to a static IP.

8. Click Finish, and you're done.

Note   *Why do we want to use static IP addresses if we're a DNS server? Because clients point to a DNS server by IP address. If the IP of the server changes, clients can't find it anymore. You can also use DHCP client reservations for the server, so it still uses DHCP, but it always gets the same address.*

The DNS MMC

DNS, like most everything else in WS03, is administered with an MMC snap-in, as shown in Figure 8-11. The DNS MMC snap-in can be opened by choosing Start | Administrative Tools | DNS.

The DNS MMC lists three components in the left pane under the name of your computer: Event Viewer, Forward Lookup Zones, and Reverse Lookup Zones.

Event Viewer

The Event Viewer section includes the DNS Events portion of the regular event viewer. This makes the DNS MMC snap-in your one-stop shop for DNS management. The management options for the Event Viewer section mirror the options in the regular event viewer.

Forward Lookup Zones

The Forward Lookup Zones section list all of the computer's Forward lookup zones for regular DNS domain entries (*A*, *SRV*, *MX*, and so on).

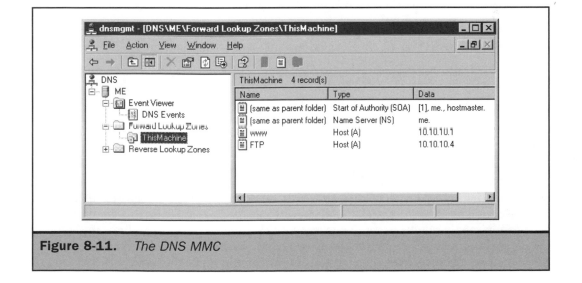

Figure 8-11.   *The DNS MMC*

Here's how to create a forward lookup zone:

1. Open the DNS MMC snap-in.
2. Right-click Forward Lookup Zones in the left pane, and choose New Zone from the pop-up menu.
3. The New Zone Wizard opens. Click Next.
4. Choose the type of zone you want to create, and then check the box to Store In Active Directory (if available).
5. Type in the zone name.
6. Choose the name of the file you want to use (if not AD).
7. Choose whether or not to allow dynamic updates.
8. Click Finish.

Now that you have created a forward lookup zone, you can create some records. The Address record is the most common type, so we'll start with that:

1. Open the DNS MMC snap-in.
2. Right-click the zone to which you want to add records, and choose New Other Records. You'll see a list of all the record types you can put in this zone.
3. Choose the record type you want to add. For this example, choose Host(A).
4. Click Create Record. The New Resource Record window appears.
5. Type in the name of the host. If you're creating a web site, more often than not, you'll choose WWW as the name of the host.
6. Type in the IP address of the host.
7. If the reverse lookup zone exists, and you want to update the reverse entry, check the box, and it will be automatically updated.
8. Click OK.
9. Click Done to close the Resource Record type window.

Reverse Lookup Zones

Reverse lookup zones contain the IP address to name mappings that allow clients to find the name associated with an IP address. This helps close the loop with name resolution, because you can resolve a name to an IP address with a forward lookup, and resolve that IP address back to a name with the reverse lookup. This is important for enabling the server to verify clients and servers, because forward and reverse lookup zones are administered separately. Someone can represent to be a certain name, but since reverse addresses are delegated separately, you can't fake the reverse. If they don't match up, it may be a bad thing.

| Tip |

It's not necessarily a bad thing, however, if reverse and forward addresses don't match up. Clients of an ISP often use generic reverse lookup names. This comes into play for commercial domains and especially for e-mail. Many e-mail servers will reject mail if the sender's e-mail server doesn't match up correctly with forward and reverse DNS.

Let's look at an example of how this works. Let's say that someone is representing to be *mail.someisp.com* and their IP address is 55.56.57.58. You check the reverse mapping and it turns out that IP belongs to *spamalot.badmail.com*. It's a pretty safe bet that there's something wrong. This is where reverse DNS comes into the picture.

How Reverse Lookup Zones Work

Reverse lookup zones are similar to forward lookup zones, with a couple of important differences. All IP addresses are part of one domain called *in-addr.arpa*. This domain is authoritative for all IP address to name lookups. These domains are delegated through IP address blocks. For example, for the class C IP block of 192.168.0.0 / 24 (192.168.0.0 – 192.168.0.255), the reverse lookup zone in DNS would be 0.168.192.in-addr.arpa. This is because the reverse zones are designated backward. The network number portion of the IP address makes up the zone, and the host (node) numbers make up the PTR records.

Here are some examples:

IP Block	Subnet Mask	Reverse Zone
10.0.0.0	255.0.0.0	10.in-addr.arpa
145.162.0.0	255.255.0.0	162.145.in-addr.arpa

Reverse DNS is delegated by an IP block, from the top block on down to the block you are using. This means that class A addresses are delegated from the first octet, class B addresses are delegated from the second octet, and class C addresses are delegated from the third octet.

Let's trace this through the path reverse DNS takes to resolve a name from IP:

1. A client wants to find out who a certain IP address is—say, 55.66.77.88. The client asks the DNS server "Who is 88.77.66.55.in-addr.arpa?"

2. Since this is a class A address, start with the first octet. The DNS server will start by asking the root servers "Who is 88.77.66.55.in-addr.arpa?"

3. The root server responds that it doesn't know, but 0.0.0.55.in-addr.arpa is delegated to MongoISP.

4. The DNS server then asks MongoISP's DNS server "Who is 88.77.66.55.in-addr.arpa?"

5. MongoISP's DNS server responds that it doesn't know, but it does own 0.0.0.55.in-addr.arpa and has delegated 0.0.66.55.in-addr.arpa to MidTierISP.

Why Delegate?

Because they are delegated from the root name servers on down, reverse delegations must be accomplished through "official" processes. This means that the root server tells the client the next server to go through in the name resolution. Since each server down the line has to be officially designated as the proper server for that reverse DNS zone, it's much harder to fake a designation.

If you're interested in diving into reverse DNS further, consult RFC 2317, entitled "Classless IN-ADDR.ARPA Delegation."

6. The DNS server then asks MidTierISP's DNS server "Who 88.77.66.55.in-addr.arpa?"

7. MidTierISP's DNS server responds that it doesn't know, but it does own 0.0.66.55.in-addr.arpa and has delegated 0.77.66.55.in-addr.arpa to HomeTownISP.

8. The DNS server then asks HomeTownISP's DNS server "Who 88.77.66.55.in-addr.arpa?"

9. HomeTownISP's DNS server responds that it knows exactly who that is: it belongs to mail.somebody.com.

This is a complicated process, because delegating uses the octet level of the IP address, especially if the subnet mask doesn't fall along clean subnet lines. However, you can delegate any subnet you want.

For example, the reverse DNS zone for the 192.168.0.128 / 26 subnet is 128/26.0.168.192.in-addr.arpa. The *128* tells you to start on that subnet, with a 26-bit subnet mask. As you can see, it can get pretty involved.

Creating a Reverse Lookup Zone

Let's step through the process of creating a reverse lookup zone.

1. Open the DNS MMC snap-in.

2. Right-click the server on which you wish to create the zone, and then choose New Zone.

3. Select the type of zone you want to create—for this example, choose Standard Primary (Not in AD).

4. Choose to create a Reverse Lookup Zone.

5. Type in the network ID of the zone you want to create. For this example, use 192.168.0. Notice how it doesn't allow you to type in the fourth octet? That's because you can't do a reverse DNS zone with that octet. In fact, if you want to create a classless (subnetted) reverse zone, you need to type in the name, instead of using the Network ID portion of the wizard.

6. You can then choose to create a zone with the given filename, choose a new one, or choose to use an existing file. Keep in mind that if you create a classless zone, a forward slash is not a valid character for Windows filenames. Use the dash (-) instead. The benefit to using an existing file is that you can use an already set up DNS file with all the records.

7. Choose whether or not you want to allow dynamic updates. If you are not using an AD integrated zone, you cannot allow only secure dynamic updates. Again, this is because you can't set ACLs on standard zones. You can, however, allow dynamic updates from any client.

8. Click Finish, and you're done.

Now that you have created a zone, you can create records inside it. For this zone, all you really care about are *PTR* records and delegations.

Creating Records in a Reverse Lookup Zone

After you've created the reverse zone, you can add the *PTR* records. Here's how to add the reverse lookup records:

1. Highlight the zone in which you wish to create the records.

2. Choose Action | New Pointer (PTR).

3. Type in the host portion of the IP Address in the text box.

4. Type in the host name.

5. Click OK.

You now have a *PTR* record for your host.

Delegating DNS Zones

Now let's walk through delegating a reverse lookup zone in DNS:

1. Highlight the reverse lookup zone for which you want to create a delegation.

2. Choose Action | New Delegation.

3. Type in the number of the subnet you want to delegate. For example, if you have the 10.10.0.0/16 subnet, and you wish to delegate 10.10.5.0/24, you would type **5**.

4. Click Next.

5. Add the name(s) of the DNS servers you want to host the zone by clicking the Add button.

6. Click Next.

7. Click Finish to exit the wizard.

You have created a delegation to that name server for this zone. You also need to create that zone on that server. What the record here does is point a client to that name server for resolution as the client resolves a DNS name.

Using Round Robin DNS

Round robin allows you to perform a crude form of load distribution across multiple web servers (or other servers, for that matter). To use round robin, you create multiple Address records for the same IP address. When a client asks for an IP address, the DNS server will return all the resource records, like this:

```
www.mycompany.com                10.10.10.1
www.mycompany.com                10.10.10.2
www.mycompany.com                10.10.10.3
```

The next time a client asks for that name, the IP address list is rotated, like this:

```
www.mycompany.com                10.10.10.2
www.mycompany.com                10.10.10.3
www.mycompany.com                10.10.10.1
```

Clients will typically take the first address in the list, so the load is distributed among these three servers. Round robin does not take into account the load of each server, or whether these servers are online. If one of these servers in this example is offline, one out of every three web page queries will fail!

Round robin also does not perform content replication, so any data stored on a server that a user needs will not be replicated to the other two servers. If you use round robin to distribute load, you will need to plan around the need for "sticky sessions," since server-side data will not persist. Because a client does keep a record in its cache for much time (only about an hour), you may not experience a problem with shorter sessions, but this still could present a problem.

With a proper DNS structure in place, name resolution for your web site will go much smoother, and you can utilize technologies such as round robin to help make your site more scalable.

Using a Hosts File for Name Resolution

In the old days, hosts files were the primary means of performing IP address to name mappings. Today, DNS is used to perform this function. However, Windows still supports the use of hosts files if you wish to use them to supplement your DNS records. A hosts file exists in the %systemroot%\system32\drivers\etc directory. You can edit this hosts file and add your own entries.

Here's how to edit the hosts file:

1. Open the hosts file using notepad.

2. Place your entry below the localhost entry in the hosts file, as shown in Figure 8-12.

3. Save and close the hosts file.

There are two fields that make up an entry in the hosts file: the IP address and the fully qualified domain name that corresponds to that IP address. These two items are all you need to make name resolution work.

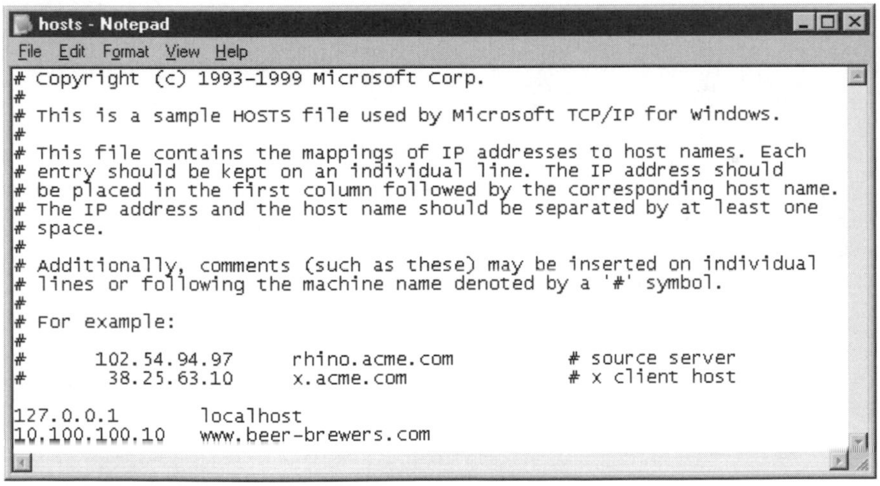

Figure 8-12. *The Hosts file*

The Complete Reference

IIS 6

Chapter 9

Administration Tasks

243

In addition to using the graphical user interface (GUI), you can administer IIS in several ways—through scripting, or even remotely, which eases administration, especially when multiple servers need to be configured. Some methods for administering IIS include the following:

- Using the IIS Microsoft Management Console (MMC) snap-in
- Editing the XML (eXtensible Markup Language) metabase file
- Using the Active Directory Scripting Interface (ADSI) provider
- Using the Windows Management Instrumentation (WMI) provider
- Using the VBScript utilities provided with IIS
- Using the Web Administration Hypertext Markup Language (HTML) interface

Note *The IIS MMC is covered in detail in Chapters 2, 3, 4, and 5, so it won't be covered in this chapter.*

Editing the XML Metabase File

The metabase can be found in *%systemroot%\system32\inetsrv\MetaBase.xml*. You can edit the metabase file using a text-based program such as Notepad. Two methods of editing the metabase can be used: editing while the server is running and editing while the server is stopped.

Editing While the Server Is Running

To edit the metabase while any IIS services are running, you must have Direct Metabase Edit enabled. This feature is found in the computer's Properties window.
To access this feature:

1. Right-click the name of the computer in the IIS MMC and choose Properties.

2. In the Properties window, place a check mark next to the box labeled Enable Direct Metabase Edit.

3. Click OK.

Note that the Metabase History option must be enabled for "edit-while-running" to be enabled. Since this option is enabled by default, it shouldn't be a problem. The Metabase History feature stores versioned copies of the metabase with each change saved on the hard disk. That way, if a catastrophic error occurs in the metabase file, you can easily restore it using an older version.

Once edit-while-running is enabled, you can open the *MetaBase.xml* file with Notepad and make the appropriate changes. They will take effect immediately upon saving.

Editing While the Server Is Stopped

To edit the metabase without Enable Direct Metabase Edit selected, you must stop all the IIS services. This pertains only to editing the *MetaBase.xml* file directly; you can edit the metabase settings at any time using the GUI, ADSI, or WMI. Once the services are stopped, and all previous metabase changes have been written to disk, you may edit the metabase using Notepad or another text editor.

If in the process of editing the metabase you make a formatting error, such as missing XML tags, it may cause IIS to fail to start. If Metabase History is enabled, IIS will recover by reverting to a previous version and will discard any changes made. Because of the risk posed by human error, directly editing the *MetaBase.xml* file isn't the best choice for making configuration changes to your web server.

Using the ADSI Provider

ADSI allows you to connect to various Windows server components as a database connection and modify an object's properties. This is commonly accomplished with VBScript, but you can also change an object's properties using any Component Object Model (COM) or .NET Framework–enabled language. For the purposes of this chapter, we'll be using VBScript.

Note *Even though the ADSI makes you think it may apply only to Active Directory, or perhaps only to domain controllers, the interface is valid for any Windows 2000 and later server.*

IIS ADSI Objects

The IIS ADSI provider includes an object for each key in the metabase. Thus, you can edit any of the keys in the metabase using ADSI. When you open the metabase file with Notepad, the leftmost keys match up with the objects. Here is the list of the keys, in alphabetical order:

- *IIsCertMapper*
- *IIsCompressionSchemes*
- *IIsCompressionScheme*
- *IIsComputer*
- *IIsCustomLogModule*
- *IIsFilter*
- *IIsFilters*
- *IIsFtpInfo*

- *IIsFtpServer*
- *IIsFtpService*
- *IIsFtpVirtualDir*
- *IIsIPSecurity*
- *IIsLogModule*
- *IIsLogModules*
- *IIsMimeMap*
- *IIsMimeType*

- *IIsWebDirectory*
- *IIsWebFile*
- *IIsWebInfo*
- *IIsWebServer*
- *IIsWebService*
- *IisWebVirtualDir*

Connecting to the ADSI Provider

To connect to the provider, create an object using the *ADsPath*. The *ADsPath* for each service can be found in the "Location" part of the key in the metabase file. For example, the location for the *IIsWebService* is */LM/W3SVC*. To connect to a specific web site, you use the *IIsWebServer* key. In the metabase file, the key location for the default web site is */LM/W3SVC/1*.

> **Note** *When you're using the location in your code, you do not need to include the /LM; it's used only in the metabase path.*

To bind to an object using ADSI, start by creating the object in your VBScript. ADSI uses Lightweight Directory Access Protocol (LDAP) for queries, so port 389 needs to be open on any firewall in the way. Additionally, you do need to be an administrator to run ADSI on a system. Here's the code to get the default web site object:

```
SET MyDefaultWebSiteObj = GetObject("IIS://mycomputer/W3SVC/1")
```

Now you can reference the default web site object with the variable *MyDefaultWebSiteObj*.

> **Tip** *You can connect to any site you wish; all you need to do is attach to the ordinal number of the site. In previous versions of IIS, these numbers were sequential, but in IIS 6, they are generated at random—although the default web site is always number 1. You can find the numbers associated with each site in several places, but the easiest way is to click Web Sites in the MMC; they're listed there.*

IIS ADSI Properties

The IIS ADSI properties correspond to the properties in the metabase. You can access the properties for an object by querying that object for particular properties. For example, the *IIsWebServer* has a *ServerComment* property. You can access that property by getting the parent object and then using that object to get the desired property.

Reading an Object's Properties

To read the properties of an object, you can reference the property name for the object in your code. Here's a simple VBScript that gets the server comment field from the metabase for the default web site and displays it on the screen:

```
option explicit
DIM MyDefaultWebSiteObj, ServerCommentProp
  SET MyDefaultWebSiteObj = GetObject("IIS://mycomputer/W3SVC/1")
  ServerCommentProp = MyDefaultWebSiteObj.ServerComment
```

```
Wscript.Echo ServerCommentProp
SET MyDefaultWebSiteObj = nothing
```

All the property names can be found in the metabase file. They are too numerous to mention in this book. As you can see in Figure 9-1, several properties exist for the web site object in the *MetaBase.xml* file. Dozens of properties exist across all the objects in the metabase.

IIS ADSI Methods

The IIS ADSI methods are used to perform actions on the associated service. The following standard ASDI methods are used:

- ■ *Get* Retrieves the value for the object property
- ■ *GetEx* Works like *Get*, but can also retrieve multivalued properties
- ■ *GetInfo* Reloads the object with the property values from the metabase
- ■ *GetInfoEx* Same as *GetInfo*, but with multivalued property support
- ■ *Put* Sets the value for an object's property
- ■ *PutEx* Sets value(s) for single or multivalued properties
- ■ *SetInfo* Writes the properties to the metabase

Let's take a look at some code that can be used to set a value in the metabase. We'll use the *ServerComment* from the previous example. This code changes the comment on the web site to *"My new site"*. You can use this code in a VBScript.

```
option explicit
DIM MyDefaultWebSiteObj, SvrComment
  SET MyDefaultWebSiteObj = GetObject("IIS://localhost/W3SVC/1")
  MyDefaultWebSiteObj.Put "ServerComment", "My new site"
  MyDefaultWebSiteObj.SetInfo
  SET MyDefaultWebSiteObj = nothing
```

You can also use ADSI methods to perform actions on the sites themselves. For example, here's some code that will start and stop the default web site:

```
option explicit
DIM DefaultWebSiteObj
  SET DefaultWebSiteObj = GetObject("IIS://localhost/w3svc/1")
 DefaultWebSiteObj.Stop
  SET DefaultWebSiteObj = nothing
```

To start the default web site, just use *Start* in place of *Stop* in this code.

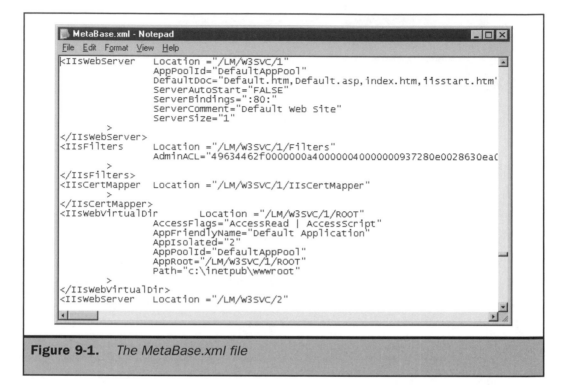

Figure 9-1. *The MetaBase.xml file*

Generally, it's better that you run these VBScripts through *cscript.exe* instead of *wscript.exe*, because any errors or messages will appear in a pop-up with *wscript* and will appear in the command window with *cscript*. You can edit anything in the metabase using the ADSI provider—it's just a matter of discovering the object that corresponds to what you want to modify.

Using the WMI Provider

WMI is an underutilized method of administering Microsoft technologies. It is gaining support, however, and all new Microsoft products are slated to have WMI support built into them. WMI uses the Common Information Model (CIM), along with some Microsoft extensions to CIM. WMI creates a repository of information that can be accessed using a single COM/DCOM (Distributed COM) API.

WMI or ADSI?

WMI has some advantages over ADSI that make it a good fit for administration scripting.

Query Support

WMI uses Structured Query Language (SQL) to select objects and properties. This is great, because you can write a detailed query that will select only the data that you want. When you create the object, you can use either the *instancesof*, which isn't supported with every WMI object, or you can use a SQL query; you then step through the query response to get your data.

Association

With WMI, you can select objects and properties that pertain to any number of items, instead of just the ADSI object to which you are linking. This allows you to write more powerful scripts that can affect multiple IIS components.

Universally Supported

As stated earlier, Microsoft is building WMI support into all its products. WMI allows you to access data from and administer all your applications through a single interface. As other vendors start to use WMI, their programs' data will appear in the WMI repository as well.

User Interface Support

You can get a program from Microsoft called the WMI Object Browser. It is available as part of the WMI SDK version 1.0. When you're looking for specific objects so you can write scripts for them, the Object Browser is handy, because it lets you graphically drill down to the item you're looking for. With ADSI, you can look in the metabase to find key names, but that's about it. With ADSI, it's not easy to find which methods you can use on an object, but they're all listed in the WMI Object Browser, shown in Figure 9-2.

Scripting with WMI

Let's explore some scripting tasks with WMI. First, you must create the object and link to the WMI provider. Here are two lines of code that will allow you to attach to the default web site. The first line attaches to the *MicrosoftIISv2* namespace. The second line connects to the default web site object.

```
SET IISConn =
GetObject("winmgmts://mycomputer/root/MicrosoftIISv2")
SET MyDefaultWebSite = IISConn.get("IIsWebServerSetting='W3SVC/1'")
```

After you've connected to the web site, you can examine any of the properties for that site and execute any of the supported methods for that site. You can connect to the site to see the properties in two ways: you can directly access the property or you can create a SQL query and then step through the results for that query.

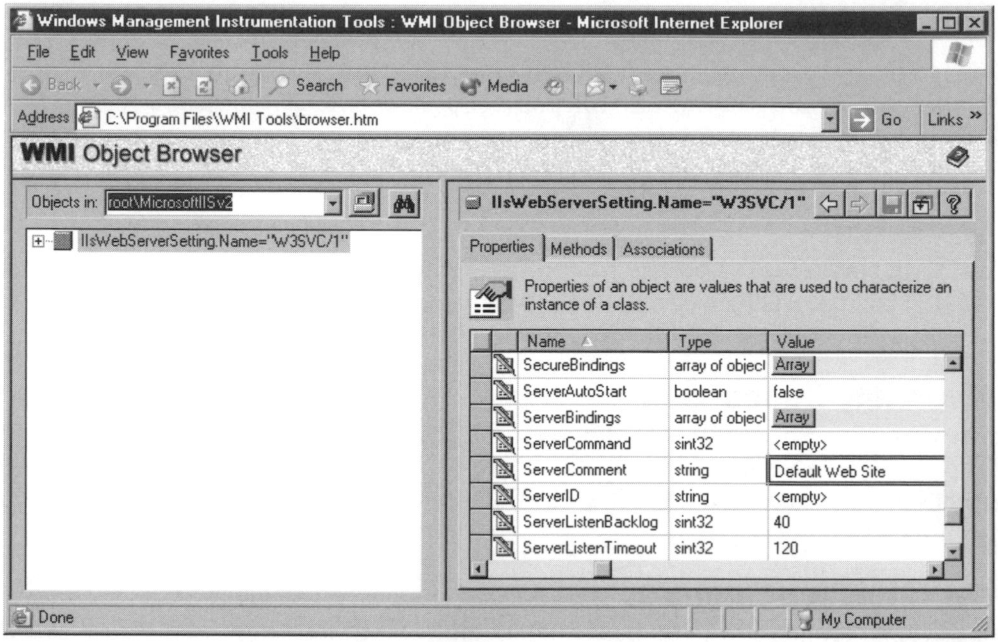

Figure 9-2. *WMI Object Browser*

Accessing Properties with WMI

Here is the code that lets you see the default web site server comment, using both connection methods. First, we'll directly access the property:

```
Option Explicit
DIM IISConn, MyDefaultWebSite
SET IISConn = GetObject("winmgmts://mycomputer/root/MicrosoftIISv2")
SET MyDefaultWebSite = IISConn.get("IIsWebServerSetting='W3SVC/1'")
    Wscript.Echo MyDefaultWebSite.ServerComment
SET MyDefaultWebSite = Nothing
SET IISConn = Nothing
```

Next, we'll use the same code, using a SQL query. The result will be the same—it's just a different way of accessing the code.

```
Option Explicit
DIM IISConnQuery, item
SET IISConnQuery = GetObject("winmgmts://mycomputer/root/MicrosoftIISv2")_
.Execquery("Select * from IIsWebServerSetting where Name='W3SVC/1'")
FOR each item in IISConnQuery
    Wscript.echo item.ServerComment
NEXT
SET IISConnQuery = Nothing
```

The neat thing about performing SQL queries is that you can select multiple values and multiple objects. Want to see a list with the web site name and the server comment for every web site on this server? Here's how:

```
Option Explicit
DIM IISConnQuery, item, ServerCommentList
SET IISConnQuery = GetObject("winmgmts://mycomputer/root/MicrosoftIISv2")_
.Execquery("Select * from IIsWebServerSetting")

FOR each item in IISConnQuery
ServerCommentList = ServerCommentList & item.Name &vbtab &_
item.ServerComment &vbcrlf
NEXT

Wscript.echo ServerCommentList
SET IISConnQuery = Nothing
```

This is where WMI really comes into its own. You can view multiple objects with one simple bit of code. With a little more effort, you can change the server comment for every site. All you have to do is set the *ServerComment* to some value, finish up with a *IISConn.Put_()*, and you're done. The IIS WMI provider can be extremely useful. At this point, not much documentation and code is out there to support it, but as support for WMI grows, it will come.

Using the VBScript Utilities Provided with IIS

IIS comes with several VBScript utilities that you can use to configure IIS from the command line. Most run under the *cscript.exe* interpreter, rather than *wscript.exe*. These scripts are ready to use right out of the box, so you don't have to write your own VBScripts to manage IIS (unless you want to). They're also written so you can administer local and remote computers using them.

These scripts are located in the *%systemroot%\System32* directory:

- **IISAPP.VBS**   Allows you to view any worker processes that are currently running. It displays them by process ID and by application pool ID.

- **IISBACK.VBS**   Allows you to back up and restore your IIS metabase and schema files.

- **IISCNFG.VBS**   Allows you to copy, import, and export your IIS configuration to and from other computers. It does this by copying the metabase and schema files.

- **IISEXT.VBS**   Allows you to enable and disable your web service extensions. You can also add, delete, and manipulate the web service extensions.

- **IISFTP.VBS**   Allows you to create, delete, stop, start, and perform other actions on FTP sites. You can also set FTP user isolation using this script.

- **ISFTPDR.VBS**   Allows you to create and delete virtual directories on FTP sites. You can also list virtual directories with this script.

- **IISVDIR.VBS**   Allows you to create and delete virtual directories on web sites. You can also list virtual directories with this script.

- **IISWEB.VBS**   Allows you to create, delete, stop, start, and perform other actions on web sites. You can also list the web sites on a machine using this script.

Two additional VBScripts are located in the *Inetpub\AdminScripts* directory:

- **ADSUTIL.VBS**   The big dog of the administration scripts, this script uses ADSI to administer IIS on this machine. It is written as the VBScript to use when you don't want to write your own scripts. If you want to configure IIS with VBScript, it's a pretty safe bet that you can use this script.

- **SYNCIWAM.VBS**   This script is designed to sync the Web Application Manager account between the Security Account Manager (SAM) database and the COM database. This is the account that was used to launch out-of-process applications. Now it is used to launch worker processes. It's not apparent whether the out-of-process issue still exists; this script may be included here for legacy purposes only.

Three more scripts are located in the *%Systemroot%\System32\inetsrv* directory:

- **IIS_SWITCH.VBS**   Allows you to switch multiple machines in an FTP or WWW cluster. It helps to manage the switch-over. It uses the following two scripts:

  - **CLUSFTP.VBS**   Includes some functions that check to see whether the FTP service is alive, and can start it if it appears not to be running.

■ *CLUSWEB.VBS*   Includes some functions that check to see whether the web service is alive, and can start it if it appears not to be running.

If you're new to scripting, the default scripts that come with IIS are an excellent place to start learning the syntax and commands that you can use to administer IIS (and Windows).

Remote Administration with the HTML Interface

The Administration web site allows you to configure your web server through an HTML interface. Unlike the HTML administration in previous versions of IIS, you can use this site even when you're not administering from the same server. Previously, you had to connect to the server through the localhost (127.0.0.1) address, which prevented you from using this site when you were not working directly on the server.

The web administration utility is an IIS component and can be loaded from the Add/Remove Windows Components Wizard. It is not loaded by default. Here's how to load the web administration utility:

1. Start the Add/Remove Windows Components Wizard by choosing Start | Control Panel | Add Or Remove Programs, and then click Add/Remove Windows Components.

2. Click Application Server, and then click Details.

3. Click Internet Information Services (IIS), and then click Details.

4. Click World Wide Web Service, and then click Details.

5. Add a check mark next to Remote Administration (HTML), and then click OK.

6. Click OK.

7. Click Next; wait, and then click Finish to complete the wizard.

The HTML administration site runs on port 8098 using Secure Socket Layer (SSL). It is also configured to run on port 8099, but no pages are configured at that Transmission Control Protocol (TCP) port. The home directory for this site is at *%systemroot%\System32\ serverappliance\web*. When Remote Administration is installed, a Remote Administration icon is added to the Start menu at Administrative Tools | Web Interface. To use this interface, you need to be an administrator on the system.

Tip   *You may experience issues using the HTML remote administration with Internet Explorer when the Internet Explorer Enhanced Security Configuration is being used. You can get around this either by changing the security settings for this site or by adding it to the Trusted Sites in Internet Explorer.*

IIS ADMINISTRATION

Using the Remote Administration Site

The remote Server Administration page (shown in Figure 9-3), can be accessed by one of two ways:

- Choose Start | Administrative Tools | Web Interface For Remote Administration.
- Open Internet Explorer and browse to http://<*servername*>:8098, where <*servername*> is the name of the server.

The remote Server Administration page includes several tabs where you can configure the web server. The tabs include options you can use to configure the server as a whole. The top of the administration site page contains the server name and the general status of the site. The options in this site are those most commonly used. Since HTML works better than remote procedure calls (RPCs) over high-latency links, HTML can be a good choice for remote administration of *very* remote servers.

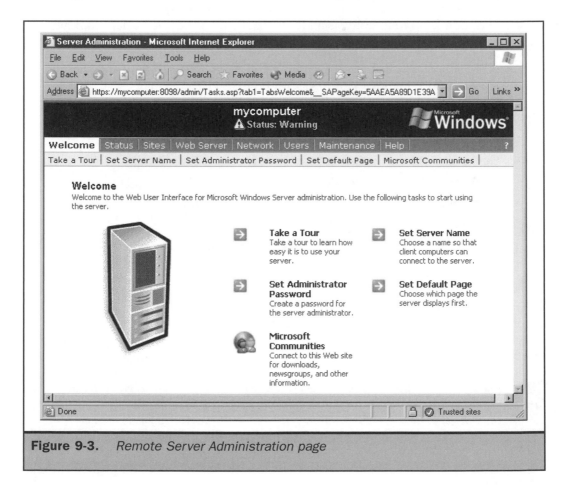

Figure 9-3. *Remote Server Administration page*

The Welcome Tab

The Welcome tab includes some wizards that allow you to configure the general options for this help site.

Take a Tour   Displays a help file that is a "how-to" for this site. It offers general information about the various options in the remote administration site.

Set Administrator Password   Allows you to set the password for the currently logged-in user. When you go to this site, you will see the name of the current user in an editable text box; however, if you try to change the password for any other user, you will be unsuccessful. You do need to know the password to change it.

Microsoft Communities   Takes you to the Microsoft Windows Server community site. The Windows Server community site has downloads, information, newsgroups, and other resources that help you learn more about WS03.

Set Server Name   Changes the name of this server. You can also change the Domain Name System (DNS) suffix of the machine. Additionally, you can join a domain or change the domain/workgroup of which this machine is a member. If you join a domain, you can also specify a user who has the ability to add a server to that domain.

Set Default Page   Chooses which tab is displayed when you first access this site. Two options are available: the Welcome tab, which is the default page, and the Status tab, which is covered next.

The Status Tab

The Status tab contains the current status and any alerts for this server. When this site is first installed, it prompts you to install a new certificate. While there is nothing wrong with the default certificate, like all certificates that do not match the site, the wizard will give you a warning message when you access this site. If this site is listed in the Trusted Sites zone in Internet Explorer, you will not receive this message. If you want to resolve this error, you can either add this site to the Trusted Sites or obtain a properly signed certificate from a certificate authority (CA) that matches this site. Note that you will need to use DNS names exclusively if a certificate is installed, or you will continue to receive a warning.

The Sites Tab

The Sites tab allows you to create, modify, delete, pause, stop, and start web sites on this server. If you've created the site with the web interface, you can modify and delete the site here. If you haven't created the site with the web interface, you can only pause, stop, and start the site.

Creating a Site Through the Web Interface   The web interface allows you to create a site. When you use the web interface, you won't be able to configure all the options that you could through the MMC, but the web interface does give you all the basic site creation options. You can go back through the MMC interface to configure application pools, SSL, Internet Server Application Programming Interface (ISAPI) filters, and so on, later. To create a site:

1. Click the Create button.
2. Type in the Site Identifier or the friendly name of the site.
3. The directory will be auto-populated; you may change it if you like.
4. Choose to create an administrator account for this site or use an existing account.
5. Click the Site Identities tab.
6. Choose the IP address of the site you wish to use, or choose All Unassigned.
7. Choose the TCP port this site will use.
8. If you want, add the host header name to the site.
9. Click the Application Settings tab.
10. Choose the execute permission level you want to use for this site.
11. Choose the name of the default page: you can accept the names already there, add your own, and modify the order in which the filenames are searched.
12. Choose whether to use FrontPage or FTP to administer content on this site. If you do not have the FrontPage server extensions and FTP installed, you will not be able to choose the respective options.
13. Choose whether to allow anonymous access to this site.
14. Click OK.

The Web Server Tab

The web server tab allows you to configure settings for both web and FTP servers. These settings apply globally, rather than on an individual site.

Web Master Settings   Configures the default settings for new web sites. You can choose the Default root directory, the ASP script default timeout, the maximum number of connections a site will allow, and whether or not FrontPage Server extensions are enabled. The ASP script Timeout setting and the Maximum Connections setting will apply to all existing sites in addition to new sites.

Web Log Settings   Changes the logging settings for web sites. The logging options are the same here as in the IIS MMC snap-in. You can configure anything that's on the General tab in the MMC. You cannot, however, change anything that appears in the Advanced tab, such as which fields are logged. Making a change here applies to all web sites on the server.

FTP Messages   Sets the welcome, exit, and maximum connections messages for all FTP sites. You can edit any or all three of the messages here. This will overwrite whatever messages you have currently set. If the FTP service is not installed, you will see a message stating so when you try to access this option.

Web Execute Permissions   Sets the default execute permissions for web sites. You can also choose to apply this setting to existing sites. Your choices are to apply this to all web sites that use the current default value (which is None, out of the box) or to apply it to all web sites regardless of their current value.

FTP Master Settings   Configures the default settings for FTP sites. You can choose the directory listing style, the maximum number of connections, and the connection timeout. Changing one of these values will affect all current FTP sites in addition to new ones. You can also enable the "Web Site Content" FTP site here. This FTP site allows you manage the content on your web site via FTP.

FTP Log Settings   Modifies the logging for FTP. Like WWW logging, this affects all FTP sites, and you can configure all the basic options for FTP logs.

The Network Tab

The Network tab allows you to configure some server options that mostly deal with administration and name resolution. Some of the options here take you to the same screens as options in the Welcome tab.

Identification   Takes you to the same screen as Set Server Name under the Welcome tab.

Interfaces   Configures the network interfaces on this server. You can configure the IP address, subnet mask, default gateway, the DNS settings, and the WINS settings for each adapter.

Administration Web Site   Configures the settings for this administration web site. You can configure the Internet Protocol (IP) addresses that are granted access to this site and the ports used for HTTP and HTTPS access. Since you are using the site that you are configuring, if you change the port numbers, you will need to start using that new port immediately.

Global Settings   Configures the DNS suffixes, the *HOSTS* file, and the *LMHOSTS* file. Changes here apply to the machine as a whole. You can modify the DNS suffixes, but you cannot change the DNS registration settings. When you change the *HOSTS* and *LMHOSTS* files, the changes take effect immediately, but there is no method to reload the NetBIOS name cache in this interface.

Administrator   Takes you to the same screen as Set Administrator Password in the Welcome tab.

Telnet   Has just one option, a checkbox to enable Telnet client access to this server. When you enable this, the Telnet service is started (it is installed but not enabled by default). Through the Telnet interface, you can run character-mode applications.

The Users Tab

The Users tab allows you to manage local users and groups on this server.

Local Users   Allows you to add, delete, and modify users on this machine. You can set the user's full name, description, and home directory here. You cannot change any of the other fields that exist in the MMC, such as login script and terminal server settings. You can also reset a user's password here.

Local Groups   Allows you to add and remove local groups on this server. You can also rename the group, change the description, and modify group memberships here.

The Maintenance Tab

The Maintenance tab configures the general options that allow you to monitor and maintain the server. You can also directly connect to the server here.

Date/Time   Allows you to set the current date and time on this server. You can also set the time zone and whether or not the computer observes daylight saving time.

Logs   Allows you to view the Application, Security, System, and Web Administration logs. In addition to viewing events, you can save a log file locally and clear the logs. In the Properties section, you can set the maximum size and overwrite settings of the log file.

Alert E-Mail   Configures the e-mail address and Simple Mail Transfer Protocol (SMTP) server address for sending alert e-mails. Three levels of alerts correspond to the appropriate event viewer alerts: you can choose to send any or all of the critical, warning, and informational categories of event viewer messages. If the SMTP service is not installed, you will get an error message stating so when you try to use this option.

Shutdown   Allows you to shut down or restart this server. You can also schedule a shutdown or restart of this server. You can schedule an event up to 27 days in advance or on a specific day and time up to a week from now.

Remote Desktop   Connects you to the server using the Terminal Services Remote Desktop Protocol (RDP). It uses the RDP ActiveX control that was formerly known as the Terminal Services Advanced Client. If Remote Desktop isn't enabled (it's not, by default), you will receive an error when attempting to connect. You cannot enable Remote Desktop through this web interface.

Language   Sets the language used on this site.

The Help Tab

The Help tab contains detailed help for the web user interface. It appears just like a normal compiled help file.

Chapter 10

Encryption

The Internet is a wonderful thing. It allows knowledge to be shared with the world. But what if you want to use the Internet to share knowledge with just one person? When web pages, e-mail, and even passwords are transferred across the Internet, they are free to be seen by anyone who cares to look. You may ask, "Who is going to be looking, anyway?" The answer, in most cases, is nobody. Anonymity can be your security. This is especially true of your Internet presence from home.

However, the situation changes when you use your credit card over the Internet, or when you are a business on the receiving end of a credit card transaction. In such cases, anonymity clearly doesn't provide enough security. Furthermore, what if you receive a sensitive document, but you are unsure if the person who sent it really is who they claim to be? How do you know that this same document wasn't tampered with between the time it was sent and the time you received it? And what if you need to protect sensitive data on your web site, or perhaps you want to protect the data in transit to the user, or authenticate the user with a stronger authentication method?

About Digital Certificates

IIS provides digital certificates to accomplish the kind of security that you may need, via the Secure Socket Layer (SSL) protocol. IIS 6 supports the SSL encryption/authentication method for web sites, and security is accomplished through the use of digital certificates.

Three types of certificates can be used:

- **Server certificates**   Provide an encryption method for data transmitted over a network (with SSL); also provide identification methods for the server, so a client can be assured the web site they are accessing is indeed what it claims to be.

- **Client certificates**   Provide identification for the client so the server knows the client is who they claim to be; also provide a stronger means of authentication than Basic Authentication. Client certificates do not provide data encryption.

- **Code signing certificates**   Provide a means to digitally "sign" your application with a digital ID that is created based on the contents of the application. If anything is modified in the application after it's signed, the ID won't match, and the user will be alerted to that fact. Code signing certificates do not encrypt the application.

Certificate Keys

Digital certificates use a technology called a *key* when they encrypt data. To understand how digital certificates work, you need to have an understanding of keys.

 A key is a piece of data used by a cipher to encrypt plaintext into cipher text. A cipher is a mathematical algorithm that does the work of encrypting or decrypting data.

There are two forms of encrypting using keys. Often they work hand in hand.

- **Symmetric-key encryption**   Uses the same key to encrypt the data that will be used to decrypt it. This form of encryption is efficient, resulting in little time lost for the user. It also provides some level of security because the receiving party has to know the key to decrypt the data. The major disadvantage to symmetric-key encryption occurs if someone were to learn the key; they could not only decrypt data, but also encrypt it and impersonate the sender.

- **Public-key encryption**   Takes keys a step further. IIS gives you the choice of DH (Diffie-Hellman) and RSA (for developers Ron Rivest, Adi Shamir, and Leonard Adleman) public-key encryption. RSA is the more common form and is the focus in this chapter. With this model, when you create a key, you are actually creating a key pair that consists of a public key and a private key.

The public key is distributed freely. The data encrypted with the public key can be decrypted only with its private-key counterpart. Since the only person to have the private key would be the owner, the only person able to see the data after it is encrypted would be the person meant to see it. Not even the person who encrypted the data can decrypt it without the private key.

The private key is kept, well, private. The private key can also be used to sign data for authenticity. The public key can be used to verify that the signature is authentic and that the data has not been tampered with. When data is encrypted with the private key, not even the person who encrypted the data can decrypt it without the public key. Again, because the only person to have the private key is the owner, theoretically, the data would be authentic. When used the other way, the private-key holder is the only one who can see that data.

When compared to symmetric-key encryption, public-key encryption requires more overhead and is not as efficient. When encrypting large amounts of data, this can have a serious impact on performance. But, you can use public-key encryption to encrypt a symmetric key, and then use a more efficient symmetric key to encrypt the rest of the data. This is exactly what SSL does.

Encryption Strength

The strength of encryption relies on the length of the key and the type of cipher used to do the encryption. Messages created with a 128-bit key are 3×10^{26} times more difficult to crack than a 40-bit key. This can shed some light on why the U.S. government previously did not allow technology to be exported that supports keys larger than 40 bits. For security proposes, the U.S. government relied on the fact that it can decipher encrypted data that has been intercepted. This is decidedly more difficult with 128-bit keys! The cipher used can also make a big difference. For example, data encrypted with symmetric-key encryption, such as Data Encryption Standard (DES) using a 64-bit key, is comparatively as secure as an RSA encrypted message using a 512-bit key.

Note	*Nowadays, the U.S. government allows 128-bit encryption to be exported to all non-embargoed countries.*

Digital Signatures

Now that you can encrypt data, how can you be sure that it came from the source that claims to have sent it and that it has not been tampered with en route? Digital signatures are the answer to both of these problems. Digital signatures are made from two components: a one-way hash and a public-key cryptosystem.

One-Way Hash Encryption   A *one-way hash* (sometimes called a *message digest*) is a set of data created by an algorithm used to verify that the document you received has not been tampered with since the hash was created. When you apply a document to the one-way hash algorithm, a set of data unique to that document is created. The document is then sent along with the one-way hash that was created. When received, the document is run through the hash algorithm again. The new hash is then compared to the one received with the document. If they are different, the document has been tampered with. Even changing one character or adding one space will completely alter the hash created. There is arguably no way to create the document from only the hash. That is why it is called a one-way hash. The two most common one-way hash algorithms are MD5 message digest algorithm from MIT professor Ron Rivest (the same person who helped develop RSA), and SHA secure hash algorithm from the National Institute of Standards and Technology (NIST) and the National Security Agency (NSA). MD5 creates a 128-bit value while SHA creates a 160-bit value.

Your private key can also be used to encrypt data that only your public key can decrypt. This normally would *not* be a good idea, however, since anyone would be able to decrypt it—except for the fact that when you decrypt something with the public key, you are in essence verifying the sender, as only its private counterpart could have sent it, and only one person has access to it. This, of course, assumes that your private key has not been compromised. The data encrypted with your private key is your public-key cipher text.

When you encrypt the one-way hash that is unique to the data that is being sent with your private key, you have just created a *digital signature*. Now the digital signature can be decrypted to verify your identity, and the one-way hash can be compared to verify integrity. Two birds with one stone, so to speak.

Certificate Authorities and Trusts   How can you know that the public key you are using to send encrypted data is trustworthy? When someone first creates a public/private-key pair for use with a web site, he is actually requesting an x.509 SSL certificate (x.509 is a standard defined by RFC 2459) from a certificate authority (CA)—a server that issues certificates. A CA can also authorize any number of subordinate CAs, and those subordinate CAs can authorize more CAs, and so on. The first CA in the chain is called the *root* CA, and only one root CA can exist in any given chain. When an SSL certificate is issued, the issuing CA verifies that the information submitted by the requesting entity is correct. The details of the verification policies are specific to each CA.

A Client Computer's Use of Certificate Authorities

A client computer will have a certain number of default CA certificates installed; these are "trusted" CAs. Which CA certificates are installed is specific to the software being used (such as Internet Explorer or Netscape). When presented with an SSL certificate from a web server, the client will look for the issuing CA's (as specified in the SSL certificate) certificate in its cache. If the certificate is located, the client will verify the issuing CA's signature on the SSL certificate with the public key found in the cache, thus authenticating the web server. If the issuing CA's certificate cannot be found in the cache, the client will request the certificate and then begin the process again by trying to verify that CA's certificate. If you reach the root CA and no CA's certificate can be authenticated, you will be warned that the SSL certificate could not be verified and you should not accept it. If at any time you reach a CA whose certificate is in your cache, the SSL certificate will be accepted.

Checking Your Browser's CA List   You can view what CAs your browser trusts. To do this in Internet Explorer (IE 6 for this example), use the following steps:

1. In Internet Explorer, choose Tools | Internet Options.
2. Click the Content tab.
3. In the Certificates section, click Certificates.
4. In the Certificates window shown in Figure 10-1, click the Trusted Root Certification Authorities tab—your trusted root CAs are listed here.

Adding a CA to Your Browser's Trusted List   If you visit a site that is trying to use a certificate for a CA that isn't trusted by your browser, your browser will let you know. You can still accept the certificate and continue with the secure communication. While you will still be encrypting your data, you have skipped one of the main functions of certificates: *authentication*. When you accept a certificate from a CA that isn't trusted, you are basically saying you don't care who they are, you just want to proceed with the transaction. If you have other means of verifying who they are, this may be acceptable. If you trust a CA that isn't trusted by your browser, such as your company's CA, you can add the trusted certificate to your browser so you won't have to view the warnings next time.

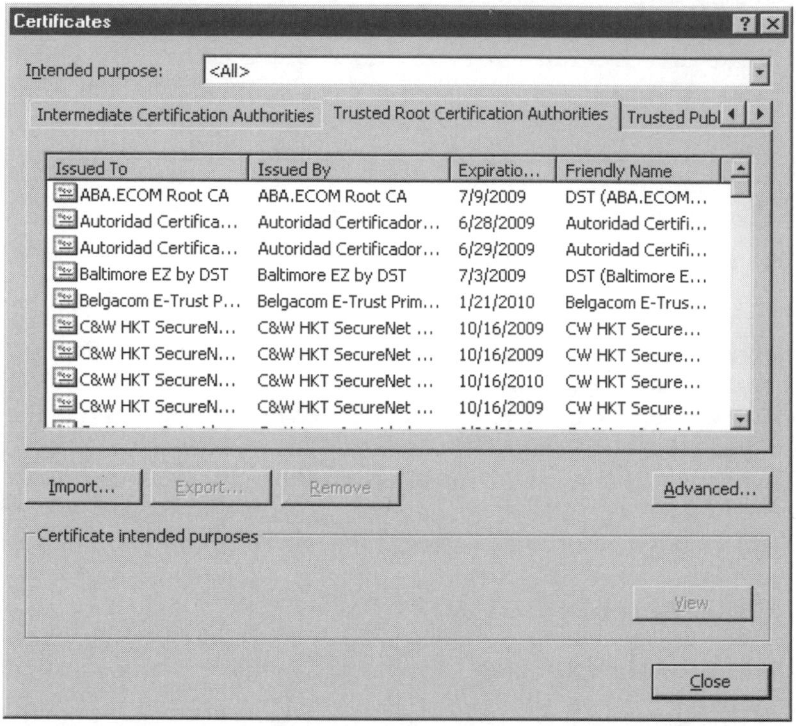

Figure 10-1. *Certificates window of IE*

Here's how to add a trusted root CA to Internet Explorer:

1. Request a CA certificate from the CA you want to trust. This is specific to the company that owns the CA, so contact the administrator.

2. Place the certificate somewhere accessible by your computer, such as a local drive or a file share.

3. Open Internet Options, either from the Control Panel or by choosing Tools | Internet Options within Internet Explorer.

4. Click the Content tab.

5. Click Certificates in the Certificates section.

6. Select the Trusted Root Certification Authorities tab.

7. Click Import, and a Certificate Import Wizard will open.

8. Click Next on the welcome screen.

9. Click Browse, and then select the CA certificate you received.

10. Click Next.

11. You can leave the defaults as is in the Certificates Store screen.

12. Click Next.

13. Click Finish. You will see a message box telling you that your import was successful.

Who Are Certificate Authorities?

Any Windows 2003 server can serve as a CA. For a public web server that is going to offer a secure area, you will not want to use certificates from your own CA, though, because the visitor's browser will not recognize your authority as a CA and the certificates you issue will be rejected. If your certificate is for a web server that serves a large amount of people, that's probably not a good thing, because most web browsers will pop up with an error message. For this sort of situation, you'll need to go to a commercial CA.

The following table lists some of the commercial certificate authorities out there:

Verisign	*http://digitalid.verisign.com/*
Thawte	*http://www.thawte.com/*
Globalsign	*http://www.globalsign.net/*
InstantSSL	*http://www.instantssl.com/*

If you want to create your own certificate, Windows Server 2003 has a certification authority that you can install. We'll get to that in "Choosing Which Type of CA to Install" a little later.

Note *A $600 certificate and a $50 certificate appear the same to your browser. The browser's only requirement is that a commercial CA be trusted.*

How Server Certificates Work with SSL

The SSL *handshake* is what brings authentication, encryption, and verification together. The following occurs during an SSL handshake:

1. The client sends the server the client's SSL version number, cipher settings, randomly generated data, and other information that the server needs to communicate with the client using SSL.

2. The server sends the client the server's SSL version number, cipher settings, randomly generated data, and other information the client needs to communicate with the server over SSL. The server also sends its own certificate.

3. The client authenticates the server as described in the Certificate Authorities and Trusts section.

4. With the information gathered so far, the client creates a premaster secret for the session, encrypts it with the server's public key, and sends it to the server.

5. Using the premaster secret, the server follows a series of steps to create the master secret; this occurs on the client.

6. The client and the server use the master secret to create the session keys.

7. The client sends a message to the server stating that the next message will be encrypted with the session key.

8. The client sends an encrypted message to the server stating that the handshake process is finished.

9. The server sends a message to the client stating that the next message will be encrypted with the session key.

10. The server sends an encrypted message to the client stating that the handshake process is finished.

11. The process is now finished. The client and the server use the session keys to encrypt data with symmetric-key encryption.

So, the client first authenticates the server using the certificate. After authentication, the client uses public-key encryption to send information that is used to created a shared key (the session key). Then the session key is used to perform the more efficient symmetrical-key encryption on the rest of the data. The shared key is specific to this session and is never used again.

How Client Certificates Work

If you want to authenticate a user who is accessing your secure site, you can use client certificates. From your CA, you can issue certificates to any client computer or to any user you like. Once a user has a client certificate installed on their machine, they can securely authenticate to your server without using passwords.

Authenticating a client using certificates adds a few steps to the SSL handshake. Let's look at the SSL handshake one more time—this time with client certificates. The added steps are in italics:

1. The client sends the server the client's SSL version number, cipher settings, randomly generated data, and other information that the server needs to communicate with the client using SSL.

2. The server sends the client the server's SSL version number, cipher settings, randomly generated data, and other information the client needs to communicate with the server over SSL. The server also sends its own certificate.

3. *The server requests the client's certificate.*

4. The client authenticates the server as described in the Certificate Authorities and Trusts section.

5. With the information gathered so far, the client creates a premaster secret for the session, encrypts it with the server's public key, and sends it to the server.

6. *Again using the information gathered so far in the handshake, the client signs a piece of data. The client sends this signed data and its certificate along with the premaster secret.*

7. The server attempts to authenticate the user using the same steps the user used to authenticate the server.

8. Using the premaster secret, the server follows a series of steps to create the master secret. This occurs on the client.

9. The client and the server use the master secret to create the session keys.

10. The client sends a message to the server stating that the next message will be encrypted with the session key.

11. The client sends an encrypted message to the server stating that the handshake process is finished.

12. The server sends a message to the client stating that the next message will be encrypted with the session key.

13. The server sends an encrypted message to the client stating that the handshake process is finished.

14. The process is now finished. The client and the server use the session keys to encrypt data with symmetric-key encryption.

Creating Your Own CA

Now that we've explored how CAs work, let's go through the process of creating your own CA.

Choosing Which Type of CA to Install

In WS03, you can choose between two types of CA servers. Because there are distinct differences between the two, one or the other may not be appropriate, depending on the circumstances.

- **Enterprise CA** Requires Active Directory. It is more automated, but because it isn't trusted, it is usually used for intranets. This is the CA you would want to install for smart card use, for example.

- **Standalone CA** Less automated than an enterprise CA, it doesn't require Active Directory, and thus it doesn't pose unnecessary security risks. This type of CA is usually used for Internet certificates or when you don't have AD installed.

> **Tip** *Your CA server and web server do not have to be the same computer. In fact, the web server shouldn't be a CA, and it should never serve as your root CA.*

The first thing to note about an enterprise CA is that it requires Active Directory to be installed. An enterprise CA's usefulness goes beyond IIS; for example, you would install an enterprise CA for use with domain logins, and it is required for use with smart cards. With that in mind, it's clear that this type of CA would probably not be suitable for issuing certificates to Internet and other external sources, because it would open your Active Directory domain to potential security issues. On the other hand, enterprise CA would be right at home issuing certificates to your intranet. When receiving a request, an enterprise CA can make a decision to issue or deny a certificate based on the security settings in Active Directory. Users can request certificates from the Certificates MMC snap-in or through the Certification Authority Web Enrollment (explained in detail later in the section "Sending a Request to Your Own CA"). The revocation list is held in Active Directory as well as in a shared folder.

A standalone CA does not require Active Directory to be installed. Because of this, a standalone CA is a little more hands-on. It does not automatically issue or deny certificates, but it marks the request as *pending*. The certificates issued from a standalone CA would not be used for logging into a domain or for using smart cards. Users would request certificates only from the Certification Authority Web Enrollment by default. The revocation list for a standalone CA is published to a shared folder.

Root and Subordinate Certificate Authorities

You must also decide whether to install a root CA or a subordinate CA. The root CA is the most trusted CA in your enterprise. It is entirely possible to have only one CA installed. The danger of this, however, is if your root CA were to fail or become compromised, your entire enterprise certificate infrastructure would be compromised. It is recommended that you install a root CA only to issue certificates to subordinate CAs that will handle issuing certificates to everyone else. You make the decision as to what kind of CA you will run during the Certificate Services install process.

> **Tip** *After you install Certificate Services, you will not be able to add or remove your server from a domain or rename it. Make sure you have that worked out before you begin this process.*

Installing the Certificate Services on Your Server

You can install Certificate Services on your server through Add or Remove Programs in the Control Panel. The procedure varies, depending on which type of CA you are creating.

Installing an Enterprise Root CA

Remember that you can install an enterprise CA only if you have Active Directory.

1. In the Control Panel, double-click Add or Remove Programs.

2. Click Add/Remove Windows Components.

3. In the Windows Component Wizard, shown in Figure 10-2, click the Certificate Services checkbox.

4. You will be warned that you will not be able to change your computer name or domain if you proceed. Click Yes in the message box.

5. Click Next.

6. Select the Enterprise Root CA radio button, and then click Next.

7. Enter some descriptive text for the name.

8. Click Next.

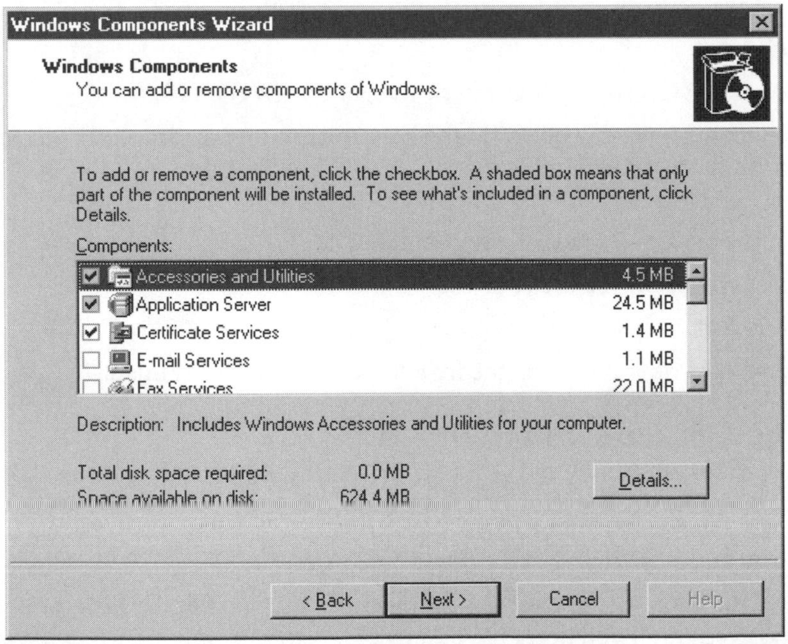

Figure 10-2. *Windows Component Wizard window*

9. The wizard will generate the key. You are then prompted with folder information. You should leave this as the default unless you know of a need to do otherwise.

10. If you are running IIS, you'll be told that you need to stop the IIS service. If you get this message, click Yes.

11. The wizard now performs the installation steps. Click Finish.

Installing an Enterprise Subordinate CA

After you install a root CA in your domain, you can install an enterprise subordinate CA.

1. In the Control Panel, double-click Add or Remove Programs.

2. Click Add/Remove Windows Components.

3. In the wizard, click the Certificate Services checkbox.

4. You will be warned that you will not be able to change your computer name or domain if you proceed. Click Yes in the message box.

5. Click Next.

6. Select the Enterprise Subordinate CA radio button.

7. Click Next.

8. Name your CA something descriptive, and then click Next.

9. The wizard will now generate the key. You are then prompted with folder information. You should leave this as the default unless you know of a need to do otherwise.

10. Select Send The Request To An Online CA.

11. Click Browse and select your root CA. Then click OK.

12. Click Next.

13. The wizard now performs the installation steps. Click Finish.

Installing a Standalone Root CA

If you choose to use a standalone CA, you will start with installing a standalone root CA. To install Certificate Services as a Standalone Root CA, follow these steps:

1. Follow steps 1–5 in the preceding procedures.

2. Select the Stand-alone Root CA radio button (notice that the Enterprise options are grayed out if you don't have Active Directory installed).

3. You'll see the option to Use Custom Setting To Generate The Key Pair And CA Certificate. Unless you have a need to do this, you should leave this unchecked. The custom settings allow you to choose the exact CSP, hash algorithm, and key length you would like to use. The default will use the Microsoft Strong Cryptographic Provider, SHA-1, and 2048, respectively.

4. Click Next.

5. Enter some descriptive text for the Common Name—for example, the domain name or computer name.

6. Click Next.

7. The key is generated. You are then prompted with folder information. You should leave this as the default unless you know of a need to do otherwise.

8. Click Next.

9. A message box will tell you that IIS must be stopped. Click Yes.

10. The wizard then performs a number of tasks; this can take several minutes. Click Finish.

Installing a Standalone Subordinate CA

Once you've installed a standalone root CA, you can install a standalone subordinate CA:

1. Follow steps 1–5.

2. Select the Stand-alone Subordinate CA radio button, and then click Next.

3. Enter a common name for the CA (such as your computer name), and then click Next.

4. You are presented with the default folder settings; unless you have a special need, you shouldn't change them. Click Next.

5. Select Send The Request Directly to a CA Already On The Network radio button.

6. Select the radio button to save the request to a file, and enter a filename. Then click Next.

7. The wizard now configures Certificate Services. You will get a message box stating "The Certificate Services installation is incomplete. To complete the installation, use the request file <c:\path\to\the\file\you\created.cer> to obtain a certificate from the parent CA."

8. Open the Certification Authority snap-in by choosing Start | Administrative Tools | Certification Authority.

9. Use Certification Authority snap-in to install the certificate by right-clicking the node with the name of the CA, and then choosing Install CA Certificate.

10. Click OK in the message box.

11. Click Finish.

12. You must submit the request via the web enrollment (explained in the section "Sending a Request to Your Own CA" later in this chapter).

IIS ADMINISTRATION

13. Approve the request on the root CA.

14. After approval, return to the web enrollment page to receive your certificate.

15. Click Download Certificate Chain.

16. Save the certificate in a location you'll remember later.

17. Open the Certification Authority snap-in by choosing Start | Programs | Administrative Tools | Certification Authority.

18. Right-click your server icon, and choose All Tasks | Start Service.

19. You are asked whether you would like to install a certificate now. Click Yes.

20. Browse to and select the certificate you just downloaded. Click Open.

21. The certificate will be installed and Certificate Services will be started.

Creating a Certificate Request with IIS

To create a certificate request, you will use the Web Server Certificate Wizard from the IIS MMC snap-in, shown in Figure 10-3.

1. Open the IIS MMC by choosing Start | Administrative Tools | Internet Information Services (IIS) Manager.

2. Click the plus (+) in front of Web Sites.

3. Right-click the web site for which you will be requesting the certificate, and choose Properties.

4. Click the Directory Security tab.

5. In the Secure Communications section, click Server Certificate.

6. The Web Server Certificate Wizard window will open. Click Next on the Welcome screen.

7. Select the Create A New Certificate radio button.

8. Click Next.

9. Select the Prepare The Request Now, But Sent It Later radio button.

10. Enter a name for you certificate; it should be something descriptive such as the URL of your web site.

11. Unless you have a need to change it, leave the bit length of the "cryptographic service provider" as the default.

12. Click Next.

13. Define your Company name and your Department as it applies to your company.

Figure 10-3.   *The Web Server Certificate Wizard*

14. Click Next.

15. Enter the Common Name for your site; this should be the fully qualified URL of the site.

16. Click Next.

17. Enter the appropriate region information, and click Next.

18. Change the location or name of the file that will contain your request. Click Next.

19. You are presented with the information you enter for confirmation. Click Next.

20. Click Finish.

Sending a Request to Your Own CA

You can request a certificate to your own CA in two ways. The Certification Authority web enrollment (Figure 10-4) works for both an enterprise CA and a standalone CA. Sending a request through the Certificates snap-in is supported only by an enterprise CA by default. If you have an enterprise CA and are requesting an SSL certificate, you will use the same wizard you use when creating a request for a commercial CA, except

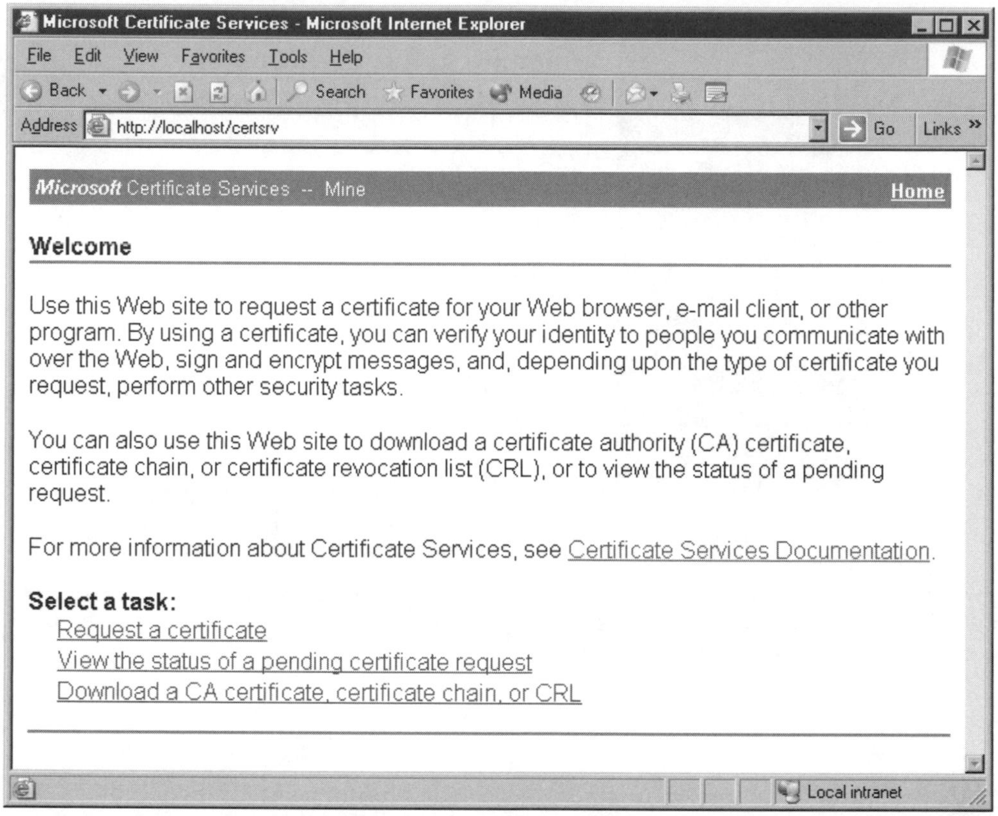

Figure 10-4. *Microsoft Certificate Services web enrollment Welcome screen*

you will select the wizard's Send The Request Immediately To An Online Certification Authority radio button. The Certification Authority MMC snap-in can be used for any other certificate request.

Here's how to use the CA web enrollment:

1. In your web browser, type **http://<*yourserver*>/certsrv** in the address bar, replacing <*yourserver*> with the IP address or URL of your CA.

2. Click Request A Certificate.

3. Click Advanced Certificate Request.

4. If you need a new certificate, you should select Submit A Certificate Request By Using A Base-64-Encoded CMC Or PKCS #10 File. If you are renewing an existing certificate, then you can select Submit A Renewal Request By Using A Base-64-Encoded PKCS #7 File.

5. Paste the contents of the certification request file into Saved Request field.

6. Click Submit.

7. If this is an enterprise CA, you will be presented with your certificate. If this is a standalone CA, you will need to return here when the request is approved.

Sending an SSL Certificate Request to a Commercial CA

The steps for sending a certificate request to a commercial CA depend on the commercial CA. Typically, the verification process for a commercial certificate is extensive. For example, to obtain a Verisign certificate, you need to complete seven steps:

1. Proof of organization.

2. Proof of domain name.

3. Generate a Certificate Signing Request (CSR).

4. Submit the CSR and select your server software.

5. Complete and submit the application.

6. Wait for processing and final verification.

7. Install your ID.

Proof of Organization

When verifying your organization, Verisign will first use your Dun and Bradstreet D-U-N-S Number (a nine character number that identifies your company). If you don't have a D-U-N-S Number or are not able to be identified using your D-U-N-S Number (if you are still in the registration process, for example), you will be asked for proof of organization using the following documents:

- Articles of incorporation
- Business license
- Certificate of formation
- Doing business as name
- Registration of trade name
- Charter Documents
- Partnership papers
- Fictitious name statement

> **Note** *Some additional steps may be required for organizations in certain countries.*

Proof of Domain Name

Verisign will then need to verify that you are the actual owner of the domain for which you want to purchase a certificate. Verisign may simply compare the company information you submitted to them in the "Proof of organization" step to the registrant information for the domain. For *.com*, *.net*, and *.org* domains, your domain information can be viewed at *http://www.netsol.com/cgi-bin/whois/whois* (among other places). If your information doesn't match for some reason, because you don't own the top-level domain name or because someone else registered it for you with another name, you can get around this in one of the following ways:

- Submit a domain authorization letter from the owner of the domain, authorizing you to use it.
- Change the registrant information and notify Verisign via e-mail.
- Submit proof of a legal family relationship between you and the owner of the domain.
- Submit proof of a legal name change from the name shown as the registrant.

> **Note** *More detail can be found on the Verisign web site (http://www.verisign.com).*

Generate a Certificate Signing Request (CSR)

This step is simply the process of creating a certificate request in IIS, as detailed earlier in the chapter. Keep in mind that the common name must be the full URL of the web site on which you will be installing the certificate; otherwise, this won't work properly. For example, if your web site is called by typing *www.beer-brewers.com* into a browser, you would define a common name of *www.beer-brewers.com*, not just *beer-brewers.com*.

Submit the CSR and Select Your Server Software

When you submit a request to Verisign, you will need to open the file you created while running the Web Server Certificate Wizard with a text editor, such as Notepad, and copy the contents into Verisign's web enrollment form. You will then choose your server software, which is IIS in our case.

Complete and Submit the Application

This step again verifies your common name (common names are important) and gets contact and payment information.

Wait for Processing and Final Verification

Verisign will now process the information you submitted and verify your payment information. This should take three to five days. The organization contact defined in the previous step will then be contacted for final verification.

Install Your ID

After all the information has been verified and processed, Verisign will e-mail your technical contact the certificate. Now it's time to install (see "Installing an SSL Certificate" a little later).

Sending a Request for a Client Certificate from the Certification Authority MMC Snap-in

You can also send a request using the Certification Authority MMC snap-in shown in Figure 10-5.

1. Open the Certification Authority MMC snap-in by choosing Start | Administrative Tools | Certificates.

2. Right-click the name of the CA (In Figure 10-5, my CA is called *Mine*), and choose All Tasks | Request New Certificate.

3. Click Next on welcome screen.

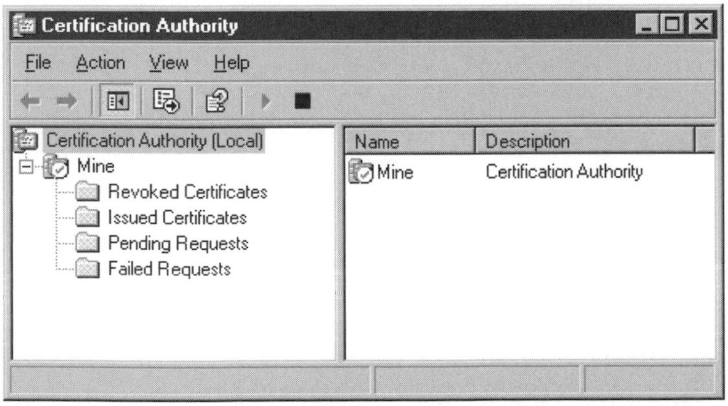

Figure 10-5. *The Certification Authority MMC snap-in*

4. Select the type of certificate you will request, and then click Next.

5. Name your certificate something descriptive, and click Next.

6. Click Finish. Your certificate should now be installed.

Sending a Request for a Client Certificate from the Web

Here's how to send a request for a client certificate from the web:

1. In a web browser, type **http://<*yourserver*>/certsrv** in the address bar, replacing <*yourserver*> with the IP address or URL of your CA.

2. Click Request A Certificate.

3. Click Web Browser Certificate.

4. Fill out the appropriate information, and then click Next.

5. If your CA is a standalone CA, you are informed that you must wait until an administrator approves your request. If your CA in an enterprise CA, you are presented with your certificate immediately.

Issuing or Denying Certificates from a Standalone CA

Once the certificate has been requested, the certificate will be in the Pending Requests folder, and all you need to do is Issue or Deny the certificate. Once issued, the certificate will be usable. Here are the steps to issue the certificate:

1. Open the Certification Authority MMC snap-in.

2. Click Pending Requests (Figure 10-6).

3. Right-click the pending certificate and choose All Tasks | Issue.

Downloading a Web Browser Certificate from the Web

Once the certificate has been issued, the requestor may install the certificate and use it. Here are the steps the requestor can use to install the certificate once it has been issued:

1. Return to **http://<*yourserver*>/certsrv**, replacing <*yourserver*> with the IP address or URL of your CA.

2. Click View The Status Of A Pending Certificate Request.

3. Click Web Browser Certificate.

4. Click Install This Certificate. The certificate is now installed.

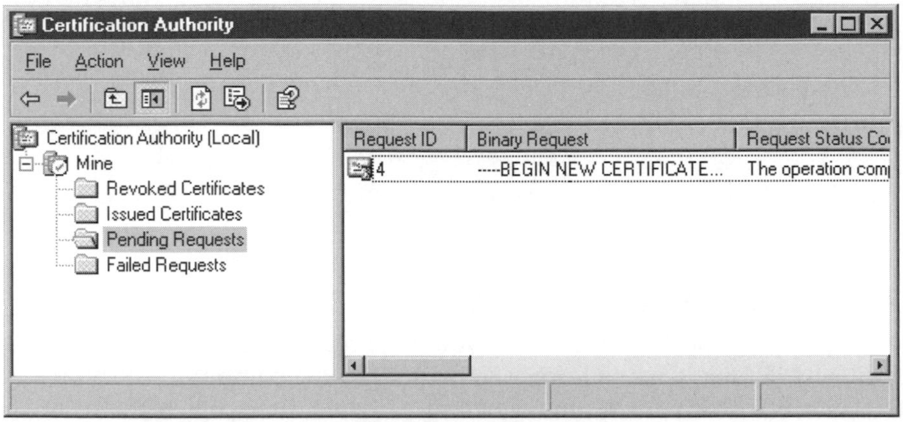

Figure 10-6.   *Certification Authority MMC snap-in*

Installing an SSL Certificate

After you receive your certificate from the CA, it is time to install it.

1. Open the IIS MMC snap-in by choosing Start I Administrative Tools I Internet Information Services (IIS) Manager.

2. Right-click the appropriate virtual server and choose Properties.

3. In the MMC, open the Directory Security tab.

4. In the Secure Communication area, click Server Certificate.

5. Click Next at the welcome screen.

6. Select the Process The Pending Request And Install The Certificate radio button.

7. Click Browse and select the certificate that was sent to you.

8. Click Next.

9. The wizard prompts you to change the SSL Port Number. The default is 443, and should not be changed unless you have a good reason to, because clients look for SSL communication on port 443 by default.

10. You are then presented with the details of your certificate. Click Next.

11. If the issuing party is not trusted, a message box appears, warning that the issuing party should not be trusted. Remember, if you create your own certificate, it will not be from a trusted party because the browser does not have your CA in its trusted CA list.

12. Click Finish.

Congratulations! Your certificate is now installed!

Configuring SSL Settings

Now that you have installed a certificate, you can offer secure communication to users of your site. By default, a web site does not require secure communications. You will need to decide whether your entire site or only a certain directory will be secure. Since encryption impacts the performance of a web site, it is a good idea to require secure communication only on the directories that absolutely need it.

You can choose any of the following options:

- Enable encryption on the entire site or individual directories.
- Require 128-bit encryption (leaving this unchecked will allow 40-bit encryption).
- Ignore, accept if offered, or require client certificates.
- Enact certificate mapping.
- Use client trust lists.

You can edit your certificate setting for a web site from the Secure Communications Properties window:

1. Open the IIS MMC snap-in.
2. Click the virtual site in which you installed a certificate.
3. Right-click the virtual host if you want to configure certificates for the entire site, or right-click a folder if you want to configure certificates for only a certain directory. Choose Properties.
4. In the Properties window, open the Directory Security tab.
5. In the Secure Communications window, shown in Figure 10-7, check the Enable Client Certification box and click the Edit button. Here you can edit your certificate settings.

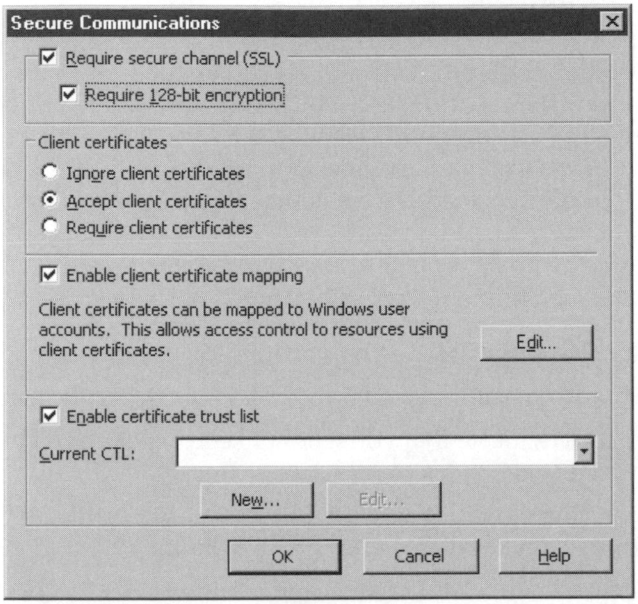

Figure 10-7.   *The Secure Communications window*

Requiring Secure Communication

In the Secure Communications window, check the Require Secure Channel (SSL)
checkbox to require encryption. You can also choose to require 128-bit encryption by
clicking the appropriate checkbox. If you require 128-bit encryption, your web server
will communicate only with web browsers that are capable of 128-bit encryption. By
clicking the Require Client Certificates radio button in the Client Certificates area, you
will deny access to any visitors that don't have a client certificate. You will not gain any
access control with client certificates until you configure client certificate mapping or
certificate trust lists.

Mapping Client Certificates to User Accounts

With IIS client certificate account mappings, you can map a client certificate to a
specific user account, or map a group of certificates that match a certain criteria to
a single user account.

One-to-One Mapping

A one-to-one mapping compares the certificate that the client sends to a certificate you have stored. If they match, the authentication is successful. Using client certificates, the server can authenticate the client, so they are useful when you're not using anonymous access. If the client creates a new certificate with the same information, the client will not be able to authenticate with the same one-to-one mapping; because the new certificate will not match the one IIS has stored, the one-to-one mapping would have to be re-created with the new certificate.

To use one-to-one mapping, you need to export the client certificates from your CA. This can be accomplished through the Certification Authority snap-in.

1. Choose Start | Administrative Tools | Certification Authority.

2. In the Certification Authority snap-in, select Issued Certificates.

3. Right-click the certificate that you would like to export, and choose All Tasks | Export Binary Data.

4. In the Export Binary Data dialog box, select Binary Certificate from the drop-down list (this should be selected by default).

5. Select the Save Binary Data To A File radio button.

6. Name the file something descriptive, such as the name of the user.

7. Save the file somewhere that the web server can access it, or save to a floppy.

8. Click Save.

Now that the client certificate has been exported, you can set up one-to-one mapping in IIS:

1. Open the IIS MMC by choosing Start | Administrative Tools | Internet Information Services (IIS) Manager.

2. Open the Properties for the web site you wish to set up client certificate mapping for by right-clicking the site and choosing Properties.

3. In the Properties window, open to the Directory Security tab.

4. In the Secure Communications section, click the Edit button.

5. In the Secure Communications window, check the Enable Client Certificate Mapping checkbox, and click the Edit button.

6. In the Account Mappings window, open the 1-to-1 tab (it should be open by default).

7. Click Add.

8. In the Open window, browse to the directory to which you saved the exported certificate and select it.

9. Click Open.

10. In the Map To Account window, name the map something descriptive.

11. Click Browse to select the account to which you want to map.

12. Select the account, click OK, and the account will populate in the Map To Account window.

13. Enter the account password.

14. Click OK.

15. Confirm the password.

16. Click OK.

You can repeat this process for as many client mappings as you like.

Many-to-One Mapping

With many-to-one mapping, you compare a set of criteria with the user certificate. If the information matches, the client is authenticated. In many-to-one mapping, you can authenticate several users with one rule. For example, you could allow all certificates issued by a particular CA to be mapped to one user account. This could be handy for authenticating all users from a sister company that uses a different CA than yours. Since many-to-one mappings are comparing information instead of certificates, if a user creates a new certificate with the same information, they would still be able to authenticate. You also don't have to extract certificates as you do in one-to-one mapping. Many-to-one rules are processed in order; the first rule that matches authenticates the user. Keeping this in mind, the last rule should always be to deny everybody (unless you have a reason not to).

Before you make some rules, it may be helpful to know what kind of fields are included in a certificate that you can use for these rules:

1. In Windows Explorer, double-click a certificate file (such as a *.cer* file).

2. Click Details.

3. In the Details tab of the Certificate window, shown in Figure 10-8, the usable information is located under Issuer and Subject.

With this in mind, you can now create the default deny rule:

1. Open the IIS MMC.

2. Open the Properties window of the web site for which you want to set up client certificate mapping, and then open the Directory Security tab.

3. In the Secure Communications section, make sure Enable Client Certificate Mapping is checked, and then click the Edit button.

4. Click the Many-to-1 tab in the Account Mappings window.

5. Click Add.

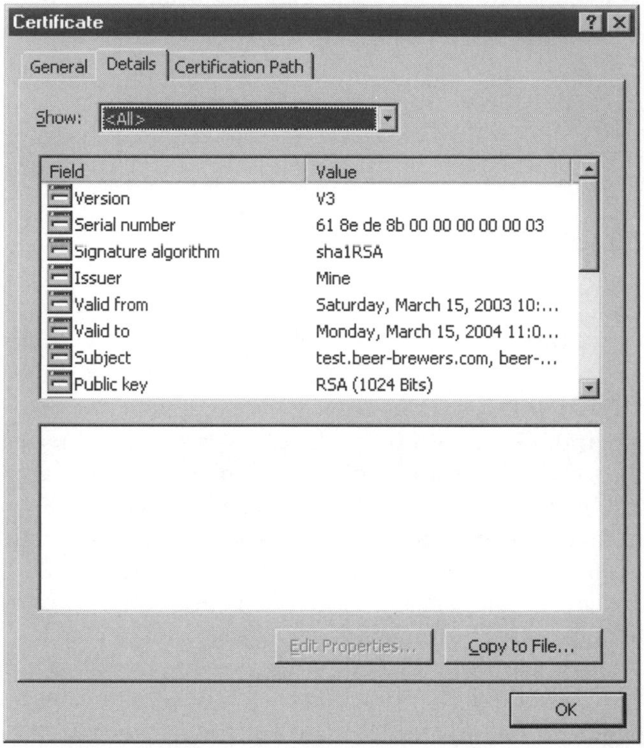

Figure 10-8.   *The Details tab of the Certificate window*

6. In the General window, name the Wildcard Matching Rule something descriptive, such as Deny All. The Enable This Wildcard Rule checkbox should be checked by default.

7. Click Next. Then click New.

8. In the Rules window, select criteria that will match every certificate, such as

   ■ Certificate field: **Issuer**

   ■ Sub field: **CN**

   ■ Criteria: * (The asterisk will catch every possible entry)

9. Leave the Match Capitalization checkbox checked.

10. Click OK, and then click Next.

11. In the Mapping window, click the Refuse Access radio button.

12. Click Finish.

Now every visitor will be denied access, regardless of his or her certificate. The next obvious step is to make some rules that will allow access:

1. In the Account Mappings window from steps 3 and 4, click Add.

2. In the General window, name the rule something descriptive, such as Engineering Department.

3. Again, leave the Enable This Wildcard Rule checkbox checked.

4. Click Next, and then click New.

5. In the Rules window, select the appropriate setting, such as

   ■ Certificate Field: **Subject**

   ■ Sub Field: **OU**

   ■ Criteria: **Engineering**

6. Remember to toggle on or off the Match Capitalization checkbox if necessary; it is checked by default.

7. If this is enough information to identify the group you are authenticating, click Next. Otherwise, click New again to add as many rules as necessary.

8. In the Mapping window, select the account name and password of the account to which you want to map.

9. Click Finish.

10. Type the password again in the Confirm Password window that pops up.

11. Click OK.

12. Make sure that you order your rules appropriately, as shown in Figure 10-9. Everything below the deny rule will be ignored. Use the Move Up and Move Down buttons as necessary to order the list.

13. Click OK to exit the Account Mappings window.

Backing Up and Restoring a Certificate

When backing up your SSL certificate, you will need to back up your private key along with the certificate from the Certification Authority snap-in.

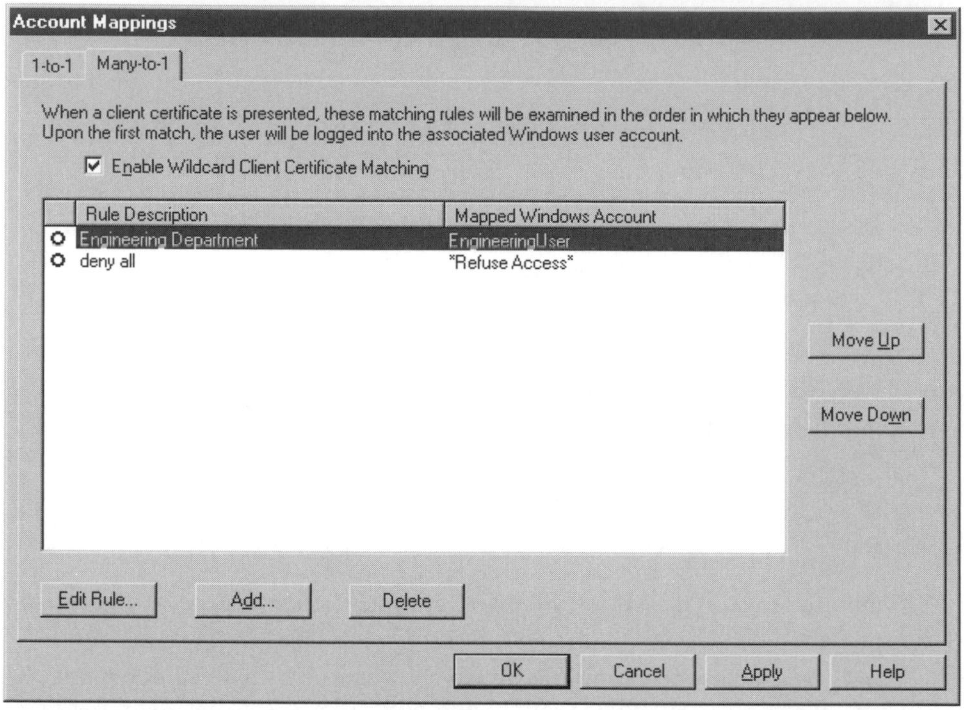

Account Mappings   ☒

1-to-1 | Many-to-1 |

When a client certificate is presented, these matching rules will be examined in the order in which they appear below. Upon the first match, the user will be logged into the associated Windows user account.

☑ Enable Wildcard Client Certificate Matching

Rule Description	Mapped Windows Account
○ Engineering Department	EngineeringUser
○ deny all	"Refuse Access"

Move Up

Move Down

Edit Rule...   Add...   Delete

OK   Cancel   Apply   Help

Figure 10-9.   *Account Mappings rules*

To back up your certificate and private key:

1. Open the Certification Authority snap-in by choosing Start | Administrative Tools | Certification Authority.

2. Click the plus (+) in front of Personal.

3. Click Certificates.

4. Right-click your certificate and select Export.

5. Click Next.

6. Select the Yes, Export The Private Key radio button, and then click Next.

7. Select the Personal Information Exchange radio button.

8. Check Include All Certificates In The Certification Path, If Possible checkbox. Uncheck everything else.

9. Click Next.

10. Chose a password, and then click Next.

11. Click Browse.

12. Name your file something descriptive, and select a directory in which to save it.

13. Click Save, then click Next, and then click Finish.

Caution *This can be dangerous if the certificate and private key backup falls into the wrong hands. Make sure this is saved in a secure location.*

To restore your certificate:

1. Open the IIS MMC.

2. Right-click the virtual server to which you want to restore a certificate, and choose Properties.

3. In the Secure Communications section in the Directory Security tab of the Properties window, click Server Certificate.

4. The Welcome To The Web Server Certificate Wizard Window pops up. Click Next.

5. Select the Import Certificate From A .pfx File radio button. Then click Next.

6. Click Browse, and select your *.pfx* file. Then click Next.

7. Enter the password. Click Next.

8. The wizard then asks for the SSL port number to use at this point. The default is 443, and should not be changed unless you have a good reason to, because clients look for SSL communication on port 443 by default.

9. Click Next.

10. You are presented with the certificate information. Click Next. Then click Finish.

The certificate has now been restored!

Chapter 11

Logging

Y ou may find it worthwhile to gather data and statistics about the people who visit your site. You can set up logging for your site to help you compile these statistics for your own use. Knowing which pages users visit most frequently can also allow you to customize your site to suit visitors' needs. The pages used most often can be expanded and supported, while the less accessed pages can be modified to better support users. If a component on the web site is causing a problem, logging can help track it down. Logging also helps you track down malicious users, by logging what pages they access or what File Transfer Protocol (FTP) files they upload or download. IIS provides logging for all its main components: FTP sites, web sites, Simple Mail Transport Protocol (SMTP) virtual servers, and Network News Transfer Protocol (NNTP) virtual servers.

In this chapter, we'll look at four different types of logging. We'll cover how to configure logging for your IIS sites and some ways to crunch the data and put it in a meaningful format for your use in examining the who, what, when, and where about people accessing your web site. As for the why—well, you'll have to get that on your own.

Although, each type of logging has favorable advantages, each does have some disadvantages, too. Both advantages and disadvantages are shown in Table 11-1.

Log Type	Advantages	Disadvantages
W3C Extended Log File Format	Most logging options and information, most common format. Logs substatus codes.	Can get unwieldy if you choose too many logging options.
Microsoft IIS Log File Format	Comma separated for easy import into other formats.	Non-customizable ASCII format, has only basic info.
NCSA Common Log File Format	Common file format that many web servers use. Compatible with non-Microsoft web server logs.	Non-customizable ASCII format; can't log FTP sites. Very basic information logged.
ODBC Logging	Log information written to database rather than flat file. Can generate reports from data.	Many third-party log file readers don't work with this logging. Doesn't log as much info as extended logging.

Table 11-1. *Log File Advantages and Disadvantages*

Log File Formats

Four types of log files are used in IIS logging:

- W3C Extended log file format
- Microsoft IIS log format
- NCSA (National Center for Supercomputing Application) Common log file format
- Open database connectivity (ODBC) logging

The W3C Extended log file format, Microsoft IIS log file format, and NCSA log file format are all ASCII text formats. The W3C Extended and NCSA formats use a four-digit year, while the Microsoft IIS format uses a two-digit year format for backward compatibility with previous IIS versions.

Enabling Logging for Your Site

Logging is configured at either the individual site level or the component level of IIS. Web and FTP sites are grouped under the Web Sites level and FTP Sites level, respectively. NNTP and SMTP sites are not grouped at the component level, and each site has its own entry in the list of sites under the local computer in the IIS MMC. If you configure logging at the component level, it will apply to all the sites on this server. If you configure logging at the individual site level, it will apply only to that site.

To enable logging:

1. Open the IIS Microsoft Management Console (MMC) by choosing Start | Administrative Tools | Internet Information Services (IIS) Manager.
2. Right-click the site or component where you wish to configure logging, and choose Properties.
3. The logging options always appear on the default tab (the one that is open by default) of the chosen component's Properties window, as shown in Figure 11-1.
4. Place a check mark in the Enable Logging box.
5. Select the type of logging you want in the Active Log Format drop-down menu.

Logging Properties Window

Click the Properties button in the Enable Logging section of the Properties window, and you'll see the Logging Properties window shown in Figure 11-2. For each type of logging (except ODBC Logging), the General tab appears pretty much the same way. The advanced tab is only visible when using W3C Extended Logging.

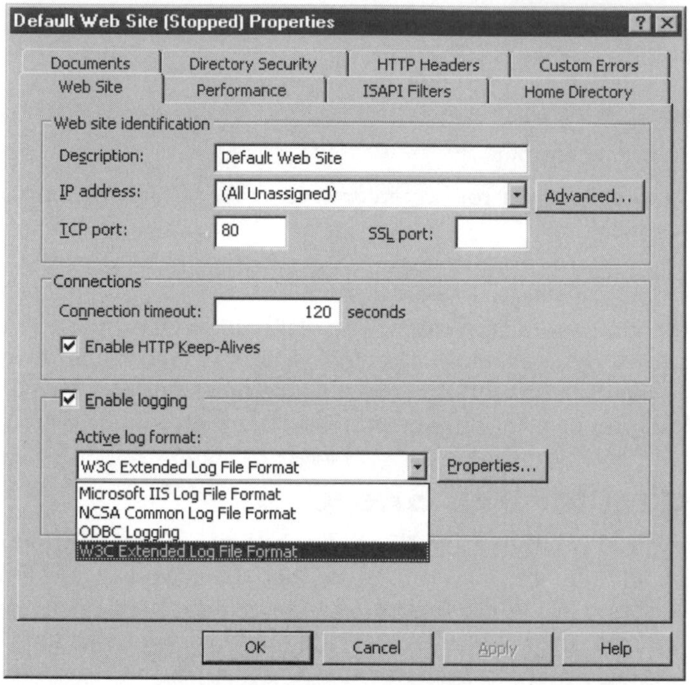

Figure 11-1.   *Web site Properties window*

New Log Schedule   In this area, choose when you want IIS to create log files. A new log file is created based on the time period you choose:

- **Hourly**   Created every hour on the hour.
- **Daily**   Created with the first entry after midnight each day.
- **Weekly**   Created with the first entry after midnight on Saturday (in other words, early Sunday morning).
- **Monthly**   Created with the first entry after midnight on the last day of the month (meaning the first day of the month).
- **Unlimited**   Always uses the same log file. Because of this, the log file can be accessed only when the service that is using that log file is stopped.
- **When The File Size Reaches**   Creates a new log file when the specified size is reached. You can choose any size from 1 MB to 4000 MB.

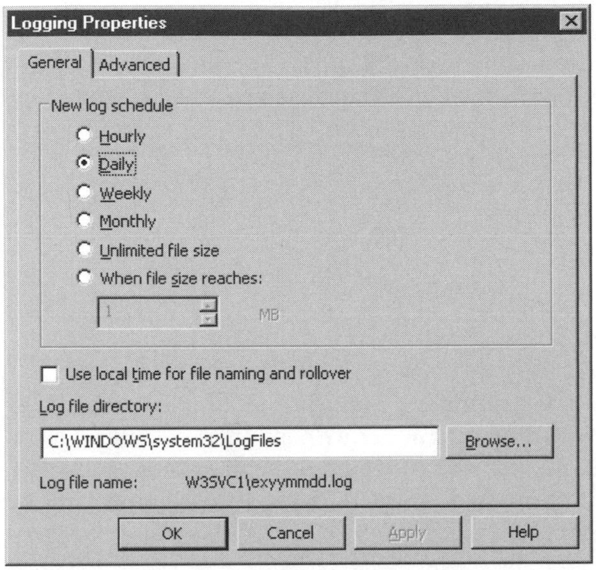

Figure 11-2. *The Logging Properties window*

Tip *Choosing a shorter time period creates more log files on the hard disk and allows you more granular control over which period of log entries you want with various logging software. A longer or unlimited time period will mean a larger log file that may take quite a while to open if it gets too large.*

Use Local Time for File Naming and Rollover This option appears only on the W3C Extended Logging Properties window. This is because all log file formats, except W3C logging, use the local time zone to determine midnight. W3C Extended logging uses Greenwich Mean Time, or GMT (also referred to as UTC, for Universal Time Format, which is in 24-hour format), for all times, including time to start a new log file. Since midnight local time is different from midnight UTC time in most cases, you may want to check this option. When the server starts a new log based on local time, it is easier for you to tell for which day the log is intended.

Tip *It's a good idea to make sure the time zone is set correctly on the server. If your time zone setting is incorrect, your logging times will be incorrect, and it will skew your data for web analysis.*

Choose the Log File Directory   You can also choose which log file directory to use. You can either type in the path or click the Browse button and navigate to the directory. By default, the directory assigned is *%systemroot%\System32\LogFiles*. Each site has its own directory under the *LogFiles* directory. The sites use the following naming conventions:

WWW sites	W3SVC#
FTP sites	MSFTPSVC#
SMTP sites	SmtpSvc#
NNTP sites	NntpSvc#

In each case, the # is a number that references the instance of that site. Each instance of a site created gets a different, randomly generated number. The default web site is always 1, so the default web site's logging directory would be *W3SVC1*. If, for example, your second web site's number is 34523453, the web logging directory for that site would be *W3SVC34523453*.

Log File Naming Conventions

The log files use a specific naming convention based on the time period being logged. This allows you to see what time period the log reflects.

The naming convention for log files is as follows for each type of logging:

Hourly	*XXyymmddhh*.log
Daily	*XXyymmdd*.log
Weekly	*XXyymmww*.log
Monthly	*XXyym*.log

In each case, the *XX* is replaced with a two-character abbreviation of the type of logging. The abbreviations are

W3C logging	*ex*
Microsoft logging	*in*
NCSA logging	*nc*

Note   *ODBC logging is covered later in the chapter in the section "ODBC Logging."*

Log Files and Disk Space

If, when IIS is attempting to add a log entry, it finds that the hard disk is full, IIS logging shuts down. Then an event is logged in the server application log. IIS will monitor the disk space, and when space becomes available again, IIS logging starts back up.

The Unlimited File Size logging and specified file size logging both use the same naming convention, which is very different based on the log file:

W3C logging	extend#.log
Microsoft logging	inetsv#.log
NCSA logging	ncsa#.log

Log File Formats

Each log file is stored in a different format, depending on its use. Let's explore the text log files and their formats.

W3C Extended Log File Format

The most common type of file format is the W3C Extended log file format. It allows for the greatest flexibility for logging options. The World Wide Web Consortium (W3C), an organization that develops specifications for web technologies, developed this format. The W3C web site is located at **http://www.w3.org**.

The W3C Extended log file format is a customizable ASCII format that allows you to choose which fields you want to be logged, thereby limiting the log file size by including only necessary entries. Microsoft's implementation of the W3C Extended format includes several extra fields. Before we start configuring extended logging, here's some background on the format.

The Extended Log Format Specifications

The extended log format was created by the W3C to address the limitations identified with the common log file format and to provide a standard for web logging, regardless of operating system or web server. The Extended log file format uses regular ASCII text. One line makes up a *directive* or an *entry*.

Log File Directives   The extended log file directives contain the information about the log file and which properties are contained in the log file. The directives appear at the beginning of the log and are preceded by a pound (#) sign.

Seven directives are available, but only Version and Fields are mandatory:

- **Version**   Defines the version of W3C logging that was used to create this log file.

- **Software**   Specifies which software package generated this log.

- **Start-Date**   Specifies the date and time this log was started.

- **End-Date**   Specifies the date and time this log ended.

- **Date**   Specifies the date and time the directives were added to the head of this log.

- **Remark**   Comments added by whomever; this entry is ignored by log analysis software.

- **Fields**   Specifies which fields are used in this log. This is the most important directive, since it details how to read the entry information. The Fields directive also contains a prefix that identifies how the data is associated with the client and/or the server.

Log File Entries   The log file entries are the records of the actual user events or process events. Each entry has a prefix and a field. The prefix appears before any of the fields to let you know the client, server, or both with which the data is associated. The prefixes are listed here:

c	Client
s	Server
r	Remote
cs	Client to server
sc	Server to client
sr	Server to remote server
rs	Remote server to server
x	Application

Note   *Microsoft's implementation of extended logging doesn't use the* sr, rs, *or* x *prefix. In the interest of completeness, they are included here.*

Each log file entry is listed on a single line, separated by white space. This gets around the issue of using a certain character, such as a comma, to delimit the entries. If a character is used, that character might appear in the entry and throw off the whole log file. If no entry appears for a certain field, a dash (–) is used to mark the space. Therefore, each log entry includes the same exact number of fields.

Table 11-2 shows the fields defined for logging by the W3C.

Because the W3C format is customizable, other fields can be added. Microsoft's implementation of W3C logging uses the additional fields shown in Table 11-3.

Field	Description
date	Date on which transaction completed. The date is recorded in YYYY-MM-DD format and is recorded using Greenwich Mean Time (GMT), rather than using local time.
time	Time when transaction completed. Time is recorded in 24-hour format and is recorded using GMT, rather than using local time.
time-taken	Time taken for transaction to complete, in seconds.
bytes	Number of bytes transferred.
cached	Records whether or not a cache hit occurred.
ip	Records IP address and, optionally, the port number (IIS uses a separate field).
dns	Records the DNS Fully Qualified Domain Name (FQDN).
status	Status, in FTP and HTTP terms.
comment	Comment associated with the status code.
method	Records the method used.
uri	The full URI (Uniform Resource Indicator).
uri-stem	The stem portion of the URI.
uri-query	The query portion of the URI.

Table 11-2.   *Standard W3C Extended Logging Properties*

Field	Description
username	The username used for this transaction
sitename	The Internet service and instance number that was accessed by a client
computername	The name of the server on which the entry was generated
port	The port number used
win32-status	The status, in Windows terms
version	The version of the protocol used for this transaction
host	The content of any host header used
user-agent	The browser used by the client
cookie	The contents of any cookie sent or received
referrer	The address of the previous site visited

Table 11-3.   *Microsoft's Extensions to the W3C Extended Logging Properties*

Note   *You may be wondering why the term URI (Uniform Resource Identifier) is used, and what happened to URL (Uniform Resource Locator)? The answer is complicated, due to the classic and modern interpretations of URIs and URLs. Even W3C and the IETF (Internet Engineering Task Force) admit there's a lot of confusion out there regarding the two acronyms. Because W3C uses URI, for the purposes of this chapter—and to simplify things—you can think of a URI as being the same as a URL.*

The Advanced Tab's W3C Extended Logging Options

The Advanced tab's Extended Logging Options screen (shown in Figure 11-3) shows the properties from which you may choose when creating your log file. After each option, its particular prefix appears in parentheses. Microsoft's implementation of W3C logging has been optimized for the most commonly used fields for logging. The extended logging format does use the W3C standard for prefixes and fields.

Use the checkboxes to select which options you want to use in your log files. The options in Microsoft W3C logging are shown in Table 11-4.

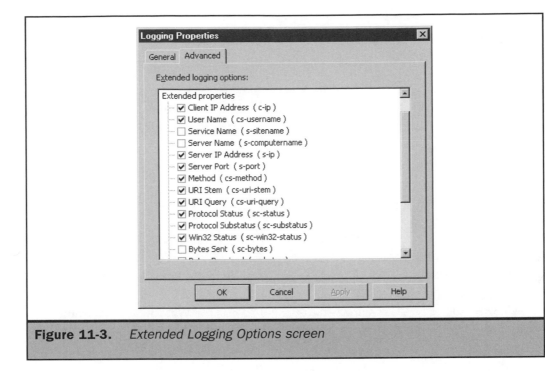

Figure 11-3. *Extended Logging Options screen*

Option	Prefix	Description
Date		Records the date of the transaction
Time		Records the time of the transaction
Client IP address	c-ip	Records the client's IP address
User Name	cs-username	Records the username the client uses to connect to the server; anonymous users are represented by a dash (–)
Service Name	s-sitename	Records the server's site name
Server Name	s-computername	Records the server's computer name
Server IP Address	s-ip	Records the server's IP address

Table 11-4. *The Extended Logging Options*

IIS ADMINISTRATION

Option	Prefix	Description
Server Port	s-port	Records the port number the site uses on the server
Method	cs-method	Records the method the client uses to access the server (such as HTTP GET)
URI Stem	cs-uri-stem	Records the URI stem the client sent to the server, the path to the document (everything after server name)
URI Query	cs-uri-query	Records the URI query the client sent to the server, if any
Protocol Status	sc-status	Records the protocol status message (such as 404, for HTTP not found)
Win32 Status	sc-win32-status	Records the Windows status from the server to the client (0 if no error)
Bytes Sent	sc-bytes	Records the bytes sent from the server to the client
Bytes Received	cs-bytes	Records the bytes sent from the client to the server
Time Taken	time-taken	Records the time taken for the transaction to complete, in seconds
Protocol Version	cs-version	Records the version of the protocol used (such as HTTP/1.1)
Host	cs-host	Records any host header used by the client to access the server
User Agent	cs(User-Agent)	Records the browser type of the client
Cookie	cs(Cookie)	Records the contents of any cookie used
Referer	cs(Referer)	The address of the previous site visited

Table 11-4.   *The Extended Logging Options* (continued)

Substatus Error Codes

W3C Extended log files can be helpful for determining errors in pages. Since IIS 6 doesn't return HTTP substatus error codes, a browser can't help you determine what an error actually is. For example, the HTTP status 404 means "File or directory not found." This error could be returned for several reasons, and the substatus codes come into play to help you determine why. For example, the HTTP status 404.2 means that the lockdown policy prevents you from getting this file. If you're after an ASP page, you need to enable the web service extension for Active Server Pages. While this full error message will appear in the log file, the client will receive only the "404" part, not the ".2" part. These substatus error codes are logged only when W3C Extended logging is used.

Figure 11-4 shows a sample of a W3C Extended log file in Notepad.

Even though the W3C Extended log file is the most complicated format, it is the most flexible one and it gives you the greatest range of logging options. In addition, most log file readers work with the W3C Extended logging format. (There's nothing worse than finding out, after logging six months' worth of data into a SQL log, that the log file reader you just purchased doesn't work with SQL logging!)

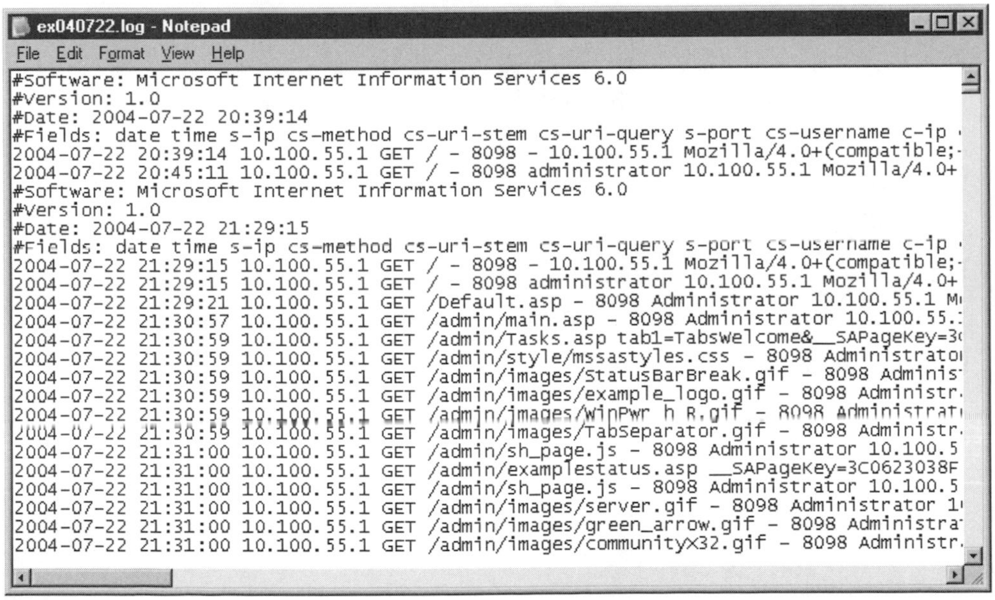

```
#Software: Microsoft Internet Information Services 6.0
#Version: 1.0
#Date: 2004-07-22 20:39:14
#Fields: date time s-ip cs-method cs-uri-stem cs-uri-query s-port cs-username c-ip
2004-07-22 20:39:14 10.100.55.1 GET / - 8098 - 10.100.55.1 Mozilla/4.0+(compatible;
2004-07-22 20:45:11 10.100.55.1 GET / - 8098 administrator 10.100.55.1 Mozilla/4.0+
#Software: Microsoft Internet Information Services 6.0
#Version: 1.0
#Date: 2004-07-22 21:29:15
#Fields: date time s-ip cs-method cs-uri-stem cs-uri-query s-port cs-username c-ip
2004-07-22 21:29:15 10.100.55.1 GET / - 8098 - 10.100.55.1 Mozilla/4.0+(compatible;
2004-07-22 21:29:15 10.100.55.1 GET / - 8098 administrator 10.100.55.1 Mozilla/4.0+
2004-07-22 21:29:21 10.100.55.1 GET /Default.asp - 8098 Administrator 10.100.55.1 M
2004-07-22 21:30:57 10.100.55.1 GET /admin/main.asp - 8098 Administrator 10.100.55.
2004-07-22 21:30:59 10.100.55.1 GET /admin/Tasks.asp tab1=TabsWelcome&__SAPageKey=3
2004-07-22 21:30:59 10.100.55.1 GET /admin/style/mssastyles.css - 8098 Administrato
2004-07-22 21:30:59 10.100.55.1 GET /admin/images/StatusBarBreak.gif - 8098 Adminis
2004-07-22 21:30:59 10.100.55.1 GET /admin/images/example_logo.gif - 8098 Administr.
2004-07-22 21:30:59 10.100.55.1 GET /admin/images/WinPwr h R.gif - 8098 Administrat
2004-07-22 21:30:59 10.100.55.1 GET /admin/images/TabSeparator.gif - 8098 Administr.
2004-07-22 21:31:00 10.100.55.1 GET /admin/sh_page.js - 8098 Administrator 10.100.5
2004-07-22 21:31:00 10.100.55.1 GET /admin/examplestatus.asp __SAPageKey=3C0623038F
2004-07-22 21:31:00 10.100.55.1 GET /admin/sh_page.js - 8098 Administrator 10.100.5
2004-07-22 21:31:00 10.100.55.1 GET /admin/images/server.gif - 8098 Administrator 1
2004-07-22 21:31:00 10.100.55.1 GET /admin/images/green_arrow.gif - 8098 Administra
2004-07-22 21:31:00 10.100.55.1 GET /admin/images/communityx32.gif - 8098 Administr.
```


Figure 11-4. *A sample W3C Extended log file*

Microsoft IIS Log Format

The Microsoft IIS log format is an ASCII format that cannot be modified. It includes basic information about each transaction. This format is comma separated, so it imports into Microsoft Excel very well. Because the fields are predefined and fixed, header information is not necessary, unlike with the W3C format. In addition, no extended properties window is available. In the log file, a blank field is represented by a dash (–). Time is represented in local time, in 24-hour format.

MS IIS Log Fields

The fields for the MS IIS log are as follows:

Field	Description
Client IP Address	The client machine IP address
User Name	Records the username the client uses to connect to the server; anonymous users are represented by a dash (–)
Date	Records the date of the transaction
Time	Records the time of the transaction
Service and Instance	Records the service and instance number of a particular site (such as W3SVC1)
Computer Name	The NetBIOS name of the server, interestingly, not the DNS name
Server IP Address	The IP address of the server
Time Taken	Time taken for transaction to complete, in seconds
Bytes Sent	Records the bytes sent from the server to the client
Bytes Received	Records the bytes sent from the client to the server
Service Status Code	Records the protocol status message (such as 404, for HTTP not found)
Windows Status Code	Records the Windows status from the server to the client (0 if no error)
Request Type	Records the method the client uses to access the server (such as HTTP GET)
Target URL	The stem portion of the URI
Parameters	Any parameters passed to a script

Figure 11-5 shows a sample of a Microsoft IIS log file.

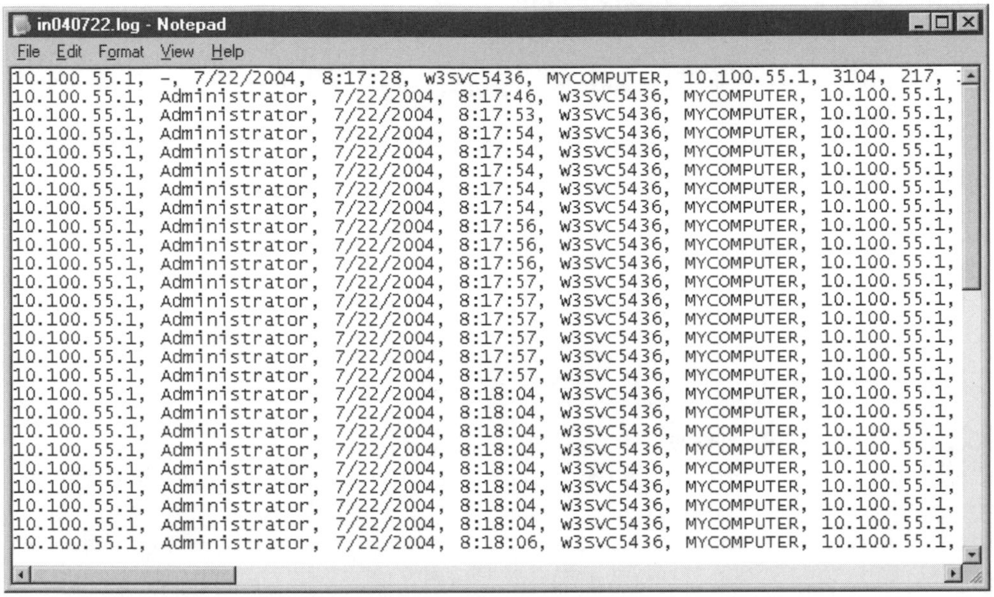

Figure 11-5. *A sample MS IIS log file*

NCSA Common Log File Format

NCSA Common format is a fixed (non-customizable) ASCII format that was designed for the CERN HTTP server, the first web server ever made. It was designed as a web server log and is not available for FTP sites. It is, however, available for IIS SMTP and NNTP sites. The NCSA log records basic information about a transaction. The fields are separated by spaces. In the log file, a blank field is represented by a dash (–). Time is represented in local time, in 24-hour format.

NCSA Common Log File Fields

The following fields are used by the log file:

Field	Description
Remote hostname or IP address	The IP address of the remote user, or the hostname if DNS is available to resolve the name
User name	The remote login name of the user

Field	Description
Authenticated name	The username used to authenticate on the server, as with password-protected pages
Date	The date, time, and GMT offset of the request
Request	The method, URI stem, and protocol used for the query
HTTP status code	Records the protocol status message (such as 404, for HTTP not found)
Bytes transferred	The bytes transferred between the client and the server

Figure 11-6 shows a sample of an NCSA log file.

Converting Log Files to NCSA Format

NCSA is the one format to which you can convert other existing log files in different formats. If you want to convert your existing log file to the NCSA common log file format, you can use a utility called *convlog.exe*, which is located in the *%systemroot%\System32* directory. When you convert a log file, any fields that aren't represented in

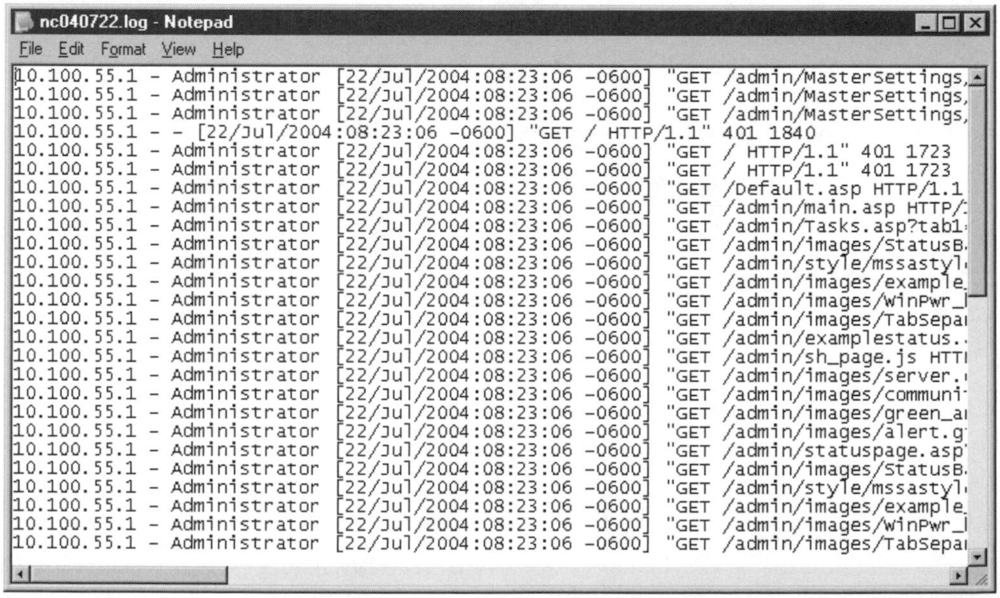

Figure 11-6.   *A sample NSCA log file*

the NCSA log format will be discarded. The remaining fields are formatted to the NCSA log standard.

Convlog is useful if you have a log file reader that works only with the NCSA format, or if you want to convert the file for compatibility because other web servers log in NCSA format. *Convlog.exe* is a command-line utility. To use convlog, simply open up a command prompt and type **convlog**. You will be shown the proper syntax to use.

The syntax of convlog is

convlog [options] [LogFile]

The options used in convlog are as follows:

Option	Description
-ii	Specifies Microsoft IIS as the input log format
-in	Specifies NCSA common logging as the input log format
-ie	Specifies W3C Extended logging as the input log format
-t ncsa:	Specifies the GMT offset (such as –0600)
-o	Specifies the output directory; the default is the current directory
-x	Specifies to save non-WWW entries to separate dump file with a *.dmp* extension
-d	Specifies to convert the IP addresses to DNS names
-l0	Specifies date as MM/DD/YY, the default (U.S. date format)
-l1 -	Specifies date as YY/MM/DD (Japanese date format)
-l2 -	Specifies date as DD.MM.YY (German date format)

Convlog Examples   Let's convert a log file in MS IIS format and then correct it for a six-hour GMT offset. The filename is *in021104.log*.

```
convlog -ii in021104.log -d -t ncsa:-0600
```

Now let's convert the *ex040211.log* from W3C Extended format to NCSA format. We'll also put it in the *logfiles* directory on a remote server called *server1*, and we'll replace the IP addresses with DNS names:

```
convlog -ie ex040211.log -d -o \\server1\logfiles
```

Convlog File Naming   When a file is converted, the new log file has the same filename. The extension used is based on whether the DNS conversion option is used. Log files converted without DNS conversion will have an *.ncsa* extension. Log files with IP addresses converted to DNS names will have an *.ncsa.dns* extension. The original log file will not be deleted.

ODBC Logging

ODBC logging is a more complicated means of logging, and it doesn't offer all the options available with W3C logging. However, if you want to use custom reporting for IIS with reports you've written, rather than an off-the-shelf package, ODBC logging may be for you. The upside to ODBC logging is that all log files for every IIS site you have can be stored in a single location. You may use any ODBC-compliant database, such as MS Access, SQL Server, or even Oracle. IIS does not set up the database for you, so you must set that up beforehand.

Note	*ODBC allows you to access a database for data storage using a standardized program interface.*

ODBC logging has fixed data fields, so it cannot be modified. You are also limited to a maximum of 255 characters in any field. Unless you have some pretty long URLs, this shouldn't be a problem. The time in ODBC logging is recorded in local time.

The ODBC Log File Format

ODBC uses the following format for fields, which are not customizable:

Field	Description
ClientHost	The IP address of the client
username	The login name of the user
LogTime	The time of the log entry
service	The IIS identifier of the service (such as W3SVC1)
machine	The machine name of the client
serverip	The IP address the client used to access the server
processingtime	The time it took to process the request, in milliseconds
bytesrecvd	Records the bytes sent from the client to the server
bytessent	Records the bytes sent from the server to the client

Field	Description
servicestatus	Records the protocol status message (such as 404, for HTTP not found)
win32status	Records the Windows status from the server to the client (0 if no error)
operation	Records the method the client uses to access the server (such as HTTP GET)
target	Records the URI stem the client sent to the server, and the path to the document (everything after server name)
parameters	Any parameters passed to a script

Creating a Database for Use with ODBC Logging

To set up the database, you must first create a new database instance. For the purposes of this example, we'll use MS Access.

1. Start Access.
2. You'll see a dialog in which you must choose whether to create a blank database, use a wizard, or open an existing file. Choose to create a blank access database. You are then asked to save the database.
3. You may choose any name and location you want, since IIS will use a DSN to connect to the database.

After the database is created, you need to create a table to hold the data, which you can do in two ways: you can use the GUI and create the table and all fields by hand, or you can use good old SQL to create the table for you. Let's choose the SQL option.

1. In the main database window, choose Insert | Query, and then choose Design View.
2. After you choose to create a new query, the Show Table screen will pop up.
3. Click Close to take you to the Select Query screen.
4. Choose View | SQL View, and the view will be changed.

Tip   *If you're testing, or using only one web site for logging, Access will work for your logging. If you're serious about logging, and multiple sites are logging to the same database, you're far better off using a more robust database. Microsoft Data Environment (MSDE) is freely available from Microsoft, and it's robust enough to handle multiple site logging. It can handle your logging database needs of up to 2 Gigabytes. For your insanely huge logging needs, use Microsoft SQL Server.*

IIS ADMINISTRATION

You can input the SQL code to create the table. Here is the code for creating the database:

```
create table inetlog (
ClientHost varchar(255),
username varchar(255),
LogTime datetime,
service varchar( 255),
machine varchar( 255),
serverip varchar( 50),
processingtime int,
bytesrecvd int,
bytessent int,
servicestatus int,
win32status int,
operation varchar( 255),
target varchar(255),
parameters varchar(255)
 )
```

This code creates a table called *inetlog*. In that table, all the columns needed for storing the data from your IIS site are created. The syntax of each table is *[tablename] [data type(max size)]*. As shown here, no field is bigger than 255 characters, and the size has to be specified only for *varchar* (text) fields.

If you would like to name your table something else—say, so that all your tables for all your sites are in one database—you can change the name of the table to be created in this SQL statement. Just remember what you've named the table, because you'll need that name when you're setting up logging in your IIS site properties.

Note   *The SQL code shown here is contained on your IIS system in the file %systemroot%\ System32\inetsrv\logtemp.sql, and it can be used to create the table for any major database package, not just for Access.*

After you've pasted the SQL code into the window, save and close the window, and name your query so you'll know what it is later. All you need to do is run the query, and the table will be created after the customary warning message. You may now close the database. Remember what you named the database and where you put it. We'll use it in the next section. Now you have created a table in your database (ours is called *inetlog*), ready for use.

Creating a DSN for Your Database

Now you'll create a Data Source Name (DSN) so that your system knows where the database is located, and so that you can refer to the database with a simple name, rather than the entire path. Here's how to create the DSN:

1. Choose Start | Administrative Tools | Data Sources (ODBC).
2. Choose the System DSN tab.
3. Click the Add button to add a new data source.
4. The Create New Data Source screen will appear. Here, you can choose which data source you want to set up. Since in our example we're using Access, we'll choose Microsoft Access Driver (*.mdb).
5. Click Finish.

After you click Finish, the ODBC Microsoft Access Setup dialog box, shown in Figure 11-7, will open. In this dialog box, you can set up the Data Source Name. You

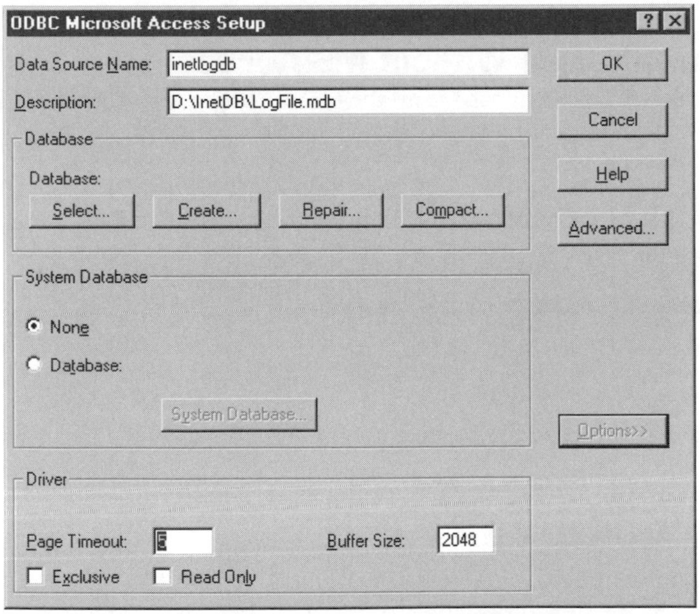

Figure 11-7. *ODBC Microsoft Access Setup*

will use this name in the ODBC Logging Properties window to connect to the database, so choose a name that you'll remember. For this example, we'll use *inetlogdb*. The description is for your use, so you may add any meaningful information here. For this example, we'll enter the path: *D:\InetDB\LogFile.mdb*.

Caution *When choosing a name for your DSN, using spaces is generally a bad idea, since some programs have issues with spaces in the DSN. Avoid using them.*

Now that you've named your data source, it's time to select the database.

1. In the ODBC Microsoft Access Setup dialog box, click Select and browse to the Access database you created earlier; in the example, we indicated the path *D:\InetDB\LogFile.mdb*.

2. Selected the Access database, and then click OK until you're out of ODBC Administrator.

If you've followed all the steps so far, you're ready to set up ODBC logging in your site properties, and you can skip to the next section. If you don't have MS Access, the next part is for you.

Creating a Database Without MS Access

You can create the Access database from the ODBC Microsoft Access Setup window. You can also perform functions on existing databases.

To access the setup window:

1. Choose Start | Control Panel | Administrative Tools | Data Sources (ODBC).

2. In the ODBC Data Source Administrator window, open the System DSN tab.

3. Click the data source you have created.

4. Click the Configure button.

5. Click the Create button.

6. In the New Database dialog box, choose a name and location for the database.

You can choose from among several options:

■ **Format** This version number refers to the version of the Jet database engine used, not the version of Access. The default for the database in this option is Version 4.x. It's not a good idea to change it, because versions 3.x and 2.x don't offer Unicode support.

■ **System Database** Choosing this option creates the database as a system DSN. If you're in the system DSN tab when you create the database, the Data Source Name will be created in the System DSN tab anyway.

- **Encryption** This checkbox allows you to encrypt the database so that text editors can't read the information in the database.

- **Network** This button allows you to map a drive to another machine, if you want to put your database there.

- **Locale** This drop-down box allows you to choose the language for this database.

When you create a database in this manner, you still need to create the table, so it's probably easier to create the database from within MS Access. If you don't have MS Access, however, you can use this procedure to create the database and then use SQL tools to create the table. MS Query, a program that comes with MS Excel, will allow you to do this, because it can run queries against an Access database. See the MS Query documentation for more information.

Setting Up Your Site for ODBC Logging

Now that the database side of ODBC logging is set up, let's set up a web site to log to the database:

1. Go to the Properties window of the site for which you want to set up ODBC logging, and choose ODBC Logging as the active log format.

2. Click Properties to open the ODBC Logging Properties window shown in Figure 11-8.

3. Type in the DSN you created earlier for your database (*inetlogdb* in our example).

4. Type in the table name used in the database (*inetlog* in our example).

   The options of the ODBC Logging Options window are shown here:

   - **ODBC Data Source Name (DSN)** Enter the name of the DSN you chose earlier. For our example, we chose *inetlogdb*.

   - **Table** Enter the name of the table created by the SQL statement here. In our SQL statement, we chose the name *inetlog*.

   - **User Name and Password** If your database requires a username and password for access, you would type them here. Our Access database does not require a username or password, so anything in this field is acceptable, or you can leave it blank.

After ODBC logging is set up here, your log is totally configured and ready for action. New data will not appear in the log database while the site is running, so if you want to open the database for viewing, stop the site that is logging to that database table first.

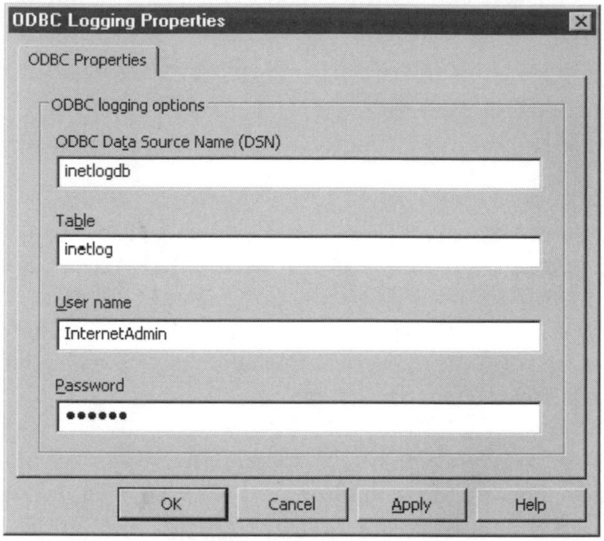

Figure 11-8. *ODBC Logging Properties window*

Using Custom Logging Modules

Custom logging modules allow you to make your own file format with completely customized fields. This is done by creating a COM object that implements the *ILogPlugin* or *ILogPluginEx* COM interface. IIS then uses your object to log entries. When you use custom logging, IIS disables the kernel-mode cache, so your system will take a performance hit if you use custom logging. More information about writing your own COM object is included in the IIS SDK documentation.

IIS, by default, writes log files to the *%systemroot%\System32\LogFiles* directory. Normally, *HTTP.SYS* handles the writing of log file information to that directory. When you have defined a custom logging module, it uses the account of the worker process in which it's running. Because worker processes run as a Network Service by default, you may experience problems writing to any files under *%systemroot%*. The best way around that is to configure your custom log module write to another directory, and grant the IIS_WPG group permissions to write to that directory.

Setting Up a Custom Logging Module with IIS

When you want to use a custom logging module, you must first register it on the system. After you've registered your custom logging module, you use its Globally

Unique Identifier (GUID) to identify the module in the metabase. After it has been identified, you can use that module in IIS by selecting it from the Active Log Format drop-down menu in the Enable Logging section in the MMC.

1. Open the *MetaBase.xml* file with Notepad (assuming you have edit-while-running enabled; see Chapter 9 for more on this option).

2. Go to the *IISLogModules* section of the metabase file, as shown in Figure 11-9.

3. Insert an entry of **IIsLogModule** for the custom logging module, using the module friendly name in the location. The module-friendly name is the name you wish the module to be listed as in the Active Log Format drop-down menu.

4. Insert the *LogModuleId*, using the *cls_id* of the COM object.

5. Insert the *LogModuleUiId*, using the *cls_id* of the UI for the COM object.

Caution   *Again, editing the metabase is dangerous, and you can disable IIS so it won't start if you inject any errors or formatting mistakes into the metabase file. Please be careful.*

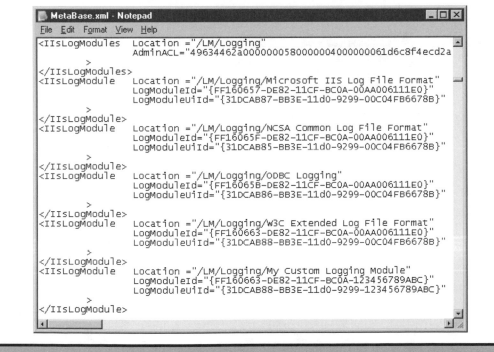

Figure 11-9.   *IISLogModule section of the metabase file*

The default COM object is *{FF160663-DE82-11CF-BC0A-00AA006111E0}*, which is the MS Custom Log Control, or *iislog.dll*.

After you've set up your custom log control, you can add it to the Active Log Format drop-down box in the IIS MMC. The list of available log modules is a "per-service property," which means, for example, that the WWW service's list would include options that aren't necessarily included on the FTP service's list. If you want to use logging for a service, you need to add logging for each service. To do this, you need to edit the metabase again.

1. Open the *MetaBase.xml* file with Notepad (assuming you have edit-while-running enabled).

2. Browse to the Info section of the registry. Each service will have its own section: *IIsWebInfo, IIsSmtpInfo, IIsNntpInfo,* and *IIsFtpinfo*.

3. Add your module to the list under the *LogModuleList* key in the metabase. The other entries are in comma-separated format.

Now you'll be able to select your custom log format in the Active Log Format drop-down box, as shown in Figure 11-10.

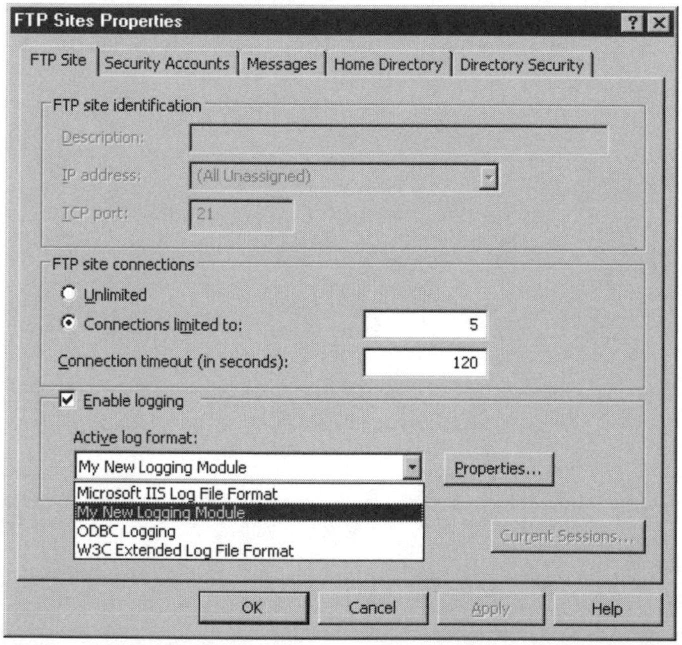

Figure 11-10.   *The Active Log Format drop-down box, with our new log module listed*

Centralized Binary Logging

With centralized binary logging, all web sites on a server write their logs to a single log file. If a large number of web sites are hosted on a server, thousands of log files can take up valuable server resources. Central logging uses a single binary file to log data, instead of a text file, which can result in performance benefits on your server.

Centralized binary logging is a server property, so when you enable it, it applies to all sites on that server. In fact, you can't even configure logging on individual sites after centralized binary logging is set up.

Setting Up Centralized Binary Logging

The easiest way to set up centralized binary logging is to use the *adsutil.vbs* script, which is located in *Inetpub\AdminScripts*.

1. Open a command prompt.
2. Navigate to the C:\Inetpub\AdminScripts directory (by default, it's on C. Your installation may vary).
3. Type in **cscript.exe adsutil.vbs set w3svc/centralbinarylogingenabled true**.
4. Press ENTER.
5. Open the Control Panel by clicking on Start | Control Panel | Services.
6. Stop and start the World Wide Publishing Service from the Services control panel.

After you've restarted the WWW service, binary logging will be active. The log file has an *.ibl* extension. Because the log is in binary format, opening it with Notepad won't help much. You'll be able to open the file, but it will be gibberish and won't be in plain text. You can extract data from the file using the parsing tool for centralized binary logging. This tool is located in the IIS 6 Resource Kit. (It probably won't be long before third-party web reporting tools have support for binary logging as well.)

Crunching the Data

Now that you've set up logging for your web site, it's time to start using that data. Log file data for your site can help you keep track of the following, along with other information:

- Where visitors to your site come from—a national ISP, a company, private ISP, a country, and so on.
- How they came to your site by looking at the referral address. This can help you determine the effectiveness of different advertisements and which ads generate traffic.

- Broken links on your site or broken links from other (referring) sites.
- Data on unauthorized or malicious access use of your site.
- Which areas of your site are the most and least popular.

The log files produced by IIS logging, while in plaintext, are not easily readable. It's difficult to analyze them just by looking at the raw text file. If you want to see a certain log entry, you could do so, but the log files don't lend themselves well to summarizing the data, especially when you have multiple web site logs to view. For reviewing log files, log file viewers are necessary. WS03 doesn't come with log file viewers that provide analysis, so you'll have to look for another program to use for this purpose. Dozens of log viewing programs are on the market—some are free and some cost money, and there are good and bad ones out there. A few programs that come to mind are

- WebTrends
- Xcavate
- Awstats
- MS Log Parser tool

If you're serious about tracking data on your web site, it may be worthwhile to look into obtaining one of them.

Part III

IIS Programming

317

The Complete Reference

IIS 6

Chapter 12

ASP Programming

A SP is an acronym for *Active Server Pages*. ASP programming enables programmers to access the Internet Information Server (IIS) application programming interface (API) using a scripting language such as *VBScript* or *JScript*. Although the next generation of ASP, called *ASP.NET*, is now available to programmers, the legacy of software using ASP is so large that Microsoft cannot abandon its support of the technology for a long time to come.

ASP enables a programmer to produce a web application quickly on a Windows server hosting IIS version 3 or higher. ASP was released to the web development community at a time that *Common Gateway Interface* (CGI) programming and *Perl* were the competitive technologies that many developers used to make web applications. ASP fits nicely with Microsoft's ActiveX strategy by providing a means of using functionality encapsulated in Component Object Model (COM) components so the developer can produce n-tier solutions using ASP and COM.

> **Note** *The code listings in this chapter are available on the author's web site as mentioned in the book's Introduction.*

Overall Architecture of ASP

ASP files are script files that are interpreted as they are requested. An Internet Server Application Programming Interface (ISAPI) extension named *ASP.DLL* is mapped in IIS to files ending in *.asp* or *.asa*, as shown in Figure 12-1. *ASP.DLL* parses the *.asp* files for tags indicating the presence of code intended for execution on the server. *ASP.DLL* sends the script code to the Windows Script Host (WSH). WSH executes the script code and returns the response to *ASP.DLL*, which returns the result of the script code executions and the content inside the ASP file itself to IIS. IIS returns the response to the requesting software. *ASP.DLL* does not execute code such as validation functions written in JavaScript that are contained in the ASP and are intended for execution in the web browser or the software requesting the ASP file.

> **Note** *For the purposes of this chapter, the client will refer to the software that is requesting a file from the web server.*

In a typical web server/web browser relationship, the web browser is the *client*. In this scenario, the client makes requests to the web server. The web server responds by returning the requested file, and if that file happens to be an ASP file, the web server will perform some work prior to returning the response to the client. As expected, the work for which an ASP is responsible generally alters the response that is returned to the client.

The ASP also offers a great mechanism for *gluing* other systems and software together. It allows the developer to manipulate the data easily to and from IIS without forcing him or her to deal with the complexities of Hypertext Transfer Protocol (HTTP)

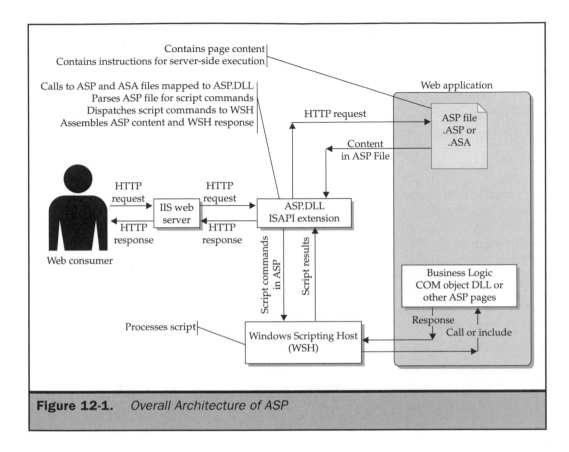

Figure 12-1. *Overall Architecture of ASP*

and IIS. The classes offered in ASP with IIS provide a nice layer of abstraction to HTTP and the web server that many competing technologies, such as Perl and CGI, fail to offer the developer.

In some cases, the business logic may be encapsulated in COM objects. If the COM object provides an interface that is accessible by VBScript or JScript, the ASP can function as a dispatching mechanism. Chapter 13 presents a greater examination of the use of ASP with COM objects.

Editing ASP files

Because ASP files are simply text files, any text editor can be used to edit and create them. *Visual Interdev Version 6* is Microsoft's tool for editing and creating ASP files. Developers commonly use other tools ranging from TextPad to Notepad to DreamWeaver. Visual Studio .NET is also a good choice for editing ASP files.

For this chapter, Visual Interdev is used to edit and create ASP files. Here's how to open a new ASP file with Interdev:

1. Open Visual Interdev, and you'll be prompted to enter a project name. Click Cancel to close the prompt, and choose File | New File.

2. Enter a filename and indicate the type of file you want to create.

3. Click the ASP File icon and then click the Open button, as shown in Figure 12-2. The editor will present an ASP with template code for a generic HTML and a processing instruction at the top that indicates that the file language is VBScript.

VBScript is the default language for ASP pages. JScript, Microsoft's implementation of JavaScript, can also be used. VBScript is probably the most popular script language used by ASP coders, however, and in this chapter, all examples are shown in VBScript.

Visual Interdev offers the developer many useful features that are not available with other editors, which makes it useful for most ASP coding tasks. Using Interdev, a developer can debug code running on the server while stepping through the code line by line as the code is executed. The Auto List Member feature of IntelliSense is another feature offered by Interdev that is useful to the developer, because it ensures that the syntax the developer uses is correct. As keywords or commands of known libraries are typed by the developer, Interdev will suggest the proper spelling of the commands, as

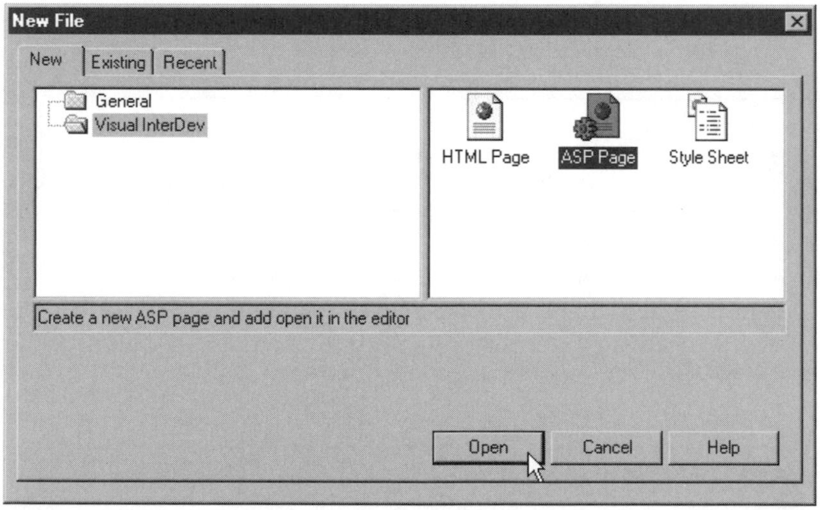

Figure 12-2. *Creating a new ASP in Visual Interdev*

shown in Figure 12-3. Interdev will finish the command for the developer if the developer presses the TAB key. Interdev also color codes text to help distinguish between commands and content.

Visual Studio .NET is also an excellent tool for editing ASP. If Visual Studio .NET is available for use, ASP.NET should be used instead of ASP, unless a compelling reason exists for not using ASP.NET—for example, if ASPs adequately serve an existing need that requires an enhancement. In such a situation, rebuilding ASP files as ASP.NET files would not be useful. ASP.NET files and ASPs may be run side by side on an IIS 6 instance, so incremental introduction of ASP.NET into an ASP solution might be a consideration if there is a need for future enhancements and you want to migrate the solution to use the .NET Framework.

The filename extensions for ASP files are different from ASP.NET files. ASP.NET filenames end in *.aspx* or *.asax*. ASP filenames end in *.asp* or *.asa*. The file extension is the means by which IIS distinguishes the file types and determines the appropriate ISAPI extension to use on the file. For example, if an ASP file named *MyAspFile.asp* was renamed *MyAspFile.aspx*, the .NET Framework would process *MyAspFile* when it was

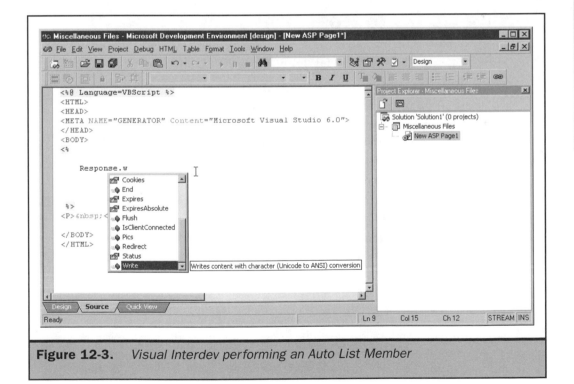

Figure 12-3.   *Visual Interdev performing an Auto List Member*

requested instead of using the ASP ISAPI extension *ASP.DLL*. The use of Visual Studio .NET and ASP.NET will be covered in greater detail in Chapter 14.

> **Note** *Although ASP and ASP.NET can be hosted on the same web server instance running side by side, they cannot share a session, because each file type is processed by different software. The ASP files are processed by ASP.DLL, which in turn uses WSH to execute the script commands. The ASP.NET files are processed by* aspnet_isapi.dll, *which in turn uses the .NET Framework to execute the code.*

The disadvantage of using Visual Interdev is primarily that it is resource intensive, so it takes a long time to open and use on simple tasks. If a developer needs to make a quick edit, for example, Notepad or Textpad will open quickly and provide enough functionality to allow the edit to be made and the file to be saved and closed. Visual Interdev is a licensed software product that must be purchased, so when it is compared to the other alternatives, it is the most expensive option.

Setting Up IIS to Host ASP

IIS 6 might not have ASP enabled if the server was just installed or if it had never been used for hosting ASP in the past. Installing support for ASP is easy, however:

1. Open the Control Panel and choose Add Or Remove Programs.

2. In the Add Or Remove Programs applet, make sure the Change Or Remove Programs icon is selected on the left side. Choose the Add Or Remove Windows Components icon and the Windows Component Wizard will be displayed.

3. Select Application Server and click the Details button.

4. After the Application Server applet opens, select Internet Information Services (IIS) and click the Details button.

5. After the Internet Information Services applet opens, select World Wide Web Service and click the Details button.

6. Finally, make sure a check appears in the checkbox for Active Server Pages in the World Wide Web Service applet, as shown in Figure 12-4, and ASP support will be installed.

A new feature of Windows Server 2003 (WS03) and IIS 6 is the restriction of all server-side programmatic support by default and the requirement that server-side programming support be explicitly enabled. Requesting a file that must be processed

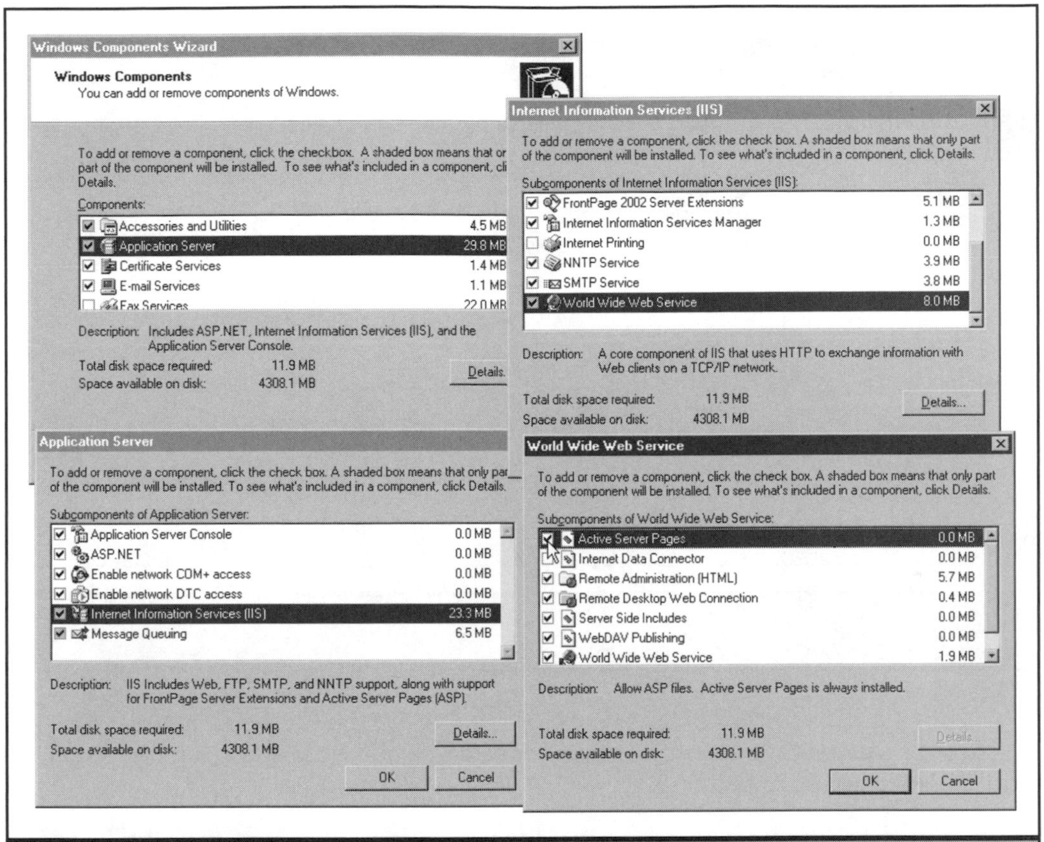

Figure 12-4. *Installing ASP support from the Windows Component Wizard*

using an ISAPI extension like ASP.DLL that is not enabled will result in a 404 error being returned. In previous versions of Windows Server, IIS came loaded with all ISAPI extensions, such as ASP.DLL, enabled. The functionality must be enabled on the server using the Web Service Extensions administrative node in the Computer Management Microsoft Management Console (MMC) snap-in, as shown in Figure 12-5. To enable the IIS to serve requests to ASP files, choose Active Server Pages in the right pane and then click the Allow button.

The web instance in IIS or the virtual directory must also have the *script* permissions set to allow ASP to run. By default, the Execute Permissions setting in the Properties

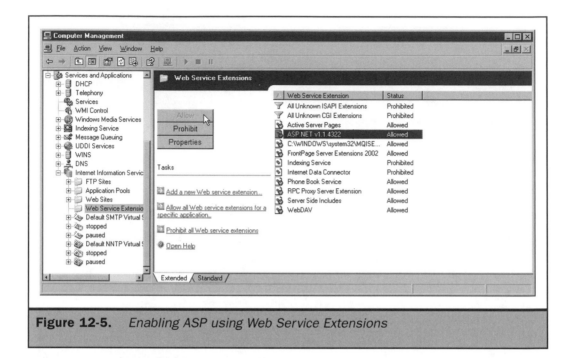

Figure 12-5. *Enabling ASP using Web Service Extensions*

window for a given IIS instance or virtual directory is not set to allow scripts to run. Here's how to access this setting:

1. Open the IIS MMC plug-in and right-click the web instance or virtual directory to expose the context menu.

2. Choose Properties to open the Properties window for the web instance or virtual directory.

3. On the Virtual Directory tab for the Properties window of a Virtual Directory or the Home Directory tab for the Properties window of a web instance in an Execute Permissions drop-down box, as shown in Figure 12-6. Select Scripts Only.

4. Click OK to close the window.

5. After you set the permissions, you can move the ASP file to the web instance or virtual directory to make ASP function properly. If everything is properly set in IIS, ASP files should be executed when requested from a browser.

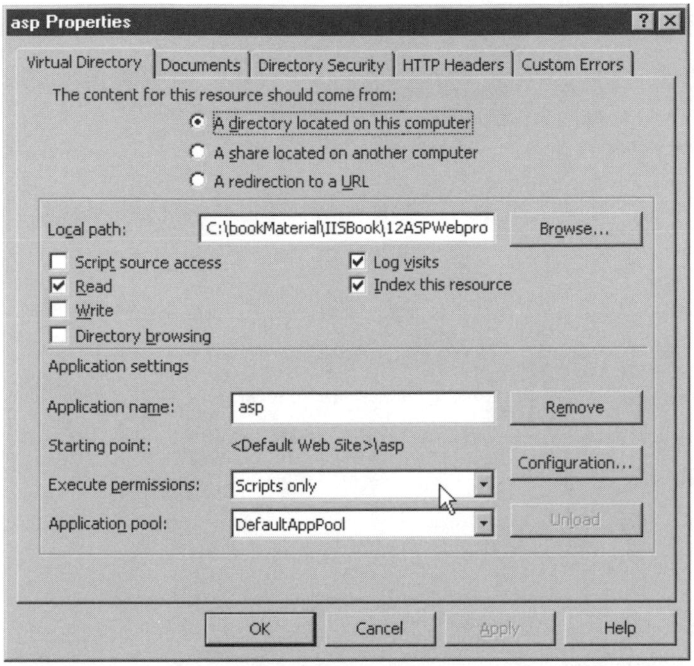

Figure 12-6. *Setting the Execute permissions for a virtual directory*

ASP Fundamentals

Using an ASP object called *Response*, ASP code can write text to the client. Any content may be written to the client, including code that is executed on the client. IIS distinguishes between code executed on the server and content being sent to the client by using the ISAPI ASP.DLL extension to parse the ASP file for the start tag <% and the end tag %> and using WSH to execute the code in between the start and end tags.

Figure 12-7 shows an example of editing an ASP page using Visual Interdev. Within the same ASP page are lines of content that are being written to the client using the response object and code being executed on the server.

The first line of code, <%@ Language=VBScript %>, tells the ASP ISAPI extension *ASP.DLL* in IIS to start looking for code to interpret. In this particular case, the language that should be used for processing the ASP is set for the ASP page, and then the %> at the end tells *ASP.DLL* to ignore subsequent lines of code except for a <% tag. *ASP.DLL*

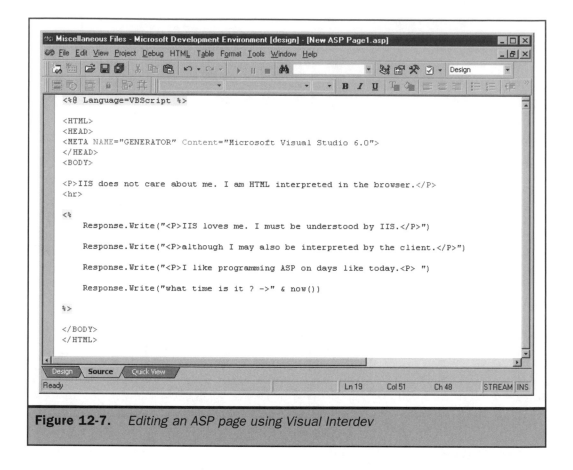

Figure 12-7. *Editing an ASP page using Visual Interdev*

does not interpret the HTML lines that follow. Referring to Figure 12-7, when *ASP.DLL* encounters the <% tag after the line that has the <hr> tag, the subsequent lines of code are interpreted by *ASP.DLL* until the ending tag %> is encountered after the line `Response.Write("what time is it ? ->" & now())`. The result of a client web browser requesting *MyAspFile1.asp*, the ASP page shown in Figure 12-7, after having been requested and displayed in a browser, is shown in Figure 12-8.

ASP Objects

ASP offers the following five objects that support the programmer's need to produce a solution that responds to a web request event:

- **Response object**   Used to write data into the HTTP response that is returned to the client

- **Application object**   Contains settings and configurations designed to affect how ASP works for a given web instance in IIS

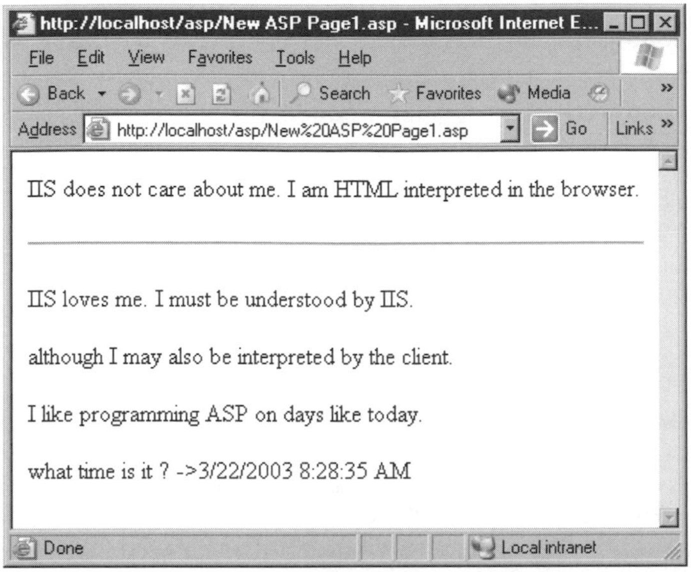

Figure 12-8.   *Running ASP that uses response.write*

- **Request object**   Contains the content of the HTTP request and offering support functionality to the developer for parsing HTTP request data
- **Server object**   Contains information about the web server and the web server instance and providing support for calling software
- **Session**   Represents the state of a given web session with a given host and client

Response Object

Like all the ASP objects, a class instance of the Response object is always available to a given ASP during a web-based request event. The purpose of this object is to support the programmer's need to write data to the client during a web request. The *Write* function of the Response object returns to the client the content of the argument passed into Write. The Response object also provides a developer the means by which to control how things are written to the HTTP response.

Application Object

The application object is used primarily in the *global.asa* file to capture events of the ASP application. Four events may be captured by the application object:

- **Session_OnStart**   Triggered on the first request from a given user for the web instance

■ **Session_OnEnd**   Triggered when the session expires for a given user

■ **Application_OnStart**   Triggered when any user requests any page for the first time

■ **Application_OnEnd**   Triggered when IIS is being shut down

The application object may also be used to store variables that will keep their state for the entire time the web site is running. Since the application object remains instantiated from the time the first request is made to the web application to the time the web server is shut down, the application object may be used to store data that must be maintained for all page requests and all web sessions.

Request Object

The Request object serves the programmer's need to obtain information from the client for a given request to the web server. The type of information available in the Request object that is useful to the developer is data that is submitted to the web server. For example, if a user's name was needed, the ASP would have to request the web user to enter it into a form and click on a submit button. After the web user clicks the button, the ASP would have to look for the information using the Request object. As shown in Listing 12-1, the Request object uses the name of the HTML input element that contains the value the web user enters for their user name.

Listing 12-1

```
AskName.asp - Sample ASP Requesting User's Name

<%@ Language=VBScript %>

<html>
<head>
<title>What is you name?</title>

</head>
<body>

<FORM METHOD = "POST" ACTION = "askname.asp" ID = "frmImage"
NAME = "getInfo" >

<%

If len(Request("UserName")) > 0 then
  Response.Write("<p>you said your name was: " & _
                  Request("UserName") & "</p>")

  Response.Write("<p>Please reenter it</p>")
```

```
else
  Response.Write( _
  "<p>Please enter you name and click the submit button.</p>")
end if

%>

<input TYPE="text" NAME="UserName" VALUE="">

<INPUT ID="subFull" NAME="subR" TYPE="submit" VALUE="Refresh" >

</FORM>

</body>
</html>
```

When the web user requests the ASP shown in Listing 12-1, he or she will be prompted to enter their name the first time. If the user types any text into the input box named *UserName* and clicks the submit button, the value entered into the input box is submitted to the web server. Clicking the submit button submits the request to the same ASP that created the page displayed to the user. The name of the ASP is *askname.asp*, as evidenced by the *FORM* element's *ACTION* attribute. When *askname.asp* is requested from the web server, it uses the Request object to seek out the value of the input box named *UserName* using the following line of code:

```
Request("UserName")
```

Collections of the Request Object

The Request object may be used to request a value from the query string, an HTTP post, or a cookie using this method of simply naming the value of the variable. The Request object avails to the programmer three collections of values:

- **Request.Cookies**   Collection of cookie names and values on the client machine
- **Request.Form**   Collection of HTML input elements names and values resulting from an HTML form submission or post to the ASP file
- **Request.QueryString**   Collection of name and value pairs in the query string used to request the ASP file

As all collections support the *Count*, *Key*, and *Item* properties, any one of these collections support the ability to refer to a value using its ordinal value. This is useful in situations for which various combinations of data could be parsed to determine the means for processing the data. Logic could be built into the ASP such that if a key of a particular name is submitted, other parameters could be sought out and processed in the request. For an example of an ASP that will list all the values in all the collections, refer to Listing 12-2.

Listing 12-2

```
ShowRequestValues.asp - ASP Listing Collection Contents

<%@ Language=VBScript %>

<%

'~~~~~~~~~~~~~~~~~~~~~~~~~~~~~~~~~~~~~~~~~~~~~~~~~~~~~~~
'sub WriteCollection
'loops through the contents of any collection object
'passed in and response.writes the index and name = value
'using HTML
'
'in
'      c = any 1 based collection
'      CollectionName = any string to describe the
'      collection
'out - nothing - writes to client
'~~~~~~~~~~~~~~~~~~~~~~~~~~~~~~~~~~~~~~~~~~~~~~~~~~~~~~~
sub WriteCollection(c, CollectionName)

    dim i                 'index for collection loop
    dim sPhrase           'phrase assembled to show values

    'draw a line
    Response.Write("<hr><p>")

    'announce the size of the collection
    Response.Write(CollectionName & " have " & c.Count & _
                                      " values:</p>")

    for i= 1 to c.Count
        'these collections are 1 based -
        'I don't know why when most all others are 0 based

        sPhrase = "#" & i & " " & c.Key(i) & _
                  " = " & c.Item(i) & "<br>"

        Response.Write(sPhrase)
    next
```

```
end sub


%>

<HTML>
<HEAD>
<META NAME="GENERATOR" Content="Microsoft Visual Studio 6.0">
<title>Tell me about the requester</title>

</HEAD>
<BODY>


<%

'show me the server time so I can verify page is not cached
Response.Write("<p>server time: " & now() & "</p>")

'write cookies collection
WriteCollection Request.Cookies, "Cookies"

'write form variables collection
WriteCollection Request.Form, "Form Variables"

'write query string collection
WriteCollection Request.QueryString, "Query String"


%>

</BODY>
</HTML>
```

Listing 12-2 features the use of a subroutine named sub WriteCollection(c, CollectionName) that takes a collection argument and prints the names and values of all the elements within the collection to the requesting browser. The collection's index must start from 1 as opposed to 0 as many other collections are indexed from. The WriteCollection subroutine is called three times from the body section of the HTML section. In each respective call, a collection of the Request object is passed into the subroutine. On running the ASP file *ShowRequestValues.asp*, Listing 12-2, the output with sample cookie values and query string values, may be seen in Figure 12-9.

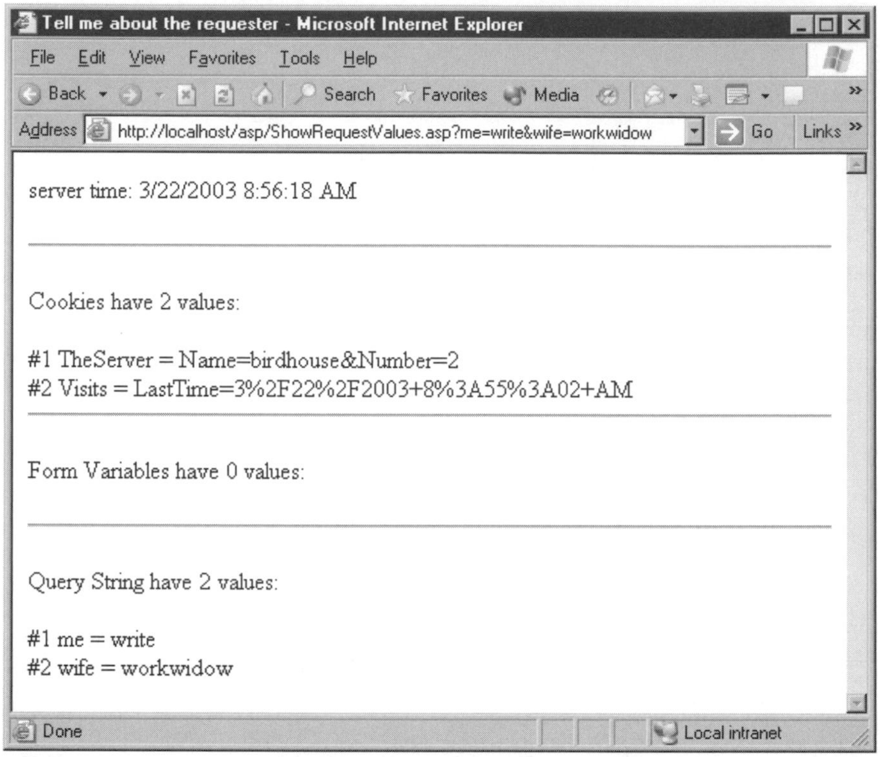

Figure 12-9. *Output of request collections*

Two cookies on the client computer made the request to *ShowRequestValues.asp* write out the following lines to the browser:

```
#1 TheServer = Name=birdhouse&Number=2
#2 Visits = LastTime=3%2F22%2F2003+8%3A55%3A02+AM
```

One cookie is named *TheServer* and the other cookie is named *Visits*. Cookie *TheServer* has multiple values, which is why the output lists the name of the cookie as being equal to the parameter named *Name*, which in turn is equal to the value *birdhouse*. This behavior exists because the *Request.Cookies* collection's *Key* property value is the name of the cookie and the *Item* property value of the cookies collection is the name/value pair. The *Request.Form* and the *Request.QueryString* collections are simply made up of name/value pairs that are contained in the *Key* and *Item* property values, respectively.

Managing Content Cache Using HTTP Headers

Web browsers occasionally cache web pages or content that is part of a web page. The reason the server time was written to the browser in Listing 12-2 was to be able to determine whether the output of *ShowRequestValues.asp* was being cached. Caching content improves performance of a web site; however, at times using caching may be undesirable. Some browsers might not write out the new data from ASP code or show the correct image if the names are the same as the files cached from a previous request from the same server and the image changed since the previous request. Using the Response object `AddHeader` command, an argument could be added to the HTTP response that is sent back to the requesting web browser telling the browser not to cache the content on the page. When the requesting web browser parses the HTTP response, it should encounter the header or headers that indicate that the content should be downloaded instead of obtained from the web browser's cache.

Refer to Listing 12-3 for a sample of the headers that should be added to the top of the ASP file to cause the web browser not to use cached content.

Listing 12-3

```
Using AddHeader Function

<%@ Language=VBScript %>

<%
'eliminate caching
Response.AddHeader "pragma","no-cache"
Response.AddHeader "cache-control","private"
Response.CacheControl = "no-cache"
%>
```

The same effect can be achieved, more simply, by adding `Response.Expires=-1` to the page.

Managing Application State Using Cookies

Cookies provide a mechanism for storing state data on the web browser's host. The data may be obtained at a later date from the user's computer. Writing cookies may be performed using the *Response.Cookies* function. Listing 12-4 shows an ASP that lists existing cookies and updates them. Cookies may be written with an expiration date. If no date is specified, the cookies last as long as the user keeps the web browser open. When the web browser is closed, the cookies are flushed from the web browser's host.

Listing 12-4

```
WriteCookies.asp - ASP Listing and Updating Cookies

<%@ Language=VBScript %>
```

IIS PROGRAMMING

```
<%
'need to do this because we are writing cookies
Response.Buffer = True
%>
<!--#include file="CommonSubs.inc"-->

<HTML>
<HEAD>
<title>Let me mark the time you were here last</title>
</HEAD>
<BODY>
<p> Here are the cookies that were here before </p>
<%

'write cookies collection
WriteCollection Request.Cookies, "Cookies"

'get time and date for right now
dim sTimeNow
sTimeNow = now()

'get previous number
dim sCookie
dim i

'get cookie value
sCookie = Request.Cookies("TheServer")("Number")

'make it a number and increment
i = cint(sCookie) + 1

%>
<hr>
<p> The Visits cookie LastTime value will be updated to
<% =sTimeNow %> </p>

<p> The TheServer cookie Number value will be updated to
 <% =i %> </p>

<%
```

```
'update cookie values
Response.Cookies("Visits")("LastTime") = sTimeNow

Response.Cookies("TheServer")("Name") = "birdhouse"

Response.Cookies("TheServer")("Number") = i

%>
</BODY>
</HTML>
```

Listing 12-4 shows an ASP file, *WriteCookies.asp*, that reads and writes cookies each time the file is called. The values of the cookies are read using the *Request.Cookies* collection and written to the browser using the *WriteCollection* subroutine for the end user to see the values. After the values are written to the browser, the ASP reads the value of the *TheServer* cookie *Number* value and increments it by one. The new value of the *TheServer* cookie *Number* value and the *Visits* cookie *LastTime* value are written using the Response.Cookies(<cookie name>)(<parameter name>) = <new value> form of the command.After the language specification code block in Listing 12-4 is the Response.Buffer = True line. This command makes certain that the entire HTTP response, including headers and content, is assembled prior to being written to the client's browser. When the page that is to be sent to the requesting browser is completely assembled, the ASP ISAPI extension *ASP.DLL* will first send the necessary headers to set the cookies and then will send the content afterward. Headers must be written prior to sending the content because of the constraints of HTTP. If the buffer setting for the Response object were not turned on, the content would be streamed to the client as it was being generated and headers could not be sent to the client. Listing 12-4 also demonstrates the use of the include file. On line 7, the command <!--#include file="CommonSubs.inc"--> inserts the contents of the file *CommonSubs.inc* into the ASP file as though it were typed in at that place on file. The subroutine *WriteCollection*, shown in Listing 12-2, was placed in the file *CommonSubs.inc*. The great advantage of using an include file in this way is that many common functions may be placed into a single file and used by many other files in a given web application without duplicating code. Maintaining a single copy of code that is common to many ASP files is much easier than writing a separate version of the same function or subroutine of code in each file. Fixing a bug to a subroutine in an include file instantly makes the fix everywhere the include file is, well, included. If separate versions of the same function or subroutine of code were used in many ASP files, the fix for the subroutine or function would require more work and there would be greater risk of introducing a new bug while attempting to fix the existing bug, because so many files would require editing.

Another ASP technique that Listing 12-4 demonstrates is the use of the = to perform a *Response.Write*. Refer to this line:

```
<p> The Visits cookie LastTime value will be updated to
<% =sTimeNow %> </p>
```

The code `<% =sTimeNow %>` opens the ASP code block in the HTML section of the ASP long enough to write the value of the variable `sTimeNow`. The = is a shorthand way of performing the `Reponse.Write` command immediately following the `<%` tag. The intention for its use is for situations such as inserting `Response.Write` in HTML code so that it is easier to follow and read.

Session Object

The Session object is a turnkey state management solution that uses cookies. The Session object manages session time and information about the end user in a way that insulates the programmer from the effort of reading and writing cookies and checking time and values for the session. If the client computer does not allow cookies to be used on the machine, the Session object will not be able to write the session cookie and it will not function properly. The cookie written by the Session object has no expiration date set, so it is flushed when the browser is closed. The Session object holds all the session data in a collection named *Session.Contents*. The Session object and the Contents collection can be managed and manipulated just like the other ASP object collections. *WriteCollection,* a custom subroutine shown in Listing 12-2, may be used to show the contents of the *Session.Contents* collection in the exact same way that the cookies, Form variables, and *QueryString* collections were written to the browser. For an example of code that uses the Session object in a way similar to the *Request.Cookies* collection, refer to Listing 12-5.

Listing 12-5

```
ReadWriteSession.asp - ASP Page Using the Session Object

<%@ Language=VBScript %>

<!--#include file="CommonSubs.inc"-->
<%


'~~~~~~~~~~~~~~~~~~~~~~~~~~~~~~~~~~~~~~~~~~~~~~~~~~~~~~~~~~
'sub UpdateSession
'Performs a simple Session object read and write
'
'obtains the current time and the previous Session
'value for Number. The value for Number is incremented.
'All new values are written to the Session.
```

```
'
'in
'      oSession = any 1 based collection - specifically
'      Session Object
'      NewTime = new time generated written to Session
'      NewNumber = new number written to Session
'
'out - nothing - writes to client.
'      NewTime, NewNumber are updated.
'~~~~~~~~~~~~~~~~~~~~~~~~~~~~~~~~~~~~~~~~~~~~~~~~~~~~~~~~~~
sub UpdateSession(oSession, NewTime, NewNumber)

    dim sSession

    'get time and date for right now
    NewTime = now()

    'get session value
    sSession = oSession("Number")

    'make it a number and increment
    NewNumber = cint(sSession) + 1

    'write the new values
    oSession("Number") = NewNumber
    oSession("LastTime") = NewTime
    oSession("Name") = "birdhouse"

end sub

%>
<HTML>
<HEAD>
<title>managing a session using the session object</title>
</HEAD>
<BODY>

<p> Here is the session prior to update</p>

<%
dim sTime
dim sNumber
```

```
'write Session collection
WriteCollection Session.Contents , "Session Contents"

'write some other sundry values
Response.Write("<br>Session.SessionID:" & Session.SessionID)
Response.Write("<br>Session.Timeout:" & Session.Timeout)

'update session and get new values that are written to session
UpdateSession Session.Contents, sTime, sNumber

'set session timeout to 1 minute - default is 20 minutes
Session.Timeout=1

%>

<hr>
<p>The session LastTime value will be updated to <% =sTime %></p>
<p>The session Number value will be updated to <% =sNumber %></p>

</BODY>
</HTML>
```

Listing 12-5 is an ASP that, when run, reads the values of the Session object, updates the values, and writes the new values to the Session object. The *WriteCollection* subroutine is in the include file specified in the line `<!--#include file="CommonSubs.inc"-->`. Two other properties unique to the Session object, *SessionID* and *Timeout,* are written to the browser. The *UpdateSession* subroutine is called using the *Session.Contents* collection, using the variables *sTime* and *sNumber* as arguments. The *sTime* and *sNumber* variables are empty variables that will be filled in the subroutine with the actual values written to the session. After *Session.Timeout* is set to 1 minute, the information about the updates made to the session are written to the browser.

In VBScript, by default, all parameters in a function or subroutine are passed *by reference*. This means that the values of the arguments will change as a result of any manipulations that take place in the function or subroutine to the arguments passed in. In the *UpdateSession* subroutine, *sTime* and *sNumber* contain no values when they are passed into *UpdateSession* as arguments. In the subroutine, *sTime* is set to the current time using the *now()* function, and the *sNumber* variable is set to the previous value and has 1 added to it. After the subroutine has completed running, both *sTime* and *sNumber* are holding the new values to which they were set in the function *UpdateSession.* Using the keyword *byval* in front of any parameter in the subroutine prototype declaration, an argument being passed in would not be changed after the subroutine completes execution.

When the ASP *ReadWriteSession.asp* shown in Listing 12-5 is run for the first time, it shows values of the Session object in the browser. The *Session.Timeout* property is set to 20 by default and no values are set in the session until the ASP completes execution. Figure 12-10 shows a sample output of the session ASP code on the first run.

Refreshing *ReadWriteSession.asp* causes the ASP to run again and update the session object with new values, and it prints the values to the web browser, as shown in Figure 12-11. The Session object can hold values associated with a name in the same way that a cookie does, thereby allowing the Session object to be used as a mechanism for maintaining application state between page requests. The cookies printed out to the browser in Figure 12-9 were added to the Session object in this example to demonstrate the similarities in functionality between storing and retrieving data from the session or a cookie. *ReadWriteSession.asp* also sets a new Session.Timeout value of 1 minute.

Session Object Limitations

The Session object has some limitations that should be considered before you build ASP state management around the exclusive use of the Session object. The session is not replicated or shared among servers working in a web farm. The session data is

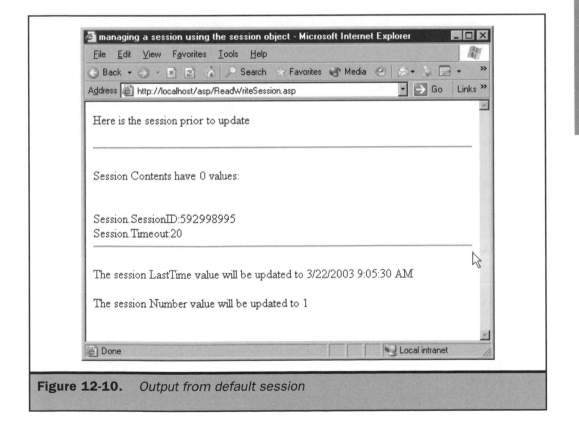

Figure 12-10.   *Output from default session*

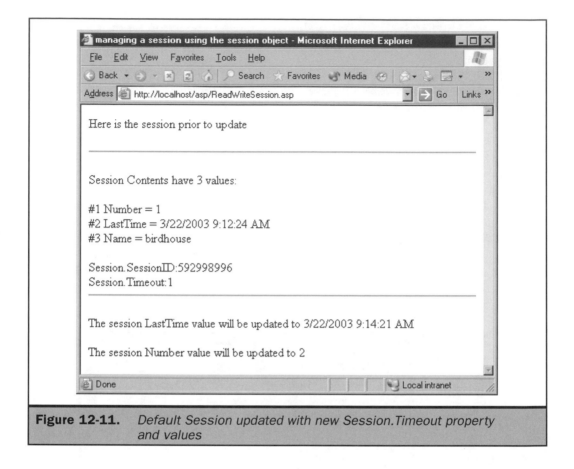

Figure 12-11.   *Default Session updated with new Session.Timeout property and values*

actually stored on the hosting server that supplied the session. When the user requests an ASP page for the first time from a given web server using the ASP session, a session cookie is written to the client's host. The session cookie holds a single value that acts as a key. When the end user requests another ASP from the web server, the ASP ISAPI extension *ASP.DLL* gets the session cookie and looks up the data that will populate the Session object using the key that was obtained from the session cookie. If the ASP is served from another web server participating in a web farm environment, the session data that was present on the web server from which the session cookie was created will not exist on that host, so the session will not be loaded.

To use the ASP Session object as it is intrinsically provided, no more than one server may be utilized. Alternatives and solutions to this problem detail the creation and use of a *session server* that maintains session data for web servers participating in a web farm. The member hosts participating in the web farm can obtain requestors' session data from the session server whenever it is needed. Details about these types of solutions are beyond the scope of this book but should be considered and examined in a web farm environment that is hosting an ASP solution using the Session object. ASP.NET does offer an easier solution that is an intrinsic part of the .NET Framework; this is covered in Chapter 14.

Server Object

A common use for ASP is to obtain some data from a data store, apply some business logic to it, and display it to the user in the web browser. Performing all of these tasks solely using ASP is possible, but many web programmers use other software libraries for this purpose. For example, ASP offers no intrinsic library for reading data sources. The *Server object* does support a function for creating an object instance of a COM object, however. The object instance can be any COM object that has an interface that is readable using VBScript. A popular COM object or set of objects useful for reading data sources is called *Active Data Objects* (ADO).

Data Access Using ADO

ADO is designed to offer a programmer a universal data access solution for all data sources. Ideally, ADO acts as a layer of abstraction between the business logic code and the data source in any solution. By changing a set of parameters that dictate the data source location, the software should still read and write to the data source without requiring a code change. Currently, ADO offers this type of abstraction among data sources of similar data structure architecture. For example, the ADO code used to read and write to and from a SQL Server database could also read and write to and from an Oracle database without requiring a code change.

Legacy Data Access Technology   Microsoft also provided other data access libraries, such as Data Access Objects (DAO) and Remote Data Objects (RDO). DAO offers a great deal of functionality for the developer to manage and parse a set of data pulled from a database, but it does not offer the ability to asynchronously query a client-server database hosted on a networked server. RDO offers less functionality for parsing and managing data pulled from a database, but it does offer a light set of software that allows a developer to pull data efficiently from a client-server database hosted on a networked server. Both DAO and RDO technologies are considered legacy and are no longer supported, so they should not be used. ADO offers the programmer the best of all situations, and it has become the marquee of the Microsoft data access technology. ADO provides the developer many options for managing and parsing data pulled from the database as well as many options for establishing the connection to the database.

Using ADO in ASP   ASP code accessing data in a database to display a recordset must use the `Server.CreateObject` command to use ADO. All COM objects have a name, and they are registered on the host server. The name feature of the COM object eliminates issues related to locating the proper library by abstracting the library location on the host from the effort of referring to the library. A COM object needs to be specified only by its name. The `Server.CreateObject` command takes the name of the COM object in the form *<library name>.<class name>* as the argument to the function. An instance of the COM object is returned to the variable that is set to the function call.

Because ADO is a group of COM objects, the `Server.CreateObject` command is used to create the various objects used in the course of connecting to a database, reading recordsets from the database, and writing the recordset values to the web browser. For a sample ASP that reads a simple recordset from a database table and writes the data to the web browser, refer to *readDB.asp* in Listing 12-6.

Listing 12-6

```
readDB.asp - ASP Opening a Recordset from a Database and Printing
the Contents to the Web Browser

<%@ Language=VBScript %>

<HTML>
<HEAD>
<title>read a database table</title>
</HEAD>
<BODY>

<%

dim myConn
dim myRecordset
dim sSQL
dim sResult
dim sConn 'For database connection string

    'create connection string
    sConn = "Provider=Microsoft.Jet.OLEDB.4.0;"
    sConn = sConn & "Data Source=C:\aspData\employees.mdb;"

    'establish connection
    Set myConn = Server.CreateObject("ADODB.Connection")
    myConn.Open sConn

    'create the recordset
    set myRecordset = Server.CreateObject("ADODB.Recordset")

    'build SQL command
    sSQL = "SELECT first_name, last_name FROM tblEmployee"

    'open the recordset from the database
```

```
myRecordset.Open sSQL, myConn

'check if there are any values in the recordset
if not( myRecordset.EOF and myRecordset.EOF) then

        'loop through the recordset until the end record
        while(not myRecordset.EOF)
            'build output string
            sResult = myRecordset("first_name") & " "
            sResult = sResult & _
                    myRecordset("last_name") & "<br />"

            'write value to browser
            Response.write(sResult)

            'advance recordset
            myRecordset.moveNext()
        wend

    else
        'let us know that there were no values
        Response.write("nothing returned")
    end if

    'shut down recordset and connection objects
    myRecordset.Close()
    myConn.Close()
%>

</body>
</html>
```

ADO Connection Object   The first object created in Listing 12-6 is an ADO connection object. The ADO library is named *ADODB* and the class is named *Connection*, so the command to create an object is

```
Set myConn = Server.CreateObject("ADODB.Connection")
```

The variable *myConn* points to an instance of the ADO Connection class. The Connection class maintains and passes the access credentials to the data source. In Listing 12-6, an Object Linking and Embedding database (OLE-DB) string was created to open a database connection to a Microsoft Access database hosted on the server.

Microsoft's Access Database   Using a Microsoft Access database on the same host as the web server is a good way to provide very fast data access on small data sets—say, data sets smaller than 300 MB. Your results for performance versus dataset size may vary considerably depending on the host and the application, so you will have to load test to determine the performance limitation. Using an Access database file costs nothing, although you do have to purchase Microsoft Access if you want to manipulate the data using a tool rather then making SQL commands in ASP code. Microsoft Access can also provide faster data access times, too, on small datasets than the costly enterprise database products like Microsoft's SQL Server or Oracle's database products.

Microsoft Access has many limitations when it is used to manage large datasets, however. Microsoft Access also does not offer the same kind of functionality as do other database products such as SQL Server or Oracle. Microsoft Access is like a glorified file read-and-write utility since the resource to query data is provided by the consuming application. In the case of an ASP, the resource to query data is drained from IIS. In stark contrast, however, the resource to perform a query in an enterprise level database will be borne by the host. The permissions to access a Microsoft Access database are set using file permissions. In the examples shown in this chapter, the IIS Windows service account named IUSER_<*machine name*> (where *machine name* is the name of the host) must be assigned read and write access to the Microsoft Access *.mdb* database file. The Microsoft Access file has an .mdb extension and may be identified in the OLE-DB connection string.

ADO Recordset Object   Another ADO object, called a *recordset*, is also instantiated. The recordset object supports the programmer's need to access the data in a dataset. It gives the programmer the ability to "touch" the data by supporting the need to read and write data to and from the data source. The recordset is opened using a SQL command and the instance of the connection object *myConn*. After the Open function of the recordset object is called, the recordset can be traversed and written to the browser. Before this exercise can be performed, however, the recordset must be validated to determine whether any records are in the recordset. A recordset is empty if the BOF (beginning of file) and EOF (end of file) conditions are both true. When a recordset is first opened, it may be safe to assume that the recordset is pointing to the first record. The recordset may be advanced using the moveNext function of the recordset object. For each call of the moveNext command, the EOF condition must be inspected. If EOF is true, the recordset has been traversed to the end. Calling moveNext after EOF is encountered will result in an error. As long as the EOF is not true, the recordset may be advanced to the next record. When the database interaction is completed, both the recordset and the connection objects should be closed.

The result of running Listing 12-6 is a display in the browser of the first name, a space, and the last name for each record in the database table *tblEmployee*. The ASP file could be improved to support end-user submission of data to the data table. Refer to

Listing 12-7 for a part of an ASP, *ReadWriteDB.asp*, that lists the data in *tblEmployee* and allows the user to submit additional data for writing into the database.

Listing 12-7

```
Part of ReadWriteDB.asp Showing Main Entry Point of ASP

<HTML>
<HEAD>
<title>read and write to a database table</title>
</HEAD>
<BODY>

<%
'~~~~~~~~~~~~~~~~~~~~~~~~~~~~~~~~~~~~~~~~~~~~~~~~~~~~~~~~~
'main entry point to ASP
'~~~~~~~~~~~~~~~~~~~~~~~~~~~~~~~~~~~~~~~~~~~~~~~~~~~~~~~~~

dim myConn 'For ADO connection
dim sSQL 'For SQL command

dim sConn 'For database connection string

    'create connection string
    sConn = "Provider=Microsoft.Jet.OLEDB.4.0;"
    sConn = sConn & "Data Source=C:\aspData\employees.mdb;"

    'establish connection to database server
    Set myConn = Server.CreateObject("ADODB.Connection")
    myConn.Open sConn

    'get parameters from user submission
    AddData myConn

    'build SQL command to show what exists in database
    sSQL = "SELECT * FROM tblEmployee"

    'show the data
    ShowUserRecordset sSQL, myConn

%>
<FORM METHOD = "POST" ACTION = "ReadWriteDB.asp"
ID = "frmFields" NAME = "getInfo" >
<%
```

```
          'build the data entry table
          MakeDataEntryTable sSQL, myConn

          'close up connection since we are done
          myConn.Close()


'~~~~~~~~~~~~~~~~~~~~~~~~~~~~~~~~~~~~~~~~~~~~~~~~~~~~~~~
'End of ASP
'~~~~~~~~~~~~~~~~~~~~~~~~~~~~~~~~~~~~~~~~~~~~~~~~~~~~~~~
%>
<INPUT ID="subFull" NAME="subR" TYPE="submit" VALUE="Add" >
</FORM>
</body>
</html>
```

The file *ReadWriteDB.asp* has three other subroutines that were excluded from Listing 12-7 for the sake of brevity. Listing 12-7 shows the main entry point of the ASP *ReadWriteDB.asp,* where the ASP.DLL ISAPI extension begins to execute the server-side code. The additional subroutines used in ReadWriteDB.asp that were excluded from Listing 12-7 are as follows:

- **sub ShowUserRecordset**   Using the SQL command and the ADO Connection object instance passed in, this subroutine prints the contents of the recordset to the browser.

- **sub MakeDataEntryTable**   Using the SQL command and the Connection object instance passed in, this subroutine prints a table with the field names for the headings and inputs for the fields to the browser.

- **sub AddData**   This subroutine checks the Request object for data submission and inserts the user submitted data into the database table *tblEmployee*.

Writing Form Submission Data to a Database: sub AddData

After the comment block labeled *main entry point to the ASP,* the ASP code will instantiate the ADO database connection object and assign a variable named *myConn* to point at the object. The ADO connection will be passed into each subroutine so that each subroutine will be able to create their own ADO objects and connect them to the data source. After the connection object is instantiated, the *AddData* subroutine, shown in Listing 12-8, is called to check for data being submitted to the ASP.

Listing 12-8

```
Part of ReadWriteDB.asp - AddData Subroutine
Writing Data to Database


'~~~~~~~~~~~~~~~~~~~~~~~~~~~~~~~~~~~~~~~~~~~~~~~~~~~~~~~
```

```
'sub AddData
'Checks Request Object for data submission and inserts
'the user submitted data into the database table
'tblEmployee
'
'in
'     oConnection = ADO connection object
'out - nothing - writes to client
'~~~~~~~~~~~~~~~~~~~~~~~~~~~~~~~~~~~~~~~~~~~~~~~~~~~~~~
sub AddData(byval oConnection)

'check for data to write
if ((len(Request("number"))< 1) or _
    (len(Request("phone"))< 1) or _
    (len(Request("first_name"))< 1) or _
    (len(Request("last_name"))< 1)) then
    exit sub
end if


dim myCommand
dim sSQL

    'create the Command object
    set myCommand = Server.CreateObject("ADODB.Command")
    set myCommand.ActiveConnection = oConnection

    'build the insert statement
    sSQL = "INSERT INTO tblEmployee ("
    sSQL = sSQL & "[number], [phone], [first_name], [last_name])"
    sSQL = sSQL & " VALUES ('" & Request("number")
    sSQL = sSQL & "','" & Request("phone")
    sSQL = sSQL & "','" & Request("first_name")
    sSQL = sSQL & "','" & Request("last_name")& "')"


    'put the command in the command object
    myCommand.CommandText = sSQL

    'execute the query
    myCommand.Execute

end sub
```

In the subroutine *AddData*, the Request object is checked for the expected parameters, which in this case are *number*, *phone*, *first_name*, and *last_name*. If any one of the parameters is missing, the subroutine is exited. The existence of the parameters is determined by checking whether the length of any one of them is less than one character. If all parameters are at least one character in length, the ADO command object will be instantiated.

Using the Command Object   The ADO command object is useful for executing SQL commands or performing other types of tasks, whereby a command is sent to the database server but a recordset response is not always needed. The command object can return a recordset, too, but as in the case whereby it is being used in this example, an Update SQL command will be passed to the database for execution. The SQL command is created by concatenating all of the parts of the string necessary to generate an update SQL statement that looks like the following:

```
INSERT INTO tblEmployee ([number],[phone],[first_name],[last_name])
VALUES ('8','444-4444','Tosa','Bergstaff')
```

The values cited in the VALUES section of the SQL command are extracted from the request object. After the SQL command is assembled, it is stuffed in the Command object's *CommandText* property and fired by using the Command object's *Execute* function. If everything goes well, the values should be written to the database. Failure generally means that some entity involved in the database transaction, like a server, was not present or identified incorrectly. This type of failure can stem from network connectivity problems or from the developer incorrectly typing the name of a table or field in the code.

Code Practices and "Hardcoding"   The subroutine *AddData* has a limited scope of service, because it has the name of the table that it updates and the parameter names that are being requested from the Request object written in the code as well. Many programmers refer to this practice as *hardcoding,* or the values may be referred to as *magic values* or *literals.* In general, the practice of hardcoding is performed for the sake of expediency and reliability of execution, but most often it should be avoided. Literals that are dependent on a given deployment of the application should be replaced and set up as configuration settings for the application that may be changed without requiring a code edit.

Reading Data from Database to Display in a Browser: sub ShowUserRecordset

After the submitted data is written to the database, *ReadWriteDB.asp* builds a SQL command to read all the data from the table *tblEmployee*. The SQL command is assigned to the variable *sSQL*. The connection object *MyConn* and the SQL command `sSQL` are both passed to the subroutine named *ShowUserRecordset*. Both arguments are passed *byval,* so there is no chance that their value will be altered in the subroutine.

ShowUserRecordset will accept any SQL command and ADO Connection object, and it will open a recordset on the SQL command and write out the values in the recordset to the browser. Refer to Listing 12-9 for the code in the subroutine *ShowUserRecordset*.

Listing 12-9

```
Part of ReadWriteDB.asp - ShowUserRecordset Subroutine
Reading Database and Showing Recordset

'~~~~~~~~~~~~~~~~~~~~~~~~~~~~~~~~~~~~~~~~~~~~~~~~~~~~~~~~~
'sub ShowUserRecordset
'Using the SQL command and the Connection object
'instance passed in, prints the contents of the
'recordset to the browser
'
'in
'      sSQL = SQL command for recordset
'      oConnection = ADO connection object
'out - nothing - writes to client
'~~~~~~~~~~~~~~~~~~~~~~~~~~~~~~~~~~~~~~~~~~~~~~~~~~~~~~~~~
sub ShowUserRecordset(byval sSQL, byval oConnection)

dim myRecordset
dim sResult
dim oField

    'create the recordset
    set myRecordset = Server.CreateObject("ADODB.Recordset")
    myRecordset.Open sSQL, oConnection

    'write out the headings
    for each oField in myRecordset.Fields
        sResult = sResult & oField.Name & "          "
    next
    Response.Write(sResult & "<br/>" )

    'check to see if there are records
    if( not myRecordset.EOF and not myRecordset.EOF) then

        'make certain that we are not at the end
        while(not myRecordset.EOF)

            'build output string
            sResult=""
```

```
                    for each oField in myRecordset.Fields
                     sResult = sResult & myRecordset(oField.Name) & " "
                    next
                    sResult = sResult & "<br />"

                    'write value to browser
                    Response.write(sResult)

                    'advance recordset
                    myRecordset.moveNext()
             wend
        else
             Response.write("No records in table <br>")
        end if

        Response.write("<hr>")

        'shut down recordset and connection objects
        myRecordset.Close()
    end sub
```

ADO Recordset Traversing Techniques   *ShowUserRecordset* in Listing 12-9 is a superior subroutine compared to *AddData* because the SQL command is passed into the subroutine instead of being hardcoded in the subroutine. *ShowUserRecordset* still has flaws because it contains literals that relate to logic display and the COM object name for the ADO recordset COM object. After an instance of an ADO recordset is created and opened using the SQL passed in via the *sSQL* parameter, the field names of the recordset are obtained and listed into a string variable named *sResult*. The purpose of *sResult* is to assemble text that will eventually be written to the browser using the Response.Write command. The ADO recordset supports a collection called *Fields*, which contains all of the fields that make up the recordset. A technique was used to loop through all of the fields in the collection that could have been used in the *WriteCollection* subroutine demonstrated in Listing 12-2. A variant may be used as an index value in a For...Next loop that uses this pseudo-code form:

```
For each <variant> in <a collection>
```

As all variables in VBScript are variants, any declared variable could act as a suitable indexing variable for a collection. The variable *oField* specifically was declared for the purposes of acting as an index in the For...Next loop used to access the *Fields* collection of *MyRecordset* in *ShowUserRecordset*. After the resulting string of field names is written to the browser, the recordset is checked for records and a While...Wend loop is started to loop through the records. Embedded in the While...Wend loop is another

For…Next loop using the *MyRecordSet* Fields Collection. The Fields Collection loop is used to specify the field name in the recordset for the purposes of obtaining a value that may be appended to the *sResult* string. Each iteration of the While…Wend results in a line being written to the browser that represents a single row from the recordset that was opened.

> **Note** *A common problem for many programmers, even after many occasions of writing software code that loops through a recordset, is that they forget to advance the recordset. The line myRecordset.moveNext() advances the recordset in Listing 12-9. If the moveNext() line was left out, the code would begin an infinite loop. This mistake is a common one, because the* moveNext () *command requires little thought on the part of the coder. It is one of those issues that requires so little thought as to the strategy for placing it that it is often forgotten.*

When the recordset has been traversed and the content of the recordset is written to the browser, the recordset should be shut down using the close() command of the recordset object. The instance of the recordset is destroyed when the variable pointing to the instance of the *myRecordset* goes out of scope. The variable goes out of scope when the subroutine *ShowUserRecordset* ends. Relying on the resources supporting the class instance being freed from memory when the variable goes out of scope is not a good idea, however, because the resource is not always freed right away when it is shut down in this manner. The close() command should be used to ensure that the database connection is closed and the resources that the connection was occupying may be used elsewhere.

Parsing ADO Recordset to Build Data Entry Form: sub MakeDataEntryTable

After the *ShowUserRecordset* subroutine is called, the *ReadWriteDB.asp* places an HTML form element on the browser page so that the end user can make a submission to the server. The purpose for the *AddData* subroutine is to accept the data submitted from the HTML form on the web page. The HTML form used for collecting the data from the end user must match the form of the dataset being updated. In this particular situation, the inputs for user submission are all named the same as the field names in the database table from which they relate. The subroutine *MakeDataEntryTable* produces the HTML table that contains the headings representing the recordset field names that are part of the recordset that is generated from the SQL statement passed into the subroutine. This subroutine uses the same looping mechanism as the subroutine *ShowUserRecordset* to build the HTML table. Refer to Listing 12-10 for a listing of the subroutine *MakeDataEntryTable*.

Listing 12-10

```
Part of ReadWriteDB.asp - MakeDataEntryTable Subroutine
Serializing a Recordset into an HTML Table


'~~~~~~~~~~~~~~~~~~~~~~~~~~~~~~~~~~~~~~~~~~~~~~~~~~~~~~~~~~~~~~~~
```

```
'sub MakeDataEntryTable
'Using the SQL command and the Connection object
'instance passed in, prints a table with the field
'names for the headings and inputs for the fields.
'
'in
'      sSQL = SQL command for recordset
'      oConnection = ADO connection object
'out - nothing - writes to client
'~~~~~~~~~~~~~~~~~~~~~~~~~~~~~~~~~~~~~~~~~~~~~~~~~~~~~~~~
sub MakeDataEntryTable(byval sSQL, byval oConnection)

dim myRecordset
dim sResult
dim oField


    'create the recordset
    set myRecordset = Server.CreateObject("ADODB.Recordset")
    myRecordset.Open sSQL, oConnection

    'build a table for user to enter values
    sResult = "<TABLE BORDER=0 CELLSPACING=0 CELLPADDING=0 >" &_
                                                        vbCRLF
    sResult = sResult & "<TR>"

    'make the headings
    for each oField in myRecordset.Fields
        sResult = sResult & "<TH>" & oField.Name & "</TH>"
    next

    'make a new row
    sResult = sResult & "</TR>" & vbCRLF & "<TR>"

    'make the user inputs
    for each oField in myRecordset.Fields
        sResult = sResult & _
                    "<TD> <input TYPE=""text"" NAME=""" & _
                    oField.Name & """ VALUE="""">"</TD>"
    next

    sResult = sResult & "</TABLE>"
```

```
    Response.Write(sResult)

    'shut down recordset and connection objects
    myRecordset.Close()

end sub
```

Running *ReadWriteDB.asp* will build a screen on the browser that shows the existing values in the database table, a line, a table with the field names and input boxes in the second row, and an Add button. Clicking the Add button without placing any data in all of the text boxes results in a screen refresh. Placing data in all four input boxes will result in data being written to the database table *tblEmployee* after the Add button is clicked. Figure 12-12 shows a screen shot of data being entered in *ReadWriteDB.asp*.

Code Practices—Logic Abstraction and Extendibility   The subroutines *ShowUserRecordset* and *MakeDataEntryTable* are both written so that they will support any recordset and connection object. They may be used in other applications where the same action and output is desired, without requiring a code edit. The database table may also change shape, and these subroutines will still function without requiring a

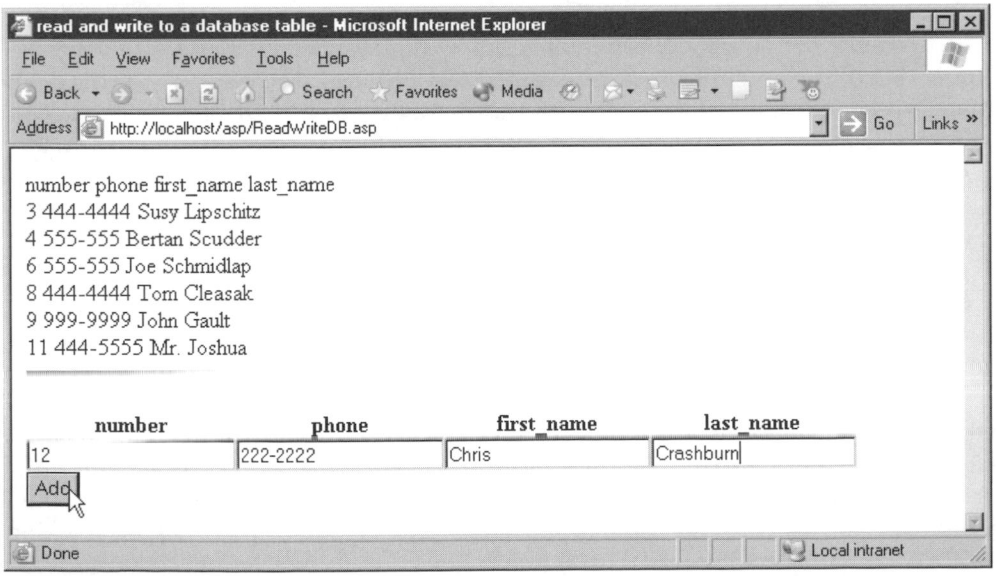

Figure 12-12.   *ReadWriteDB.asp displayed in browser before update*

code edit. The subroutines are still quite limited in terms of their usefulness in other applications, however, because they contain display logic. Most other needs for a web application require an alternative user interface. Abstracting the presentation logic from the subroutines would make them much more useful across a wide scope of applications. Code that is useful across multiple scopes of application is called *extendible* code. Abstracting various portions of logic generally affords greater extendibility in code but usually at the expense of performance and speed of development.

Using XML

One technology that is useful for abstracting display logic is XML. XML is not a type of code, although many programmers say that they know how to program in XML. Instead, XML is a hierarchical format used for describing data using text. Data described using XML has many benefits over other formats for data storage. XML is portable among operating systems. Text is a format that all operating systems can understand and parse. XML may be validated by software using a set of rules. XML should also be readable by a human being. XML may also be parsed and constructed using a common set of rules that may be documented or described to many potential consumers of the XML so that they can reliably parse the XML to perform data manipulation activities on the data.

XML has some disadvantages, too, in that it requires much more storage space than any of the comparative technologies it seeks to replace such as comma delimited or fixed width text. XML also requires a great deal of resources to parse and serialize. To illustrate the benefits and disadvantages of XML, it can be compared to a comma-delimited text file. Both the comma-delimited text file and XML file are text based, and as such, both are usable on any operating system. Both can be the result of the data stored in a database table serialized into each respective data format. The XML file will be three to five times larger than the comma-delimited version of the same data set, because no descriptors are used in the comma-delimited file for each row and field value of data, as would exist in an XML file. Parsing the XML will take much longer as well, based on its sheer size difference alone over the comma-delimited version.

Given a scenario in which an XML file and a comma-delimited file are sent for use to other third-party consumers, however, what would happen if another column was added to the database table that was the source of the two respective files? The comma-delimited file would likely end up with another column added to either side or somewhere in the middle, depending on the export logic used to create the comma-delimited file. The XML file would also have additional data, but since each data value in an XML document is explicitly defined and generally XML is parsed in an explicit way, there would likely be no failures arising from a consumer as long as the rules for creating the XML were followed. In contrast, the software parsing the comma-delimited file will likely fail because the format is not what the software was designed to expect.

Making a Transformation Using XSL

XML can provide abstraction of display logic by allowing the display logic to exist in another file. Using software that combines the XML and the display logic using a known instruction set, the XML may be transformed into any other type of document, such as an HTML document. Some of the known instruction sets in use are Extensible Stylesheet Language (XSL) or Extensible Stylesheet Language Transformation (XSLT). The display logic resides in the XSL sheet or XSLT sheet. The abstraction of display logic enables programmers to develop web applications from the perspective of producing XML documents that are meant to describe data or some object. The user interface may change as needed without necessitating a code change anywhere but in the XSL or XSLT file.

For an example of a simple transformation performed in an ASP, refer to Listing 12-11.

Listing 12-11

```
XMLToHTML.asp - Simple XML to HTML Transformation
Performed in an ASP

<%@ Language=VBScript %>
<HTML>
<HEAD>
</HEAD>
<BODY>
<%

dim oXMLDoc
dim oXMLXSL

    Set oXMLDoc = Server.CreateObject("Microsoft.XMLDOM")
    Set oXMLXSL = Server.CreateObject("Microsoft.XMLDOM")

    oXMLDoc.load(Server.MapPath("employees.xml"))
    oXMLXSL.load(Server.MapPath("employeesDisplay.xsl"))

    Response.Write( oXMLDoc.transformNode(oXMLXSL) )

%>
</BODY>
</HTML>
```

The ASP page named *XMLtoHTML.asp,* shown in Listing 12-11, creates an instance of the *XMLDOM* class. The *XMLDOM* class is part of Microsoft's MSXML library that is used to convert XML and XSL or XSLT into HTML. MSXML is a collection of classes and other software that also provides XML parsing, validation, construction, and other useful XML functions. The load function of the *XMLDOM* class is called using the complete filename as the argument to the function. The file being loaded resides in the web root, so the *Server.MapPath* function was called to get the whole physical path and filename to the XML file. The load function of the *XMLDOM* class can accept a string that contains an XML document as the argument or a string that contains the complete filename as the argument.

Refer to Listing 12-12 for the contents of the XML file that was loaded in this example.

Listing 12-12

```
employees.xml - tblEmployee Data Serialized into an XML Document

<?xml version="1.0"?>
<Recordset Table = "MyMembership"
           Command = "Select * From tblEmployee">
    <Row number = "3" phone = "444-4444"
         first_name = "Susy" last_name = "Lipschitz" />
    <Row number = "4" phone = "444-555"
         first_name = "Bertan" last_name = "Scudder" />
    <Row number = "6" phone = "444-4444 "
         first_name = "Joe" last_name = "Schmidlap" />
    <Row number = "8" phone = "444-4444 "
         first_name = "Tom" last_name = "Cleasak" />
</Recordset>
```

This document is a simple XML document that describes the employees that were extracted from the *tblEmployee* table in Listing 12-10.

The same effort that was devoted to creating the class instance and loading the XML document was also performed on the XSL style sheet. XSL is also an XML document, so the *XMLDOM* class treats the file the same as the XML document. Refer to Listing 12-13 for the contents of the XSL file that was loaded in this example.

Listing 12-13

```
employeesDisplay.xsl - XSL Stylesheet to Make HTML from tblEmployee
XML Document

<?xml version="1.0"?>
<xsl:stylesheet xmlns:xsl="http://www.w3.org/TR/WD-xsl">
```

```xml
<xsl:template match="/">

<xsl:for-each select="Recordset">

<P><xsl:value-of select="@Table"/>
<br/><xsl:value-of select="@Command"/><br/>
</P>

<TABLE BORDER="1" CELLSPACING="0" CELLPADDING="0">
    <TR>
        <TH>Number</TH>
        <TH>Phone</TH>
        <TH>First Name</TH>
        <TH>Last Name</TH>
    </TR>

    <xsl:for-each select="Row">
        <TR>
            <TD><xsl:value-of select="@number"/></TD>
            <TD><xsl:value-of select="@phone"/></TD>
            <TD><xsl:value-of select="@first_name"/></TD>
            <TD><xsl:value-of select="@last_name"/></TD>

        </TR>
    </xsl:for-each>

</TABLE>
</xsl:for-each>

</xsl:template>
</xsl:stylesheet>
```

Once both the XSL and the XML documents are loaded into their own separate class instances of the *XMLDOM* class, the *transformnode* function is called from the *XMLDOM* instance that contains the XML document. The *XMLDOM* class instance that contains the XSL document is used as the argument to the *transformnode* function call, and the resulting string that is returned from *transformnode* is an HTML document. The product of the XSL and the XML document as it is displayed in a web browser can be seen in Figure 12-13.

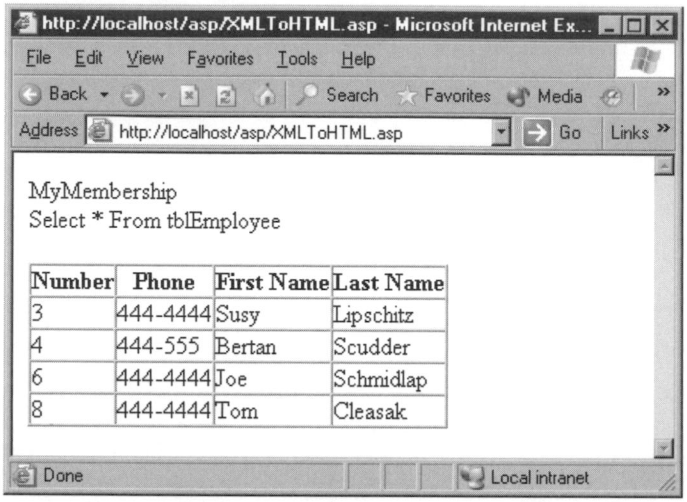

Figure 12-13.   *Resulting display of transformed XML into HTML in web browser*

The HTML that was created from the XML shown in Listing 12-12 and the XSL shown in Listing 12-13 being transformed is shown in Listing 12-14.

Listing 12-14

```
HTML Resulting from XSL employeesDisplay.xsl and
XML employees.xml Document Transformation

<HTML>
<HEAD>
</HEAD>
<BODY>
<P>MyMembership
<br />Select * From tblEmployee<br />
</P>
<TABLE BORDER="1" CELLSPACING="0" CELLPADDING="0">
<TR>
<TH>Number</TH>
<TH>Phone</TH>
<TH>First Name</TH>
<TH>Last Name</TH>
</TR>
```

```
<TR>
<TD>3</TD>
<TD>444-4444</TD>
<TD>Susy</TD>
<TD>Lipschitz</TD>
</TR>
<TR>
<TD>4</TD>
<TD>444-555</TD>
<TD>Bertan</TD>
<TD>Scudder</TD>
</TR>
<TR>
<TD>6</TD>
<TD>444-4444</TD>
<TD>Joe</TD>
<TD>Schmidlap</TD>
</TR>
<TR>
<TD>8</TD>
<TD>444-4444</TD>
<TD>Tom</TD>
<TD>Cleasak</TD>
</TR>
</TABLE>

</BODY>
</HTML>
```

Chapter 13

COM Web Programming

Component Object Model (COM) is a specification developed by Microsoft and used for building software components that can be consumed by programs or existing Windows-based programs to enhance functionality. Using COM, software written in one language (such as C++) can also use software written in another language (such as Visual Basic) without having to recompile either piece of software. This means, for example, that a dynamic-link library (DLL) written in C++ code could be called by an executable written in Visual Basic, or in the case of Active Server Pages (ASP), VBScript could call a function from a COM object written in VB, C++, or any language. COM web programming is accomplished by using ASP to call functions in COM objects.

The *D* in *DCOM* stands for *distributed*. DCOM works the same way as COM from the software construction and consumption perspective, and it differs from COM only in terms of deployment and server configuration. Using DCOM simply means that COM objects hosted on other physical hosts are *consumed*.

Note Consumed, *or "to consume," is the term that is often used when referring to software calling functions in a DLL other type of library. You can view it as an adaptation of the client-server terminology used to describe the interaction with a database client (software that requests data or inputs data) and a database. The terms* consumer *and* provider *have become the nomenclature used to describe the software entities that exist in an interaction between software that relies on other software to function and software that is designed to serve other software.*

Constrasted to conventional ASP programming (described in Chapter 12), COM web programming uses ASP as a dispatching system. ASP marshals Hypertext Transfer Protocol (HTTP) requests into commands, consumes COM objects that perform work, and returns a response to the client. The advantage of this system is that the software in the COM object is encapsulated as a single discrete entity that may be added or removed from a system as a whole. The software may be coded, tested, documented, and deployed so that other programmers can use the software and not change it, as the source code is not available in the software distribution. Depending on the language that was used to build the COM object, the machine instructions inside are likely to be binary instructions that are executed with greater performance than can be expected with a scripting language such as VBScript in an ASP.

The architecture of a typical COM web application is shown in Figure 13-1.

The most common way that COM web programming is used today is by writing ActiveX DLLs using Visual Basic version 6 (VB6). Although COM objects can be written in many different languages, this chapter will feature the use of VB6. VB6 will compile into a native language binary, and the programmer is totally insulated from the complexities of working with the COM Interface Description Language (IDL) or managing the architecture of the object itself. VB6 is a well-known language, and the VB Integrated Design Environment (IDE) is easy enough to use that anyone can write, compile, and run the program without being very astute in the ways of building software.

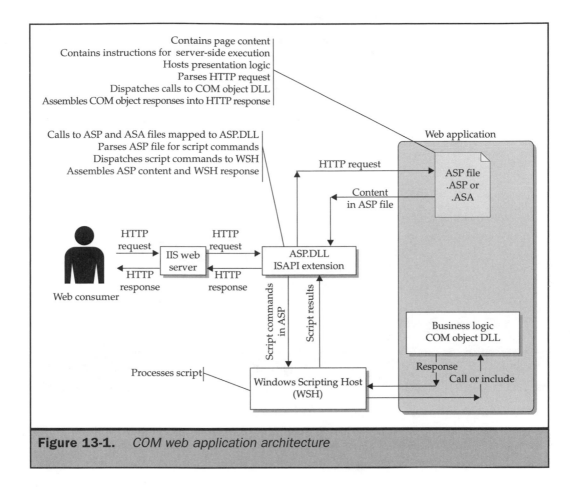

Contains page content
Contains instructions for server-side execution
Hosts presentation logic
Parses HTTP request
Dispatches calls to COM object DLL
Assembles COM object responses into HTTP response

Calls to ASP and ASA files mapped to ASP.DLL
Parses ASP file for script commands
Dispatches script commands to WSH
Assembles ASP content and WSH response

Web application

HTTP request

Content
in ASP file

ASP file
.ASP or
.ASA

HTTP
request

HTTP
request

HTTP
response

HTTP
response

IIS web
server

ASP.DLL
ISAPI extension

Web consumer

Script commands
in ASP

Script results

Business logic
COM object DLL

Processes script

Windows Scripting Host
(WSH)

Response

Call or include

Figure 13-1.   *COM web application architecture*

IIS PROGRAMMING

Note   *An Active X DLL is a project template in VB6 that allows a programmer to produce a COM object.*

Introduction to VB6

After you open VB6, a New Project dialog box (Figure 13-2) prompts you to choose a project type. For building COM objects for use with a web application, choose ActiveX DLL and then click Open.

VB6 allows you to create many other types of projects, ranging from executables to ActiveX controls. Most of the project types, such as ActiveX EXE and Standard EXE (executables), are best suited for desktop development. An executable project will be used later in this chapter for generating a test harness for an ActiveX DLL. An ActiveX Control project will generate an ActiveX control that may be deployed to a web browser

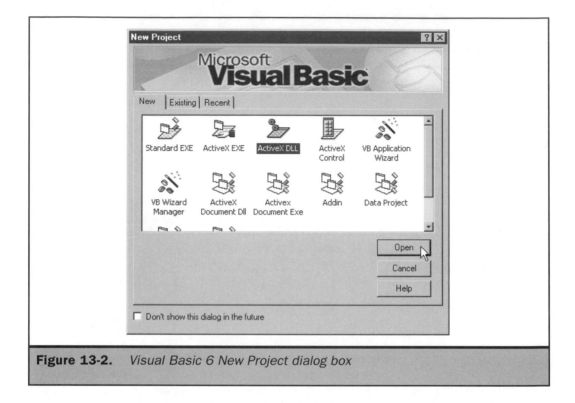

Figure 13-2. Visual Basic 6 New Project dialog box

or used in desktop applications. Due to the constraints of deployment with the VB runtime, ActiveX controls written in VB are not well suited for web deployment, since a restart is often required after installation for the client to use the new Active X control.

Setting Up an ActiveX DLL Project

After you choose to create an ActiveX DLL project, VB6 will create a new project named *Project1* and a new class named *Class1*. If the project were to be compiled immediately, the default name for the DLL would be *Project1.dll* and the class identifier, or CLSID, that would be used to identify the class in the ASP command *Server.CreateObject* would be *Project1.Class1*. The class and the project names, however, should be meaningful rather than these nondescript default names. The class should be named after a real-world entity that is part of the solution that is being built. The project should be named in a way that defines the container or deployment file within which the class will reside.

Note *All COM Objects made from an Active X DLL project in VB6 have .dll as a file extension.*

In this example, suppose the web application is part of a web-based furniture configuration project named *ConfigSeat*. A chair object was identified in the requirements-gathering effort, and the class being built is to represent the chair that might be part of the software's business logic. A good name for this class is *clsChair*. The *cls* prefix is useful because it identifies the object as a class. The Auto List Members of Visual Basic's IntelliSense shows the names of the parts of a project and will not distinguish between classes and other types of files that could exist in a given VB project, such as a module. Using the *cls* prefix will help make the task of identifying the class in the Auto List Members list easier to identify.

To change the default class name, open the Properties window by choosing View | Properties Window, and select the class in the Project Explorer. Change the name *Class1* in the Name section to *clsChair*, as shown in Figure 13-3. (The other properties in the Properties window should remain unedited. Changing the values of these settings requires advanced knowledge of VB ActiveX development and is beyond the scope of this chapter.)

In addition to the class name change, the project name can also be changed. Right-click the project name in the Project Explorer and choose Properties. In the Project Properties dialog box, under the General tab, is a Project Name text box, in which the

Figure 13-3.   *Properties window for class clsChair*

default name *Project1* should appear. For this example project, *ConfigSeat* is a good project name. Delete the name *Project1* and type **ConfigSeat** in the text box, as shown in Figure 13-4.

Many programmers are unaware of the automatic version numbering capabilities offered by VB6. The benefits of this feature are great, and the effort to enable it is minimal. The version number helps to determine which version of the DLL is the latest and provides a unique identifier as to the version of the DLL that should be used. Each time the software is compiled, the version number will be advanced. As is often the case, a COM object will be deployed multiple times to a host. Since you only want one version being used by the software consumers, the version number helps to ensure that there is only one version and that the version used will be the latest version, which has the highest number. If there are no version numbers, the file date is used to determine the newest version. Sometimes there are situations that occur, especially when there are multiple programmers working on a given project, where the host will not use the latest version and the file date is not an accurate identifier of the latest version. To enable automatic versioning, click the Make tab in the Project Properties dialog box. Choose the Auto Increment checkbox. It generates a new version number for the project each time it is compiled. Not checking this box does *not* cause any failure to occur in the software. Even though the Auto Increment checkbox is not checked by default, it should be checked for every project as a matter of good practice.

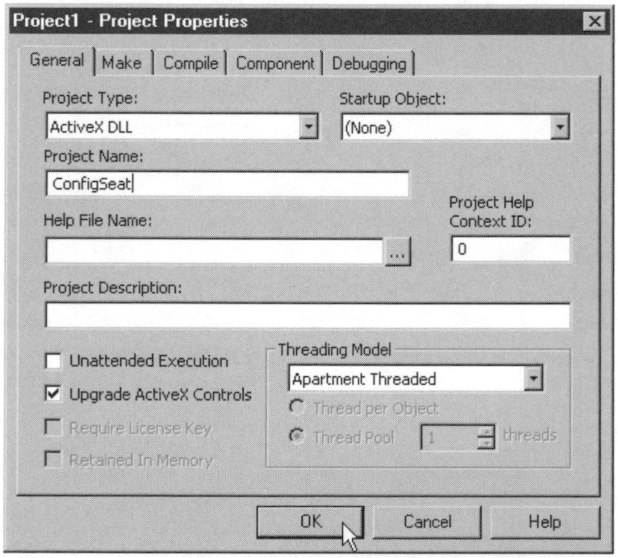

Figure 13-4. *Project Properties dialog box with the new name ConfigSeat*

Creating a Class Interface in an ActiveX DLL

The chair object also has some attributes, such as color, height, and whether or not wheels are attached. These attributes can be added to the class as *properties*. Here's how to enhance the class *clsChair* by adding a property for color:

1. Choose Tools | Add Procedure.
2. Type the name of the property in the Name text box, as shown in Figure 13-5.
3. Choose Property in the Type area.
4. Choose Public in the Scope area.
5. Click OK and code should appear in the code window, showing framework code for *Let* and *Get* properties.

Object Browser

A *property* is a special pair of functions that are designed to emulate a single attribute for the class when other software is consuming it. One function is used for reading the value and the other function is used for writing the value. Press the F2 button to open a special viewer called the Object Browser, which shows the interface to all of the software that is being used in the project open in the VB IDE. In Figure 13-6, the *ConfigSeat* library is selected in the top-left combo box, and the class *clsChair* is listed in the Classes list on the left side of the window.

Select the *clsChair* class to reveal the newly added property named *color* in the right pane. Select the *color* property, and the summary area at the bottom of the window describes the property in detail, identifying the type of parameter that *color* must be and the class and library to which it belongs.

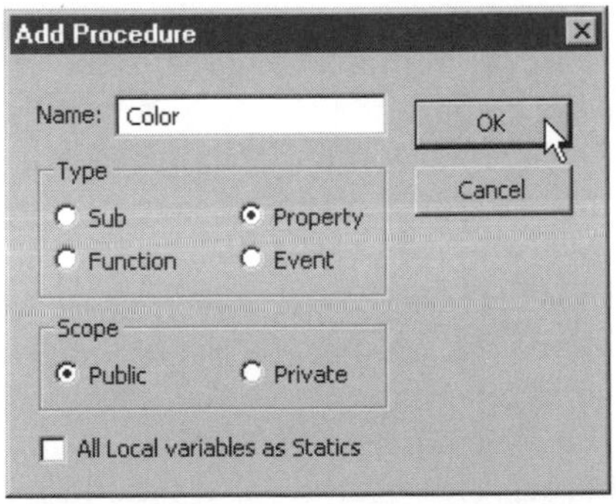

Figure 13-5. Add Procedure dialog box, with Color property

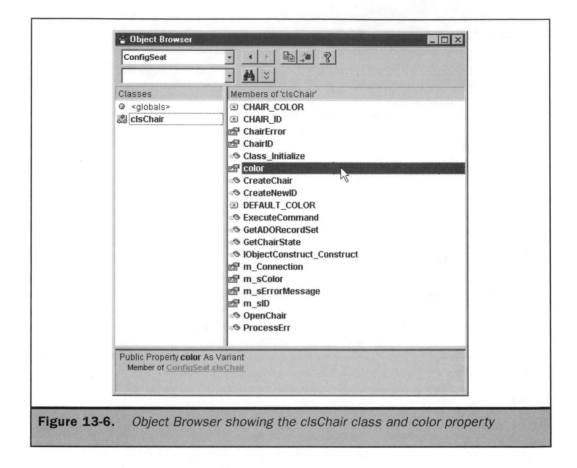

Figure 13-6. *Object Browser showing the clsChair class and color property*

The *color* property as it currently exists in the *clsChair* class is pretty worthless, because no variables have been set to hold the value of the property. Without variables, setting a value for the property or getting a value from it will result in nothing being stored or acquired from the property. Because the property is used to change a value in the class that will exist in memory while the class is instantiated, a local variable must be declared that has scope over the entire class.

The *color* values are strings that describe the color of the chair, so a private string variable named *m_sColor* will be declared at the top of the class listing. This variable will hold the value of the chair's color. The keyword *private* makes the variable inaccessible by software outside of the class itself. The scope *private* is useful to control how consumers access class members, properties, subroutines, and functions. The class may need to change other values or validate the color when it is set, and if the local variable *m_sColor* were public, the consumer of the class could change the value of *m_sColor* and the class would not know it.

It is a good practice to always use a property to allow an attribute in a class to be set or read. In the short term, it adds an additional burden to the programmer to code it and may also increase the complexity of the solution, but doing this will pay off by making changing the class less difficult in the future. If the business rules for the class were to change in the future, updates to the COM object would be much easier behind the COM public interface because code hidden behind the property functions could be used to alter the meaning of the class attribute without changing the public interface to the class. Changing the interface of the class requires the consumers of the class to be changed also, so the long-term burden for not maintaining this abstraction between the class's internal members and the class's external interface can be greater than the initial burden.

Listing 13-1 shows the code that creates the class *clsChair*.

Listing 13-1

```
clsChair With Support to Read and Write the Color to the Instance
Option Explicit


'~~~~~~~~~~~~~~~~~~~~~~~~~~~~~~~~~~~~~~
'    constants to class

Private Const DEFAULT_COLOR = "Brown"


'~~~~~~~~~~~~~~~~~~~~~~~~~~~~~~~~~~~~~~
'    locals to class

'holds the color of the chair
Private m_sColor As String


'~~~~~~~~~~~~~~~~~~~~~~~~~~~~~~~~~~~~~~

Public Property Get color() As Variant
    color = m_sColor
End Property
Public Property Let color(ByVal vNewValue As Variant)
    m_sColor = vNewValue
End Property

Private Sub Class_Initialize()
    'set default color on instantiation
    m_sColor = DEFAULT_COLOR
End Sub
```

It is a good practice in VB to place the statement *Option Explicit* at the top of each code file. This statement causes VB to check for undeclared variables being used in the code at compile time. If any undeclared variables are found, VB will fail to complete the compile and provide an error message. This statement helps the programmer by enforcing the use of declared variables so that if a variable was misspelled, for example, VB would catch it—the misspelled version would likely not be declared. You might spend hours attempting to figure out why a variable does not contain a value when it should, only to discover that the variable that was assigned the value was misspelled in a critical line of code. Tracking these types of bugs is difficult, so the *Option Explicit* command is useful at eliminating these types of situations. You can set VB to add this statement automatically to the top of every code file by choosing Tools | Options, opening the Editor tab, and checking the Require Variable Declaration checkbox.

Building a Test Harness

All software should be tested, and the VB IDE offers a great mechanism for testing. Click the Start button on the toolbar in VB, or press F5, to cause VB to compile and run the software being coded in VB.

Because the project *ConfigSeat* is an ActiveX DLL, it cannot execute; instead, it must be consumed by another program that can execute. To test the class *clsChair*, another project should be created in the same IDE instance in which *clsChair* is being edited. The project needs to be an executable software program whose sole purpose is to test the class *clsChair*. A program that tests another program is often referred to as a *test harness*.

1. In Visual Basic, choose File | Add Project to open the Add Project dialog box.

2. In the New tab, choose the project template Standard Exe. A new project is created, called *Project1*, that includes a form called *Form1*.

3. In the Project Explorer, right-click the new project and choose Set As Start Up.

4. Rename the project *clsChairTester*.

5. Currently, the *clsChair* class is not accessible in the test harness *clsChairTester* because the test harness does not have a reference to the *ConfigSeat* project. To set this reference, choose Project | References to open the project's References dialog box shown in Figure 13-7.

6. Choose the reference for the library *ConfigSeat* by checking the box next to it, and then click OK.

Remember *Opening the References dialog box will open the references for the currently selected project only. Editing the references applies to the currently selected project only. Other projects within a project group might become the currently selected project if a code file is selected from the respective project by an inadvertent slip of the mouse. The name of the active project window is also shown in the References dialog box title bar. Be sure to verify that the appropriate References dialog box is opened before you make any changes.*

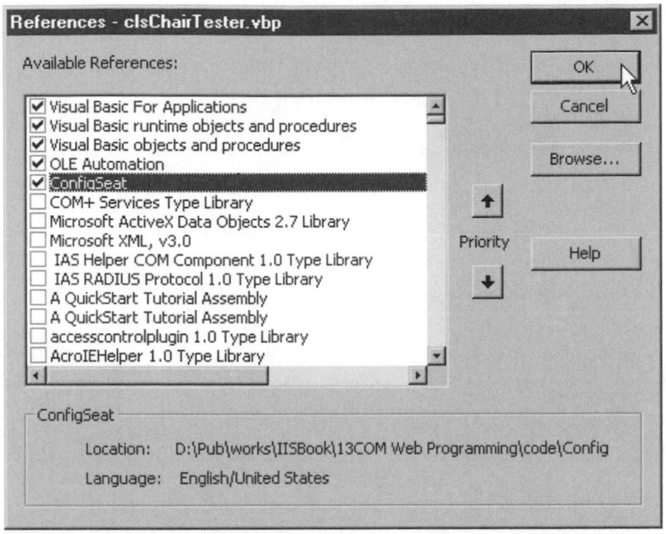

Figure 13-7.   *Project References dialog box*

The *form1* may be manipulated to show how various parts of the class *clsChair* function. A good strategy is to represent all class properties as text boxes and all functions as buttons, with text boxes for the arguments on the test harness form for the respective class. The test harness should be stored with the source code for the class that it tests, since it may be useful to future efforts to enhance or fix the class.

Note   *This test harness,* clsChairTester, *is stored with the source code of this chapter and will be made available on the author's web site as mentioned in the book's Introduction.*

Because only one property exists to the class *clsChair*, the test harness will simply show and set the value of the property to the user. After pasting a few text boxes and a command button on the form, and writing code to create and manipulate the class *clsChair* according to the user interaction, you can test the chair component using the test harness.

1. Press F5 to start the test harness. The output shows that the object was created successfully and the color of the chair is set to *Brown*.

2. Type in a new color and click the Set New Color button.

Please refer to Figure 13-8 to see the test harness demonstrating the color property being changed successfully in a few tests.

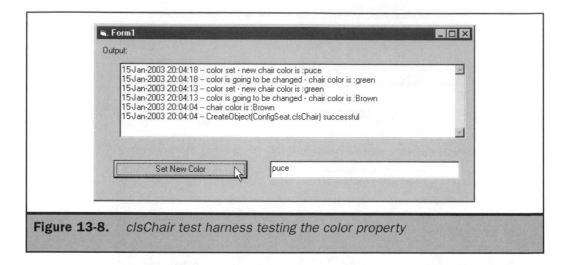

Figure 13-8.   *clsChair test harness testing the color property*

Deploying a COM DLL

Now that the *clsChair* class has passed the unit test in the test harness, it's almost ready to be used in a web application. Before it can be used, however, the class must be compiled and placed on the hosting server. Here's how to deploy class *clsChair*:

1. In the Project Explorer, choose the *ConfigSeat* project.
2. Choose File | Make ConfigSeat.dll.
3. The Make Project dialog box will open and prompt you for the file name and the location for the new DLL. Edit the filename or the file path if you want and click OK.

   VB will compile the ConfigSeat project and produce a *.dll* file based on the name and location specified in step 3. The DLL will also be automatically registered on the host so you can use the new DLL immediately. (Registering a DLL will be covered in the next section.)

4. Copy the new DLL to the host server. The DLL does not have to reside under the web root; you can place it anywhere on the host, but it is a good idea to choose a directory that is not under the web root and that is clearly designated as a storage location for binary components for the web application. Placing COM binaries under the web root also exposes an unnecessary risk if a failure occurred in the configuration of the web server, allowing the possibility of the COM binary to be accessed and downloaded by a web user.

Using regsvr32

After copying *ConfigSeat.dll* to the server, the DLL must either be registered or loaded into Component Services as a COM+ application. To register a component, Microsoft created a command-line utility called *regsvr32.exe*. Here's how to run the utility:

1. Open a command window, or choose Start | Run.

2. Type **regsvr32 *<name of COM DLL>*** (replacing *<name of COM DLL>* with the COM DLL filename). If you kept the name ConfigSeat.dll, then the command would be **regsvr32 ConfigSeat.dll** if your command window cursor was at the same directory that ConfigSeat.dll resides. If you are running regsvr32 from another location on the server other than the location where the COM DLL is located, you will have to type the whole file path to the *.dll* file in the command. For example, if ConfigSeat.dll were placed at C:\bin\, the command that should be executed is **regsvr32 C:\bin\ConfigSeat.dll**.

3. Press ENTER to register the COM DLL.

4. A message should pop-up in a dialog box indicating a successful registration occurred. Click OK to dismiss the dialog box.

If you want to remove the COM object DLL or replace it with another COM object DLL, you should unregister the COM object DLL and delete the file. Unregistering a COM object DLL removes the CLSID entry for the COM object DLL from the registry, thereby minimizing the entries in the registry. You can perform this action using the same steps for registering except that you must use the /u switch in the command. For example, if the file C:\bin\ConfigSeat.dll needed to be unregistered, the command would be **regsvr32 /u C:\bin\ConfigSeat.dll**. If you want to see the available switches for the regsvr32 command, execute the command without any parameters as follows: **regsvr32**. A pop-up dialog box will display the switches and how they affect the execution of regsvr32.

Using *regsvr32* is not complicated, and it works without a hitch. It is an ideal solution for scenarios that don't require management and overview of the COM object. Registering COM objects using *regsvr32* is a perfectly acceptable solution for a desktop application.

Using Component Services

Deploying a COM object in Component Services is a better strategy than using *regsvr32* for web applications, because the components used in a web application often require future management and component updates. Any software loaded in Component

Services is called a component. Component Services provides many more features to manage a component, such as the following:

- Updating a component without interrupting consumer utilization of the component
- Providing statistical information about the utilization of the component
- Masquerading operation of the component under a given set of user's credentials
- Distributing the component's functionality to other hosts
- Rolling back database transactions

To load a COM object into Component Services, a COM+ application must first be created. A COM+ application contains one or more COM objects or components. A COM+ application in Component Services should be thought of as an ideal deployable unit—*ideal* in terms of the consumer of the component. A COM+ application can be consumed by another process, or Component Services could provide a process under which the COM+ application could run. Starting and stopping a COM+ application will respectively enable or prohibit all of the components in the COM+ application from functioning. If you have reliable components loaded with unreliable components, the reliable components should be moved to another COM+ application that does not require as many administrative changes as the COM+ application containing the problematic DLLs. This strategy will minimize the down time for parts of the application that may not need to be taken out of commission due to the failure of one bad component. Likewise, you will be able to better manage the deployment of a component if it is isolated from the rest of the other reliable components until it proves its reliability.

Adding a New COM+ Application to Component Services

Here's how to add a new application to Component Services:

1. Open the Component Services MMC snap-in, and expand the tree view on the left so that the COM+ Applications folder is open under the computer that will host the component.

Note   *The Component Services MMC can also manage Components Services on a remote host if you have administrative credentials that are valid for the remote host. Loading a component on a remote host requires that the component file reside on the remote host, however. The Component Services MMC will not move the component file to the remote host.*

2. Right-click the COM+ Applications folder and choose New | Application (as shown in Figure 13-9) to launch the COM+ Application Install Wizard.
3. In the first wizard screen, click the Next button.

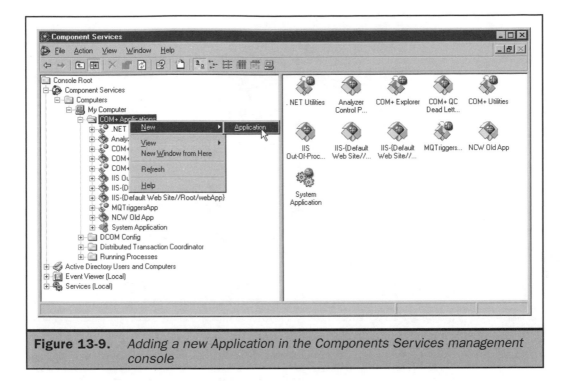

Figure 13-9. *Adding a new Application in the Components Services management console*

4. In the Install Or Create A New Application screen shown in Figure 13-10, click Create An Empty Application and the wizard will advance to the Create Empty Application screen automatically.

5. On the Create Empty Application screen, shown in Figure 13-11, enter the name of the COM+ Application; in this case, enter **New ConfigSeat Web**. The name of the COM+ application has little significance programmatically; the name identifies the COM+ application in the Component Services MMC.

6. Because the DLL *ConfigSeat* is a new component, select the default, Server Application, for activation type. The Activation Type setting has a profound effect on the COM+ application's performance and reliability. For more information about this setting, please refer to the sidebar "Background on Windows Architecture and Component Services Applications." Click the Next button to continue.

7. In the Set Application Identity screen shown in Figure 13-12, the default setting is Interactive User. You can also choose either of the built-in accounts Local Service or Network Service or you can establish an account for the COM+ application to run under. The Interactive User selection causes the COM+ application to run under the current logged-on user. You should not use Interactive User for

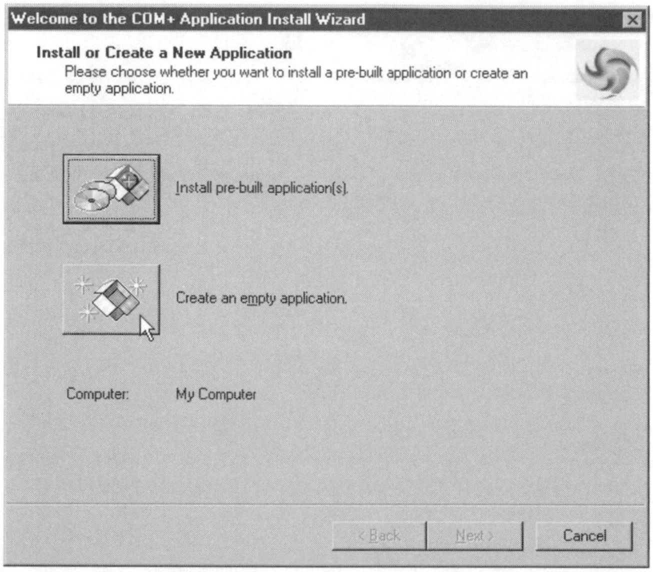

Figure 13-10. *Install Or Create A New Application screen of the COM+ Application Install Wizard*

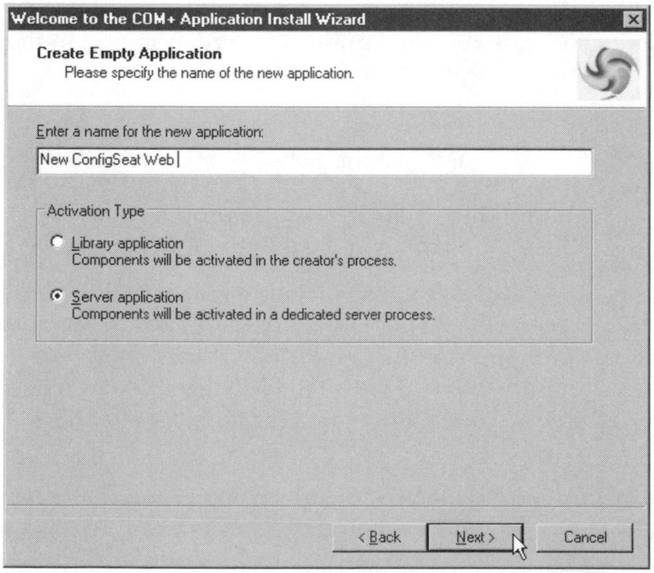

Figure 13-11. *Create Empty Application screen in the COM+ Application Install Wizard*

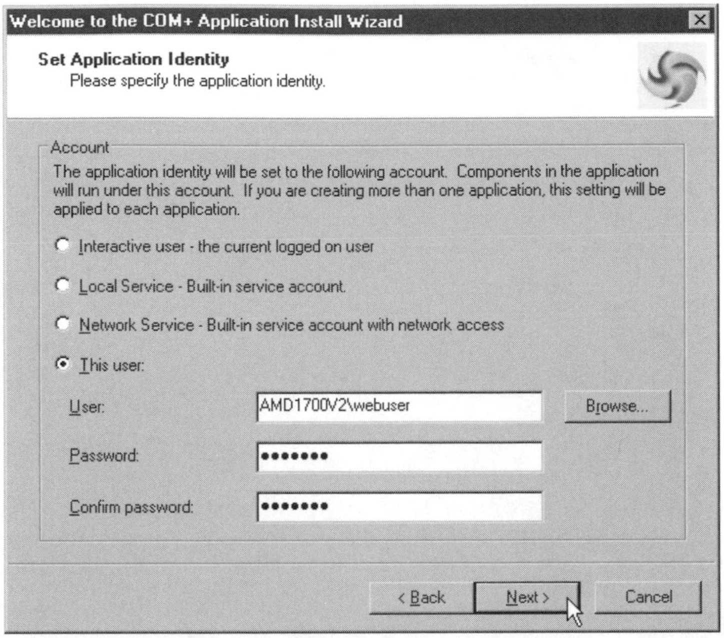

Figure 13-12. *Set Application Identity screen in the COM+ Application Install Wizard*

a COM+ application hosting components that are used in a web application because the COM+ application will not run after the current logged-on user logs off from the host.

The Network Service account is the default Windows user account for worker processes in IIS to run under. The Local Service account is more restrictive than the Network Service account. Both the Local Service or Network Service Windows user accounts are quite restrictive and are, therefore, very safe Windows user accounts to run applications under. For this example, a specified Windows user account will be used for the application to run under. The Windows user account named *webuser* was created to handle web-related services. The Windows user account *webuser* belongs to the *users* group. After the *webuser* password is entered and confirmed, click the Next button.

8. The Add Application Roles screen appears, as shown in Figure 13-13. As complexities of web applications increase, programmers are forced to define roles in addition to providing access control to content. Role-based security and extendible access control systems are complicated and difficult to build. Defining roles and assigning Windows user accounts to the roles as they pertain to a given COM+ application is one way that you can exploit Component Services.

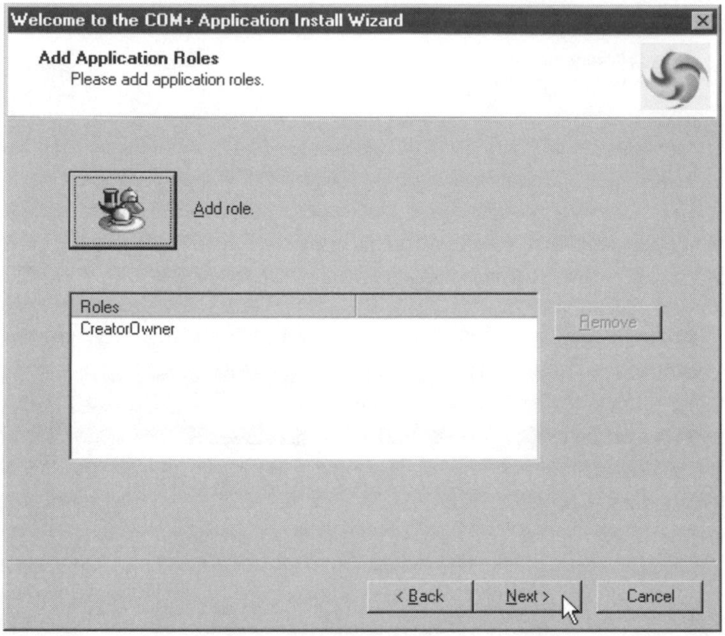

Figure 13-13. *Add Application Roles screen in the COM+ Application Install Wizard*

Roles can be created with associated Windows user accounts that enable the web application to support sophisticated access control and security schemes. You can click the Add Role button to add more roles to the COM+ application. In this case, a default role has been added, called *CreatorOwner*. This role is more than adequate to serve the needs of the COM+ application in this example. Click Next to continue.

9. In the Add Users To Roles screen, shown in Figure 13-14, Windows user accounts can be added to the roles that were defined in the Add Application Roles screen. By default, your Windows user account will be used for each role defined in the previous screen. You will probably never use your user account to act as a user for a role. The Windows user accounts that are added to roles are likely established to provide credentials under which processes can run. The *webuser* Windows user account will be the only Windows user account added to the role *CreatorOwner*, as shown in Figure 13-14. Click Next to continue.

10. Finally, the finish screen of the wizard is presented. Click Finish, and a COM+ application is now set up and ready for a COM DLL to be placed inside.

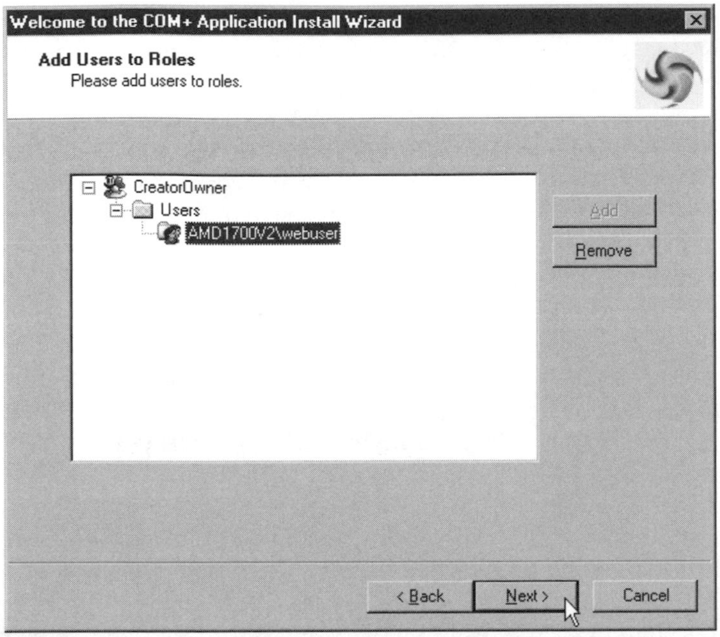

Figure 13-14.   *Add Users To Roles screen in the COM+ Application Install Wizard, with the webuser Windows user account added to the CreatorOwner role*

Background on Windows Architecture and Component Services Applications

To understand the difference between a server application and a library application in Component Services, you must understand the terms and some of the mechanics of Windows architecture. A *process* is an executable program that is running. The Windows operating system provides slices of time to the processor to each spawned process. A *thread* is work being performed within a process. A process can support more than one running thread at a time. When no threads are running in a process, the process is done, and Windows no longer provides the process with slices of time to the processor.

The more processes running, the more resources the computer utilizes to support the processes. Starting a process initially requires a great deal of server resources. Shutting down a single process has no effect on any other process, unless other processes require the shut-down process to function. Shutting down processes is usually a graceful action that does not risk the stability of the system, so distributing more work among processes uses more machine resources but offers greater reliability.

In an effort to minimize the system resource drain caused by starting and maintaining processes, programmers try to design software to load into memory under an existing process instead of requiring the computer to create a new process for the software. The comparison of Common Gateway Interface (CGI) web applications versus ASP web applications illustrates this difference. Early versions of CGI web applications generally consisted of an executable that was launched to handle each web server page request. That means that if 10 hits per minute occurred on a web page that required a CGI application to perform some work, regardless of how simple or difficult the work being performed, the server would have launched the CGI executable 10 times a minute, or 600 times per hour.

If an ASP page were performing the same functional purpose as the CGI executable, zero processes would be launched over the same period of time. Actually, only one process is launched to support an ASP to run, and the process is launched when the server starts—the process is IIS itself. ASP is an Internet Server Application Programming Interface (ISAPI) extension called ASP.DLL that runs under the process space of IIS. In the past, problems may have caused IIS to stop working after some prolonged period of time for no apparent reason. IIS failures of this sort were likely due to the fact that the IIS process had become corrupted in some way after an exception had destabilized it, after a memory leak, or following unreleased pointers. These failures were likely the result of DLLs that contained a defect being loaded into the IIS process space. This inherit design feature (or flaw) in Windows architecture has contributed to IIS being perceived as unreliable compared to other less sophisticated systems that use CGI primarily.

To produce a solution that offered greater reliability without sacrificing as much performance, as would be the case if all software was written to run under its own independent process, Microsoft created Microsoft Transaction Server (MTS) for Windows NT 4. MTS became Component Services or COM+ on the Windows 2000 platform. With each new platform, Component Services provides a few more features. The primary benefit, however, is that Component Services acts as a DLL server. A COM object DLL may be loaded into a COM+ application in Component Services and can be run in its own process, or can be run in the process space of the consuming software. A COM+ server application runs in its own process space and a library application runs in the consuming process's space. If the DLLs being consumed are reliable and do not need to be changed or updated often, they should be hosted in a library application in Component Services because the overall software solution will benefit by using less server resource and functioning with greater performance. If the DLLs are new or unreliable, or they need to be changed often, they should be hosted in a server application in Component Services because the overall software solution will benefit by not crashing if a failure occurs in the component or will not require the entire solution to be stopped in order to make an update.

Adding a New Component to a COM+ Application in Component Services

The purpose for creating the COM+ application was to enable Component Services to serve instances of the classes inside *ConfigSeat.dll*. The next step to deploy *ConfigSeat.dll* to the host server is to add *ConfigSeat.dll* to the COM+ application *New ConfigSeat Web* that was just created.

1. From the Component Services management console, right-click the Component folder under COM+ Application *New ConfigSeat Web*, and choose New | Component, as shown in Figure 13-15.

2. The welcome screen to the COM+ Component Install Wizard opens. Click the Next button to continue.

3. In the Import Or Install A Component screen, click the Install New Components button.

4. In the file selection dialog box, select the *ConfigSeat.dll* file and click Open.

5. The next screen, Install New Components, summarizes the components that are being added to the new COM+ application, as shown in Figure 13-16. This

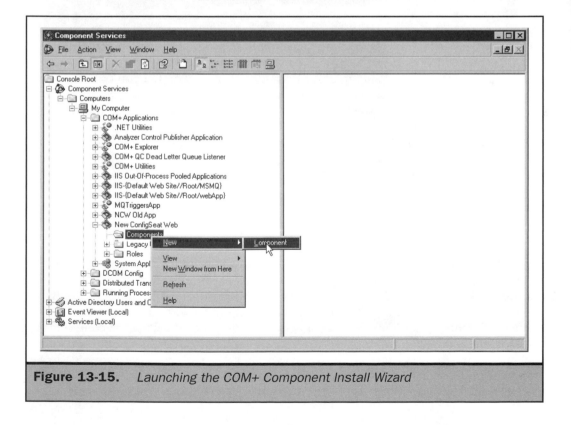

Figure 13-15.   *Launching the COM+ Component Install Wizard*

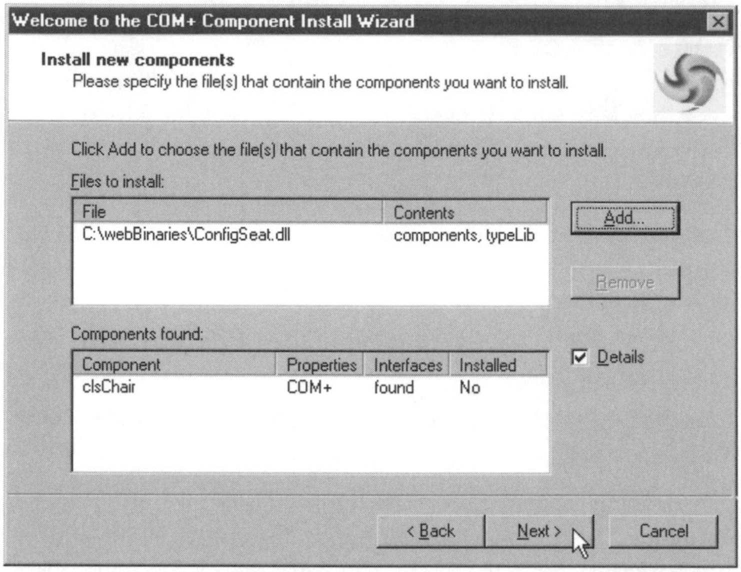

Figure 13-16.   *Install New Component Screen of the COM+ Component Wizard, showing the result of ConfigSeat.dll being loaded*

screen seems to have no other purpose than to allow you to open other COM DLLs to load into the COM+ application and to show you what has been chosen. You can click the Add button to get the same file selection dialog box presented in step 4. Selecting other COM DLLs will add them to lists of files and components displayed in this screen. Click Next.

6. Click Finish. The COM+ Component Install Wizard will finish and the *ConfigSeat.dll* should be added to the COM+ application *New ConfigSeat Web* in Component Services.

Using Component Services for Role-Based Access

Component Services enables role-based access to any component loaded into a COM+ application. Windows user accounts are assigned to a role. Requests to a component in Component Services is made using Windows user account credentials. Component Services associates the consumer to a role using the Windows user account credentials provided by the consuming software. If the roles associated with the Windows user account credentials provided are associated with the requested part of the component, the consuming software will function as expected; otherwise, the consuming software will not be able to access the component as expected. The roles may be associated to a component loaded in a COM+ application at the following four levels:

- **COM+ application**   All components placed in the COM+ application
- **Component**   A specific COM object loaded into a COM+ application
- **Component's interfaces collectively**   All of the methods for a COM object loaded in a COM+ application
- **Component's method**   A specific method in a specific COM object loaded in a COM+ application

You have to enable the role access starting from the highest level of definable access and descend the levels until the desired access control is achieved. The lowest discrete functionality that access control may be defined as a method of a component. To enable role-based access, you have to perform the following steps:

1. Enable component-level access checks for the COM+ application.
2. Enable component-level access checks for the component.
3. Assign a role or roles to any of the following parts of the component:
   - The component itself
   - A method of the component
   - All methods of the component

To enable component-level access checks for a COM+ application, do the following:

1. From the Component Services management console, right-click the COM+ Application and choose Properties.
2. Select the Security tab in the Properties window.
3. Click the Enforce Component-Level Access Checks checkbox.
4. Click OK.

To enable component-level access checks for a component, you must enable component-level access checks for the COM+ application prior to performing these steps.

1. From the Component Services management console, right-click the component and choose Properties.
2. Select the Security tab in the properties window.
3. If you want to assign a role to the component as a whole, check the role in the list labeled Roles Explicitly Set For Selected Item(s). All the methods of the component will inherit this role.

   If you want to assign roles to specific methods within the component, click the Enforce Component-Level Access Checks checkbox. This will enable you to further assign roles to methods of the component.
4. Click OK.

In the case of the component *ConfigSeat.clsChair* that was added to the COM+ application named *New ConfigSeat Web,* role-based access is not required. Enforce component-level access checks will not be turned on for *ConfigSeat.clsChair.* The COM+ application *New ConfigSeat Web* will be set to enforce access checks, however, so component-level access checks will be selected. If IIS was running under the default guest user account created by Windows (for example, *IUSR_MyMachineName*), an ASP creating the *ConfigSeat.clsChair* object will fail since the Internet guest account does not have access to the *ConfigSeat.clsChair* component. If the IIS Internet guest account were changed to a different Windows user account that had access to the *ConfigSeat.clsChair* component, the ASP would run correctly. To make an ASP consume the *ConfigSeat.clsChair* component, the web instance or virtual web instance within IIS will be set to run using the *webuser* account credentials.

You can configure this access by doing the following:

1. Open the Properties window for a web instance or virtual web instance, and select the Directory Security tab.

2. Click the Edit button under the Authentication And Access Control area to open the Authentication Methods window.

3. By default, the Enable Anonymous Access checkbox is selected, and the credentials of the default guest user account are placed in the User Name and Password text boxes. Type the login name **webuser** into the User Name text box and enter the password for *webuser* in the Password text box.

4. Click OK repeatedly until all of the windows that were opened from the property pages window for the web instance or the virtual web instance are closed.

The ASP pages will execute under the Windows user account *webuser.* When the ASP creates the *ConfigSeat.clsChair* component, the credentials for the webuser Windows user account will be presented to Component Services for the request. Component Services will verify that *webuser* is allowed to create and use the component, and the ASP will consume the functions in the *ConfigSeat.clsChair* component.

Unit Test a COM DLL

To test the deployment of *ConfigSeat.dll*, a simple ASP can be created that creates a class instance of *clsChair*, prints the value of *color* to the browser, and changes the value of *color* in the class instance. The ASP file *DescribeChair.asp*, as shown in Listing 13-2, can be placed in a web application on the server hosting the *ConfigSeat.dll*. The ASP file could be placed under the default web site created by IIS when it is installed. If the server has not been configured to run ASP files, it will need to be configured. Refer to Chapter 12 for instructions on enabling IIS 6 to run ASP.

Listing 13-2 ASP *DescribeChair.asp* used to test the COM component ConfigSeat.DLL

```
<%@ Language=VBScript %>
<HTML>
<HEAD>
</HEAD>
<BODY>
<%
dim o

    Response.Write("<p>start Test</p>")

    'create the object since this is hard work
    set o = Server.CreateObject("ConfigSeat.clsChair")

    'demonstrate that values were changing
    Response.Write("<p> color=" & o.color & "</p>")
    Response.Write("<p>change color to blue</p>")
    o.color = "blue"
    Response.Write("<p> color=" & o.color & "</p>")

    'destroy object so it can be created again
    set o = nothing
%>
</BODY>
</HTML>
```

To demonstrate the ability of Component Services to show the status of a given COM object being consumed, the *DescribeChair.asp* needed to be run many times. The stress caused to the web server by a human requesting the ASP file cannot provide enough demand on the COM component or the server hosting the component to cause Component Services to register any resource demand. Microsoft offers two tools designed to provide some load-testing capabilities:

- Microsoft Application Center Test
- Microsoft Web Application Stress (WAS) test

WAS is freeware, and Microsoft Application Center Test is part of Visual Studio .NET Enterprise Edition.

To create a resource drain on the ASP to see how it will respond, a simple script was created in the Microsoft Application Center Test tool that simulates 100 concurrent users for 5 minutes. This demand was significant enough to observe the Component Services being stressed in the effort of serving out instances of *clsChair*. To meet the demand,

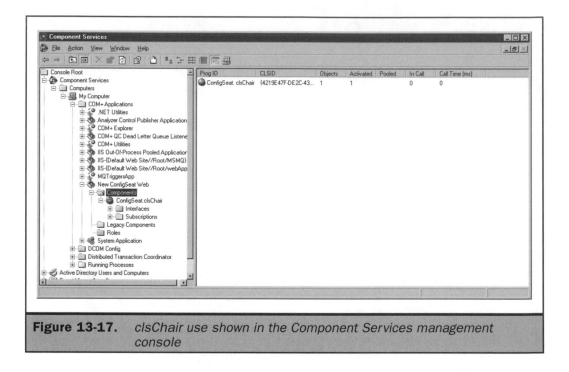

Figure 13-17. *clsChair use shown in the Component Services management console*

zero to five instances of *clsChair* were created at any given time to support a demand of 175 page requests per second. Figure 13-17 shows the Component Services management console indicating the status of *clsChair* during the load test.

Using VB in COM

The construction of an extremely simple COM web application from start to finish, including all the steps that should be a part of the development effort, has been demonstrated. A more realistic COM object would feature a set of classes that mimic the objects discovered in a requirements gathering exercise with greater reality. Among the features likely to exist in a COM web application are the ability to store data related to the objects discovered, read data for the objects discovered, serialize the object data into XML, and format it for display in a web browser. For the purposes of this chapter, many of the steps related to requirements gathering are skipped. Refer to Chapter 18 for an overview of the effort that is included in a software development cycle.

Object-oriented (OO) design and analyses is likely one of the greatest deficits that exists in the web software development community today. Web software is no less complex or unconfined by the realities of engineering and design than any other complex engineering effort, so the conventions and efforts of good practice and design should not be ignored. It seems, however, that OO design is not performed often prior to a programmer embarking on creating a web application.

Organizations often perform design and analyses *after* the product is built and they realize that the product has to be rebuilt for each enhancement. In any project, providing time for analyses and design is critical to increasing the chances that the software effort will exhibit greater adherence to meeting projected development timelines, accommodate future enhancements with less problems, and increase team moral on the project.

There is a problem with OO analyses and design and VB6, however. VB6 cannot employ a true OO software solution. It does not support implementation inheritance. The lack of true polymorphism and some other deficiencies in the extendibility of the language limits its effective use in providing software applications that offer longevity, especially in regard to the extendibility of an existing solution. COM objects can be built with other languages that do support true OO capabilities, however, such as C++ and Java.

VB6 supports many of the other features found in a truly polymorphic language, but the ability to inherit another class is an important feature that it lacks. You should not confuse the inheritance that VB6 claims to possess as being *true* inherence. Microsoft VB6 literature describes VB6 as an object-oriented language that can inherit from another class using the *implements* command. However, the *implements* command offers only what might be construed as *interface inheritance*. In the practical sense, interface inheritance simply means that the VB6 IDE will reconstruct the interface of the *superclass* in the child class and force the programmer to support the entire interface of the superclass in the subordinate class. The programmer must still write all of the code of the inherited functions from the superclass in the child class.

VB6 in its simplicity does offer the programmer the ability to develop reliable components quickly that offer functionality that may be associated with a class instance. The classes may consume other classes, which is useful. Probably the best case scenarios for using VB6 are in a project for which the requirements gathering exercise did not identify too many objects, or for a project in which little potential exists for extending the solution in the future and for which the development cycle must be short. VB6 offers a legitimate alternative to using a truly polymorphic language such as C++, which requires an advanced programmer skill set, and a high maintenance script solution such as a VBScript ASP.

Building a COM Object in VB6 with Data Access Support

Taking the chair object introduced earlier in this chapter a step further in the development process, the *clsChair* class will be enhanced to read and write chair data to a database and serialize the state of the class instance into an XML document. The following functions will be added to the *clsChair* class:

- *OpenChair(ID as string)* **as Boolean** Opens an existing record for a chair and populates the object with the values
- *CreateChair()* **as Boolean** Generates a new ID, populates object with the new ID, and writes a record to the database
- *GetChairState()* **as XMLDOM** Serializes the object state into XML DOM to look like this: *<Chair ID="" Color="" />*

The following properties will be added to class *clsChair*:

- *ChairID* **as String - Read only** Identifier used to uniquely identify a given chair
- *ChairError* **as String - Read only** Description of the last identified error that occurred in the class *clsChair*

The interface still is not that complicated, but the class reflects an interface that is more consistent with a class found in a real OO-designed solution. Other functions, such as *delete* and *save,* ought to supplement the interface, but for the sake of brevity necessary in a book example, these functions are not included.

The name *chair* prefixes the names of the functions in *clsChair*. Creating an interface to an object that uses the name of the object itself is not a good practice but a necessity based on the limitation of the technology. Unfortunately, the terms *open* and *create* are keywords that are reserved in VB, so they cannot be used as user-defined functions in a class instance. Note as well that the interface to the class contains no logic other that what pertains to describing the chair itself or pertains to things a chair would do in our software scenario. For example, no remnants of data logic or presentation logic exist, such as a database connection string or HTML output.

The public interface of the entire chair as it now stands shown in Listing 13-3 possesses the following function declarations, excluding implementation code:

Listing 13-3

```
clsChair Prototypes

Public Property Get color() As Variant
End Property
Public Property Let color(ByVal vNewValue As Variant)
End Property

Public Property Get ChairError() As String
End Property
```

```
Public Property Get ChairID() As String
End Property

Public Function OpenChair(ID As String) As Boolean
End Function

Public Function CreateChair() As Boolean
End Function

Public Function GetChairState() As DOMDocument30
End Function
```

Properties in Classes

Properties in VB are simply functions designed to facilitate value assignment and access. The programmer could place code in the property subroutine to make the program perform work. It is considered best practice, however, to build functions or subroutines for situations in which work is performed by the software. A good example of a function in *clsChair* that might have been a read-only property is *GetChairState()*. *GetChairState()* did perform work to produce the XML, so it was placed in a function that returned the instance to the class. If the *DOMDocument30* class were stored in a variable local to the class and was instantiated after the *Open()* or *Create()* function was called, using a read-only property would be a better choice for returning the instance of class *DOMDocument30*.

Because the properties *ChairError* and *ChairID* are read-only, if consuming software attempts to write a value to the function, an error will be thrown. The property *color* is the only property that supports read and write capability, as evidenced by the fact that two property prototypes exist—*Get* and *Let*. Because *ChairError* and *ChairID* are read-only, they have a *Get* prototype only.

A quirk of VB that was not demonstrated in any of the code snippets presented in this chapter is still worth noting. A property can accept and return a class instance argument. If a property prototype is used to accept a class instance, it must use the keyword *Set* and not *Let*. For example, if the *clsChair* class had a write property called *ChairState* that took an XML DOM class instance as the argument, the prototype would look like this.

```
Public Property Set ChairState(ByVal vNewValue As DOMDocument30)
End Property
```

Database Connection Credentials

A common problem of many VB applications is that the abstraction of logic is not maintained properly. If a class such as *clsChair* were made to read and write data to and

IIS PROGRAMMING

from a data source such as a database, the programmer might place a property called *Connection* in the class, for example. The *Connection* property would become the means for providing the class instance with the information necessary to connect to the database. This is a bad practice that causes VB web applications to experience extendibility issues. The interface of the class does not imitate reality because the chair does not have a *Connection* attribute in real life. By placing the *Connection* property in the interface, the programmer is implying that the consumer of the class should know how the class interacts with a data source. *Connection* and other similar technical implementation attributes should not poison the interface. The proper solution is to abstract from the business logic anything not related to the object as the object exists in the real world.

How, then, does the programmer keep the logical abstraction of the class pure and get the class to communicate with the database? Hard coding the connection information into the class is certainly not a good idea, because a change in deployment will require a change to the code. All software should have state settings that are sought out on initialization or construction. In the case of software deployed on a Windows server, the *registry* is the mechanism of choice for storing settings. All Windows support utilities and services ultimately utilize the registry for the storage of state data or initialization data. The .NET Framework has adopted the use of XML files for storing deployment data and state data for web applications.

Any system works as long as the software, through convention, knows the host context for storing initialization data. The Windows registry is found in the same way no matter on what host it resides. Software does not have to seek out the registry on the C:\ drive and run the risk that some server elsewhere might not have a C:\ drive. The registry has a context that is associated with the host itself as opposed to a file location on the host, a location within a server, or a location within a server on a separate host. In web applications, the web root can serve as a common host of context. Content or files may be referred to in the context of the web root. The web root could be located on the C:\ drive or on the D:\ drive, but if the context is always stated in terms of the web root, a problem finding a given initialization parameter value will not be encountered. The .NET platform has adopted such a standard for storing deployment data in XML files named *Web.config*, which may be located on any given directory within a web directory structure. Please refer to Chapters 14 and 15 for more information about .NET web applications and using the *web.config* file.

Because the class *clsChair* was designed to be hosted in a COM+ application, an interface was added to obtain the database connection credential from the COM+ component settings. The interface is called *IObjectConstruct*. To use this interface, a reference to the class project references was added called COM+ Services Type Library. (Figure 13-7 shows the project References dialog box, where the references can be viewed.)

The interface *IObjectConstruct* was implemented in the class using the *Implements* command and an event subroutine was added to the class called *IObjectConstruct_ Construct*. The *IObjectConstruct_Construct* event subroutine occurs on class instantiation and passes in an object instance to a class represented by the parameter *pCtorObj*. The class instance pointed at by *pCtorObj* has the property *ConstructString*. The value of

ConstructString was used to instantiate the Active Data Objects (ADO) Connection object that is used throughout the class *clsChair*. Listing 13-4 shows the *IObjectConstruct_ Construct* event subroutine implementation.

Listing 13-4

```
IObjectConstruct_Construct event subroutine implementation in clsClass
Option Explicit
Implements IObjectConstruct


'~~~~~~~~~~~~~~~~~~~~~~~~~~~~~~~~~~~~~~~~
' *****   constants to class *****
'~~~~~~~~~~~~~~~~~~~~~~~~~~~~~~~~~~~~~~~~

'old style connection string in case nothing else works
Private Const DEFAULT_CONSTRUCTION_STRING = _
"driver={Microsoft Access Driver (*.mdb)};" & _
"dbq=D:\aspData\employees.mdb"


Private Const DEFAULT_COLOR = "Brown"
Private Const CHAIR_ID = "ID"
Private Const CHAIR_COLOR = "Color"


'~~~~~~~~~~~~~~~~~~~~~~~~~~~~~~~~~~~~~~~~
' ***** locals to class *****
'~~~~~~~~~~~~~~~~~~~~~~~~~~~~~~~~~~~~~~~~
'holds the color of the chair
Private m_sColor As String

'Chair ID for class instance
Private m_sID As String

'holds the ADO Connection to the data
'source that the object interacts with
Private m_Connection As ADODB.Connection

Private m_sErrorMessage As String


Private Sub IObjectConstruct_Construct(ByVal pCtorObj As Object)

On Error GoTo Sub_Error_Handler
Const ERROR_MESSAGE_INFO = "IObjectConstruct_Construct"

Dim sConnection As String

    sConnection = pCtorObj.ConstructString

    'make certain there is something
```

```
    If Len(sConnection) < 1 Then
        sConnection = DEFAULT_CONSTRUCTION_STRING
    End If

    'establish connection to database server
    If m_Connection Is Nothing Then
        Set m_Connection = CreateObject("ADODB.Connection")
    End If

    m_Connection.Open sConnection 'DEFAULT_CONSTRUCTION_STRING
    'establish connection to database server
    Set m_Connection = CreateObject("ADODB.Connection")
    m_Connection.Open sConnection '"DSN=ASPExample"


'~~~~~~~~~~~~~~~~~~~~~~~~~~~~~~~~~~~~~~~~~~~~~~
sub_Exit_Done:
    Exit Sub

Sub_Error_Handler:
    'record the error in class instance and rethrow
    'for consuming software to learn of issue
    ProcessErr ERROR_MESSAGE_INFO & _
    " Failure obtaining database connection information." & _
    " Class will not connect to database"
End Sub
```

The value of the property *ConstructString* is set in the Component Services Properties window for the component being hosted. In the case of *clsClass*, the connection string was set on the Properties window Activation tab's Constructor String text box for the component *ConfigSeat.clsClass*, as shown in Figure 13-18. When using this mechanism for storing initialization state, the deployment for class *clsChair* may be configured using the native services of Windows Server that any network engineer managing a Windows server should be familiar with.

Note *Windows data access technology using open database connectivity (ODBC) or OLE-DB provides automatic database connection pooling. The ADO connection class instance stored in* m_Connection *is local to the class* clsChair, *as shown in Listing 13-4. This means that the connection is open as long as the class instance of* clsChair *exists. When the instance of* clsChair *is destroyed, the instance of the ADO connection is destroyed in the class, but ODBC or the OLE-DB provider will keep an instance of the connection available for the next requester. Take care not to attempt to create a cache of connection objects or a situation in which a cache is created, since Windows is already performing this function.*

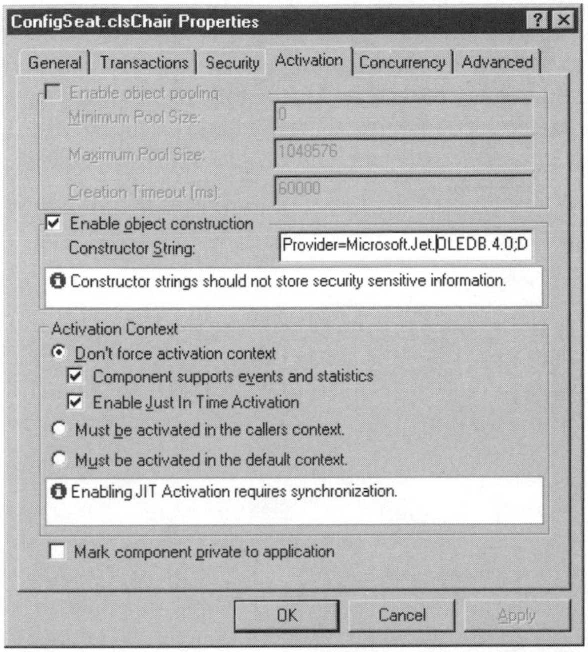

Figure 13-18. *Activation tab for the ConfigSeat.clsClass Properties window in Component Services*

Error Handling

Interacting with a database introduces a new level of complexity to the application that demands greater respect in terms of exception situations. Proper error handling should always exist in any code that is subject to conditions that might cause a subroutine to fail, such as data entry from a user or communication with heterogeneous systems or environments.

Visual Basic offers an error handling system that is easy to invoke and manipulate. Errors are always bubbled up to the consuming code until the error is handled. If the error is never handled, the user is shown a nasty message and the program shuts down. In a web application where the COM object is consumed by an ASP page, the end user may see the error message if IIS is set up to display these messages.

Each exception that occurs in the *clsChair* class is written to the event log and stored in the local variable for the *ChairError* property. The code is written to dump out of the function after the error information is obtained. Error handling in *clsClass* is implemented using the same basic framework in all functions and subroutines. The error handler is established on entry to the function or subroutine to go to a specified line within the function or subroutine. Two lines that play a role in the exit strategy for error handling are specified: *sub_Exit_Done* and *Sub_Error_Handler*. The line *sub_Error_Handler* is the strategy that is followed in an exception condition as specified by the *On Error* statement. The code that follows line *sub_Exit_Done* is the normal exit strategy for the function or subroutine if the routine executes without any exception occurring. Listing 13-5 shows a generic framework listing of the error handling that was employed in *clsClass*.

Listing 13-5

```
Error Handling Framework

On Error GoTo Sub_Error_Handler
Const ERROR_MESSAGE_INFO = "This Function's name"

Part of the function
that actually does something
    here

'~~~~~~~~~~~~~~~~~~~~~~~~~~~~~~~~~~~~~~~~~~~
sub_Exit_Done:
    'return success value

    On Error Resume Next
    'destroy objects
    Exit Function

Sub_Error_Handler:
    ProcessErr "message about the failure in terms of function"
```

The *ProcessErr* subroutine called from the exception strategy in all of the functions and subroutines is a routine that processes the VB error or any other error condition that might exist. *ProcessErr* performs two purposes:

- Logs error information to the Windows event log for forensic analyses
- Places the error in the local error variable for the class so that the consuming software could access it

The event logging will not occur until the component is compiled due to a constraint of VB and Windows security. Running the component while in the VB IDE will not produce event logs.

Listing 13-6 shows the code that consists of subroutine *ProcessErr*.

Listing 13-6

```
ProcessErr Subroutine - Error Logger and Formatting

'~~~~~~~~~~~~~~~~~~~~~~~~~~~~~~~~~~~~~~~~~
```

```
'ProcessErr
'formats error and stores it in error local
'then write to event log. Event logging
'will not function in IDE - only in compiled.
'
'in: vsMessage - usually denoting function
'out: nothing
'~~~~~~~~~~~~~~~~~~~~~~~~~~~~~~~~~~~~~~~~~~
Private Sub ProcessErr(ByVal vsMessage As String)

Const ERROR_SEPARATOR = "  --  "
Const NOW_TIME_FORMAT = "yyyy mmm d   hh:mm:ss"
Const A_SPACE = " "
Const ERROR_NUM = " Error #"
Const ERROR_BY = " was generated by "

Dim sDateTime As String

    'get a time data stamp
    sDateTime = CStr(Format(Now, NOW_TIME_FORMAT)) & _
                                    ERROR_SEPARATOR

    'construct the error entry
    vsMessage = sDateTime & vsMessage

    'add err object data to the error entry
    m_sErrorMessage = vsMessage & ERROR_NUM & Err.Number _
    & ERROR_BY & Err.Source & A_SPACE & Err.Description & vbCrLf

    'write to event log
    App.LogEvent m_sErrorMessage, vbLogEventTypeError

End Sub
```

ProcessErr records the time and appends it to the error description. The properties of the VB *Err* class are concatenated into a string that will become a part of the error that is logged and stored in the local error variable.

Writing to Database

The implementations of the *CreateChair* and *OpenChair* functions both require interaction with a database. The function *CreateChair* inserts data for a new chair into the database, and *OpenChair* populates the state of the class instance based on the values read from the database for a particular chair instance. The *CreateChair* function generates an ID for the chair, builds a SQL command, and writes the new values to the database using a SQL *INSERT* statement. Listing 13-7 shows a listing of function *CreateChair*.

Listing 13-7

```
Function CreateChair


'~~~~~~~~~~~~~~~~~~~~~~~~~~~~~~~~~~~~~~~~~~~~~
'CreateChair
'Generates a new ID, populates object with
'the new ID, writes record to DB
'
'in: nothing
'out: returns true on success and false otherwise
'~~~~~~~~~~~~~~~~~~~~~~~~~~~~~~~~~~~~~~~~~~~~~
Public Function CreateChair() As Boolean

On Error GoTo Sub_Error_Handler
Const ERROR_MESSAGE_INFO = "CreateChair"

Const COMMAND_PREFIX = "INSERT INTO tblChair" & _
                       " ([ID], [Color]) VALUES ('"
Const COMMAND_CONJUNCTION = "', '"
Const COMMAND_SUFFIX = "')"

Dim sNewID As String
Dim sSQL As String

    'get new ID
    sNewID = CreateNewID

    'build the insert statement
    sSQL = COMMAND_PREFIX & sNewID & _
    COMMAND_CONJUNCTION & m_sColor & COMMAND_SUFFIX

    'perform database update
    If Not ExecuteCommand(sSQL) Then
        Err.Raise 1001, ERROR_MESSAGE_INFO, _
        "Failure updating database table for Chair ID = " & sNewID
    End If

    'set new ID to local setting
```

```
        m_sID = sNewID


'~~~~~~~~~~~~~~~~~~~~~~~~~~~~~~~~~~~~~~~~~~~~~~
sub_Exit_Done:
    'return success value
    CreateChair = True

    On Error Resume Next
    'destroy objects
    Exit Function

Sub_Error_Handler:
    ProcessErr " Failure Creating Chair. ID = " & sNewID

End Function
```

Calling a function named *CreateNewID* generates the new chair ID. *CreateNewID* simply calls the *Now()* function, formats the value into a number that should be unique, and converts it into a string. Listing 13-8 shows the function *CreateNewID* source code. The algorithm has a huge shortcoming, however. It will generate a unique ID string only if the request occurs more than 1 second from the last ID requested. Much better ways can be used for obtaining unique values, such as using the Windows Globally Unique Identifier (GUID) function or other homegrown functions using the random number generator. This flaw was left in place to cause the class *clsChair* to generate an error reliably when writing the data to the database. The error will occur because the chair ID is a primary key in the database table that stores the chair data. Attempting to write a row that has the same value for ID as a previously written value will result in an ADO update error.

Listing 13-8

```
Function CreateNewID

'~~~~~~~~~~~~~~~~~~~~~~~~~~~~~~~~~~~~~~~~
'CreateNewID
'creates a new ID for a new chair
'
'in: nothing
'out: returns string ID for Chair
'~~~~~~~~~~~~~~~~~~~~~~~~~~~~~~~~~~~~~~~~
Private Function CreateNewID() As String

Const NOW_TIME_FORMAT = "yyyymmddhhmmss"
```

```
Dim sDateTime As String

    'get a time data stamp
    sDateTime = CStr(Format(Now, NOW_TIME_FORMAT))
'~~~~~~~~~~~~~~~~~~~~~~~~~~~~~~~~~~~~~~~~~~~~~~~~~~
'Note: This algorithm has a huge flaw.
'It does not create unique IDs if more than
'one is requested in a given second.
'~~~~~~~~~~~~~~~~~~~~~~~~~~~~~~~~~~~~~~~~~~~~~~~~~~


    'return value
    CreateNewID = sDateTime

End Function
```

After the ID is generated, a SQL statement is constructed using constants that make up part of the SQL update statement that will result in the new data being written to the database. The value for *color* that was being used is actually the local value *m_sColor*. The property *color,* as in *me.color,* could also have been used in place of the local *m_sColor* and should have been used. If *color* needed to be validated or changed from how it is actually stored in memory in the class instance, the property would be a useful mechanism for making a simple code change in a single location but as it is now, a code edit may be required in both the property and the function using the variable *m_sColor*.

After the SQL command is constructed, the *ExecuteCommand* function sends the SQL command to the database for execution, as shown in Listing 13-9. *ExecuteCommand* is a function that sends SQL to a data source for execution, and it does not expect a return value from the event. *ExecuteCommand* uses ADO to perform the operation.

Before ADO may be used in VB, a reference to ADO must be set in the project references for *ConfigSeat*. ADO is installed from the Microsoft Data Access Components (MDAC) package. MDAC installs many software libraries that support Microsoft's data access software including ADO. ADO is listed in the Visual Basic references as Microsoft ActiveX Data Objects *x* Library, where *x* is the version number of the version of MDAC. The latest version is 2.7 as of this writing, but 2.6 may be used as well. If the software must reside on an NT 4 host, version 2.6 must be used.

Listing 13-9

```
Function ExecuteCommand

    '~~~~~~~~~~~~~~~~~~~~~~~~~~~~~~~~~~~~~~~~~~~~~~~
    'ExecuteCommand
    'sends a SQL command text to the datasource
    'without expectation of return value
```

```
'
'in: vsSource - SQL string to execute
'out: returns true on success, false otherwise
'~~~~~~~~~~~~~~~~~~~~~~~~~~~~~~~~~~~~~~~~~~~~~~
Private Function ExecuteCommand(ByVal vsSource As String) _
As Boolean

On Error GoTo Sub_Error_Handler
Const ERROR_MESSAGE_INFO = "ExecuteCommand"

Dim cmdRequested As ADODB.Command

    'establish connection
    If m_Connection.State <> adStateOpen Then
        Err.Raise 1001, ERROR_MESSAGE_INFO, _
     "Connection Object is not open. Database connect be opened."
    End If

    'establish command
    Set cmdRequested = CreateObject("ADODB.Command")
    Set cmdRequested.ActiveConnection = m_Connection

    'set up command object
    cmdRequested.CommandType = adCmdText
    cmdRequested.CommandText = vsSource

    'run SQL
    cmdRequested.Execute

'~~~~~~~~~~~~~~~~~~~~~~~~~~~~~~~~~~~~~~~~~~~~~~
sub_Exit_Done:
    'return success value
    ExecuteCommand = True

    On Error Resume Next
    'destroy objects
    Set cmdRequested = Nothing
    Exit Function

Sub_Error_Handler:
    ProcessErr " Failure executing SQL command."

End Function
```

In most of the *Err.Raise* calls that are made in the exception scenarios, error number *1001* is issued. Any number may be entered, but I chose 1001 for simplicity. Numbers less than 65,535 and greater than 1000 should be used, since this range is designed for custom error numbers. The ADO *Command* object is used to make the call to the database server. If a Recordset was expected from a *Command* object sending a SQL statement to the database server, the *Execute* function could return an ADO Recordset. Because *ExecuteCommand* was not built to handle returning a Recordset, the Recordset object that is returned from the *Command* object is ignored.

ExecuteCommand verifies that the local connection object *m_Connection* has been set and is alive. After *m_Connection* is verified, the *Command* object is created and set up to send the SQL command to the server. If an error occurs at any time during the execution of *ExecuteCommand*, the error handler will log the error thrown and dump out of the function, returning false. All Boolean variables in VB are false unless set otherwise, so it is necessary to include code that deliberately sets the function to *True* after success is assured. Code to return the value *False* in any sort of failure condition is not required.

The function *OpenChair* opens an ADO Recordset based on a known chair ID being passed into the function and populates the class instance based on the results of moving to the first record of the Recordset. Listing 13-10 shows the source code in function *OpenChair*. Since the chair ID is unique in the database, due to the constraints of the data design, it would be safe to assume that no more than one row of data will ever be returned in this function, and using the first row is likely the desired row. The Recordset is checked to ensure that data exists in it by ensuring that the *BOF* (beginning-of-file) and *EOF* (end-of-file) are both not true. If the record has BOF and EOF equal to true, no records are in the Recordset. Attempting to issue a *MoveFirst* command on an empty Recordset will result in an error. The *EOF* or *BOF* properties, depending on the direction of traversing, should always be checked before advancing the Recordset in either of the respective directions using the respective navigational command *MoveNext* or *MovePrevious*.

Listing 13-10

```
Function OpenChair

'~~~~~~~~~~~~~~~~~~~~~~~~~~~~~~~~~~~~~~~~~~~~~~
'OpenChair
'Opens an existing record for a chair and
'populates the object with the values
'
'in: Chair ID to open
'out: returns true on success and false otherwise
'~~~~~~~~~~~~~~~~~~~~~~~~~~~~~~~~~~~~~~~~~~~~~~
Public Function OpenChair(ID As String) As Boolean
On Error GoTo Sub_Error_Handler
Const ERROR_MESSAGE_INFO = "OpenChair"
```

```vb
Const COMMAND_PREFIX = "SELECT * FROM tblChair WHERE ([ID]='"
Const COMMAND_SUFFIX = "')"

Dim sSQL As String
Dim rs As ADODB.Recordset

    'build the insert statement
    sSQL = COMMAND_PREFIX & ID & COMMAND_SUFFIX

    'get Recordset
    Set rs = GetADORecordSet(sSQL)

    'make certain we got a valid Recordset
    If rs Is Nothing Then
        Err.Raise 1001, ERROR_MESSAGE_INFO, _
        "Failure Opening Chair ID = " & ID
    End If

    'make certain that we got a Recordset
    'with at least 1 value
    If rs.EOF And rs.BOF Then
        Err.Raise 1001, ERROR_MESSAGE_INFO, _
        "Failure - record for Chair does not exist. ID = " & ID
    End If

    rs.MoveFirst

    'set new ID to local setting
    m_sID = rs(CHAIR_ID)

    'set new color to local setting
    color = rs(CHAIR_COLOR)

'~~~~~~~~~~~~~~~~~~~~~~~~~~~~~~~~~~~~~~~~~~~~~~
sub_Exit_Done:
    'return success value
    OpenChair = True

    On Error Resume Next
    'destroy objects
```

```
    Set rs = Nothing
    Exit Function

Sub_Error_Handler:
    ProcessErr "Failure Opening Chair ID = " & ID

End Function
```

The Recordset obtained for *OpenChair* was produced by another ADO helper function called *GetADORecordSet*. Like *ExecuteCommand*, *GetADORecordSet* takes a SQL statement as a parameter and opens a Recordset from the data source set in the local *Connection* object instance *m_Connection*. The Recordset object is passed back to the calling function. Listing 13-11 shows the source code of function *GetADORecordSet*.

Listing 13-11

```
Function GetADORecordSet

'~~~~~~~~~~~~~~~~~~~~~~~~~~~~~~~~~~~~~~~~~~~~
'GetADORecordSet
'Sends SQL command to datasource and returns
'an ADO Recordset to the function consumer
'

'in: vsSource - SQL string to execute
'out: returns true on success, false otherwise
'~~~~~~~~~~~~~~~~~~~~~~~~~~~~~~~~~~~~~~~~~~~~
Private Function GetADORecordSet(ByVal vsSource As String) _
As ADODB.Recordset

On Error GoTo Sub_Error_Handler
Const ERROR_MESSAGE_INFO = "GetADORecordSet"

Dim rsRequested As ADODB.Recordset
Dim cmdRequested As ADODB.Command

    'establish connection
    If m_Connection.State <> adStateOpen Then
        Err.Raise 1001, ERROR_MESSAGE_INFO, _
      "Connection Object is not open. Database connect be opened."
    End If

    'establish command
```

```
    Set cmdRequested = CreateObject("ADODB.Command")
    Set cmdRequested.ActiveConnection = m_Connection

    'set up command object
    cmdRequested.CommandType = adCmdText
    cmdRequested.CommandText = vsSource

    'Create instance of Recordset object
    Set rsRequested = cmdRequested.Execute

    'return Recordset
    If Not rsRequested Is Nothing Then
        If rsRequested.State = adStateOpen Then
            Set GetADORecordSet = rsRequested
        Else
            'rsRequested state is not open
            Err.Raise 1001, ERROR_MESSAGE_INFO, _
             " Recordset state is not open " & vsSource
        End If
    Else
        'rsRequested is nothing error
        Err.Raise 1001, ERROR_MESSAGE_INFO,  _
          " Recordset object is nothing " & vsSource
    End If


'~~~~~~~~~~~~~~~~~~~~~~~~~~~~~~~~~~~~~~~~~~~~~~
sub_Exit_Done:
    'return value
    On Error Resume Next
    'destroy objects
    Set rsRequested = Nothing
    Set cmdRequested = Nothing
    Exit Function

Sub_Error_Handler:
    ProcessErr " Failure obtaining Recordset."

End Function
```

Many opportunities exist for improving the function *GetADORecordSet*. A better approach might be to set an ADO Recordset as a parameter to the function passed in *ByRef* and return true or false based on the success of pulling the Recordset. The software will expend resources on the creation of the ADO Recordset only once, and the function will tell the calling function whether or not the Recordset is good. The *ExecuteCommand* and *GetADORecordSet* could also be combined into a single function.

Serializing into XML

The function *GetChairState* produces an XML document that describes the class instance of *clsChair*. The XML is a simple, single-element XML document. The element *Chair* contains two attributes, *ID* and *Color*. To use the XML object, a reference must be added to the project for the MSXML library. (Figure 13-7 shows the References dialog box.)

For use in this project, the Microsoft XML v3.0 library was chosen, but many other versions exist. At the time of publication, version 4 existed as well. The subroutine could have also used string concatenation to build the XML and return the string from the class. However, there is danger in using string concatenation for the purposes of constructing XML, since most XML parsers will fail easily if any portion of the XML is malformed. Creating the XML using the parser will ensure that the XML is built perfectly. Listing 13-12 shows the source code in the function *GetChairState*.

Listing 13-12

```
Function GetChairState

'~~~~~~~~~~~~~~~~~~~~~~~~~~~~~~~~~~~~~~~~
'   ChairID - read only
'~~~~~~~~~~~~~~~~~~~~~~~~~~~~~~~~~~~~~~~~
Public Property Get ChairID() As String
    ChairID = Trim(m_sID)
End Property


'~~~~~~~~~~~~~~~~~~~~~~~~~~~~~~~~~~~~~~~~
'GetChairState
'serializes object state into XML DOM
'to look like this <Chair ID="" Color="" />
'
'in: nothing
'out: returns DOMDocument30 object filled
'~~~~~~~~~~~~~~~~~~~~~~~~~~~~~~~~~~~~~~~~
Public Function GetChairState() As DOMDocument30
On Error GoTo Sub_Error_Handler
Const ERROR_MESSAGE_INFO = "GetChairState"

Const CHAIR_ELEMENT = "Chair"
Const CHAIR_ID_ATTRIBUTE = "ID"
```

```vb
Const CHAIR_COLOR_ATTRIBUTE = "Color"

Dim xmlChair As MSXML2.DOMDocument30
'~~~~~~~~~~~~~~~~~~~~~~~~~~~~~~~~~~~~
'note : Constructing the XML using
'string concatenation and using the
'XML object to validate is another
'strategy often times used.
'~~~~~~~~~~~~~~~~~~~~~~~~~~~~~~~~~~~~

    'refresh the object
    OpenChair Me.ChairID

    'build XML document
    Set xmlChair = New DOMDocument30

    'create the element for Chair
    Set xmlChair.documentElement = _
        xmlChair.createElement(CHAIR_ELEMENT)

    'add the Chair attributes
    xmlChair.documentElement.setAttribute _
                            (CHAIR_ID_ATTRIBUTE), ChairID
    xmlChair.documentElement.setAttribute _
                            (CHAIR_COLOR_ATTRIBUTE), color


'~~~~~~~~~~~~~~~~~~~~~~~~~~~~~~~~~~~~~~~~~~~~~~
sub_Exit_Done:
    'return object
    Set GetChairState = xmlChair

    On Error Resume Next
    'destroy objects
    Set xmlChair = Nothing

    Exit Function

Sub_Error_Handler:
    ProcessErr " Failure serializing chair into XML. "

End Function
```

After observing the code in Listing 13-12, it is clear why you might want to use string concatenation as a means of building XML. The use of the DOM Document is not intuitive and seems like a lot of work to build a formatted string. Version 1 of *MSXML.DLL*, the XML library, was an extremely slow and resource intensive as well. A savvy programmer could produce XML much faster by concatenating strings together. In addition, VB is inefficient at performing string concatenation. Minimizing the changes that occur in a string as much as possible will greatly improve performance. Because the technologies related to XML are rather new, the software that supports the technology is fluxing a great deal as well. Testing the hypotheses of manufacturer's claims and author's assertions in articles and books is a must for the programmer working with this technology because of the continuous changes occurring.

Enhanced Test Harness

The new *clsChair* may be unit tested after the test harness shown in Figure 13-8 is enhanced to test the new interface recently added. Command buttons Get XML, Open a new chair instance, and Create New chair instance were added to the test harness, as shown in Figure 13-19. Before you click the Open button, a chair ID argument must be entered into the text box.

Setting Binary Compatibility in VB

If the *ConfigSeat.dll* is recompiled and the test harness is not compiled after *ConfigSeat.dll* is compiled, the test harness might fail to create a class instance. This condition may exist for any COM object if the COM object is recompiled and the other software that uses the COM object has references to the COM object inside it. In VB, an ActiveX DLL project is set to have *project* compatibility by default in the Project Properties window's Component tab. If the ActiveX DLL project in question is recompiled, the compatibility is not set to binary compatibility, and other software with references compiled to the DLL in question is run, the software referencing the ActiveX DLL will fail.

To illustrate this point, consider this scenario: *ConfigSeat.dll* was compiled at 0900 this morning. At noon, a test harness named *testconfigseat.exe* was compiled. The test harness *testconfigseat.exe* has specific references to *ConfigSeat.dll* and it names the class specifically in the class instantiation code. At 1800, the *ConfigSeat.dll* project was recompiled and project compatibility was set. When *testconfigseat.exe* was run at 1808, it failed because it could not find *ConfigSeat.dll* because the CLSID was different. Each time *ConfigSeat* is compiled without binary compatibility, a new CLSID is generated. Setting the component to use binary compatibility, as shown in Figure 13-20, will make VB use the same CLSID each time the DLL is recompiled, so all other dependent software will continue to function.

An application consuming an ActiveX DLL expects an interface for a given CLSID. Changing a class's interface in any way except to add a new function or property will cause consuming applications that rely on the class to fail. New functions may be

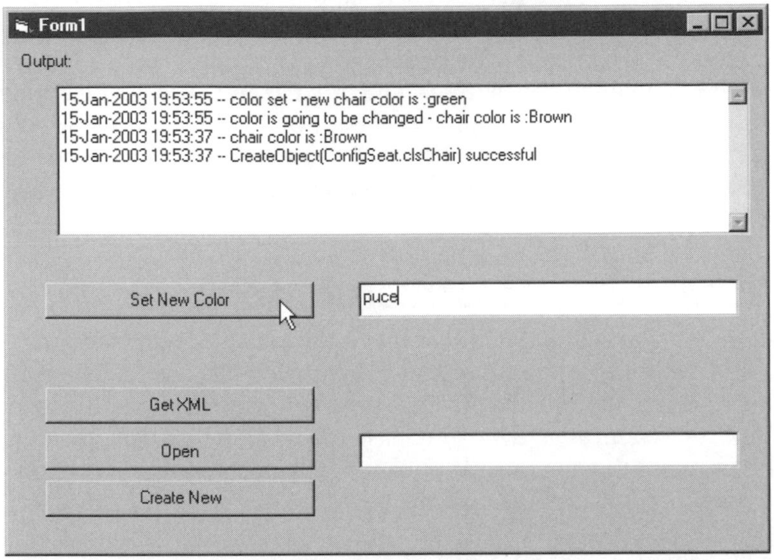

Figure 13-19. *Enhanced test harness for clsChair*

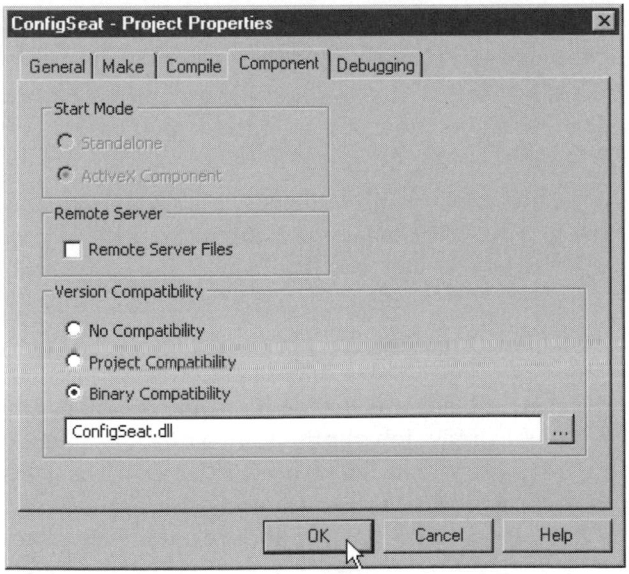

Figure 13-20. *Component tab of the Project Properties window with Binary Compatibility set*

added, but nothing in existence may be changed or removed. The CLSID must also remain the same for the name of the library and class, which is what compiling with binary capability will accomplish. The benefit of using project compatibility is that the programmer can reference an ActiveX DLL project and change the interfaces of the classes inside easily during a development effort. Since the interface may change during development, project compatibility will cause VB to allow the changes to take place without warning the programmer of breaking compatibility if a public function is deleted or changed.

Deploy to COM+ with Constructor String

ConfigSeat.dll may be copied to the next server environment and placed into the COM+ application, replacing the previous version of *ConfigSeat.dll*. The COM+ application in Component Services might have the DLL locked. Performing a shutdown on the application in Component Services will release the DLL so that it can be deleted. If the DLL were participating in a web application, the web server would no longer be utilizing the *clsChair* class after the classes in the DLL are deleted from the COM+ application.

The next effort that should take place is to load the new version of *clsClass* to the COM+ application *New ConfigSeat Web*.

1. From the Component Services management console, delete the old version of the *ConfigSeat.clsClass* by right-clicking the component and choosing Delete.

2. Add the new version of the component the same way that the first version was added, by using the COM+ Component Install Wizard.

3. After the wizard is finished, right-click the class in the Component Services management console and choose Properties to open the Properties window for the *ConfigSeat.clsClass* class.

4. Select the Activation tab and check the box Enable Object Construction. Then enter the text that the class should obtain from the event subroutine *IObjectConstruct_Construct* that was shown in Listing 13-4. In the specific case of *ConfigSeat.clsClass*, the constructor string must be set to an acceptable ADO connection string so that *ConfigSeat.clsClass* can access the data in the database, as shown in Figure 13-18.

5. Verify that the class *clsChair* was loaded by running a quick unit test on it. The test harness might do a nice job of providing a quick unit test clarification of the class's functionality within the new environment. The executable could be copied to the host and started up. A simpler test could also be run using the *DescribeChair.asp* (see Listing 13-2) and adding a few new function calls to stress the component. Listing 13-13 shows an enhanced version of *DescribeChair.asp* called *DescribeChairFinal.asp*.

Listing 13-13   DescribeChairFinal.asp used to
demonstrate added interface of clsChair.

```
<%@ Language=VBScript %>
<HTML>
<HEAD>
</HEAD>
<BODY>
<%
dim i
dim o
dim oXML

    Response.Write("<p>start Test</p>")

    'create the object since this is hard work
    set o = Server.CreateObject("ConfigSeat.clsChair")

    'demonstrate that values were changing
    Response.Write("<p> color=" & o.color & "</p>")
    Response.Write("<p>change color to blue</p>")
    o.color = "blue"
    Response.Write("<p> color=" & o.color & "</p>")

    if o.CreateChair() then
     Response.Write("<p> new id=" & o.ChairID & "</p>")
    else
     Response.Write("<p> possible error=" & o.ChairError & "</p>")

    end if

    set oXML = o.GetChairState()

    Response.Write("<p> xml=" & oXML.XML & "</p>")

    Response.Write("<p> open new chair</p>")

    if not o.OpenChair("20021129095221") then
     Response.Write("<p> possible error=" & o.ChairError & "</p>")
    end if

    Response.Write("<p> new chair color should be purple</p>")
    Response.Write("<p> new chair color =" & o.color & "</p>")
```

```
        'destroy object so it can be created again
        set o = nothing
%>
</BODY>
</HTML>
```

Run the load test script for the Microsoft Application Center Test tool that was created earlier in this chapter, and the results demonstrate that the work of the ASP to COM to database application was much more demanding than the simple ASP to COM web application. The previous version of *clsChair* did not possess any interaction with a database, and the database is hosted on the same server that hosts the ASP and the COM object *clsChair*. Simulating the same 100 concurrent users for 5 minutes, the application was able to maintain an average demand of 45 page requests per second.

Figure 13-17 shows Component Services displaying the status of the previous test. In the first test performed on the previous version of *clsChair*, the In Call and Call Time headings never registered any value other than 0. In the latest version of *clsChair*, the In Call showed 0 to 1 consistently and the Call Time was as high as 15 milliseconds during the load test. Clearly, the performance of the component dropped significantly from the load test run previously. As expected, the additional burden of reading the database diminishes the efficiency of the web application.

Integrating XML and XSL

Class *clsChair* supports the ability to abstract the presentation logic. The *GetChairState* function delivers a serialized version of the chair object to a consumer that can render a page. Typically, COM web applications use the ASP page for parsing the HTML submission, instantiating the classes, and facilitating the page rendering by stuffing the XML objects with the XML documents necessary to construct the page. In the COM – ASP – XSL (Extensible Stylesheet Language) or XSLT (Extensible Stylesheet Language Transformation) scenario, a multitiered web application may be created that abstracts the types of logic and technology summarized in Table 13-1.

Tier Name	Supporting Technology
Presentation Logic	XSL or XSLT sheet
Business Logic	VB COM and ASP
Data Access Logic	ADO
Data Logic	SQL Server

Table 13-1.   *Tiers and Technology in COM Web Application*

The ASP page is a unique part of the solution, because it glues together the business logic and presentation logic. In the solution presented earlier in this chapter, the ASP is not a pure abstraction from either the business tier or the presentation tier, since it contains aspects of each. Listing 13-14 shows the source code to the dispatching ASP that was used with *clsChair*. *XMLCOMChair.asp* contains no HTML. All the page display is in the XSL sheet. Regardless of the way the data from *clsChair* is displayed in the browser, the ASP will not require any editing. Because the ASP does have to know something about the interface of the class *clsChair,* some business logic is included. If the class *clsChair* is updated with more functions or properties, the ASP will need to be edited. The ASP could be easily parameterized to accommodate a configurable class launching system. In that particular case, the ASP would be fully abstracted from the business logic and the presentation logic.

Listing 13-14

```
Source Code for XMLCOMChair.asp object dispatcher

<%@ Language=VBScript %>
<%
'~~~~~~~~~~~~~~~~~~~~~~~~~~~~
' Drawpage
'     handles XML transformation
'~~~~~~~~~~~~~~~~~~~~~~~~~~~~
sub Drawpage(sXML)

CONST XSL_FILE = "formatChair.xsl"

dim oXML
dim oXMLXSL

    Set oXMLXSL = Server.CreateObject("Microsoft.XMLDOM")
    Set oXML = Server.CreateObject("Microsoft.XMLDOM")

    'load XML
    oXML.loadXML(sXML)

    'load the XSL
    oXMLXSL.load(Server.MapPath(XSL_FILE))

    'write the page
    Response.Write(oXML.transformNode(oXMLXSL))

    'destroy object
    set oXML = nothing
```

IIS PROGRAMMING

```
        set oXMLXSL = nothing
end sub


'~~~~~~~~~~~~~~~~~~~~~~~~~~~~
' main
'     dispatches calls
'~~~~~~~~~~~~~~~~~~~~~~~~~~~
sub Main()

dim o
dim XMLDOM

    'create the object chair
    set o = Server.CreateObject("ConfigSeat.clsChair")

    'check for color setting
    if len(Request("color"))>0 then
        o.color = Request("color")
    end if

    'decide what to do
    select case Request("Action")
        case "New"
                o.CreateChair
        case "Open"
                o.OpenChair Request("ID")
    end select

    'get the object state
    set XMLDOM = o.GetChairState()

    'write the page
    Drawpage XMLDOM.XML

    'destroy object
    set o = nothing
    set XMLDOM = nothing

end sub

'~~~~~~~~~~~~~~~~~~~~~~~~~~~
```

```
' Script entry point
'~~~~~~~~~~~~~~~~~~~~~~~~~~
Main()

%>
```

After the class instance for *clsChair* has performed the business logic it was dispatched to do, the state of *clsClass* is serialized into XML and used to build the HTML page. The name of the XSL sheet, *formatChair.xsl*, is stored in the ASP code, but it could be obtained through another means such as HTTP arguments in form submissions or links. The *Drawpage* subroutine takes a string argument that contains XML and draws the entire web page output. The XSL sheet defines how the web page is built and how the values in the XML will be displayed. Other data may be placed in the XSL sheet, too, such as JavaScript routines that are meant to run in the web browser. Listing 13-15 shows the XSL sheet *formatChair.xsl*.

Listing 13-15

```
Source code for formatChair.xsl

<?xml version="1.0"?>
<xsl:stylesheet xmlns:xsl="http://www.w3.org/TR/WD-xsl">
<xsl:template match="/">

<xsl:comment>
~~~~~~~~~~~~~~~~~~~~~~~~~~~~~~~~~~~~~~~~~~~~~~~~~~~~~~
XSL Sheet primarily for the purposes of building an
HTML page to allow a user to open or create a new
chair and see the results with the presentation
logic abstracted completely
~~~~~~~~~~~~~~~~~~~~~~~~~~~~~~~~~~~~~~~~~~~~~~~~~~~~~~

</xsl:comment>



<xsl:comment>      Start the HTML page here </xsl:comment>
<HTML>
    <HEAD>
        <TITLE>XML COM page</TITLE>
    </HEAD>
<BODY>

<xsl:comment>
```

```
~~~~~~~~~~~~~~~~~~~~~~~~~~~~~~~~~~~~~~~~~~~~~~~~~~~~
build table for chair data
~~~~~~~~~~~~~~~~~~~~~~~~~~~~~~~~~~~~~~~~~~~~~~~~~~~~
</xsl:comment>

<xsl:for-each select="Chair">
    <P>current</P>
    <TABLE BORDER="1" CELLSPACING="0" CELLPADDING="0">
        <TR>
            <TH>ID</TH>
            <TH>Color</TH>
        </TR>
        <TR>
            <TD><xsl:value-of select="@ID"/></TD>
            <TD><xsl:value-of select="@Color"/></TD>
        </TR>
    </TABLE>
</xsl:for-each>

<xsl:comment>
~~~~~~~~~~~~~~~~~~~~~~~~~~~~~~~~~~~~~~~~~~~~~~~~~~~~
XSL parts are completed

Please never forget, all HTML must be well formed
also. XSL is also case sensitive.
~~~~~~~~~~~~~~~~~~~~~~~~~~~~~~~~~~~~~~~~~~~~~~~~~~~~
</xsl:comment>


<P>command </P>
<xsl:comment>
~~~~~~~~~~~~~~~~~~~~~~~~~~~~~~~~~~~~~~~~~~~~~~~~~~~~
build table for commanding new chair data
~~~~~~~~~~~~~~~~~~~~~~~~~~~~~~~~~~~~~~~~~~~~~~~~~~~~
</xsl:comment>

<FORM METHOD = "POST" ACTION = "XMLCOMChair.asp" ID = "frmImage"
NAME = "getInfo" >
    <TABLE BORDER="1" CELLSPACING="0" CELLPADDING="0">
        <TR>
            <TD>Action</TD>
            <TD>
          <input TYPE="text" NAME="Action" VALUE="Open or New">
          </input>
            </TD>
        </TR>
        <TR>
```

```
               <TD>ID</TD>
               <TD><input TYPE="text" NAME="ID" VALUE=""></input></TD>
        </TR>
        <TR>
               <TD>color</TD>
               <TD>
          <input TYPE="text" NAME="color" VALUE="puce">
          </input>
               </TD>
        </TR>
     </TABLE>
     <input ID="subFull" NAME="subR" TYPE="submit" VALUE="Go"></input>
</FORM>


</BODY>
</HTML>

</xsl:template>
</xsl:stylesheet>
```

A few issues should be considered during the coding of XSL. All XSL must be *well formed*, which means that it must comply with the standards for properly formed XML according to the World Wide Web Consortium (W3C) organization. Well-formed errors are generally caused from the following problems in the XML:

- **Element tags do not match**   Make certain that the tags used include matching beginning and ending tags—including the HTML tags.

- **Inappropriate Spacing between characters**   The proper amount of spaces between certain parts within an element must be maintained. An extra space between a / character and a > character could make the XML not well-formed.

- **Special Characters encountered**   An element's and an attribute's values must have the special characters escape coded. Please see the sidebar "Escape Coding XML" for more information about escaping characters.

XML editors can greatly improve your ability to eliminate well-formed errors in XML. You should consider using an XML editor to help diagnose errors in a solution that uses XML or for the purposes of developing software that constructs XML. If any XML document is not well formed, virtually nothing that requires the XML document will work. The existing XML parses do not offer a great deal of information about the point of failure, so finding the problem can be difficult.

When the whole solution is deployed to a server and the *XMLCOMChair.asp* is requested in a browser, the page should be drawn in the browser, as shown in Figure 13-21.

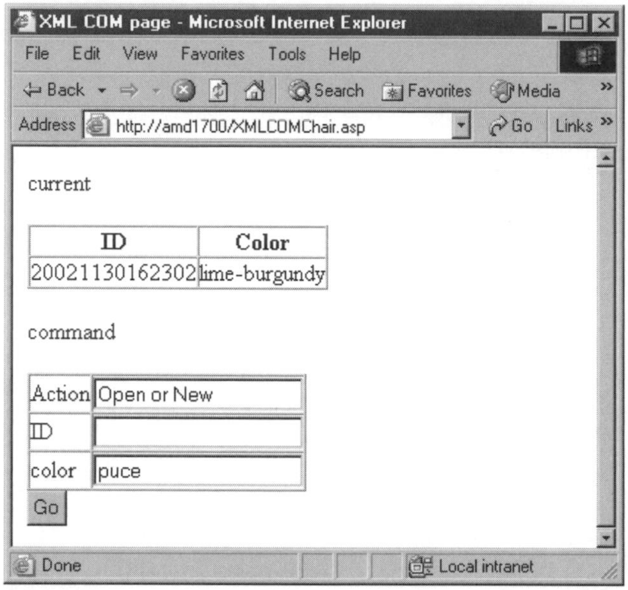

Figure 13-21. XMLCOMChair.asp using the clsChair and formatChair.xsl to draw a web page

Escape Coding XML

Since XML uses plain text to describe data, problems may arise deciphering the data from the XML structure. For example, what would happen if you had an employee named O'Brien and your software put a list of the employees into an XML document to be rendered in the browser? The XML element might read as follows: <employee name="O'Brien">. If the apostrophe found in O'Brien were not escape coded, the XML parser would bomb when XML was loaded because an apostrophe is considered a special character. If the XML were escape coded, the XML element should read as follows: <employee name="O'Brien">.

Many characters require escape coding. Special characters may be escaped using the numeric character references from the ISO/IEC 10646 character set. Some characters were provided special escape sequences, called general entities, that use an escape sequence similar to the characters themselves, as shown here:

Character	General Entity Escape Sequence
&	&amp;
<	&lt;

Character	General Entity Escape Sequence
>	>
'	'
"	"

For example, the numeric character reference for the & symbol is & but you could also use &. The numeric character reference for the = symbol is =. There is no general entity escape sequence available for this symbol. Please refer to the Appendix for more characters and equivalent escape sequences. For more information on XML, please visit http://www.w3.org/TR/REC-xml to see the W3C specification on XML.

Chapter 14

ASP.NET Web Forms

A SP.NET is Microsoft's latest set of tools and technology for web programmers to use in their quest to produce extendible web applications. The editor used by many developers for writing solutions that capitalize on ASP.NET is Visual Studio .NET. The language in which ASP.NET applications may be written varies. Visual Basic or C# are the most common languages of choice, and C# is featured in this chapter.

Visual Basic is a popular language used for programming on the Microsoft platform. Microsoft has been adding new features and options to Visual Basic through version 6 without sacrificing backward compatibility. Version 7 of Visual Basic ships with Visual Studio .NET; with this version, support for legacy versions of the language has been abandoned. A VB6 snippet of code will not likely compile in Visual Basic .NET (version 7). Visual Basic .NET does offer a great deal of new functionality, such as true inheritance, making it a true object-oriented (OO) language.

Given that the C++, Java, and JavaScript style languages seem to have a large influence on the web programming community, it would seem that a language that closely resembles the style of syntax emulated in those languages would be better suited as a web programming language. C#, a new language offered by Microsoft with Visual Studio .NET, attempts to offer the programmer the benefits of existing languages such as C++ and Java, while excluding legacy aspects of each respective language that diminish from the language's value. As a result, C# will be used to demonstrate the production of ASP.NET web forms in this chapter.

Because VB programmers will need to learn a new language syntax and some architecture to advance to the Visual Studio. NET Integrated Design Environment (IDE), C# would seem a logical choice for expanding their language horizons. Although C# is a Microsoft technology–specific language, so is Visual Basic. However, C# follows a convention that is more familiar to programmers accustomed to using languages such as Java.

Overview of the Web Forms Architecture

An ASP.NET web form page filename uses an *.aspx* suffix and in this chapter is referred to as an *ASPX file*. Each ASP.NET web form has a class associated with it. The classes for any given ASPX file exist in a "code-behind-the-form file," or *Codebehind file*. The Codebehind's filename is specified as follows: *<filename>*.aspx.*<language extension>*, where *<filename>* is the filename used for the related ASPX file and *<language extension>* is the two-letter extension associated with the language that is used in the Codebehind file. So, for example, if the ASPX file were named *Webform.aspx*, the Codebehind filename would be *Webform.aspx.cs* if it was written in C# and *Webform.aspx.vb* if the Codebehind file was written in Visual Basic. An ASPX file hosts the visual elements of the web form, and the Codebehind file hosts the logic behind the web form. All of the Codebehind files are compiled into a project dynamic link library (DLL) that is deployed with the related ASPX pages. The project DLL, also known as the assembly, is named after the project, by default.

When an ASPX is requested from IIS, it is processed through the .NET Framework ASP.NET Internet Server Application Programming Interface (ISAPI) extension, *aspnet_isapi.dll*. The .NET Framework generates another temporary DLL based on the ASPX during the first request of the file. The temporary DLL that is generated will contain a class that inherits from the respective web form class that was generated for the web form in the Codebehind file and is hosted in the project DLL, as shown in Figure 14-1.

This system provides an abstraction between the presentation logic and business logic that is more intrinsic than the ASP architecture. The Codebehind file should contain business logic and the ASPX should contain presentation logic of the web form. The system of having these two files and the capabilities each offer the programmer

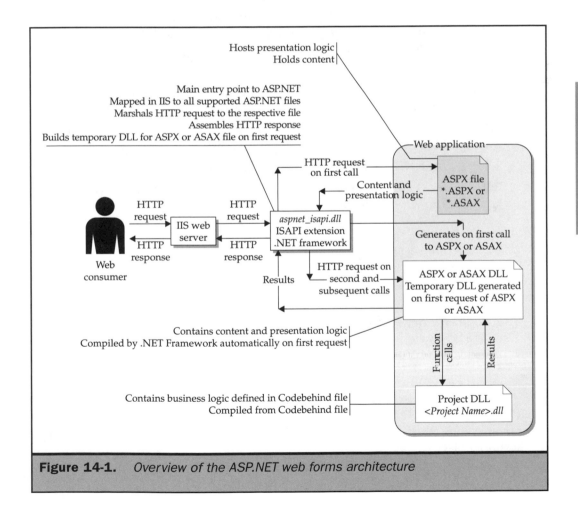

Figure 14-1. *Overview of the ASP.NET web forms architecture*

IIS PROGRAMMING

encourage the abstraction of the presentation logic and business logic. The ASPX files are XML files that contain HTML elements and elements representing server-side controls which create HTML. A programmer could put business logic in the ASPX files but doing so requires extra effort. The Codebehind files are code files, and placing presentation logic in the Codebehind file requires more effort than using the ASPX files. In sharp contrast, abstracting business logic and presentation logic in ASP required more effort. ASP encouraged the programmer to mix presentation logic and business logic, because to abstract them requires more effort to design the solution and the abstraction.

Getting Started in Visual Studio .NET

Open Visual Studio .NET, and a start page will be displayed (unless it has been configured not to display the start page). Like the previous version of Vision Studio, a project template splash screen is provided by default, but this can be disabled. Let's create a new ASP.NET web forms project:

1. Click the New Project button on the splash screen and the New Project window will open displaying project types and the corresponding project templates.

2. Select the Visual C# Projects node in the left list. The project templates that correspond to C# will be displayed in the right list.

3. Select the ASP.NET Web Application project template.

4. Enter a project name other than the default name offered in the location text box. The server name may also be specified using the Uniform Resource Locator (URL), as shown in Figure 14-2, or using a Universal Naming Convention (UNC) file path to the web root. The default server name, *localhost,* could be specified in the URL if you wanted to host the solution on your workstation during the initial code and unit test phase. In this example, the name *SimpleWF* was chosen.

5. Click the OK button. Visual Studio .NET will connect to the hosting server and generate the project files. Visual Studio .NET alters the web instance on port 80 on the host when a new project is added by creating a virtual directory in the instance that maps to the file directory where the web files reside for the web forms project. If no IIS web instance appears on port 80 or if IIS is not running, Visual Studio .NET will fail to generate the web application project.

If Visual Studio .NET was able to successfully connect to the server specified in the New Project window, the following files will be generated by a default ASP.NET web application project:

- *AssemblyInfo.cs*
- *Global.asax*

■ *Global.asax.cs*

■ *Global.asax.resx*

■ *SimpleWF.csproj*

■ *SimpleWF.csproj.webinfo*

■ *SimpleWF.vsdisco*

■ *Web.config*

■ *WebForm1.aspx*

■ *WebForm1.aspx.cs*

■ *WebForm1.aspx.resx*

After Visual Studio .NET completes the creation of the web form application on the host, the editor will display a blank web form named *WebForm1*, which is prepared for editing in design view, as shown in Figure 14-3.

All web forms in Visual Studio .NET are edited using the Web Forms Designer. The Web Forms Designer lets you switch the web form to HTML view at any time to reveal the XML and HTML code that is in the ASPX file by clicking the HTML button at the lower-left corner of the web form window. Switching back to design view is easily

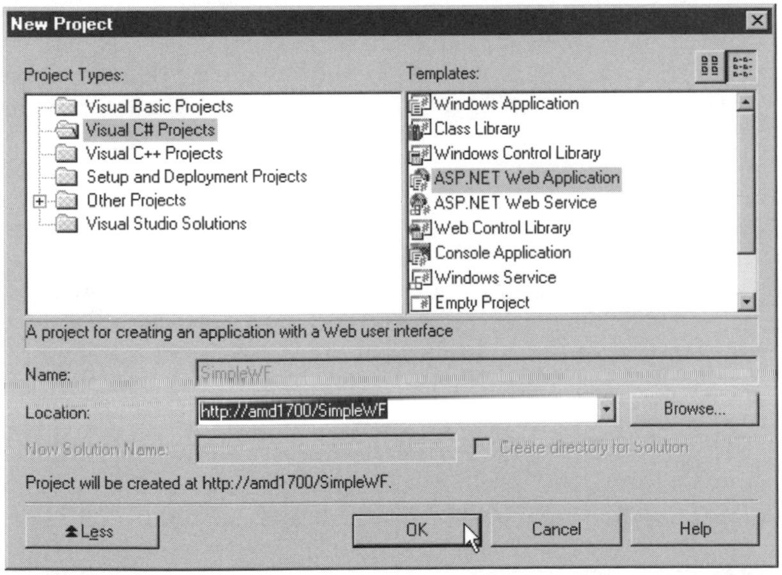

IIS PROGRAMMING

Figure 14-2. *Naming the SimpleWF ASP.NET web application project*

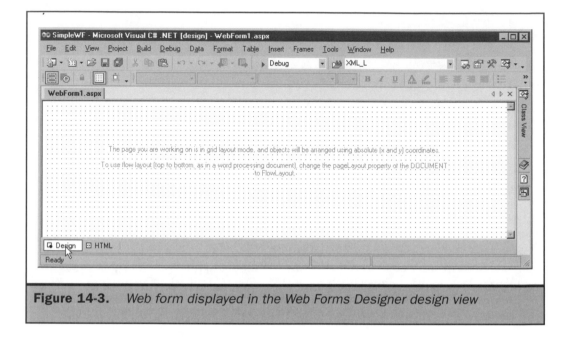

Figure 14-3. *Web form displayed in the Web Forms Designer design view*

accomplished by clicking the Design button next to the HTML button. The Web Forms Designer is smart enough to reflect changes made manually to the HTML view. The developer does not have to update the web form using the design view exclusively. The ASPX file may be edited using either view in the Web Forms Designer interchangeably.

Web Form File—ASPX

The ASPX file is the most visible file in an ASP.NET web application. The end user will request the ASPX file in their web browser to consume all of the programmatic functionality that supports the ASP.NET web application. If an end user wants to view the web form shown in that file from IIS, he or she would request *http://<myhostURL>/ <my virtual web directory>/WebForm1.aspx* in the web browser's address field.

The virtual web directory created is the same name as the project, by default. All ASP.NET web applications generate a virtual web directory when they are deployed to IIS. The files *WebForm1.aspx.cs* and *WebForm1.aspx.resx* are used to produce the project DLL or assembly that will result from the *WebForm1.aspx* being compiled. The *aspx.cs* could be thought of as the implementation code file of the ASPX file, and the ASPX file could be thought of as a header file of sorts. The *.aspx.cs* file contains all the code behind the ASPX file and the *aspx.resx* is the resource file for the web form.

Listing 14-1 shows the HTML view of an ASPX file for an ASP.NET web form file. You can edit the HTML and client side javascript in the ASPX file using the HTML view, but by using the ASP.NET web form controls in the design view, you can build a sophisticated web page without writing any HTML code. The design view of the Web Forms Designer in Visual Studio .NET is a "what you see is what you get" (WSYWIG) editor that abstracts you from the HTML code and provides a medium for building web pages that works like an Integrated Development Environment (IDE) for desktop applications like Visual Basic 6. If you are more comfortable coding the ASPX file in the HTML view, you can use the HTML section of the toolbox to get HTML elements.

Listing 14-1

```
HTML View for requestSomething.aspx

<%@ Page language="c#" Codebehind="requestSomething.aspx.cs"
AutoEventWireup="false" Inherits="SimpleWF.requestSomething" %>
<!DOCTYPE HTML PUBLIC "-//W3C//DTD HTML 4.0 Transitional//EN" >
<HTML>
  <HEAD>
   <title>requestSomething</title>
  <meta name="GENERATOR" Content="Microsoft Visual Studio 7.0">
  <meta name="CODE_LANGUAGE" Content="C#">
  <meta name="vs_defaultClientScript" content="JavaScript">
  <meta name="vs_targetSchema"
content="http://schemas.microsoft.com/intellisense/ie5">
  </HEAD>
  <body MS_POSITIONING="GridLayout">
   <form id="requestSomething" method="post" runat="server">
    <asp:TextBox id="txtYourself" style=
     "Z-INDEX: 101; LEFT: 193px; POSITION: absolute;
     TOP: 46px" runat="server" Width="330px"
     Height="25px">
    </asp:TextBox>
    <asp:Label id="Label1" style=
     "Z-INDEX: 102; LEFT: 26px; POSITION: absolute;
      TOP: 41px" runat="server" Width="155px"
      Height="43px">
      Tell me about yourself and click submit:
    </asp:Label>
    <asp:TextBox id="txtResponse" style=
     "Z-INDEX: 103; LEFT: 57px; POSITION: absolute;
      TOP: 148px" runat="server" Width="435px"
      Height="101px" ReadOnly="True"
      TextMode="MultiLine">
    </asp:TextBox>
```

```
<asp:Button id="Button1" style=
  "Z-INDEX: 104; LEFT: 298px; POSITION: absolute;
   TOP: 79px" runat="server" Width="131px"
   Height="43px" Text="Submit">
</asp:Button>
<asp:Label id="Label2" style=
  "Z-INDEX: 105; LEFT: 66px; POSITION: absolute;
   TOP: 116px" runat="server" Width="138px"
   Height="27px">You Said:
</asp:Label>
</form>
</body>
</HTML>
```

The first line of *requestSomething.aspx* identifies the Codebehind file *requestSomething.aspx.cs*. The *Global.asax* uses the same filename convention as the *requestSomething.aspx* file by referencing a Codebehind file called *Global.asax.cs*. The *Global.asax* file serves the same purpose that it did in legacy ASP—it provides a file location where code may be written, which is accessible by all the web forms in the given project and allows the developer to capture application-specific events. For example, just as the *Global.asa* file in ASP provides events for application start and end and session start and end, the *Global.asax* file provides a class named *Global* that inherits *System.Web.HttpApplication* and has member functions that provide the same events. As an added benefit, *Global.asax* also provides new events that capture the start and end of a given resource request, authentication, and application errors.

The web form *requestSomething.aspx* includes three web form controls. The web form controls were added in design view using the Web Forms part of the toolbox. The Web Forms Designer in Visual Studio .NET offer developers a unique opportunity to work with web forms as though they were writing code for desktop applications. The toolbox in Visual Studio .NET allows developers to paste controls onto the web form just as if they were creating a desktop application form in Visual Basic or Visual C++. The interfaces to the controls are almost identical to the control counterparts found in desktop software.

Developers can write code behind the web forms in a similar way that code was written behind form classes in the Visual Basic or Visual C++ desktop development environment. The properties view for each control is formatted into XML and placed in the ASPX file. The .NET Framework uses the XML to initialize the respective control and produce HTML that is eventually returned to the consumer. The Visual Studio .NET toolbox also provides developers a selection of HTML elements. For example, both the *DataGrid* control and the HTML table element will produce results that display a table in the web browser. The web forms *DataGrid* control provides greater programmatic control of the population and configuration of the table versus the HTML table. Listings 14-2 and 14-3 illustrate the differences in the ASPX file between the *DataGrid* web form control and the HTML element. Listing 14-2 shows the XML placed in the ASPX file for a *DataGrid* control.

Listing 14-2

```
<asp:DataGrid id="DataGrid2"
style="Z-INDEX: 104; LEFT: 88px; POSITION: absolute; TOP: 258px"
runat="server">
</asp:DataGrid>
```

Listing 14-3 shows an HTML element created when you paste a table from the HTML part of the toolbox onto the web form.

Listing 14-3

```
<TABLE id="Table1" style="Z-INDEX: 103; LEFT: 191px;
POSITION: absolute; TOP: 291px" cellSpacing="1"
cellPadding="1" width="300" border="1">
  <TR>
   <TD></TD>
   <TD></TD>
   <TD></TD>
  </TR>
  <TR>
   <TD></TD>
   <TD></TD>
   <TD></TD>
  </TR>
  <TR>
   <TD></TD>
   <TD></TD>
   <TD></TD>
  </TR>
</TABLE>
```

In the overly simple web form *requestSomething.aspx*, shown in Figure 14-4, the end user can type in some personal information and click the Submit button. After the web form is submitted, the form responds to the end user with the contents typed in the text box labeled Tell Me About Yourself And Click Submit and also typed in the You Said text box. Figure 14-4 shows the *requestSomething.aspx* form after some information has been submitted to the server.

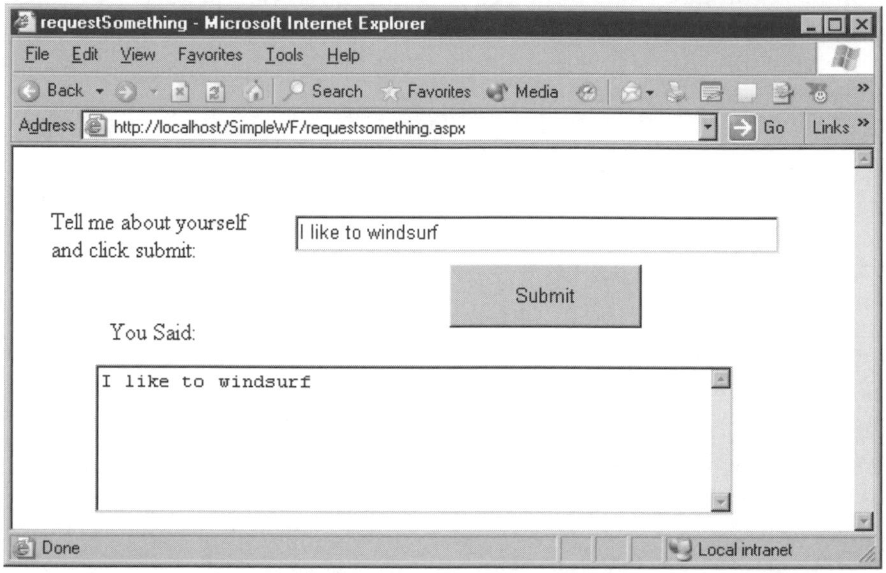

Figure 14-4.   *Web form requestSomething.aspx in action*

Web Form Codebehind File—aspx.cs

Using classic ASP, the developer places code in the ASP file to extract the posted data typed into a text box after the end user clicks the Submit button. After the data is extracted from the Request object, the data is placed in the value attribute for the other text box that displays what the end user submitted. The following line of code can achieve the result in an ASP file:

```
<textarea name="txtResponse" ><% =Request("txtYourself") %>
</textarea>
```

The ASP.NET web form achieves the result with more code but with greater organization and better form than the ASP. Listing 14-4 shows the code behind the web form *requestSomething.aspx* in the Codebehind file *requestSomething.aspx.cs*. The Visual Studio .NET Web Forms Designer automatically generates the majority of the code shown in Listing 14-4. If you open the file *requestSomething.aspx* in the design view and double-click the control named *txtYourself*, which is the top text box control, the Web Forms Designer will create an event in the Codebehind file *requestSomething.aspx.cs* named *txtYourself_TextChanged*. The Web Forms Designer will open the file *requestSomething.aspx.cs* to the event function created for the web form control *txtYourself*. Although the Web Forms Designer may generate much of the code within the Codebehind file, you can edit code within the file as needed because the Codebehind file is the intended location for the supporting code for the ASPX file.

Listing 14-4

```
Source Code for the requestSomething.aspx CodeBehind File
requestSomething.aspx.cs

using System;
using System.Collections;
using System.ComponentModel;
using System.Data;
using System.Drawing;
using System.Web;
using System.Web.SessionState;
using System.Web.UI;
using System.Web.UI.WebControls;
using System.Web.UI.HtmlControls;
namespace SimpleWF
{
  /// <summary>
  /// Summary description for requestSomething.
  /// </summary>
  public class requestSomething : System.Web.UI.Page
  {
   protected System.Web.UI.WebControls.Button Button1;
   protected System.Web.UI.WebControls.TextBox txtYourself;
   protected System.Web.UI.WebControls.TextBox txtResponse;
   protected System.Web.UI.WebControls.Label Label2;
   protected System.Web.UI.WebControls.Label Label1;

   private void Page_Load(object sender, System.EventArgs e)
   {
    // Put user code to initialize the page here
   }
   #region Web Form Designer generated code
   override protected void OnInit(EventArgs e)
   {
    //
    // CODEGEN: This call is required by the
    // ASP.NET Web Form Designer.
```

```
    //
    InitializeComponent();
    base.OnInit(e);
}

/// <summary>
/// Required method for Designer support - do not modify
/// the contents of this method with the code editor.
/// </summary>
private void InitializeComponent()
{
  this.txtYourself.TextChanged += new
  System.EventHandler(this.txtYourself_TextChanged);

  this.Load += new
  System.EventHandler(this.Page_Load);
}
#endregion
private void txtYourself_TextChanged
    (object sender, System.EventArgs e)
{
  this.txtResponse.Text = this.txtYourself.Text;
}
}
}
```

The event handler for the web form is called when the value in *txtYourself* is changed and submitted in a form to the web server. When the form submission is made to the server, the code in the Codebehind file for the web form *requestSomething.aspx* determines that a value was submitted for the text box named *txtYourself* and calls the event function *txtYourself_TextChanged*. In this particular event, one line of code was actually written to place the value submitted into the text box *txtResponse*:

```
this.txtResponse.Text = this.txtYourself.Text;
```

Both text boxes are treated like controls or class instances in a normal software application, abstracting the programmer entirely from the details of the HTML. Because the programmer can paste controls in the design view and edit code that relates to the behavior of the control after clicking the specific control, the programmer is almost completely removed from ever having to edit in HTML.

AssemblyInfo.cs File

The ASP.NET project that Visual Studio .NET created, named *SimpleWF,* results in an assembly being created. The *assembly* is the deployment package for the web form files that make up the project, which is simply a DLL. When an ASPX file is requested for the first time from IIS, the assembly is produced. The Codebehind file and the resource file that are referenced in the ASPX file are compiled in Microsoft instruction language (MISL), which has a similar format to assembly code not unlike binary products of other conventional compilers. The MISL is produced only for the code subroutines that are executed. The MISL will not be produced for functions or subroutines that were not executed.

The files *AssemblyInfo.cs, SimpleWF.csproj, SimpleWF.csproj.webinfo,* and *SimpleWF.vsdisco* all provide information for the compiler to produce the assembly that hosts the MISL generated from the ASP.NET files. The *AssemblyInfo.cs* file contains information that describes the assembly, such as version and name. You can also use the file to sign your assemblies by assigning a key. Assembly signing provides a mechanism that will protect your assembly from being reverse-engineered. Listing 14-5 shows a blank *AssemblyInfo.cs* file. You can edit the assembly file directly, and you do not have to be comprehensive. You can edit the values that are known and leave other parts blank.

Listing 14-5

```
Blank AssemblyInfo.cs file

using System.Reflection;
using System.Runtime.CompilerServices;
[assembly: AssemblyTitle("")]
[assembly: AssemblyDescription("")]
[assembly: AssemblyConfiguration("")]
[assembly: AssemblyCompany("")]
[assembly: AssemblyProduct("")]
[assembly: AssemblyCopyright("")]
[assembly: AssemblyTrademark("")]
[assembly: AssemblyCulture("")]
[assembly: AssemblyVersion("1.0.*")]
[assembly: AssemblyDelaySign(false)]
[assembly: AssemblyKeyFile("")]
[assembly: AssemblyKeyName("")]
```

Project File—csproj

The *csproj* file is an XML file that contains information about the dependencies of the project and some compilation settings for the creation of the assembly. Visual Studio

.NET updates this file as web forms, and references are added or removed from the project. You should not edit the *csproj* file in the normal course of working on an ASP.NET project. If you do open it however, you will see a file that describes all of the settings and elements that contribute to the project, such as filenames, deployment settings, and assembly references.

Project WebInfo File—csproj.webinfo

The *csproj.webinfo* file is an XML file that describes where the project file is located or hosted. Listing 14-6 shows the *SimpleWF.csproj.webinfo* file contents. This file is also generated and updated by Visual Studio .NET, and you should not edit it directly.

Listing 14-6

```
Contents of File SimpleWF.csproj.webinfo

<VisualStudioUNCWeb>
 <Web URLPath = "http://amd1700/SimpleWF/SimpleWF.csproj" />
</VisualStudioUNCWeb>
```

Discovery Information File—vsdisco

The *vsdisco* file identifies searchable paths on a development web server to enable ASP.NET to seek and find ASP.NET web services. The *SimpleWF.vsdisco* file is the default file generated for the project *SimpleWF*. Listing 14-7 shows the source of *SimpleWF.vsdisco*. You should edit the *vsdisco* file to help ASP.NET find other assemblies in a development environment by setting web directories that should not be searched. The default version of the *vsdsico* excludes the FrontPage extension directories because an assembly will not be located within any of those directories under normal circumstances.

Listing 14-7

```
Source of SimpleWF.vsdisco

<?xml version="1.0" encoding="utf-8" ?>
<dynamicDiscovery xmlns=
     "urn:schemas-dynamicdiscovery:disco.2000-03-17">
  <exclude path="_vti_cnf" />
  <exclude path="_vti_pvt" />
  <exclude path="_vti_log" />
  <exclude path="_vti_script" />
  <exclude path="_vti_txt" />
  <exclude path="Web References" />
</dynamicDiscovery>
```

Web Configuration File—web.config

The *web.config* file is a deployment configuration file for IIS. The programmer can use the *web.config* file as a means of setting IIS to run in a particular way during development. When the ASP.NET project gets rolled to production, the instance or virtual directory of IIS is immediately configured according to the configuration described in the *web.config* file. The settings in the file pertain to all subdirectories that exist subordinate to the directory in which it was placed unless another *web.config* file is encountered. This means that a web application can be made up of multiple *web.config* files. If there is no *web.cong* file found in a web application, the *machine.config* file located in the *$:\WINDOWS\Microsoft.NET\Framework\v1.1.4322\CONFIG* folder will be used as a default. The v1.1.4322 portion of the file path is subject to reflect the version of the .NET Framework that you are hosting on your server. Listing 14-8 shows the default *web.config* file that was produced in the ASP.NET project *SimpleWF*.

Listing 14-8

```
Source Code of web.config file
<?xml version="1.0" encoding="utf-8" ?>
<configuration>
 <system.web>
 <compilation
  defaultLanguage="c#"
  debug="true"
 />
 <customErrors
 mode="RemoteOnly"
 />
 <authentication mode="Windows" />
 <trace
  enabled="false"
  requestLimit="10"
  pageOutput="false"
  traceMode="SortByTime"
   localOnly="true"
/>
 <sessionState
   mode="InProc"
   stateConnectionString="tcpip=127.0.0.1:42424"
   sqlConnectionString=
       "data source=127.0.0.1;user id=sa;password="
   cookieless="false"
   timeout="20"
 />
```

IIS PROGRAMMING

```
<globalization
  requestEncoding="utf-8"
  responseEncoding="utf-8"
/>
</system.web>
</configuration>
```

The application settings are set as child elements to the *appSettings* element, which is a child element of the *configuration* element. A *web.config* file will not contain any application settings by default. Application settings are typically added by the dynamic properties for controls pasted on web forms in the Web Forms Designer or manually by the developer. Application settings contain initialization values for components in the application. Utilization of the *web.config* file for storing and extracting application settings will be covered in greater detail in Chapter 15.

The *system.web* element has child elements that contain settings that control the mechanics of the web application itself. If child elements are not present, the application will use the settings found in the *machine.config* file. Although not a comprehensive list of potential settings, the following six child elements of the *system.web* element are found in a *web.config* file created by Visual Studio .NET by default:

- **compilation**   Defines the default compilation parameters for the application
- **customErrors**   Defines the error reporting configurations
- **authentication**   Defines the authentication method that should be used
- **trace**   Defines the means whereby the .NET Trace service will function
- **sessionState**   Defines how the session will function and by what mechanism it will be maintained
- **globalization**   Defines the character set parameters, encoding, and cultural settings

Building Web Forms

Displaying data from a database in an HTML table is usually performed using the web form *DataGrid* control. In design view, after adding a new web form to a given project, choose the *DataGrid* from the toolbox and paste it onto the web form. (The web form must be displayed in the design view. If HTML code is visible, the HTML view is being displayed. Figure 14-3 shows a web form in design view.) After the *DataGrid* is pasted on the web form, the name may be edited in the Properties window for the newly created *DataGrid* control. In Figure 14-5, the name of the *DataGrid* was set to *dgChair*.

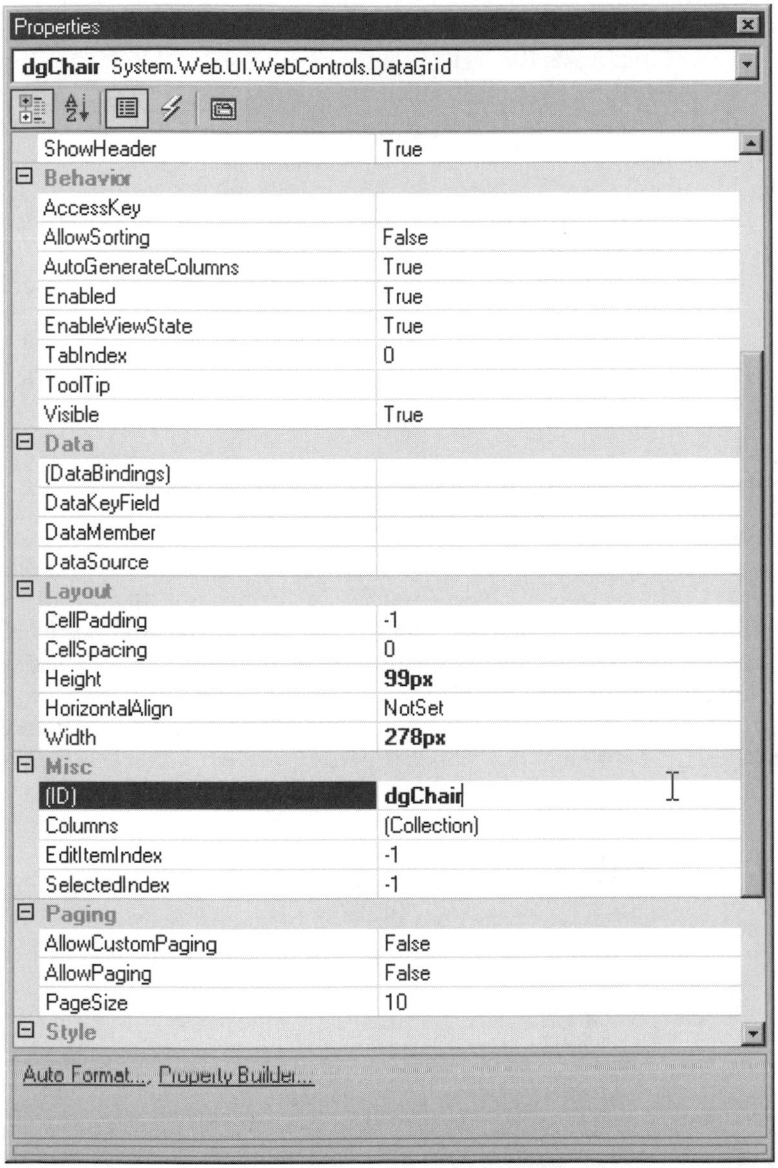

Properties	
dgChair System.Web.UI.WebControls.DataGrid	
ShowHeader	True
Behavior	
AccessKey	
AllowSorting	False
AutoGenerateColumns	True
Enabled	True
EnableViewState	True
TabIndex	0
ToolTip	
Visible	True
Data	
(DataBindings)	
DataKeyField	
DataMember	
DataSource	
Layout	
CellPadding	-1
CellSpacing	0
Height	**99px**
HorizontalAlign	NotSet
Width	**278px**
Misc	
(ID)	**dgChair**
Columns	(Collection)
EditItemIndex	-1
SelectedIndex	-1
Paging	
AllowCustomPaging	False
AllowPaging	False
PageSize	10
Style	

Auto Format..., Property Builder...

Figure 14-5. *Properties window for dgChair DataGrid control*

Running the web form at this point in Visual Studio .NET will cause the web form to be compiled into an assembly on the development server. In this example, the development server that hosts the web form is named *amd1700*. To compile the web form and run it in debug mode in Visual Studio .NET, press the F5 key. Visual Studio .NET will compile the web form and enter into a debugging mode, just as the previous editions of Visual Studio ran a Visual Basic or Visual C++ executable.

After the compilation is complete on the server, the web browser on your workstation will spawn and open the web form. After the development server grinds away at the effort to deliver the web page for a short period of time, the browser will display a blank page. If you close the browser, the debug session will end and Visual Studio .NET returns to the edit mode. In this specific exercise, the browser displays a blank page because the *DataGrid dgChair* is not loaded with any data. In order for the *DataGrid* to display any data, you will have to write code in the Codebehind file that obtains a *DataSet* and places the data from the *DataSet* into the *DataGrid* control, *dgChair*.

Editing Code for a Data-Oriented Web Form

To edit the Codebehind file for the web form hosting the *DataGrid dgChair*, right-click the web form file in the Solution Explorer or right-click the file itself in design view, and select View Code. By default, Visual Studio .NET does not display all files in the Solution Explorer that are part of the solution. Select the Show All Files icon at the top of the Solution Explorer to display all the files in the Solution Explorer so that the Codebehind file may be chosen directly.

The Codebehind file will be displayed with *using* directives for the classes that are required to make the web form function, the namespace, and the class framework. The namespace has the same name as the project. The class name is the name of the web form. Listing 14-9 shows the source code of the Codebehind file for the web form *showGrid*. The web form *showGrid* was created to demonstrate the use of the *DataGrid* control and as such, the Web Forms Designer placed a protected member in the class *showGrid* to represent the *DataGrid* that was pasted on the web form and named *dgChair*. The *using System.Data.OleDb* reference was added to provide an easy means of referring to ADO.NET classes.

Listing 14-9

```
Source Code for showGrid.aspx.cs
after DataGrid Added in Design View

using System;
using System.Collections;
using System.ComponentModel;
using System.Data;
using System.Data.OleDb; //for the OleDbclasses
```

```
using System.Drawing;
using System.Web;
using System.Web.SessionState;
using System.Web.UI;
using System.Web.UI.WebControls;
using System.Web.UI.HtmlControls;
namespace SimpleWF
{
  /// <summary>
  /// Summary description for showGrid.
  /// </summary>
  public class showGrid : System.Web.UI.Page
  {
   protected System.Web.UI.WebControls.DataGrid dgChair;
   private void Page_Load(object sender, System.EventArgs e)
   {
   }
   #region Web Form Designer generated code
   override protected void OnInit(EventArgs e)
   {
    //
    // CODEGEN: This call is required by the
    // ASP.NET Web Form Designer.
    //
    InitializeComponent();
    base.OnInit(e);
   }

   /// <summary>
   /// Required method for Designer support - do not modify
   /// the contents of this method with the code editor.
   /// </summary>
   private void InitializeComponent()
   {
    this.Load += new System.EventHandler
           (this.Page_Load);
   }
   #endregion
  }
}
```

If the desired result is to fill the *DataGrid dgChair* with data that is hosted in a database table, an ADO.NET *DataSet* must be obtained that is filled with data from a database. The *DataSet* may be used to populate the *DataGrid dgChair* when the web page is requested from the web server. When the page is loaded from the web server, the *Load* event of the *Page* object is triggered. The class *showGrid* inherits from *System.Web.UI.Page*, as evidenced by the class declaration in Listing 14-9, so the class *showGrid* inherits the *Load* event from *System.Web.UI.Page*. When *Load* is executed, it can execute code that will obtain a *DataSet* and fill the *DataGrid*. Listing 14-10 shows a subroutine named *LoadGrid* that will fill a *DataGrid* with a *DataSet*.

Listing 14-10

```
Source Code for Subroutine LoadGrid

private void LoadGrid(DataGrid dg)
{
  //set the connection credentials
  string DataSetName = "myChairs";
  string ConnectionString =
      "Provider=Microsoft.Jet.OLEDB.4.0;" +
    "Data Source=C:\\aspData\\employees.mdb;";

  //make the DB connection
  OleDbConnection myConn = new
   OleDbConnection(ConnectionString);

  //make a data set to hold chairs
  DataSet myDataSet = new DataSet(DataSetName);

  //make a data adaptor
  OleDbDataAdapter myAdapt = new
   OleDbDataAdapter("Select * From tblChair", myConn);

  //fill the dataset
  myAdapt.Fill(myDataSet);

  //get a view in the dataset
  DataView myDataView = new DataView(myDataSet.Tables[0]);

  //show the data view in the Grid
  dg.DataSource = myDataView;
  dg.DataBind();
}
```

LoadGrid is a member function of class *showGrid*. The function is called by placing the following call in the *Page_Load* event function for *showGrid.aspx*:

```
LoadGrid(dgChair);
```

ASP.NET Security

When the page *showGrid.aspx* is loaded, the *Load* event is captured and the *LoadGrid* function is called. When *LoadGrid* is called, the database connection data is set to a string variable and the ADO Connection object is instantiated using the connection string.

> **Note**   *It should be pointed out that coding the literal connection string arguments in the code, as demonstrated in Listing 14-10, is an extremely bad practice. This technique was used to explicitly show the connection credentials that were used and how they applied to the Connection object. A better method for obtaining the database connection credentials is to place the database connection string in the* web.config *file. See Chapter 15 for more information on obtaining initialization data from the* web.config *file.*

In Listing 14-10, the data source being utilized is Microsoft Access 2000. The host server file permissions for the Access *.mdb* data file must be configured to allow the ASP.NET web form to read and write the Access database file. If an enterprise database like SQL Server or Oracle were utilized, *integrated security* could be used to send credentials to the database server when the ASP.NET web form queries the database. The *integrated security=sspi* argument in the database connection string specifies the use of integrated security so the Windows .NET Server credentials under which the web form is running are presented to the data source. The Windows user account that an ASP.NET application runs under varies based on the following criteria:

- **Authentication established for your ASP.NET application**   Anonymous or non-anonymous

- **IIS Isolation mode being used**   IIS 5.0 isolation mode or worker process isolation mode

Depending on the authentication you establish for your application in IIS, the possible Windows user account being used by ASP.NET is as follows:

- **IIS guest Windows user account for anonymous access**   *IUSER_<machine name>*

- **Application pool identity**   Windows user account established in the application pool identity. Default accounts include: Network Service, Local Service, and Local System.

- **Windows user account of the authenticated user consuming the application**   Credentials presented by the end user during authentication to the ASP.NET server application.

If you set up IIS to allow anonymous access to the site, and the default application isolation mode is set for the server (which is worker process isolation mode), ASP.NET will use the identity established in the application pool being used for the web application. If you were using IIS 5.0 isolation mode for backwards compatibility, the IIS guest user account will be used as an identity for your application. If your application were set to use one of the authentication modes available in IIS so that the end user presents credentials, IIS by default will use the credentials as an identity. The default identities used by an IIS application are summarized in Table 14-1.

Your application can use identities other than the default identities IIS will use. For example, you could use forms authentication to authorize the end user access to the application and still use a special user account for all queries to a database.

In the case of the web form *showGrid.aspx*, worker process isolation mode will be assumed since that is the default mode for IIS 6. Anonymous access will be allowed so the credentials of the application pool's Windows user account will be the credentials used to access the data source. For the Microsoft Access database file, the host server file permissions must be set to allow the Windows user account to read, write, and modify the *.mdb* file. In the case of the enterprise database, the Windows user account must be provided the appropriate access to the database within the database server.

Note   *Don't forget that the* web.config *file contains an element named* authentication. *The default* mode *for authentication is* Windows. *Since many programmers use a Windows user account that belongs to the administrators group, it is possible to develop a false sense of confidence in the ASP.NET web form functioning because the programmer's user account will have the rights to do most anything to the development environment. When the application is migrated to a staging or production server that has restricted access, the web form may no longer work.*

Authentication	Application Isolation Mode	Windows User Account Used by ASP.NET
Anonymous	IIS 5.0 isolation	*IUSER_<machine name>*
Anonymous	Worker process isolation	Application pool identity for web application
Non-anonymous	IIS 5.0 isolation	Credentials presented by the user during authentication
Non-anonymous	Worker process isolation	Credentials presented by the user during authentication

Table 14-1.   *Default Identities for an ASP.NET Application*

ADO.NET Overview

Since ADO.NET will be used to fill the *DataGrid dgChair* with data from the database table, a namespace must be added to the file *showGrid.aspx* for the data classes required to access the data source. The web forms by default include the namespace *System.Data* that is the core namespace of ADO.NET. Other namespaces subordinate to *System.Data* support a given data source type. The subordinate namespaces native to *System.Data* are as follows:

- *System.Data.Common*
- *System.Data.OleDb*
- *System.Data.SqlClient*
- *System.Data.SqlTypes*

The *SqlClient* provides an interface to a managed provider of SQL Server. This namespace provides the programmer with the most efficient means of communicating with SQL Server 2000. The namespace *System.Data.OleDb* supports an interface that is similar to legacy ADO and is not as efficient to use as the *SqlClient* namespace when communicating with SQL Server 2000. *System.Data.OleDb* is a good choice to use on data sources other than SQL Server 2000 that have an OLE-DB Provider. The namespaces *System.Data.Common* and *System.Data.SqlTypes* provide supporting interfaces for SQL Server and the common interfaces between SQL Server and OLE-DB classes.

ADO.NET ships as a single assembly named *System.Data.dll*. If support of an ODBC data source is necessary, Microsoft offers another assembly that can be downloaded and will provide a namespace for ODBC classes.

Since the data source used in the examples in this chapter is Microsoft Access 2000, the *OleDb* namespace will be used. If SQL Server 2000 was being used, *SqlClient* namespace would be used since it is the most efficient way to communicate with SQL Server 2000. The following line of code must be added at the top of the file *showGrid.aspx* along with the other namespace directives:

```
using System.Data.OleDb; //for the OleDb classes
```

Using ADO.NET Classes to Fill a Web Form Data Grid Control

After the connection is created, an ADO.NET Dataset instance named *myDataSet* is requested for the table *tblChairs* in the database. The *DataSet* is assigned the name *myChairs* when it is instantiated. The ADO.NET *Adaptor* object named *myAdapt* is instantiated for the purpose of filling the *DataSet* instance *myDataSet*. After *myDataSet* has been filled, an ADO.NET *DataView* object named *myDataView* is instantiated using *myDataSet*'s first table. Finally, the argument for the *DataGrid*, named *dg*, which was passed into the subroutine, has the data source property set to the *DataView* instance *myDataView* and the *DataBind* method of *dg* is called to fill the *DataGrid* instance *dg* with the data from the contents of table *tblChairs*.

The use of the *DataView* class is not required if the entire *DataSet* is to be displayed. In Listing 14-10, the entire *DataSet* that is created is displayed in the *DataGrid dg*. Since the entire *DataSet* is displayed in the grid, it would have been possible to skip the following line:

```
DataView myDataView = new DataView(myDataSet.Tables[0]);
```

The *DataSource* property of the *DataGrid dg* could have been set to the *Tables[0]* property of the *DataSet myDataSet*. The line assigning the *dg.DataSource* to *myDataView* could be changed to the following:

```
dg.DataSource = myDataSet.Tables[0]
```

When you press F5, the page *showGrid.aspx* should compile and the browser instance will open, displaying the results of the data in table *myChairs*, as shown in Figure 14-6.

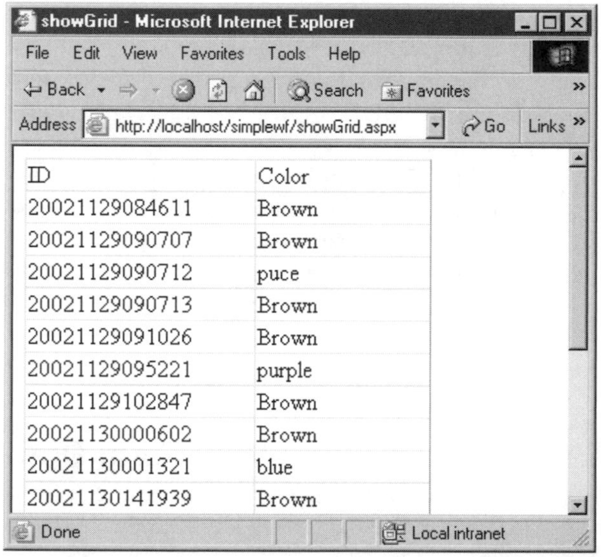

Figure 14-6.   *Results of showGrid.aspx shown hosting DataGrid*

Using the DataList Control

In addition to the *DataGrid*, other types of data controls may be used to display database data. The *DataList* control is useful for displaying data in a format other than a tabular form. Listing 14-11 shows the source code to *datalist.aspx.cs*, a web form with a *DataList* control being filled with data using an ADO.NET *DataSet*.

Listing 14-11

Web Form Featuring the Use of the DataList Control

```csharp
using System;
using System.Collections;
using System.ComponentModel;
using System.Data;
using System.Data.OleDb; //for the OleDb classes
using System.Drawing;
using System.Web;
using System.Web.SessionState;
using System.Web.UI;
using System.Web.UI.WebControls;
using System.Web.UI.HtmlControls;
namespace SimpleWF
{
  /// <summary>
  /// Summary description for datalist.
  /// </summary>
  public class datalist : System.Web.UI.Page
  {
    protected System.Web.UI.WebControls.DataList dlChair;

    private void LoadList(DataList dl)
    {
      //set the connection credentials
      string DataSetName = "myChairs";
      string ConnectionString =
        "Provider=Microsoft.Jet.OLEDB.4.0;" +
"Data Source=C:\\aspData\\employees.mdb;";

      //make the DB connection
      OleDbConnection myConn = new
       OleDbConnection(ConnectionString);

      //make a data set to hold chairs
      DataSet myDataSet = new DataSet(DataSetName);
```

```
    //make a data adaptor
    OleDbDataAdapter myAdapt = new
     OleDbDataAdapter("Select * From tblChair", myConn);


    //fill the dataset
    myAdapt.Fill(myDataSet);

    //show the data in the data list
    dl.DataSource = myDataSet;
    dl.DataBind();
    }
private void Page_Load(object sender, System.EventArgs e)
{
 LoadList(this.dlChair);
}
#region Web Form Designer generated code
override protected void OnInit(EventArgs e)
{
 //
 // CODEGEN: This call is required by the
 // ASP.NET Web Form Designer.
 //
 InitializeComponent();
 base.OnInit(e);
}

/// <summary>
/// Required method for Designer support - do not modify
/// the contents of this method with the code editor.
/// </summary>
private void InitializeComponent()
{
 this.Load += new System.EventHandler(this.Page_Load);
}
#endregion
  }
}
```

The *DataList* uses another mechanism to sculpt the *DataSet,* called a *template.* The template describes how the data is to be displayed in the *DataList* control. Right-click the *DataList* and select any of the template editing selections under the context menu's Edit Template command to enable you to edit the template's properties. Items such as field headings or names may be set in the template to format how the data should be displayed. Headers, footers, and titles can also accompany a *DataList*. To specify data from an intended *DataSet*, the template must be edited in HTML view. The tags <%# and %> denote a data binding expression in a web form page. Inside the template code, the data binding fields may be specified. Listing 14-12 shows the HTML view of *datalist.aspx*.

Listing 14-12

HTML for datalist.aspx Featuring Data Binding Expressions

```
<%@ Page language="c#" Codebehind="datalist.aspx.cs"
 AutoEventWireup="false" Inherits="SimpleWF.datalist" %>
<!DOCTYPE HTML PUBLIC "-//W3C//DTD HTML 4.0 Transitional//EN" >
<HTML>
  <HEAD>
   <title>datalist</title>
  <meta name="GENERATOR" Content="Microsoft Visual Studio 7.0">
  <meta name="CODE_LANGUAGE" Content="C#">
  <meta name="vs_defaultClientScript" content="JavaScript">
  <meta name="vs_targetSchema"
   content="http://schemas.microsoft.com/intellisense/ie5">
  </HEAD>
  <body MS_POSITIONING="GridLayout" bgColor="#ffffff">
   <form id="datalist" method="post" runat="server">
    <asp:DataList id="dlChair" style=
     "Z-INDEX: 102; LEFT: 18px; POSITION: absolute;
      TOP: 34px" runat="server" Height="301px"
      Width="316px">
     <ItemTemplate>
     <DIV style="PADDING-RIGHT: 15px;
        PADDING-LEFT: 15px; PADDING-BOTTOM:
        15px; FONT: 12pt verdana;
        COLOR: black; PADDING-TOP: 15px"
        align="left">ID:</DIV>
     <%# DataBinder.Eval(Container.DataItem, "ID")%>
     <DIV style="PADDING-RIGHT: 15px; PADDING-LEFT:
        15px; PADDING-BOTTOM: 15px;
        FONT: 12pt verdana;
        COLOR: black; PADDING-TOP: 15px"
        align="left">Color:</DIV>
     <%# DataBinder.Eval(Container.DataItem, "Color")%>
     </ItemTemplate>
    </asp:DataList>
   </form>
  </body>
</HTML>
```

The *DataList* is denoted by the HTML elements `<asp:DataList>`. Inside the *DataList* element tags are the template tags denoted by the `<ItemTemplate>` tag. The template properties in the Web Forms Designer generate the tags inside the `<ItemTemplate>` tags, but you can edit them by hand using the HTML view of the web form. The data binding tags may be strategically placed inside the template at locations where you want the respective field of the *DataSet* to be displayed. Listing 14-12 shows two fields from the *DataSet* being displayed—*ID* and *Color*. The binding tag for field *ID* is `<%# DataBinder.Eval(Container.DataItem, "ID")%>` and the binding tag for field *Color* is `<%# DataBinder.Eval(Container.DataItem, "Color")%>`.

When *datalist.aspx* is run, the same *DataSet* that was generated for the *DataGrid* example shown in Figure 14-6 was generated for the *DataList* in *datalist.aspx*. As seen in Figure 14-7, however, the data format is much different given that it is formatted according to the template shown in Listing 14-12.

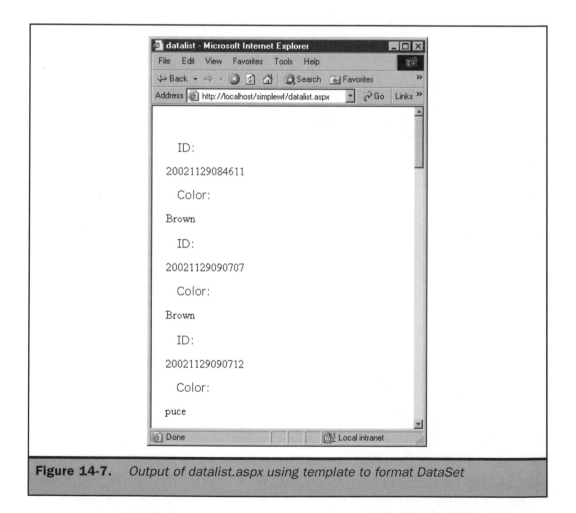

Figure 14-7.   *Output of datalist.aspx using template to format DataSet*

Data Form Wizard

The Web Forms Designer also offers a wizard to use for creating web forms that display *DataSet*s from a data source. Here's how to use the Data Form Wizard:

1. In Solution Explorer, right-click and select Add New Item.

2. In the Add New Item dialog box, many types of files are listed that can be added to the project. All file types are displayed in the right panel, but if the directory tree on the left is expanded, the child roots of the tree will offer categorical sorts that will change the items displayed in the right panel.

3. Select Data Form Wizard and type in a filename, as shown in Figure 14-8.

4. Click the Open button and a new web form will be created in Visual Studio .NET. In this example, the name *employees.aspx* was given to the new web form that was created.

5. The Data Form Wizard opens with the introduction page, informing you of the actions that will take place. Click Next.

6. In the Choose The Dataset You Want To Use step, the wizard will prompt you to choose an existing dataset or create a new *DataSet*. In this example, a *DataSet* named *dsEmps* will be created, as shown in Figure 14-9. All *DataSet*s that are created in this wizard become an item in the project and may be used by other web forms or web services within the same project. The *DataSet* file has an *.xsd* extension.

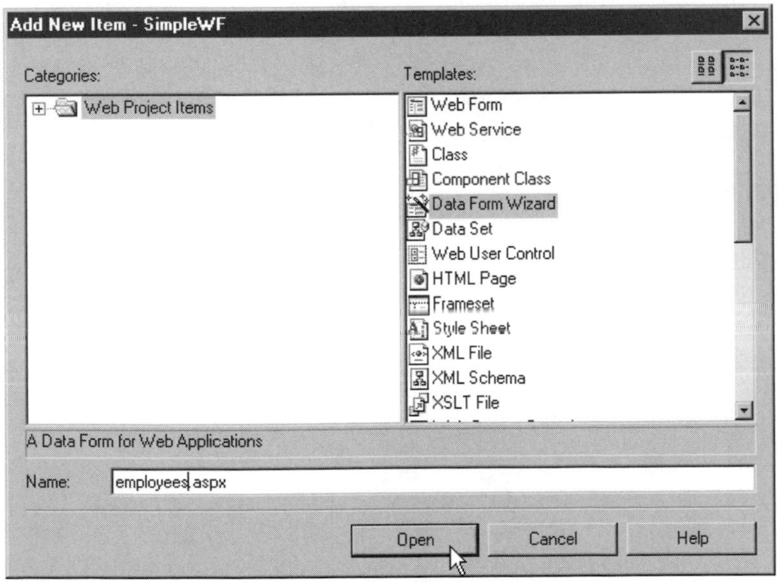

Figure 14-8.   *Choosing Data Form Wizard*

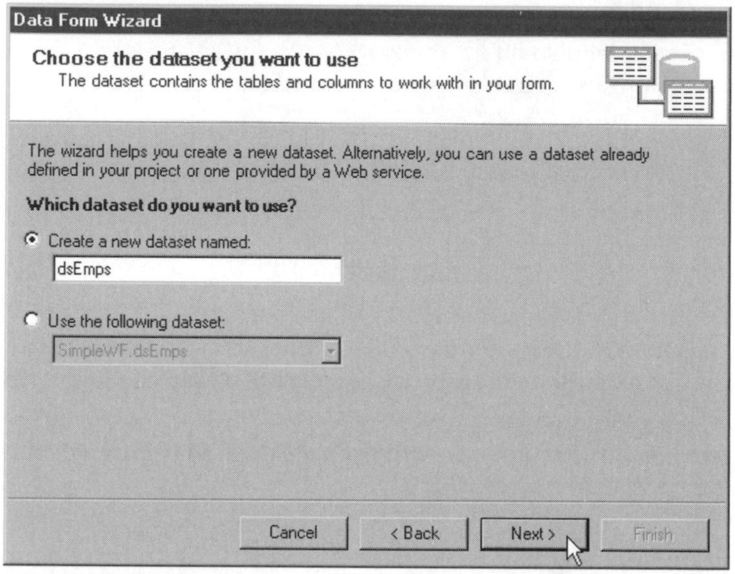

Figure 14-9.   *Choose The Dataset You Want To Use step of the Data Form Wizard*

7. Click the Next button, and the Choose A Data Connection step will display, as shown in Figure 14-10. Existing connections that were established in the project previously are listed in the drop-down combo box. You can choose an existing connection or configure a new connection in this step of the wizard. In this example, the existing connection *ASPNETExample* is chosen.

8. Click the New Connection button to open the Data Link Properties window, through which a new connection to a database can be configured.

9. Click the Next button to see the Choose Tables Or Views step. The wizard will open the data connection provided in the previous step and find the database. You can select the tables to which the web form should connect in the data source. Any tables or views that are to be shown in the web form should be selected in the left panel and placed in the right panel by clicking the right arrow (>) button. In this example, the *tblEmployee* table is chosen, as shown in Figure 14-11.

10. Click the Next button, and the Choose Tables And Columns To Display On The Form step is displayed. The wizard will open the tables or views that were chosen in step 9 and display the tables and views along with each respective column that is available for display in a dual list select box.

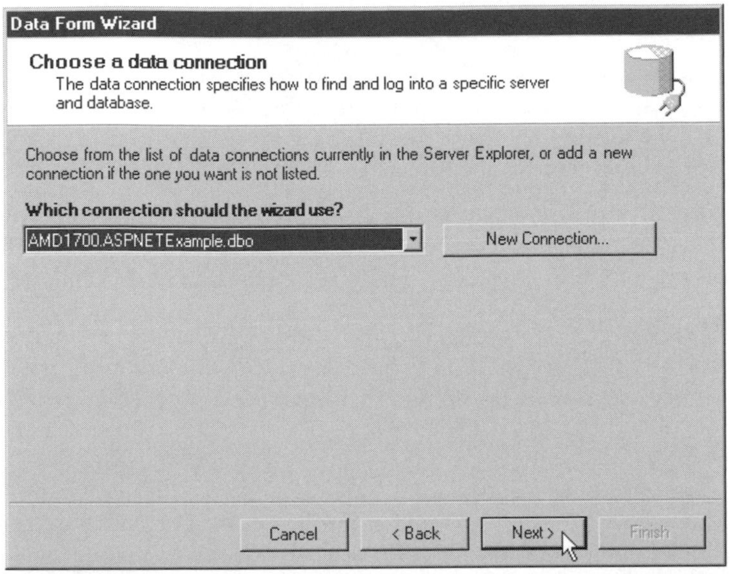

Figure 14-10.   *Choose A Data Connection step of the Data Form Wizard*

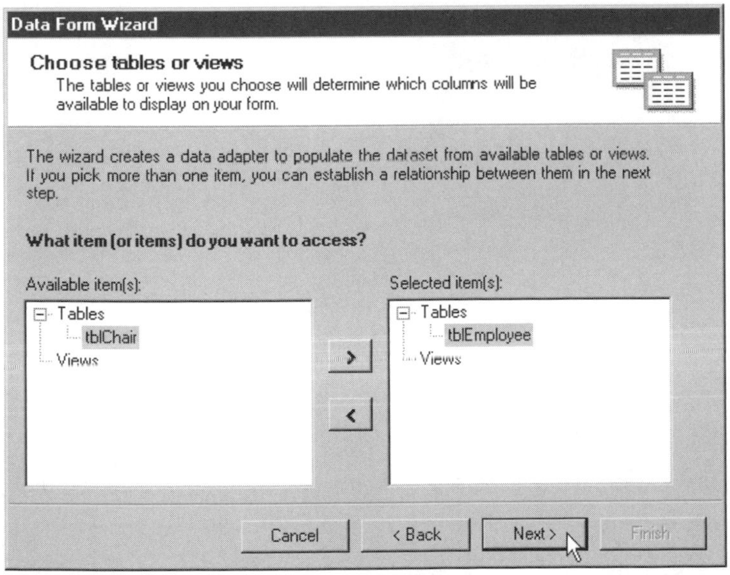

Figure 14-11.   *Choose Tables Or Views step of the Data Form Wizard*

11. Place a check mark next to a column name to tell the wizard the columns that should appear on the web form.

    If more than one table was chosen, the Create A Relationship Between Tables screen will appear, where you can define the relationship between the tables selected by choosing the keys and table relationships. In this example, all of the columns in table *tblEmployee* are selected for display, as shown in Figure 14-12.

12. Click Finish, and Visual Studio .NET will generate a completed web form named *employees.aspx* with all of the necessary code in the Codebehind file and controls pasted on the form to display the data in table *tblEmplyee*.

Figure 14-13 shows the web form *employees.aspx* in design view. The controls may be moved around to be displayed or to fit as desired. The code behind the form is actually quite good quality as far as wizard-generated code goes, since it even has error handling!

If *employees.aspx* is set as the start page, you can press F5 to compile *employees.aspx* to start the web browser requesting the web form. The page will display a Load button with no data shown in the web browser initially. Click the Load button, and data will be displayed in the web browser, as shown in Figure 14-14.

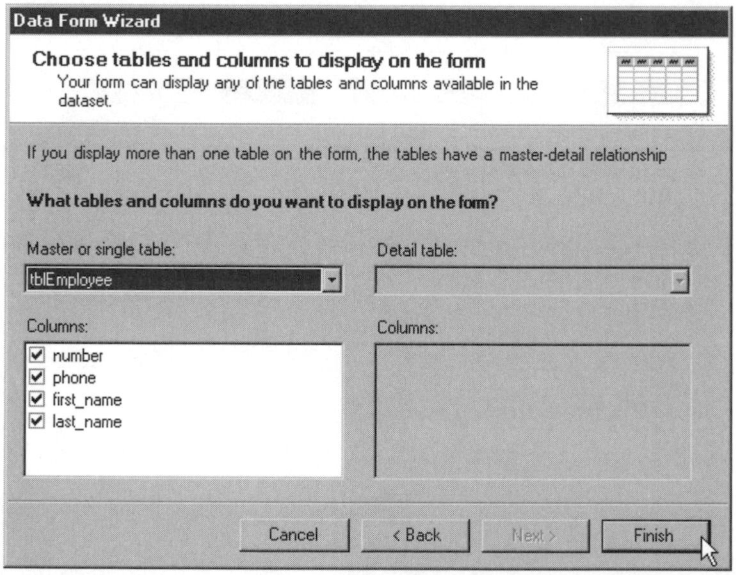

Figure 14-12. *Choose tables and columns to display on the form*

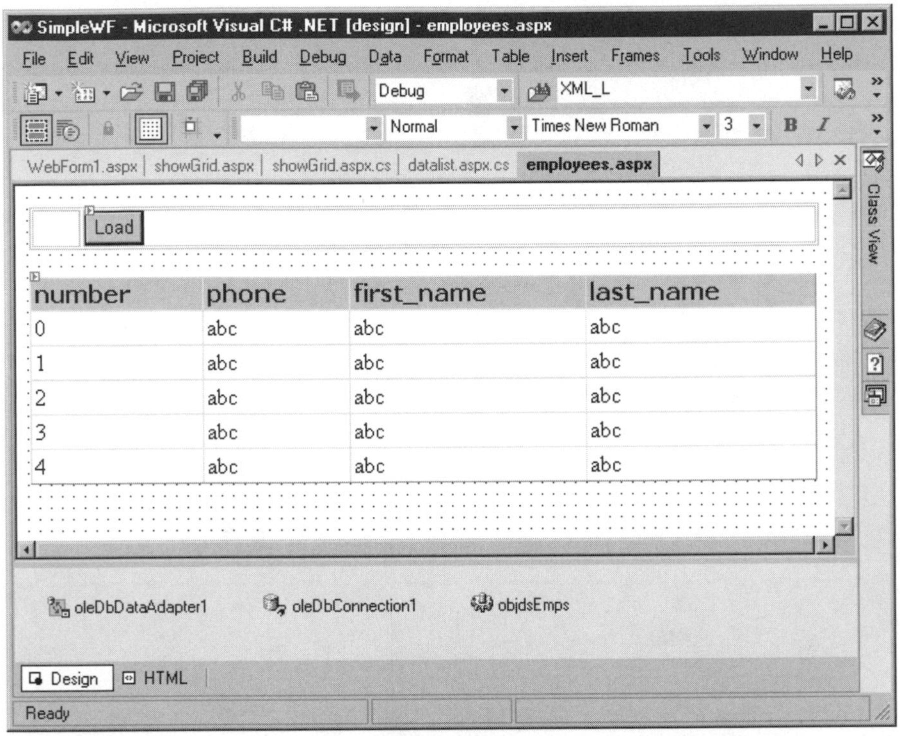

Figure 14-13. *Resulting web form generated from Data Form Wizard, shown in design view*

Using XML

Web forms offer an XML control that will perform XML and Extensible Stylesheet Language (XSL), or XSL Transformations (XSLT). To create a web form that will host an XML to XSL transformation, create a new web form, and while in design view, paste the XML web control onto the form, as shown in Figure 14-15. The best use for the XML control is for integrating the use of web forms in a legacy application that used XSL to encapsulate the presentation logic.

The XML control may be configured using the Properties window, as shown in Figure 14-15. The XML file and the XSLT or XSL file may be specified in the Properties window, and when the page is opened, the XML and XSL to HTML transformation will occur. If files are specified in the control, they must be a part of the project displayed in the Solution Explorer.

Figure 14-14. Data Form Wizard–generated web form employees.aspx displaying tblEmployee data

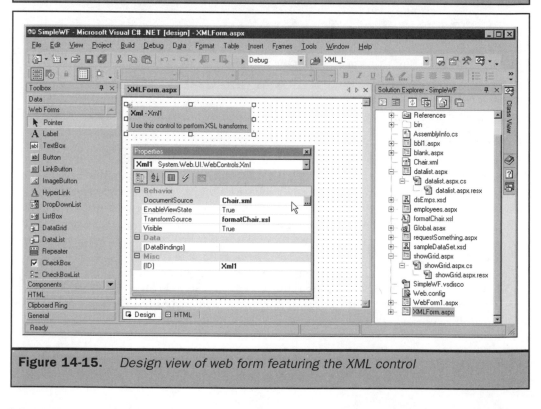

Figure 14-15. Design view of web form featuring the XML control

Placement of the XML control is restricted on a web form. You can paste other web form controls on the web form around the XML control. The Web Forms Designer allows for the XML control to reside in the upper-left corner of design view only, as shown in Figure 14-15, although certain controls may be squeezed in above, on the right side, and below the XML control. Since the Web Forms Designer can have no real understanding of the page construction that could be placed in the XSL or XSLT document, its ability to represent the page look in the design view is greatly diminished, which might explain why the Web Forms Designer restricts the placement of the XML control.

Chapter 15

ASP.NET Web Services

SP.NET offers the programmer two basic web application project types: web *forms* and web *services*. Web forms are designed to provide presentation logic while consuming business logic or data logic. Web services are designed to provide business logic across the Internet and consume data logic. A web services project does not offer the programmer any presentation logic controls. Most web services are designed to be consumed by another web service, by software hosted on an alternative platform, or by a web form prior to an end user receiving any data processed by the web service.

Web Services Architecture

An ASP.NET web service consists of a dynamic link library (DLL), an ASMX file, and the Codebehind file, which contains a class specifically designed to support the needs of the web service. The ASMX file is analogous to the ASP.NET web form ASPX file. Requests to a web service occur via an ASMX file. You can think of the web service as a class with an integrated HTTP interface. For this reason, the web service and the web service's class are essentially the same entity, and as such will be referred to in a collective manner in this chapter. Other classes may be added to the project, but they do not require creation of another ASMX file, since they are not web services themselves. When another class is added, only one file is created to host the code for the class, and it is named *<class name>.cs* or *<class name>.<language extension>*.

A web service project in Visual Studio .NET can contain many web services. When a web service project is compiled, the resulting assembly will be written into a single DLL. Many ASMX files could have their class hosted in the same DLL. The DLL can contain many classes in addition to the classes used to support a web service ASMX file.

The ASMX file is mapped to the .NET Framework *aspnet_isapi.dll* Internet Server Application Programming Interface (ISAPI) extension in IIS, so when a respective ASMX file is requested from IIS, *aspnet_isapi.dll* marshals the Hypertext Transfer Protocol (HTTP) request to the related web service DLL, as shown in Figure 15-1. An ASMX file is associated with a single DLL at any given time. Typically, the web services projects in Visual Studio .NET place the DLL in a bin directory subordinate to the directory hosting the ASMX files.

An ASP.NET web service project uses the same assembly configuration files used by an ASP.NET web form project. The ASP.NET web service also has the same IIS deployment configuration files as the ASP.NET web form project. The ASP.NET web service files that are used by the compiler to make a web service in the assembly are named *<my web Service Name>.asmx,* as contrasted to the ASP.NET web form files, which are named using the *.aspx* extension. The ASP.NET web service also follows the same architecture, as far as the types of files that relate to a given web service within a project. For example, the ASMX file is the addressable entry point to the web service, and like a header file, it provides processing directives for the web service compilation. The ASMX file describes the files that contribute to the ASP.NET web service, and it can host the code itself. It's likely that the associated code for the ASP.NET web service is hosted in a Codebehind file. The *<myservice>.asmx.cs* Codebehind file contains the

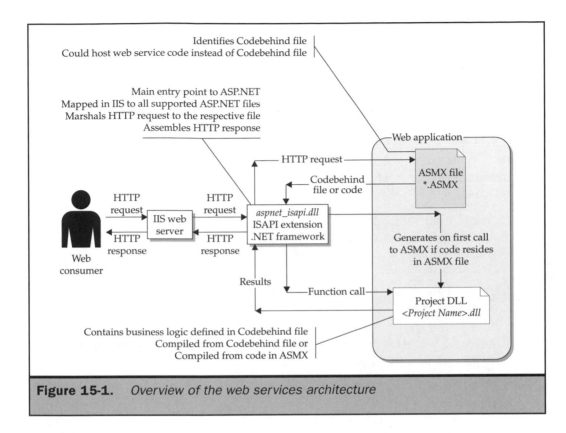

Figure 15-1.   *Overview of the web services architecture*

source code to the web service, and the *<myservice>.asmx.resx* file is the resource file that serves the Codebehind file.

Note   *The ASMX file could also host the code instead of using a Codebehind file for this, but Visual Studio .NET uses the Codebehind file in the web service project template by default. If the ASMX file does not use a Codebehind file, the .NET Framework will compile the file and produce the DLL automatically on the first request.*

Creating a Web Service Using Visual Studio .NET

To demonstrate how a web service may be constructed and used by other web services and web forms, a simple date scheduling application is presented in this chapter. This date scheduling system is made up of the following three classes:

■ *anEvent*   A class representing an event that takes place at a given time and day

- *Events*   A class representing a collective group of instances of class *anEvent*
- *EventClient*   A web form that consumes *Events* and *anEvent* instances

The *Events* class is a web service, *anEvent* is a class used by the *Events* web service, and the *EventClient* class is a web form that uses *anEvent* and *Events*. All the classes reside under the same namespace, called *myPortal*. The assembly created when compiled is *myPortal.dll*. An *Events.asmx* file will point to a class within the *myPortal.dll*. The *myPortal.dll* will also host the class for the web form *EventClient* and the class *anEvent*. The *EventClient.aspx* file will direct the .NET Framework to *myPortal.dll* for the compiled code containing the associated class.

Let's create a new ASP.NET web service project:

1. Open Visual Studio .NET, and a start page will be displayed (unless it has been configured not to display the start page). Like the previous versions of Visual Studio, a project template splash screen is provided by default, but this can be disabled.

2. Choose File | New Project to open the New Project window and the New Project window will open displaying project types and the corresponding project templates.

3. Select the Visual C# Projects node in the left list. The project templates that correspond to C# will be displayed in the right list.

4. Select the ASP.NET Web Service project template.

5. The default name assigned to a new web service in any project is *Service1*. In this example, the project will be named *myPortal*, as shown in Figure 15-2. The server name may also be specified using the Uniform Resource Locator (URL) or using a Universal Naming Convention (UNC) file path to the web root. The default server name, *localhost*, could be specified in the URL if you wanted to host the solution on your workstation during the initial code and unit test phase.

6. Click OK.

Visual Studio .NET will attempt to connect to the web server specified in the New Project dialog box. If Visual Studio .NET connects successfully, it will create a new virtual directory and it will copy the default web services files to the new virtual directory.

After Visual Studio .NET has completed generation of all of the project files for the web service being created, the design view of the newly generated web service, *Service1*, is presented and prepared for editing. Visual Studio .NET assigns a default name to the web service files created in the project so they will be renamed.

1. Open the Solution Explorer from the menu View | Solution Explorer.

2. Right click on the file *Service1.asmx* and select *Rename*.

3. Delete the name *Service1* and enter the name **Events**.

4. Press the ENTER key and the filename for the ASMX file, the Codebehind file, and the resolution file should change to *Events.asmx*, *Events.asmx.cs*, and *Events.asmx.res*, respectively.

The class supporting the web service will still be named *Service1*, however. The web service will function properly with the different names but let's change the class to be the same as the web service name.

1. Select the *Events.asmx* file in the Solution explorer and click the View Designer button at the top of the Solution Explorer. The *Events.asmx.cs* file will be displayed in the Visual Studio .NET Component Designer.

2. Right-click on the *Events.asmx.cs* file as it is displayed in the Visual Studio .NET Component Designer and select Properties.

3. After the Properties window opens, the value *Service1* should be in the Name property. Delete the value.

4. Enter the value **Events** in the name property. The Component Designer will change each occurrence of the class name in the Codebehind file automatically.

The purpose of the *Events* web service is to add, open, or delete instances of class *anEvent* to and from the portal. The data for a given instance of *anEvent* will be stored in a database. Because the *Events* class will interact with a database, components from

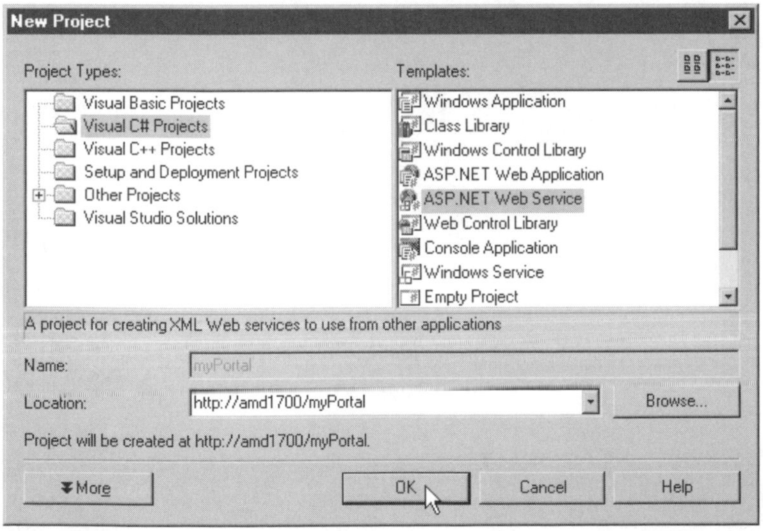

Figure 15-2.   *New project* myPortal *being created in the New Project dialog box*

the toolbox that will aid in the acquisitions and submission will be used in the course of building the web service, as shown in Figure 15-3. The components will be pasted on the design view of the *Events* web service.

Using the Component Designer

The toolbox provides many types of components that you can add to a web service. Some of the components are available in both web forms and web services, but the components that serve to produce a graphical user interface (GUI) for the end user are not available in the web service project. Pasting web service components on the design view for the *Events* web service has no effect on the *Events.asmx* file. The ASMX is just like the web form ASPX file in that it associates the language, class, Codebehind, and resource files to the web service. The ASMX differs from the ASPX file in that it does not contain any other information pertaining to display.

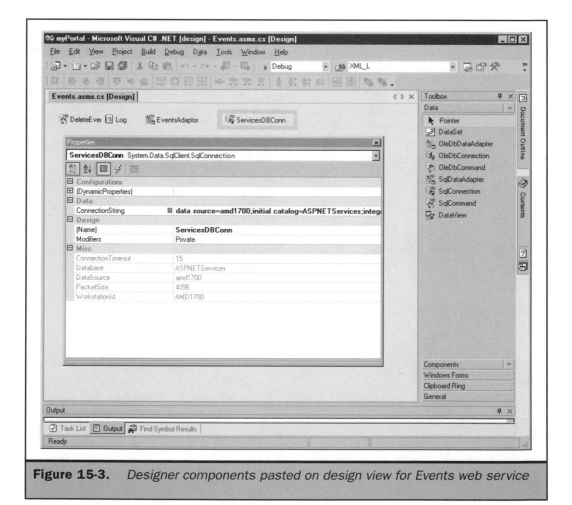

Figure 15-3.   *Designer components pasted on design view for Events web service*

The content of *Events.asmx* is shown in Listing 15-1. If Listing 15-1 were for a web form, it would contain more XML (eXtensible Markup Language) and HTML (Hypertext Markup Language) code designating display configurations; however, because this code is for a web service, it consists of only a single line of text.

Listing 15-1

```
Source Code of Web Service Events - File Events.asmx

<%@ WebService Language="c#" Codebehind="Events.asmx.cs"
Class="myPortal.Events" %>
```

When the connection component or any component is pasted on the design view of the web service, the properties for the component may be set in the Properties window. For each value set in the Properties window, the Visual Studio .NET Component Designer produces initialization code in the Codebehind file for the web service. A preprocessor region command is defined, called Component Designer–generated code. Preprocessor commands in C# are similar to the preprocessor commands in C++ and C. The preprocessors commands in C# differ from those of C++ and C in the following ways:

■ C# preprocessor commands are not interpreted by a preprocessor that is separate from the compiler. The compiler and the preprocessor are the same.

■ C# preprocessor commands cannot specify macros.

The # region command specifies an area that can be expanded or collapsed within the Visual Studio .NET editor. The # region command has no functional effect on the solution.

Within the Component Designer–generated code region, Visual Studio .NET declares three items:

■ A reference to *IContainer* named *components*

■ A subroutine named *InitializeComponent*

■ A function named *Dispose*

All components pasted on the design view of the web service are initialized in the subroutine *InitializeComponent*. A call to the *InitializeComponent* subroutine is automatically placed in the constructor for the web service. Any properties that are set in the Properties window, as shown in Figure 15-3, will be assigned to the respective component to which they belong. The comments the Visual Studio .NET Component Designer places within this region warn you not to edit code manually. The Component Designer–generated code region appears as a section devoted to supporting Component Designer design view interaction for the web service.

The *IContainer* components instance is used by the *Dispose* function. The components instance contains references to all of the instances of components within the web service. The *Dispose* method of the components instance will release any resources claimed by the web services container.

Configuring a Database Connection Component

Because the intended data source for the *Events* web service is a SQL Server 2000 database, a *SQLConnection* component from the toolbox will be pasted into the design view. If support for another type of database were required, the *OleDBConnection* component could be used instead. *SQLConnection* offers some advanced management capabilities and efficiencies over the *OleDBConnection* component, however, so the *OleDBConnection* should be used only when necessary. An open database connectivity (ODBC) provider is also available if no OLE-DB provider is available for the data source, but the former ships in a separate assembly that must be downloaded from Microsoft.

The *ConnectionString* property from the Properties window will offer the developer the option of selecting previous connections that have been configured on the workstation or the opportunity to create a new connection. For this example, a new connection will be created, as shown in Figure 15-4.

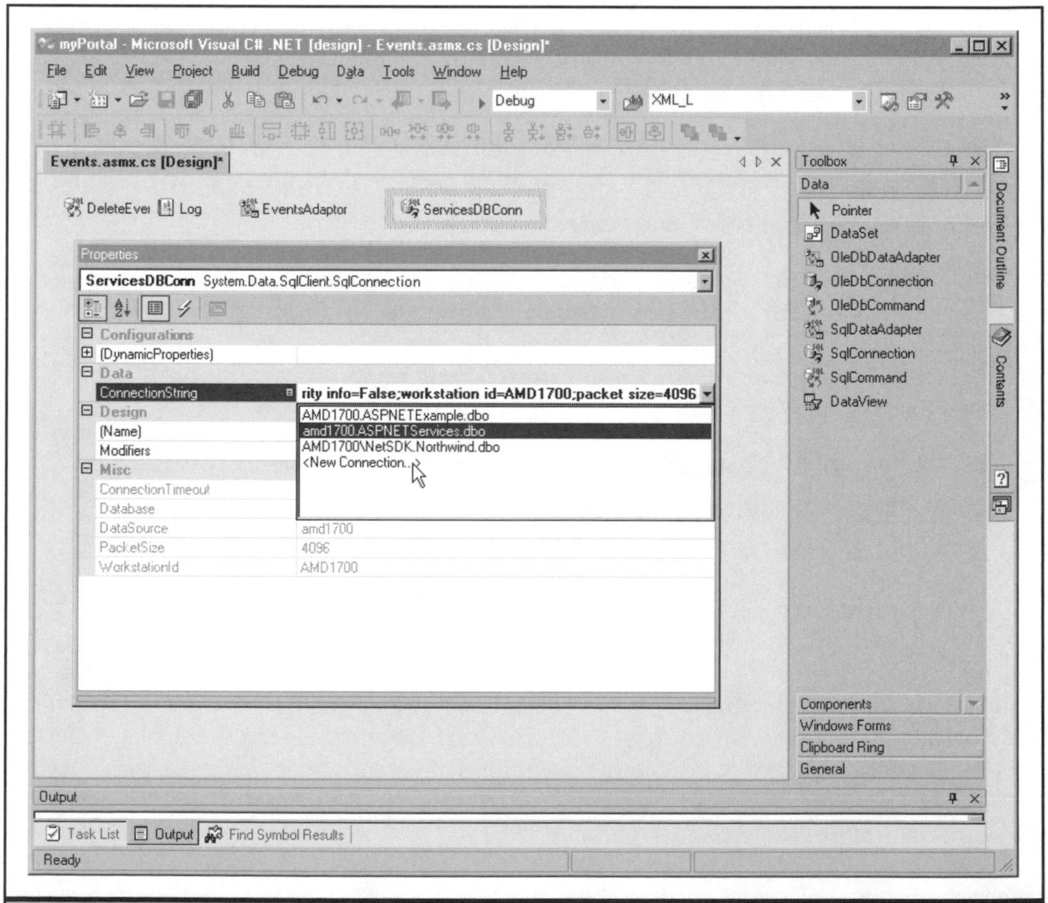

Figure 15-4. *Selecting a new connection for the ConnectionString property of the SQLConnection component*

The Data Link Properties window will open after you select *<New Connection…>* from the *ConnectionString* property setting. Almost all of the possible settings that could be represented in an ADO.NET connection string may be established using the Data Link Properties window. The Data Link Properties window is a common window used by Visual Studio anytime you configure an ADO connection string. For the *Events* web service, the database server hosted on the server named *AMD1700* and the database named *ASPNETServices* will be utilized, as shown in Figure 15-5.

The name of the *SQLConnection* component will be changed to *ServicesDBConn* from the default *SQLConnection1* so that is has a user-friendly name. After the *SQLConnection* is configured and created, it may be used anywhere within the web service, and it will not have to be created again. The *Events* class inherits from *System.Web.Services.WebService*, which provides the class many of the web-oriented classes and functions required to interact with HTTP communication. Listing 15-2 shows the source code generated by Visual Studio .NET for the class *Events*.

Listing 15-2

```
Source Code of Class Events after SQLConnection Component
Added and Configured

/// <summary>
/// Summary description for Events.
/// </summary>
public class Events : System.Web.Services.WebService
{
    public Events()
    {
        //CODEGEN: This call is required by the
        //ASP.NET Web Services Designer
        InitializeComponent();
    }

    private System.Data.SqlClient.SqlConnection ServicesDBConn;

    #region Component Designer generated code

    //Required by the Web Services Designer
    private IContainer components = null;

    /// <summary>
    /// Required method for Designer support - do not modify
    /// the contents of this method with the code editor.
    /// </summary>
    private void InitializeComponent()
    {
        this.ServicesDBConn = new
                        System.Data.SqlClient.SqlConnection();
        //
        // ServicesDBConn
        //
        this.ServicesDBConn.ConnectionString =
```

```
                "data source=amd1700;initial catalog=ASPNETServices;" +
                "integrated security=SSPI;persist security info=False;" +
                "workstation id=AMD1700;packet size=4096";

        }

        /// <summary>
        /// Clean up any resources being used.
        /// </summary>
        protected override void Dispose( bool disposing )
        {
            if(disposing && components != null)
            {
                components.Dispose();
            }
            base.Dispose(disposing);
        }

        #endregion
}
```

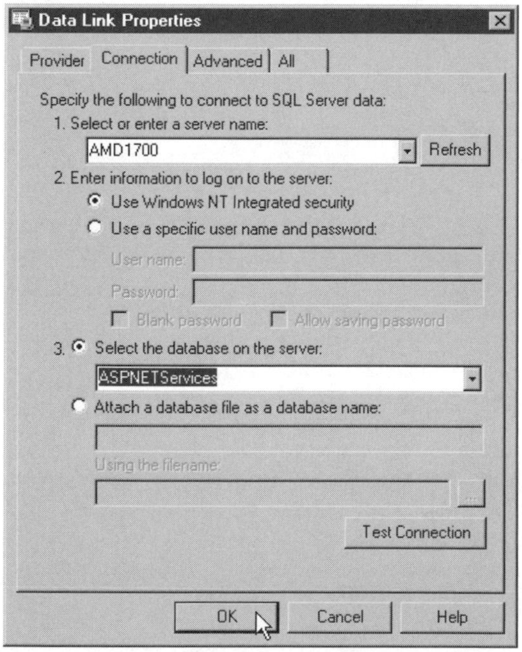

Figure 15-5.   *Setting a new data link for the Events web service*

The use of the Visual Studio .NET Component Designer on web services components is not obligatory in terms of using the web service controls. The controls can also be added to a given web service by declaring and constructing them in the Codebehind file, as with any other variable or class. For example, a *SQLConnection* object instance could also have been created and initialized in the constructor for the *Events* class. The code in Listing 15-3 demonstrates the creation and use of a local instance of the *SQLConnection* object without using the Visual Studio .NET Component Designer and the *SQLConnection* component from the toolbox.

Listing 15-3

```
Using SQLConnection Object without the Designer and Obtaining
Connection String from the web.config File

public class Events : System.Web.Services.WebService
{
    //locals to class
    private System.Data.SqlClient.SqlConnection myConn;

    public Events()
    {
        //CODEGEN: This call is required by the
        //ASP.NET Web Services Designer
        InitializeComponent();

        System.Configuration.AppSettingsReader
            myAppSettings =
            new System.Configuration.AppSettingsReader();

        //get the connection string from web.config
        string sConnect =
            ((string)
            (myAppSettings.GetValue
            ("ProductionDB.ConnectionString",
            typeof(string))));

        //make the DB connection
      myConn = new System.Data.SqlClient.SqlConnection(sConnect);
    }

    #region Component Designer generated code

    //Required by the Web Services Designer
    private IContainer components = null;

    /// <summary>
```

```
/// Required method for Designer support - do not modify
/// the contents of this method with the code editor.
/// </summary>
private void InitializeComponent()
{
}
/// <summary>
/// Clean up any resources being used.
/// </summary>
protected override void Dispose( bool disposing )
{
    if(disposing && components != null)
    {
        components.Dispose();
    }
    base.Dispose(disposing);
}

#endregion
}
```

In Listing 15-3, the *myConn* instance is declared local to the *Events* class. The connection string is obtained from the *web.config* file and used as a constructor for the *myConn* instance. After the *myConn* instance is created in the *Events* constructor, *myConn* may be used elsewhere throughout the class as needed.

Reading Application Settings from web.config

The *web.config* file is a great place to obtain initialization data specific to a web application deployment. This enables a developer to produce a solution that obtains arguments that pertain to the specific deployment without making a code change for other deployments. Using the *AppSettingsReader* class, data may be read from the *<appSettings>* section of the *web.config* file. The w*eb.config* file that contains the database connection string that Listing 15-3 obtained in the *Events* constructor is shown in Listing 15-4.

Listing 15-4

web.config File With <appSettings> Element That Contains Database Connection String

```
 <?xml version="1.0" encoding="utf-8" ?>
<configuration>
  <system.web>
    <compilation defaultLanguage="c#" debug="true"/>
    <customErrors mode="RemoteOnly" />
  </system.web>
```

```
<appSettings>
  <add key="ProductionDB.ConnectionString"
        value="data source=amd1700;
                initial catalog=ASPNETServices;
                integrated security=SSPI;
                persist security info=False;
                workstation id=AMD1700;
                packet size=4096"
  />
 </appSettings>

</configuration>
```

The Visual Studio .NET Component Designer also has a mechanism that uses the *appSetings* element of the *web.config* file. If the Properties window for an existing connection component that is hosted on the design view of a given web service were accessed, the *ConnectionString* setting could be configured as a property set using *DynamicProperties,* as shown in Figure 15-6.

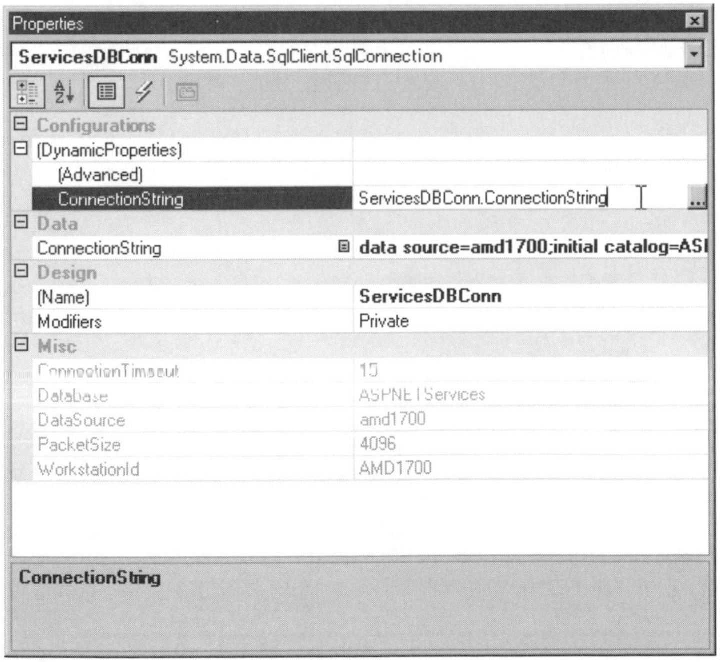

Figure 15-6.   *Connection component properties using DynamicProperties to obtain ConnectionString*

By default, the *ConnectionString* property is not enabled to use *DynamicProperties*. The specific property must be mapped to a key in the *web.config* file. The key is an attribute named *key* located in an *add* element subordinate to the *appSettings* element, as seen in Listing 15-4. Clicking the ... button in the *ConnectionString* property under the *DynamicProperties* will open a dialog box where the developer can choose a key, as shown in Figure 15-7.

The Data Adaptor Component

After the data connection has been established, the web service knows what data source it will communicate with and what credentials need to be supplied to the data source. Next, the web service must send a request to the data source to get the data. ADO.NET offers another component for this purpose, called a *data adaptor*. A version of the data adaptor for SQL Server 2000 uses the SQL Server .NET provider called *SQLDataAdaptor*. *OledbDataAdaptor*, the version for OLE-DB, is available for legacy versions of SQL Server or other databases that do not have a specific provider. The data adaptor may be created, set, and used as any other class in ADO.NET. ASP.NET provides a component in the toolbox that may be used instead, if the developer wishes. In the Visual Studio .NET Component Designer, the data adaptor component may be pasted on the design view of the web service and configured via the Properties window.

When the data adaptor component is pasted on the design view of a web service, the Data Adaptor Configuration Wizard opens, inviting the programmer to configure the component instance. The Data Adaptor Configuration Wizard may be dismissed and the properties may be set manually if desired.

Here's how to use the Data Adaptor Configuration Wizard:

1. In the opening screen, click Next to start the effort of gaining information about setting up the instance of the data adaptor component pasted on the web service.

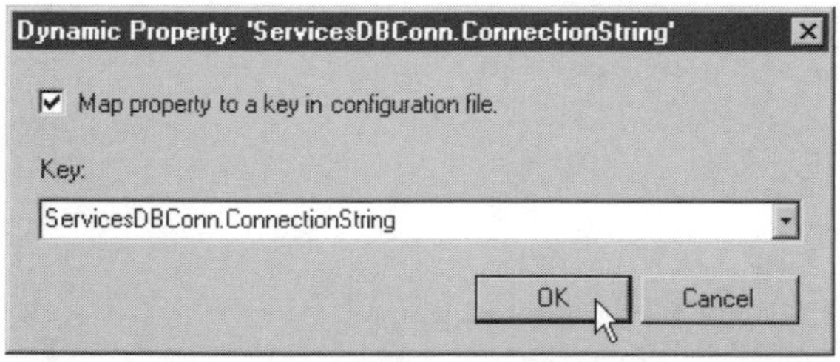

Figure 15-7. *Mapping the ConnectionString property to a key in the configuration file*

2. In the Choose Your Data Connection screen as shown in Figure 15-8, you can select from the drop-down combo box a data connection that has already been configured for the project. If you click the New Connection button to configure a new connection, the same Data Link Properties window shown in Figure 15-5 will open and you can configure a new connection. In this example, a previously configured connection will be chosen.

3. After you select the data connection, click the Next button and the wizard will prompt you for the means whereby data will be requested from the data source, as shown in Figure 15-9, in the Choose A Query Type screen.

   Choose Use SQL Statements and the wizard will generate a set of command objects (using either *SQLCommand* or *OledbCommand* classes, depending on the respective connection class being utilized) in the *InitializeComponent* function of the web service class. The command objects will be set with SQL commands that use aliases for each field name. Referring the alias name in the command object instance, values may be set in the command object to represent the value for a given field.

   Choose either Create New Stored Procedures or Use Existing Stored Procedures and the wizard will ask for more information about the data tables so that the stored procedures may be built or mapped, respectively.

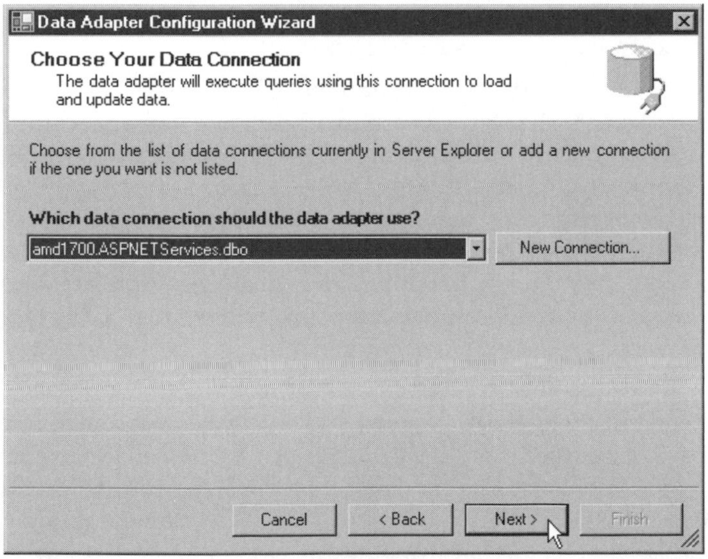

Figure 15-8.   *Data Adaptor Configuration Wizard—Choose Your Data Connection*

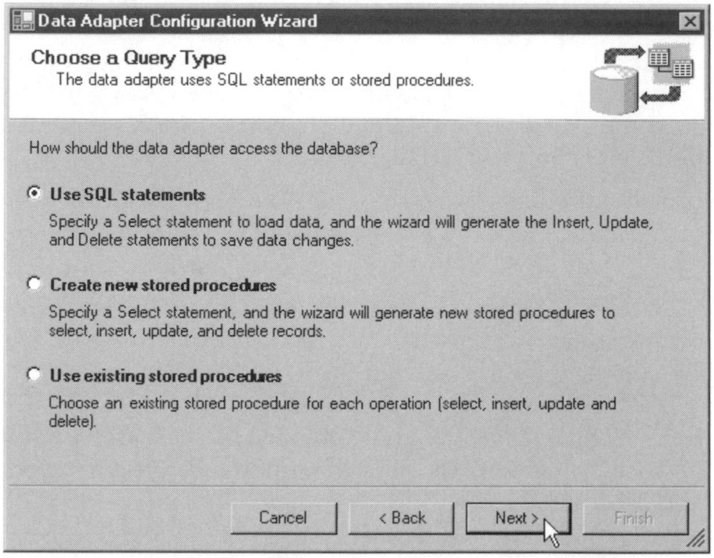

Figure 15-9. *Data Adaptor Configuration Wizard—Choose a Query Type*

4. For this example, choose Use SQL Statements.

5. Click the Next button to continue, and the wizard will open a Generate The SQL Statements screen. Here you'll type in a Select SQL command for the dataset that the adaptor should use as a model dataset to construct the SQL statements, as shown in Figure 15-10. The *SQLDataAdaptor* and the *OledbDataAdaptor* both support an interface for executing *Select*, *Insert*, *Delete*, and *Update SQL* statements. The wizard generates the SQL commands for the data manipulation commands that are to be set in the data adaptor. The wizard prompts for this Select SQL statement to produce the command text that will be used in the respective *Select*, *Insert*, *Delete*, and *Update SQL* commands that will be set in the respective SQL commands for the data adaptor.

6. After typing the Select SQL statement **select * from tblEvents** in the box, click the Next button to see the View Wizard Results confirmation screen, as shown in Figure 15-11. This screen describes what will be performed on the web service code. If the wizard had difficulty parsing the SQL statement that was entered in the previous step, this confirmation would not show all of the possible SQL comments shown in Figure 15-11. The developer can click the Back button and revise the SQL command that was entered or even choose to have stored procedures created in the database server.

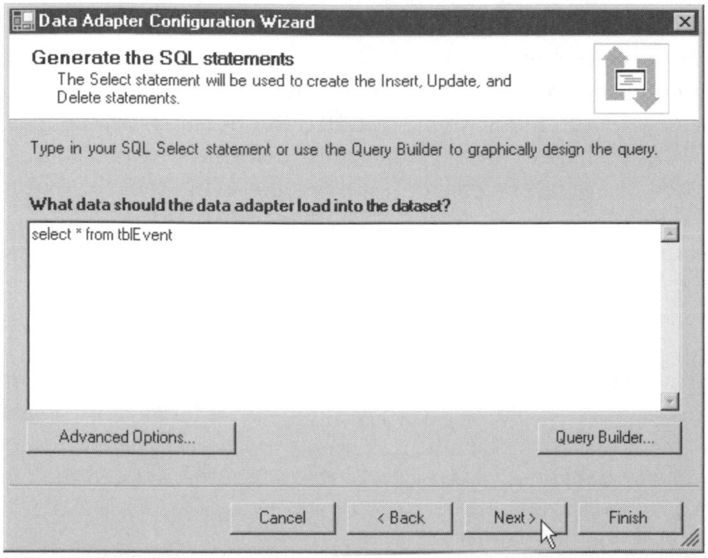

Figure 15-10. *Data Adaptor Configuration Wizard—Generate The SQL Statements*

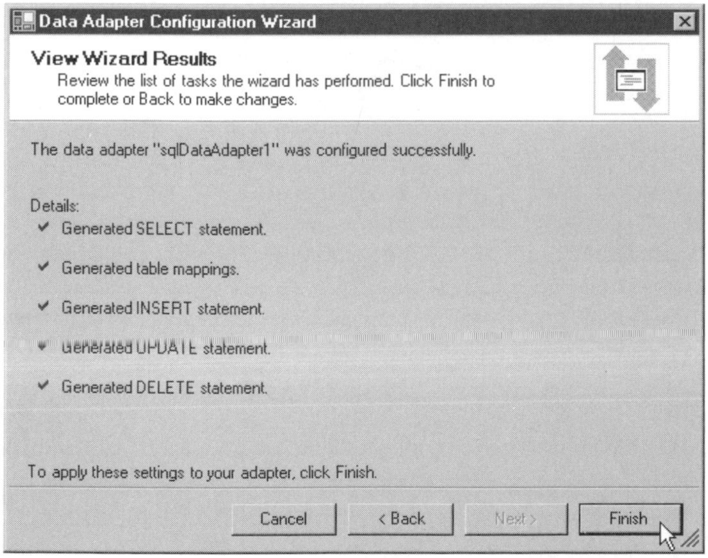

Figure 15-11. *Data Adaptor Configuration Wizard—View Wizard Results*

IIS PROGRAMMING

In this example, the data adaptor was named *SQLDataAdaptor1*, since the Visual Studio .NET Component Designer provides this name as a default name for any *SQLDataAdaptor* component being pasted in the design view. This name can be changed at any time, however, and the associated wizard-generated code in the *InitializeComponent* subroutine of the web service will automatically be updated by theVisual Studio .NET Component Designer if the Name property in the Properties window is edited. In this example, the *SQLDataAdaptor* name was changed to *EventsAdaptor* using the name property of the Properties window.

The *SQLCommand* objects generated by the Data Adaptor Configuration Wizard were named *SQLSelectCommand1*, *SQLDeleteCommand1*, *SQLInsertCommand1*, and *SQLUpdateCommand1*. To make them more appropriate to their context, the names for the command objects were changed to *SelectEvent*, *DeleteEvent*, *InsertEvent*, and *UpdateEvent*, respectively. The Properties window for the SQLDataAdaptor was used for this purpose by editing the name property found subordinate to the *Dynamic Properties* of each specific command object. Listing 15-5 shows the code generated by the designer for the *EventsAdaptor* data adaptor and the *ServicesDBConn* data connection object.

Listing 15-5

```
Initialization Code Generated by the VS Designer for a
Data Adaptor and a Data Connection

private void InitializeComponent()
{
    System.Configuration.AppSettingsReader
    configurationAppSettings = new
    System.Configuration.AppSettingsReader();

  this.ServicesDBConn = new System.Data.SqlClient.SqlConnection();

  this.EventsAdaptor = new System.Data.SqlClient.SqlDataAdapter();

  this.SelectEvent = new System.Data.SqlClient.SqlCommand();

  this.InsertEvent = new System.Data.SqlClient.SqlCommand();

  this.UpdateEvent = new System.Data.SqlClient.SqlCommand();

  this.DeleteEvent = new System.Data.SqlClient.SqlCommand();

    //
    // ServicesDBConn
    //
     this.ServicesDBConn.ConnectionString =
                    ((string)(configurationAppSettings.GetValue
```

```
                ("ServicesDBConn.ConnectionString", typeof(string))));

//
// EventsAdaptor
//
this.EventsAdaptor.DeleteCommand = this.DeleteEvent;

this.EventsAdaptor.InsertCommand = this.InsertEvent;

this.EventsAdaptor.SelectCommand = this.SelectEvent;
```

Listing 15-5 features part of the subroutine *InitializeComponent*, demonstrating the SQLCommand components that were created by the Visual Studio .NET Component Designer after they were renamed. After the *AppSettingsReader* class was created to get the application settings form the *web.config* file, the connection, data adaptor, and command classes are created. After the connection class is initialized with the connection string obtained from the *web.config* file, the data adaptor class has each of the *SQLCommand* object instances assigned to their respective command property. For example, the *DeleteEvent* command instance is assigned to the *DeleteCommand* property of the *SQLDataAdaptor* instance named *EventsAdaptor*.

The Visual Studio .NET Component Designer generated a considerably large amount of code for setting the SQL command text and parameters to each of their respective command object instances, which is not shown in Listing 15-5. The designer also identified each field in the dataset with an alias in the SQL command. The aliases were set as parameters in the command object. Listing 15-6 shows the source code setting the SQL command text and the parameters for the *InsertEvent* command object.

Listing 15-6

```
Initialization Code Generated by the VS Designer for a
InsertEvent SQLCommand Object in Subroutine InitializeComponent();

//
// InsertEvent
//
this.InsertEvent.CommandText = "INSERT INTO tblEvent" +
        "(Name, StartDate, Description) " +
       "VALUES (@Name, @StartDate, @Description); "+
       "SELECT Name, StartDate, Description, ID " +
       "FROM tblEvent WHERE (ID = @@IDENTITY)";

this.InsertEvent.Connection = this.ServicesDBConn;

this.InsertEvent.Parameters.Add(
```

```
                              new System.Data.SqlClient.SqlParameter
               ("@Name", System.Data.SqlDbType.VarChar, 50, "Name"));

this.InsertEvent.Parameters.Add(
                         new System.Data.SqlClient.SqlParameter
               ("@StartDate", System.Data.SqlDbType.DateTime,
                    8, "StartDate"));

this.InsertEvent.Parameters.Add(
                         new System.Data.SqlClient.SqlParameter
               ("@Description", System.Data.SqlDbType.VarChar,

                                   200, "Description"));
```

Data Reader Class

By observing the aliases that were generated by the Visual Studio .NET Component
Designer, code may be written to set the parameters and fill a *DataReader* object. For
example, the *Add* function of the *Events* web service uses the *InsertEvent* command class
instance to add a new event. The aliases of the database table field names established in
the *InsertEvent* class initialization are used by the *Parameters* method to assign a value
to the field that the alias represents in the *Insert* SQL command that the *InsertEvent* class
uses to update the database table. Listing 15-7 shows the *Add* function.

Listing 15-7

```
Add Function in Events Web Service

/// <summary>
/// Adds a new event to system
/// </summary>
[WebMethod]
public bool Add()
{
     System.Data.SqlClient.SqlDataReader myEvent;

  try
  {
   //set state for the command object instance
   InsertEvent.Parameters["@Name"].Value =mEvent.Name;

   InsertEvent.Parameters["@StartDate"].Value =mEvent.DateTime;
```

```
InsertEvent.Parameters["@Description"].Value =mEvent.Description;

 //open the connection object
ServicesDBConn.Open();

//run query
myEvent = this.InsertEvent.ExecuteReader();

//must advance to first record
myEvent.Read();

//fill local properties
mEvent.ID =  myEvent.GetInt32(3);

//shut down record
myEvent.Close();
}
catch(System.Exception Err )
{
//log error
this.LogMessage(Err.ToString() , true);

//rethrow for client consumption
throw Err;
}

//success if we get this far
return true;
}
```

A class instance of the *SQLDataReader* was created to access the data returned from the *SQLCommand* class instance *InsertEvent*. Because *InsertEvent* was set as a property of the *SQLDataAdaptor EventsAdaptor,* and has an instance of the connection object *servicesDBConn, InsertEvent* can return data to the *SQLDataReader* object instance *myEvent.* A local instance of *anEvent* named *mEvent* is used to hold the current state of the event for the *Events* web service. Listing 15-8 shows the source for class *anEvent.*

Listing 15-8

```
Source Code for Class anEvent

/// <summary>
/// a single event
```

```csharp
/// </summary>
public class anEvent
{

    private long CurrentID;
    private string CurrentName;
    private string CurrentDescription;
    private DateTime CurrentDateTime;

    public anEvent()
    {
    }

    /// <summary>
    /// ID for opened event
    /// </summary>
    public long ID
    {
        get
        {
            return CurrentID;
        }
        set
        {
            CurrentID = value;
        }
    }

    /// <summary>
    /// Date and time of actual event
    /// </summary>
    public DateTime DateTime
    {
        get
        {
            return CurrentDateTime;
        }
        set
        {
            CurrentDateTime = value;
        }
    }
```

```
/// <summary>
/// description of event
/// </summary>
public string Description
{
    get
    {
        return CurrentDescription;
    }
    set
    {
        CurrentDescription = value;
    }
}


/// <summary>
/// Name for opened event
/// </summary>
public string Name
{
    get
    {
        return CurrentName;
    }
    set
    {
        CurrentName = value;
    }
}
}
```

As shown in Listing 15-8, class *anEvent* simply holds the data that makes an *Event*. The web service *Events* reads and writes the values of an event to and from the database data source so a local instance of *anEvent* was declared for the class *Events* and created in the *Events* constructor.

When the *Add* function in Listing 15-7 sets the parameters for the *Name*, *Date*, and *Description*, it uses the respective property values for the *anEvents* instance *mEvent*. The properties for *mEvent* are set in the *Events* web service either from a consumer's input or from the database values for the *Event* that might be loaded in the web service at any given moment. Once the parameters for the *InsertEvent* command are set, the connection is opened, and the command is executed and the results are read into the *myEvent* instance using the *ExecuteReader* command of the *InsertEvent SQLCommand* object. The Read command of the *SQLDataReader* object advances the dataset to the next row, which happens to be the first row on a freshly opened dataset. If *myEvent* is read without advancing to the first row, an error would be raised by ADO.NET. The local instance of *anEvent* is updated with the new ID since the database generates the ID for any given *anEvent* in the system.

Many programmers familiar with ADO versions previous to ADO.NET may be horrified by the use of the ordinal position of the ID field being referenced to obtain the value of the ID for the *mEvent* instance. The ordinal value of any field should *not* be used to refer to a value in a recordset. The *SQLDataReader* is very much like an ADO recordset. If the database table were updated with the addition of a new column, the ADO recordset might start pulling the wrong field value depending on where in the table definition the new column was added. In ADO.NET, however, this is not a problem, since the ordinal position is defined in terms of the data adaptor instance. The data adaptor provides the layer of abstraction from the data layer so that the programmer may refer to the ordinal position if he or she chooses to do so without fear that database table changes will break the software, as he or she would if the code were abstracted properly using named fields in legacy ADO.

Event Log Component

All the database interaction code in Listing 15-7 is inside the *Try* section of a *Try .. Catch* block. If an exception scenario occurs, the *Catch* block is executed. The *System.Exception* class instance is passed as an argument to the *Catch* function, and it should have information about the error that occurred in the *Try* block. In Listing 15-7, the *System.Exception* class instance is serialized into a string using the *ToString* function. The *ToString* function is a common function that is found among many classes, since the function is inherited from the *object* class. The string representation of the error message is passed to the *LogMessage* function, which writes the error to the Application Log in the Event Viewer, and then the error is rethrown so that the consuming application can catch the error.

The *LogMessage* function is designed so that any information may be written to the Application log of the host server. The Application log also supports a means for identifying the type of message that is written to the log. The *LogMessage* function writes messages that are type *error* or type *information* depending on the value of the *Error* parameter that is passed. If the *Error* parameter is true, *LogMessage* identifies the message in the Application log as an *error*; otherwise, the message is *information*. Listing 15-9 shows the code for the *LogMessage* function.

Listing 15-9

LogMessage Function of the Events Class

```
/// <summary>
/// logs messages to event log
/// in: string that contains message of error
///         or information that ought to be logged
```

```
///
///     out: returns true if successful write,
///          rethrows the error if failure occurs
/// </summary>
///
[WebMethod]
public bool LogMessage(string Message, bool Error)
{
    System.Diagnostics.EventLogEntryType MessageType;

    try
    {
        //determine the type of message
        if (Error )
        {
            MessageType =
                    System.Diagnostics.EventLogEntryType.Error;
        }
        else
        {
            MessageType =
            System.Diagnostics.EventLogEntryType.Information;
        }

        //make the write
        this.Log.WriteEntry(Message, MessageType);
    }
    catch (System.Exception eLogWrite)
    {
        //nothing else left to do except throw the raw error
        throw eLogWrite;
    }
    //we have success if we get to this line
    return true;
}
```

The object instance named *Log* represents the application log for the host server. The Visual Studio .NET Component Designer toolbox provides a component that represents any log in the host server Event Viewer. Simply paste the control onto the design view of the web service and the properties for the log may be set to establish the log on the host that messages should be written to using the instance of the component. Of all the possible logs that could be utilized, the Application log is probably the best choice for writing messages to, since it was designed for application information logging.

Logging Status and Errors

In all web services, status and errors should always be logged on the local host server. Quite often, web projects seem to be produced without adequate error handling code or diagnostic information about what the code is doing. When the application begins to fail in production, and the error condition cannot be duplicated in a development environment, the inclination often seems to be to allow a developer access to the production environment to diagnose and debug the code in production. However, the application should *never* be diagnosed in a production environment, and because developers can examine messages written to the Application log and easy ways of writing the information to the Application log exist, there is no reason for a developer to take such measures at diagnosing the failure. Allowing a developer access to a production environment should be considered a huge failure of the application and is easily preventable with good error handling and diagnostic logging.

Application Security

Writing to the event log does require modification of the rights under which the web service runs. Among the new features of IIS6 are two new built-in accounts for worker processes called Network Service and Local Service. In previous versions of IIS, the worker processes for IIS ran under the Local System account. The Network Service account is the default account for worker processes in IIS to run. Network Service is more restrictive than the Local System account, and Local Service is more restrictive than Network Service. A custom user account could be created that caters to the specific functional and security needs of the application as well.

To configure an application to run under a different account, you create a new application pool and set it to run under the credentials of the Local System account.

1. Open the Computer Management Microsoft Management Console (MMC) snap-in by choosing Start | Administrative Tools.

2. Open the Internet Information Services (IIS) Manager node, and then open the Application Pools folder node. All the defined application pools should be listed as icons in the tree subordinate to the Application Pools folder. An application pool named *DefaultAppPool* should exist; if it is expanded, all the web sites that use it will be listed below it, as shown in Figure 15-12.

3. The Default Web Site that is created when IIS 6 is installed uses *DefaultAppPool*. As seen in Figure 15-12, the Default Web Site is listed as one of the many web applications using the *DefaultAppPool*. To set the application pool that a web site uses, open the Properties page for the web instance or virtual directory by right-clicking on the node and selecting Properties.

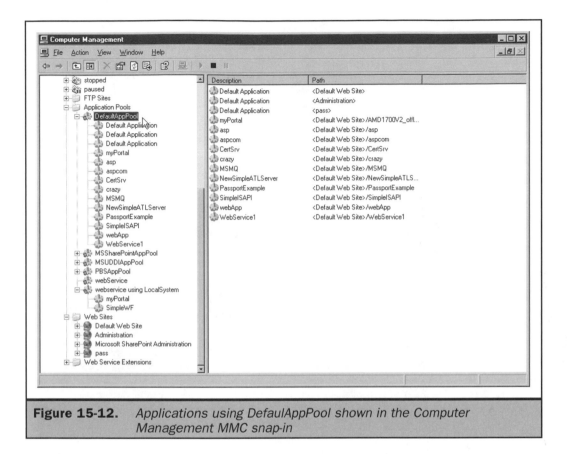

Figure 15-12.   *Applications using DefaulAppPool shown in the Computer Management MMC snap-in*

4. Select the Home Directory tab for a web instance, or the Virtual Directory tab for the virtual directory. In the Home Directory tab, the Application Pool combo box shown in Figure 15-13 displays the available application pools that can be selected.

   The *Events* web service is running under a virtual directory called *myPortal*, which is located in the Default Web Site. The virtual directory *myPortal* was set to use *DefaultAppPool*, which runs under the credentials of the Network Service account. When the *Events* web service attempts to write to the event log, it will fail because the Network Service account does not have adequate rights to write to the application event log. If the *Events* web service were running on a previous version of IIS, it would write to the application event log without any problems. To solve the access problem, a new application pool will be created that uses the Local System account, and *myPortal* will be set to use the new application pool.

5. Right-click the Application Pools icon in the Computer Management MMS and choose New | Application Pool.

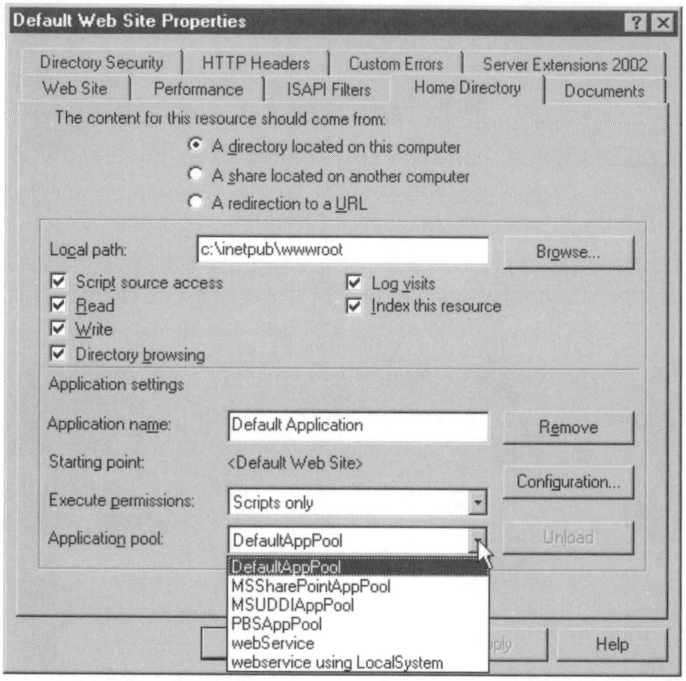

Figure 15-13. *Home Directory tab for the Default Web Site Properties page*

6. In the Add New Application Pool dialog box, shown in Figure 15-14, you can see that the Application Pool ID is set to *webservice using LocalSystem.* The default settings for a new application pool will be used.

7. Click the OK button, and the new application pool will be created.

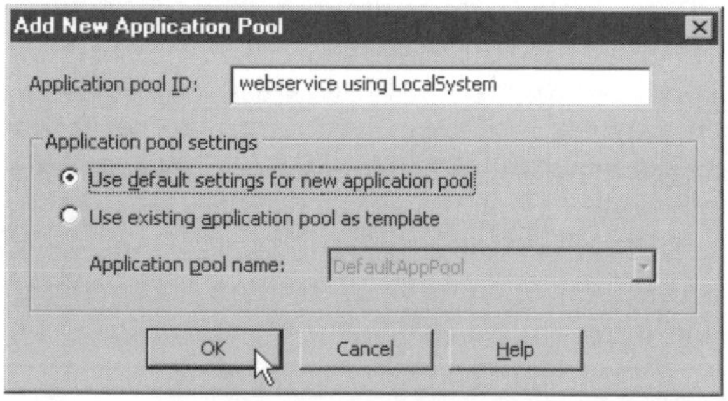

Figure 15-14. *Add New Application Pool dialog box*

Here's how to change the identity of the application pool *webservice using LocalSystem:*

1. Open the Properties window by right-clicking the newly created node labeled *webservice using LocalSystem* in the Computer Management MMC under the Application Pools node and choosing Properties.

2. In the Properties window, choose the Identity tab and select Local System from the Predefined security account selection, as shown in Figure 15-15.

3. Click OK or Apply. A box will appear warning you of the dangers of running an application pool under the Local System. If you're concerned about the web service running under the Local System account, you can configure a user account that betters suits your security requirements and allows the web service to write to the application event log.

After the application pool is created, the virtual directory, *myPortal,* may be set to use the *webservice using LocalSystem* application pool. Open the Properties window for *myPortal,* and on the Directory tab, select the new application pool, as shown in Figure 15-16.

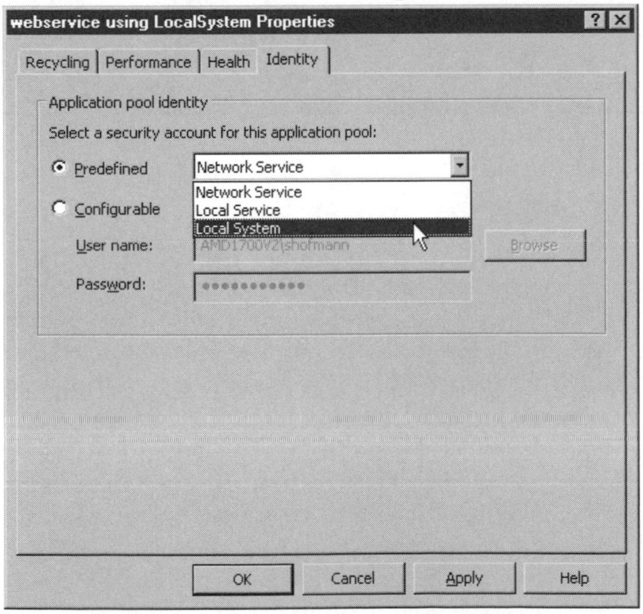

Figure 15-15.   *Set the identity for the application pool*

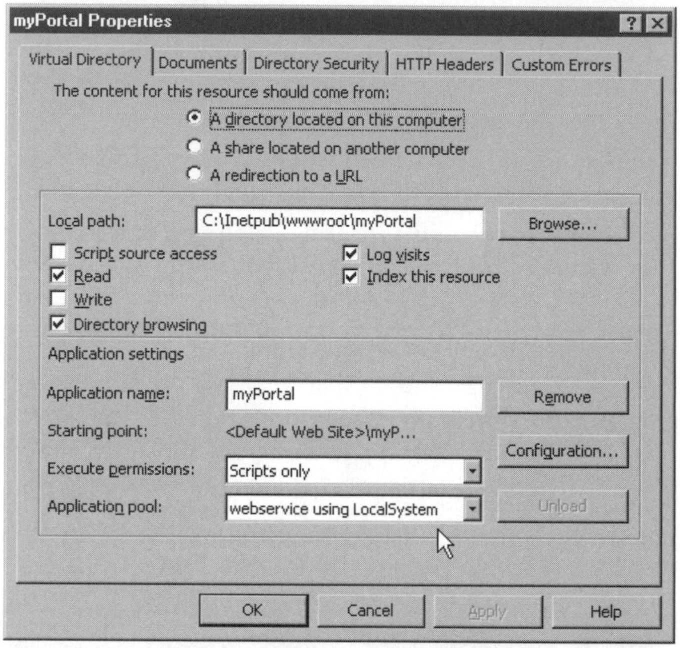

Figure 15-16.   *Selecting the new application pool webservice using LocalSystem for myPortal*

Testing the Web Service

In addition to the *Add* method shown in Listing 15-7 and the *LogMessage* function shown in Listing 15-9, the *Events* web service contains three other public web methods called *Delete*, *Open*, and *HelloWorld*. *Delete* and *Open* are similar to the *Add* function in that they perform some data read or write function based on end-user submitted data. *HelloWorld* is the default method that Visual Studio .NET Component Designer places in all new web services to demonstrate how to make a method in the web service available to web access.

If the ASMX for the web service is set as the startup file, the web service can be run and debugged in Visual Studio .NET. Press F5 to start the compiler; if no errors are found, the web browser will open with a default web service test harness provided by the .NET Framework, as shown in Figure 15-17.

Click any of the method calls to open a new page that displays a data entry form based on the parameters of the method. The HTTP and SOAP request and response are defined and described under the data entry fields for the method being described.

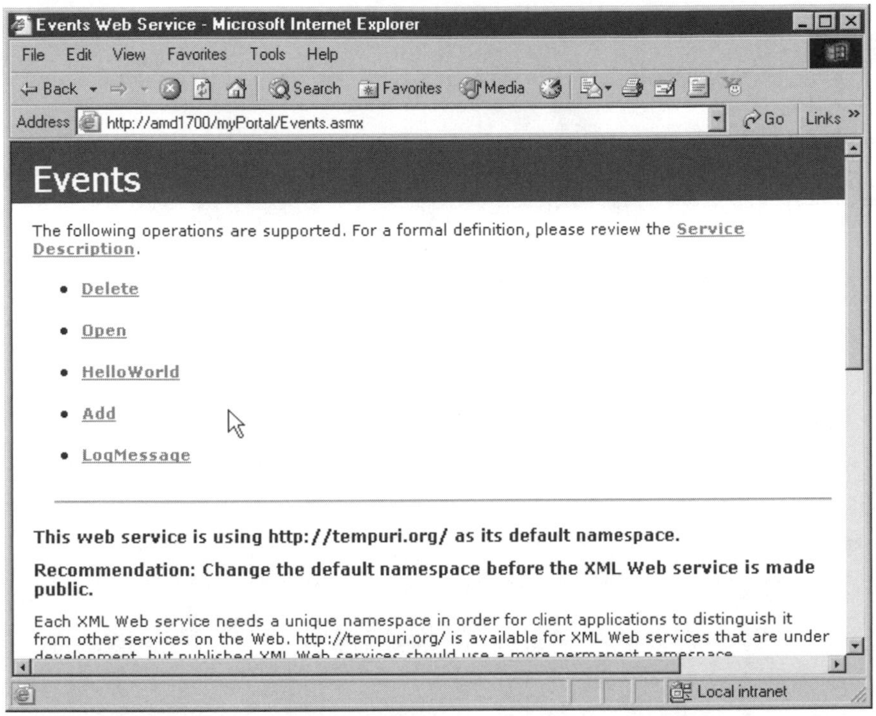

Figure 15-17. *Requesting a web service using a web browser*

Data placed in the text boxes presented in the test screen will be passed as arguments for the method's parameters after you click the Invoke button. Figure 15-18 shows the *Open* method test screen in the web browser.

Set the ID with a value of 13 and click the Invoke button, and another web browser instance will open with the result of the call to the *Open* method formatted into XML. Because the *Open* method returns true or false depending on the success or failure of the function to execute, the response is quite minimal and does not help demonstrate whether the web service really opened the record correctly; however, the feedback does indicate that the web service believes it functioned correctly, since it returned a value of true, as shown in Figure 15-19. It would be much more useful to see the data being pulled from the data source, so the default test harness provided by the .NET Framework may not be very suitable for unit testing your web service.

IIS PROGRAMMING

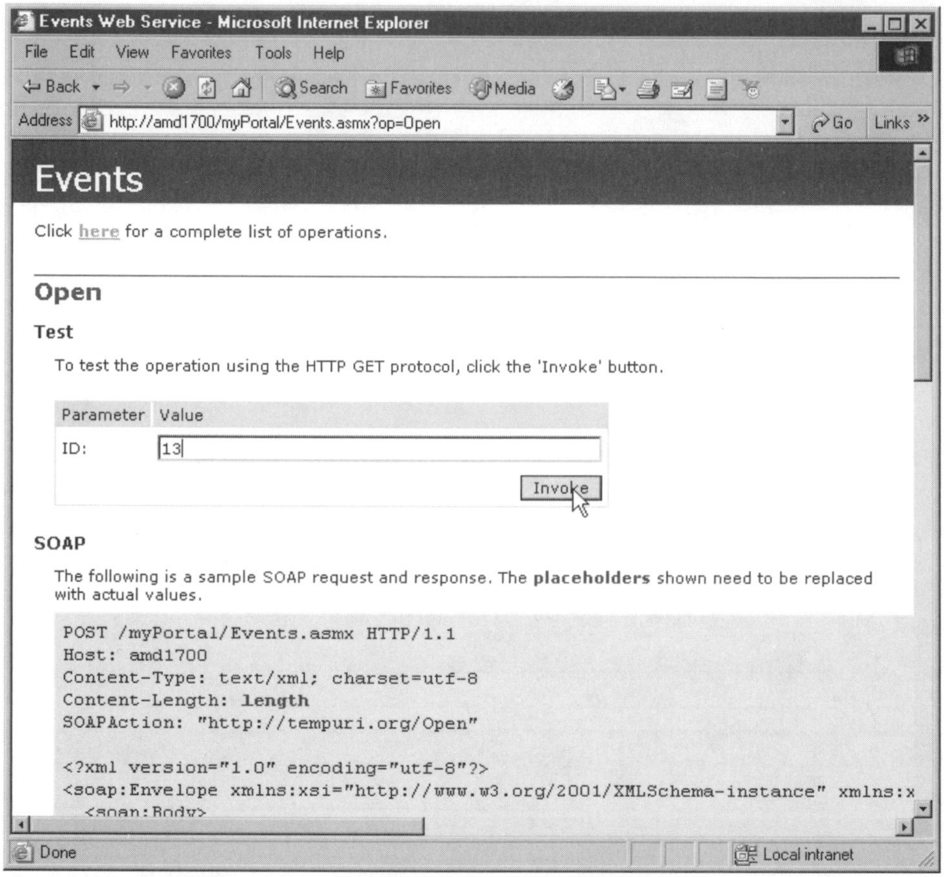

Figure 15-18. Open method of the Events web service requested from web browser

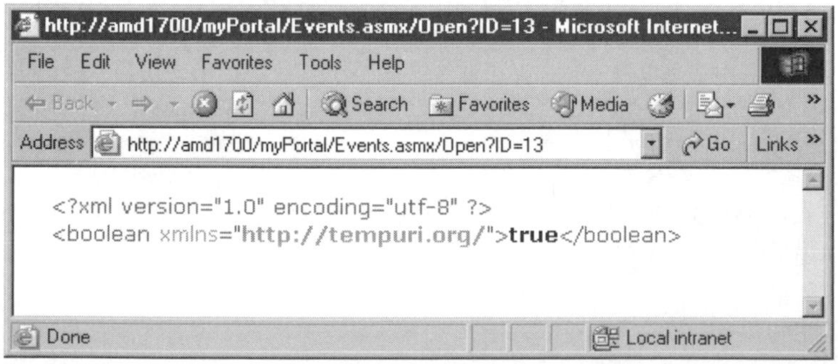

Figure 15-19. Response of Open method in web browser

Writing a Test Harness

The actual value that was opened on the *Open* method is stored in the *Events* class property called *Event*. The intended use of the *Events* class is for a consumer to call a method such as *Open* or *Add* and have a value returned that indicates whether or not the call was successful. If the call is successful, the *Event* data could be obtained from the *Event* property.

The test harness provided by the .NET Framework does not display the values in a web service property, and a property cannot be identified as a web method using the *[WebMethod]* identifier. The *WebMethod* identifier is placed above any public method that should be exposed as an XML web service. In this case, a test harness should be written to use the web service and display the results so that it can be verified that the code functioned properly.

Web forms are great mechanisms for producing a web service test harness. For the *Events* class *Add* method, a web form that adds an event was produced called *EventClient* *.aspx*. Web forms offer a calendar control to the developer that is ideal for capturing the date from the end user. Two text boxes for the name and description of the event may be pasted on a web form, along with the calendar control. To show the resulting ID of the new event after the *Add* function is successfully executed, a text box that displays the ID and the Submit button is added so that the web form will know when to respond to the end user. Figure 15-20 shows a calendar control *Add* method after an event was added.

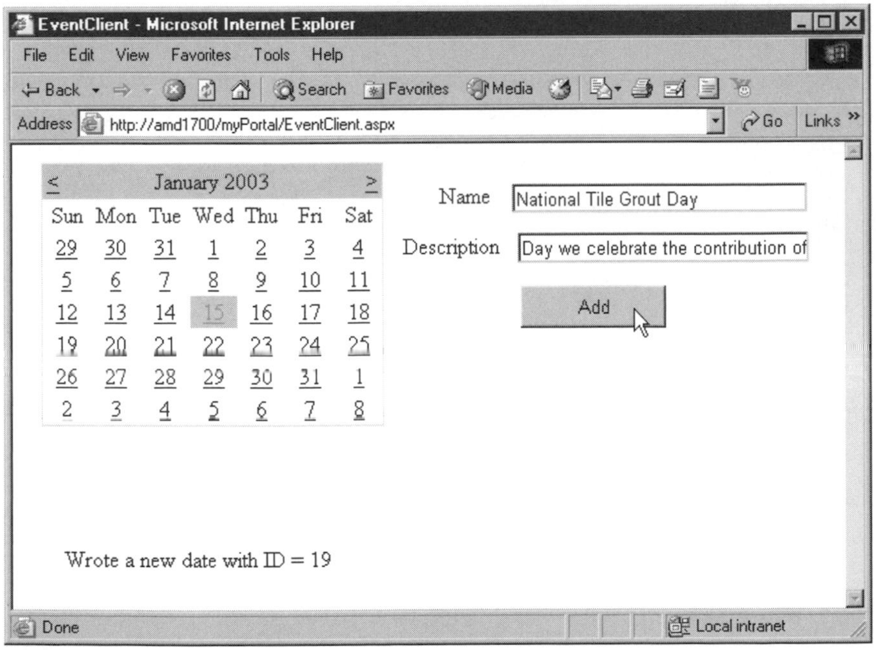

Figure 15-20.   *Add method web form test harness*

The code behind the web form *EventClient.aspx*, shown in Listing 15-10, is simple. As shown in Figure 15-20, a control on the form exists for each property of the class *anEvent*. The Submit button is used to trigger the event of calling the *Add* event. The code behind the *EventClient.aspx* web form consists mostly of the button click event function for the *btnAdd* control. The web form *EventClient.aspx* should be run in the same web application that hosts the web service. The sole purpose of the web form *EventClient.aspx* is to unit test the code and make certain that the functions in the web service *Events* work properly, so it was kept as simple as possible and provides the developer useful feedback about the performance of *Events* web service.

Listing 15-10

```
Source Code for Events Add Function
Test Harness - Web Form EventClient.aspx

/// <summary>
/// Summary description for EventClient.
/// </summary>
public class EventClient : System.Web.UI.Page
{
    protected System.Web.UI.WebControls.Calendar Calendar1;
    protected System.Web.UI.WebControls.TextBox txtName;
    protected System.Web.UI.WebControls.Label Label1;
    protected System.Web.UI.WebControls.Label Label2;
    protected System.Web.UI.WebControls.TextBox txtDescription;
    protected System.Web.UI.WebControls.Label lblFeedback;
    protected System.Web.UI.WebControls.Button btnAdd;

    private void Page_Load(object sender, System.EventArgs e)
    {
        //don't show the feedback text box until
        //there is a good reason
        this.lblFeedback.Visible = false;

        //make the numbers red that are selected in calendar
        this.Calendar1.SelectedDayStyle.ForeColor =
            System.Drawing.Color.Red;
    }

    #region Web Form Designer generated code
    override protected void OnInit(EventArgs e)
    {
    //
    // CODEGEN: This call is required by the
```

```
    // ASP.NET Web Form Designer.
    //
      InitializeComponent();
        base.OnInit(e);
    }

    /// <summary>
    /// Required method for Designer support - do not modify
    /// the contents of this method with the code editor.
    /// </summary>
    private void InitializeComponent()
{
  this.btnAdd.Click += new System.EventHandler(this.btnAdd_Click);
  this.Load += new System.EventHandler(this.Page_Load);

}
    #endregion

    private void btnAdd_Click(object sender, System.EventArgs e)
    {
        Events myEvents = new Events();
        anEvent myEvent = new anEvent();

        //get the name
        myEvent.Name = this.txtName.Text;

        //get the date/time
        myEvent.DateTime = this.Calendar1.
            SelectedDate.Date;

        //get the description
        myEvent.Description = this.txtDescription.Text;

        myEvents.Event = myEvent;

        //add it
        if (myEvents.Add())
        {
            this.lblFeedback.Visible = true;
            lblFeedback.Text = "Wrote a new date with ID = " +
                myEvent.ID;
```

IIS PROGRAMMING

```
        }
        else
        {
            this.lblFeedback.Visible = true;
            lblFeedback.Text = "Unable to write date";
        }
    }
}
```

The Visual Studio .NET Component Designer added the *Click* event automatically when the control *btnAdd* was double-clicked in design view. A class instance for *anEvent* and the *Events* web service are created in the beginning of the *Click* event. Since these classes all exist in the same namespace, there is no need to refer to the namespace or place a using directive at the top of the source code for the namespace *myPortal*. The event being added is represented by an instance of *anEvent* named *myEvent*. The *Events* instance is named *myEvents*. The properties for *myEvent* are obtained from the calendar *txtDescription* and *txtName* controls. When *myEvent* is filled with the end-user submitted data, it is placed in the *event* property of the instance *myEvents*. The *myEvents Add* function is called, and if successful, the success message is written to the *lblFeedback* control; otherwise, a failure message is written to the *lblFeedback* control.

It should also be pointed out that no error handling exists in this code. Because this code is designed to test for failure and not serve in a production capacity, it is better not to have error handling. The test harness is for the developer to analyze failure. Allowing unhandled errors to occur will provide better data for developers to help them understand the robustness of features of the code.

The test harness should be kept and stored in the same way that other source code for the web service is stored. The harness will help to provide a future means of reference showing how the solution works, and it may be used to test future enhancements to the web service.

Chapter 16

ATL Server

A TL Server is a set of classes that are part of Microsoft's Visual Studio .NET offering and a mechanism for using them in an Internet-related context. The classes are used in developing C++ application projects for the web. When Microsoft decided to produce ASP.NET, it started with ATL Server. Many of the features that ASP.NET Web Forms and Web Services provide are truncated forms of functionality found within the ATL Server classes. In addition to all of the classes that are afforded in a web service, ATL Server offers the developer classes that control memory utilization, session management, resource caching, and thread management of IIS and Hypertext Transfer Protocol (HTTP) requests. ATL Server also offers many new classes that are devoted to file management—classes that were previously unavailable to ISAPI (Internet Server Application Program Interface) developers. ATL Server gives a developer a great deal of command and control in producing web-based solutions, and it provides the ease and convenience of access to many classes oriented toward the production of web-based solutions.

ATL Server could also be viewed as a nice enhancement for ISAPI. In the same way that the Active Template Library (ATL) was produced to help developers interact with the Microsoft Foundation Classes (MFC) and the Windows application programming interface (API), ATL Server was produced to aid the programmer in working with the IIS API or ISAPI. ATL Server allows developers to produce web solutions that are either managed via the .NET framework or unmanaged. ATL Server also provides many intricate options for controlling interactions with IIS that are not available in the managed languages such as Visual C# and Visual Basic. ATL Server is also a great alternative to using ISAPI directly, because many of the classes provided in ATL Server would likely be classes that developers would have to produce themselves if they were working with ISAPI.

ATL Server Architecture Overview

ATL Server associates classes and functions stored in dynamic link libraries (DLLs) with tags placed in text files in such a way that requests to IIS can call the functions within the DLLs and return to the requesting client the text file contents along with the results from the function calls. ATL Server uses ISAPI to establish the calling mechanism between the text files, IIS, and the DLLs using a tag style command system that is enabled by the .NET Framework. The simplest ATL Server solution comprises the following:

- ISAPI extension DLL
- Web Application DLL or Request Handler DLL
- Server Response File (SRF)
- Internet Information Services (IIS)

As requests are sent to IIS for a resource that happens to be an ATL Server source, IIS will associate the call to the ISAPI extension DLL. After IIS hands the request to the ISAPI extension DLL, the requested web application DLL or server response file is opened by the ISAPI extension DLL and processed. If the requested resource is a server response file, the *replacement tag* indicating a function located in the web application DLL is called and the results are pasted into the server response file at the location of the replacement tag. The combination of the results of the calls placed to the web application DLL and the contents of the server response file are returned to the requester. If the web application DLL is requested directly, the ISAPI DLL makes the appropriate call(s) and returns the result to the browser.

Figure 16-1 provides an architecture overview of ATL Server.

Because an ISAPI extension DLL could reside on the host server in a file location other than within the web root, IIS has to know what to do with the ISAPI extension file and the files associated with the ISAPI extension DLL, such as the server response files and the web application DLL. To illustrate the situation with a common web solution that requires the use of text files to be processed by an ISAPI extension, Active Server Pages (ASP) will be used to contrast the mechanism by which IIS associates files and ISAPI extensions. IIS knows how to process ASP files because all filenames ending with the extension *.asp* are processed using an ISAPI extension named *ASP.DLL*. The code within *ASP.DLL*

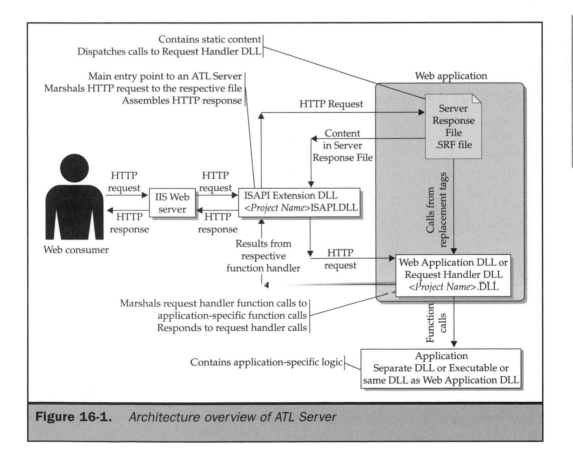

Figure 16-1.   *Architecture overview of ATL Server*

opens the associated ASP file and interprets the code in the ASP tags. Web forms and web services using the *.aspx* and *.asmx* files, respectively, use the same mechanism, except they use the .NET Framework instead of using ASP.DLL to interpret code and tags within the respective files.

ATL Server uses the ISAPI extension DLLs to interpret code embedded in server response file tags and call functions identified with replacement tags in the web application DLL. When a developer is building a web application using ASP files, they would never consider recompiling the ASP.DLL so that it would contain code only useful for processing the ASP functions that they used in their ASP files. The ASP.DLL does not change from ASP application to ASP application—in essence, providing a *one size fits all* interpreting ISAPI extension DLL. In contrast, however, ATL Server makes a customized interpreter for the solution being built that is optimized for the solution. The customized interpreter is the ISAPI extension DLL that is part of the ATL server project. The developer has the luxury of changing it to meet the needs of their application rather then accepting the default configuration.

To make IIS use the ISAPI extension DLL, the server response files and the application DLL files must be mapped to the respective ISAPI extension DLL. Just as filenames ending in *.asp* are mapped to the ASP.DLL ISAPI extension DLL or filenames ending in *.aspx* are mapped to the .NET Framework interpreter named *aspnet_isapi.dll*, so must the filename extension *.srf* for server response files and *.dll* for web application DLLs be mapped to their respective ISAPI extension DLL.

Here's how to map filename extensions to ISAPI extensions:

1. Open the Microsoft Management Console (MMC) snap-in for IIS.

2. Click the Web Site folder icon in the tree to expand the list of web server instances on the server, and then click the web site instance that should be configured to expand the contents within the instance.

3. Open the Properties window for any given web instance, or virtual directory (by right-clicking the web instance or directory), and click the Configuration button found on the Home Directory tab, or the Virtual Directory tab, respectively. The Application Configuration applet shown in Figure 16-2 will open.

4. Associate the file and path location of the desired path location of the ISAPI extension DLL on the host. Once this effort is complete, the instance of IIS should be restarted.

The location of the web application DLL used by the server response file is identified in the server response file itself. The web application DLL must reside within the virtual directory root. The server response file contains a handler tag that identifies the relative location of the web application DLL. (See the section "Server Response Files" for more on handler tags.) When an HTTP request is sent to IIS for the server response files or the web application DLL, IIS will know from the file mapping where to find the ISAPI extension DLL to process and interpret the request.

Because none of the DLLs involved are Component Object Model (COM) DLLs, the mechanism used by IIS and the parts of ATL Server to find the proper DLLs consists of physically locating the DLLs on the host, based on actual file locations. As many of you

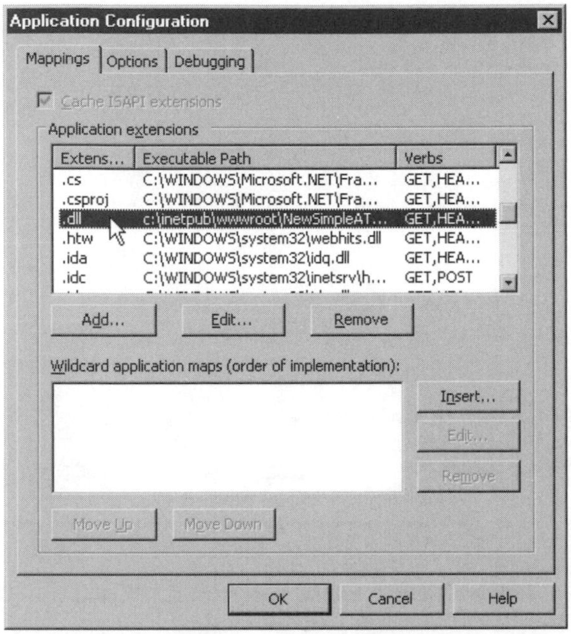

Figure 16-2. *Application Configuration applet for mapping files to extensions*

may recall, a COM object's location on a host is known by associating a unique identification number (CLSID) with the file path of the DLL. This information is stored in the Windows registry where any software requesting the use of the COM object DLL would be able to use the functionality it offered. Although accessing a DLL by physically locating it and loading it may be viewed as somewhat antiquated when contrasted to the post-COM architecture, this solution offers some benefits from a maintenance perspective. The file mappings in IIS are based on filename extensions. The web application DLL is specified using a relative path. Moving files to another server would disrupt a file mapping for IIS to the ISAPI extension DLL, but the other files could be moved as though they were static content, as long as their locations relative to one another are maintained.

Create a Simple ATL Server Project

Let's create an ATL Server project.

1. Open Visual Studio .NET.
2. Choose File | New | Project to open the New Project dialog box, shown in Figure 16-3.

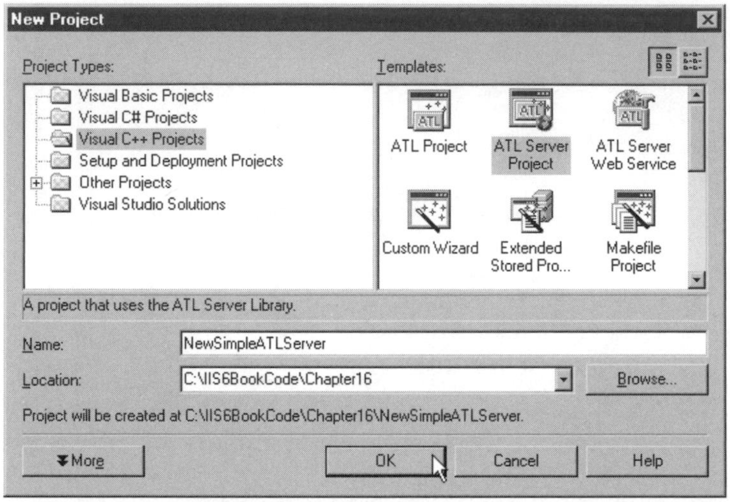

Figure 16-3. *New Project dialog box with ATL Server project template*

3. Visual Studio .NET offers many ATL templates for web solutions or ATL solutions, but for this exercise, select the ATL Server Project template. Be careful not to choose the ATL Project template since it does not offer a web component. As it always has, however, the ATL Project template will provide the framework for producing a classic ATL DLL or executable that utilizes ATL Libraries.

The ATL Server Web Service template will produce a Web Service project that is similar to web service project templates produced in Visual Basic and C#, except, of course, the project is coded in C++. An associated ISAPI extension is produced for the web service that may be deployed and managed separately from the Web Service DLL. Just as the web services in C# had the *.asmx* file that acted as a dispatching mechanism to the web service DLL, the ATL Server Web Service uses HTML files for this purpose.

4. Enter the name of the project, and then click the Next button to start the ATL Server Project Wizard, which opens with an overview of the project that will be produced.

5. The ATL Server Project Wizard is a one-step wizard with four separate screens that may be used to change project settings of the ATL Server prior to the point at which the files are actually generated. The settings are summarized as part of the wizard's Overview (Figure 16-4) screen for the project. If the default settings are known and desired, you can click the Finish button, and the project files will be created.

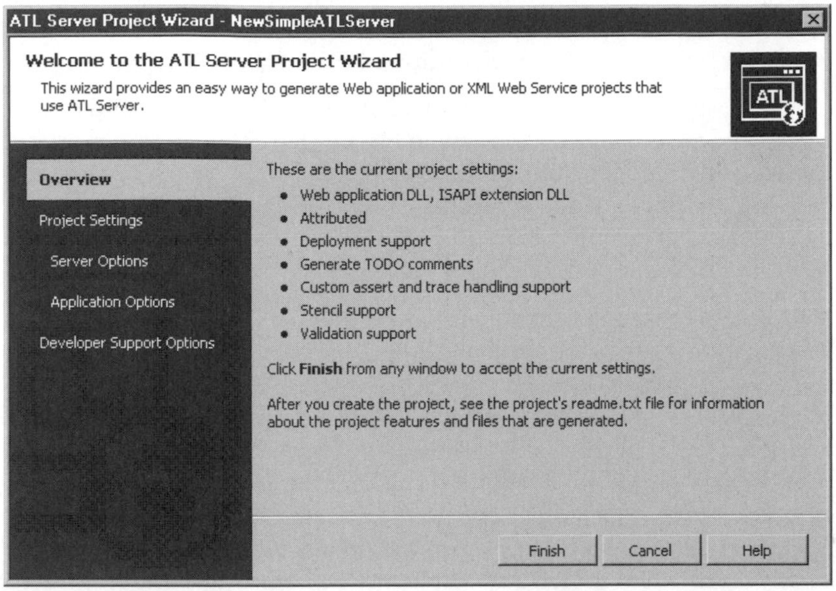

Figure 16-4.   *Overview screen for ATL Server Project Wizard*

After you click the Finish button of the ATL Server Project Wizard, Visual Studio .NET will begin to generate the files according to the default settings of the ATL Server Project Wizard. Either of the ATL Server project templates mentioned in step 3 (ATL Server Web Service or ATL Server Project) will generate two projects in Visual Studio .NET. The start-up project is the main project whose name you provided in the New Project dialog box. The second project that is generated uses the same name as the start-up project, but *ISAPI* is concatenated to the end of the filename. For example, in Figure 16-3, the name *NewSimpleATLServer* was given to the ATL Server project being created. Visual Studio .NET provides a window, called the Solution Explorer, for examining projects and the associated files. The Solution Explorer window displays the projects and files in a hierarchical tree format that are associated with the currently opened solution. The Solution Explorer may be opened from the Visual Studio .NET menu View | Solution Explorer. In the Solution Explorer, the project *NewSimpleATLServer* will exist and a second project named *NewSimpleATLServerISAPI* will also exist. The *NewSimpleATLServer* project contains the application-specific code. The product of the *NewSimpleATLServer* project is a Web Application DLL and Server Response File (SRF). The product of the *NewSimpleATLServerISAPI* project is a single ISAPI DLL.

Unlike the web service templates for C# and Visual Basic, a virtual directory is not automatically added to the local instance of IIS. Visual Studio .NET can be set up to deploy the files that make up your ATL Server solution to IIS. The first IIS web instance loaded in IIS, however, is the only instance that Visual Studio .NET will deploy to. If you need to deploy to another web instance other than the first one, which usually is the default web site, you will have to perform this operation manually. To configure Visual Studio to deploy the ATL Server solution to IIS automatically, follow these steps:

1. Select Project | Properties from the Visual Studio .NET menu and the property pages window will open, as shown in Figure 16-5. An ATL server project actually consists of two projects (unless the project was configured to use a single DLL). The property pages window will display the properties for the currently selected Visual Studio project. The currently selected project may be changed by selecting the project in the Solution Explorer window.

2. After the property pages window opens, select the Web Deployment node in the left panel of the window at the bottom. Each of the nodes in the left panel of the window is identified with a folder icon. Selecting any node in the left panel of the property pages window will cause the window to refresh the contents of the right panel so that the controls that are used to edit configurations related to the selected node in the left panel are displayed.

3. Select the ISAPI extension DLL project from the Solution Explorer. Unless the project name was changed from the project template default, this project usually has the phrase *ISAPI* appended to the name given the ATL Server project.

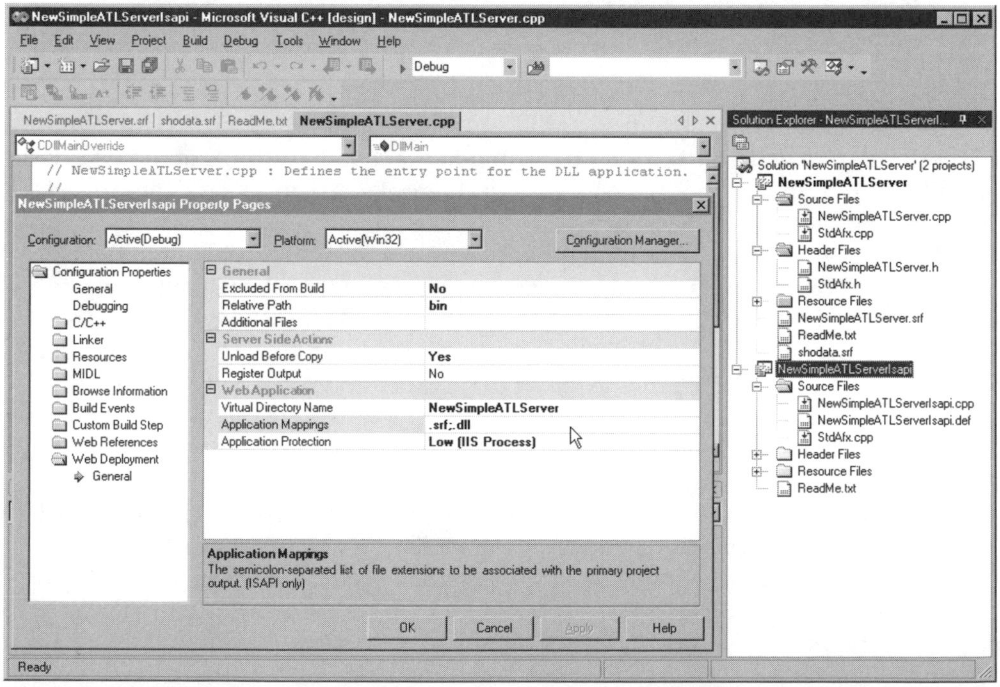

Figure 16-5. *Project property pages window and solution explorer*

4. For the *Relative Path* property displayed in the right panel, type the value **bin**. This will cause the ISAPI extension DLL to be placed in a subdirectory named bin subordinate to the directory that the IIS virtual directory points to. If you want a different name than *bin*, any name you would like the files to be deployed to will do.

5. Set the *Virtual Directory Name* property to the name of a virtual directory you would like the ATL server project files to be deployed to in IIS. If the virtual directory does not exist, it will be created. The drop-down list box provides an option to simply choose the name of the project for the setting.

6. The *Application Mappings* should be set to *.srf;.dll*. The virtual directory created will have these mappings set.

7. Now, select the project for the web application dll in the Solution Explorer so that the property pages window will refresh with the settings for the web application dll project.

8. Just as was done for the ISAPI project, select the Web Deployment node in the left panel of the window at the bottom if it is not already selected.

9. Make the same settings as described in steps 4 and 5. The virtual directory name must be the same name used for the ISAPI project. The relative path property can be set to a different path than the ISAPI project's relative path. The application mappings should not be set to any value for the web application dll project.

10. Click the OK button to keep the configuration changes and dismiss the window.

After the relative path, virtual directory name, and application mappings are set for the projects in an ATL server solution, the files will be deployed after the first build is performed.

Pressing the F5 key, regardless of what window in Visual Studio .NET is selected, will cause Visual Studio .NET to begin to build, deploy, and run *NewSimpleATLServer*. A prompt will appear, informing you that the files are out of date and requesting permission to recompile. After the binaries for the request handler DLL and the ISAPI extension are compiled successfully, they will be moved along with the sample SRF to a location within the web root of the default web server instance in IIS. Visual Studio .NET will attempt to attach itself to IIS and provide step-through code debugging, and the likely result will be that you will be presented with the following error message:

Remember *The name of the StartUp project in any given Visual Studio .NET solution is identified in boldface font in the Solution Explorer. For a solution that contains multiple projects, the project template will likely automatically set the proper project as the StartUp project. If multiple projects are being added to a given solution, however, the developer will need to ensure that the desired project is set as the StartUp because Visual Studio .NET will establish a StartUp project arbitrarily. To set a project as the StartUp, right-click the project in the Solution Explorer and choose Set As StartUp Project from the context-sensitive menu.*

By default, Visual Studio .NET does not install with support for ATL Server debugging in place. *Full Remote Debugging* is installed by default, and it will support the debugging requirements of managed code solutions such as Visual Basic and C# web forms and web services. C++ solutions require the use of *Native Remote Debugging*. The Visual Studio .NET installation program may be used to add the support, as shown in Figure 16-6. Simply access the install program that was used to install Visual Studio .NET on your workstation and start the installation process. When the window shown in Figure 16-6 is displayed, choose Native Remote Debugging.

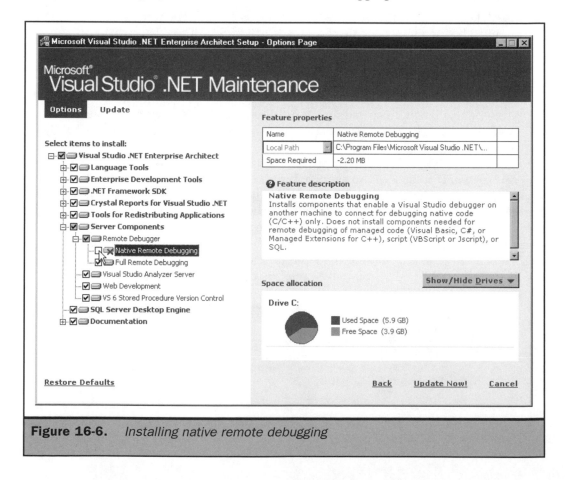

Figure 16-6. *Installing native remote debugging*

If native remote debugging is in place and everything is set up properly, a browser instance should have been opened showing the phrase, *This is a test: Hello World!* The only other likely failure that might occur at this point is if the file extensions *.dll* and *.srf* are not mapped to the associated ISAPI extension DLL for the project in a given IIS instance or virtual directory. If you believe this might be the case, open the application mappings for the IIS instance or virtual directory as shown in Figure 16-2 and inspect the mappings to see if the *.srf* and *.dll* files are mapped to the proper ISAPI extension DLL.

Because of the complicated ATL Server configuration required to get a *Hello World* program to run, the developer must have an intricate knowledge of the workings of IIS and the .NET Framework. Harnessing the power of the ATL Server can benefit the development shop a great deal, but the learning curve is a formidable consideration.

> **Tip**   *Whenever something does not function properly when you're working with IIS and ATL Server, and you can find no apparent reason for it not to work, you might try restarting the web services. This is especially true when a developer or system engineer has to map an ISAPI extension manually or after configuration changes for the IIS instance or the virtual directory are made.*

Using the ATL Server Project Wizard

The ATL Server Project Wizard provides options for changing the way the project will be created. Although the wizard is a one-step wizard, it offers many potential scenarios for creating an ATL Server project. Some items may be changed in the project property pages window after the project is created, and others must be set in the wizard since they cannot be changed later. Visual Studio .NET does allow you to change any given project into another type of project, but the effort to perform such a task manually is time consuming. If you want to change a project from one type to another type of project, many problems can be avoided simply by saving the desired code and pasting it in to a project generated by the proper project template in Visual Studio .NET. Knowing what options are available in the ATL Server Project Wizard can save you time and help you become familiar with and reliably use the options that are available in ATL Server.

Project Settings

The Project Settings tab in the ATL Server Project Wizard (shown in Figure 16-7) allows you to set the virtual directory to which the project will be deployed when compiled, but this directory may be changed any time using the project property pages window. The project names and directories may also be changed after the ATL Server Project Wizard generates the solution files, but the ability to generate a single DLL to host both the ISAPI code and the web application code should be set prior to finishing the wizard.

A savvy developer could probably edit the project settings well enough to change any given project into any other project type, but for the sake of making the change reliably and saving time, it is far easier to change the wizard settings for some configurations that pertain to the production binary file type. Names of projects and parts of the

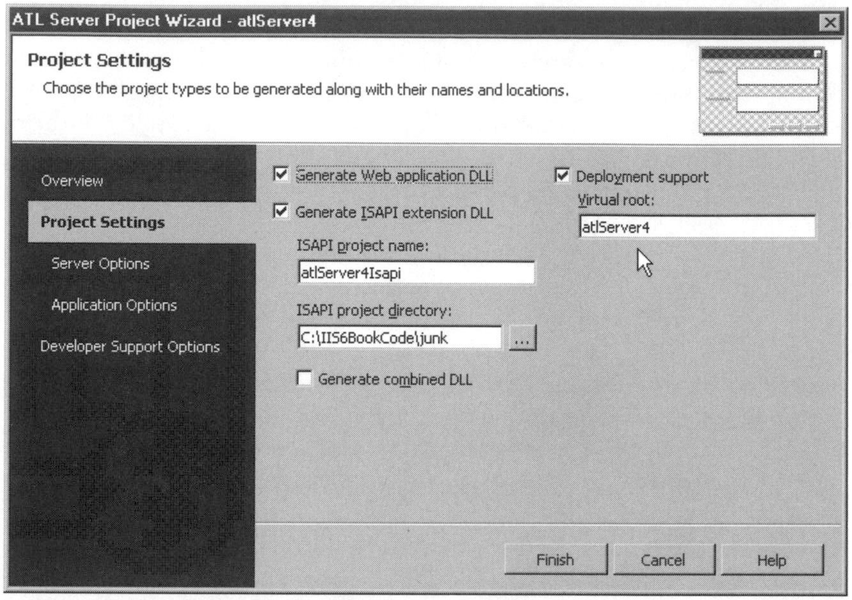

Figure 16-7. *Project Settings in the ATL Server Project Wizard*

solution and file path changes are easily made in the project property pages window at any time, and sometimes small edits are required elsewhere in the project.

Server Options in the ATL Server Project Wizard

The Server Options tab in the ATL Server Project Wizard (shown in Figure 16-8) provides support for some advanced integration with server host services and session management. For session management, a session may be written to a data source that has an OLE DB provider, such as a database. Such is the case in a web cluster deployment, where placing session data inside a data source is necessary if other servers participating in hosting the web solution must access the session.

If the ATL Server project is designed to operate on a single server, or the solution requires no collaboration with other web servers using the session, the Memory-Backed Session State Services option can be chosen, and it offers greater performance. The OLE DB-Backed Session State Services option provides greater extendibility of the solution since the solution may be deployed to a distributed hardware environment without making any changes to the code. If the solution's requirement calls for any sort of session support, check the checkbox for the Session Services. The respective OLE DB-Backed or Memory-Backed selection may be chosen based on the desired level of support.

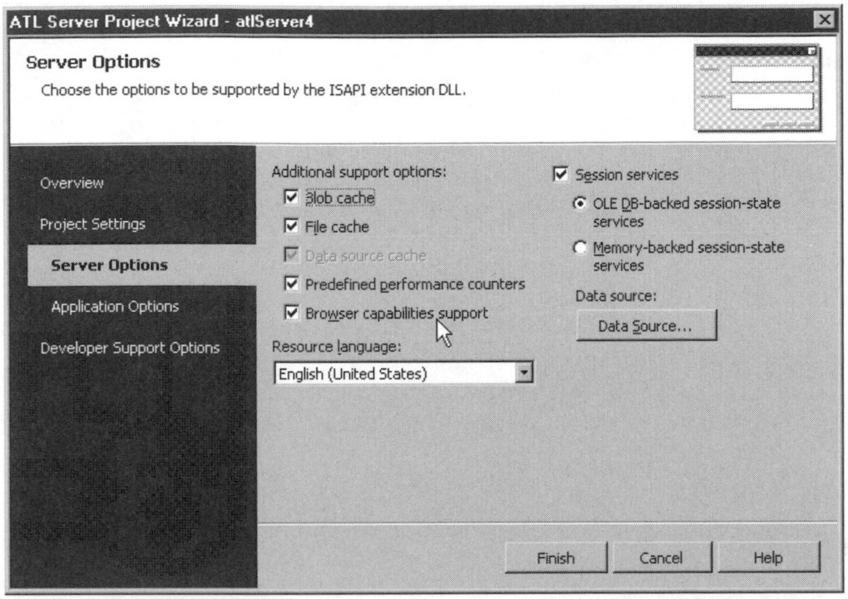

Figure 16-8.   *Server Options tab in the ATL Server Project Wizard*

When the ATL Server Project Wizard generates the code, a class with the same name as the project, but prefixed with a *C* and suffixed by the phrase *Handler*, is created. This class is designed to be the web application interface to IIS by hosting the tag handlers. For example, if the project shown in Figure 16-7 is named *atlServer4*, the class that is created by the wizard for hosting the tag handlers is named *CatlServer4Handler*.

Checking any of the following checkboxes on the Server Options tab of the wizard causes code to be included in the handler class that declares and initializes the pointers to each respective supporting class:

■ **Blob Cache**   Adds a pointer for a class instance of *IMemoryCache* to the project for managing arbitrary chunks of memory.

■ **File Cache**   Adds a pointer for a class instance of *IFileCache* to the project for managing filenames.

■ **Data Source Cache**   Adds many classes to the ATL Server project and the ISAPI project for managing per-thread caching of OLE DB connections.

■ **Predefined Performance Counters**   Add classes for integrating the project with *perfmon* performance counters.

■ **Browser Capabilities Support**   Adds a pointer for a class instance of *IBrowserCapsSvs* to the project for managing browser capacities.

For example, if the server options for File Cache, Blob Cache, and Browser Capabilities Support were selected in the wizard, and the project was named *SimpleATLServer*, the class named *CSimpleATLServerHandler* would be generated and written to the header file *SimpleATLServer.h*. In the private section of the class *CSimpleATLServerHandler*, the following declarations would be generated with comments in front of the code:

```
    // File cache support
//      CComPtr<IFileCache> m_spFileCache;

    // Blob cache support
//      CComPtr<IMemoryCache> m_spBlobCache;

    // Data Source cache support
//      CComPtr<IBrowserCapsSvc> m_spBrowserCaps;
```

Note   *In the preceding code, the Browser Capabilities Support pointer is incorrectly identified by the comment as "Data Source cache support" as a result of a minor bug in the ATL Server Project Wizard template.*

If the developer decides to utilize the pointers for File Cache, Blob Cache, and Browser Capabilities Support, each respective pointer must be uncommented. The pointers are initialized in the public function named *ValidateAndExchange*. Each handler class generated by the ATL Server Project Wizard is provided a *ValidateAndExchange* function unless the Validation Support checkbox under the Application Options tab is not checked (see the next section). The initialization snippets for each respective pointer must also be uncommented if the developer decides to utilize the support.

```
HTTP_CODE ValidateAndExchange()
{
    // TODO: Put all initialization and validation code here

    // Set the content-type
    m_HttpResponse.SetContentType("text/html");

    // uncomment the service initialization(s) if you want to use
    // a service that was generated with your ISAPI extension


    // Get the IFileCache service from the ISAPI extension
//      if (FAILED(m_spServiceProvider->QueryService
//              (__uuidof(IFileCache),
//              &m_spFileCache)))
//          return HTTP_FAIL;
```

```
        // Get the IMemoryCache service from the ISAPI extension
//      if (FAILED(m_spServiceProvider->QueryService
//              (__uuidof(IMemoryCache),
//              &m_spBlobCache)))
//          return HTTP_FAIL;

        // Get the IBrowserCapsSvc service from the ISAPI extension
//      if (FAILED (m_spServiceProvider->QueryService
//              (__uuidof(IBrowserCapsSvc),
//               &m_spBrowserCaps)))
//          return HTTP_FAIL;

        return HTTP_SUCCESS;
}
```

The associated ISAPI extension also has code added to it to provide the support for the items selected in the Server Options tab of the wizard. Unlike the code in the handler class, however, the support code in the ISAPI extension is not commented out and is left as part of the solution regardless of whether or not it is used. Support for functionality that is not absolutely required should not be chosen; this minimizes the resources that might be otherwise devoted to unnecessary functionality.

The file cache support provides a class pointer that supports functions for managing file pointers as they relate to reading and writing to files. Actual file content is not stored in the cache class, but rather the information that relates to the files location, name, and size is stored. When items are removed from the cache, they are removed from the hard drive, so the file cache is not meant to manage files other than temporary files.

The blob cache is a memory-caching system designed to deal with memory chunks of varying sizes. The other memory caching classes offered in ATL Server are designed to support memory chunks of a consistent size. The blob cache fills that void by supporting the need to cache memory of variable sizes.

The data source cache provides a similar type of functionality to the other cache classes except for the purpose of storing data source connections.

Choosing the Predefined Performance Counters option places code in the ISAPI extension so that the ISAPI counters for *perfmon* are updated based on the web application interaction with IIS. This particular feature requires no coding on the part of the developer to make it function. The wizard generates all the code necessary to support the functionality in the ISAPI extension implementation file.

The predefined performance counters are as follows:

- **Active Threads**   Active threads being used by the web application process
- **Average Response Time**   Average response time for the web application to return an HTTP response
- **Current Queued Requests**   HTTP requests awaiting processing

- **Maximum Queued Requests**   Running maximum of the queued HTTP requests
- **Server Failed Requests**   Requests that failed including file not found (404) or forbidden (403) error
- **Server Requests Per Second**   Requests per second made to the IIS web site
- **Server Total Requests**   Running total number of requests made to the IIS web site

The browser capabilities support provides a class pointer to *IbrowserCapsSvc* and initialization to set up the pointer to *IbrowserCapsSvc*. If a pointer to a pointer to *IbrowserCaps* is passed into the *IbrowserCapsSvc GetCaps* function along with a pointer to the server context, the instance of *IbrowserCaps* will allow the developer to query the web user's browser's capabilities. Information about the web browser's capabilities are determined by the class instance of *IbrowserCaps* by comparing the HTTP User Agent (*HTTP_USER_AGENT*) value that is sent with the HTTP request to the web server to corresponding capabilities cited in the *browsercap.ini* file that is usually located at *$(windows)\system32\inetsrv*. The *browsercap.ini* file is formatted such that the HTTP User Agent is cited and the known capabilities are defined. For example, the capabilities cited for Internet Explorer (IE) 5 in *browsercap.ini* are as follows:

```
;;;;;;;;;;;;;;;;;;;;;;;;;;;;;;;;;;;;;; IE 5.0
[IE 5.0]
browser=IE
Version=5.0
majorver=5
minorver=0
frames=True
tables=True
cookies=True
backgroundsounds=True
vbscript=True
javaapplets=True
javascript=True
ActiveXControls=True
Win16=False
beta=True
AK=False
SK=False
AOL=False
Update=False

[Mozilla/4.0 (compatible; MSIE 5.*; Windows 95*)]
```

```
parent=IE 5.0
platform=Win95
beta=True

[Mozilla/4.0 (compatible; MSIE 5.*; Windows 98*)]
parent=IE 5.0
platform=Win98
beta=True

[Mozilla/4.0 (compatible; MSIE 5.*; Windows NT*)]
parent=IE 5.0
platform=WinNT
beta=True

[Mozilla/4.0 (compatible; MSIE 5.*; Windows 2000*)]
parent=IE 5.0
platform=Win2000
beta=True

[Mozilla/4.0 (compatible; MSIE 5.*)]
parent=IE 5.0
```

The Resource Language option in the Server Options tab provides support for other languages to be used to generate copy text in the resource files for the project. Visual Studio .NET must be installed with the language support for the respective resource that is desired for the option to make itself available in the drop-down box labeled *Resource Language*.

Application Options in the ATL Server Project Wizard

The Application Options are mostly based on the differences of the originally chosen project template (see Figure 16-9). If you wanted to build a web service using ATL Server, the Create As Web Service option box would be checked. This option is mutually exclusive to all other options on the Application Options tab, so no other options may be selected if the project is to be a web service. If the project is an ATL Server, all other options are available for selection. If the Stencil Processing Support option is not selected, the two items subordinate to the Options for the initial server response file section are not available for selection.

Validation Support provides a function named *ValidateAndExchange* in the handler class header file. Other wizards will insert initialization code in the *ValidateAndExchange* function. *ValidateAndExchange* is a member function of the base class *CRequestHandlerT* that's intended to be overridden with custom initialization and validation code that relates to the given web application DLL. The web application DLL inherits from

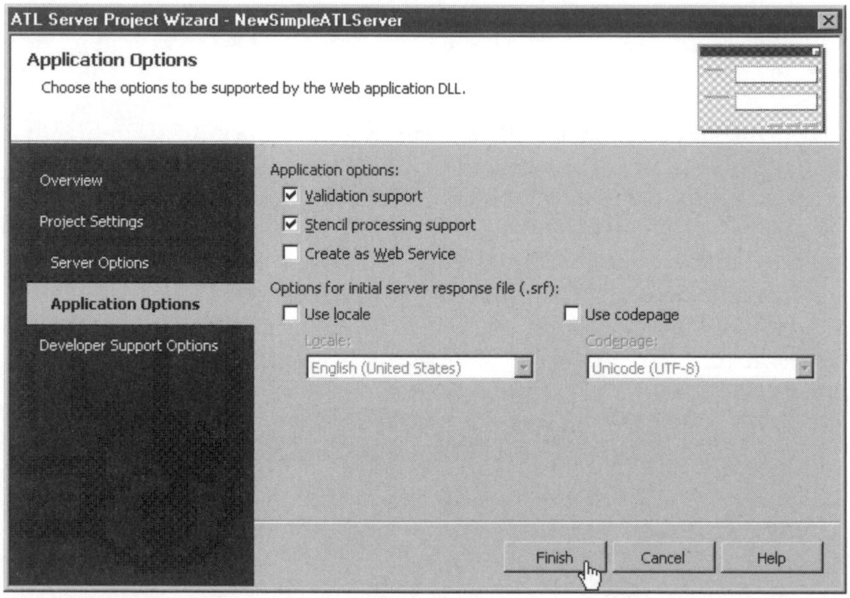

Figure 16-9.   *Application Options tab in the ATL Server Project Wizard*

CRequestHandlerT, which is one of the reasons that the web application DLL is also referred to as the *Request Handler DLL* (see Figure 16-1). *CRequestHandlerT* provides many of the basic HTTP interactions between the request handler DLL and ISAPI by providing a layer of abstraction to the ISAPI. Among the other features allotted to the request handler DLL that inherits *CRequestHandlerT* are the class instances *m_HttpResponse* and *m_HttpRequest.* Both classes provide the developer with a mechanism to read and write the HTTP request or response.

Stencil Processing Support places a sample *hello world* function and a sample tag handler for the *hello world* function. The Options For The Initial Server Response File become available when Stencil Processing Support option is checked, allowing for the settings to be made on the initial SRF generated by the wizard.

Not checking any options in the Application Options tab will generate a code framework that is similar to a simple ISAPI extension project. For many programmers who have dabbled in ISAPI and have no desire for the SRF functionality, this might be a preferred route. The ATL Server does not require the SRF file in order to function since calls directly to the response handler DLL may be performed at any time. In fact, choosing the Generate Combined DLL option under the Project Settings tab and not selecting any options in the Application Options tab will produce a framework for a solution that is similar to a generic ISAPI extension project that is free of many of the ATL support features.

The class framework code for a request handler DLL without any Application Options selected is as follows:

```cpp
// singleDLLNoOptions.h :
//Defines the ATL Server request handler class
//
#pragma once

[ request_handler("Default") ]
class CsingleDLLNoOptionsHandler
{
private:
    // Put private members here

protected:
    // Put protected members here

public:
    // Put public members here

public:
    HTTP_CODE HandleRequest(AtlServerRequest *pRequest,
                            IServiceProvider *pProvider)
    {
        // Initialize the CHttpResponse
        CHttpResponse Response;
        BOOL bRet = Response.Initialize(
                            pRequest->pServerContext);
        if (!bRet)
            return HTTP_FAIL;

        // Set the content-type
        Response.SetContentType("text/html");

        // TODO: Add your handler code here
        // Write the response
        Response <<
            "<html><body><H1>Hello World!</H1></body></html>";
        return HTTP_SUCCESS;
    }
}; // class CsingleDLLNoOptionsHandler
```

Developer Support Options in the ATL Server Project Wizard

The Developer Support Options tab in the ATL Server Project Wizard provides three checkboxes, as shown in Figure 16-10:

- **Generate TODO Comments**   Places comments in the code that tell the developer what he or she should do in a given section

Note
TODO comments are hints and phrases that the wizard places in the code to provide the developer with some instruction about the intent of the section of code that is being described.

- **Attributed Code**   Provides support for using the attribute tags to specify function calls
- **Custom Assert And Trace Handling Support**   Provides a globally accessible class instance of *CDebugReportHook* for capturing information from ATL debugging macros

The Attributed Code option causes the familiar tag handlers to be placed in the request handler DLL to map the tags that may be used in the SRFs to the functions

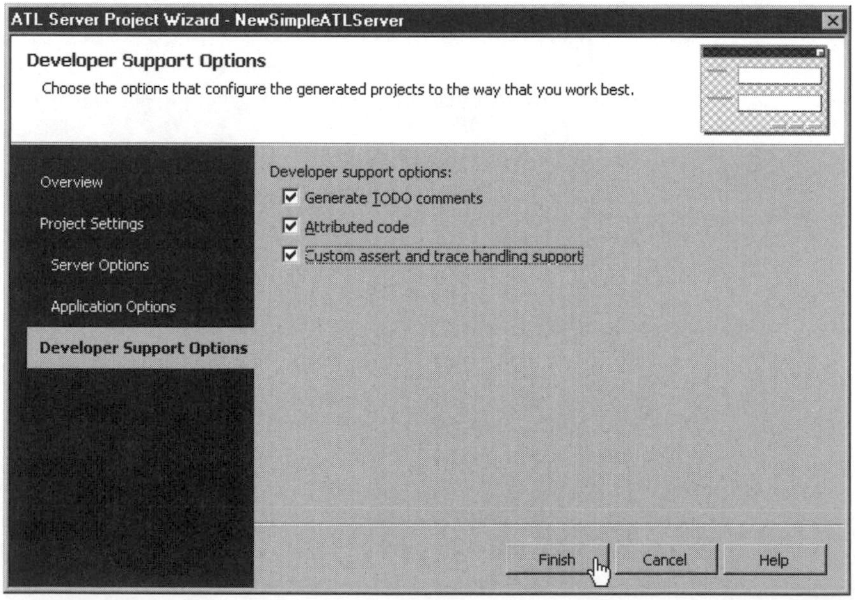

Figure 16-10.   *Developer Support Options tab in the ATL Server Project Wizard*

in the request handler DLL that are to be called when the tag handler is encountered. For example, the sample *hello world* method with attributed code is as follows:

```
[ tag_name("Hello") ]
HTTP_CODE OnHello(void)
{
     m_HttpResponse << "Hello World!";
     return HTTP_SUCCESS;
}
```

The nonattributed code still supports tag handler names in the SRFs being mapped to a given function. The code simply uses the *REPLACEMENT_METHOD_ENTRY* macro to assign the tag name to the function name. Not using attributes may be a preferred means of assigning tag handlers to functions in large code projects. The request handler DLL is spared the cluttering of the bracketed tag handler syntax and the functions that have tags are all identified in the same location. The following listing shows a snippet of code that uses nonattributed tag handlers for the *OnHello* function:

```
// TODO: Add additional tags to the replacement method map
BEGIN_REPLACEMENT_METHOD_MAP(CNonAttributedCodeHandler)
     REPLACEMENT_METHOD_ENTRY("Hello", OnHello)
END_REPLACEMENT_METHOD_MAP()

HTTP_CODE ValidateAndExchange()
{
     // TODO: Put all initialization and validation code here

     // Set the content-type
     m_HttpResponse.SetContentType("text/html");

     return HTTP_SUCCESS;
}

protected:
// Here is an example of how to use
//a replacement tag with the stencil processor
HTTP_CODE OnHello(void)
{
     m_HttpResponse << "Hello World!";
     return HTTP_SUCCESS;
}
```

The Custom Assert And Trace Handling Support feature declares a globally accessible class instance of *CDebugReportHook* in the ISAPI extension DLL. Using *ATLTRACE* and other related macros allows the developer to write code into a request handler DLL that is executed only in the debug build and provides output only to a program designed to read named pipes, such as *WebDbg.exe*. In the following code listing, the declaration of *CDebugReportHook* is valid only when the *_DEBUG* macro is defined:

```
// For custom assert and trace handling with WebDbg.exe
#ifdef _DEBUG
CDebugReportHook g_ReportHook;
#endif
```

ATL Server Project Wizard Completion

When the ATL Server Project Wizard finishes generating the code for the ATL Server project, the code may be run immediately. As long as a function exists in the request handler DLL, the project can be compiled and deployed. Using a project with all of the default settings from the ATL Server Project Wizard, a project would be generated with the following options:

- Separate DLLs for the ISAPI extension and the request handler DLL
- Nothing selected from the Server Options tab
- Validation support
- Stencil processing support
- Generate TODO comments
- Attributed code
- Custom assert and trace handling support

Server Response Files

The next task that you will likely want to perform with any web application is to parse information from a web user, make some decision about the data, and return a response to the web user. Taking the *NewSimpleATLServer* project and adding some code, the SRF may be changed from the Hello World web application to a web application that either prompts the web user for his or her name and favorite color or tells the web user what his or her name and favorite color are. After the SRF has been established, the request handler DLL class may be edited to provide the necessary functionality to support the needs of the SRF.

Tags in Server Response Files

The SRF provides many features that make it an attractive alternative to Extensible Stylesheet Language (XSL) or Extensible Stylesheet Language Transformation (XSLT), as well as ASP.NET web forms, in terms of offering a mechanism to format and display

ATL Server output while abstracting the presentation logic from the business logic. The design view, as shown in Figure 16-11, in ATL server provides a layer of abstraction for accessing the request handler DLL and writing HTML code. Through the use of tags placed throughout the SRF, you can perform simplified scripting that's optimized for dispatching function calls to request handler DLLs, similar to the XSL or XSLT files that parse and manipulate the content of XML. Just as an XSL or XSLT file has some type of processing instruction at the top to indicate how the file should be used, so, too, does the SRF. The SRF also supports simplified amounts of looping and decision capabilities, as with an XSL and XSLT file.

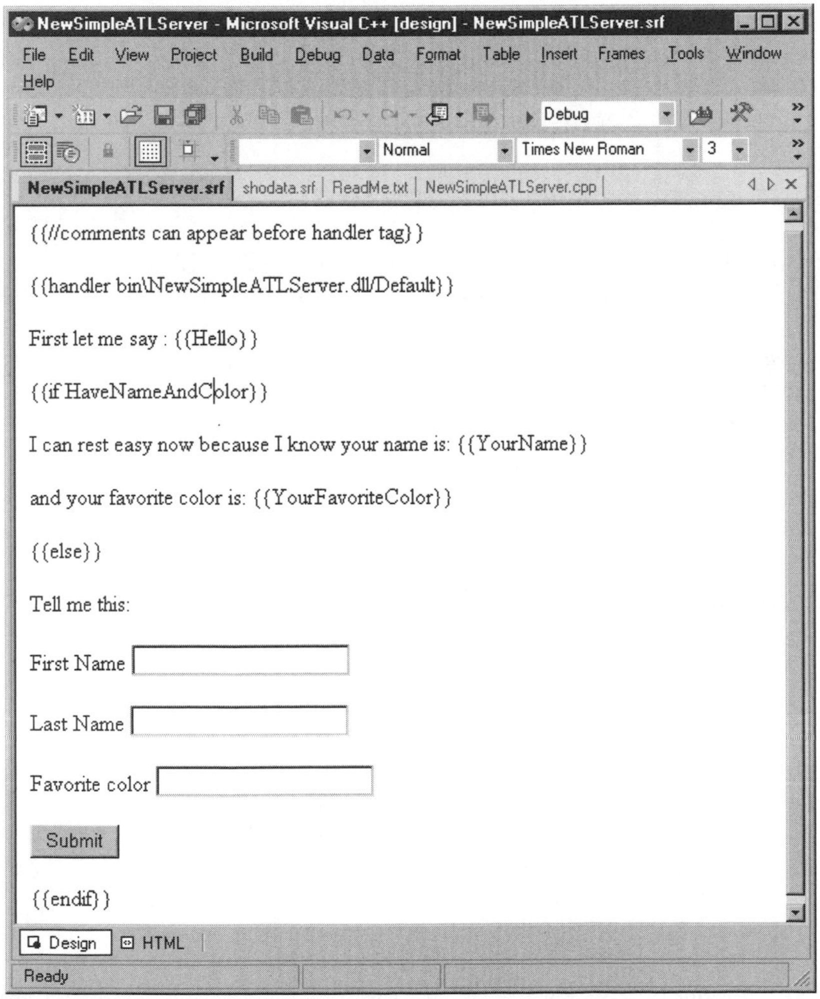

Figure 16-11. *Design view of NewSimpleATLServer.srf*

Tags in a SRF are designated by two pairs of curly brackets that enclose the argument, which most often correlates to a tag attribute inside the request handler DLL. Tag attributes within the request handler DLL are mapped to functions that perform some task and return some data that will be inserted into the SRF. A single SRF may call many request handler DLLs. The SRF may also include other SRFs using the *include tag*, and SRF files support code comments.

Handler and Subhandler Tags

The first tag that any SRF likely contains is the *handler tag*. The handler tag specifies the request handler DLL that will be accessed when searching for the functions specified by the replacement tags in the SRF. A *subhandler tag* may also be specified. A single SRF may call functions from one or more request handler DLLs. Aliases may be specified in the handler or subhandler tag. Using the aliases, replacement tags may be formed to call functions from a given request handler DLL using the *alias.function* name. The default syntax for a handler tag is as follows:

```
{{handler <handler name>.dll/Default}}
```

By default, Visual Studio .NET will always deploy the DLL files in the same directory as the SRFs. Because placing binaries usually represents a particular layer of abstraction that is different from the code that is hosted in the SRFs, it is often preferable also to deploy the binary files in a separate directory on the server. A common choice is a subdirectory from the web root or virtual directory root named *bin*. (The phrase *bin* is short for the word *binary*.) Given the scenario of using a *bin* subdirectory to store the DLLs, the handler tag appear as follows:

```
{{handler bin\<handler name>.dll/Default}}
```

Replacement Tags

The *replacement tag* is the most often used SRF tag. Replacement tags in SRFs are the developer's point of access to the functions contained in the request handler DLLs. The replacement tag will request the response from the request handler DLL that hosts the desired function and insert the response at that point in the SRF in which the replacement tag exists. Replacement tags also support instructions for calling functions, and they can pass arguments to functions in the request handler DLL. For example, an *if..else..endif* situation may be established using the command `{{if <FunctionName>}}` to start the *if* portion of the execution. *Else* and *endif* are specified by `{{else}}` and `{{endif}}`, respectively.

In the *NewSimpleATLServer* project, the SRF checks a function with an attribute name *HaveNameAndColor*, as shown in the following source code for *NewSimpleATLServer.srf*. If *HaveNameAndColor* returns a value of *true*, the name and favorite color entered by the web user is displayed. If any one of the items are not known, *HaveNameAndColor* will

return a *false* and the SRF will prompt the user for his or her first name, last name, and
favorite color. Replacement tags also support *while..endwhile* instructions for looping.

```html
<html>
<HEAD>
</HEAD>
<BODY>
<P>{{//comments can appear before handler tag}}</P>
<P>{{handler bin\NewSimpleATLServer.dll/Default}}</P>
<P>First let me say : {{Hello}}<br>
</P>
<P>{{if HaveNameAndColor}}
</P>
<P>I can rest easy now because I know your name is:
{{YourName}}</P>
<P>
and your favorite color is: {{YourFavoriteColor}}
<P>
{{else}}
<P>Tell me this:</P>
<FORM id="Form1" action="NewSimpleATLServer.srf" method="post">
<P>First Name <INPUT id="Text1" type="text" name="firstname"></P>
<P>Last Name <INPUT id="Text2" type="text" name="lastname"></P>
<P>Favorite color <INPUT id="Text3" type="text" name="color"></P>
<P>
<INPUT id="Submit1" type="submit" value="Submit" name="Submit1">
</P>
</FORM>
<P>{{endif}}</P>
</BODY>
</html>
```

Caution   *Replacement tags in SRFs that refer to a nonexistent attribute in the request handler DLL will return an HTTP 500 Internal Server Error. This appears to be a difficult error to catch, because many conditions can cause HTTP 500 Internal Server Errors. No auto complete feature is available in Visual Studio .NET to show the available attributes in the request handler DLL when a developer is editing a SRF, so the chances of misspelling a request handler tag are quite likely.*

As shown in the source code listing for *NewSimpleATLServer.srf*, the SRF code behind the design view shown in Figure 16-11, the file is an HTML document. The only difference between an HTML file and the SRF is the presence of tags enclosed by the curly bracket pairs: { { } }. None of the server controls that are afforded the web service or web form projects are available in the ATL Server project by default. Since the file extension for the SRF is mapped to the ISAPI extension DLL, it is possible to map HTM, HTML, or any file to the ISAPI extension DLL and have it processed as though it were a SRF with the file extension *.srf*.

Note   *The ability to comment in the SRF is not as robust as it is for other types of solutions, such as code in an executable program or a web service. Sometimes spaces placed before or after replacement tags will cause the SRF to fail. Comments may be placed before the handler tag. The HTML (! - -) or the C++ (//) styles of comment may be used to specify the tags. Comments cannot appear on the same line of code with other tags, such as replacement tags. For example, the following line will cause the SRF to return an HTTP 500 Internal Server Error: {{endif // if HaveNameAndColor }}.*

Request Handler DLL

The request handler DLL produced by the ATL Server Project Wizard is designed so that the developer edits code in a header file named after a project name. The prototype for a class named C<Project Name>*Handler* is in the header file. In the case of the project *NewSimpleATLServer*, the class was named *CNewSimpleATLServerHandler*. In the following code listing for *NewSimpleATLServer.h*, this class is designed to be the gateway between the classes that are the web application software you are making and the SRFs. All the code could be placed in the handler class, but it would make the code unmanageable. The best strategy is to use this class to host only the attributes for SRF replacement tags and to build classes for the system according to the software design.

```
// NewSimpleATLServer.h : Defines the ATL Server request handler class
//
#pragma once

[ request_handler("Default") ]
class CNewSimpleATLServerHandler
{
private:
     //locals for holding the state of the class
     CString FName;                    //first name
     CString LName;                    //last name
     CString FavoriteColor;       //name of color

     //flag to identify if color and name are known
     bool HaveNameandColor;

public:
     //initialization function
     HTTP_CODE ValidateAndExchange()
     {
```

```
        //for debug purposes
        ATLTRACE("ValidateAndExchange started \n");

        //used to validate data passed in
        CValidateContext c;

        //assume that we have everything
        HaveNameandColor = true;

        //get the form fields
        const CHttpRequestParams& Formdata =
              m_HttpRequest.GetFormVars();

        //Check validation failures
        if (VALIDATION_S_OK !=
         Formdata.Validate("firstname", &FName, 1, 10000, &c))
                  HaveNameandColor = false;

        if (VALIDATION_S_OK !=
         Formdata.Validate("lastname", &LName, 1, 10000, &c))
                  HaveNameandColor = false;

        if (VALIDATION_S_OK !=
        Formdata.Validate("color", &FavoriteColor, 1, 10000, &c))
                  HaveNameandColor = false;


        // Set the content-type
        m_HttpResponse.SetContentType("text/html");

        ATLTRACE("ValidateAndExchange completed \n");
        return HTTP_SUCCESS;
 }

protected:
 [ tag_name(name="Hello") ]
 HTTP_CODE OnHello(void)
 {
        ATLTRACE("OnHello started \n");

        m_HttpResponse << "Hello World!";

        ATLTRACE("OnHello completed \n");
        return HTTP_SUCCESS;
 }

 [ tag_name(name = "HaveNameAndColor") ]
 HTTP_CODE OnHaveNameAndColor(void)
```

```
{
      ATLTRACE("OnHaveNameAndColor started \n");

      if (HaveNameandColor)
            return HTTP_SUCCESS;
      else
            return HTTP_S_FALSE;
}

[ tag_name(name = "YourName") ]
HTTP_CODE OnYourName(void)
{
      m_HttpResponse << FName + " " + LName;

      return HTTP_SUCCESS;
}

[ tag_name(name = "YourFavoriteColor") ]
HTTP_CODE OnYourFavoriteColor(void)
{
      m_HttpResponse << FavoriteColor;

      return HTTP_SUCCESS;
}

}; // class CNewSimpleATLServerHandler
```

In addition to satisfying the purpose of hosting the replacement tag attributes, the class *CNewSimpleATLServerHandler* exists primarily for the following purposes:

■ Saying Hello World

■ Validating the user input

■ Reporting back to the user his or her name and favorite color

All the implementation code for the project *NewSimpleATLServer* is in header file for the sake of simplifying the demonstration of this example. The *ValidateAndExchange* function is the first function called when a request is processed through the handler DLL, so the *m_HttpRequest* class instance will be inspected for HTTP-posted data using the *m_HttpRequest.GetFormVars* function and placing the data into an instance of *ChttpRequestParams* using a reference named *Formdata*. The *Validate* function of *Formdata* will determine whether the specified input value was submitted, will determine whether it meets the range specified, and will place the value in a variable. For example, the first name input value is validated using the following line in the code snippet

```
Validate("firstname", &FName, 1, 10000, &c)
```

where *FName* is a CString variable in which the first name will be placed if it is longer than 1 character and shorter than 10,000 characters.

The *ATLTRACE* macro is sprinkled throughout the listing for *CNewSimpleATLServer Handler* with various debugging phrases as the argument. The *ATLTRACE* will place the argument in the WebDbg window if it is running on the host, as shown in Figure 16-12. WebDbg is a utility that ships with the Visual Studio .NET tools. The start link is usually found under the Visual Studio .NET Tools program group and is labeled *ISAPI Web Debug Tool* in the Start menu.

After it is started, WebDbg needs to be attached to the pipe name *AtlsDbgPipe*, after you choose File | Select Pipe | Pipe Name. The process that is being debugged must have the permission to write to the named pipe. The credentials under which IIS is running should be set by choosing File | Permissions. Allowing the group *Everyone* to have permission to write to the pipe should work if WebDbg is running on the same machine as the web site, but if the web site is running remotely, the credentials for the specific machine or domain will likely need to be specified as well.

Once WebDbg is running, it listens to the pipe for messages from software writing to the pipe. As the messages are written, they appear instantly in the WebDgb window. Although stepping through the code using the Visual Studio .NET IDE (Integrated Development Environment) is a good way to test the code initially, the *trace* commands may be useful for environments in which the software will be hosted after it is moved from the development server environment. The *ATLTRACE* works only in the *debug*

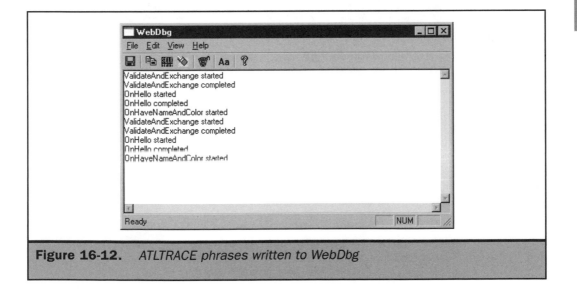

Figure 16-12.   *ATLTRACE phrases written to WebDbg*

configuration. If the solution was compiled in the *release* configuration, the *ATLTRACE* macros are ignored, so there is no need to remove any of the debug code. Running the project *NewSimpleATLServer* will tell the user *hello world* because it always tells the user *hello world*. The second function called is the *OnHaveNameAndColor* function using the *HaveNameandColor* replacement tag in the SRF. *OnHaveNameAndColor* simply checks the value of the local variable *HaveNameandColor* to see whether or not it returns true and returns the corresponding answer so that the SRF can either display the information or prompt the user for his or her name and favorite color. Figure 16-13 shows an example of *NewSimpleATLServer* running after the user entered information. In the figure, the SRF checked the value returned from *HaveNameandColor* and since it was positive, the *OnYourFavoriteColor* and *OnYourName* functions were called using the replacement tags *YourFavoriteColor* and *YourName*, respectively.

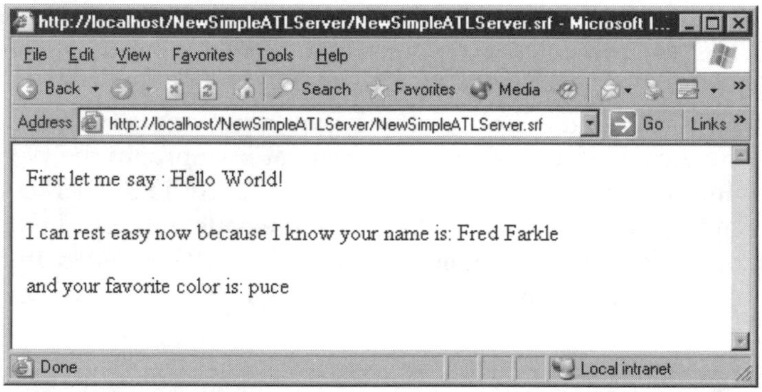

Figure 16-13. *NewSimpleATLServer running after the user entered information*

Chapter 17

ISAPI Extensions

Internet Server Application Program Interface (ISAPI) comprises the API of Internet Information Services (IIS). ISAPI consists of supporting classes and structures that aid in the programmatic exploitation of IIS. Web applications that use ISAPI to interact with IIS interact in the most efficient way possible on a Windows web server. The layers of supporting software or interpretation between IIS and the web application are greatly diminished when the developer uses ISAPI. All Microsoft web application software uses ISAPI technology, either directly or indirectly. For example, Microsoft's Application Server Pages (ASP) and .NET Framework are built as ISAPI applications.

Originally, ISAPI was marketed toward Common Gateway Interface (CGI) programmers as an alternative to writing CGI programs or as an easy upgrade from a CGI executable. Because many CGI executables were written in C++ or C, integrating an existing CGI web application would be quite simple. Converting a CGI web application to use ISAPI would also provide a great performance boost to the web application. CGI spawns a new process with each HTTP request; as a result, the technology demands a large amount of resources from the host server to create and destroy the CGI processes. Since ISAPI extensions are loaded in the process space of IIS, the host bears no burden associated with spawning a new process with each HTTP request. Because Windows loads a dynamic link library (DLL) into memory space once on the initial call to a function in the DLL and keeps it in memory for an indefinite amount of time, the ISAPI extension would remain loaded and likely not removed until an IIS server shutdown or unless the instance or virtual directory was unloaded. In this way, Microsoft offered a compelling reason for programmers to adopt the use of ISAPI in lieu of CGI and an easy upgrade path from CGI.

ISAPI is a good choice for developers who are producing software or have already written a software application in C++ for a product that is being distributed on the open market. If performance is critical and a development time longer than the typical web script file effort can be accommodated, ISAPI should be considered. In addition, ISAPI can perform some sophisticated tasks on the host server that cannot be performed with any other technology. ISAPI software can also be written to execute in such a manner that other web applications written in scripted languages that used other ISAPI extensions for interpretation, such as the .NET Framework or ASP.DLL, would be oblivious to the tasks being performed by the ISAPI extension.

On the downside, ISAPI is complicated to work with and difficult to debug. Stepping through code in the Visual Studio .NET Integrated Design Environment (IDE) is difficult, and since IIS is running as a multi-threaded process, unpredictable results can occur while debugging. The slightest bug in an ISAPI application can have a catastrophic result on IIS performance. Compared to all other development environments, ISAPI is the most unforgiving technology to use to build a web application.

In addition, ISAPI must be written using unmanaged C++ code. The new features offered by Visual Studio .NET for managed C++ code through the .NET Framework cannot be used in an ISAPI project.

| Note | *If a program is written using* managed *code, that means that the software is written with code that uses the .NET Framework. C# and Visual Basic both use the .NET Framework. The term* managed *is representative of the fact that the .NET Framework manages memory cleanup, memory allocation, and other low-level resource management. Software written in C++ does not use the .NET Framework unless you use* Managed Extensions for C++. *Managed C++ means that the software uses the .NET Framework through the introduction of Managed Extensions for C++. C++ code written as usual, without using the* Managed Extensions for C++, *is unmanaged C++ and does not use the .NET Framework.* |

ISAPI Architecture Overview

ISAPI applications are DLLs that interact with IIS API directly. ISAPI software can be an extension or a filter. ISAPI extensions are DLLs that are called from a qualified request to IIS. ISAPI filters are called indiscriminately from all requests to IIS. HTTP requests may be sent directly to an ISAPI extension using a uniform resource locator (URL) link or using an HTTP post via an HTML form submission. An ISAPI extension can be called indirectly by mapping a file to a particular ISAPI extension in IIS, so that when a file is requested from IIS with a filename that matches the mapping value, the respective ISAPI extension will be called on the file request. The file mapping technique is the same process that ATL Server uses (see Chapter 16) to associate Server Response Files (SRFs) to a particular ISAPI extension. ISAPI filters can be set to respond to requests according to a priority, as compared to other filters loaded in IIS. Filters are good options for specialized applications involving IIS and are usually related to the following tasks:

- Encryption
- Logging
- Authentication
- Data compression

ISAPI extensions are the most common implementation of ISAPI. ISAPI filters are rather difficult to produce and limited in their scope of usage. They are beyond the scope of this chapter and, therefore, will not be covered.

URL Anatomy

A URL defines the entire string used to denote a particular resource on a server located on the Internet. A URL is formed according to the following syntax:

<scheme>://<user>:<password>@<host>:<port>/<url-path>/<extra-info>

For example, the following URL requests an ISAPI DLL named *SEUX.dll*. Parameters named *parm1* and *parm2* are also specified in the URL. In Table 17-1, this URL is broken down into its parts to show how a typical URL requesting an ISAPI DLL will be identified.

Many of the terms for the URL parts will be useful for the purposes of describing server variable values, which are presented later in this chapter. Note that the fields that are not in the example, as noted in the table, are rare to find in a URL. The example used is of a common URL, which you're more likely to encounter.

```
http://amd1700v2/simpleisapi/folder1/folder2/SEUX.dll/PATH_INFO?
parm1=value1&parm2=value
```

If an ISAPI DLL is requested via a URL link directly, the filename of the ISAPI extension DLL is identified in the *url-path* section. The *parameter = value* pairs are located in the *extra-info* section of the URL, as shown in Table 17-1. Data may be sent in the form of *parameter = value* pairs, which may be passed to the ISAPI extension using the URL *extra-info* section or using HTTP posts via an HTML form submission.

ISAPI Extensions Interacting with IIS

When IIS receives the request and deems that it is necessary to use the ISAPI extension, either because a file was requested that was mapped to the ISAPI extension or because the ISAPI extension itself was requested, IIS will pass the HTTP request along to the ISAPI extension. For the ISAPI extension to receive the HTTP request, a certain programmatic interface must be implemented by the ISAPI extension. As expected, your ISAPI application must include the ISAPI header files that define the structures and classes. The ISAPI extension will receive the request through the implemented API, and the HTTP request data will be loaded in the structures and classes that are a part of ISAPI.

URL Part	Value from Example
scheme	*http*
user	Not present in example URL
password	Not present in example URL
host	*amd1700v2*
port	Not present in example URL but assumed to be 80
url-path	*simpleisapi/folder1/folder2/SEUX.dll/PATH_INFO*
extra-info	*?parm1=value1&parm2=value*

Table 17-1. *Sample URL Parts*

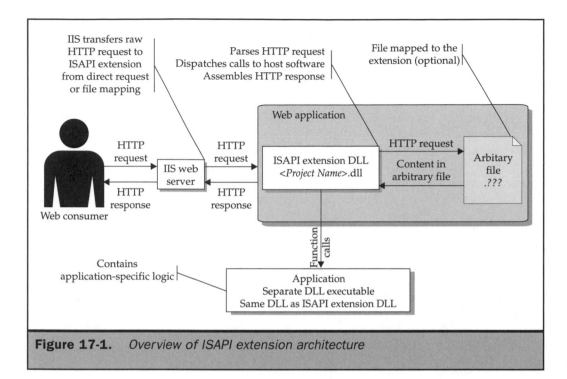

Figure 17-1. *Overview of ISAPI extension architecture*

The ISAPI extension will parse the HTTP request data and could dispatch calls to other software, such as the business layer software, as shown in Figure 17-1. Responses from the business layer will be formed into an HTTP response and returned to the IIS. IIS will take the ISAPI extension response and return it to the web consumer that placed the initial request to IIS.

The architecture shown in Figure 17-1 represents two possible ways that an ISAPI extension might be used, but it should not be viewed as an exclusive implementation of the technology. The only definite aspect of the implementation of an ISAPI extension is the call into the ISAPI extension on an HTTP request and the presence of the structures and classes that contain the HTTP request and support the programmatic interaction with the HTTP response and the HTTP request. It is up to you to architect the logic abstraction. Dispatching calls to a business logic DLL may not be necessary if the business logic is inside the ISAPI extension itself. Because ISAPI writes data back to the HTTP request directly, you should consider making an architectural design that abstracts the presentation logic so that you do not have to recompile your ISAPI DLL when the presentation logic is changed.

ISAPI Compared to ATL Server

When comparing ATL Server and ISAPI, a major difference is that ISAPI offers the developer less infrastructure support and provides less of an implied architecture than ATL Server. The ISAPI for extensions (as opposed to filters) consists of a few API functions and a few structures and classes that are the parameters of the API functions. In contrast, ATL Server provides many new support classes, macros, and functions. ATL Server plays much the same role to ISAPI that Microsoft Foundation Classes (MFC) did to the Windows API—ATL Server acts as an additional layer of code to help the developer better utilize the technology. ATL Server helps support the developer who chooses to produce software that interacts with the ISAPI by pointing the developer in a direction that will likely help and offering supporting software. The developer can choose which software to use, but sometimes that, too, can be difficult. In such circumstances, ISAPI may seem like an attractive alternative. Unlike ATL Server, ISAPI offers no abstraction of any type of logic, and not much has been written about how to use ISAPI. You can use ATL Server classes in an ISAPI application without using an ATL Server project template. Alternatively, configuring an ATL Server project template to use a single DLL and no options will provide a project framework that is quite similar to a typical ISAPI project framework.

Building a Simple ISAPI Extension

ISAPI extensions are so minimal in their stature that they may be written with no support from MFC or Active Template Library (ATL). An ISAPI extension may be written with the ISAPI extension include file *httpext.h* and a DLL *definition export file* (DEF) exporting the following two functions:

- *HttpExtensionProc*
- *GetExtensionVersion*

Each ISAPI extension must export these two functions. An ISAPI extension can optionally export the *TerminateExtension* function, too. After the DLL project is set up with these requirements, the extension should be usable by IIS. Visual Studio .NET provides a project template for an ISAPI project that launches the ISAPI Extension Wizard. This ISAPI Extension Wizard creates a class named after the project that inherits the *CHTTPServer* class and contains the required ISAPI functions. The ISAPI Extension Wizard also uses header files that provide more support from MFC and ATL than *httpext.h* offers to get the ISAPI classes and structures.

The use of the ISAPI Extension Wizard will be covered later in this chapter. Let's examine the technique for producing an ISAPI extension with the least amount of MFC and ATL support to gain an understanding of the minimum requirements for producing a simple ISAPI extension without using the ISAPI Extension Wizard:

1. In Visual Studio .NET select File | New | Project and the New Project dialog box will open.

2. In the New Project dialog box, click the Visual C++ Projects node in the left side of the dialog box and select the Win32 project template. Name your project *HelloWorld* and select a location for the project to be created.

   If you click the *More* button, the New Project dialog box will display more information about where the project will be created. The button will also change its name to *Less*. By default, Visual Studio creates a directory named the same name as the project in the directory set in the Location text box. All of the project files are placed in the newly created directory. As shown in Figure 17-2, the Location text box is set to *C:\bookMaterial\IISBook\17ISAPIExtention\code* and the project name is *HelloWorld*.

3. Click the OK button and the Win32 Application Wizard will open as shown in Figure 17-3.

4. Click the Application Settings tab on the left side of the Win32 Application Wizard.

5. Click DLL for application type as shown in Figure 17-4.

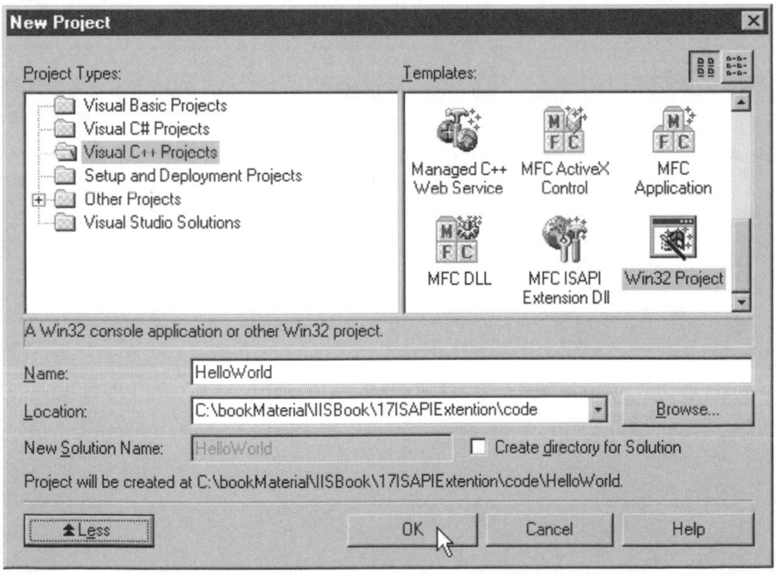

Figure 17-2.   *New Project dialog box with Win32 Project selected*

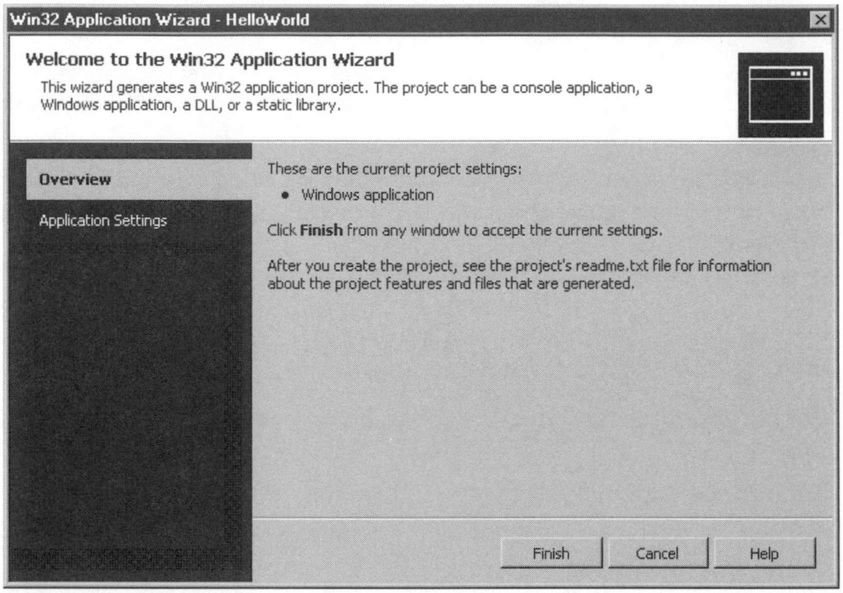

Figure 17-3. *Overview in the Win32 Application Wizard*

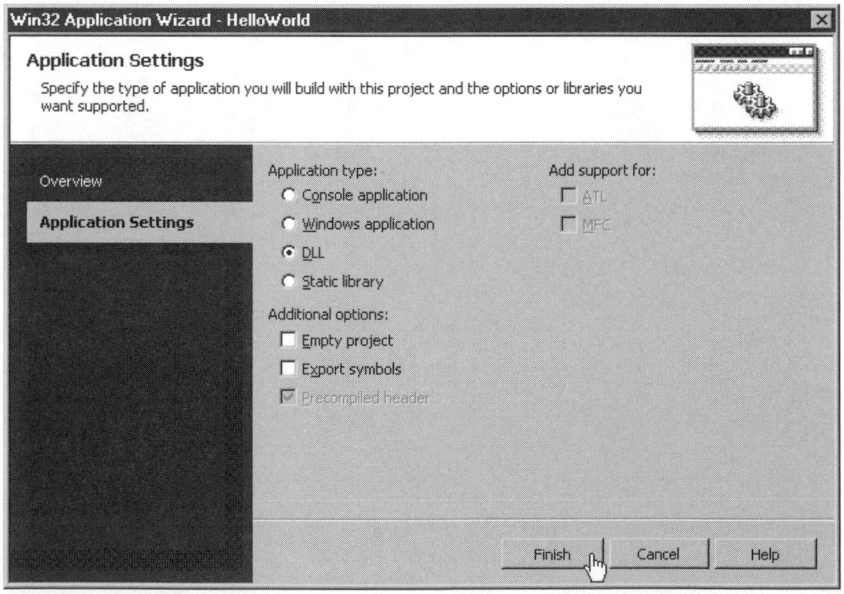

Figure 17-4. *Creating a Win32 DLL project*

6. Click the Finish button of the Win32 Application Wizard and Visual Studio will create the directory *C:\bookMaterial\IISBook\17ISAPIExtention\code\HelloWorld* and place the project files in the new directory.

7. After you have created the DLL project, select the menu Project | Properties and the Property Pages window will open.

8. Select the Precompiled Header node under the C/C++ node in the left side of the Property Pages window and Visual Studio will display the properties.

9. Visual Studio .NET does not provide a project template that will produce the project without the precompiled header, so you have to choose the Win32 project template, make the project a DLL, and delete the precompiled header setting. Select the value *Not Using Precompiled Headers* in the Create/Use Precompiled Header property drop-down combo box as shown in Figure 17-5.

10. Click OK on the Property Pages window. The Solution Explorer window should already be open but if it is not, select View | Solution Explorer from the menu.

11. Since the precompiled header will not be used, the *stdafx* files produced by the Visual Studio .NET to support the precompiled header must be removed. Select the *stdafx* header and implementation files in the Solution explorer, right-click and select Remove as shown in Figure 17-6.

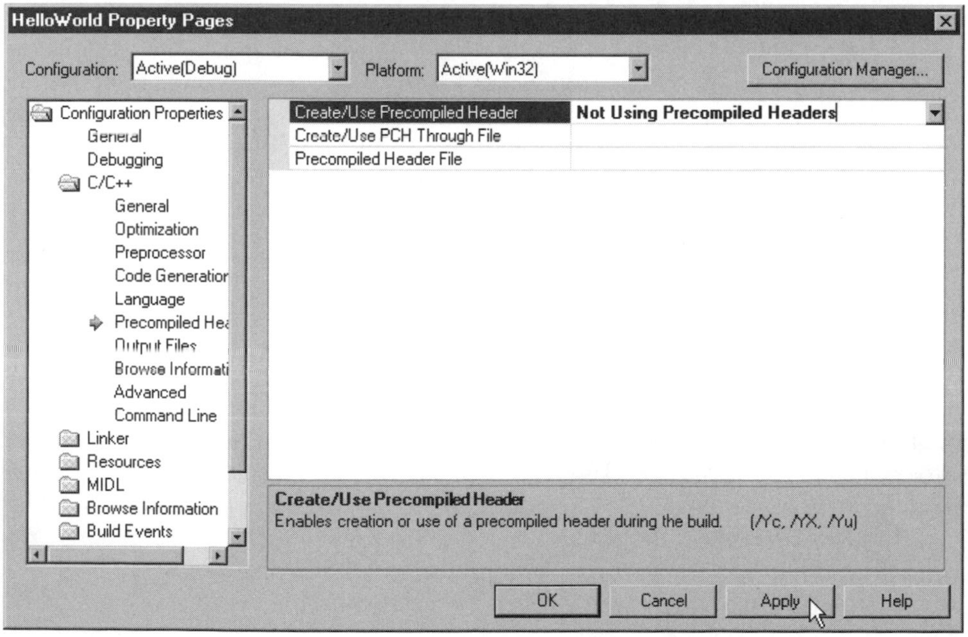

Figure 17-5.   *Changing the precompiled header property for the project*

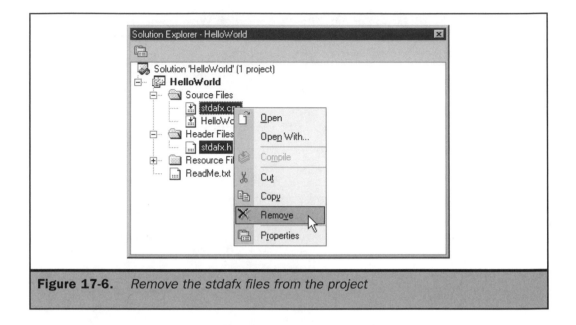

Figure 17-6.   *Remove the stdafx files from the project*

12. Next, add a DEF to the project. To do this, right-click the project name in the Solution Explorer and choose Add | Add New Item.

13. In the Add New Item dialog box, select DEF File, and name the file *HelloWorld* to match the project name as shown in Figure 17-7. The filename must match the DLL name otherwise the C++ compiler will throw a warning that the filenames do not match. This DEF file (definition export file) describes what functions will be exported from the DLL so that another application can load the DLL and be able to find the address of the functions.

14. Click the Open button on the Add New Item dialog box to add the new DEF file to the project.

The Visual Studio project templates use an intrinsic mechanism through MFC to export functions and make the ISAPI extension DLL usable by a consuming application like IIS. Visual Studio .NET does not provide a project template that will produce the project without the precompiled header, so you have to choose the Win32 project template, make the project a DLL, and delete the files and settings that are not needed. By creating a project without the MFC support, you expose yourself to some of the complexities that MFC hides. MFC also introduces some complexities of its own, however, so small projects that perform limited activities like this example, can be simplified by eliminating MFC.

The next step necessary to make the ISAPI extension usable by IIS is to configure the DEF file.

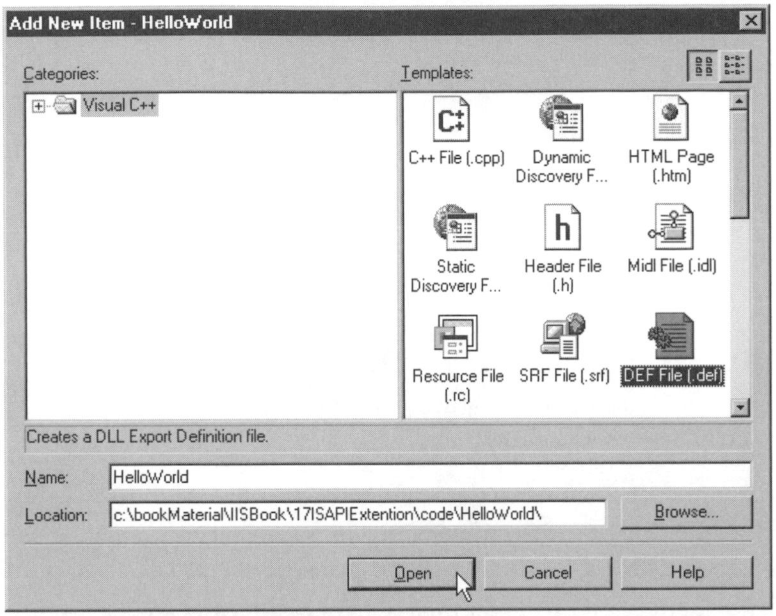

Figure 17-7.   *Adding a definition export file to the project*

Definition Export File

After the DEF is added to the project, the library name in the file will have the same name as the project. Visual Studio .NET will issue a warning if the library name is different from the DLL name. In the case of this project, it should read

```
LIBRARY     HelloWorld
```

A *DESCRIPTION* block may also be added to the DEF to describe the purpose of the DLL. The description should be enclosed be single quotes. The *DESCRIPTION* block is not necessary, but an *EXPORTS* block *is* necessary. The function names must follow the *EXPORTS* block. In Listing 17-1, only *HttpExtensionProc* and *GetExtensionVersion* will be exported. Listing 17-1 shows the definition export file that is used for this project. The functions may be listed in any order, but they must match the names in the implementation of the extension.

Listing 17-1

```
HelloWorld.def Content

LIBRARY     HelloWorld

DESCRIPTION 'Demonstration of a simple Hello World ISAPI extension'

EXPORTS
    HttpExtensionProc
    GetExtensionVersion
```

ISAPI Extension Main Entry Point

The *HelloWorld.cpp* file must be configured to support the functions required to make the ISAPI extention work as follows:

1. In Visual Studio .NET open the *HelloWorld.cpp* file for editing by double-clicking on the filename in the Solution Explorer.
2. Delete the existing *DLLMain* function because it will not be used in this example.
3. Add the include preprocessor directive for header file *httpext.h* and *<string>* at the top of the code file, as shown in Listing 17-2.
4. Add the *GetExtentionVersion* Function (shown in Listing 17-2).
5. Add the *HttpExtensionProc* function (shown in Listing 17-2).

Listing 17-2

```
Source Code for HelloWorld.cpp

// HelloWorld.cpp : Defines the entry point for
//the DLL application.

#include <httpext.h>      //for ISAPI classes and structures

// tell the compiler to shut up about using STL
#pragma warning(disable:4786)
#include <string>        //to build response to send back to user
using namespace std;


/*~~~~~~~~~~~~~~~~~~~~~~~~~~~~~~~~~~~~~~~~~~~~~~~~~~~~~~~~~~~~~~~~~~~~~~
Name:GetExtensionVersion
```

In: pVer - Pointer to ISAPI structure HSE_VERSION_INFO.

Out: Returns true if you want IIS to use the extension, otherwise
   if another value is returned, IIS will not use the extension

Purpose:
   Called when the extension is loaded into IIS. The member
   variables of HSE_VERSION_INFO, dwExtensionVersion and
   lpszExtensionDesc should be filled with the extension
   version and description.

   Other initialization functionality could be called from this
   function to set up the server to use this extension.

```
/*~~~~~~~~~~~~~~~~~~~~~~~~~~~~~~~~~~~~~~~~~~~~~~~~~~~~~~~~~~~~~~~~~~~~*/
BOOL WINAPI GetExtensionVersion(HSE_VERSION_INFO *pVer)
{
   //ISAPI version
   const DWORD VERSION_NUMBER = 0.9;
   const char* VERSION_NAME = "Hello World";

    pVer->dwExtensionVersion = VERSION_NUMBER;

    strncpy(   pVer->lpszExtensionDesc,
            VERSION_NAME,
            HSE_MAX_EXT_DLL_NAME_LEN);

    return TRUE;
}


/*~~~~~~~~~~~~~~~~~~~~~~~~~~~~~~~~~~~~~~~~~~~~~~~~~~~~~~~~~~~~~~~~~~
Name:HttpExtensionProc
```

In: pECB - pointer to the Extension control block structure

Out: DWORD - HSE status code

Purpose:
   main entry point for HTTP request

```
   the possible return codes are:
   HSE_STATUS_SUCCESS    - everything worked great
   HSE_STATUS_SUCCESS_AND_KEEP_CONN - same as HSE_STATUS_SUCCESS
                              since IIS 4
   HSE_STATUS_PENDING - wait until effort completed
   HSE_STATUS_ERROR    - sends a 500 error code
/*~~~~~~~~~~~~~~~~~~~~~~~~~~~~~~~~~~~~~~~~~~~~~~~~~~~~~~~~~~~~~~~~*/
DWORD WINAPI HttpExtensionProc(EXTENSION_CONTROL_BLOCK *pECB)
{
   //HTTP headers
   const char* BASIC_HEADER = "Content-type: text/html\r\n\r\n";
   //output values
   const DWORD BUFFER_LENGTH = 4096;
   TCHAR szTempBuffer[BUFFER_LENGTH];
   DWORD dwBufferSize = BUFFER_LENGTH;
   string sResponse;

   //start our HTML document
   sResponse = "<HTML><HEAD></HEAD><BODY><P>";
   sResponse += "Hi! Hello World";
   sResponse += "</P></BODY></HTML>";

   // set content-type header
   strcpy(szTempBuffer, BASIC_HEADER);
   DWORD dwHeaderSize = strlen(szTempBuffer);
   pECB->ServerSupportFunction(pECB->ConnID,
                     HSE_REQ_SEND_RESPONSE_HEADER,
                     NULL,
                     &dwHeaderSize,
                     (LPDWORD) szTempBuffer);

   //write value to http response
   DWORD dwLength=sResponse.length();
   pECB->WriteClient(   pECB->ConnID,
                  (PVOID)sResponse.c_str(),
                  &dwLength,
                  0);

   //return a success code
   return HSE_STATUS_SUCCESS;
}
```

GetExtensionVersion Function

The *GetExtensionVersion* function takes a pointer to the *HSE_VERSION_INFO* structure as the parameter and returns a *BOOL* value depending on whether or not IIS should use the ISAPI extension. If true is returned from *GetExtensionVersion*, the ISAPI extension will be used. If false is returned, the ISAPI extension will not be used by IIS. The *GetExtensionVersion* function is called when the ISAPI extension is loaded into the process space of IIS. After the ISAPI extension is loaded into IIS, *GetExtensionVersion* will not be called again. This function is an excellent place for code that performs a license key check or initialization procedures that will validate whether or not the extension should be used. In Listing 17-2 of *HelloWorld.cpp*, the *GetExtensionVersion* function is used only to set the version information for the ISAPI extension.

The *HSE_VERSION_INFO* structure contains two member variables named *dwExtensionVersion* and *lpszExtensionDesc*. The expectation is that the values for these member variables in the *HSE_VERSION_INFO* structure will be filled when the *GetExtensionVersion* function is called. In the case of the Listing 17-2, the *DWORD* of *0.9* is placed in *dwExtensionVersion* and the value of *HelloWorld* is placed in *lpszExtensionDesc*. True is always returned from this function because the ISAPI extension should always be loaded into IIS. Because this ISAPI extension is a "Hello World" program for demonstration purposes, no situation exists for which this ISAPI extension should not be loaded. If you had an ISAPI extension that required a dependency such as a valid license file, presence of another software library, or a special configuration, then you could perform that check in this function and return a value of false if the dependency check failed.

HttpExtensionProc Function

The *HttpExtensionProc* function takes one of the most important structures in ISAPI as a parameter. A pointer to the *Extension Control Block* (ECB) structure is passed into *HttpExtensionProc*. This structure contains the following:

- All the data about the HTTP request
- Data about the web instance of IIS that the request came through
- Support functions to parse the HTTP request
- Support functions to manage the HTTP response

In the case of Listing 17-2, however, the pointer to the ECB block is used only to send a response header to the client and to write the phrase *Hi! Hello World* to the client. The C++ code looks a little *C-like* in the structures and support functions, likely because ISAPI has not changed a lot since IIS was first produced and there was a desire to maintain backward compatibility. As a result, ISAPI has not been changed much, other than adding new functionality. The difficulty with working with ISAPI is the fact that some of the API is unsophisticated and requires that you code using some C-like conventions.

The first function called in the ECB block in the *HelloWorld* extension is the *ServerSupportFunction*. It is used to set a header in the HTTP response to indicate that the content type is text or HTML using the following string:

```
Content-type: text/html\r\n\r\n
```

Two pairs of carriage returns and linefeeds should follow all HTTP response headers. That's why, in this *Content-type* header, the escape characters for newline and carriage return (\n and \r) are added to the end of the header twice.

The next function called using the ECB is the *WriteClient* function. The phrase *Hi! Hello World* is written to the web browser using this function by passing a *char* pointer (*char**) of the string variable that holds the HTML and the phrase *Hi! Hello World*. *WriteClient* requires a void pointer (*void**), however, so the *char* pointer is cast into a void pointer using the *PVOID* macro.

Deploy the HelloWorld ISAPI

If the DLL compiles, the ISAPI extension may be deployed to a web server. If you set the file location for the DLL output to a web server instance or virtual directory root, you can request the file from IIS immediately after the DLL is built. If you try to debug the DLL by pressing F5 to start the build and debug process, Visual Studio .NET will not start up your web browser and automatically request the ISAPI DLL from IIS as it would if you were debugging an ASP.NET web service. Visual Studio thinks that the project is simply a DLL so it will request that you assign an executable to consume the DLL.

Remember *If the developer builds an ISAPI extension DLL and then tests the DLL by requesting it through IIS, the second build of the ISAPI DLL in Visual Studio .NET will likely fail to write the DLL. IIS locks the ISAPI extension DLL when it is requested from IIS, and IIS keeps it locked since the DLL is loaded into the IIS process space. The instance of the web site or the virtual directory must be unloaded or the application must be recycled to free up the ISAPI DLL. After the ISAPI DLL is freed, you can overwrite it in the build process.*

When the ISAPI DLL is requested from IIS 6 for the first time on Windows Server 2003 (WS03), the server will likely return a 404 error. A new feature of WS03 and IIS6 is the restriction of all server-side programmatic support by default, unless explicitly enabled. In previous versions of Windows Server, IIS would come loaded with all of the server-side programmatic support enabled, such as ASP. The functionality must be enabled on the server using the Web Service Extensions administrative applet in the Computer Management Microsoft Management Console (MMC) plug-in, as shown in Figure 17-8.

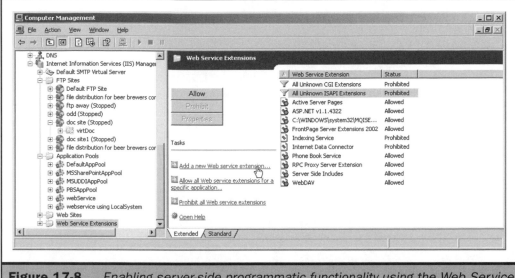

Figure 17-8.   *Enabling server-side programmatic functionality using the Web Service Extensions applet*

Let's set up IIS to allow requests for the *HelloWorld* ISAPI extension.

1. From the Web Service Extensions administrative applet in Computer Management, click the link labeled Add A New Web Service Extension. A New Web Service Extension dialog box will open.

2. Enter a name in the Extension Name text box that you want to display in the Web Service Extensions administrative applet. As shown in Figure 17-9, the name *HelloWorld* was entered.

3. Click the Add button to add the file path for the ISAPI extension. The Add File dialog box will open and you can enter the file path directly or use the Browse button to open the Open File dialog box.

4. Set a file path for the ISAPI extension, click OK on the Add File dialog box, and the ISAPI extension file path will appear in the New Web Service Extension dialog box.

5. Check the Set Extension Status To Allowed checkbox and click OK.

The HelloWorld extension will appear in the Web Service Extensions administrative applet in Computer Management and the status will show Allowed.

Alternatively, you can set the All Unknown ISAPI Extensions web service extension to be Allowed. This setting allows any request to any ISAPI extension to be allowed.

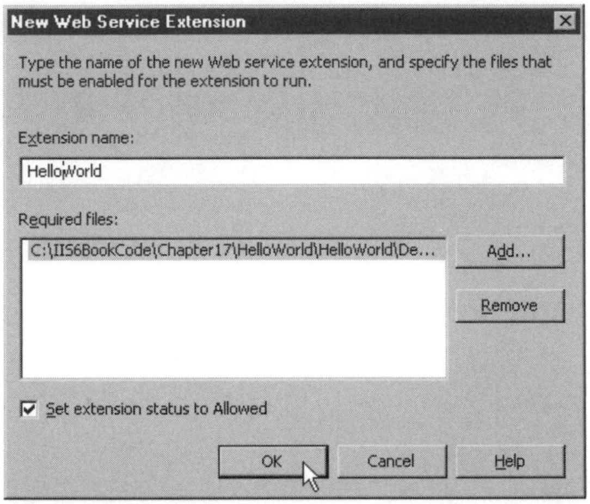

Figure 17-9.   *New Web Service Extension dialog box*

From a security perspective, enabling this setting exposes the server to unnecessary risk, so it should be used only in environments that are isolated, such as in a development environment.

The web instance in IIS or the virtual directory must also have its execute permissions set to allow ISAPI DLLs to run. By default, the setting Execute Permissions on the Properties window for an IIS web instance or virtual directory is not set to allow scripts and executables to run.

1. Open the IIS Computer Management MMC plug-in, and right-click the web instance or virtual directory to expose its context menu.

2. Choose Properties to open the Properties window for the web instance or virtual directory.

3. Under the Virtual Directory tab for the Properties window of a virtual directory or the *Home* Directory tab for a web instance is an Execute Permissions combo box, as shown in Figure 17-10. Make sure that Scripts And Executables is selected.

If everything is set properly in IIS, the *HelloWorld* ISAPI should function. Simply request the ISAPI DLL in the URL of your web browser as though it were an HTML file, and the DLL should run. The result of the *HelloWorld* ISAPI sample running is shown in Figure 17-11.

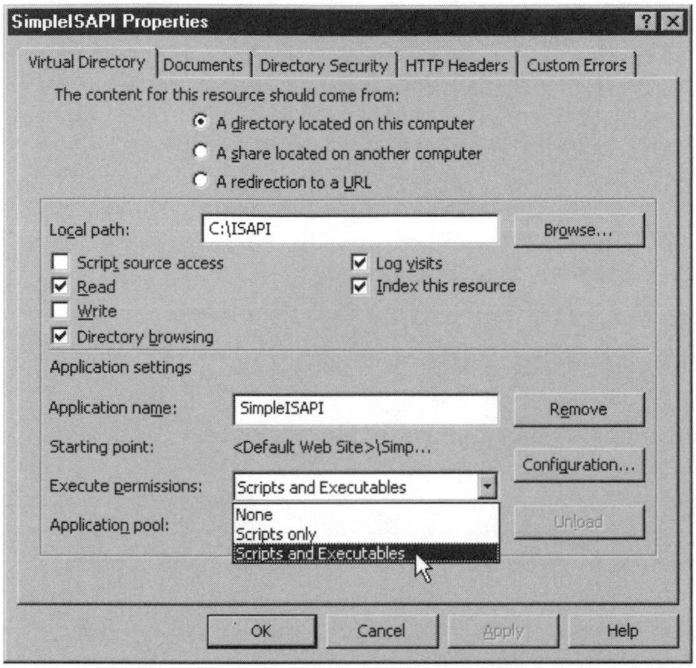

Figure 17-10. *Setting the execute permissions for a virtual directory*

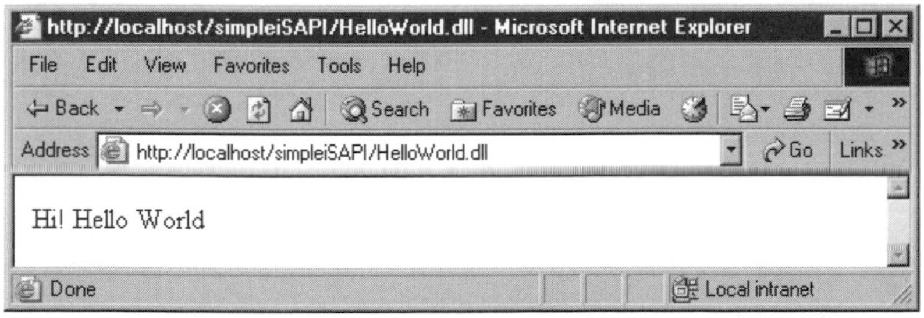

Figure 17-11. *Running the HelloWorld ISAPI extension*

Extracting Information from IIS

The ECB is commonly used to extract information about the HTTP request and the server instance of IIS so that the ISAPI extension can perform some programmatic effort based on the request event. In Listing 17-3 from the ISAPI extension *SEUX* (*Simple Extension Using XML*), the *HttpExtensionProc* function is used to perform the following tasks:

- Build an XML document with many of the common server variables obtained from the *GetServerVariable* function.
- Add properties of the ECB into the XML document.
- Return the XML document to the requester.

Listing 17-3

HttpExtensionProc Function Building XML Document in
SEUX ISAPI Extension

```
/*~~~~~~~~~~~~~~~~~~~~~~~~~~~~~~~~~~~~~~~~~~~~~~~~~~~~~~~~~~~~~~~~~~~~~
Name:HttpExtensionProc

In:        pECB - pointer to the Extension control block structure

Out:    DWORD - HSE status code

Purpose:
    main entry point for HTTP request

    the possible return codes are:
    HSE_STATUS_SUCCESS     - everything worked great
    HSE_STATUS_SUCCESS_AND_KEEP_CONN - same as HSE_STATUS_SUCCESS
                                       since IIS 4
    HSE_STATUS_PENDING - wait until effort completed
    HSE_STATUS_ERROR    - sends a 500 error code
/*~~~~~~~~~~~~~~~~~~~~~~~~~~~~~~~~~~~~~~~~~~~~~~~~~~~~~~~~~~~~~~~~~~~~~*/
DWORD WINAPI HttpExtensionProc(EXTENSION_CONTROL_BLOCK *pECB)
{
    string sDoc;

    //start our XML document
    sDoc = string(HEAD) + string(NEW_LINE) + string(XML_L) +
               string(MAIN_ELEMENT_NAME) + string(XML_R) +
               string(NEW_LINE);
```

```
//START THE ECBServerVariable VARIABLES
sDoc += string(XML_L) +
    string("ECBServerVariable") + string(XML_R) +
    string(NEW_LINE);
//GET the ALL_HTTP
sDoc += string(XML_L) + string("ALL_HTTP");
GetALLHTTPHeader(pECB, &sDoc);
sDoc += string(XML_R_END) +
    string(NEW_LINE);//end the first main element

GetECBElement(pECB, string("AUTH_TYPE"), &sDoc);
GetECBElement(pECB, string("APPL_MD_PATH"), &sDoc);
GetECBElement(pECB, string("APPL_PHYSICAL_PATH"), &sDoc);
GetECBElement(pECB, string("CONTENT_LENGTH"), &sDoc);
GetECBElement(pECB, string("CONTENT_TYPE"), &sDoc);
GetECBElement(pECB, string("GATEWAY_INTERFACE"), &sDoc);
GetECBElement(pECB, string("HTTP_ACCEPT"), &sDoc);
GetECBElement(pECB, string("HTTPS"), &sDoc);
GetECBElement(pECB, string("HTTP_AUTHORIZATION"), &sDoc);
GetECBElement(pECB, string("LOGON_USER"), &sDoc);
GetECBElement(pECB, string("AUTH_PASSWORD"), &sDoc);
GetECBElement(pECB, string("AUTH_TYPE"), &sDoc);
GetECBElement(pECB, string("AUTH_USER"), &sDoc);
GetECBElement(pECB, string("APPL_PHYSICAL_PATH"), &sDoc);
GetECBElement(pECB, string("INSTANCE_ID"), &sDoc);
GetECBElement(pECB, string("INSTANCE_META_PATH"), &sDoc);
GetECBElement(pECB, string("PATH_INFO"), &sDoc);
GetECBElement(pECB, string("PATH_TRANSLATED"), &sDoc);
GetECBElement(pECB, string("QUERY_STRING"), &sDoc);
GetECBElement(pECB, string("REMOTE_ADDR"), &sDoc);
GetECBElement(pECB, string("REMOTE_HOST"), &sDoc);
GetECBElement(pECB, string("REMOTE_USER"), &sDoc);
GetECBElement(pECB, string("REQUEST_METHOD"), &sDoc);
GetECBElement(pECB, string("SCRIPT_NAME"), &sDoc);
GetECBElement(pECB, string("SERVER_NAME"), &sDoc);
GetECBElement(pECB, string("SERVER_PORT"), &sDoc);
GetECBElement(pECB, string("SERVER_PORT_SECURE"), &sDoc);
GetECBElement(pECB, string("SERVER_PROTOCOL"), &sDoc);
GetECBElement(pECB, string("SERVER_SOFTWARE"), &sDoc);
GetECBElement(pECB, string("URL"), &sDoc);
```

```
//End THE ECBServerVariable VARIABLES
sDoc += string(XML_L_END) +
    string("ECBServerVariable") + string(XML_R) +
    string(NEW_LINE);

//START THE ECBProperties
sDoc += string(XML_L) +
    string("ECBProperties") + string(XML_R) +
    string(NEW_LINE);

GetElement(string("lpszLogData"),
        string(pECB->lpszLogData),&sDoc);
GetElement(string("lpszMethod"),
        string(pECB->lpszMethod),&sDoc);
GetElement(string("lpszQueryString"),
        string(pECB->lpszQueryString),&sDoc);
GetElement(string("lpszPathInfo"),
        string(pECB->lpszPathInfo),&sDoc);
GetElement(string("lpszContentType"),
        string(pECB->lpszContentType),&sDoc);

//end THE ECBProperties
sDoc += string(XML_L_END) +
    string("ECBProperties") + string(XML_R) +
    string(NEW_LINE);

    //end our XML document
sDoc += string(XML_L_END) +
    string(MAIN_ELEMENT_NAME) + string(XML_R) +
    string(NEW_LINE);

//write it!
SendResponse(pECB,sDoc);

return HSE_STATUS_SUCCESS;
}
```

Note *The source code for SEUX is available on the author's web site as mentioned in the book's Introduction.*

Building XML Representing the Server Variables Values

The first task that the code in Listing 17-3 does is to start the XML document by appending some constants that represent parts of an XML document. Since the XML is being built manually, constants are declared for common parts of the XML document because they are used many times in many places. The XML document is placed in a string variable named *sDoc*. The XML constants are as follows:

```
//xml parts
const char* MAIN_ELEMENT_NAME = "HTTPRequestRaw";
const char* QUOTE        ="\"";
const char* XML_L        ="<";
const char* XML_R        =">";
const char* XML_L_END    ="</";
const char* XML_R_END    ="/>";
const char* NEW_LINE     ="\n";
const char* HEAD = "<?xml version=\"1.0\"?>";
```

Because this particular ISAPI extension builds XML manually, the parts of an XML document that are represented by the constant *char* pointers (*const char**) are commonly used in many places. This XML document is also simple, so building it manually using string concatenation is not difficult. If the document were more complex, the use of an XML parsing library, such as MSXML, might be considered.

After the XML document is started, the effort of grabbing all of the server variables and placing them into XML elements will begin. The XML document that is produced has a parent element called *HTTPRequestRaw*. Within *HTTPRequestRaw* are two child elements called *ECBServerVariable* and *ECBProperties*. For each server variable value requested from the ECB, a child element will be created under the *ECBServerVariable* element, regardless of whether or not a value is obtained for the respective server variable. For each ECB property requested, a child element will be created under the *ECBProperties* element to hold the value, regardless of whether or not a value for the property was obtained. When the ISAPI extension *SEUX* is called using Internet Explorer (IE) version 6.0, the XML document will be displayed, as shown in Figure 17-12. Other browser versions may display the XML differently or not at all.

Special Case of ALL_HTTP Server Variable

The first server variable that a value is obtained for is the *ALL_HTTP* variable that represents all of the HTTP headers that were passed in the HTTP request. All the other server variables requested result in a number or a string that fits into XML quite easily, but the *ALL_HTTP* server variable returns all of the headers in the same server variable. Since

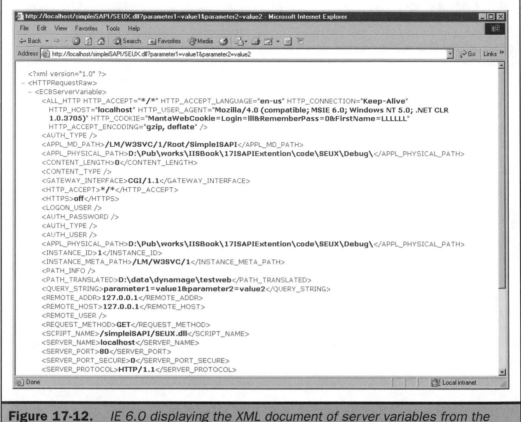

Figure 17-12. IE 6.0 displaying the XML document of server variables from the SEUX ISAPI extension

the headers in the value returned from the *ALL_HTTP* server variable are delimited using linefeeds, some additional parsing is required to make each header fit into an XML element as an attribute. The function *GetALLHTTPHeader* performs this task by using the ECB's *GetServerVariable* function, as shown in Listing 17-4.

Listing 17-4

```
GetALLHTTPHeader Function Building XML Element in
SEUX ISAPI Extension


/*~~~~~~~~~~~~~~~~~~~~~~~~~~~~~~~~~~~~~~~~~~~~~~~~~~~~~~~~~~~~~~~~~~~~~
Name:GetALLHTTPHeader
```

```
In:    pECB - pointer to the Extension control block structure

    psElement - string pointer to XML document being built that
                will be updated with the element for the ALL_HTTP
                server variable value.

Out:   nothing returned but the string psElement points to
       will be updated.

Purpose:
    Updates the XML document string by adding an element
    for the ALL_HTTP server variable. This variable contains
    all of the http headers so some additional parsing must
    take place on the headers to format them into XML.

/*~~~~~~~~~~~~~~~~~~~~~~~~~~~~~~~~~~~~~~~~~~~~~~~~~~~~~~~~~~~~~~~~~~~~*/
void GetALLHTTPHeader(EXTENSION_CONTROL_BLOCK *pECB,
                      string *psElement)
{
    TCHAR szTempBuffer[BUFFER_LENGTH];
    DWORD dwBufferSize = BUFFER_LENGTH;
    const string EQUAL("=");
    const string SPACE(" ");

    string sAllHeaders;    //used to cut up 'all headers' returned
    int nNewLinePos = 0;
    int nEndLinePos = 0;
    string sName;
    string sValue;


    //pull the whole HTTP header
    if (pECB->GetServerVariable(    pECB->ConnID,
                                    "ALL_HTTP",
                                    szTempBuffer,
                                    &dwBufferSize))
    {
       //if the whole http header was pulled then parse it
        sAllHeaders.assign(szTempBuffer);

        //get the name / value pairs
```

```
      while (GetHeaderValuePair(     sAllHeaders,
                                     nNewLinePos,
                                     &sName,
                                     &sValue,
                                     &nEndLinePos))
    {
        //add the attribute to the element
        psElement->append(     SPACE + sName + EQUAL +
                               QUOTE +
                               ValidateValue(sValue) +
                               QUOTE);

        //reset the newline to the last endline
        nNewLinePos = nEndLinePos;

        //dump the values
        sName.erase();
        sValue.erase();
    }
  }
}
```

GetServerVariable Function

The *GetServerVariable* function returns true on a successful execution and returns false if an error was encountered, as shown in the following function prototype:

```
BOOL WINAPI GetServerVariable(
  HCONN hConn,
  LPSTR lpszVariableName,
  LPVOID lpvBuffer,
  LPDWORD lpdwSizeofBuffer
);
```

The prototype of *GetServerVariable* as shown here requires that four parameters be passed in:

- *hConn*   Connection handle obtained from the ECB
- *lpszVariableName*   Null terminated string of the server variable that is being requested

- *lpvBuffer*   Void pointer to a buffer that should be filled with the resulting value of the variable name and 1 null terminating byte

- *lpdwSizeofBuffer*   Pointer to a DWORD that indicates the size of the buffer

If *GetServerVariable* is successful, the function returns a value of true. The pointer *lpvBuffer* should be pointed to a value of the requested server variable, and *lpdwSizeofBuffer* should be pointed to a new *DWORD* value that indicates the actual size of the value *lpvBuffer* points to including the null terminating byte. If the *GetServerVariable* function is not successful, it will return a false value. If false is returned, the *GetLastError* function may be called. *GetLastError* returns a *DWORD* value representing an error code that may be referenced against a library to determine the error description. Four possible errors are thrown by *GetServerVariable*, as shown in Table 17-2. The values in Table 17-2 are constants that are defined in the ISAPI extension support header file.

Server Variable Values

Many of the possible server variables that could be requested are shown in Listing 17-3, the *HttpExtensionProc* function in the SEUX ISAPI extension, as arguments in the *GetECBElement* calls. The values of server variables can change at various points during a given HTTP request event in IIS, and often no value will be assigned to a variable. Server variables may have values only under certain IIS configurations as well. Table 17-3 summarizes many of the server variables that may be queried using the *GetServerVariable* function.

Error Constant	Description of Error
ERROR_INVALID_PARAMETER	The value of *hConn* is no good or closed or the server variable parameters are invalid.
ERROR_INVALID_INDEX	The server variable being requested is not a supported variable.
ERROR_INSUFFICIENT_BUFFER	The size of *lpdwSizeofBuffer* is too small to contain the value of the server variable being requested.
ERROR_NO_DATA	The server variable being requested is not available.

Table 17-2.   *Summary of GetServerVariable Errors*

Variable	Description
ALL_HTTP	All of the HTTP headers (separated by linefeeds) that were passed in the HTTP request in a null-terminated string. The headers are in the form of *<header name> : <value>*.
ALL_RAW	All of the HTTP headers in an unaltered form as they were sent from the HTTP requester. The result will be similar to the value of *ALL_HTTP*.
APPL_MD_PATH	Metabase path of the web application. For example, */LM/W3SVC/1/Root/SimpleISAPI*.
APPL_PHYSICAL_PATH	Physical path of the web root for the web application. For example, *C:\ISAPI*.
AUTH_PASSWORD	Password entered by the web end user in the generic authentication dialog box spawned by the web browser if Basic Authentication is set.
AUTH_TYPE	Type of authentication used. Empty for no authentication or returns a value that correlates to Kerberos, user, SSL/PCT, Basic, or integrated Windows authentication.
AUTH_USER	User name entered by the end user in the generic authentication dialog box spawned by the web browser if Basic Authentication is set.
CERT_COOKIE	Unique ID of the client certificate.
CERT_FLAGS	Bit flags about the certification authority (CA) of the client certificate. If bit0 is set to 1, a client certificate is present. If bit1 is set to 1, the CA is not on this server's list of recognized CAs so it is considered invalid.
CERT_ISSUER	Contains the issuer's distinguished name of the client certificate. For example, *O=Schmidlaps, OU=House, CN=user name, C=USA*.
CERT_KEYSIZE	Key size of the Secure Sockets Layer (SSL) connection in bits.

Table 17-3.   *Summary of Server Variables that May Be Queried Using the GetServerVariable Function*

Variable	Description
CERT_SECRETKEYSIZE	Key size of the server certificate private key in bits.
CERT_SERIALNUMBER	Serial number of the client certificate.
CERT_SERVER_ISSUER	Issuer's distinguished name of issuer of the server certificate.
CERT_SERVER_SUBJECT	Issuer's distinguished name of subject of the server certificate.
CERT_SUBJECT	Subject of the client certificate.
CONTENT_LENGTH	The number of bytes, not including headers for the HTTP request.
CONTENT_TYPE	The content type of a POST HTTP request.
LOGON_USER	If the end user successfully authenticated to Windows, the login account used.
HTTPS	Returns the value *off* if HTTPS is not being used via SSL and returns a value of *on* otherwise.
HTTPS_KEYSIZE	Key size of the SSL connection in bits.
HTTPS_SECRETKEYSIZE	Key size of the server certificate private key in bits.
HTTPS_SERVER_ISSUER	Issuer's distinguished name of issuer of the server certificate.
HTTPS_SERVER_SUBJECT	Issuer's distinguished name of subject of the server certificate.
INSTANCE_ID	Server instance number. Value of the server ID in the metabase. For example, *1*.
INSTANCE_META_PATH	Metabase path for web instance. For example: LM/W3SVC/1.
PATH_INFO	Part of the URL that is between the ISAPI DLL and the start of the extra-info section of the URL. Normally nothing is between the ISAPI DLL and the extra-info section of the URL unless the requesting software put a value in place.

Table 17-3. *Summary of Server Variables that May Be Queried Using the GetServerVariable Function* (continued)

Variable	Description
PATH_TRANSLATED	Path of the web instance as it is mapped to the physical hard drive and the value of PATH_INFO concatenated.
QUERY_STRING	String of the characters that follow the ? in the extra-info section of the URL.
REMOTE_ADDR	IP address of the requesting software's host or gateway.
REMOTE_HOST	Host name of the requesting software's host or gateway if reverse DNS is enabled; otherwise, the value of the IP address of the requesting software's host or gateway is returned.
REMOTE_USER	User name supplied HTTP requester and authenticated by the host server. This value is an empty string when the end user is anonymous.
REQUEST_METHOD	HTTP request method verb.
SCRIPT_NAME	Name of the binary being executed. For example, the ISAPI DLL or the CGI executable.
SERVER_NAME	Host's server name, or IP address.
SERVER_PORT	TCP/IP port on which the request was received.
SERVER_PORT_SECURE	Value of either 0 or 1. Secure port requests return a value of 1; otherwise a value of 0 will be returned.
SERVER_PROTOCOL	Name and version of the request protocol. For example, HTTP/1.1.
SERVER_SOFTWARE	Name and version of IIS under which the ISAPI extension DLL program is running. For example, *Microsoft-IIS/6.0.*
URL	Value of the *url-path* part of the URL excluding the PATH_INFO value. For example, */simpleisapi/folder1/folder2/SEUX.dll.*

Table 17-3. *Summary of Server Variables that May Be Queried Using the GetServerVariable Function* (continued)

To demonstrate the values described in Table 17-3, Listing 17-5 shows an XML document produced from the *SEUX.DLL* ISAPI extension. In this example, the host server and IIS were configured so that many of the values for server variables would be obtained during the HTTP request. The hosting server is named *amd1700v2*. IIS 6 on amd1700v2 was configured with the following settings and file locations:

■ **Physical location of the ISAPI extension SEUX.DLL**   *C:\ISAPI\folder1\folder2 \SEUX.dll*

■ **Web instance root**   *C:\inetpub\wwwroot*

■ **Virtual directory mapped to**   *C:\ISAPI*

■ **Anonymous access**   Not enabled for the virtual directory

■ **Basic authentication**   Checked for the virtual directory

The *SEUX.DLL* ISAPI extension was requested from amd1700v2 using the following data using a web browser hosted on a separate computer:

■ User logged into web site with user name *normaluser*

■ User logged into web site with password *normaluser*

■ URL placed in browser:
   http://amd1700v2/simpleisapi/folder1/folder2/SEUX.dll/PATH_INFO?parm1= value1&parm2=value

Listing 17-5

```
SEUX.DLL Output from
http://amd1700v2/simpleisapi/folder1/folder2/SEUX.dll/PATH_INFO?
parm1=value1&parm2=value

<?xml version="1.0" ?>
<HTTPRequestRaw>
 <ECBServerVariable>
  <ALL_HTTP HTTP_CONNECTION="Keep-Alive"
   HTTP_ACCEPT=
 "image/gif, image/x-xbitmap, image/jpeg, image/pjpeg,
application/vnd.ms-powerpoint, application/vnd.ms-excel,
application/msword, */*"
   HTTP_ACCEPT_ENCODING="gzip, deflate"
   HTTP_ACCEPT_LANGUAGE="en-us"
   HTTP_AUTHORIZATION="Basic bm9ybWFsdXNlcjpub3JtYWx1c2Vy"
   HTTP_COOKIE="ASPCLIENTDEBUG=1" HTTP_HOST="amd1700v2"
   HTTP_USER_AGENT=
 "Mozilla/4.0 (compatible; MSIE 6.0; Windows NT 5.0; .NET CLR
1.0.3705)" />
```

```
   <AUTH_TYPE>Basic</AUTH_TYPE>
   <APPL_MD_PATH>/LM/W3SVC/1/Root/SimpleISAPI</APPL_MD_PATH>
   <APPL_PHYSICAL_PATH>C:\ISAPI\</APPL_PHYSICAL_PATH>
   <CONTENT_LENGTH>0</CONTENT_LENGTH>
   <CONTENT_TYPE />
   <GATEWAY_INTERFACE>CGI/1.1</GATEWAY_INTERFACE>
   <HTTP_ACCEPT>image/gif, image/x-xbitmap, image/jpeg, image/pjpeg,
application/vnd.ms-powerpoint, application/vnd.ms-excel,
application/msword, */*</HTTP_ACCEPT>
   <HTTPS>off</HTTPS>
   <HTTP_AUTHORIZATION>
Basic bm9ybWFsdXNlcjpub3JtYWx1c2Vy
   </HTTP_AUTHORIZATION>
   <LOGON_USER>normaluser</LOGON_USER>
   <AUTH_PASSWORD>normaluser</AUTH_PASSWORD>
   <AUTH_TYPE>Basic</AUTH_TYPE>
   <AUTH_USER>normaluser</AUTH_USER>
   <APPL_PHYSICAL_PATH>C:\ISAPI\</APPL_PHYSICAL_PATH>
   <INSTANCE_ID>1</INSTANCE_ID>
   <INSTANCE_META_PATH>/LM/W3SVC/1</INSTANCE_META_PATH>
   <PATH_INFO>/PATH_INFO</PATH_INFO>
   <PATH_TRANSLATED>c:\inetpub\wwwroot\PATH_INFO</PATH_TRANSLATED>
   <QUERY_STRING>parm1=value1&parm2=value</QUERY_STRING>
   <REMOTE_ADDR>169.254.176.147</REMOTE_ADDR>
   <REMOTE_HOST>169.254.176.147</REMOTE_HOST>
   <REMOTE_USER>normaluser</REMOTE_USER>
   <REQUEST_METHOD>GET</REQUEST_METHOD>
   <SCRIPT_NAME>/simpleisapi/folder1/folder2/SEUX.dll</SCRIPT_NAME>
   <SERVER_NAME>amd1700v2</SERVER_NAME>
   <SERVER_PORT>80</SERVER_PORT>
   <SERVER_PORT_SECURE>0</SERVER_PORT_SECURE>
   <SERVER_PROTOCOL>HTTP/1.1</SERVER_PROTOCOL>
   <SERVER_SOFTWARE>Microsoft-IIS/6.0</SERVER_SOFTWARE>
   <URL>/simpleisapi/folder1/folder2/SEUX.dll</URL>
 </ECBServerVariable>
 <ECBProperties>
  <lpszLogData />
  <lpszMethod>GET</lpszMethod>
  <lpszQueryString>parm1=value1&parm2=value</lpszQueryString>
  <lpszPathInfo>/PATH_INFO</lpszPathInfo>
  <lpszContentType />
 </ECBProperties>
</HTTPRequestRaw>
```

Parsing the Header–Value Pair

After the *ALL_HTTP* header is obtained from the *GetServerVariable* function in Listing 17-4, the string must be parsed for SEUX to be able to display the contents in XML. The headers are delineated by a linefeed and a carriage return. The colon (:) is used to separate the header name from the value. *GetHeaderValuePair* is designed to begin searching in a given position and return the name and associated value for a given header along with the position that the function stopped looking for headers. *GetHeaderValuePair* searches for one header value pair at a time.

As shown in Listing 17-6, the function *GetHeaderValuePair* takes the entire HTTP header and looks for a colon starting at position *nStart* in the string *sHeader*. The value of *nStart* is a counter that starts at zero. If a colon does not exist after the position *nStart* in the HTTP header, the function exits, returning a value of false. If a colon is found, this means a header exists, and *sHeader* is searched for a new line starting from the position at which the colon was found. The search is performed using the *find* function of the Standard Template Library (STL) string with the newline escape character \n as an argument along with the colon location as the start position. The newline position becomes the end position that is returned in the parameter *pnEnd* pointer, so that the calling function will know where the search stopped. Using all of the position parameters that are discovered from the find function calls to the *sHeader* string, the header name and value are extracted into the memory locations that are associated with pointers *psName* and *psValue*.

IIS PROGRAMMING

Listing 17-6

```
Source Code for Function GetHeaderValuePair


/*~~~~~~~~~~~~~~~~~~~~~~~~~~~~~~~~~~~~~~~~~~~~~~~~~~~~~~~~~~~~~~~~~~~~~~
Name: GetHeaderValuePair

In: sHeader - string HTTP Header
    nStart - integer search start location
    psName - pointer to name of header that is being sought
    psValue - pointer to string that will be filled if
                value found
    pnEnd - pointer to integer of the final search position

Out: bool    true returned if the header was found,
             false returned otherwise
Purpose:
        Searches through the HTTP header passed in for a
        header value. Returns data about the search
        parameters if found or not.
```

```cpp
/*~~~~~~~~~~~~~~~~~~~~~~~~~~~~~~~~~~~~~~~~~~~~~~~~~~~~~~~~~~~~~~~~*/
bool GetHeaderValuePair(const string &sHeader,
                        const int &nStart,
                        string *psName,
                        string *psValue,
                        int *pnEnd)
{
    const string sColon(":");

    //determine if header is a post header
    string::size_type idxColonPosition = nStart;

    //start looking at beginning
    idxColonPosition = sHeader.find(sColon, idxColonPosition);

    if (idxColonPosition == string::npos)//no more headers found
        return false;//this is failure

    //get the name
    psName->assign(sHeader.substr
                   (nStart, idxColonPosition - nStart));

    //find next newline
    string::size_type idxNewLine;
    idxNewLine = sHeader.find('\n', idxColonPosition);

    //get the end even if it means not found
    *pnEnd = idxNewLine;

    if (idxNewLine == string::npos)    //a newline was not found
        return true;//not a failure - might be the last header

    //get the value
    //adjust colon position so we do not assign colon in value
    idxColonPosition = idxColonPosition +1;
    psValue->assign(sHeader.substr(idxColonPosition,
        idxNewLine - idxColonPosition));

    return true;
}
```

Assembling the Remaining XML Elements

After the *HttpExtensionProc* function parses the *ALL_HTTP* header value, the remaining server variables are all processed using *GetECBElement*, as shown in Listing 17-7. Each server variable passed into *GetECBElement* is extracted using the *GetServerVariable* function and serialized into an XML element that is appended to a string pointed to by *psElement*. The pointer *psElement* points to the XML document that is being constructed in *HttpExtensionProc*.

Listing 17-7

```
Function GetECBElement


/*~~~~~~~~~~~~~~~~~~~~~~~~~~~~~~~~~~~~~~~~~~~~~~~~~~~~~~~~~~~~~~~~~
Name:GetECBElement

In:    pECB - Pointer to the extension control block for the
       purposes of calling the GetServerVariable function.

    sName - string name of the server variable that is
           being sought.

    psElement - string pointer to XML document being built that
               will be updated with the name and value for the
               server variable extracted from the extension
               control block.

Out:    nothing returned but the string psElement points to
        will be updated.

Purpose:
    appends a string of an XML element to the string psElement
    points to. The XML element that is created is in the form of
<Server Variable Name>Server Variable Value</Server Variable Name>

    for example:
 <GATEWAY_INTERFACE>CGI/1.1</GATEWAY_INTERFACE> + newline


/*~~~~~~~~~~~~~~~~~~~~~~~~~~~~~~~~~~~~~~~~~~~~~~~~~~~~~~~~~~~~~~~~~*/
void GetECBElement(    EXTENSION_CONTROL_BLOCK *pECB,
                                const string &sName,
                                string *psElement)

{
```

```
TCHAR szTempBuffer[BUFFER_LENGTH];
DWORD dwBufferSize = BUFFER_LENGTH;

    //get the server variable value
    if (pECB->GetServerVariable(      pECB->ConnID,
                        (LPSTR)sName.c_str(),
                        szTempBuffer,
                        &dwBufferSize))
    {
        //build the XML element and
        //add it to the XML document passed in
         psElement->append(string(XML_L) + sName + string(XML_R));

         psElement->append(ValidateValue((string)szTempBuffer));

         psElement->append(string(XML_L_END) + sName + string(XML_R) +
             string(NEW_LINE));
    }

}
```

The *ValidateValue* function is used to make certain that special characters are escaped. The function is applied to a string before the string is set as an element value. *ValidateValue* could also be used to validate an attribute value. XML cannot tolerate certain special characters in a value position unless they are escaped. As shown in Listing 17-8, the characters that are used to make an XML structure, such as the equal sign or the greater than or less than symbols, are replaced with an acceptable equivalent escape version of the character.

Listing 17-8

```
Function ValidateValue

/*~~~~~~~~~~~~~~~~~~~~~~~~~~~~~~~~~~~~~~~~~~~~~~~~~~~~~~~~~~~~~~~~~~~
Name: ValidateValue

In: Constant reference to a string variable sValue. sValue is the
    value being checked to see if it has a character requiring
    escaping

Out: returns a string with the escaped characters in place
```

```
Purpose:
    blindly replaces all special characters
    with the escape sequence character so that XML will
    be valid.


/*~~~~~~~~~~~~~~~~~~~~~~~~~~~~~~~~~~~~~~~~~~~~~~~~~~~~~~~~~~~~~~~~~~~~*/
string ValidateValue(const string &sValue)
{
    string sReturn;
    sReturn = sValue;

    FindAndReplace(&sReturn, &string("&"),&string("&amp;"));
    FindAndReplace(&sReturn, &string("="),&string("&#61;"));
    FindAndReplace(&sReturn, &string("<"),&string("&lt;"));
    FindAndReplace(&sReturn, &string(">"),&string("&gt;"));
    FindAndReplace(&sReturn, &string("'"),&string("&apos;"));
    FindAndReplace(&sReturn, &string("\""),&string("&quot;"));

    return sReturn;
}
```

The *FindAndReplace* function is a utility function that may be used to replace all the occurrences of a string. In the case of the SEUX ISAPI extension, it acts as a perfect mechanism to replace a phrase inside a string with another phrase. The arguments are pointers to the strings that represent the following:

- The containing string that is being edited, otherwise known as the *container*
- The string that needs to be replaced within the *container*, otherwise known as the *target*
- The string that will be replacing the *target* within the *container*, otherwise known as the *replacement*

The STL string provides a *find* function and a *replace* function that the *FindAndReplace* function uses to search the container for all occurrences of the target, as shown in Listing 17-9. Each time the target is found in the container, it is replaced and a new search begins at the end of the replacement. When *FindAndReplace* completes, the container is updated with the replacements if any exist.

Listing 17-9

```
/*~~~~~~~~~~~~~~~~~~~~~~~~~~~~~~~~~~~~~~~~~~~~~~~~~~~~~~~~~~~~~~~~~~~~
Name: FindAndReplace
```

```
In: psContainer - pointer to a string that will be searched
                  and edited if a value is discovered.
    psTarget - pointer to a string that is being sought for
               replacement.
    psReplacement - pointer to a string that will replace the
                    the string pointed to in psTarget.

Out: nothing - but psContainer will be changed

Purpose:
    searches string psContainer pointer for the string that
    psTarget points to and replaces it with the string that
    psReplacement points to.


/*~~~~~~~~~~~~~~~~~~~~~~~~~~~~~~~~~~~~~~~~~~~~~~~~~~~~~~~~~~~~~~~~~~~*/
void FindAndReplace(string *psContainer,
                    string *psTarget,
                    string *psReplacement)
{

    string::size_type idx;
    idx = psContainer->find(*psTarget);
    while (idx != string::npos)//an instance was found
    {
        //are we at the end of the string
        if (psContainer->size() == idx)
        {
            *psContainer += *psReplacement;
            break;
        }
        else
        {
            psContainer->replace
                    (idx, psTarget->size() , *psReplacement);

            //advance beyond the current character
            idx += psReplacement->size();
        }

        //look for next occurance
        idx = psContainer->find(*psTarget, idx);
    }

}
```

The *GetElement* function works almost exactly the same as *GetECBElement*. It is called from the *HttpExtensionProc* function to concatenate elements from the properties of the ECB. The properties are extracted from the ECB, and then they are passed along with their names and the XML document to the function *GetElement*. *GetElement* places the ECB property and the respective value placed into an XML element and concatenates it to the XML document pointer passed into *GetElement*. The following properties are queried:

- *lpszLogData* Buffer the size of *HSE_LOG_BUFFER_LEN* that can be used to place information that will be added to the log file for the given HTTP request transaction.

- *lpszMethod* Property that contains a string value of the HTTP method used. For example, *GET* or *PUT* or *HEAD*.

- *lpszQueryString* Property that contains a string value of the characters in the *extra-info* section of the URL excluding the ? character. This is the same value as the server variable *QUERY_STRING*.

- *lpszPathInfo* Property that contains a string value of the part of the URL that is between the ISAPI DLL and the start of the *extra-info* section of the URL. Normally there is nothing between the ISAPI DLL and the *extra-info* section of the URL unless the requesting software put a value in place. This is the same value as the server variable *PATH_INFO*.

- *lpszContentType* Property that contains a string value of the content type of an HTTP Post. This is the same value as the server variable *CONTENT_TYPE*.

When the *HttpExtensionProc* function finishes contributing the content for all of the possible server variables and properties of the ECB, the XML document is capped off with the proper enclosing XML tags and sent to the *SendResponse* function. *SendResponse* writes the string value passed into the function to the requesting software. As shown in Listing 17-10, the content type header is sent to the requesting client using the ECB *ServerSupportFunction*. The header that is sent is represented by the constant *BASIC_HEADER*, which equals the following string: *Content-type: text/html\r\n\r\n* . HTTP headers are to be followed by two carriage returns and linefeeds so the *text/HTML* header is specified in the header since the return data is text. XML could be specified, but if the Multipurpose Internet Mail Extensions (MIME) types on the requesting web browser were registered to XML, the registered program may open to display the XML.

Listing 17-10

```
Function SendResponse

/*~~~~~~~~~~~~~~~~~~~~~~~~~~~~~~~~~~~~~~~~~~~~~~~~~~~~~~~~~~~~~~~~~~~~~
Name: SendResponse

In:    pECB - pointer to the extension control block
       sValue - string reference to the value to be
```

IIS PROGRAMMING

```
                    written to the HTTP response

Out:    nothing

Purpose:
        writes the intended value to the HTTP response
/*~~~~~~~~~~~~~~~~~~~~~~~~~~~~~~~~~~~~~~~~~~~~~~~~~~~~~~~~~~~~~~~~~~~~*/
void SendResponse(EXTENSION_CONTROL_BLOCK *pECB, string &sValue)
{
    TCHAR szTempBuffer[BUFFER_LENGTH];
    DWORD dwBufferSize = BUFFER_LENGTH;

    // set content-type header
    strcpy(szTempBuffer, BASIC_HEADER);
    DWORD dwHeaderSize = strlen(szTempBuffer);
    pECB->ServerSupportFunction(pECB->ConnID,
                                HSE_REQ_SEND_RESPONSE_HEADER,
                                NULL,
                                &dwHeaderSize,
                                (LPDWORD) szTempBuffer);

    //write value to http response
    DWORD dwLength=sValue.length();
    pECB->WriteClient(    pECB->ConnID,
                        (PVOID)sValue.c_str(),
                        &dwLength,
                        HSE_IO_SYNC);
}
```

After the return header is sent, the actual content passed is sent using the *WriteClient* function. As shown in the following function prototype, the handle to the connection *ConnID* is passed during the write to the client. The existing value obtained from the current instance of the ECB pointer was used in Listing 17-10. The content is sent with the *WriteClient* function using a void pointer in the *Buffer* parameter. The content to which the *Buffer* pointer refers must be sized in terms of the number of bytes being passed to the client and referenced in the *lpdwBytes* parameter. After the call is completed, *lpdwBytes* will contain the number of bytes that were sent unless the write was performed asynchronously. The value of the *dwSync* parameter determines how the write will occur to the client. Listing 17-10 specifies a value of *0x00000001* using the *HSE_IO_SYNC* macro, which means that the write will be performed synchronously and the memory space referenced by the pointer *lpdwBytes* will be updated after the *WriteClient* completes with the number of bytes written to the client. If the macro

HSE_IO_ASYNC, which represents the value *0x00000002*, were used, the data written to the client and a callback function would capture the client write event data. Using *WriteClient* asynchronously requires the callback function to be declared and the *ServerSupportFunction* also must send a *HSE_REQ_IO_COMPLETION* value to set up the asynchronous write transaction with the client.

The *WriteClient* function is a member function of the ECB. As such, it might seem odd that the handle to the ECB being used must be passed into the function. Since IIS is a multi-threaded application, however, there could be many ECB instances in use at any given time, and it is conceivable that you might want to write in an instance of the ECB to another instance of the ECB. The prototype for WriteClient is as follows:

```
BOOL WriteClient(
  HCONN ConnID,
  LPVOID Buffer,
  LPDWORD lpdwBytes,
  DWORD dwSync
);
```

ISAPI Project Template Wizard

If you want to produce an ISAPI extension using more of the support that is afforded in MFC, the ISAPI Project Template Wizard should be used. The wizard will set up the project with the necessary support for ISAPI libraries and make a class that inherits from *CHttpServer*. The following MFC classes are provided for ISAPI:

- *CHttpArgList*   Class containing functions and structures for parsing a URL.
- *CHtmlStream*   Class useful for managing memory of data that is intended for writing to the client.
- *CHttpFilter*   Class that extends the interface of IIS to produce an ISAPI filter. Filters are a type of ISAPI application that is called on each request to IIS, so they respond to events inside IIS.
- *CHttpFilterContext*   Class provided as a parameter in the functions that are provided by *CHttpFilter* to process the content of a given HTTP event. *CHttpFilterContext* provides member functions, which are primarily designed to process data related to a given HTTP event passing through the filter.
- *CHttpServer*   Class that extends the interface of IIS for a given HTTP request event.
- *CHttpServerContext*   Class provided with the *CHttpServer* class that provides member functions useful for manipulating data related to a given HTTP event.

The classes provided in MFC offer a nice layer of abstraction to the raw interaction with ISAPI structures and functions shown previously. MFC allows the developer to have access to the raw ISAPI, but some classes are provided that make it easier to parse the headers and HTTP data that was being performed manually in the SEUX ISAPI extension. The wizard will produce a class that is named using the following schema: C<*ProjectName*>*Extension*. A function called *Default* acts as the main entry point for the ISAPI DLL and has the following prototype:

```
void Default(CHttpServerContext* pCtxt);
```

Function *Default* will take the place the of the *HttpExtensionProc* function that was used in the SEUX ISAPI extension for the main entry point. The pointer to the *CHttpServerContext* class that is passed into *Default* provides functionality and serves the need of the developer to manipulate data and the HTTP transaction that the ECB served in the SEUX ISAPI extension.

Creating an ISAPI Extension in Visual Studio .NET

To create an ISAPI extension using the Visual Studio .NET project template, open Visual Studio .NET and choose File | New | Project. The New Project dialog box will open, as shown in Figure 17-13. Choose the MFC ISAPI Extension DLL project template, enter a name for the project, and click the OK button.

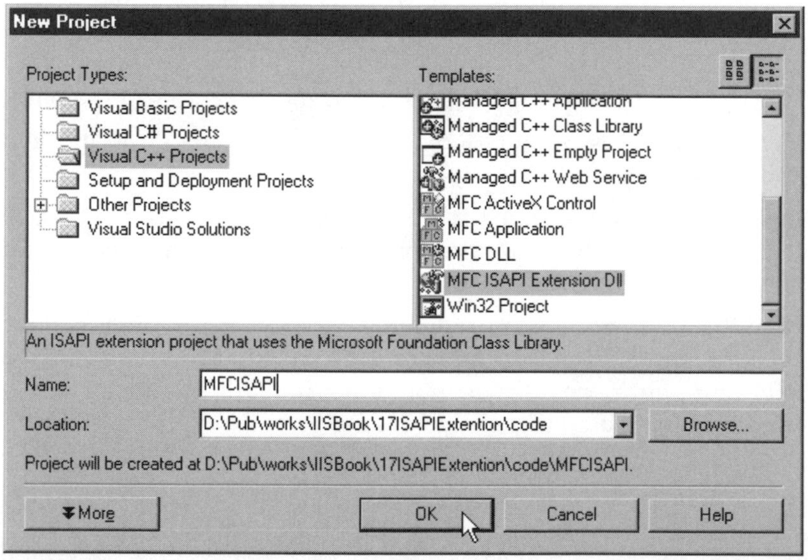

Figure 17-13. *Choosing an MFC ISAPI Extension DLL project template in Visual Studio .NET*

Note   *The New Project dialog box shown in Figure 17-13 shows icons that are much different from the New Project dialog box shown in Figure 17-2. The versions of Visual Studio .NET used in each figure are exactly the same. In Figure 17-2, the Large Icons button in the upper-right corner was selected. In Figure 17-13, the Small Icons button was selected. The Large Icons and the Small Icons buttons are mutually exclusive choices, and they affect the project template icons that are displayed in the right pane of the New Project dialog box.*

Much like the ATL Server Project Wizard discussed in Chapter 16, the ISAPI Extension Wizard is a one-step wizard that can be completed immediately by clicking the Finish button, as shown in Figure 17-14. The wizard summarizes the project settings in the Overview section. The default project type created is an ISAPI extension DLL with MFC in a shared DLL. Most ISAPI projects will conform to these specifications. These options may be changed in the Object Settings section.

The Object Settings section provides for a means for changing the class names that are generated by the wizard, and it provides options to allow the ISAPI extension to link to MFC statically or dynamically. By choosing the Use MFC In A Shared DLL option, as shown in Figure 17-15, MFC will be linked dynamically in the ISAPI DLL that is generated at compile time. This option assumes that MFC will exist in the intended

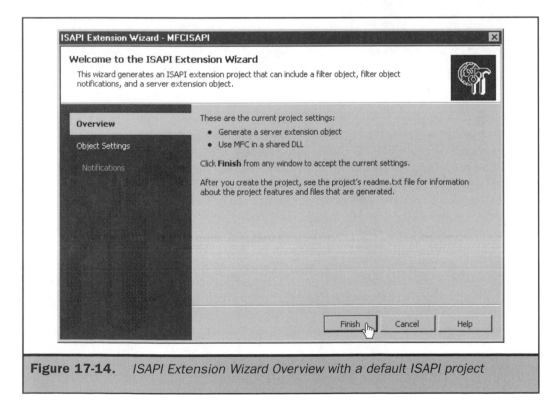

Figure 17-14.   *ISAPI Extension Wizard Overview with a default ISAPI project*

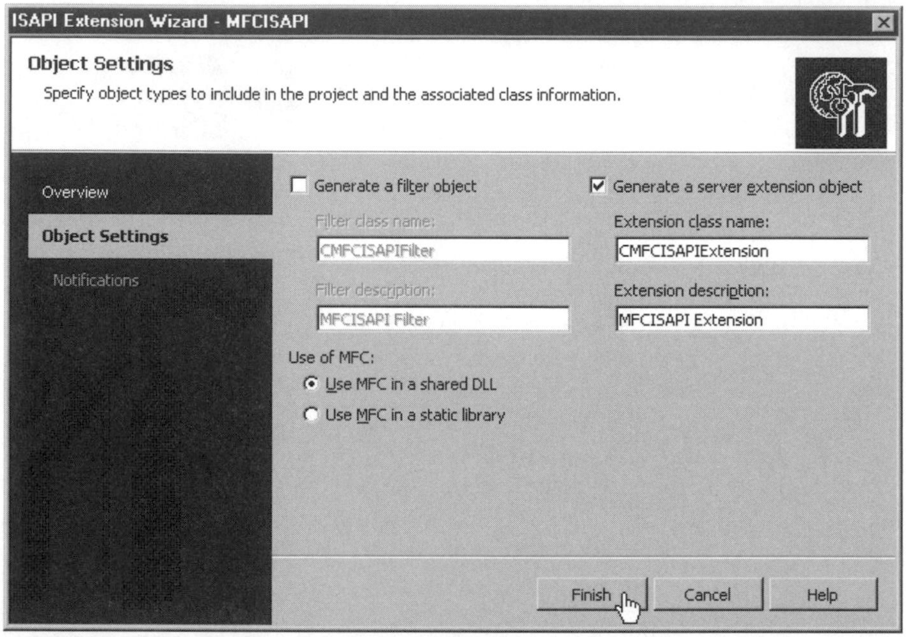

Figure 17-15.   *ISAPI Extension Wizard Object Settings section with a default ISAPI project*

deployment environment by not including the content of MFC in the ISAPI DLL. If Use MFC In A Static Library is selected, the components of MFC that are needed by the ISAPI DLL are compiled into the DLL and linked statically. This option assumes that MFC does not exist in the deployment environment. The size of the DLL under static linking is much larger than in dynamic linking. In most cases, MFC should exist in the target environment since it is a Windows server. In the case of WS03, dynamic linking can be assumed to be adequate since MFC will exist on the server.

You can also generate a filter object by checking the Generate A Filter Object checkbox. Filters may be loaded into IIS to respond to every request that is handled by IIS. Filters function in much the same way as an ISAPI extension would function if it were mapped to every file that exists in the web root. A filter and an extension are not mutually exclusive options, either. A single DLL can host an extension and a filter, thereby allowing state to be shared by each through global variables.

ISAPI filters are difficult to produce and test, however. Because filters are invoked with each request to IIS, great care must be taken to ensure that they are efficient and built properly. They can easily utilize resource in a way that greatly diminishes from server efficiency as well as crash the server in the event that a problem occurs with the way the filter uses memory.

After you click the Finish button and the wizard completes the process of generating
the files, the project may be compiled and run as soon as the DLL is deployed to the server.
If it runs correctly, the following message should be displayed in the browser, with the class
name that is consistent with the chosen name for the class:

```
This default message was produced by the Internet Server DLL
Wizard. Edit your CMFCISAPIExtension::Default() implementation
to change it.
```

The Complete Reference

IIS 6

Part IV

IIS Extras

The Complete Reference

IIS 6

Chapter 18

Software Process and Methodology for Web Applications

Somebody has hired you to build a web site or a software solution. You're tasked with determining what the client or owner wants in terms of a site, and you have to get the owner to agree to provide you a certain amount of time and money to produce the web site and make certain that the team performing the work will deliver the same web site that the owner wants. The challenge of such an effort is that often the owner does not know what he or she wants, and often the owner wants it done in less time than is reasonable. The team building the site does not know exactly what the owner wants, nor do they always know how to produce the desired outcome, even when the outcome is known.

Many development managers or technical leads follow a pattern called the *Unified Process* to help them deliver software solutions. The Unified Process plan is divided into phases that should be performed during any software development cycle. The goal of the process is to reduce the risk of software being delivered that does not meet the needs of the owner and client. The spirit of the process is meant to identify any unknowns, assumptions, or risks, and to measure the effort required to deliver a quality software solution by the most efficient means possible.

Many processes have evolved from the Unified Process, but their implementations may vary somewhat. Companies have built software to help encourage a particular utilization of the Unified Process, too, such as Rational Software, which refers to its version as the Rational Unified Process.

Definition of Terms

In this chapter, the following terms will be used and are defined here.

Owner refers to the recipient of the web site. The term *client* refers to the consumer of a server. This convention will be used to reduce the confusion that can result from the interchangeable use of the two synonyms. An owner may be internal to your organization. Owners may be your boss, a member of the sales team, or a marketing representative. Although the motives for each owner may be different, in the end, all owners are acting as a surrogate for the end user, at the very least. The owner always wants the web site to perform some desired task with the lowest expenditure of resources.

The term *end user* represents the human consumer of some software solution. For example, a person using a web browser to view a web site or a person receiving a file e-mailed from a Simple Mail Transport Protocol (SMTP) server are two examples of an end user consuming a solution. The end user interacts with the solution.

The terms *software solution*, *automated solution*, and *solution* are interchangeable. In this chapter, *solution* is used to represent all three. The solution represents the combination of software and hardware required to perform some amount of work.

The *project manager* is generally the individual who controls the project from the point that the owner decides to obligate the resource to build the solution to the time of delivery. The project manager manages client expectations and generally bears the ultimate responsibility of meeting project timelines. If the project is being executed as a time and materials contract, the project manager is the advocate for profit on the project.

The *business analyst* acts as the owner's functional advocate and defines how the solution should work. This person typically owns the functional specification. Individuals who serve in other capacities, such as the project manager or a developer, may serve in this role as well.

Development is a term that represents developers, technical leaders, development managers, and system architects. Many titles and roles within development mean different things to different organizations. In general, the individuals in this role generally write code but do not manage or configure hardware.

Systems professionals manage the hardware. They act as the hardware's advocates—they're usually responsible for managing, configuring, and maintaining the hardware and the operating system. They will configure solutions but they do not produce code.

The *UI developer* produces the presentation logic for a particular software solution. The *Object developer* produces the business logic and data logic code.

UML is an acronym for *Unified Modeling Language*, in which drawings are used to document software, although it can be used to document any process.

Use case is a description of a business event or process that may be performed by the software.

QA is an acronym for *Quality Assurance* and refers to members of the software team who are responsible for testing the software.

The Unified Process

The Unified Process identifies four phases and five workflows for completing a software effort. An *iteration* consists of the following four phases:

- **Inception**   Determine objectives that the software should meet and the tasks the software should perform.
- **Elaboration**   Design the solution that will fulfill the objectives.
- **Construction**   Code, document, and configure the software.
- **Transition**   Roll the code to production or deliver it.

Workflows are subordinate to a phase. Each phase could contain all five possible workflows:

- **Requirement collection**   Perform investigation for determining the requirements and objectives.
- **Analysis**   Examine the data gathered for the purposes of creating a design.
- **Design**   Design the solution.
- **Implementation**   Roll or move to the desired environment within which the solution should be executed.
- **Test**   Make certain the solution meets the identified requirements and objectives.

An Adaptation of the Unified Process

Because the Unified Process describes a generalized methodology for software development of any sort, this chapter presents a specific variation based on the Unified Process that has been used to produce web portal software. This process is based on the author's personal experience and has no further basis for acceptance other than the fact that it is a variation of the Unified Process. This process may be modified or changed to accommodate the specific environment, based on the needs of the parties involved.

At the beginning of any project, a *scope* is defined that describes an overview or summary of the desired outcome. If all parties agree to pursue the scope, a *requirements gathering* exercise will ensue, which results in a *functional design*. On completing the requirements gathering, a *technical design* will be performed to determine how to build the solution, resulting in a *technical specification*. The *functional design* can be referred to as defining the "what," and the *technical design* can be referred to as defining the "how" of the solution. Once a solution is described in such a way that a programmer can build the solution, it is assigned to development to build and test against the technical specification. After development is completed, the solution must be *tested* against the functional specification. After the software passes the tests, it will be rolled to *production* and the project is completed. Figure 18-1 shows the overall process for building a web site.

Many new methodologies challenge or enhance the Unified Process, such as *Extreme Programming* or *Agile*. These alternative methodologies offer the development organization many opportunities to optimize the process for building a software

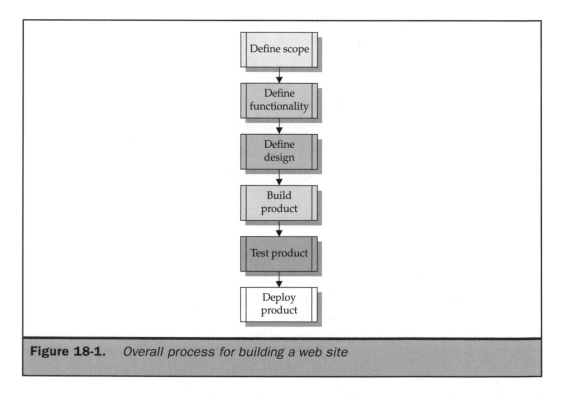

Figure 18-1. *Overall process for building a web site*

product. For example, Extreme Programming proposes such techniques as eliminating documentation, reducing the time of a development cycle, and coding in pairs. Elements of Extreme Programming are presented in the methodology discussed in this chapter, since they have been demonstrated to be effective in the web development effort.

Each step has a deliverable or set of deliverables that provide a basis for the efforts that will take place later in the project. For a software effort, deliverables are generally documentation or code. The scope generally results in a document summarizing the owner's expectations and an estimate for delivering a solution that meets those expectations. The requirements gathering process will result in a functional specification that describes the way the product should work and look. The technical design step results in a technical specification document. Development and coding will result in a unit-tested group of files that meets the requirements of the technical specification and an install program for the solution. The test product step will result in a document that indicates that the code effort produced a solution that meets the needs described in the functional specification. Finally, the deployment step should result in an invoice, an announcement to the user base, and product instructions.

Note	*Samples of the documents described in this chapter are available on the author's web site as mentioned in the book's Introduction.*

The passing of deliverables among steps and teams in the software project is often the cause of great strife among the collaborating parties. A project's success is often dependent on the effective collaboration of sales, marketing, business analysts, and software engineers. Given the diverse background of these types of professionals, collaboration is often difficult to obtain. An effective strategy for producing greater synergy among professionals is to challenge all involved to act as though they are always serving the needs of an owner in the course of producing the deliverables. The measure of their performance is based on the satisfaction of the owner they serve.

For the software project team, their teammates are their "customers." For example, if the functional specification does not make the desired outcome clear to the software engineer reading it, the business analyst should improve the document rather than suggest that the software engineer is not astute enough to understand the document. If the installation of the software cannot be performed properly after it is coded, the developer who wrote the installation program or script should improve it so that the systems personnel can install the software without failure. In this way, the developer is the business analyst's customer and the systems personnel are the developer's customer. The responsibility for the recipient effectively utilizing the deliverable should be the measure of a professional's effectiveness to the team. If their "customers" love their product then they are performing effectively. If this culture is established immediately in a software project, success will be more likely regardless of the interpersonal skills of the members on the team.

Another source of strife among parties involved in a software production process is the length of time it takes to produce the product. Typically, the longer it takes to produce a project, the more functionality and software is produced. The original requirements will likely change over time, so reducing the time of delivery will tend to reduce the likelihood that the owner's requirements will change and increase owner satisfaction. It will also reduce the stress among a software development team, because the total burden in moving or managing a single given effort is much smaller.

One might argue, however, that the owner sets the requirements rather than the development team. Attempting to reduce the length of time needed to deliver a solution can be satisfied only by reducing scope or increasing the labor supporting the effort. Clearly, the owner must set the requirements, so choosing not to deliver required functionality does not please the owner. The best way to manage this problem is to reduce scope but not the overall scope of the solution—that is, the project should be broken up into smaller projects. You still may not be able to complete the project within the time frame the owner desires, but you will be able to provide the owner with a plan for everything they want. According to the Unified Process, these smaller projects are called *iterations*. When all of the iterations are completed, the final project is delivered. Producing a project with several iterations, rather than a few, is the preferred manner in which a project should be executed. One big effort to deliver a piece of software is always more difficult and poses more risk than a series of small efforts that result in the same piece of software.

Define Project Scope

The goal of the scope process is to get the owner to commit to providing resources to fund the solution. A proposal for a solution is presented to the owner, and if successful, the owner is obligated to provide the resources needed to build the solution. A proposal consists of the following:

- A brief statement of work
- A qualified schedule for delivery

Because there is no assurance that the potential owner will agree to fund the entire effort, the project manager must define what's appropriate to include in the proposal. The effort applied to preparing the proposal should be consistent with the relationship that your organization has with the potential owner. For example, the potential owner told the account manager that they are willing to accept the proposal if particular information is included. In this case, great effort should be made to ensure that the proposal meets the owner's expectations, because the chances are quite high that the owner will accept it. In another situation, you may have little or no insight into the owner's motives regarding the proposal and, therefore, devoting a great deal of effort to producing the proposal is more likely to be a waste of time—especially if there are many competitors proposing solutions.

You should also consider the risk of obligating your organization when all of the facts are not clearly known. If no opportunity exists to revise the schedule after the requirements gathering has been performed, than certain efforts performed in the *define functionality* step should be performed in the *scope* step. The owner should be made aware of the qualifications that shroud the proposal and understand that functionality beyond the qualifications will add to the expense and execution time of the effort.

After an account manager produces the statement of work, development produces a qualified estimate based on the statement of work. Next, the project manager assembles a plan to determine whether the work can be performed, when it can be completed, and date constraints, deliverables, and milestones.

After being presented with the proposal, the owner will hopefully agree to the terms in writing. Then the next step of the process begins—defining functionality. Table 18-1 summarizes the deliverables in the scope step and the party responsible for their production.

Statement of Work

At the beginning of many software solution engagements, an owner has some ideal that is presented to an organization that will create the solution. Alternatively, an account manager could approach an owner to determine whether new work could be contracted. In any case, either the owner or the account manager defines the outcome of the work, which is set as the statement of work. The statement of work could be described in a 15-minute phone conversation, written on a couple sheets of paper, or summarized in a 15-word sentence. The following represents a sample statement of work:

Sample Statement of Work

The owner wants a web site that will allow a manager to post a recipe to a web site. The employees under the manager need to be able to post comments about the recipe. Everyone can read the comments for a recipe posted by their respective manager.

Owner needs a host for the application.

They want it in three weeks to meet a 22 June date for beer brewing trade show.

Execution Order	Deliverable	Responsible Party
1	Description of owner's expectations - statement of work	Account manager
2	Qualified estimate for scope	Development
3	Qualified project plan for scope	Project manager
4	Owner acceptance of the scope and proposed delivery date	Project manager

Table 18-1.   *Summary of Deliverables for the Scope Step*

Scope Estimate

The goal of a scope estimate is to produce a qualified basis for the development time that may be necessary for completing a project. Development creates a scope estimate to inform the team the development resources required from a technical perspective. The qualifications in the estimate serve to offer the team more information about what the development staff thinks the owner wants. Qualifications also cover the points that should be understood about the product or how it will be delivered to the owner. Many programmers consider the effort of providing a scope estimate risky and difficult, since the known requirements are undefined at this point. Clearly, the sample statement of work shown previously is vague, and the solution could require three weeks of work or three years of work, depending on the exact requirements of the project.

An effective strategy for producing a scope estimate is to identify all of the deliverables that are necessary for producing the solution. After the deliverables are identified, they should be qualified in terms of the assumptions surrounding their production and the risks associated with production. The deliverables should also be identified to the extent possible in terms of the scoped requirements they fulfill. The team participating in the estimate may view a developer's qualifications in an estimate as a counterproductive effort that the developers use to protect themselves. Qualifications should be viewed as the initial framework for how the solution can function. Likewise, developers should qualify the estimate as much as possible to communicate to the team the issues they believe will affect the resources required to produce the solution. In Figure 18-2, the sample statement of work document was used as the basis for a web site that maintains beer-brewing recipes in a local brewer's supply store.

Scope Project Plan

To help reduce the risk of an owner building impossible expectations, a qualified scope project plan should be produced. The scope project plan at this point should be an overview of the steps of the unified process with the dates based on the project starting date and the development estimate for the deliverables. Milestones for the owner's participation should also be included, such as dates that the owner must provide feedback or acceptance of parts of the project. Figure 18-3 shows a sample project plan Gantt chart. (If you're not familiar with Gantt charts, see the following sidebar.)

What Is a Gantt Chart?

Predicting the future is complicated. You have to figure out what tasks need to be performed and who should perform them. You also have to consider the dependencies for completing tasks. For example, you cannot back a car out of the garage until you open the garage door.

The Gantt chart is designed to graphically display the following:

- The tasks in a project
- Who is responsible for completing the tasks
- The dependencies tasks have on other tasks or events
- The dates expected for completion of the tasks

The Gantt chart is useful for showing your prediction of the future. Although a Gantt chart may not help you see the future exactly, it does make your predictions easier for others to visualize.

Gantt charts may be built using project management software. Microsoft Project is the most popular software tool used for this purpose, but other tools like Visio can also be used. The chart shown in Figure 18-3 was prepared using Microsoft Project.

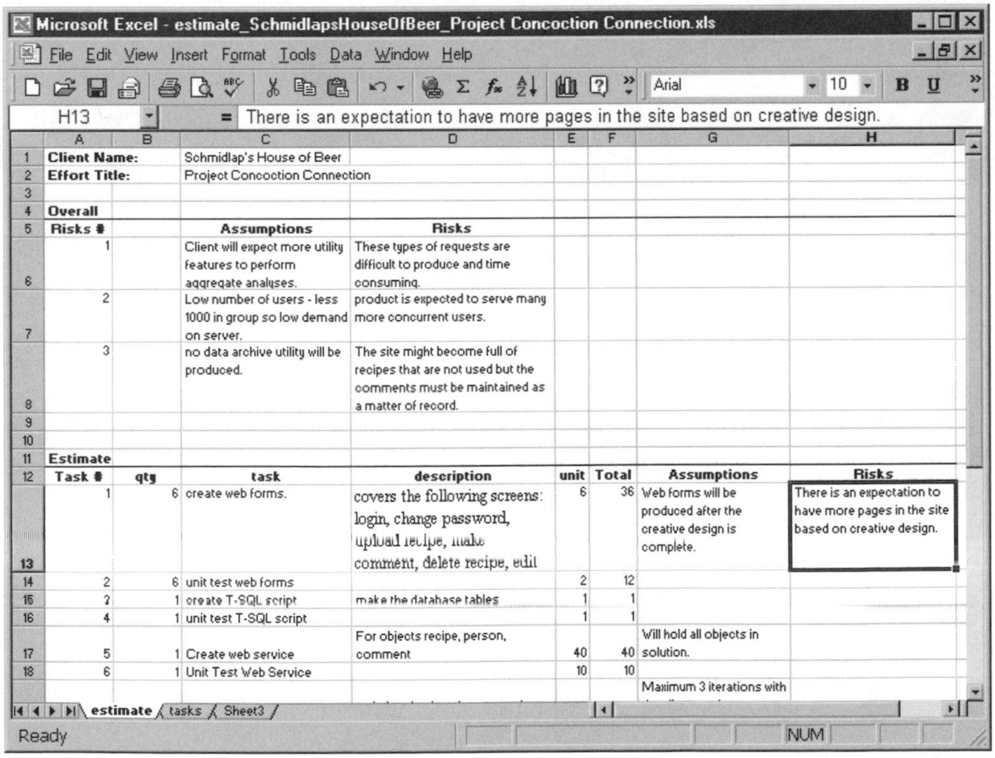

Figure 18-2.   *Spreadsheet example of a scope estimate*

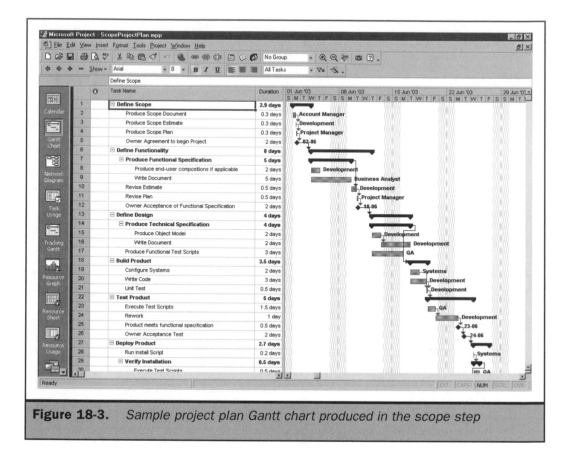

Figure 18-3. *Sample project plan Gantt chart produced in the scope step*

The scope project plan also serves an important role in providing an initial understanding as to the size of the work. If the scope estimate's assumptions were correct and the plan demonstrated that the work could not physically be performed within the required time frame, an alternative strategy would have to be adopted that might require the owner to accept an alternative scope, a phased approach to the delivery of the solution by increasing the iterations, or an alternative design to be pursued by the development staff.

When the plan and all proposal related materials are completed, the proposal can be assembled and delivered to the owner. If the owner accepts the proposal, the project will likely be tuned over to the project manager to complete. If the owner does not accept the proposal, the account manager may have to present other versions of the scope document and the project plan.

Define Functionality

The goal of defining the functionality is to determine enough detail from the owner's perspective to define a successful outcome for the solution. Following are the goals of the define functionality step:

- Determine the way the desired solution should exist and function so that a developer with limited expertise could produce a solution without having to ask the owner any further questions or seek further clarification.

- Establish an expectation with the owner as to what will be received from the effort in terms of how the solution will exist and function on delivery and when it will be delivered.

- Reestablish an estimate for the amount of work that needs to be completed and the expected delivery date for the solution.

- Obtain the owner's acceptance of how the solution will exist and function on delivery and when it will be delivered.

As described previously, the way a solution exists and functions is the functional requirement for the solution. Since the interpretation of the phrase "the way a solution exists and functions" is given to great creative license, you need to narrow the scope of the functionality to the context of the solution. Asking the owner the following questions should help provide answers to clarify the functional requirements relative to a web-based solution:

- *How will the solution be hosted?* The solution might need to be hosted at the owner's site or on a third-party's site. The platform (operating system, web server, or other portal enhancement product) might already be chosen or required for use with the solution that needs to be produced. If the owner does not know the answers to this question, then you have to make a recommendation.

- *What clients need to be served?* Web-based solutions do not always support a web browser client. Other means may be necessary to support software solutions that are located elsewhere on the Internet with data that requires processing prior to consumption by an end user. You must identify all of the consumers of data and functionality.

- *What does the solution need?* Web-based solutions might also service other servers elsewhere on the Internet. The solution might be expected to obtain data from another system prior to processing the data. You must identify all of the providers of data and functionality.

- *Who interacts with the system?* The end users should be examined in terms of what they do to the solution and what they need from the solution. What are the roles that exist in the workflow and what responsibilities are associated with the roles?

- *What real-world entities can be represented in the solution?* The object model of the solution must be discovered and documented. The objects in the system and their attributes need to be defined and modeled in total abstraction to the technical constraints of the system. A good strategy is to identify all of the nouns that are used to describe what the solution should do.

- *What does the solution need to do?* Ultimately, the software must do something to data prior to delivering it to a client. The objects identified must have their interactions modeled and documented. After identifying objects in a system by nouns used to describe the system, identifying the verbs in a system can help lead to the understanding of how the objects must interact with each other and thereby describe what actions the objects perform.

In the course of defining the way the solution exists and functions, a great deal of information will be communicated to the owner. Often, the owner is not aware of exactly what they want. The requirements gathering effort is a great opportunity for communicating expectations to the owner by allowing them to arrive at the conclusions themselves. Through the effort of defining the solution, the owner discovers the deliverables and the resources needed to fulfill the solution.

The solution should be documented as it is being defined, in terms of what the owner expects as the outcome. This document is called the *functional specification*. After the functional specification is complete, the estimate should be reexamined and revised if needed based on the functional specification.

A project plan with milestones and project dates should be specified as part of the functional specification. The owner should be able to review the functional specification and the estimate with the understanding that the work cannot begin until the owner indicates approval, in writing, of the functionality described in the specification. Table 18-2 summarizes the deliverables required for the define functionality step.

Functional Specification

The functional specification describes the expected outcome from the owner's perspective. This specification is a prerequisite to the technical design and the test scripts, and it serves to define for the owner what will be delivered. It should describe what the solution should do. Owner-visible deliverables should be itemized and described so that a developer with limited expertise could produce the solution without having to ask the owner any further questions or without seeking further clarification. The functional specification should be written from a technically abstracted perspective and should not contain technical instructions for producing the solution. The functional

Execution Order	Deliverable	Responsible Party
1	Functional specification	Business analyst
2	Qualified estimate for functional requirements	Development
3	Qualified project plan for functional requirements	Project manager
4	Owner acceptance of the defined functional requirements and delivery dates in plan	Project manager

Table 18-2. *Summary of Deliverables for the Define Functionality Step*

specification also should not contain information about functionality not required by the client, except to describe functionality that is out of scope.

The functional specification, which should be less than 30 pages in length, should provide the following elements:

- Identification of every functional requirement so that development and QA can reference parts of the specification in the technical specification and test scripts
- Pictures or diagrams for each screen that is referenced or presented to the end user
- Change control record
- Table of contents
- Cover page with owner name and project name
- Footer with your company name, confidential info, and print date
- Identification of the project with a memorable name

A good way to make each item in a functional specification uniquely identifiable is to number all prose that describes how each part should work. This method works well for describing subordination of functional specifications. Figure 18-4 shows an example of prose in a document that uses hierarchical numbering to identify functional specifications.

Making your functional specification 30 pages or less is recommended because it is generally a size that team members can readily review prior to planning and designing. Creating your specification to adhere to an arbitrary size requirement may seem ridiculous. After all, stuffing an elephant into a shoebox will not be possible just because you say that it should. If your set of functional requirements requires more than 30 pages to describe, don't truncate it but, rather, create more than one functional specification so

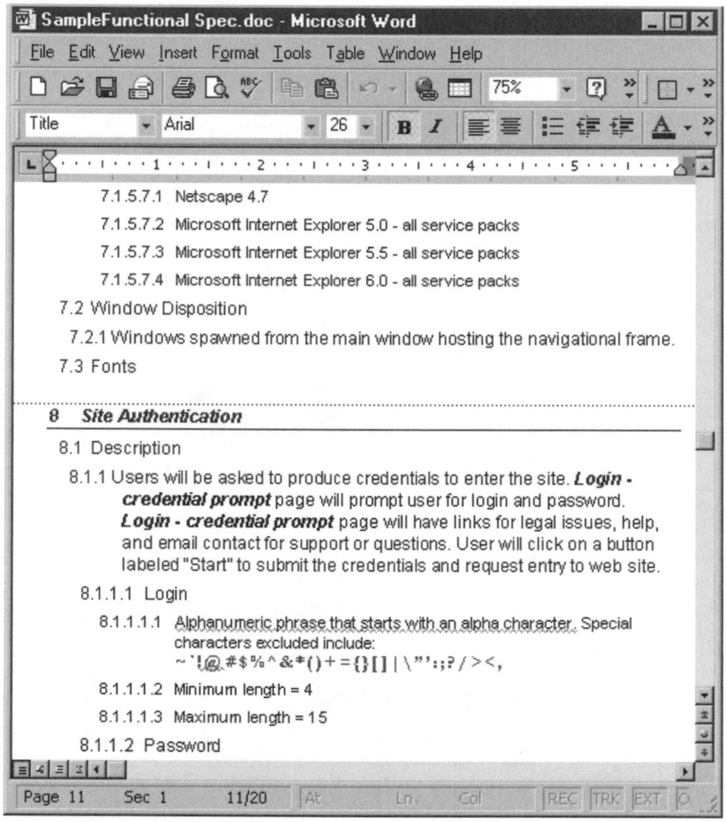

Figure 18-4. Uniquely identified functional requirements using hierarchical numbering

that all of the functional requirements are defined. By having multiple small functional specifications as opposed to a single large functional specification, you are instilling more iterations in your project. The functional specification could be considered the scope of the iterations. The functional specification defines an atomic piece of the project that the owner should be able to relate to or understand.

Development always responds to the functional requirements. By having more iterations of the project, you reduce the length of your development cycle, and shorter development cycles reduce the chance that development will build the solution incorrectly. More iterations for a project also creates more deliverables for the owner to see. An owner typically will have greater satisfaction seeing many positive developments in their project over a given period of time versus a single delivery of the solution. Delivering a project in multiple iterations will also keep the owner occupied with positive project events. If you always deliver functionality when you speak to the owner, you are setting the project's agenda. When a project produces deliverables that the owner cannot see or understand, or if the deliverables occur after long periods of time, the owner tends to speculate negatively about the project's progress.

The front page of the functional specification should convey enough information to tell someone whether or not they need to open and read the document. The owner name, project name, change control section, footer section, and table of contents should all be placed on the cover page of the specification. The owner name and project name clearly indicate the project's origins. The footer section tells the reader which company produced the document, when it was printed, and the fact that this is a confidential document.

The confidential statement has a legitimate legal function if the document is provided to another organization that does not have permission to view the document. When a contract for services is arranged with a software company, the owner is usually asked to honor a nondisclosure agreement that forbids the owner from providing the materials that they receive in the course of the contract execution to another organization. By marking the documents confidential, all recipients may assume some legal responsibility by reading the document if they are not legally entitled. The owner should exercise great care with the distribution of the document and the recipient should understand the confidentiality requirements before reading the document.

A change control section on the front cover should identify the date, an incremented version number, summarized changes made to the document, and who made the change. For an example of a functional specification cover page, see Figure 18-5.

Note *Many word processors such as Microsoft Word or WordPerfect offer a feature to generate a table of contents automatically. It is important that predefined styles be used for the text so that the table of contents generator works properly. For example, the table of contents shown in Figure 18-5 was produced from all Heading 1 and Heading 2 styles. A mistake that many specification authors make is to write an entire document using a word processor and ignore the use of its formatting capabilities.*

Note *The Word document used for the sample functional specification is available with the source code on the author's web site.*

Developing a functional specification template or common outline is a good way to maintain a consistent approach that will enable all the consumers of the document to know where to look for certain pieces of information based on their knowledge of the last functional specification they examined. The danger in this approach, however, is that you may be destined to make the same failures over and over again.

The best means for striking a balance among the objectives of consistency and providing documentation that meets the needs of the organization is to focus on the *spirit* of the document's purpose. The template is the default setting, and you should stray from it as required to make the document best describe how the solution should

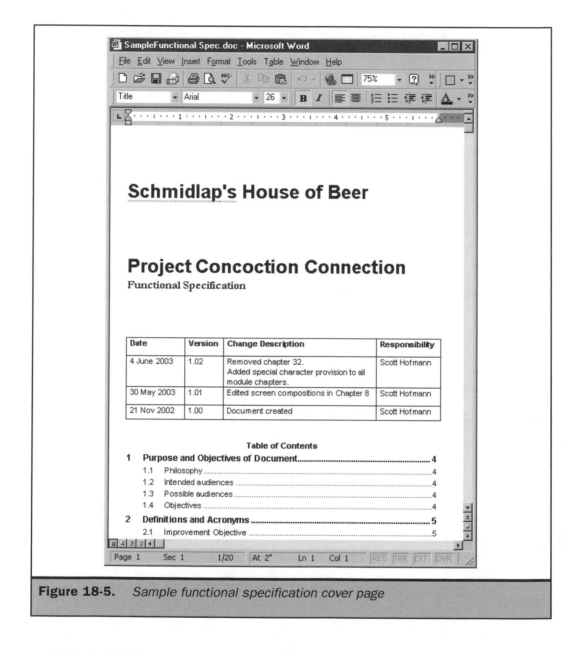

Figure 18-5. *Sample functional specification cover page*

work. If you find that the document template must be changed in the same way for each project, alter the document template. A good outline for the functional specification follows.

Definitions and Acronyms

■ Define any potentially confusing terms that are used in this document or in the owner's industry.

■ Define acronyms used throughout the document or in the owner's industry.

This section is helpful in defining terms to avoid confusion and misunderstanding, and it's also useful for establishing a project nomenclature. Names will be used consistently to describe an entity to prevent using multiple terms to refer to the same entity or concept.

Functional Objectives

■ List all features of the site (avoid too much detail in this section).

■ List what should be delivered in business terms.

This section is meant to serve as a summary of what the solution will do in terms of the owner. This section is useful for establishing brief terms to represent types of functionality in a given solution that are consistently used by all of the participants in the project. This section should strongly resemble the items identified in the scope document.

Out of Scope

■ List features that normally belong in the functional objectives section but were removed from the solution.

■ List features that normally are included in a solution but will not be included in this solution.

■ List features that seem like they ought to be in this solution.

■ List features that are not included in this phase of the solution but will appear in a future phase.

This section is the opposite of the functional objectives section, because it lists the functional objectives that are not included in this solution. This section helps to manage the expectations of all those involved in the project so that they understand exactly what the solution won't deliver. Functional objectives cited in the previous section may imply certain things to certain readers. If the reader does not perform a comprehensive examination of the entire functional specification, he or she may not understand the exact meaning of a particular functional objective.

IIS EXTRAS

Assumptions

■ State any new information that would help others understand some of the solution's details that are affecting decision making.

This section allows the specification author to highlight certain situations or conditions that may have been agreed to by the owner. For example, the owner may already have contracted with a graphics art agency for the images that are to be displayed on the site. If these images do not fit in the user interface that is produced while building the solution, the firm creating them will be responsible for changing them to fit as needed.

Affected Screens

■ List all screens that are part of the solution. These screen names should be used throughout the document.

This section offers a way of naming or identifying all the screens that will be changed or created in the course of completing the solution. One of the most common errors incurred in functional specifications is that they do not make sense in terms of the site's navigational possibilities. Performing the exercise of identifying all othe screens in the beginning reduces this type of failure.

Site Style

■ Describe the look and feel (font style, browser usage, and window disposition) for the whole site.

This section is optional. Many organizations have a style guide that governs how their site must look and the behavior for responding to certain circumstances or window disposition. For example, the following guide defines a type of window disposition:

Prompting the end user for parameters for a query requires that a new web browser be spawned; otherwise, all content should appear within the same browser that hosts the site navigation. At no time should more than two browser instances remain open for any proper use of the site.

Functional Objective Sections

■ Describe the functional objectives in detail.

■ Describe how the functional objective should work from the client's perspective.

■ Describe compositions of all screens involved in the functional objective.

- Describe all possible response scenarios to intended end-user interactions.
- Describe exceptions to all possible responses to unintended end-user interactions.

For each functional objective identified in the section Functional Objectives, there should be a functional objective section. This section is devoted to describing each functional objective in detail. It describes the actual business logic for the functional objective to which it pertains, and it describes how the parts of the solution that belong to this functional objective should work from the owner's perspective. Screen flow or process flow should be defined and plotted. A composition for each screen should also be presented. The scenarios for success and failure should be defined. A common failure in functional specifications is the lack of consideration of what should happen under all success or failure events that can occur. Explicitly describing what end-user events are allowed or planned and what the expected results should be will leave little room for failure to identify functionality. For example, a matrix may be assembled that describes the event and the expected solution response to the event, as shown in Figure 18-6.

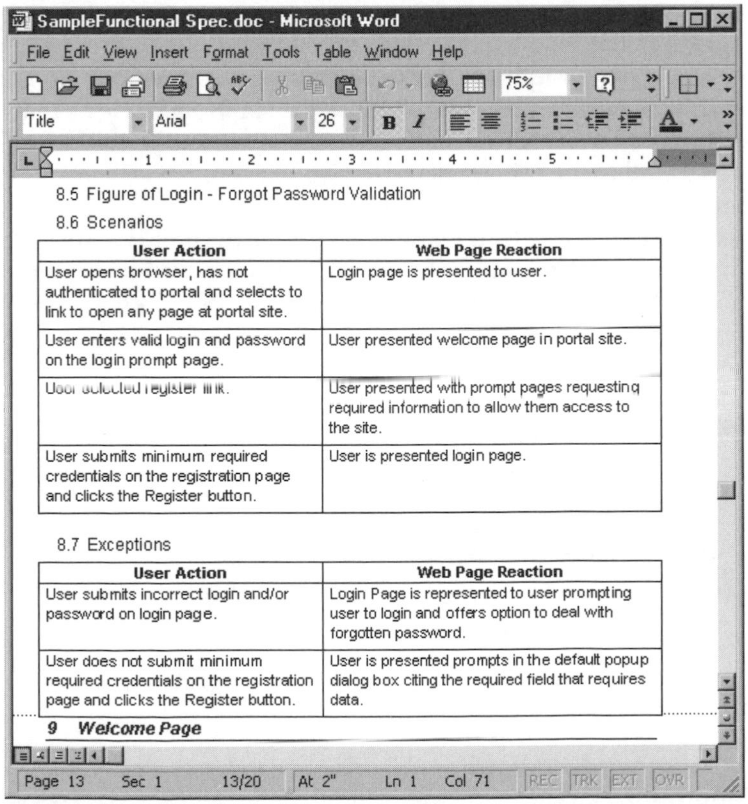

8.5 Figure of Login - Forgot Password Validation

8.6 Scenarios

User Action	Web Page Reaction
User opens browser, has not authenticated to portal and selects to link to open any page at portal site.	Login page is presented to user.
User enters valid login and password on the login prompt page.	User presented welcome page in portal site.
User selected register link.	User presented with prompt pages requesting required information to allow them access to the site.
User submits minimum required credentials on the registration page and clicks the Register button.	User is presented login page.

8.7 Exceptions

User Action	Web Page Reaction
User submits incorrect login and/or password on login page.	Login Page is represented to user prompting user to login and offers option to deal with forgotten password.
User does not submit minimum required credentials on the registration page and clicks the Register button.	User is presented prompts in the default popup dialog box citing the required field that requires data.

9 Welcome Page

Figure 18-6. *Sample functional specification scenarios and exceptions*

Appendix

- Present use cases.
- Present other useful information germane to the project functionality.

The appendix can be thought of as the place for miscellany. If you think that the material is important to the project and that it may need to be referred to by most of the team involved in the project, the material should be placed in the appendix.

Gathering Functional Requirements

To write the functional specification, the author must know the functional requirements. The author must perform a requirements gathering investigation, which involves consulting with the business analyst, who has discussed the solution's functionality with the owner. The success of the investigation is dependent on the disposition of the owner, who may be organized and available to work with the business analyst or uncooperative in providing the necessary information. The business analyst must help the owner focus only on information that is important or useful to the project and not to offer technical details for how the solution should be built.

The business analyst must parse all of the data that the owner provides and assemble a detailed functional specification that describes the solution in a way that satisfies the owner so that the development team can efficiently produce the solution. The analyst must try to identify all the requirements of the software solution, starting from the scope documents.

After the requirements are documented, the use cases of the business processes should be diagrammed using UML. Like many of the other tasks presented in this chapter, the use cases should be produced with as much detail as possible to enable the exact business process to be described. UML diagrams make the use case simple and easy for all to understand and verify.

After the business analyst is satisfied that all of the appropriate use cases have been collected, the use cases should be documented in a form or table so that they may be analyzed. The template or form for documenting a use case should include the following items:

- **Name of the use case**   Short descriptive name
- **ID of the use case**   Alphanumeric code that is unique
- **Actors**   All of the end users who participate in the use case
- **Preconditions**   How much of the environment must exist for the use case to take place
- **Flow**   What takes place during the use case
- **Post Conditions**   What is the environment like after the use case occurs

For example, a use case could be described as follows:

Name: Search Recipe
ID: UC001
Actors: User
Preconditions: User must have successfully logged on to web site.
Flow:
1. User clicks on link "Search Recipe"
2. Search Recipe screen is displayed in web browser
3. User enters keyword in search keyword dialog box that may be in their desired recipe
4. User presses Enter key
5. Screen is refreshed with results from search
6. If User observes desired recipe name
6.1. User clicks on link to observe recipe
6.2. Recipe is displayed in web browser
7. Else if User does not observe desired recipe
7.1. User enters new search criteria in search keyword dialog box
7.2. User performs search until desired recipe discovered

Post Conditions: User has desired recipe presented in web browser.

This type of analyses is extremely helpful to the design effort. It should be clear that the use case template follows the template of a code function. The Flow section of the use case is an algorithm that may become part of the software that is to be built.

After the use cases are validated by the owner and documented, they may be correlated to the requirements that the owner identified. If use cases are included that do correspond to the requirements, those use cases must either be thrown out or other requirements must be defined according to the particular use cases.

After the functional specification is complete, the estimate and plan presented in the scope step should be revised, if necessary. If changes must be made, supporting functional requirements should be identified that may contribute to the addition of time or expenditure of resources. If the owner agrees to the new schedule, it is time to move on to the next step of the project. If the owner does not agree to the revised schedule, the scope must be altered to make the solution fit the delivery requirement.

Define the Design

A *design* is an instruction for building the solution. It provides an understanding for how the solution should fit into the host and defines the tasks required to build the solution. Deliverables of the build process are also itemized in the design. The design describes what code efforts need to be performed and what configurations need to take place on the hosting platforms. In an ideal world, the design would provide enough information for a programmer to write the code necessary to build the software.

A design consists of diagrams, text, pictures, pseudo-code, or any other means necessary to convey technical specifications. The deliverables of the design step process are called a *façade*, functional test scripts, and a technical specification, as summarized in Table 18-3.

What Is a Façade?

A façade in this context is *not* an object-oriented design pattern. Instead, it could be better described as a *limited prototype* or a *creative mock-up mixed with a little reality*. The façade effort is a step that was introduced to help an owner view a solution before the final product is received. It helps to demonstrate the way that a creative mock-up described in the functional specification might appear in action in a web browser.

Designing the solution takes place after the requirements are gathered and summarized in a functional specification. This implies that the owner knows what they want and that these desires have been rendered on paper. Realistically, however, although the owner may describe what they want in the form of a document, they are likely to want something else after they see the solution begin to take shape. After the objectives in the functional specification come to life in the form of a dynamic software application that works, new requirements often come to light.

In many web-based projects, the owner's primary concern is the way the end user interacts with the software. The functional specification defines what the software should be, and it should be defined by the way it looks to the end user. The façade plays a role in the design and build process by asking the owner or business analyst to verify how they want the software to look and to function. Web portal software projects generally consist of the following deliverables:

- Data source configurations and scripts
- Binary and script code files that obtain data and apply business rules
- Script files used to apply presentation logic

Execution Order	Deliverable	Responsible Party
1	Façade	Business analyst and development
2	Technical specification	Development
3	Functional test scripts	Quality assurance

Table 18-3. *Summary of Deliverables for the Define Design Step*

Why not build the presentation logic before building anything else? As long as the solution supports abstraction from the business logic and the presentation logic, the presentation logic may be produced first. The technology that supports this abstraction is the Extensible Markup Language (XML). For the purposes of this chapter, it will be assumed that data is formatted in XML.

The collaborative effort of the business rules code and script and the data sources involved in the process builds the XML that the presentation logic needs to create the desired output. Prior to building the data source or the software that applies business rules, the developer writes a technical specification that establishes the way these items should work, including the XML they will produce. This means that the XML should be produced and be designed prior to building the software. If the XML is established prior to building the supporting software, why not validate the XML design prior to building the data source or the software that applies the business rules? The script files used to apply presentation logic must be written, and they may be written before the supporting software is written—or, they may be written after the supporting software is written. If requirements change, changing a presentation logic script file is less work than changing a compiled code business object. If the presentation logic is embodied in Extensible Stylesheet Language (XSL), XSL Transformations (XSLT), or some other presentation technology such as ASP.NET web forms, static XML documents representing the desired output for every given command to the solution may be produced and used to test the presentation logic script file.

Given the amount of work required to develop a technical specification and build the software, validating the functional specification is a valuable effort toward ensuring that the design and technical specification are valid. The façade part of the design process is performed with that goal in mind. Following are the goals of the façade portion of the design process:

- Establish the XML document for every given solution event to the portal project.

- Build the presentation logic

- Demonstrate visually to the decision makers how the product will function and verify that it is correct.

Once the façade is completed, the rest of the work of building the business rules code and the data source may be completed. The owner may also be shown the façade. Although the façade is not totally functional, it does demonstrate progress and provides reassurance to the owner. The owner/decision maker feels included in the process and accepts some responsibility for the outcome of the development effort.

The façade presentation logic files that were produced do not need to be changed in the build effort except to support other web browser versions or other client platforms. The business rules software and data source efforts, which generally require the most amount of work to produce or alter, may be built with greater confidence that the final product will meet the owner's expectations.

Produce the Façade

The effort to build the façade requires the cooperation of the players involved with defining and building the solution. The business analyst, the developer coding the presentation logic, and the developer writing the business logic or data solution will interact with one another until they are satisfied that the product is presentable to the owner. In this discussion, the developer producing the presentation logic will be referred to as the *UI developer* and the developer producing the business logic and data logic code will be referred to as the *object developer*.

The façade process begins by examining the screens required, as indicated by the functional specification and producing edge case XML. Each unique screen identified in the functional specification results in an XML document. The UI developer and the object developer work together to develop *edge case* XML documents for each screen. Edge case XML documents represent the scenarios that are specified in the functional specification. The goal of an edge case is to choose a set of test data that is likely to force the developer to code based on the worst case data and thereby produce code that is likely to be more reliable. As the edge case XML is created, the UI developer will produce functioning presentation logic code based on the edge case XML.

> **Note** *Many of the objects in .NET stream the state of an object into XML automatically. This functionality shifts the effort of defining XML to defining objects to use in the solution, which is a huge benefit since ultimately the objects producing the XML will need to be built. Specifically, ASP.NET affords many conveniences for producing XML and displaying XML. Please refer to Chapters 14 and 15 for more information about ASP.NET technologies.*

The following deliverables will be produced with any façade:

- One or more edge case XML specifications for each screen identified in the functional specification
- Presentation logic code for each screen in the functional specification

The UI developer performs most of the work directly related to this stage of the façade effort by attempting to duplicate the desired UI specified in the functional specification. Because the business analyst has produced the functional specification by the time the façade process begins, the analyst will likely perform the least amount of work at this point. The analyst's role in the façade is to clarify issues in the specification and to revise the functional specification as needed during the process. The object developer should examine the existing solution, if it exists, for sources of the XML that hosts the objects or data being identified as required content in the edge case XML. As mentioned previously, this search could include .NET Framework classes if the .NET Framework is to be a part of the solution. If the UI developer is intimately familiar with the output XML of the existing solution, the object developer may also start laying groundwork code or performing feasibility analyses on parts of the new solution that reliably will not change after the façade review.

The façade is finished when the screens may be shown in a web browser using the edge case XML documents, although the links and ability to navigate from one façade screen to another is likely not possible. The presentation logic may also need to be tweaked prior to actual deployment.

Presenting the Façade

Presenting the façade to the owner requires the ability to display the screen in a web browser. Microsoft Internet Explorer version 5.5 and higher performs XML to HTML transformation using XSL and XSLT. Because IE is free to use and is widely used, it serves as a great platform for presenting the façade on a computer running any version of Windows. Often, the presentation of the façade would take place at the owner's established place of business, where Internet connectivity may not be easily accessible. Although the façade could be set up on a server that performs the XML and XSL/XSLT transformation, using the browser to perform the transformation always provides a sure means for allowing the owner to observe the desired output.

To get IE to perform the XML to HTML transformation using XSL or XSLT, add the processing instruction shown in Listing 18-1 at the top of the XML. The XML containing the processing instruction will be transformed using the XSL sheet named *MyXSLSheet.xsl*. If the XML originates from a web server, the specified XSL sheet must come from the same web server. In the case presented in Listing 18-1, the file *MyXSLSheet.xsl* could reside in the same file directory as the XML file itself.

Listing 18-1

```
Processing Instruction to Transform XML into HTML

<?xml version="1.0"?>
<?xml-stylesheet type="text/xsl" href="MyXSLSheet.xsl" ?>
```

The façade presentation shows the owner how the screens look in a web browser, and the transition from one page to another may be scripted or mocked up to demonstrate flow between screens. After the owner sees the façade for the first time, they usually have some suggestions or demands for change.

The façade generally results in scope change, or *scope creep*, but the scope creep is performed in a preemptive fashion because you are setting the ground for change. Scope creep is dangerous because it often occurs in the project during a time that causes great difficulty in delivering the project. Scope creep happens because the solution in the web browser looks different from that of the functional specification. Using scope creep to your advantage, the façade may also harness the owner's creative energy and desire to micromanage the design process by helping them focusing on the *requirements*. As any owner/decision maker should know, change is not without cost—that is, change

IIS EXTRAS

usually results in a new and later delivery date. If the owner is against changing delivery dates, the façade may make the case easier to sell. After all, if what the owner requested is presented in the façade, how could the development staff be blamed for delivering what was requested? If change must take place, however, the following may occur:

- Make simple changes on the current solution early on in the process.
- Up-sell more services in the immediate future on the current solution.
- Start gathering requirements for a phase 2 project.

Why Produce a Façade?

A façade is the visible representation of some structure. The façade best represents the part of design that many developers refer to as *prototyping*. Many infer that prototype efforts require additional work to determine how something should be built. The need for a prototype may also imply that the owner doesn't understand what development is trying to build, or that developers don't understand what the owner needs. The prototype can also be seen as a huge effort that requires a large amount of resources to generate something that cannot be sold. However, a façade, as presented here, differs from the prototype by offering alternative features that a prototype cannot offer.

Some owners can actually interfere with the development process by presuming that developers need to be micromanaged or that they do not understand the scope of the project. Rather than fight the owner's desire to participate in the process at various stages, the façade development strategy attempts to embrace the owner's participation for the positive benefits that can be gained from it.

Owners may doubt the developers' ability to deliver on time or within budget—and sometimes for good reason. Software projects are routinely delivered late or over budget, and many development problems are not revealed until close to the delivery date. Part of the solution for this problem entails notification of risks to delivery and making the owner aware of any problems as soon as possible. Another more predominant reason why developers' ability is questioned is because the requirements may not have been adequately identified, or the functional requirements may have been changed while the software was being built. The software developer leading the effort may erroneously conclude that the owner is aware of the consequences of these changes. The owner can blame developers if the product is seen as "flawed."

Involving the owner/decision maker throughout the process solves your problem. This does not mean that they are included in technical design; rather, owners must be included in the parts of the process that mean something to them. They want to see implementation of the items they requested. The façade offers a solution that allows the owner to be involved in the process and to have some say regarding issues that arise in the development process.

The façade presentation is generally a positive experience. Developers may demonstrate their talents by offering suggestions for alternative means of providing the desired functionality. The programmers receive validation for their work from individuals outside the development world as well as the confidence gained by knowing that they were trusted to present the façade to an owner/decision maker.

Note   *A developer should exercise caution to make suggestions that fit within the global architectural considerations of the site. In the heat of the moment, an ambitious developer may obligate the delivery of a solution that works in some cases but violates a greater constraint that is not often considered.*

Write the Technical Specification

After the façade is presented, the functional specification is changed (if required), and if the owner is satisfied with the façade, the design may be completed. The edge case XML produced in the façade effort defines the data model for the solution. The XML elements within the edge case XML specifications represent object instances serialized into XML. However, no code may exist to produce the objects that are serialized into XML. The remaining effort of the design step is to describe how to configure existing solutions or build a new solution that provides objects that may be instantiated to represent the objects identified in the façade effort so that they may be serialized into XML.

The technical specification should be detailed enough so that a programmer or team can produce the desired solution as specified. Documenting the design also tests the validity of the design by forcing the developer to reduce his or her thoughts to paper. In addition, the technical specification serves to enhance the functional specification as an as-built plan of the software. Much like the functional specification, the technical specification should provide the following elements:

- Identification of every technical requirement so that development can reference parts of the specification in correspondence
- Change control record
- Table of contents
- Cover page with owner name and project name
- Footer with your company name, confidential info, and print date
- Reference of the functional specification name, title, and version that were used to produce the technical specification

The same hierarchical numbering strategy that was used in the functional specification should be used in the technical specification. (Refer to Figure 18-4.) The front page of the technical specification should be produced in much the same way as the cover page for the functional specification.

IIS EXTRAS

Technical Specification Template

A technical specification template or common outline should be created, considering the dangers of consistency for the sake of consistency. The template is the default setting, and you should stray from it as required to make the document meet the needs of describing the design. If you find that the document template must be changed in the same way for each project, alter the document template. A good outline for the technical specification follows:

Introduction

- Summary of the Solution
- List of items that need to be built (such as scripts, components, database scripts)
- List of items or files that might be changed or edited in an existing solution
- Definitions and acronyms
- Definition of any potentially confusing terms that are used in this document or the technical environment
- Definition of acronyms used throughout the document or in the owner's industry
- Out of scope
- List of things that a developer might think they should do but that should not be done
- Assumptions

This section should set the stage regarding the circumstances surrounding the production of the specified solution. The introduction should not restate parts of the functional specification; rather, it should describe the project as though the developer were familiar with the functional specification. The danger in restating information from the functional specification is that this document is generally updated or owned by someone other than the technical specification author. The functional specification might be updated to prepare for some future enhancement to the solution. If the technical specification has information in the introduction section that was changed in the functional specification as a result of an update, the technical specification would contain incorrect information.

Object Model

- Results from façade

This section represents the actual instances that were discovered in the façade exercise. This section should offer a summary diagram for how these objects relate to one another in the real world. The purpose of this section is to document the analyses that resulted from the façade exercise and also offer the supporting basis for the class model that is created for this solution.

Class Diagram

- Description of each class's purpose
- Relationship to other classes (Inheritance, Composition, and Aggregation)
- Functions in the object (Purpose, Description of interface, Parameters, Data types)
- Initialization state settings that apply to the solution and related objects
- Pseudo-code of the functions

This section contains the code that will support the object instances described in the object model. These two sections may seem similar, but the difference is that certain classes may represent more than one object-instance. The class model offers an abstraction from real-world entities to the actual code structures that represent real-world entities.

Data Diagram

- Description of container or tables
- Description of all fields or attributes in a table or container
- Description of keys among tables

This section simply describes the data layer or how the data is stored in the system. One could think of the class diagram as the in-memory storage and the data diagram as the hardware-based storage system. This section will likely describe a database design, but it could describe files or directory items.

Unit Testing

- Description of test harness for solution
- Edge case data that should be used in unit test to validate code

This section describes what the solution must demonstrate the ability to perform if it was produced properly. It might include a test or set of tests that must be coded to test the solution and describe whether the solution ran correctly. This section should also describe the data that provides an edge case scenario for unit testing the solution. Edge case data might include dealing with strings that contain all of the special characters, such as ~ ` ! @ # $ % ^ & * ( ) _ + - { } [ ] \ | ; : ' " < > ? / . , .

Other edge case data might include a data set of bogus data that is meant to test the execution time on the largest data set that the solution was meant to encounter.

Deployment

- Deployment diagram
- Description of perquisites required in host (Libraries, Versions)
- Script for deployment (Steps that need to be performed, Order of execution, Host configuration)
- Validation that the deployment was successfully executed
- Uninstallation steps

This section describes how the solution must be rolled or moved into a production environment. The deployment diagram demonstrates the files with which classes and functions will be hosted. For example, because a solution is likely to consist of one or more DLLs, the diagram should identify existing DLLs or new DLLs that will host the classes or functions. The solution's dependencies should also be identified by version and name. Install and uninstall instructions should also be provided, along with steps for verifying that the installation worked properly.

Functional Test Scripts

Because the functional test scripts are based on the content of the functional specification, they are included as a deliverable in the design step. The test scripts document the actions that the solution must perform flawlessly to demonstrate that the solution meets the needs of the functional specification.

The functional test scripts should be documented so that an individual responsible for the development or business requirements can execute the test script. Much like the other documents associated with the solution development process, the script should include the following elements:

- Change control record
- Cover page with owner name and project name
- Footer with your company name, confidential info, and print date

The format of the test script should be a table that includes the following fields:

- **Sequence Number**   Number to uniquely identify the step in the script
- **Action Item**   Title or name of the step; a good name to use is where the action begins or the section in which the action takes place
- **User Action**   A description of the action the tester should perform on the solution
- **Inputs**   A description of what the tester does to make the solution respond
- **Expected Results**   What the solution should produce

- **Actual Results**   What the solution actually produced
- **Pass or Fail**   Boolean value indicating whether or not the test passed

Build the Solution

Building the solution generally consists of the developer writing code or scripting software configurations to meet the requirements set forth in the technical and functional specifications. As an ancillary set of steps, the developer will perform unit testing and maintain code in a form of code control. When required, end-user documentation is also produced in this step. Table 18-4 summarizes the deliverables in the design step.

When the developer writes the code, he or she should be using the technical specification and the functional specification as a guide. If problems are encountered during the coding effort that correlate to the technical design or the functional design, they should be elevated to the respective document owner—the developer for technical specification or the business analyst for the functional specification. When problems are encountered, the coding developer should always provide a specific reason for the need to alter or change a design. The developer should also always recommend a solution. This encourages ownership in the solution on the part of all those involved.

The developer's duties while coding are generally as follows:

- Write code that meets the technical specification's requirements.
- Check code into the code control storage system on a routine basis.
- Unit test the code.
- Integration test the code.

The developer writes code on his or her desktop computer. The developer should also perform unit testing on the desktop as well. The purpose of the unit test is to ensure that the functions and classes all work properly. If the solution fails, the unit test should also help the developer determine whether defects exist in the logical algorithms or whether deviations from the specification have occurred.

If the unit test is successful, the solution should be migrated to the next environment for integration testing. This type of testing validates that the solution works with the software with which the solution must collaborate. If the solution fails, the unit test

Execution Order	Deliverable	Responsible Party
1	Code	Development
2	Documentation	Development

Table 18-4.   *Summary of Deliverables for the Build the Solution Step*

IIS EXTRAS

should also help the developer determine whether defects exist in the logical algorithms or deviations from the specification have occurred.

If the solution meets the requirements of both types of testing, the solution should be migrated to a separate environment for functional testing to verify that the solution meets the requirements specified in the functional specification.

As the solution is migrated along the testing environments in the development process, the environments must be managed with great control. The following environments generally exist in a web development environment:

- Developer workstation
- Development
- QA
- Staging
- Production

The developer workstation should have the least controlled environment. The purpose of the developer workstation is to provide an environment for code production and unit testing. Developers need to perform the necessary analyses, experimentation, and diagnoses to remain knowledgeable and familiar with the technology with which they are required to work.

The development environment is a server environment that should offer a high degree of developer access to install solutions for testing. The environment should serve the needs of developers to test their solutions. Installation of dependency software should be restricted so that only the versions and types of software that exist on the production environment exist on the development environment. This environment should also have restricted access to or from the Internet. Because the development environment provides a "loose" environment, the potential for hacker abuse is high. Because performance on this environment is not important, resources should not be devoted to providing high performance.

The QA environment should be separate from the development environment so that solutions may be tested while other development efforts take place simultaneously. The primary consumer of this environment is the QA solution functional testing. The QA environment must also closely represent the environment in which the solution is expected to function. Developer access should be restricted so that only senior level developers or the QA team can install solutions. The danger in allowing too many people access is that the testing scripts become corrupted if a change takes place during a test. This environment should also be restricted from Internet access, since the environment does not host production level code. Performance on this environment is not important, so resources should not be devoted to high performance. This environment should support the same physical boundaries as the production environment. For example, if the solution must function in a distributed environment or a load balanced environment, the physical boundaries should be replicated so that the QA process can test the solution in an environment that best represents the situation that might produce a failure.

The stage environment offers an environment for testing the solution for the owner's acceptance after it has passed the functional testing. The owner is the primary consumer of the stage environment. The stage environment also can be used for the following purposes:

■ Sales and training

■ Production backup

■ Performance testing

The stage environment should be entirely restricted from developer access. The changes to the environment should be managed entirely by a member of the Systems group.

The production environment is the host for the client-visible product. The primary consumer of production is the end user. Performance of the production environment is important. The production environment should also be restricted to Systems personnel to mange the environment.

Test the Solution

After the solution passes the unit testing and integration testing, a QA team member or other professional involved in the effort will execute the functional scripts to test the solution. The purpose of this testing is to

■ Verify that the solution meets the requirements and objects described in the functional specification

■ Find defects in the solution algorithms

■ Find deviations in the solution's ability to meet the requirements

If a tester discovers any deviations or defects, the tester will stop executing the test script, record the output of the failure event, and send it to development. Depending on the severity and priority of the bug, development will make a fix to include in a patch or fix the solution at a later date in the next release. Table 18-5 summarizes the deliverables in the test step.

Execution Order	Deliverable	Responsible Party
1	Execute test script	QA
2	Bug description	Tester
3	Bug fix patch	Development

Table 18-5.   *Summary of Deliverables for the Test Step*

IIS EXTRAS

Most development organizations use a bug tracking software package to record, queue, and track bugs. A good bug tracking system supports the following features:

- Customizable e-mail notification of responsible parties
- Ability to attach screen captures or other pertinent files
- Customizable status levels
- Customizable priority levels
- Reporting capabilities to perform aggregate analyses on bug data
- Ability to scan bug data in user-defined sort orders

Usually, a solution never passes a functional test without encountering errors. Quite often, situations arise that require a decision to be made about passing the solution so that it might be rolled to the production environment. The owner or responsible authority must be provided reports from testing to decide what is the best course of action. The combination of bug reports and test script information should be made available to help support a decision that is made in full knowledge of the consequences of the action.

Deploy the Solution

The last step in the process is the deployment. In a web software solution, this usually means that a member of systems installs the software to the web server and other applicable hosts. The install should be scripted using software if possible so that systems may execute an automated install program instead of having to copy files manually to locations on the host.

A few software packages offer some ease in building an installation program executable, such as the Visual Studio .NET installation project templates, InstallShield, or Wyse. Building an installation program for deploying a web solution might seem like an excessive amount of work, but it does help to eliminate the potential of failure during an installation effort. The install program should be built as part of the solution and tested accordingly. As part of the installation, a test should be executed to verify that the solution was installed correctly so that the installer will know whether a problem occurred. The software should include an uninstall script.

Another activity that takes place and that is not always considered is the promotion and documentation of the new solution to the end users. This effort may require strict adherence to a release date, and the deployment may be required to occur exactly on the date without failure.

After the Project Completion

After the project is completed, analyses should be performed to determine how the process methodology served the organization. The process presented in this chapter was the result of this type of analyses in the course of producing web portal software. For example, the façade step was introduced because sales and marketing did not understand the functional specification and needed to see the screen in the web browser to understand how it functioned. The development cycles generally lasted six months, but the organization wanted the site to be enhanced more often. As a result, development shortened the cycles to three months and also discovered that they could produce the enhancements with greater reliability because there was less work to do.

Analyses should be performed to answer the following questions:

- *What were the differences between the actual and planned milestone or delivery exchange dates in the plan?* This question helps the organization optimize the estimation process that took place in the project for the next project. Drastic variances in these items might also indicate an inability to predict or measure the organization's resource.

- *Were there great differences between the amount of resources required to make deliverables versus the estimated resources?* This question helps the organization optimize the estimation process that took place in the project for the next project.

- *Was the owner satisfied with the solution?* If the owner is not pleased, some improvement in the strategy with managing owner expectations may be necessary.

- *Was the owner satisfied with the way the solution was delivered?* Deployment issues are often overlooked in the requirements gathering process. If the owner was not pleased with the delivery, some additional effort may be required to prevent this dissatisfaction with future owners.

- *What failures were encountered and why are they failures?* Are the problems anomalies or systematic and thereby indicative of a required change in process?

- *Was the project profitable?* This answer might help the business decision makers decide to pursue these types of projects in the future.

- *Are there opportunities to capitalize on the solution that were built in an effort to sell it to other organizations?* Many time and materials software companies found their niche in the product market by asking this question. If one owner wants the solution, others might be willing to pay for it also.

- *Can a repeatable and profitable business process be observed?* If an owner keeps coming back for more work, there might be an opportunity to up-sell an automated solution to the owner to save them maintenance costs.

Note *Take care to change processes based on issues that are systematic and not just anomalies. A process is not an indication of personal success or failure, and it's unreasonable to identify a process's success as a failure simply because some situations did not execute flawlessly. To make progress under these circumstances (which can be very stressful), the process should not be changed unless the issues are observed on other occasions under other circumstances.*

Chapter 19

Bringing It All Together: Creating Your Own Web Site Using IIS

Now that we've covered all the individual components of IIS, we'll show you how to create your own web site from the ground up. We'll start with a server loaded up with WS03 and end up with a fully functional web site. The site we create will be a simple ASP site with an Access database back end in which users can input their names and other information so we can send out a monthly home brewer's newsletter. Simple programming in this chapter is designed to let you see how this all interconnects.

We'll follow these steps to create our site. (Depending on the type of site you make, your steps may be different.)

1. Get a domain name.

2. Get an Internet Protocol address.

3. Set up the Domain Name System (DNS) entries.

4. Prepare the server.

5. Add the web sites to IIS.

6. Enable Active Server Pages.

7. Configure the application pool.

8. Write the code.

9. Make a database.

10. Get a certificate for the test site.

11. Get a certificate for the production site.

12. Set up web site security.

13. Test the code.

14. Roll into production.

Get a Domain Name

The first step in the process is to choose and obtain a domain name. With most domain name registrars you must first determine whether a name is available, then you can register online. While many domain names are already taken, you can still find available names—one trick is to use multiple words or dashes in the name. For example, if *beerbrewers.com* is already taken, you could choose another name, such as *beer-brewers.com, sudsbrewers.com,* or *beerbrewerz.com*. Or you can use another extension, such as *beerbrewers.org* or *beerbrewers.biz*. Some registrars have restrictions on the usage of their Top Level Domains (TLDs); you can check the registrar's web site to see if these exist.

Let's say that *beer-brewers.com* sounds good, and it's available. Now that we've chosen our domain name, we need to register it. Each registrar uses a slightly different process, so check out its web site. Most of them will need the following information:

- Name
- Address
- Phone/fax
- Technical contact information
- Administrative contact information
- Username and password for registration site
- Name and IP address of the DNS (Domain Name Service) server that will host the records
- Payment information

Registrars keep information only for the DNS server that will host the records for your domain; they don't hold any information about the A records in the zones you created in that domain. Therefore, you need to provide only the name of the primary and secondary DNS servers that host records for that domain. When you set this up, it's a good idea to have separate DNS servers hosting your site's records. Often, if you have a major Internet connection (at least a T1), your Internet service provider (ISP) will act as your secondary DNS server with the registrar.

Note   *As you may recall from Chapter 8, A zone is a part of the DNS domain. Typically, the term zone is used to refer to a part of the domain as it pertains to the DNS server. The term subdomain is used to describe the section of the domain that a zone handles. When only one zone exists in a domain, either term can be used. An A record is a DNS Address record. This record type is used to identify a host resource record. It maps a DNS domain name to an IPv4, 32-bit address.*

Get an IP Address

Our next step is to obtain two IP addresses from our ISP (or choose from the block of addresses you already have available). Then we can assign the two addresses to the server: one IP address for the test site, and the other IP address for the production site. It's important that you get static IP addresses that won't change, because changing IPs will cause the web site to be inaccessible until the DNS is updated.

After we have our static IP addresses, we can then assign them to the server:

1. In the Control Panel, open Network Connections.
2. Double-click the connection that will use this IP address. Depending on your machine, you may have one or more connections listed here.
3. In the Status dialog box that pops up, click on the Properties button.
4. The Properties window for this connection will pop up. In the Properties window, select Internet Protocol (TCP/IP), and then click Properties.

IIS EXTRAS

5. Click the Advanced button in the Internet Protocol (TCP/IP) Properties window that pops up to access the Advanced TCP/IP Settings window.

6. In the IP Addresses section of the IP Settings tab (the default), click the Add button.

7. Type in the IP address and subnet mask for the test site in the TCP/IP Address window, and then click Add.

8. Repeat steps 6 and 7 to add the IP address for the production site.

9. Add the default gateway for this connection if it's not already there.

10. Click OK twice, and then click Close.

You can assign multiple IP addresses to a single interface. Now that the IPs are assigned, remember them, because we'll use them again later.

Note   *If you're asking, "What about host headers? Don't they allow us to use multiple web sites on a server?" that's a good question. Normally, we would want to use host headers, because they save IP addresses. Unfortunately, however, the Secure Socket Layer (SSL) protocol and host headers don't get along very well. Since the header information is encrypted in the SSL transmission, it's tough to decrypt that way. So our workaround is to use another IP address.*

Set Up DNS

Now that we have registered our domain name, we need to create a zone and set up the DNS records for our server. Let's use the Microsoft DNS server that comes with WS03 for this. (Refer to Chapter 8 for instructions on installing DNS server.)

To create a forward lookup zone:

1. Open the DNS MMC by choosing Start | Administrative Tools | DNS.

2. Right-click Forward Lookup Zones, and choose Select New Zone.

3. The New Zone Wizard pops up. Click Next.

4. We want to create a primary zone, so choose that, and click Next.

5. Type in the zone name (**beer-brewers.com**). Since our DNS server isn't a domain controller, we won't be storing it in Active Directory.

6. The default zone filename is OK, so click Next.

7. Choose whether or not you want to allow dynamic updates. It's not important to update our records dynamically because they will change infrequently. Choose not to allow dynamic updates, and then click Next.

8. Click Finish.

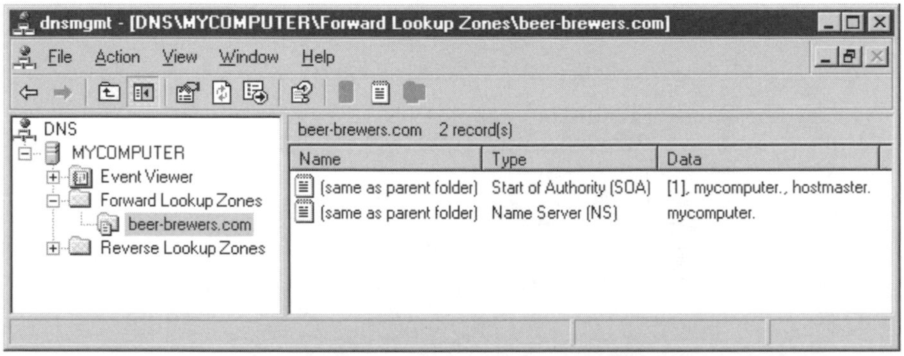

Figure 19-1. *Our DNS zone*

Now that we have a forward lookup zone, let's create our DNS records. As you can see from Figure 19-1, the Start of Authority (SOA) and Name Server (NS) records are already populated. What we need are a couple of A records so people can access *www.beer-brewers.com* and *test.beer-brewers.com*.

1. Right-click the beer-brewers.com zone in the left pane, and choose New Host (A).

2. The name of our host is "www," since that's what everyone uses on the web. Type in **www** in the name field, as shown in Figure 19-2.

3. Type in the IP address for this site—this is the IP address that is assigned to the server hosting IIS, which we chose previously. We will also assign this same IP address to the web site. For the WWW record, use the production IP address.

4. We won't create a Pointer Resource Record (PTR) for this record, since we aren't hosting the reverse lookup zone for this IP block. We can send the IP address and PTR record name to our ISP to add a reverse zone entry later.

5. Click Add Host.

6. Click Done.

7. Repeat these steps to create another A record for the test site. The Name of the Host Record for the test site will be "test."

We now have created an A record in our zone that allows clients to use www as a host name. From now on, when people type in *http://www.beer-brewers.com* in their browser window, they'll connect to our DNS server, which uses the IP address associated with that URL.

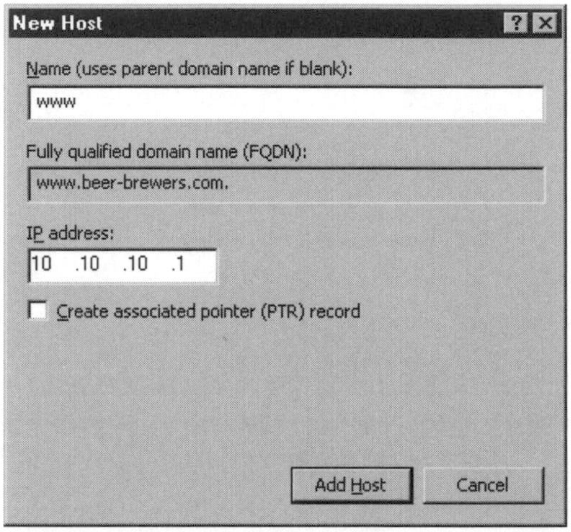

Figure 19-2. *The New Host window for the www.beer-brewers.com zone*

Prepare the Server

Now we'll prepare the server for the web site. This involves the following:

- Checking server hardening
- Setting up the directory for the web site
- Securing the NT File System (NTFS) permissions for the site

Checking Server Hardening

When your server is exposed to the Internet, it's important that it is secured. Chapter 6 details how to develop a security methodology. For this server, we'll use a basic security checklist. Use this list as a template for a basic security checklist:

- Are all the appropriate operating system and application patches installed, especially security patches?
- Is auditing enabled on this server in the local security policy?
- Do all the accounts on this server have difficult passwords?
- Did you enable only the options you needed in IIS?
- Are you using NTFS, and are the permissions secure?
- Are you using elevated privileges for any components?
- Is there a process in place to evaluate and update the security on this server continually?

Setting Up the Directory for the Web Site

By default, IIS is installed to the *C:\Inetpub* directory. You will probably want to separate the operating system files from the application files installed on your machine. When you create a web site, you can put it on another drive, such as D:, or you can create a Web Site folder on the E: drive, and place the web site files there. That way, you can secure that folder and the permissions will propagate. Additionally, any upgrades, formatting, or loss of the C: drive won't affect the data stored on the D: or E: drive.

Securing the NTFS Permissions for the Site

When you create and format a new drive with an NTFS, it has the following permissions:

Security Principal	Permissions
Local Administrators Group	Full control
SYSTEM	Full control
CREATOR OWNER	Full control
Users	Read & execute, create folders / append data, create files / write data
Everyone	Read & execute

These permissions may be more than you want to allow for your web site. In addition, the Internet Guest Account doesn't have any easily controllable rights to this folder (just what it gets from Everyone and Users). While it's not the best practice to assign resources directly to a specific account, you do want to have more control over what the anonymous account sees than what permissions for the Everyone and Users groups can offer. The answer is to create a local group, assign the NTFS rights to that group, and put the anonymous user into that group. That way, if you want to grant permissions to another user account, you can just add it to this group.

Here's how to set up a folder with permissions:

1. Open the Computer Management MMC by choosing Start | Administrative Tools | Computer Management.

2. Expand Local Users and Groups.

3. Click the Groups container.

4. Create a new group by choosing Action | New Group. The New Group window will appear.

5. Call the Group Name *Anonymous Access for BeerBrewers Site*. That is acceptable for the description as well, as shown in Figure 19-3.

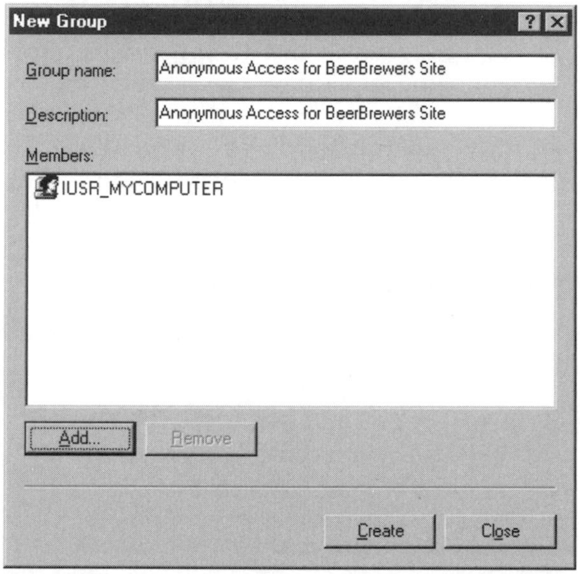

Figure 19-3.   *Anonymous Access for BeerBrewers Site group*

6. Add the Internet Guest Account to that site by clicking the Add button and typing in the name of the Internet Guest Account in the Select Users window. As we learned in Chapter 2, this account is created when IIS is installed and is named IUSR_*computername*. In this example, the account is called IUSR_MYCOMPUTER.

7. Click OK to add the account to the Members of the group.

8. Click Create to finish creating the group and then click Close to close the New Group window.

Once you've created the group, you can add that group to the security permissions of the folder in which the web site will reside. Since this is a brand-new site, first we need to create the folder.

1. Create the appropriate folder on the E: drive using Windows Explorer. Let's name it *BeerBrewers Site*.

2. Open the Properties window for that folder by right-clicking the folder and choosing Properties.

3. Go to the security tab for that folder, as shown in Figure 19-4. The first thing we need to do is remove the permissions inheritance, which is done by clicking the

Advanced button and removing the check mark from the Allow Inheritable Permisions From The Parent To Propagate To This Object And All Child Objects box.

4. When you uncheck the box, a Security dialog box will open, asking you to copy or remove the permissions. Click the Copy button to copy the permissions.

5. Click OK to get out of the Advanced Security Settings window.

6. Remove Creator Owner and Users objects from the Group Or User Names list by clicking the name, and then clicking the Remove button.

7. Our Anonymous group will have Read & Execute, List Folder Contents, and Read permissions by default, as shown in Figure 19-4. That is acceptable for our site.

We have created a folder that Administrators and the Operating System have rights to manage, but anyone else has read and execute rights. Repeat the second section (steps 1-7) to make a development area for the development web site called "BeerBrewers Test Site." You can use the same group for permissions—in fact, it's better that way.

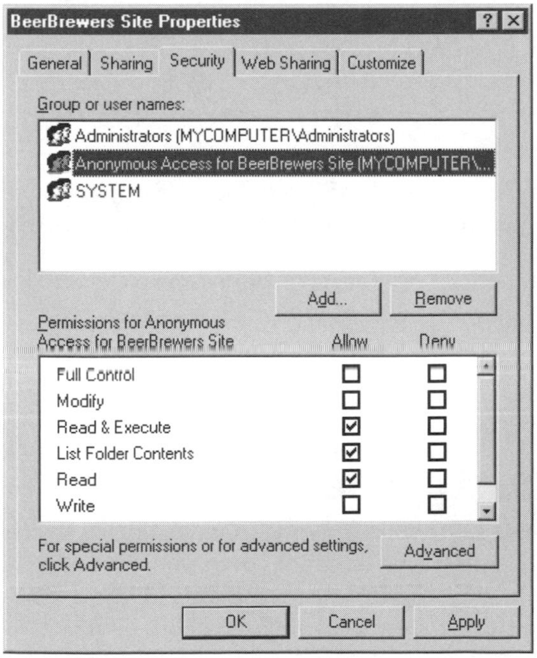

Figure 19-4.   *The Security tab of the Site Properties window*

IIS EXTRAS

Add the Web Sites to IIS

Next we'll create a test site on this server. It's important that you have a place to test the code before releasing it into production. The test site will reside on the same server, in the directory we just created.

1. In the IIS MMC, highlight Web Sites.
2. Choose Action | New | Web Site.
3. The Web Site Creation Wizard will open. Click Next.
4. Type in the description (**beer-brewers.com test site**).
5. Click Next.
6. In the IP addresses and Port Settings window, choose the IP address in the drop-down field.
7. Click Next.
8. In the Web Site Home Directory window, browse to the test site folder, and select it.
9. Click Next twice, and then click Finish.

Repeat these steps to create the production web site.

Enable ASP

When a web server is first installed, ASP is turned off as part of Microsoft's "Off By Default" mentality. Therefore, we're going to need to enable ASP for our web server.

1. In the IIS MMC, click Web Service Extensions to expand the folder.
2. Highlight Active Server Pages, and then click Allow.

Simple enough. Now ASP is enabled for all the web sites on this server.

Configure the Application Pool

Now that we have created our sites, it's time to make an application pool. The test site won't have much traffic, so it can stay in its own pool. We will make an application pool for the production site, however. At the moment, there's no great need for an application pool, since our site is just an ASP form, but as it grows and we start to use more complex components, such as an ActiveX DLL or two, the need to recycle worker processes grows. This also separates the process for our production site from all the other sites.

To create an application pool for our site:

1. In the IIS MMC, highlight Application Pools.
2. Choose Action | New | Application Pool.
3. In the Add New Application Pool window, type in the name of the application pool (**beer-brewers app pool**).
4. Click OK.

For now, the default settings for this application pool are fine. Now we need to assign this application pool to the site:

1. In the IIS MMC, highlight the production site.
2. Choose Action | Properties.
3. In the Web Site Properties window, open the Home Directory tab.
4. Choose the new application pool in the Application Pool drop-down list.
5. Click OK.

Make the Code

This code will create a simple web site with a default page and a menu at the top with three links: Home, About Us, and the registration page. The registration page will have a form to fill out, which will submit information to a database so we can send out the monthly newsletter. This site will have six files, as detailed in Figure 19-5.

Here is the sample code for each of the files.

Default.htm

```
<HTML>
 <HEAD>
   <TITLE>
     Beer Brewers Home Page
   </TITLE>
 </HEAD>
<frameset rows="60,*">
  <frame name="banner" scrolling="no" noresize target="main" src="top.htm">
    <frame name="main" src="about:blank">
  </frameset>
  <noframes>
<BODY>
<p>This page uses frames, but your browser doesn't support them.</p>
</BODY>
  </noframes>
</HTML>
```

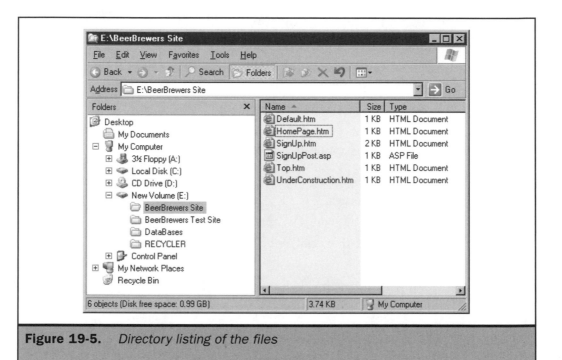

Figure 19-5. *Directory listing of the files*

HomePage.htm

```
<HTML>
 <HEAD>
   <TITLE>
     Beer Brewer's Home Page
   </TITLE>
 </HEAD>
<BODY>
Welcome to the Beer Brewer's site.  Please sign up for the newsletter.
</BODY>
</HTML>
```

SignUp.htm

```
<HTML>
 <HEAD>
   <TITLE>
```

```
      Sign up for the newsletter!
    </TITLE>
  </HEAD>
<BODY>
This form will sign you up to receive the Beer-Brewers.com newsletter.
You can get the newsletter by email and postal mail.<br>
<form METHOD="POST" target="main"
ACTION="https://www.beer-brewers.com/SignUpPost.asp">
  <table BORDER="0">
    <tr>
      <td><b>First Name</b></td>
      <td><input TYPE="TEXT" NAME="FirstName" SIZE="50">
    </tr>
    <tr>
      <td><b>Last Name</b></td>
      <td><input TYPE="TEXT" NAME="LastName" SIZE="50">
    </tr>
    <tr>
      <td><b>Street Address</b></td>
      <td><input TYPE="TEXT" NAME="Address" SIZE="50">
    </tr>
    <tr>
      <td><b>City</b></td>
      <td><input TYPE="TEXT" NAME="City" SIZE="50">
    </tr>
    <tr>
      <td><b>State</b></td>
      <td><input TYPE="TEXT" NAME="State" SIZE="50">
    </tr>
    <tr>
      <td><b>Zip Code</b></td>
      <td><input TYPE="TEXT" NAME="Zip" SIZE="50">
    </tr>
    <tr>
      <td><b>Country</b></td>
      <td><input TYPE="TEXT" NAME="Country" SIZE="50">
    </tr>
    <tr>
      <td><b>Email Address</b></td>
      <td><input TYPE="TEXT" NAME="Email" SIZE="50">
    </tr>
  </table>
  <br>
  <input TYPE="Submit" value="Submit">
</form>
</BODY>
</HTML>
```

SignUpPost.asp

```
<HTML>
 <HEAD>
   <TITLE>
     Server
   </TITLE>
 </HEAD>
<BODY>
<%
' Set up and open the database using the DSN

Set conn = Server.CreateObject("ADODB.Connection")
Set rs = Server.CreateObject("ADODB.Recordset")
conn.open "DSN=BeerBrewersDSN;"
rs.open "BeerBrewersTable", conn, 2, 3

' Add a new record using all the fields in the form
  rs.addnew
  rs("FirstName") = request("FirstName")
  rs("LastName") = request("LastName")
  rs("Address") = request("Address")
  rs("City") = request("City")
  rs("State") = request("State")
  rs("Zip") = request("Zip")
  rs("Country") = request("Country")
  rs("Email") = request("Email")

' Update the records and close the connection
  rs.update
  rs.close
  conn.close

' Always close out the objects to eliminate memory leaks
SET conn = Nothing
SET rs = Nothing
%>


Your information has been updated. You will receive the newsletter in 4-6 weeks

Thanks!

</BODY>
</HTML>
```

Top.htm

```html
<html>
<body leftmargin="0" topmargin="0" marginwidth="0" marginheight="0">
  <table width="100%" height=60 border="0" cellspacing="0" cellpadding="0">
    <tr>
      <td valign="middle" align="center">
      </td>
      <td valign="middle" align="center">
        <p align="center"><a target="main" href="homepage.htm">Home</a></p>
      </td>
      <td valign="middle" align="center">
        <p align="center"><a target="main"
href="https://www.beer-brewers.com/signup.htm">Sign up for the newsletter</a></p>
      </td>
      <td valign="middle" align="center">
        <p align="center"><a target="main"
href="https://www.beer-brewers.com/NewsLetter.htm">Current Newsletter</a></p>
      </td>
      <td valign="middle" align="center">
        <p align="center"><a target="main" href="UnderConstruction.htm">About
Us</a></p>
      </td>
    </tr>
</table>
</body>
</html>
```

UnderConstruction.htm

```html
<HTML>
 <HEAD>
   <TITLE>
     Under Construction
   </TITLE>
 </HEAD>
<BODY>
  This page is under construction.  Please come back later.
</BODY>
</HTML>
```

This code applies to the production site. The data for the production and test sites is the same, except for the database table name and URL of the test site. One set of these files would be in the production directory, and one set would be in the test directory. The *newsletter.htm* page is just the newsletter and doesn't have any relevant code, so it's not listed here.

Make a Database

The database will hold all the information we can use to send out the newsletter. We'll need to identify all the fields we want in the database, so we can design it accordingly. Here are the fields we want to put into this database:

Information	Field Name	Field Type	Field Length
First Name	FirstName	Text	255
Last Name	LastName	Text	255
Street Address	Address	Text	255
City	City	Text	255
State	State	Text	255
Zip Code	Zip	Text	255
Country	Country	Text	255
E-mail Address	Email	Text	255

That should about do it. The next step is to create the database. Since the database will need to have write access for the anonymous user, we will need to add that to the NTFS permissions. Because of this, it's a good idea to store the database in a directory that's different from the directory the web site is stored in. When it's in the same directory as the web site, it's too easy to modify the permissions so that no one can write to the database—or even worse, so that the permissions on the entire directory are open. When Microsoft Access opens a file, it creates a *.LDB* file, which is a lock file. Unless the anonymous user has the ability to create and destroy files in the directory that holds the database, you'll experience issues.

Let's create a directory on our E: drive, as we did earlier for the web site, and call it "Databases." Make sure the Anonymous access group has modify rights to this directory.

To create the database, you can use either the GUI (graphical user interface) in Microsoft Access or a SQL statement. Let's call the database *BeerBrewersDB.mdb*, and the table in that database can be called *BeerBrewersTable*. The GUI is pretty much self-explanatory, so here's the SQL statement that's used to create this table:

```
create table BeerBrewersTable
(
FirstName varchar(255),
LastName varchar(255),
Address varchar(255),
City varchar(255),
```

```
State varchar(255),
Zip varchar(255),
Country varchar(255),
Email varchar(255)
)
```

Now that the database is created, we need to create the DSN for the database.

1. Choose Start | Administrative Tools | Data Sources (ODBC).

2. In the Data Sources Administrator, choose the System DSN tab.

3. Click the Add button to add a new data source.

4. The Create New Data Source screen will appear. Choose Microsoft Access Driver (*.mdb).

5. Click Finish.

6. Type in the data source name: **BeerBrewersDSN**.

7. Click Select and browse to the Access database you created earlier (*E:\Databases\BeerBrewersDB.mdb*).

8. Once you've selected the Access database, click OK until you close the ODBC Administrator.

Now perform these same actions for a test database for the test site. If you like, you can create another table in the *BeerBrewersDB.mdb*. That way, you don't have to create a directory or make a new DSN, and you can just insert a new table with the same specs.

Tip   *If you use Microsoft Access to make the table, you may want to make sure that the fields are all set to "Allow Zero Length = Yes". The default is No, but this setting will cause an error if all the fields are not filled out.*

Get a Certificate for the Test Site

Since we'll be collecting names, addresses, and other personal information on our site, it's a good idea to encrypt the traffic traveling across the Internet. Also, a certificate will prove our identity on the Internet and help people be more at ease that we are indeed a real entity. For the test site, a "homegrown" certificate will suffice. For the production site, we'll need to get a commercial certificate.

As discussed in Chapter 10, the best practice for having your own CA (Certification Authority) is to make an offline root CA, and then delegate a certificate to a subordinate CA. You can then use the subordinate CA to issue certificates without risk of your entire certification system being compromised. Since this certificate is for a test site that no end users will ever see, and we are using the certificate only for this site, it's simpler to just make a CA and issue a certificate from there. It is still a good idea to issue the CA from another machine. (After all, we're using the test certificate just to make sure we have the code for SSL set up correctly.)

Obtaining and installing the test certificate is a three-step process.

1. Request the certificate in the IIS MMC.
2. Grant the certificate request, generate the certificate in the CA MMC, and export the certificate.
3. Process the request and install the export certificate back in the IIS MMC.

Here's how to request the test certificate:

1. Install Certificate Services to another machine.
2. Open the Properties window for the test web site.
3. On the Directory Security tab, click Server Certificate.
4. The Web Server Certificate Wizard pops up. Click Next.
5. Choose to create a new certificate, and then click Next.
6. Choose to Prepare The Request Now, But Send It Later, and click Next.
7. Type in the name for the certificate: **beer-brewers.com test site**.
8. Choose the bit length—1024 should be sufficient.
9. Click Next.
10. Type in the organization: **beer-brewers.com** is fine.
11. The organization unit is for organizations that have multiple departments or divisions. For our purposes, **beer-brewers.com** is fine to use here.
12. Click Next.
13. The common name is important; it needs to be the DNS name of the site. So for this site we use **test.beer-brewers.com**.
14. Click Next.
15. Select the Country/Region, State/Province, and City/Locality. Remember not to use any abbreviations.
16. Click Next.
17. Select the name you wish to use for this certificate request. Remember this name and location; we'll need to find this file in the next section.
18. Click Next twice.
19. Click Finish.

Now that we have created a certificate request, we can issue the certificate:

1. Open the Certification Authority MMC.
2. Highlight the CA name, and choose Action | All Tasks | Submit New Request.
3. Browse to the location of the certification request. If it's on a machine that is not accessible over the network, you may need to copy the request to a floppy and take it to the machine.
4. Highlight the file, and click Open.
5. Our certification request is now in the Pending Requests folder. Now we need to issue the certificate. Highlight the request in the Pending Requests folder, and choose Action | All Tasks | Issue.
6. The certificate will then move to the Issued Certificates folder. Now we can export the certificate to send to the web server. Highlight the certificate in the Issued Certificates folder, and choose Action | All Tasks | Export Binary Data.
7. Choose to export the Binary Certificate, and save the binary data to a file.
8. Click OK.
9. Select the name you wish to use for this certificate. Remember this name and location; we'll need to find this file in the next section. It's a good idea to use the *.cer* extension.

Now that we have a certificate export, we can go back into IIS and process the request for use

1. In the IIS MMC, start the Web Server Certificate Wizard for the test site.
2. Click Next.
3. Choose to process the pending request, and click Next.
4. Select the certificate file, and click Next.
5. Choose the SSL port you will use for this certificate. The default, 443, is fine Click Next.
6. Click Next, and then click Finish.

We now have a fully installed certificate for our test site, and we can use this certificate to test our code. When you are finished, make sure that you delete both the request file and the certificate export. If someone were to obtain those files, our certificate could be compromised.

Get a Certificate for the Production Site

For a production site, it's important that you get a commercial certificate, especially when dealing with the public. If you're on an intranet, you can have a certificate from your own CA, because you can add that CA to the browsers of all the clients. That just can't be done on the Internet. Although you can use your own CA to issue the certificate, it will send a warning message to all clients when they try to access any sites using SSL and it may discourage them from accessing your site. Also, issuing your own certificate from your own CA is risky, especially if the root CA were ever compromised. For these reasons, it's best to go to a commercial CA for publicly accessible sites.

The process for obtaining a production certificate is the same as that for the test certificate, except you have to request the certificate from a commercial CA and send it the request file.

1. Request the certificate in the IIS MMC.

2. Go online and request a certificate from a commercial CA.

3. Send the online CA the request file we generated in IIS.

4. Process the request by installing the CA's response file.

Each commercial CA will have a slightly different process. The important thing to remember is that the certificate request information needs to match what your organization information uses. For a larger company, a D-U-N-S Number goes a long way. Since we're not a corporation, a letter from the president of the club on official letterhead will do nicely to identify us. Other than the commercial CA portion, follow the same steps as the test site to install the certificate.

Note *See Chapter 10 for more on issuing certificates.*

Set Up the Web Site Security

The newsletter page of this server will be password-protected. This means that everyone who accesses that page will need to provide a username and password to access the site. To set this up, you need to perform the following tasks.

Create a User Account

When a user signs up, you can create an account on the web server for that user and e-mail the user their username and password. You can create a group as well to make NTFS permissions easier to manage.

Creating the Group

Here's how to create a group:

1. Open the Computer Management MMC.

2. Highlight Groups under Local Users and Groups.

3. Choose Action | New Group.

4. Type in the name of the group: **BeerBrewers Newsletter Group**.

5. Click Create.

Creating the Users

Now we'll create a user for the group:

1. In the MMC, highlight Users under Local Users and Groups.

2. Choose Action | New User.

3. Type in the username and password for the new user.

4. Uncheck the User Must Change Password At Next Logon checkbox.

5. Click Create.

Adding a User to the Group

Here's how to add a new user to the group:

1. In the MMC, open Groups under Local Users and Groups.

2. Double-click the BeerBrewers Newsletter Group.

3. Click Add.

4. Choose the user account you wish to add to this group.

5. Click OK, and then click OK again.

Set Up NTFS Permissions

After you have created the group, you will need to assign that group the rights to the file system. We assigned the anonymous group rights earlier; now it's time to add the beerbrewers site group to the list. You need to add the group only to the file(s) that you want secured. In this case, it's *newsletter.htm*.

1. In Windows Explorer, locate the *newsletter.htm* file.

2. Right-click the file, and choose Properties.

3. Open the Security tab.

4. Click Add.

5. Locate the BeerBrewers Newsletter Group.

6. Click OK.

7. Grant the BeerBrewers Newsletter Group read and execute permissions to the file.

8. Click OK.

Set Up the Authentication Options

Now that the NTFS permissions are set, it's time to set up the security options in IIS. These permissions will need to be set up for both the test and production sites here, so you'll need to perform this procedure twice.

1. Open the IIS MMC and locate the *newsletter.htm* file.
2. Right-click the file, and choose Properties.
3. Open the File Security tab.
4. Click the Edit button under Authentication And Access Control.
5. Uncheck the Enable Anonymous Access option.
6. For this site, we'll use Basic authentication only, so check Basic Authentication, and uncheck Integrated Windows Authentication.
7. Click OK once; this will keep the File Security tab open.

Stop right there!

You: Hey, wait, a sec. Isn't basic authentication really bad because it sends the plaintext password?

Me: Normally, yes. But, we have a certificate! All the traffic to this page will be encrypted.

You: OK, we do have a certificate, but how do you force people to use that?

Me: That's next.

Here's how to force SSL so we're not sending plaintext passwords around the Internet:

1. Click the Edit button under Secure Communications.
2. Click the option to Require Secure Channel (SSL).
3. If you want, you can require 128-bit encryption, but that will mean that browsers that don't have 128-bit encryption installed will not be able to access the site.
4. Click OK.
5. Click OK again.

Now this file will be password protected, and the password will be protected, too.

Test the Code

Now that everything is in place, it's important that you test and verify the code before rolling it into production. You need to create a detailed plan before you start testing, and a checklist is also useful—for this site, it would look something like this:

- Did I go into each page to make sure it is functioning properly?
- Do all the site links work?
- Are there any broken or unneeded site links?
- Is the DSN set up and functional?
- Can I produce an error message by not filling out all the fields?
- Is the security setup too much, too little, just right?
- Is SSL functioning correctly?
- Do my binary certificate and request files exist on this machine?
- Are the file system permissions set up correctly?
- Can I break the system by inputting malformed data?

Note   *In this web site, no error checking occurs for the fields, so it is possible to enter malformed data into the fields. In the real world, it's a good idea to perform field validation on form fields.*

Roll into Production

After you've fully tested the code and verified it according to your test plan, it's time to roll the code into production. It's important to test any future changes in the test environment and prove them out before rolling it into production. It appears, then, that we have a fully functional web site!

Note   *Everything in this chapter is completely fictional and is for demonstration purposes only. Any resemblance to any other site, real or imagined, is purely coincidental.*

IIS EXTRAS

The Complete Reference

IIS 6

Chapter 20

Troubleshooting

Troubleshooting in IIS 6 can be an involved process. In previous versions of IIS, all the functionality and all the components of IIS were enabled in a default installation. With Microsoft's new "off by default" mentality, you need to take care to make sure that all the necessary components are enabled. IIS is integrated into the operating system and touches many parts of it. If you find that you need to do some troubleshooting, you may need to look at the following to find the source of the problem:

- Log files
- MIME mappings
- Dynamic web content
- Permissions issues
- Worker processes
- Web service shutdown

Log Files

Needless to say, consulting log files can help enormously when you're troubleshooting issues with your IIS server. The two main log files you'll be concerned with are the IIS log file (hopefully the W3C, or World Wide Web Consortium Extended version) and the Windows Event Viewer.

About W3C Logging

Since W3C logging has the most complete set of fields that are logged, it is the most useful log to consult when you're troubleshooting issues. If you are not using W3C Extended logging, you may want to switch your logging type temporarily while trying to track down issues, but only if you aren't using site logging data for something important. The W3C Extended log can provide some great information about your site.

Which Account Is a Client Using to Access the Site?   If you are troubleshooting permissions issues, it's helpful to know which account the client is using to access the site. If you've set up Integrated Windows Authentication, the browser does not prompt the user for login information, so it is difficult to determine from the user which account they are using. Luckily, it's right there in the log file.

Which Browser Is a Client Using to Access the Site?   Some browsers do not support certain features. For example, Integrated Windows Authentication is supported only on Internet Explorer browsers. If you have anonymous access turned off and the client has no other choice but to use Integrated Windows Authentication, only IE users will be able to access the site. Taking a look at the log files, you can see which browsers are being used to access the site.

Which HTTP Status Codes Are Being Transmitted?   When IIS sends out an error message, it does not send a specific error message—rather, it sends a general error. This means that the client does not receive the substatus code. If the lockdown policy prevents a client from accessing the file, the client will receive a generic "404 not found" error, while the extended log file will contain the full 404.2 error message. In addition to this, since the *stats* codes are on the same line as the time/date, user, Internet Protocol (IP), browser, and so on, it is much easier to tie a specific error message to a specific client.

The basic list of HTTP status codes is defined by RFC 2616. These codes are extensible, so different vendors can add to this list. Microsoft has added the substatus codes in its implementation. Table 20-1 lists both sets combined and the basic meaning of each code.

Code	Meaning
100	Continue
101	Switching protocols
200	OK
201	Created
202	Accepted
203	Non-authoritative information
204	No content
205	Reset content
206	Partial content
300	Multiple choices
301	Moved permanently
302	Found
303	See other
304	Not modified
305	Use proxy
307	Temporary redirect
400	Bad request

Table 20-1. *HTTP Status Codes and Their Meanings*

IIS EXTRAS

Code	Meaning
401	Unauthorized
401.1	Unauthorized: Access is denied due to invalid credentials.
401.2	Unauthorized: Access is denied due to server configuration favoring an alternative authentication method.
401.3	Unauthorized: Access is denied due to an Access Control List (ACL) set on the requested resource.
401.4	Unauthorized: Authorization failed by a filter installed on the web server.
401.5	Unauthorized: Authorization failed by an Internet Server Application Programming Interface/Common Gateway Interface (ISAPI/CGI) application.
401.7	Unauthorized: Access denied by URL authorization policy on the web server.
402	Payment required
403	Forbidden
403.1	Forbidden: Execute access is denied.
403.2	Forbidden: Read access is denied.
403.3	Forbidden: Write access is denied.
403.4	Forbidden: Secure Sockets Layer (SSL) is required to view this resource.
403.5	Forbidden: SSL 128 is required to view this resource.
403.6	Forbidden: IP address of the client has been rejected.
403.7	Forbidden: SSL client certificate is required.
403.8	Forbidden: Domain Name System (DNS) name of the client is rejected.
403.9	Forbidden: Too many clients are trying to connect to the web server.
403.10	Forbidden: Web server is configured to deny Execute access.
403.11	Forbidden: Password has been changed.
403.12	Forbidden: Client certificate is denied access by the server certificate mapper.
403.13	Forbidden: Client certificate has been revoked on the web server.

Table 20-1. *HTTP Status Codes and Their Meanings* (continued)

Code	Meaning
403.14	Forbidden: Directory listing is denied on the web server.
403.15	Forbidden: Client access licenses have exceeded limits on the web server.
403.16	Forbidden: Client certificate is ill-formed or is not trusted by the web server.
403.17	Forbidden: Client certificate has expired or is not yet valid.
403.18	Forbidden: Cannot execute requested URL in the current application pool.
403.19	Forbidden: Cannot execute CGIs for the client in this application pool.
403.20	Forbidden: Passport logon failed.
404	Not Found
404.1	File or directory not found: Web site not accessible on the requested port.
404.2	File or directory not found: Lockdown policy prevents this request.
404.3	File or directory not found: Multipurpose Internet Mail Extensions (MIME) map policy prevents this request.
405	Method not allowed
406	Not acceptable
407	Proxy authentication required
408	Request timeout
409	Conflict
410	Gone
411	Length required
412	Precondition failed
413	Request entity too large
414	Request Uniform Resource Identifier (URI) too large
415	Unsupported media type
416	Requested range not satisfiable
417	Expectation failed

Table 20-1. *HTTP Status Codes and Their Meanings* (continued)

IIS EXTRAS

Code	Meaning
500	Internal server error
500.11	Server error: Application is shutting down on the web server.
500.12	Server error: Application is busy restarting on the web server.
500.13	Server error: Web server is too busy.
500.14	Server error: Invalid application configuration on the server.
500.15	Server error: Direct requests for GLOBAL.ASA are not allowed.
500.16	Server error: Universal Naming Convention (UNC) authorization credentials incorrect.
500.17	Server error: URL authorization store cannot be found.
500.18	Server error: URL authorization store cannot be opened.
500.19	Server error: Data for this file is configured improperly in the metabase.
500.20	Server error: URL authorization scope cannot be found.
500.100	Internal server error: ASP error.
501	Not implemented
502	Bad gateway
503	Service unavailable
504	Gateway timeout
505	HTTP version not supported

Table 20-1. *HTTP Status Codes and Their Meanings* (continued)

The Windows Event Viewer

The Windows Event Viewer can also log events that pertain to IIS. The Event Viewer has three—or four, if DNS is installed—components:

- **The Application log** Contains information about the applications that are running on the server. Most Component Object Model (COM) objects will send informational and error messages to the Application log.

- **The Security log** Contains all the auditing information that the server collects. We'll set that up in a moment.

- **The System log** Contains information about the operating system itself. Services also send information to the System log.

- **The DNS server log** Present only if the Microsoft DNS server component is installed, and contains events pertaining to the DNS server.

Note *Applications can add their own logs as well. The list of logs you have may vary, depending on any other applications you may have installed. For example, the DNS server log only appears if the DNS server component is installed.*

Some of the Event Viewer messages you will see include the following:

- Service start and stop
- Application errors
- COM object activity
- Service errors
- Application Pool errors
- News feed information

You can also set up auditing and view the information in the Security log. You can set up auditing in a security policy and Group Policy Objects. Here's how to set up auditing in the Local Security Policy for an individual server.

1. Open Start | Administrative Tools | Local Security Policy.

2. In the Local Security Settings window shown in Figure 20-1, select Local Policies, and then select Audit Policy.

3. To enable auditing for an item, double-click the item in the right pane.

4. Choose to audit Success, Failure, or both.

5. Click OK.

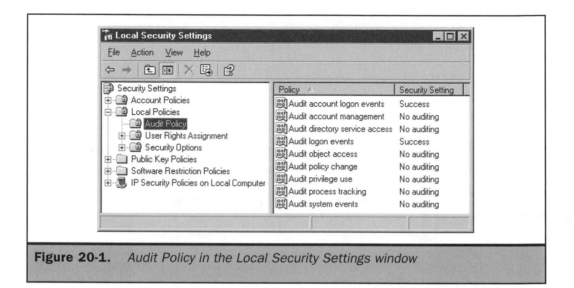

Figure 20-1.   *Audit Policy in the Local Security Settings window*

MIME Mappings

If you're having trouble with static files, check the registered MIME types. By default, IIS will serve up only HTML and text files. If an unknown file type is requested, IIS sends the client a 404 error and, if available, logs a 404.3 error in the W3C Extended log file. If you encounter this issue, check the IIS log, and if you see the 404.3, add the MIME mapping to the list. Here's how:

1. Open the IIS MMC by choosing Start | Administrative Tools | Internet Information Services (IIS) Manager.

2. Right-click on the component (at the global, site, or directory level) that you wish to change the MIME types for, and choose Properties.

3. Open the HTTP headers tab, and click the MIME Types button in the MIME Types section.

4. Click New in the MIME Types window that pops up.

5. In the MIME Type window, type the extension of the file you wish to add in the Extension text box.

6. Type the MIME type in the text box provided.

7. Click OK. You will then see that your extension has been added to the list of Registered MIME Types.

8. Click OK again.

9. Click OK one last time.

If you don't set up the MIME type properly, but the extension appears in the Registered MIME Types list, IIS will still serve up the file—it just won't know what to do with it. IE users will be prompted to choose a program to use to open this file.

 Don't know which MIME type is the correct one? They're all assigned and listed by the Internet Assigned Numbers Authority (IANA). Check them out at http://www.iana.org.

Dynamic Web Content

If you're having trouble with dynamic content, remember that by default, IIS serves up only static content. All dynamic content must be enabled in the Web Service Extensions portion of the IIS Microsoft Management Console (MMC). If you're using Active Server Pages (ASP), and you don't enable it, when clients try to access an ASP file they will receive a generic "404 not found" error. If you're using extended logging, the IIS log file will contain a 404 error with a substatus code of 2, which means "File or directory not found: Lockdown policy prevents this request."

To enable dynamic content, go to the Web Service Extensions section of the IIS MMC. Here, you will be able to add web service extensions and allow them to run.

The following web service extensions are predefined:

- All unknown ISAPI extensions
- All unknown CGI extensions
- Active Server Pages
- BITS server extensions (if installed)
- FrontPage Server Extensions 2002 (if installed)
- Internet data connector
- Internet printing
- Server-side includes
- WebDAV

To enable a web service extension, highlight it in the MMC and click Allow. If the extension you need is not listed here, you can add it and then click Allow.

A great tool for troubleshooting Web Service Extensions is the Allow All Web Service Extensions For A Specific Application hyperlink. You can use this to ensure that all the extensions on which a particular extension is dependent are enabled.

Permissions Issues

Setting the wrong NT File System (NTFS) permissions can wreak havoc with your web site. Not only do you have to be concerned about the permissions on the site, but you must ensure that any COM objects that are used are also accessible. The permissions on the site are straightforward enough, but most dynamic link libraries (DLLs) are in the *System32* directory. That's where it can get tricky.

If you have an ISAPI DLL with an ACL on it that the IIS worker process identity can't access, all requests for that DLL will receive a "503 Service Unavailable" error. It's important that you make sure that the worker process identity can load all the DLLs that you use on your site.

When troubleshooting permissions issues—and especially when you're not even sure it *is* a permission issue—the easiest way to determine the problem is to elevate the permissions. If you access the site using an account with Administrator credentials and the problem still exists, the problem is most likely *not* a permissions issue. If you can access it as an Administrator, but not as the Internet Guest Account, the problem *must* be permissions based.

Caution   *Right now you're thinking, "Haven't I heard at least 30 times in this book not to use elevated permissions?" True enough, but it is the quickest way to narrow down whether a problem is a permissions issue. Elevated permissions do need to be strictly controlled. You definitely don't want to do this when the site is in production. Instead, make the site inaccessible to everyone else, and then test it. When you're done, you need to set the permissions back to their appropriate settings. You don't want to run everything as Administrator.*

Worker Processes

In IIS 5, applications ran in-process using the *LocalSystem* account by default. This account has a higher level of rights than IIS 6 worker processes do, since they run as a network service. If your application that runs just fine under IIS 5 experiences issues under IIS 6, you can check out a few of the following things.

Worker Process Identity

You can change the identity assigned to a worker process. If you want to troubleshoot application permission issues, you can assign the worker process to run under *LocalSystem*. This is not recommended for production use, but it is a good way to test to see whether the issues stem from the way the application interacts as a network service. If you find that the application works well as *LocalSystem*, you have identified the issue, and you can redesign the application around the worker processes or check permissions on a DLL to see if they are too restrictive.

Here's how to change the identity of the worker processes in an application pool:

1. Highlight the application pool in the IIS MMC.
2. Choose Action | Properties.
3. Go to the Identity tab.
4. Choose a predefined identity (Network Service, Local Service, or Local System), or select a user account from the local machine or a trusted domain.

Worker Process Recycling

Not all applications work well with worker process recycling. Most do, but some can have issues. The following four issues can cause an application to have problems running under application isolation mode:

- Multi-instance ISAPIs that are written to be used multiple times simultaneously by different processes
- Read raw-data filters that would try to grab all the data before it hits a web site
- In-process session state variables, because they are lost every time a worker process is recycled
- Applications that farm out work to their own worker processes

Web Service Shutdown

In a couple of instances, a client can receive an HTTP error 503. When 503 errors are sent out, an event is logged in the Windows Event log. Check the Event Viewer to see whether the error was in *HTTP.sys* or in the WWW service. If the error is in *HTTP.sys*, check the application pool queue length. It may be that too many requests have been received. You can modify the application pool queue length manually:

1. In the IIS MMC, highlight the application pool you want to modify.
2. Choose Action | Properties, and go to the Performance tab.
3. Under the Request Queue Limit, increase the value for the number of requests.
4. Click OK.

If the error message is in the WWW service, it's possible that IIS has detected multiple errors in the worker processes and has initiated the *rapid-fail* protection. This causes the afflicted application pool to stop serving requests, and it is designed to protect the server from harm by misbehaving applications. If you experience this once, it may be an anomaly. If you experience this multiple times, and frequently, you will want to check out the application configuration, since it appears that something is amiss. You can increase the failure count and time period, but that does not attack the root problem.

IIS EXTRAS

Here's how to modify the rapid-fail settings:

1. In the IIS MMC, highlight the application pool you want to modify.

2. Choose Action | Properties, and go to the Health tab.

3. Increase the settings for the failures and/or for the time period that IIS monitors worker process failures.

4. Click OK.

Performance Monitoring

Monitoring the performance of your IIS server is important. You can have the best-written code in the world, but if the server hosting that code is underpowered, you will have performance issues. The Windows Performance Monitor, shown in Figure 20-2, allows you to log data to a file and then crunch that data later to see if you experience performance problems. Windows has more than 50 performance objects you can monitor. Performance Monitor allows you to monitor your system in real-time, generate logs to view later, and generate alerts based on thresholds you set. The counters you'll be most interested in logging for an IIS server are discussed next.

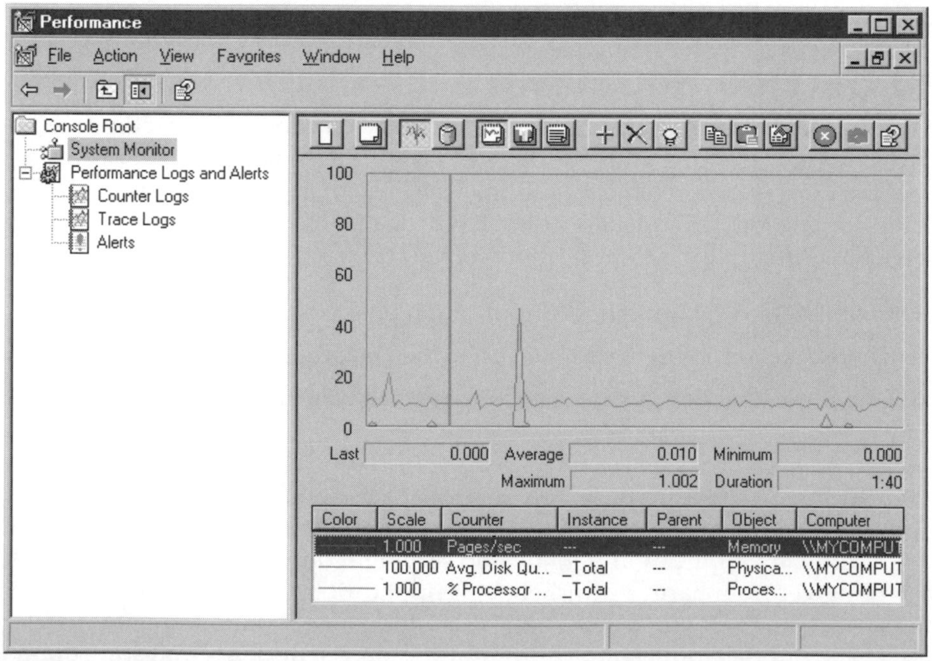

Figure 20-2. *Performance Monitor*

Active Server Pages   The Active Server Pages counters help you count errors in ASP scripts, template caches, various statistics regarding requests, and much more.

FTP Service   The FTP Service counters keep track of total bytes, connections broken down by users and logons, and file transfers.

Internet Information Services Global   The IIS global counters keep track of such information as binary large objects (BLOBs) and file and URI caching statistics.

Memory   The Memory counters keep vital statistics on system memory usage, along with how well paging is performing on the system.

Network Interface   The Network Interface counters keep track of the bytes transferred, bandwidth used, and how well packets are being transferred, including errors.

NNTP Commands   The Network News Transfer Protocol (NNTP) Commands counters keep statistics on how many of each type of NNTP commands are being received by the server.

NNTP Server   The NNTP Server counters keep track of information such as bytes, users, connections, and feed statistics.

Physical Disk   The Physical Disk counters keep track of vital statistics on the hard disk data transfers. These statistics can help you determine whether you are becoming I/O bound on the server.

Processor   The Processor counters keep track of the percentage of time the processor is working on commands, and which state the processor is in.

Server   The Server counters keep statistics on the page file, logon traffic, errors, and more.

SMTP NTFS Store Driver   The Simple Mail Transfer Protocol (SMTP) NTFS Store Driver keeps track of the number of messages allocated, deleted, enumerated, and queued.

SMTP Server   The SMTP Server object has more than 100 counters to log information on a large number of message statistics.

Web Service   The Web Service object has about 85 counters that track all the different types of HTTP requests and errors, CGI/ISAPI requests, and connection statistics.

Web Service Cache   The Web Service Cache counters keep track of all the caching statistics for the web server component, including hits and misses for each of the various types of items the web service uses. Most of the counters deal with URI caching.

IIS EXTRAS

Real-Time Monitoring

You can monitor your server in real-time using the System Monitor:

1. Open the Performance MMC by choosing Start | Administrative Tools | Performance.

2. Click System Monitor (it should be selected by default).

3. On the toolbar at the top of the monitor, click the plus (+) sign.

4. In the Add Counters dialog box, choose which computer you want to monitor; the default is this computer.

5. Use the drop-down box to choose which Performance object to use.

6. Select the individual counter from the list.

7. If more than one instance is possible (for example, if you have multiple processors), choose the instance you wish to monitor, or choose Total for all the instances.

8. Click Add. The counter will be added, even though the Add Counters dialog box is still active.

9. Repeat steps 3-7 for each counter you wish to add.

10. When you have added all the appropriate counters, click Close.

This will help you to monitor in real-time, but it doesn't give you any long-term information. That is what counter logs are for.

Using Counter Logs

Counter logs allow you to monitor a system over a great length of time and keep the data in log files that you can analyze later. This makes counter logs useful in determining intermittent performance issues. Here's how to set up a counter log:

1. In the Performance MMC, highlight Counter Logs under Performance Logs and Alerts.

2. Choose Action | New Log settings.

3. In the New Log Settings window, type in a name for the log you wish to create.

4. Click OK. The properties window will open.

At this point, you are in the Properties window for this log, which offers three tabs: General, Log Files, and Schedule.

The General Tab

In the General tab, shown in Figure 20-3, you can add objects and counters to this log file, and configure how it gathers data.

Objects are the performance objects that Windows has defined. You can add an entire object to the log file, and it will automatically gather data for every counter in that object. It also takes more disk space that way. To add an object, click the Add Objects button, and select all the objects that you wish to monitor in the Add Objects dialog box. When you have added all the objects, click Close.

Counters are individual performance counters that are contained in an object. You can choose to monitor an individual counter, and it will take less disk space. Your log file will not be as detailed as it would be if you monitored the entire object. To add a counter, click the Add Counters button, and in the Add Counters dialog box, select all the counters from the objects that you wish to monitor. When you have added all the counters, click Close.

Typically, if you have the disk space and spare CPU cycles, add objects rather than counters. You can't go back after the fact and gather data on additional counters, so just

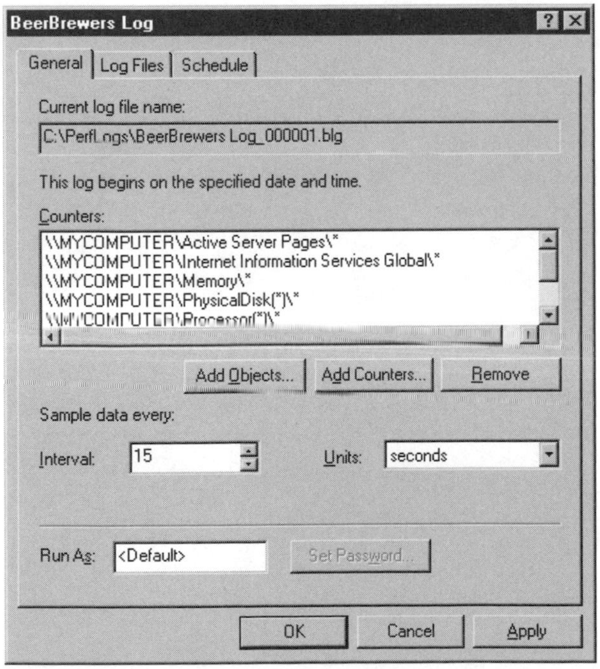

Figure 20-3.   *The General tab*

get the information right up front. If you're after something specific, use the counters; otherwise, use the objects.

The Sample Data Every area allows you to change the interval at which data is collected. At every interval, performance monitor queries all the defined performance counters to get their data at that moment. It then puts that data into the log file. As you might guess, the more often you gather data, the larger your log file will be—and the more detailed your data will be. Choose a time interval that gives you a good balance between size and detail. You can choose any interval between 1 second and 45 days. (Just a tip: 45 days might be a little weak on the detail side of that equation.)

In the Run As text box, you can specify a user account under which to run the Performance Monitor. This allows Performance Monitor to run, regardless of who is logged in.

The Log Files Tab

The Log Files tab, shown in Figure 20-4, allows you to configure the type of file that Performance Monitor will log data to.

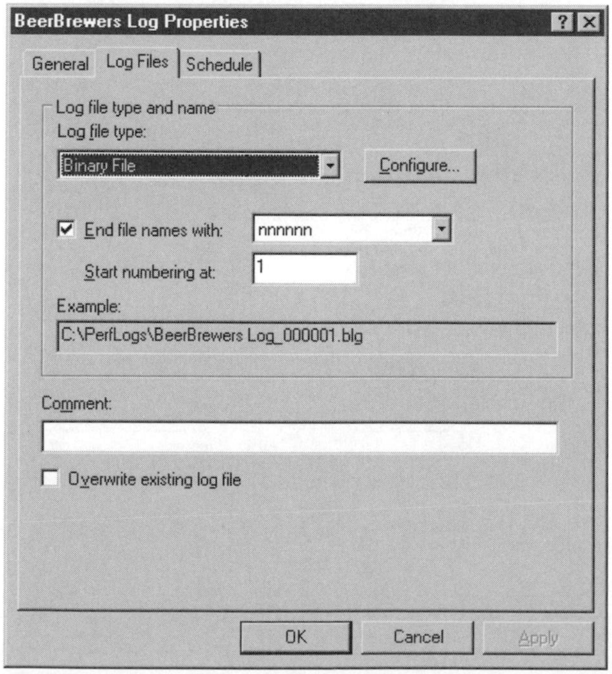

Figure 20-4. *The Log Files tab*

Your choices are as follows:

- Text File (Comma Delimited)
- Text File (Tab Delimited)
- Binary File
- Binary Circular File
- SQL Database

You can also choose how to increment the log files. This is especially helpful when you are logging on a periodic basis. You can choose to append the log file with various forms of the date and time, or just use incremented numbers for each log file. You can also add a log file comment and choose to overwrite existing log files.

The Schedule Tab

The Schedule tab, shown in Figure 20-5, allows you to configure the time period when the log file will collect data.

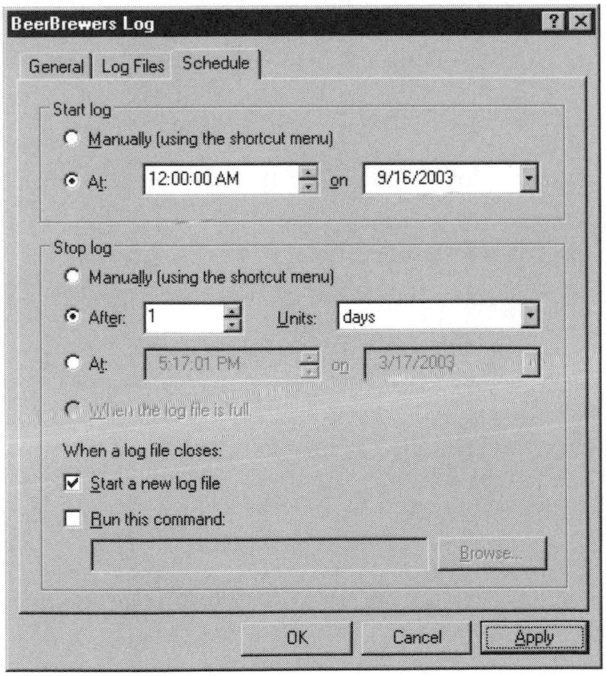

Figure 20-5. *The Schedule tab*

In the Start Log area, you can either kick off the log file manually or start it at a scheduled date and time.

In the Stop Log area, you can stop the log based on one of four criteria:

- Manually
- After a certain time period has passed
- At a specific data and time
- When the log file is full

When the log file closes, you can opt to start a new log file. If Start A New Log File is enabled, a new log file will be created based on the increment specified in the Schedule tab. You can also specify a certain command to run when the log file closes. This could be a script that processes the data—or anything you want, really.

After you've collected the data, it can help you determine system bottlenecks and thereby help you ensure that your IIS server is meeting the system needs.

Using Alerts in Performance Monitor

Performance Monitor has configurable thresholds that, when reached, will trigger a response. This allows you to monitor the health of a server, letting you know if something is amiss.

Here's how to create an alert:

1. In the Performance Monitor, click Alerts in the left pane under Performance Logs and Alerts.

2. Choose Action | New Alert Settings.

3. In the New Alert Settings window, type in the name of the alert settings you wish to create—this is a friendly name.

4. Click OK.

5. After you click OK, the Properties window will open. Use the three tabs (General, Action, and Schedule) of the Properties window to configure the alerts you wish to create.

The General Tab

The General tab, shown in Figure 20-6, allows you to choose which counters you want to monitor and set the threshold. You can select specific counters from an object to monitor here.

Comment   Type a description for this counter. This is a friendly name, so type in a name that will help you remember this counter later.

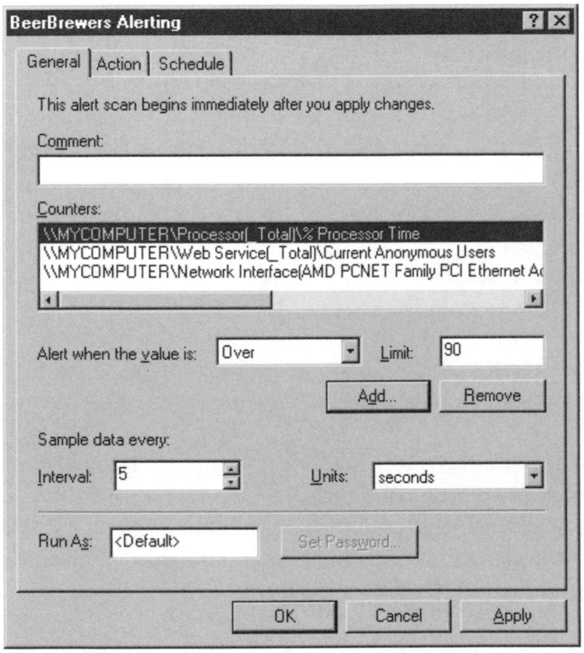

Figure 20-6. *The Alerting General tab*

Counters View the counters that have been selected and to which instance that each counter applies, if applicable.

Alert When The Value Is Over/Under Limit Configure the threshold for this counter. For example, for the % Processor Time, you can choose to alert when the value is larger than a certain percentage, such as 90 percent. When this threshold is reached, the action specified on the Action tab is triggered. This threshold is a one-time trigger, rather than occurring over a specific time period. If the processor utilization reaches 90 percent just once, the threshold is triggered. Because of this, processor triggers may not be the best use of the alerting feature, because momentary spikes up to 100 percent are normal. A sustained 100 percent processor, however, would be a good alert trigger.

Sample Data Every Change the interval at which data is collected. At every interval, Performance Monitor queries all the defined performance counters to get their data at that moment.

Run As Specify a user account under which to run the Performance Monitor. This allows Performance Monitor to run regardless of who is logged in.

IIS EXTRAS

The Action Tab

The Action tab, shown in Figure 20-7, lets you configure which action is performed when an event is triggered. You can select one or multiple events to perform.

Log An Entry in the Application Event Log   Writes an event detailing the alert counter, the value that triggered the alert, and the threshold. The source of the event is *SysmonLog*.

Send A Network Message To   Sends a network message using the messenger service to the name you enter in the text field.

Start Performance Data Log   Starts the defined log specified in the drop-down box. That log will run until schedule to stop, or until stopped manually.

Run This Program   Executes the specified command. You can use this to start a debugger, run a script, send an e-mail, or really do just about anything. The application is started with the command line arguments you specify. A great use of this would be to run a VBSript with some specified arguments, and that VBScript could be written to do just about anything you needed to have done.

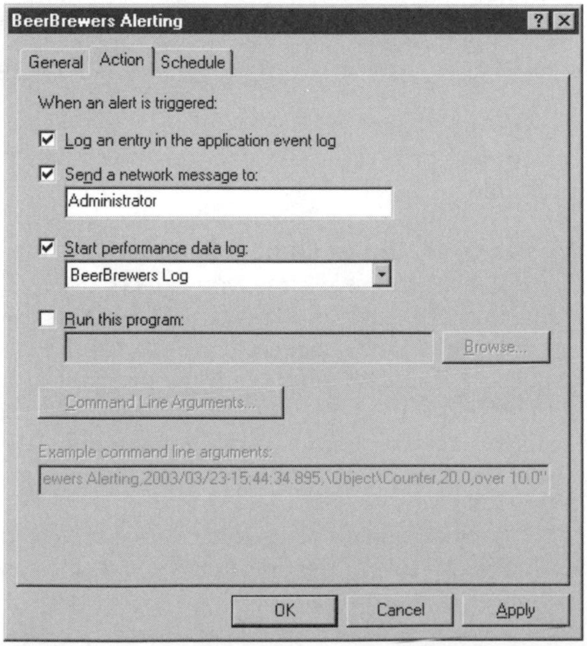

Figure 20-7.   *The Action tab*

Command Line Arguments   Click this button to configure which parameters are sent to the application when it is run. Seven arguments are available:

- Single argument string
- Date/time
- Measured value
- Alert name
- Counter name
- Limit value
- Text message

The Single argument string option puts the string into a comma-separated format, instead of listing each variable individually. The Text message allows you to type in any text you want to send. This is great; since you're configuring the alert, you know what is being triggered and you add in the text message for the variable you need to kick off the VBScript you wrote to fix this issue.

The Schedule Tab

The Schedule tab is used exactly as it is used in the other areas of Performance Monitor. Since it's been covered already, it won't be covered here as well. Turn back a few pages to see the details about the Schedule tab.

Appendix

XML Escape Values

The following fives tables provide escape sequences from the ISO/IEC 10646 character set of common characters that may be used in XML and HTML. The tables are as follows:

- **Table A-1: Latin ISO 1 Character Set**   The ASC II character set of letters and symbols
- **Table A-2: Greek Characters**   Letters of the Greek alphabet
- **Table A-3: Arrows**   Arrow symbols
- **Table A-4: Mathematical Operators**   Common mathematical symbols
- **Table A-5: Miscellaneous Symbols and Characters**   Other odd symbols and characters

Character	Numeric Character Reference	General Entity Escape Sequence	Description
	&#00;		NA
	&#01;		NA
	&#02;		NA
	&#03;		NA
	&#04;		NA
	&#05;		NA
	&#06;		NA
	&#07;		NA
	&#08;		NA
	&#09;		Horizontal tab
	&#10;		Line feed
	&#11;		NA
	&#12;		NA
	&#13;		Carriage return
	&#14;		NA
	&#15;		NA
	&#16;		NA
	&#17;		NA
	&#18;		NA
	&#19;		NA
	&#20;		NA
	&#21;		NA
	&#22;		NA
	&#23;		NA
	&#24;		NA

Table A-1.   *Latin ISO 1 Character Set*

Character	Numeric Character Reference	General Entity Escape Sequence	Description
	&#25;		NA
	&#26;		NA
	&#27;		NA
	&#28;		NA
	&#29;		NA
	&#30;		NA
	&#31;		NA
	&#32;		Space
!	&#33;		Exclamation mark
"	&#34;	&quot;	Quotation mark
#	&#35;		Number sign
$	&#36;		Dollar sign
%	&#37;		Percent sign
&	&#38;	&amp;	Ampersand
'	&#39;		Apostrophe
(	&#40;		Left parenthesis
)	&#41;		Right parenthesis
*	&#42;		Asterisk
+	&#43;		Plus sign
,	&#44;		Comma
-	&#45;		Hyphen
.	&#46;		Period
/	&#47;		Slash
0	&#48;		Number 0
1	&#49;		Number 1

Table A-1. *Latin ISO 1 Character Set* (continued)

Character	Numeric Character Reference	General Entity Escape Sequence	Description
2	&#50;		Number 2
3	&#51;		Number 3
4	&#52;		Number 4
5	&#53;		Number 5
6	&#54;		Number 6
7	&#55;		Number 7
8	&#56;		Number 8
9	&#57;		Number 9
:	&#58;		Colon
;	&#59;		Semicolon
<	&#60;	&lt;	Less than
=	&#61;		Equals sign
>	&#62;	&gt;	Greater than
?	&#63;		Question mark
@	&#64;		At symbol @
A	&#65;		Capital letter A
B	&#66;		Capital letter B
C	&#67;		Capital letter C
D	&#68;		Capital letter D
E	&#69;		Capital letter E
F	&#70;		Capital letter F
G	&#71;		Capital letter G
H	&#72;		Capital letter H
I	&#73;		Capital letter I
J	&#74;		Capital letter J

Table A-1.   *Latin ISO 1 Character Set* (continued)

Character	Numeric Character Reference	General Entity Escape Sequence	Description
K	&#75;		Capital letter K
L	&#76;		Capital letter L
M	&#77;		Capital letter M
N	&#78;		Capital letter N
O	&#79;		Capital letter O
P	&#80;		Capital letter P
Q	&#81;		Capital letter Q
R	&#82;		Capital letter R
S	&#83;		Capital letter S
T	&#84;		Capital letter T
U	&#85;		Capital letter U
V	&#86;		Capital letter V
W	&#87;		Capital letter W
X	&#88;		Capital letter X
Y	&#89;		Capital letter Y
Z	&#90;		Capital letter Z
[	&#91;		Left square bracket
\	&#92;		Backslash
]	&#93;		Right square bracket
^	&#94;		Caret
_	&#95;		Underscore
`	&#96;		Acute accent
a	&#97;		Small letter a
b	&#98;		Small letter b
c	&#99;		Small letter c

Table A-1. *Latin ISO 1 Character Set* (continued)

Character	Numeric Character Reference	General Entity Escape Sequence	Description
d	&#100;		Small letter d
e	&#101;		Small letter e
f	&#102;		Small letter f
g	&#103;		Small letter g
h	&#104;		Small letter h
I	&#105;		Small letter i
j	&#106;		Small letter j
k	&#107;		Small letter k
l	&#108;		Small letter l
m	&#109;		Small letter m
n	&#110;		Small letter n
o	&#111;		Small letter o
p	&#112;		Small letter p
q	&#113;		Small letter q
r	&#114;		Small letter r
s	&#115;		Small letter s
t	&#116;		Small letter t
u	&#117;		Small letter u
v	&#118;		Small letter v
w	&#119;		Small letter w
x	&#120;		Small letter x
y	&#121;		Small letter y
z	&#122;		Small letter z
{	&#123;		Left curly brace
|	|		Vertical bar

Table A-1.   *Latin ISO 1 Character Set* (continued)

APPENDIX

Character	Numeric Character Reference	General Entity Escape Sequence	Description
}	&#125;		Right curly brace
~	&#126;		Tilde
	&#127;		NA
			Nonbreaking space
¡	&#161;	&iexcl;	Inverted exclamation
¢	&#162;	&cent;	Cent sign
£	&#163;	&pound;	Pound sterling
¤	&#164;	&curren;	General currency sign
¥	&#165;	&yen;	Yen sign
¦	&#166;	¦ or &brkbar;	Broken vertical bar
§	&#167;	&sect;	Section sign
¨	&#168;	¨ or ¨	Diæresis/Umlaut
©	&#169;	&copy;	Copyright
ª	&#170;	&ordf;	Feminine ordinal
«	&#171;	&laquo;	Left angle quote, guillemot left
¬	&#172;	&not;	Not sign
	&#173;	&shy;	Soft hyphen
®	&#174;	&reg;	Registered trademark
¯	&#175;	¯ or &hibar;	Macron accent
°	&#176;	&deg;	Degree sign
±	&#177;	&plusmn;	Plus or minus
²	&#178;	&sup2;	Superscript two
³	&#179;	&sup3;	Superscript three
´	&#180;	&acute;	Acute accent

Table A-1. *Latin ISO 1 Character Set* (continued)

Character	Numeric Character Reference	General Entity Escape Sequence	Description
μ	&#181;	&micro;	Micro sign
¶	&#182;	&para;	Paragraph sign
·	&#183;	&middot;	Middle dot
،	&#184;	&cedil;	Cedilla
¹	&#185;	&sup1;	Superscript one
º	&#186;	&ordm;	Masculine ordinal
»	&#187;	&raquo;	Right angle quote, guillemot right
¼	&#188;	&frac14;	Fraction one-fourth
½	&#189;	&frac12;	Fraction one-half
¾	&#190;	&frac34;	Fraction three-fourths
¿	&#191;	&iquest;	Inverted question mark
À	&#192;	&Agrave;	Capital letter A, grave accent
Á	&#193;	&Aacute;	Capital letter A, acute accent
Â	&#194;	&Acirc;	Capital letter A, circumflex
Ã	&#195;	&Atilde;	Capital letter A, tilde
Ä	&#196;	&Auml;	Capital letter A, diæresis / umlaut
Å	&#197;	&Aring;	Capital letter A, ring
Æ	&#198;	&AElig;	Capital letter AE ligature
Ç	&#199;	&Ccedil;	Capital letter C, cedilla
È	&#200;	&Egrave;	Capital letter E, grave accent
É	&#201;	&Eacute;	Capital letter E, acute accent
Ê	&#202;	&Ecirc;	Capital letter E, circumflex
Ë	&#203;	&Euml;	Capital letter E, diæresis/umlaut

Table A-1.   *Latin ISO 1 Character Set* (continued)

Character	Numeric Character Reference	General Entity Escape Sequence	Description
Ì	&#204;	&Igrave;	Capital letter I, grave accent
Í	&#205;	&Iacute;	Capital letter I, acute accent
Î	&#206;	&Icirc;	Capital letter I, circumflex
Ï	&#207;	&Iuml;	Capital letter I, diæresis/umlaut
Ð	&#208;	&ETH;	Capital letter Eth, Icelandic
Ñ	&#209;	&Ntilde;	Capital letter N, tilde
Ò	&#210;	&Ograve;	Capital letter O, grave accent
Ó	&#211;	&Oacute;	Capital letter O, acute accent
Ô	&#212;	&Ocirc;	Capital letter O, circumflex
Õ	&#213;	&Otilde;	Capital letter O, tilde
Ö	&#214;	&Ouml;	Capital letter O, diæresis/umlaut
×	&#215;	&times;	Multiply sign
Ø	&#216;	&Oslash;	Capital letter O, slash
Ù	&#217;	&Ugrave;	Capital letter U, grave accent
Ú	&#218;	&Uacute;	Capital letter U, acute accent
Û	&#219;	&Ucirc;	Capital letter U, circumflex
Ü	&#220;	&Uuml;	Capital letter U, diæresis/umlaut
Ý	&#221;	&Yacute;	Capital letter Y, acute accent
Þ	&#222;	&THORN;	Capital letter Thorn, Icelandic
ß	&#223;	&szlig;	Small sharp s, German sz
à	&#224;	&agrave;	Small letter a, grave accent
á	&#225;	&aacute;	Small letter a, acute accent
â	&#226;	&acirc;	Small letter a, circumflex

Table A-1. *Latin ISO 1 Character Set* (continued)

Character	Numeric Character Reference	General Entity Escape Sequence	Description
ã	&#227;	&atilde;	Small letter a, tilde
ä	&#228;	&auml;	Small letter a, diæresis/umlaut
å	&#229;	&aring;	Small letter a, ring
æ	&#230;	&aelig;	Small letter ae ligature
ç	&#231;	&ccedil;	Small letter c, cedilla
è	&#232;	&egrave;	Small letter e, grave accent
é	&#233;	&eacute;	Small letter e, acute accent
ê	&#234;	&ecirc;	Small letter e, circumflex
ë	&#235;	&euml;	Small letter e, diæresis/umlaut
ì	&#236;	&igrave;	Small letter i, grave accent
í	&#237;	&iacute;	Small letter i, acute accent
î	&#238;	&icirc;	Small letter i, circumflex
ï	&#239;	&iuml;	Small letter i, diæresis/umlaut
ð	&#240;	&eth;	Small letter eth, Icelandic
ñ	&#241;	&ntilde;	Small letter n, tilde
ò	&#242;	&ograve;	Small letter o, grave accent
ó	&#243;	&oacute;	Small letter o, acute accent
ô	&#244;	&ocirc;	Small letter o, circumflex
õ	&#245;	&otilde;	Small letter o, tilde
ö	&#246;	&ouml;	Small letter o, diæresis/umlaut
÷	&#247;	&divide;	Division sign
ø	&#248;	&oslash;	Small letter o, slash
ù	&#249;	&ugrave;	Small letter u, grave accent
ú	&#250;	&uacute;	Small letter u, acute accent

Table A-1. *Latin ISO 1 Character Set* (continued)

Character	Numeric Character Reference	General Entity Escape Sequence	Description
û	&#251;	&ucirc;	Small letter u, circumflex
ü	&#252;	&uuml;	Small letter u, diæresis/umlaut
ý	&#253;	&yacute;	Small letter y, acute accent
þ	&#254;	&thorn;	Small letter thorn, Icelandic
ÿ	&#255;	&yuml;	Small letter y, diæresis/umlaut

Table A-1.   *Latin ISO 1 Character Set* (continued)

Character	Numeric Character Reference	General Entity Escape Sequence	Description
Α	&Alpha;	&#913;	Greek Capital letter alpha U0391
Β	&Beta;	&#914;	Greek capital letter beta U0392
Γ	&Gamma;	&#915;	Greek capital letter gamma U0393 ISOgrk3
Δ	&Delta;	&#916;	Greek capital letter delta U0394 ISOgrk3
Ε	&Epsilon;	&#917;	Greek capital letter epsilon U0395
Ζ	&Zeta;	&#918;	Greek capital letter zeta U0396
Η	&Eta;	&#919;	Greek capital letter eta U0397
Θ	&Theta;	&#920;	Greek capital letter theta U0398 ISOgrk3
Ι	&Iota;	&#921;	Greek capital letter iota U0399
Κ	&Kappa;	&#922;	Greek capital letter kappa U039A
Λ	&Lambda;	&#923;	Greek capital letter lambda U039B ISOgrk3
Μ	&Mu;	&#924;	Greek capital letter mu U039C
Ν	&Nu;	&#925;	Greek capital letter nu U039D
Ξ	&Xi;	&#926;	Greek capital letter xi U039E ISOgrk3

Table A-2. *Greek Characters*

Character	Numeric Character Reference	General Entity Escape Sequence	Description
O	&Omicron;	&#927;	Greek capital letter omicron U039F
Π	&Pi;	&#928;	Greek capital letter pi U03A0 ISOgrk3
P	&Rho;	&#929;	Greek capital letter rho U03A1
Σ	&Sigma;	&#931;	Greek capital letter sigma U03A3 ISOgrk3
T	&Tau;	&#932;	Greek capital letter tau U03A4
Y	&Upsilon;	&#933;	Greek capital letter upsilon U03A5 ISOgrk3
Φ	&Phi;	&#934;	Greek capital letter phi U03A6 ISOgrk3
X	&Chi;	&#935;	Greek capital letter chi U03A7
Ψ	&Psi;	&#936;	Greek capital letter psi U03A8 ISOgrk3
Ω	&Omega;	&#937;	Greek capital letter omega U03A9 ISOgrk3
α	&alpha;	&#945;	Greek small letter alpha U03B1 ISOgrk3
β	&beta;	&#946;	Greek small letter beta U03B2 ISOgrk3
γ	&gamma;	&#947;	Greek small letter gamma U03B3 ISOgrk3
δ	&delta;	&#948;	Greek small letter delta U03B4 ISOgrk3

Table A-2. *Greek Characters* (continued)

Character	Numeric Character Reference	General Entity Escape Sequence	Description
ε	&epsilon;	&#949;	Greek small letter epsilon U03B5 ISOgrk3
ζ	&zeta;	&#950;	Greek small letter zeta U03B6 ISOgrk3
η	&eta;	&#951;	Greek small letter eta U03B7 ISOgrk3
θ	&theta;	&#952;	Greek small letter theta U03B8 ISOgrk3
ι	&iota;	&#953;	Greek small letter iota U03B9 ISOgrk3
κ	&kappa;	&#954;	Greek small letter kappa U03BA ISOgrk3
λ	&lambda;	&#955;	Greek small letter lambda U03BB ISOgrk3
μ	&mu;	&#956;	Greek small letter mu U03BC ISOgrk3
ν	&nu;	&#957;	Greek small letter nu U03BD ISOgrk3
ξ	&xi;	&#958;	Greek small letter xi U03BE ISOgrk3
o	&omicron;	&#959;	Greek small letter omicron U03BF NEW
π	&pi;	&#960;	Greek small letter pi U03C0 ISOgrk3
ρ	&rho;	&#961;	Greek small letter rho U03C1 ISOgrk3
ς	&sigmaf;	&#962;	Greek small letter final sigma U03C2 ISOgrk3

Table A-2. *Greek Characters* (continued)

Character	Numeric Character Reference	General Entity Escape Sequence	Description
σ	&sigma;	&#963;	Greek small letter sigma U03C3 ISOgrk3
τ	&tau;	&#964;	Greek small letter tau U03C4 ISOgrk3
υ	&upsilon;	&#965;	Greek small letter upsilon U03C5 ISOgrk3
φ	&phi;	&#966;	Greek small letter phi U03C6 ISOgrk3
χ	&chi;	&#967;	Greek small letter chi U03C7 ISOgrk3
ψ	&psi;	&#968;	Greek small letter psi U03C8 ISOgrk3
ω	&omega;	&#969;	Greek small letter omega U03C9 ISOgrk3
ϑ	&thetasym;	&#977;	Greek small letter theta symbol U03D1 NEW
ϒ	&upsih;	&#978;	Greek upsilon with hook symbol U03D2 NEW
ϖ	&piv;	&#982;	Greek pi symbol U03D6 ISOgrk3

Table A-2.   *Greek Characters* (continued)

Character	Numeric Character Reference	General Entity Escape Sequence	Description
←	&larr;	&#8592;	Leftward arrow U2190 ISOnum
↑	&uarr;	&#8593;	Upward arrow U2191 ISOnum
→	&rarr;	&#8594;	Rightward arrow U2192 ISOnum
↓	&darr;	&#8595;	Downward arrow U2193 ISOnum
↔	&harr;	&#8596;	Left right arrow U2194 ISOamsa
↵	&crarr;	&#8629;	Downward arrow with corner leftward, =carriage return U21B5 NEW
⇐	&lArr;	&#8656;	Leftward double arrow U21D0 ISOtech
⇑	&uArr;	&#8657;	Upward double arrow U21D1 ISOamsa
⇒	&rArr;	&#8658;	Rightward double arrow U21D2 ISOtech
⇓	&dArr;	&#8659;	Downward double arrow U21D3 ISOamsa
⇔	&hArr;	&#8660;	Left right double arrow U21D4 ISOamsa

Table A-3. *Arrows*

Character	Numeric Character Reference	General Entity Escape Sequence	Description
∀	&forall;	&#8704;	For all U2200 ISOtech
∂	&part;	&#8706;	Partial differential U2202 ISOtech
∃	&exist;	&#8707;	There exists U2203 ISOtech
∅	&empty;	&#8709;	Empty set, =null set, =diameter U2205 ISOamso
∇	&nabla;	&#8711;	Nabla, =backward difference U2207 ISOtech
∈	&isin;	&#8712;	Element of U2208 ISOtech
∉	&notin;	&#8713;	Not an element of U2209 ISOtech
∋	&ni;	&#8715;	Contains as member U220B ISOtech
∏	&prod;	&#8719;	*n*-ary product, =product sign U220F ISOamsb
−	&sum;	&#8722;	*n*-ary sumation U2211 ISOamsb
−	&minus;	&#8722;	Minus sign U2212 ISOtech
∗	&lowast;	&#8727;	Asterisk operator U2217 ISOtech
√	&radic;	&#8730;	Square root, =radical sign U221A ISOtech
∝	&prop;	&#8733;	Proportional to U221D ISOtech

Table A-4. *Mathematical Operators*

Character	Numeric Character Reference	General Entity Escape Sequence	Description
∞	&infin;	&#8734;	Infinity U221E ISOtech
∠	&ang;	&#8736;	Angle U2220 ISOamso
⊥	&and;	&#8869;	Logical and, =wedge U2227 ISOtech
⊢	&or;	&#8870;	Logical or, =vee U2228 ISOtech
∩	&cap;	&#8745;	Intersection, =cap U2229 ISOtech
∪	&cup;	&#8746;	Union, =cup U222A ISOtech
∫	&int;	&#8747;	Integral U222B ISOtech
∴	&there4;	&#8756;	Therefore symbol U2234 ISOtech
~	&sim;	&#8764;	Tilde operator U223C ISOtech
≅	&cong;	&#8773;	Approximately equal to U2245 ISOtech
≅	&asymp;	&#8773;	Almost equal to U2248 ISOamsr
≠	&ne;	&#8800;	Not equal to U2260 ISOtech
≡	&equiv;	&#8801;	Identical to U2261 ISOtech
≤	&le;	&#8804;	Less than or equal to U2264 ISOtech
≥	&ge;	&#8805;	Greater than or equal to U2265 ISOtech

Table A-4. *Mathematical Operators* (continued)

Character	Numeric Character Reference	General Entity Escape Sequence	Description
⊂	⊂	⊂	Subset of U2282 ISOtech
⊃	⊃	⊃	Superset of U2283 ISOtech
⊄	⊄	⊄	Not a subset of U2284 ISOamsn
⊆	⊆	⊆	Subset of or equal to U2286 ISOtech
⊇	⊇	⊇	Superset of or equal to U2287 ISOtech
⊕	⊕	⊕	Circled plus U2295 ISOamsb
⊗	⊗	⊗	Circled times U2297 ISOamsb
⊥	⊥	⊥	Up tack U22A5 ISOtech
·	⋅	⋅	Dot operator U22C5 ISOamsb

Table A-4. *Mathematical Operators* (continued)

Character	Numeric Character Reference	General Entity Escape Sequence	Description
ƒ	&fnof;	&#402;	Latin Small letter f with hook, =function, =florin U0192 ISOtech
•	&bull;	&#8226;	Bullet U2022 ISOpub
…	&hellip;	&#8230;	Horizontal ellipsis U2026 ISOpub
′	&prime;	&#8242;	Prime U2032 ISOtech
″	&Prime;	&#8243;	Double prime U2033 ISOtech
‾	&oline;	&#8254;	Overline U203E NEW
/	&frasl;	&#8260;	Fraction slash U2044 NEW
℘	&weierp;	&#8472;	Script capital P U2118 ISOamso
ℑ	&image;	&#8465;	Black letter capital I U2111 ISOamso
ℜ	&real;	&#8476;	Black letter capital R U211C ISOamso
™	&trade;	&#8482;	Trademark sign U2122 ISOnum
ℵ	&alefsym;	&#8501;	Alef symbol cardinal U2135 NEW

Table A-5.   *Miscellaneous Symbols and Characters*

Index

Symbols and Numbers

N

S

INTERNATIONAL CONTACT INFORMATION

AUSTRALIA
McGraw-Hill Book Company Australia Pty. Ltd.
TEL +61-2-9900-1800
FAX +61-2-9878-8881
http://www.mcgraw-hill.com.au
books-it_sydney@mcgraw-hill.com

CANADA
McGraw-Hill Ryerson Ltd.
TEL +905-430-5000
FAX +905-430-5020
http://www.mcgraw-hill.ca

GREECE, MIDDLE EAST, & AFRICA
(Excluding South Africa)
McGraw-Hill Hellas
TEL +30-210-6560-990
TEL +30-210-6560-993
TEL +30-210-6560-994
FAX +30-210-6545-525

MEXICO (Also serving Latin America)
McGraw-Hill Interamericana Editores S.A. de C.V.
TEL +525-117-1583
FAX +525-117-1589
http://www.mcgraw-hill.com.mx
fernando_castellanos@mcgraw-hill.com

SINGAPORE (Serving Asia)
McGraw-Hill Book Company
TEL +65-6863-1580
FAX +65-6862-3354
http://www.mcgraw-hill.com.sg
mghasia@mcgraw-hill.com

SOUTH AFRICA
McGraw-Hill South Africa
TEL +27-11-622-7512
FAX +27-11-622-9045
robyn_swanepoel@mcgraw-hill.com

SPAIN
McGraw-Hill/Interamericana de España, S.A.U.
TEL +34-91-180-3000
FAX +34-91-372-8513
http://www.mcgraw-hill.es
professional@mcgraw-hill.es

UNITED KINGDOM, NORTHERN,
EASTERN, & CENTRAL EUROPE
McGraw-Hill Education Europe
TEL +44-1-628-502500
FAX +44-1-628-770224
http://www.mcgraw-hill.co.uk
computing_europe@mcgraw-hill.com

ALL OTHER INQUIRIES Contact:
McGraw-Hill/Osborne
TEL +1-510-420-7700
FAX +1-510-420-7703
http://www.osborne.com
omg_international@mcgraw-hill.com